15.95

Budgeting:
Profit Planning and Control.

FOURTH EDITION

Glenn A. Welsch, *Ph. D., C. P. A.*

The John Arch White
Professor of Business Administration
and Professor of Accounting

The University of Texas
Austin, Texas

Prentice-Hall, Inc., Englewood Cliffs, New Jersey

Library of Congress Cataloging in Publication Data

WELSCH, GLENN A
 Budgeting: profit planning and control.

 Includes bibliographical references and index.
 1. Budget in business.   I. Title.
HF5550.W443 1976   658.1'54   75-33686
ISBN 0-13-193391-4

© 1976, 1971, 1964, 1957 by Prentice-Hall, Inc.,
Englewood Cliffs, N.J.

Printed in the United States of America

10   9   8   7   6   5   4   3   2   1

Prentice-Hall International, Inc., *London*
Prentice-Hall of Australia Pty. Limited, *Sydney*
Prentice-Hall of Canada, Ltd., *Toronto*
Prentice-Hall of India Private Limited, *New Delhi*
Prentice-Hall of Japan, Inc., *Tokyo*
Prentice-Hall of Southeast Asia Pte. Ltd., *Singapore*

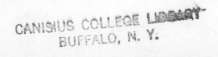

Contents

ILLUSTRATIONS   xi

SCHEDULES   xv

PREFACE   xix

chapter one

THE MANAGEMENT PROCESS   1

Plan of the Book, 2
Comprehensive Profit Planning and Control Defined, 3
The Role of Management, 4
The Management Planning Function, 11
The Control Function Related to Profit Planning and Control, 16
Coordination, 19
A Word of Caution, 20
Summary, 22
DISCUSSION QUESTIONS, 23
CASES, 24

chapter two

THE FUNDAMENTALS OF PROFIT PLANNING AND CONTROL   28

Fundamental Distinctions, 29
Managerial Evaluation of Alternatives in Planning, 49
Application of Profit Planning and Control to Various Types of Firms, 50
Advantages and Disadvantages of Profit Planning and Control, 50
Establishing the Foundation for Profit Planning and Control, 53
DISCUSSION QUESTIONS, 54
CASES, 55

chapter three

COMPREHENSIVE PROFIT PLANNING
AND CONTROL OUTLINED   60

Components of a Comprehensive Profit Planning and Control Program, 61
Summary, 73
Frequency and Time Dimensions in Profit Planning and Control, 74
Line and Staff Responsibilities, 76
Planning Perspectives, 80
Summary, 83
DISCUSSION QUESTIONS, 84
CASES, 84

chapter four

COMPREHENSIVE PROFIT PLANNING
AND CONTROL ILLUSTRATED   92

Case Background, 92
Summary of the Profit Planning and Control Manual, 94
Evaluation of Relevant Variables and Strengths and Weaknesses Illustrated, 97
Statement of Broad Objectives Illustrated, 97
Statement of Specific Goals Illustrated, 100
Statement of Basic Strategies Illustrated, 100
Planning Premises Illustrated, 101
Project Planning Illustrated, 103
Strategic and Tactical Profit Plans Illustrated, 103
DISCUSSION QUESTIONS, 126
CASES, 126

chapter five

SALES PLANNING AND CONTROL   139

Long-Range and Short-Range Sales Planning Compared, 140
Comprehensive Sales Planning, 142

Consideration of Alternatives, 146
Pricing Policy in Sales Planning, 147
Product Line Considerations, 149
Managing Sales Planning, 150
Considerations in Selecting Approaches for Planning Sales, 151
Steps in Planning Sales, 152
Methods of Projecting Sales, 154
The Concern's Capabilities and Its Sales Plan, 165
Control of Sales and Related Costs, 166
The Sales Plan Illustrated, 167
DISCUSSION QUESTIONS, 170
CASES, 171

chapter six

PLANNING PRODUCTION: FINISHED GOODS AND WORK IN PROCESS INVENTORY REQUIREMENTS   182

Responsibility for Production Planning, 183
General Considerations in Planning Production and Inventory Levels, 185
Time Dimensions of Production Planning, 186
Developing the Production Plan, 186
Setting Inventory Policies, 192
Setting Production Policies, 196
Adequacy of Manufacturing Facilities, 197
Availability of Raw Materials and Labor, 198
Length of the Production Period, 198
The Production Budget as a Planning, Coordinating, and Control Tool, 199
The Production Plan Illustrated, 201
DISCUSSION QUESTIONS, 203
CASES, 204

chapter seven

PLANNING AND CONTROLLING MATERIALS USAGE AND PURCHASES   211

The Materials Budget, 213
The Purchases and Materials Inventory Budgets, 217
Estimating Raw Material Unit Costs, 219
Cost of Materials Used Budget, 220
Planning, Coordination and Control Aspects of Raw Materials Budgeting, 220
The Materials Budgets Illustrated, 224
DISCUSSION QUESTIONS, 228
CASES, 233

chapter eight

PLANNING AND CONTROLLING DIRECT LABOR COSTS   240

Approaches in Planning Direct Labor Costs, 241
Planning Direct Labor Hours, 242
Planning Wage Rates, 244
Organizing the Direct Labor Budget, 246
Planning and Control Features of the Direct Labor Budget, 246
The Direct Labor Budget Illustrated, 248
DISCUSSION QUESTIONS, 249
CASES, 253

chapter nine

PLANNING EXPENSES—MANUFACTURING OVERHEAD,
DISTRIBUTION AND ADMINISTRATIVE EXPENSES   260

Some Relevant Distinctions, 261
Planning Expenses, 264
Planning Manufacturing Overhead, 265
Planning Distribution Expenses, 272
Construction of Distribution Expense Budgets, 273
Planning Administrative Expenses, 276
Expense Budgets Illustrated, 277
DISCUSSION QUESTIONS, 290
CASES, 290

chapter ten

DEVELOPMENT AND APPLICATION
OF VARIABLE BUDGETS OF EXPENSE   302

Concepts Underlying the Variable Budget, 303
Fixed Costs Defined, 305
Variable Costs Defined, 306
Semivariable Costs Analyzed, 309
Selecting the Measure of Activity, 309
Determining the Relevant Range of Activity, 314
Methods for Determining Cost Variability, 314
Direct Estimate Methods, 316
Budgeted High and Low Point Method, 318
Correlation Methods, 319
Negative Values in Cost Analysis, 327
Participation by Supervisors in Developing Variable Budgets, 327
Cost-Volume Considerations, 328
Methods of Expressing Variable Budgets, 329

Utilization of Variable Budgets, 331
Use of the Concept of Cost Variability, 336
Comprehensive Illustration of the Development and Utilization
of Variable Budgets, 336
DISCUSSION QUESTIONS, 341
CASES, 341

chapter eleven

PLANNING AND CONTROLLING CAPITAL EXPENDITURES   355

Management Planning for Capital Expenditures, 357
Responsibility for Budgeting Capital Expenditures, 360
Control of Capital Expenditures, 361
Management Evaluation of Proposed Capital Expenditures, 363
Discounted Cash Flow Methods, 367
Capital Expenditures Budget Illustrated, 377
DISCUSSION QUESTIONS, 380
CASES, 380

chapter twelve

PLANNING AND CONTROLLING CASH   385

Time Horizons in Cash Planning and Control, 386
Methods of Developing the Cash Budget, 387
Cash Receipts and Disbursements Method of Estimating Cash Receipts, 388
Estimating Cash Receipts Illustrated, 388
Estimating Cash Payments, 391
Estimating Cash Payments Illustrated, 392
Determination of Financing Needs, 398
Income Statement Cash Flow Method, 400
Control of the Cash Position, 403
DISCUSSION QUESTIONS, 405
CASES, 408

chapter thirteen

COMPLETION AND APPLICATION OF THE PROFIT PLAN   416

Completion of the Annual Profit Plan, 417
Consideration of Alternatives in Developing the Profit Plan, 418
Implementing of the Profit Plan, 424
Development of the Budgeted Financial Statements Illustrated, 426
DISCUSSION QUESTIONS, 443
CASES, 443

chapter fourteen

TECHNIQUES AND MANAGERIAL APPLICATION OF COST-VOLUME-PROFIT ANALYSIS (BREAKEVEN ANALYSIS)   449

The Concept of Cost-Volume-Profit Analysis, 450
Basic Assumptions Underlying Cost-Volume-Profit Analysis, 454
The Principle of Cost Variability As Applied to
Cost-Volume-Profit Analysis, 455
Identification of Fixed and Variable Cost Components, 455
Straightline Variability, 456
Sales Price and Sales Mix Considerations, 457
Management Policies, 460
Evaluation of Assumptions, 460
Special Problems in Breakeven Analysis, 461
Breakeven Analysis and Inventory Change, 463
Use and Application of Cost-Volume-Profit Analysis, 467
Evaluating the Effect of Changing Variables, 469
Cost-Volume-Profit Analysis by Organizational Subdivision or Product, 471
Margin of Safety, 474
Cost-Volume-Profit Analysis Illustrated for Superior
Manufacturing Company, 474
DISCUSSION QUESTIONS, 479
CASES, 479

chapter fifteen

PERFORMANCE REPORTS FOR MANAGEMENT CONTROL   487

Performance Reports as a Communication Tool, 489
Essential Features of Performance Reports, 490
The Basic Format of Performance Reports, 491
Adapt Performance Reports to Requirements of User, 494
Keep Reports Simple and Essential, 497
Minimize the Time Gap Between the Decision and the Reporting, 500
Management Follow-Up Procedures, 501
Technical Aspects of Control Reports, 501
The Integrated Performance Report, 503
January Performance Report for Superior Manufacturing Company, 506
DISCUSSION QUESTIONS, 508
CASES, 508

chapter sixteen

ANALYSIS OF BUDGET VARIANCES   513

Analysis of Sales Variances, 515
Analysis of Raw Material Variances, 517
Analysis of Direct Labor Variances, 520
Analysis of Manufacturing Overhead Variances, 522

Use of Variance Analysis, 527
DISCUSSION QUESTIONS, 528
CASES, 528

chapter seventeen

PROFIT PLANNING AND CONTROL
RELATED TO THE ACCOUNTING SYSTEM   535

Variable Costing Related to Profit Planning and Control, 536
The Distinctive Features of Variable Costing, 537
Standard Costs Related to Profit Planning and Control, 541
The Standard Cost Specification, 541
Standard Costs for Material—Accounting and Budgeting Procedures, 543
Standard Costs for Direct Labor—Accounting and Budgeting Procedures, 546
Standard Costs for Overhead—Accounting and Budgeting Procedures, 547
The Standard Cost Income Statement, 550
Variable Expense Budgets Related to Standard Costs, 551
Integration of Standard Costs and Budgeting, 551
DISCUSSION QUESTIONS, 553
CASES, 553

chapter eighteen

BUDGET PLANNING AND CONTROL
FOR NONMANUFACTURING CONCERNS   565

General Considerations, 566
The Merchandise Budget, 567
Markup Considerations, 573
Open-to-Buy Planning, 575
Budgeting Expenses, 577
Budgeting Capital Additions, 578
Budgeting Cash, 578
Budget Summaries, 578
Budget Control, 579
DISCUSSION QUESTIONS, 579
CASES, 579

chapter nineteen

AN OVERVIEW   583

Budget Adaptation, 583
System Installation, 585
Management Flexibility in Using Profit Plans, 586
Some Behavioral Implications, 589
Impact of Mathematical Models and Data Processing Systems, 593

INDEX   595

Illustrations

CHAPTER 1

1 Planning and Controlling Inflows and Outflows for Profit   *6*
2 Identification and Evaluation of Variables   *8*
3 Philosophy of the Role of Management   *9*
4 Levels of Planning   *14*
5 Planning and Control Responsibilities by Position   *15*

CHAPTER 2

6 Time Dimensions in Profit Planning and Control   *42*

CHAPTER 4

7 Organization Chart—Superior Manufacturing
Company   *94*
8 Statement of Broad Objectives—Superior Manufacturing
Company   *98*
9 Statement of Specific Goals—Superior Manufacturing
Company   *99*
10 Summary of Basic Strategies—Superior Manufacturing
Company   *100*

11 Planning Premises Letter—Superior Manufacturing Company   *101*

12 Project Proposal Summary—Superior Manufacturing Company   *104*

13 Strategic Long-range Plan (Profits)—Superior Manufacturing Company   *105*

CHAPTER 5

14 Summary of Tactical and Strategic Sales Plan   *141*

15 Worksheet—Economic Rhythm Method   *161*

CHAPTER 6

16 Planning Manufacturing Operations   *183*

17 Production and Finished Goods Inventory Budgets   *189*

18 Sales, Production, and Inventory Budgets—Proposal A   *190*

19 Sales, Production, and Inventory Budgets—Proposal B   *190*

20 Sales, Production, and Inventory Budgets—Proposal C   *191*

CHAPTER 7

21 Raw Material and Product Flow—Superior Manufacturing Company   *225*

CHAPTER 10

22 Variable Budget for Department 42   *304*

23 Fixed Costs Graphed   *307*

24 Variable Costs Graphed   *310*

25 Semivariable Costs Graphed   *311*

26 Semivariable Costs (curved) Graphed   *312*

27 Graphic Cost Analysis—Indirect Materials, Department Z   *321*

28 Indirect Material, Department Z, Least Squares   *325*

29 Typical Improvement in Cost Variability with Budget Control   *329*

30 Variable Budget—Table Method   *330*

31 Variable Budget—Formula Method   *331*

32 Expense Budget for Department 42   *332*

33 Department 42 Cost Targets for Work   *334*

34 Performance Report, Department 42   *335*

CHAPTER 11

35 Time Dimensions in Capital Expenditures Budget—Carter Company *356*

36 Long-range Capital Expenditures Budget *359*

37 Present Value Analysis—Machine A *373*

CHAPTER 12

38 Income Statement Cash Flow Method—Short Term *401*

39 Income Statement Cash Flow Method—Long Term *404*

40 Report of Cash Position Daily *407*

41 Report of Cash Position Monthly *406*

CHAPTER 13

42 Worksheet to Estimate Probable Profit *421*

43 Worksheet for Ratio Tests *423*

CHAPTER 14

44 Breakeven Chart, XYZ Company (volume in units) *451*

45 Breakeven Chart, XYZ Company (volume in dollars) *452*

46 Detailed Breakeven Chart, XYZ Company *453*

47 Breakeven Charts—Sales Mix *458*

48 Breakeven Chart—With Other Incomes and Expenses *463*

49 Breakeven Chart—Economic Characteristics *468*

50 Change in Cost Structure *470*

51 Change in Unit Sales Price *472*

52 Breakeven Analysis by Sales Districts *473*

CHAPTER 15

53 Organization Chart—SP Manufacturing Company *492*

54 Performance Reports—SP Manufacturing Company *493*

55a Graphic Presentation—Sales and Profits *498*

56a Graphic Presentation—Sales and Profits *498*

55b Tabular Presentation—Sales and Profits *499*

56b Tabular Presentation—Sales and Profits *499*

57 Departmental Performance Report *504*

58 Performance Report, List of Schedules—Superior Manufacturing Company *507*

CHAPTER 17

59 Income Statement—Variable Cost Approach   *538*

60 Simplified Standard Cost Flow Chart   *542*

61 Standard Cost Specification—Able Company   *543*

62 Income Statement—Standard Cost Approach   *550*

CHAPTER 18

63 Simplified Organization Chart of a Department Store   *566*

64 Distribution of Planned Net Sales by Month   *568*

65 Distribution of Planned Net Sales by Department   *569*

66 Computation of BOM Stock Levels   *571*

67 Computation of Purchases at Retail   *572*

68 Computation of Purchases at Cost   *573*

CHAPTER 19

69 Illustrative Data for Estimation of Future Performance   *588*

70 Estimation of Future Performance   *589*

Schedules

(for Superior Manufacturing Company)

CHAPTER 4

1 Sales Plan Summary By Product, By District   *108*
2 Production Budget Summary By Product Units   *109*
3 Direct Materials Budget Summary in Units By Material,
   By Product, By Department   *109*
4 Purchases Budget Summary   *110*
5 Direct Labor Budget Summary By Product, By Department   *111*
6 Building Services Budget Summary   *112*
7 Manufacturing Overhead Budget Summary By Department   *114*
8 Budget of Initial and Final Inventories   *115*
9 Cost of Goods Sold Budget Summary   *116*
10 Distribution Expense Budget Summary   *117*
11 Administrative Expense Budget Summary   *117*
12 Budget of Other Incomes and Expenses   *118*
13 Statement of Planned Income   *118*
14 Statement of Planned Retained Earnings   *118*
15 Capital Additions Budget Summary   *119*
16 Cash Flow Budget Summary   *120*
17 Projected Balance Sheet   *121*
18 Variable Expense Budget—Manufacturing Division   *122*
19 Sales Performance Report by District, By Product   *124*
20 Performance Report on Factory Overhead   *125*

CHAPTER 5

21 Marketing Plan (Detailed) By Product, Time, and District   *169*

CHAPTER 6

22 Production Plan (Detailed) By Product, By Time   *202*
23 Finished Goods Inventory Budget   *203*

CHAPTER 7

24 Materials Budget—Unit Requirements for Raw Materials
    By Material, Product, By Time Periods   *226*
25 Materials Budget—Unit Requirements for Raw Materials
    By Product, Department and Time   *227*
26 Purchases Budget   *228*
27 Raw Material Inventory Budget in Units and Dollars   *229*
28 Estimated Cost of Materials Used for Production   *230*
29 Estimated Cost of Materials Used for
    Production—Summary   *232*

CHAPTER 8

30 Direct Labor Budget   *250*
31 Budgeted Direct Labor Hours   *252*

CHAPTER 9

32 Expense Budget—Building Services   *279*
33 Factory Expense Budgets (Service Departments)   *280*
34 Factory Expense Budgets (Producing Departments)   *282*
35 Computation of Planned Overhead Rates   *284*
36 Manufacturing Expenses Applied by Product   *287*
37 Budgeted Overhead Over/Under Applied   *289*
38 Promotion Plan Summary   *289*
39 Selling Expense Budgets   *290*
40 Administrative Expense Budgets   *292*

CHAPTER 10

41 Variable Budget—Manufacturing Division
    (Service Department)   *337*
42 Variable Budget—Manufacturing Division
    (Producing Department)   *338*

43 Variable Budget—Sales Division   *339*
44 Variable Budget—Administrative Division   *340*
45 Least Squares Worksheet—General Sales Overhead   *342*

CHAPTER 11

46 Annual Capital Expenditures Budget   *378*
47 Schedule of Budgeted Depreciation   *379*

CHAPTER 12

48 Cash Inflow from Sales and Accounts Receivable   *389*
49 Planned Cash Inflows from Other Incomes   *390*
50 Summary of Budgeted Cash Inflows   *391*
51 Budgeted Cash Required for Purchases of Raw Materials   *392*
52 Budgeted Cash Required for Expenses   *395*
53 Cash Requirements for Accrued Items, Deferred Items, Dividends, and Income Taxes   *396*
54 Summary of Cash Requirements   *397*
55 Comparison of Estimated Cash Receipts and Disbursements   *398*
56 Budgeted Short Term Financing Requirements   *399*
57 Final Cash Budget   *400*

CHAPTER 13

58 Estimated Cost of Goods Manufactured—Detailed   *428*
59 Estimated Cost of Goods Manufactured—Summary   *429*
60 Budget Worksheet—Cost of Goods Sold and Finished Goods Inventory   *430*
61 Budgeted Cost of Goods Sold   *433*
62 Budgeted Cost of Goods Sold—Summary   *434*
63 Finished Goods Inventory Budget   *435*
64 Budgeted Income Statement—By Time Periods   *436*
65 Budgeted Income Statement—By Sales Districts   *437*
66 Budgeted Income Statement—By Product   *438*
67 Budget Worksheet   *439*
68 Budgeted Balance Sheet—January   *441*
69 Budgeted Changes in Working Capital Balances   *442*
70 Budgeted Flows of Working Capital   *442*

CHAPTER 14

71 Income and Cost Data for Cost-Volume-Profit Analysis   *476*
72 Breakeven Chart   *478*

Preface

The fourth edition is designed for (a) a one-semester, or term, course in managerial accounting where the primary focus is on the broad aspects of comprehensive profit planning and control; (b) a course in management accounting emphasizing the broad processes of planning and control; (c) supplementary materials in a wide range of management, industrial engineering, and management accounting courses; and (d) executive development programs. In addition, the book has been revised to be particularly useful to a wide range of managers in industry, government, and nonprofit enterprises. It focuses on general management and not on accounting, decision models, or technical topics. Therefore, at the end of each chapter there is included a series of discussion questions that follow the sequential development in the chapter and a series of short cases designed to involve the student in broad applications of the subject matter of the chapter. The instructor's manual includes appropriate responses to the questions and extensive discussion suggestions for each case. This edition has been especially written for those who are not sophisticated in the subject, and an attempt has been made to present the subject matter clearly and simply so that the reader will be in a position, whether in the classroom or in practice, to move immediately to higher levels of sophistication in understanding and application. This book is designed, not for the expert, but for those interested in the practical application of this dynamic approach to managing as opposed to being designed for those interested in highly theoretical and complex excursions in areas of disagreement. Although the behavioral implications of profit planning and control and the significance of mathematical models are pinpointed throughout the book, no effort has been made to treat either of these subjects in detail. The objective is to provide a complete explanation of the profit planning and control process and how it is applied. This gives the instructor ample time to enrich the course in other ways, such as with the use of cases, the relevant contributions by behavorial science and decision models. This is not a book in management science; the reader who is interested in exploring the highly significant mathematical models and computer applications in profit planning and control is provided selected references for further study. Because of the practical focus of the discussions, many instructors turn to publications by Chamberlain and Ackoff for conceptual expansion of the subject (see Footnote 4 to Chapter 1).

Dynamic profit planning and control is a broad approach to accomplishing the management function; its development and usefulness have significantly increased in recent years. It is especially significant in that the functional areas of management are brought into focus, creating a mutual enrichment of functions between management and the measurement of performance that is a vital feature in the successful life of progressive enterprises. Its full potential frequently is limited by a gap between the mechanics of the system and its conceptual sophistication and pervasive applications. In developing the essential features of a comprehensive profit planning and control program, this book focuses on the usefulness of profit planning and control in aiding management in accomplishing the basic functions of planning, coordination, and control. The book strives to provide a broad view of the subject with a minimum of attention to mechanics, the intricacies of accounting, and non-essential details. The conceptual foundations and their practical application are the core of the subject matter. The concepts and techniques in current use by eminently successful enterprises are introduced as general concepts and then explained in sufficient detail to permit application to the particular management problems in large and small enterprises. Explicit in the exposition, however, is the realization that a profit planning and control program must be tailor-made to fit each particular situation and that the real essence of management is the human factor as opposed to a particular set of concepts or techniques.

A typical comprehensive profit planning and control program is outlined and illustrated throughout the book to provide continuity for the reader and to emphasize the interrelationship of the areas, concepts and techniques. The illustrative problem is continuous from chapter to chapter.

A significant feature of the fourth edition is the deletion of practically all "pencil-pushing" problems and the inclusion of cases designed to require the student to think imaginatively, to identify a problem, to weigh the various factors bearing on it, to evolve alternatives, to take a position, and finally to be prepared to defend his position. In class, the student should be required to explain his point of view, to defend it, to understand and appraise the positions espoused by his classmates, to recognize viable alternatives, and to decide what alternatives appear to be the more realistic in the light of the situation. Practice in doing these things helps to increase the competence of the students to resolve problems as opposed to completing a series of "cookbook" computations. Additional case materials may be found in my book on *Cases in Profit Planning and Control* (Englewood Cliffs, N.J.: Prentice-Hall, Inc., 1970).

I express my gratitude to the educators, graduate students, and businessmen who have provided numerous suggestions for improving the materials in the fourth edition. I also wish to thank Richard Ratliff for editorial and substantive suggestions for the manuscript.

Comments from executives, accountants, and teachers will be sincerely appreciated by the author.

Glenn A. Welsch

Profit Planning and Control and the Management Process

chapter one

Since the turn of the century substantial advances have been made in the art and science of managing group efforts in industry, government, and other endeavors. The focus of this work is primarily on the management process in profit-oriented enterprises, although the concepts and procedures discussed have wide application in other characteristically related activities of our society. Fundamentally, management is the coordination of human effort, that is, the accomplishment of goals by utilizing the efforts of other people. The effectiveness with which an endeavor is managed has come to be recognized in most instances as perhaps the single, most essential ingredient to long-range success of that endeavor. The management process may be viewed as the total management effort operating in a particular endeavor that includes decision-making, the application of selected techniques and procedures, and the motivation of individuals and groups to accomplish specified objectives. One of the more important approaches that has been developed for facilitating effective performance of the management process is comprehensive profit planning and control (managerial budgeting). The concepts and techniques of profit planning and control, as discussed in this book, have wide application in individual business enterprises, governmental units, charitable organizations, and virtually all group endeavors.

Both business and nonbusiness endeavors necessarily must have objectives and goals. In business endeavors there is the multiple objective of profit and contribution to the economic and social improvement of the broader environment. Likewise, nonbusiness endeavors have relatively precise objectives, such as the accomplishment of a given mission or effect, generally within specified cost constraints. In both cases it is absolutely essential that the management of the endeavor, as well as other properly interested parties, know the objectives and goals; otherwise, effective managerial guidance of the activities and measurement of the effectiveness with which desired activities are performed are impossible. Thus, the planning, coordination, and control responsibilities of management are fundamentally identical in business and nonbusiness enterprises; the broad management process essentially conforms to a common pattern, whatever the type of endeavor.

In many diverse situations today a high degree of managerial efficiency is obvious to a perceptive observer. Competitive pressures, whether in business or nonbusiness endeavors, impose upon management the necessity to employ, in a sophisticated way, managerial approaches and techniques that have been developed and validated as especially relevant in accomplishing the management process with maximum long-range effectiveness. One does not need to look far into the available literature—management development programs currently being conducted or records of conferences devoted to the subject of general management—to observe that the broad concept of profit planning and control in recent years has been accorded a unique and relevant role. In order to keep pace with the competition among profit-making enterprises, modern management has found that it must chart its course in advance and use appropriate techniques to assure coordination and control of operations. By following a planning and control approach, attainment of enterprise goals is more likely. As a consequence, the concept of comprehensive profit planning and control has found wide acceptance in recent years in the better-managed companies. Surveying well-managed companies, researchers generally find that practically all those companies utilized a comprehensive profit planning and control program on a continuing basis.

PLAN OF THE BOOK

The first four chapters present the basic foundations and an overview of the broad subject of profit planning and control. Chapters 5 through 13 focus on the development of profit plans and variable budgets. These chapters discuss the topics, starting with sales planning, in an order that tends to parallel the actual planning and control cycle. Chapter 14 focuses on the important concept of cost-volume-profit analysis. Chapters 15 and 16 discuss performance reports and variation analyses. Chapter 17 deals with the accounting system including contribution accounting and standard costs as related to the profit planning and control program. Chapter 18 considers some special planning and control problems of department stores. The final chapter is a summary, emphasizing the broad impacts of the computer revolution and behavioral factors.[1]

COMPREHENSIVE PROFIT PLANNING AND CONTROL DEFINED

In recent years the phrase "comprehensive profit planning and control" has been used extensively in the literature of business. Other terms sometimes used in the same context are *comprehensive budgeting, managerial budgeting,* and *budgeting.* The term comprehensive profit planning and control may be broadly defined as a systematic and formalized approach for accomplishing the planning, coordination, and control responsibilities of management. Specifically, it involves the development and application of (1) broad and long-range objectives for the enterprise; (2) specification of enterprise goals, (3) a long-range profit plan developed in broad terms; (4) a short-range profit plan detailed by relevant responsibilities (divisions, products, projects); (5) a system of periodic performance reports detailed by assigned responsibilities; and (6) follow-up procedures. Implicit in the concept of profit planning and control are realism, flexibility, and continuing attention to the planning and control functions of management. This definition recognizes management as the critical success factor in the long-run destiny of the enterprise. Also implicit is the confidence that a competent management can plan for, manipulate, and control in large measure the *relevant variables* that dominate the life of the enterprise. In many of the better-managed companies, comprehensive profit planning and control has been identified as a "way of managing." It focuses directly upon a rational and systematic approach to *management by objectives* and realistic *flexibility* in performing the management process. It is the only comprehensive approach to managing so far developed that, if utilized with sophistication and good judgment, fully recognizes the dominant role of the manager and provides a framework for implementing such fundamental aspects of scientific management as management by objectives, effective communication, participative management, dynamic control, continuous feedback, responsibility accounting, management by exception, and managerial flexibility. The definition also implies the application of profit planning and control principles and procedures to all phases of the operations of an enterprise. In summary, profit

---

[1] Although the discussions in this book do not require an in depth background in management accounting, the following supplemental sources are recommended: As background, Robert N. Anthony and Glenn A. Welsch, *Fundamentals of Management Accounting* (Homewood, Ill.: Richard D. Irwin, Inc., 1974); As supplemental, Charles T. Horngren, *Cost Accounting: A Managerial Emphasis*, 3rd ed. (Englewood Cliffs, N.J.: Prentice-Hall, Inc., 1972).

planning and control means the development and acceptance of objectives and goals and moving an organization efficiently to achieve the objectives and goals.

In order to gain a sophisticated understanding of the broad concept of comprehensive profit planning and control, one must realize that it approaches the total systems concept that integrates all the functional and operational aspects of an enterprise. Throughout, this book emphasizes the integration and interrelationship of the various functions and subfunctions in a business that are essential for effective management. Wide participation of all levels of management from all the subdivisions of the enterprise also is emphasized as being fundamental to effective profit planning and control. Although profit planning and control is related to accounting—as it is to the other functions of the business—it cannot be properly classified as an accounting technique; rather, it is a *management system*. Comprehensive profit planning and control does have a unique relationship to the accounting system in the enterprise in the following respects: (1) accounting provides inputs of historical data (usually quantitative) that are particularly relevant for analytical purposes in the development of enterprise plans; (2) the financial component of a profit plan generally is structured in an accounting format; (3) actual data utilized in the measurement of performance (actual data are compared with planned data) are provided in large measure by the accounting system. A comprehensive profit planning and control program can be developed and adapted to any particular accounting system. However, it will be emphasized here that in many business enterprises a financial planning and control approach built around the following concepts has particular relevance: (1) profit planning; (2) responsibility accounting; (3) contribution accounting (direct costing); (4) standard costs; (5) variable expense budgets; and (6) comprehensive performance reports.

In order to gain a depth of understanding of the concept of comprehensive profit planning and control one must recognize that it is not a "separate technique" that can be thought of and operated independently of the total management process. Rather, the broad concept of profit planning and control entails an integration of numerous managerial approaches and techniques that might be exploited, such as sales forecasting, sales quota systems, capital budgeting, cash flow analysis, cost-volume-profit analysis, variable budgets, time and motion study, standard cost accounting, strategic planning, production planning and control, inventory control, management by objectives, organizational planning, manpower planning, and cost control.

THE ROLE OF MANAGEMENT

Comprehensive profit planning and control is justified only to the extent that it serves to facilitate performance of the management process. Accounting, which reports historical data, can also be justified by reasons of public information, stockholders' rights, government reports and requirements, creditors' demands, and others; in contrast, profit planning and control is strictly internal in its scope. Therefore, in order for a comprehensive profit planning and control program to be justified, it must result in relevant benefits directly related to the effective accomplishment of the basic responsibilities of management. How, then, is comprehensive profit planning and control related to the functions of management? A response to this question suggests a brief consideration of the basic functions of management and the nature of the management process.[2]

Technological advances and the evolution of scientific management have been perhaps the two most significant factors in the economic development of the United States since the turn of the century. Scientific management does not involve a formalized, highly complex system but is based rather upon the idea that a scientific approach—investigation, analysis, and systematic decision-making approaches—should be used to carry out effectively the managerial process.

Fayol, one of the more perceptive observers of the management process, wrote that all activities of an industrial undertaking could be divided into six groups:[3] (1) technical (production), (2) commercial (buying, selling, and exchange), (3) financial (search for, and use of capital), (4) security (protection of property and persons), (5) accounting (including statistics), and (6) managerial (planning, organization, command, coordination, and control).

Fayol very perceptively identified a *managerial activity*, basically viewed as the effort required to assure accomplishment of the other five activities listed. He noted that the other activities were accomplished by managers *through people*; thus, people is the basic subject of management—not land, buildings, or raw materials. Koontz and O'Donnell called attention to the fact that in "classifying" the functions of management, one must distinguish clearly those of *operation*, such as selling, manufacturing, accounting, engineering, and purchasing. These differ from one enterprise to another, but the *functions of the manager* are common to all. Koontz and O'Donnell state further that "the most useful method of classifying managerial functions is to group them around the activities of *planning, organizing, staffing, directing,* and *control.* It is not always possible in practice to slice all managerial functions neatly into these categories, since the functions tend to coalesce; however, this classification is a helpful and realistic tool for analysis and understanding." Throughout this book the five-category classification of the functions of

[2] For an excellent treatment of management theory see: Harold Koontz and Cyril O'Donnell, *Principles of Management, An Analysis of Managerial Functions,* 5th ed. (New York: McGraw-Hill Book Co., Inc. 1972) and George A. Steiner, *Top Management Planning* (New York: The Macmillan Company, 1969).

[3] H. Fayol, *General and Industrial Administration* (London: Sir Issac Pitman & Sons, Ltd., 1949). Also see interpretive comments in Koontz and O'Donnell, *Management,* p. 22.

management by Koontz and D'Donnell listed above will be utilized with primary emphasis on the planning and control functions.

The essence of the planning and control functions of management rests upon some fundamental or philosophical views of the real role of management in an endeavor. In harmony with some of these views, profit planning and control rests upon the conviction that a management can plan and control the long-range destiny of the enterprise by making a continuing stream of well-conceived decisions; the concept speaks to planned prosperity as opposed to unplanned happenstance. Thus, the thrust of the comprehensive profit planning and control concept goes to the very heart of managing, that is, the decision-making process. Specifically, for long-range success the stream of managerial decisions must generate plans and actions to provide the essential inflows that are necessary to support the planned outflows of the enterprise so that realistic profits and return on investments are earned. Continuing generation of profits by managerial manipulation of the inflows and outflows provides the substance of profit planning and control. These relationships are presented simply in Illustration 1. In Illustration 1, it may

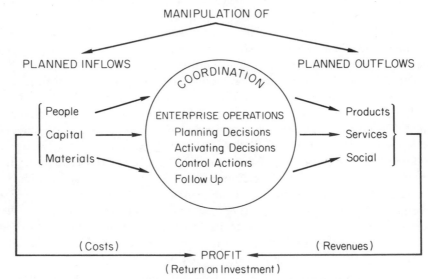

ILLUSTRATION 1. Planning and Controlling Inflows and Outflows for Profit

be noted that the essential inflows are people, capital, and materials and that they are generally cost-incurring factors. On the other hand, the planned outflows are products, services, and social contributions that the enterprise generates. The planned outflows of products and services generally are revenue-generating factors. Now the essential responsibility of management is to manipulate, through the management process, the combinations of planned inflows and planned outflows so that the long-range objectives of the enterprise are attained. In a profit-making situation, the principle measure of the accomplishment of long-range objectives must be in terms of profit and return on investment. In the discussions to follow, manipulation of the relevant variables by a management implies a stream of well-conceived decisions directed toward accomplishment of the *specified* long-range objectives of the enterprise. The managerial decisions must be both *purposive* and *futuristic*. By *futuristic* we mean that the important managerial decisions must be fundamentally concerned with the long-range future in contrast to "spur-of-the-moment" decisions. By *purposive* we mean that the stream of important managerial decisions must be primarily concerned with developing purpose, that is, enterprise objectives, and with devising realistic strategies to attain those objectives. The stream of decisions must demonstrate implicit managerial self-confidence that the destiny of the firm can be effectively planned and controlled. Decision-making first and foremost requires imagination and courage; each major decision of management involves an effort to create or seize a positive opportunity or to escape the onset of decline. The decision-making process must be rational and systematic yet responsive to the uniqueness of the environment surrounding each major decision.

Fundamentally, then, managerial decision-making entails the tasks of (1) manipulating the relevant *controllable variables* and (2) taking advantage of the relevant *noncontrollable variables* that may influence long-run operational success. Illustration 2 is presented to reflect in a direct manner how a management may initially—and periodically—approach the problem of identifying and evaluating the *relevant variables* for its particular firm. The analysis is designed to provide some initial insights essential to developing realistic plans and strategies for the enterprise. The relevant variables affecting the firm are presented in a three-way classification scheme in Illustration 2: external v. internal; time dimension; and controllability v. noncontrollability. The last column, Strategy and Planning Reference, provides a key to the plans and strategies devised with respect to each variable. Of particular relevance is the classification of each variable as to controllability or noncontrollability in the short-, intermediate-, or long-range time horizons. It is this classification in particular that provides the management with insights that may suggest desirable strategies for the future. An especially salient generalization may be made at this point. The *controllable variables* are those that can be actively planned and manipulated by the management. In direct contrast, the *noncontrollable variables* cannot be influenced by the management, yet this does not mean that effective planning with respect to them is not possible. Significantly, the noncontrollable variables must be projected and "planned for" so as to take full advantage of their anticipated favorable impacts and to minimize their unfavorable impacts. Thus, we observe that managerial planning is necessary with respect to all of the relevant variables. Herein lies a subtle trap for many managements—that is, to assume that

ILLUSTRATION 2. Identification and Evaluation of Variables

RELEVANT VARIABLES*	MANIPULATION BASIS						STRATEGY AND PLANNING REFERENCE
	SHORT-RANGE		INTER-MEDIATE		LONG-RANGE		
	Ct	NCt	C	NC	C	NC	
External:							
Population		x		x		x	
GNP		x		x		x	
Industry sales		x		x	x		
Competitive activities		x		x		x	
Industry (in which to compete)		x		x	x		
Product lines		x	x		x		
etc.							
Internal:							
Employees—quality		x	x		x		
Employees—quantity	x		x		x		
Capital—sources	x		x		x		
Capital—amount	x		x		x		
Research—nature		x	x		x		
Research—cost	x		x		x		
Advertising	x		x		x		
Pricing product		x	x		x		
Sales methods	x		x		x		
Production methods		x	x		x		
Operating costs—fixed	x		x		x		
Operating costs—variable	x		x		x		
etc.							

*Illustrative only; classification unique to each situation
†C—Controllable; NC—Noncontrollable

they should plan for and consider primarily the controllable variables since "we can't do anything about the uncontrollable variables." To restate this important point in a different way, management, to be effective, also must anticipate the noncontrollable variables, evaluate their potential effects, and make plans consistent with those evaluations. Additionally, an evaluation and analysis is important so that the interrelationships between the controllable and noncontrollable variables may be taken into account. For example, the impact of certain noncontrollable variables on one or more of the controllable variables may be both significant and pervasive in a particular situation.

The preceding paragraph aims to pose the fundamental question of the real role of management. There are conceptual or philosophical disagreements as to the real role of management in both business and nonbusiness entities. A brief look at the opposite extremes of conceptual disagreements may add to our insights. One extreme pole has been labeled as the *market theory*, and at the opposite end of the spectrum is the *planning and control theory.*[4] These two opposing philosophies are presented in a direct way in Illustration 3. Observe that the market theory, in the extreme sense, views the managerial role basically as comprising reactive decisions that respond to environmental events as they occur. This view accords a passive role to management. In direct contrast, the planning and control theory views the

ILLUSTRATION 3. Philosophy of the Role of Management

MARKET THEORY	PLANNING AND CONTROL THEORY
Conceptual:	
1. Management is solely at the whim of the prevailing economic, social, and political forces (environment).	1. The future destiny of the enterprise can be manipulated; hence, it can be planned and controlled by the management.
2. As a consequence, management essentially fills the role of a fortune teller—reading the environment.	2. Good managers can contrive realistic means to achieve the objectives.
3. When the environment is read the reactive managerial decisions are made.	3. Management can manipulate the controllable variables and plan for the non-controllable variables.
4. Therefore, managerial competence (success) depends on the ability to read the environment and to react wisely.	4. Therefore, the quality of managerial planning decisions determines managerial competence.
Reactive (Ex Post) Decisions	Active (Ex Ante) Decisions
(Management reads events that are happening and then reacts to them.)	(Management anticipates future events and plans accordingly.)

management role essentially as an active one that attempts to condition the state of the enterprise. The latter theory obviously maximizes the importance of the planning function of management. The concept of comprehensive profit planning and control rests firmly upon the planning and control theory, that is, that the primary success factor in an enterprise is the competence of management to plan and to control enterprise activities. This notion says that a management earns its "bread and butter" only if it can, in fact, plan and control in ways that determine the long-range destiny of the enterprise. The foundation for profit planning and control then is that the management must have absolute confidence in its ability to establish realistic objectives and to devise efficient strategies to attain those objectives for the enterprise.

[4] The following three sources are highly recommended for their excellent conceptual exposition of these and numerous related theories mentioned throughout this book: Neil W. Chamberlain, *The Firm: Micro-Economic Planning and Action* (New York: McGraw-Hill Book Co., Inc., 1962); also by the same author and publisher: *Enterprise and Environment: The Firm in Time and Place* (1968); and Russell L. Ackoff, *A Concept of Corporate Planning* (New York: John Wiley & Sons, 1970).

The market theory argues very little for the concept of profit planning and control.

In the real world, enterprise management normally must operate somewhere between the two conceptual extremes represented in Illustration 3. Clearly, some companies from time to time find themselves in situations where the noncontrollable variables appear dominant enough to determine the destiny of the firm. This observation is particularly true in many situations when viewed in the short run. However, such situations do not deny the profit planning and control theory; there are many variables in practically every situation that an enlightened and imaginative management can manipulate that will have a dominant impact on the long-range future success of the endeavor. For example, a competent management, finding itself in an environment (industry, market area, product line, geographical location, political situation) where the long-range destiny of the enterprise is dominated by the noncontrollable variables, very quickly will devise avenues for moving to environments where the controllable variables tend to dominate. Competent managers, and rational investors as well, generally are not interested in operating in an environment that is completely random. Thus, it would appear that the closer to the planning and control theory that a management can operate, the greater the opportunities to reduce the "randomness" and the greater the significance of managerial competence.

In this context we can elaborate on the five management functions identified by Koontz and O'Donnell (see page 5):

1. Planning
   a. Evaluate relevant variables.
   b. Establish enterprise objectives.
   c. Disaggregate enterprise objectives as specified goals.
   d. Develop strategies for attaining the specified objectives and goals.
   e. Operationalize objectives, goals, and strategies by developing a profit plan.
2. Organizing
   a. Develop a structure (subdivision) of the tasks to be performed in accomplishing the enterprise objectives and plans.
   b. Identify structural tasks with specific individuals through assignment of authorities and responsibilities.
3. Staffing
   a. Assess and define manpower requirements consistent with the enterprise objectives and plans.

    b. Employ competent people and develop training programs for increasing that competence.

4. Directing

    a. Exert dynamic leadership in activating and executing the plans and strategies.

    b. Develop a work situation that provides positive motivation for the individual and groups.

5. Controlling

    a. Continually measure performance and compare actual results with the plans and standards of performance.

    b. Continually use supervision and feedback to improve performance through corrective action.

We will now focus on the planning and control functions of management.

THE MANAGEMENT PLANNING FUNCTION

We have viewed the broad role of management in a philosophical way. It is now appropriate to focus on the management planning function. This section will attempt to explain the broad concept, to indicate its importance, and to introduce some approaches and techniques in accomplishing it.

Management planning has been defined as the design of a desired future state for an entity and of effective ways of bringing it about.[5]

A fundamental purpose of management planning is to provide for a *feedforward process*. The concept of feedforward is to provide each manager with guidelines for making operational decisions on a day-to-day basis. The approved plans constitute the primary element of feedforward (also see Chapter 15). Planning is generally recognized as the most difficult task facing the manager, and it is one on which it is very easy to procrastinate.

The above definition clearly indicates that planning is a decision-making process. Since it is a decision-making process of the highest order, it requires management time and dedication, and a systematic approach. The decisions made in the planning process are: (1) anticipatory, since they are made some time in advance of action, and (2) interrelated, since they comprise broad groups of interdependent choices (from an array of alternatives) by the management. Ackoff presents a particularly useful distinction between strategic and tactical planning. (Perhaps a more frequent, but less funda-

---

[5] Adapted from Russell L. Ackoff, *A Concept of Corporate Planning* (New York: John Wiley & Sons, Wiley-Interscience Division, 1970), p. 1.

mental, distinction is between long-term and short-term planning.) The distinction between strategic and tactical planning is related to three dimensions, which may be outlined as follows:

		DIMENSIONS	
CLASSIFICATION	TIME	SCOPE OF ENTITY ACTIVITIES	ORIENTATION
Strategic	Long-term	Broad View of Activities	Objectives and Goals
Tactical	Short-term	Detailed View of Activities	Means to Attain Goals

Since the description for each of the three dimensions is in relative terms, there are some arbitrary distinctions. Generally, strategic planning is viewed as planning beyond one year; deals with the broad subdivisions of the entity (such as divisions but not departments); and focuses on objectives and goals that extend over the long term. Throughout the discussions to follow we will use the terms *strategic* and *long-term*, and *tactical* and *short-term*, interchangeably. The distinction between strategic and tactical planning is important in structuring the planning process for an entity.

Planning rests upon the belief that the future state of an entity can be enhanced by continuous management action. It presupposes that an entity can be more successful, in terms of its broad objectives, because of planned management decisions (to implement the *feedforward concept*) than it can if there were no planned intervention by the management. On this basis Ackoff suggests that the management of an entity, during the planning process, should engage in three different types of "projections" as follows:[6]

1. A reference projection—an attempt to specify what the future state of the entity would be if nothing new is done; that is, if there is no planned intervention by the management.

2. A wishful projection—a specification of the "hopes and dreams" as to the future state of the entity; that is, essential fulfillment of all of the aspirations of the entity.

3. A planned projection—a specification of how closely the entity can attain the wishful projection realistically. The planned projection tends to be a realistic compromise between the reference and wishful projections. The planned projection, then, would represent the planned objectives and goals (for example, the future state) to be attained during the time covered by the planning process.

Therefore, planning should start with a reference projection, coupled with a wishful projection, and conclude with a planning projection that

[6] Ibid., Chapter 5.

represents the management plan. Obviously, the planning projection would be more formal than the others.

Management planning is a continuous process, as opposed to a periodic endeavor, since a planned projection can never be considered as the final and ultimate product. It must be revised as conditions change and new information becomes available.

From another viewpoint, management planning may be approached with absolute informality at one extreme, or from complete formality at the other extreme. Formality is used here to indicate the extent to which (1) the planning process is structured (or systematized), and (2) the planning decisions are expressed in the form of written plans and standardized financial results (as in a budget). Numerous studies have shown that the better-managed companies strike a reasonable balance on this point, with a strong tendency toward a systematic approach to planning and expression of the results in a comprehensive profit plan and related expressions. However, these managements clearly appreciate the serious hazards of making a fetish of overformalization.

The planning decisions are interacting ones and must be partitioned to accord with the operational (or organizational) subdivisions of the entity. Therefore, planning follows the lines of authority and responsibility in the enterprise. This subdivision means that there is a subset of planning decisions (and a consequent plan) for each manager in the entity (for each area of responsibility) from the highest level to the lowest management level. It makes possible effective and integrated application of the feedforward concept.

Let us return to the previously discussed concepts of strategic and tactical planning and the management function of planning. Each facet of planning must encompass an evaluation, or re-evaluation, of the relevant variables (both controllable and noncontrollable) since they will have significant impacts on the planning of realistic objectives and goals. The establishment of *enterprise objectives* represents the most fundamental level of decision making in the planning process. Objectives represent an expression of the broad, long-range future state desired. For example, the objectives for a manufacturing company would relate to such basic issues as breadth of product lines, quality of product, growth expectations, responsibilities to the owners, economic expectations, relationships (attitudes) with respect to employees, and social responsibilities. Objectives express the desired future states and the end results of entity activities.

In contrast, the next level is known as *goals*, which represent the broad objectives brought into sharper focus by explicitly specifying (a) time dimensions for attainment, (b) quantitative measurements, and (c) subdivision of responsibilities. For example, the goals would explicitly state such items as: in Year 3 the new product will be introduced; in Year 1 the return investment goal is 15 percent; and in the upcoming year the profit goal for Plant A is 5 percent of sales.

In order to establish the foundation for attainment of the enterprise objectives and the specific goals, the management must develop *strategies* to be pursued by the entity. Strategies specify the "how;" they represent the plan of attack to be used in pursuing the goals operationally. For example, in a manufacturing company the strategies may include expansion of sales territory, low selling price to attract higher volume, increased advertising, and financing expansion with debt rather than equity.

Finally, the most detailed level of planning occurs when the management *operationalizes* the objectives, goals, and strategies by developing one or more *profit plans*. A profit plan is a financial and narrative expression of the expected results from the planning decisions. It is called the profit plan (or the budget) because it explicitly states the goals in terms of time expectations and expected financial results (return on investment, profit, costs) for each major segment of the entity. Typical profit plans follow the format of the internal accounting reports in respect to operations, inputs, outputs, and financial position used in the entity for monthly reporting to the management.

Two concurrent profit plans are typically developed; one strategic (long-range) and one tactical (short-range). The strategic profit plan is broad and usually encompasses five or more years in the future. The tactical profit plan normally is quite detailed and encompasses a one-year time horizon—the upcoming year. These and certain related concepts are summarized in Illustration 4.

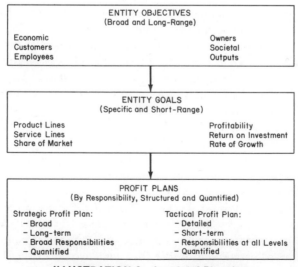

ILLUSTRATION 4.   Levels of Planning

The planning function should vary in scope and intensity with the level of management—top management has a much broader planning responsibility than lower management—yet each level of management should have definite planning responsibilities. A generalized expression of the relationship between planning and control responsibilities related to the structural position of the individual manager is depicted in Illustration 5.

ILLUSTRATION 5. Planning and Control Responsibilities by Position

POSITION	PROPORTION OF TIME SPENT ON—
Chairman President Executive Vice President Vice President Division Head Department Head Assistant Department Head Supervisor Foreman Assistant Foreman Worker	The Planning Function The Control Function

One of the salient features of comprehensive profit planning and control is the fact that it establishes a basis for participative management. This term has been used widely to suggest the relevance of bringing all levels of management directly into the planning process because of the behavioral implications. The profit planning and control approach establishes a systematic approach for the involvement of all management levels in the planning process. The relevant approaches for accomplishing this goal will be discussed in subsequent chapters; at this point we are primarily concerned with the underlying behavioral reasons. There are at least three basic principles involved. First, the active participation of all managerial levels in shaping the desired goals and the plans for achieving them has a positive behavioral effect on interest, enthusiasm, and morale. Second, active participation by all members of management makes them aware of how their particular responsibilities fit into the total operation of the enterprise and of the necessity for interdepartmental cooperation. Members of middle management, for example, can appreciate how arbitrary decisions based on narrow considerations of single departments may create crucial problems in other departments. Such decisions, within the narrow departmental scope, may appear to be the most logical, but their overall effect on the enterprise may actually be detrimental. Third, junior members of management, having participated in the planning function, are more fully informed of the future with respect to objectives, problems, and other considerations. Thus, we note a positive behavioral approach to enhancing communication in the enterprise. It is discouraging and damaging to the morale of a lower-level supervisor to be "in the dark" about what is expected in the future and the goals of his particular function. Under such circumstances, which are not uncommon, lower supervisory personnel find it almost impossible to make effective and adequate plans for their departmental operations or to make day-to-day decisions with confidence. These conditions can best be corrected by bringing all management levels into the planning process in a continuing and meaningful way; the behavioral implications are enormous.

THE CONTROL FUNCTION RELATED TO PROFIT PLANNING AND CONTROL

Control may be defined simply as the action necessary to assure that objectives, plans, policies, and standards are being attained. Control presupposes *feedforward*; that is, that objectives, plans, policies, and standards have been developed and communicated to those managers who have performance responsibility for their accomplishment. Consequently, effective control necessarily must rest upon a firm foundation of management planning. Control also is based upon the concept of feedback, which requires performance measurements and triggers corrective action designed to assure attainment of the objectives. When plans become operational, control must be exercised in order to measure progress. In some cases control also results in revision of prior plans and goals or even in the formulation of new plans, changes in operations, and reassignment of people. Control approaches must be tailored to the characteristics of the operation and to the individuals involved. All of these aspects suggest that there is a *control* process that encompasses the following:

1. Measurements of performance against predetermined objectives, plans, and standards.
2. Communication (reporting) of the results of the measurement process to the appropriate managers.
3. An analysis of the deviations from the objectives, plans, policies, and standards in order to determine the underlying causes.
4. Consideration of alternative courses of action that may be taken to correct indicated deficiencies and to learn from successes.
5. Choice and implementation of the most promising alternative.
6. Follow-up to appraise the effectiveness of the corrective action and a feedback of information to the planning process to improve future planning and control cycles.[7]

[7] In contrast, Ackoff (see footnote 4 in this chapter) states that the control process involves four steps: (1) Predicting the outcomes of decisions in the form of performance measures;

An important aspect of control that is frequently overlooked is its relationship to the point of action. Control cannot be *ex post facto*; for example, an expenditure already made or an inefficiency already committed can hardly be undone. Thus, effective control must be exercised at the point of action or at the time of commitment. This concept implies that the manager responsible for certain actions must engage in a form of prior control (*ex ante*); to do this, the predetermined objectives, plans, policies, and standards must have been communicated to the manager and fully understood by the manager in advance. With such information at hand the manager is in a position to exercise control at the point of action (the decision point). This fact emphasizes why the concept of feedforward is so fundamental.

The comparison of actual results with planned goals and standards constitutes *measurement of the effectiveness of control* during a specified *past period* that provides the basis for effective feedback. The facts shown in a performance report cannot be changed; however, the historical measurement may lead to improved control in the future. The significant concept involved here is that objectives, policies, and standards fulfill two basic requirements in the overall control process, namely: (1) feedforward—to provide a basis for control at the point of action (the decision point); and, (2) feedback—to provide a basis for measurement of the effectiveness of control after the point of action.

We have said that control implies measurement, and it must be approached in a systematic and consistent manner. Obviously, control in the broad sense may be attained in an enterprise by utilization of a number of different approaches. The most important approach is based upon the fact that control is attained through people and not "things." Therefore, the first and foremost essential in control is to assure *management quality*. Direct supervision of people and operations represents another primary approach to control. Aside from these two "direct" controls, there are a number of technical approaches that may be used, depending upon the nature of the problem. In respect to overall control in an enterprise and in each of the subunits, the concept of comprehensive profit planning and control has gained wide acceptance in the better-managed companies.

A comprehensive profit planning and control program aids control in many ways; underlying these is the measurement of actual performance against planned objectives, goals, and standards and the reporting of that measurement in what is commonly referred to as *performance reports*. This measurement and reporting extends to all areas of operations and to all responsibility centers in the enterprise. From the point of view of method-

---

(2) Collecting information on actual performance; (3) Comparing actual results with predicted performance, and (4) when a decision is shown to have been deficient, correcting the procedure that produced it and correcting its consequences where possible.

ology, it involves reporting (1) actual results, (2) budget or planned results, and (3) the differences (variations) between the two. This type of reporting represents an effective application of the well-recognized management → *exception principle*. As applied to this situation, the exception principle holds that the manager should devote detailed attention chiefly to the exceptional or unusual items that appear in daily, weekly, and monthly events, thereby leaving sufficient managerial time for overall policy and planning considerations. It is the out-of-line items that need managerial attention; the items that are not out-of-line need not utilize extensive management time. In order to implement the exception principle, techniques and procedures must be adopted to call the attention of the manager to the unusual and exceptional items. Conventional accounting reports tend to present a mass of figures with no provision for calling attention to the unusual or exceptional items. Alternatively, *performance reports*, since they include a comparison of actual results with plans, emphasize in a meaningful way the deviations or variations and the out-of-line items stand out. It is with these items that the busy executive should be presently concerned.

   ⅃ A basic problem of control confronting managers from time to time involves the evaluation of performance data presented to them. Evaluation of an actual result must be based upon some standard of performance, either specified or unspecified. For example, a report may show January sales of $100,000 in Sales District A, and another report may show January indirect labor costs in Producing Department X of $18,000. The pertinent problem facing the manager is whether or not these amounts represent good or indifferent performance. The absolute actual amount, standing alone, certainly sheds little light on the matter; some standard or yardstick against which to measure is necessary if performance is to be evaluated.

   The traditional accounting approach has been that of comparing current actual results with the actual results of some past period. For example, assume sales in District A above for the preceding January were $90,000; and indirect labor in Department X was $20,000. Do these additional facts suggest satisfactory current performance in District A and Department X? The answer must be that there is still no adequate basis for evaluating performance. It may be that because of changes in conditions since last January, the prior sales and cost performances are not satisfactory as a reliable standard. To extend the example, because of increased advertising, more salesmen, or an increase in size of territory, changes in product prices, or product lines, the sales goal in District A was set at $110,000 for the current period. Or, in the case of indirect labor and changes in Department X operations, the goal for labor costs was set at $16,000; thus both performances were unsatisfactory. It is assumed that these latter amounts represent realistic goals; thus the example serves to suggest that a comparison of actual results for the current January with the actual results of a prior

January did not provide effective measurement of performance, whereas comparison with a reliable standard provided a valid measurement. A comparison of current actual results with those of some past period has value perhaps in that trends are revealed; however, the comparison is generally inadequate for control purposes. Comparison with the actual results of a prior period is defective for the following reasons: (1) conditions may have changed—reorganization, new products, new methods, price changes, volume differentials, technological improvements, increased labor efficiency; (2) accounting classifications utilized may be different; and (3) performance in the prior period may have been unsatisfactory. On the other hand, assuming the planned goals are attainable and represent efficient performance in relation to the situation, a valid and meaningful comparison or measurement of actual performance is possible. The profit planning and control approach thus makes it possible for management to feel the pulse of the enterprise throughout the year—to know specifically where there is satisfactory or unsatisfactory progress toward the overall company objectives and the more specific goals.

Progress or lack of progress must be recognized and evaluated throughout the period rather than at the end of the year, because it is then too late to take corrective action. Accordingly, performance reports for control purposes in the better-managed companies normally are prepared and communicated on a monthly basis.[8]

COORDINATION

Some authorities list coordination as a separate function of management; however, most view it as an effect that ensues when the managerial functions of planning, organizing, staffing, directing, and controlling are accomplished. Coordination is the synchronization of individual actions (goal congruence) with the result that each subdivision of an entity effectively works toward the common objectives, with due regard for all other subdivisions and with unity of effort. It means developing and maintaining the various activities within the enterprise in proper relationship to each other. This harmony of effort toward the enterprise objectives is one of the central tasks of management since it involves a reconciliation of differences in effort, timing, policies, and aggregations of resources. Frequently, one observes a lack of coordination in an enterprise when an aggressive department head is permitted to expand the department out of proportion to others or to base major decisions on the specific needs of the department only, although the decision may negatively affect other departments and alter their relative effectiveness.

[8] For an excellent discussion of control see: Koontz and O'Donnell, *Management*, Chapters 28–31.

For example, there must be very close coordination between the sales and production departments—sales should not plan to sell more than production can provide, and vice versa. There must be coordination at all vertical levels as well as on a horizontal basis; this dimension of coordination is especially difficult for management to attain in a large enterprise.

How is coordination attained? In the preceding paragraph it was stated that coordination fundamentally was attained through effective performance of the management functions. However, certain of those functions have particular relevance in this respect. Coordination involves the interpersonal relationships of people in the work situation as they exchange views, ideals, prejudices, and other attitudes. When managers at all levels understand how their particular functions contribute to the overall enterprise objectives, a basic foundation for coordination is established. It is important that each member of management from the top to the lowest level knows well in advance what is planned and how, when, and by whom it is to be accomplished. Planning decisions that are made sufficiently in advance, and with the care and detail necessary to meet coordination needs, must take into account the objectives, problems, potentialities, and other considerations of each subdivision of the enterprise and of the enterprise as a whole.

Fundamentally, the control function has, as its objective, assurance of conformance with predetermined objectives and plans of the enterprise and each of its subdivisions. Control, thus, is designed to check on the effectiveness with which those plans are being accomplished. Management must know whether or not policies and plans are being followed throughout the organization; they must have indicators (reports) of defects in the plans and early warnings of deviations from established goals. Thus, the control process must be effective if coordination is to be attained on a continuing basis.

In planning and implementing the organizational structure and related assignments of responsibilities, another important foundation for synchronization of effort is established. Communication, both vertically and horizontally, is fundamental to coordination. The need for continuous interchange of plans, policies, and ideas, as well as for alterations affecting them, is essential. A comprehensive profit planning and control program, since it emphasizes goal congruence through realistic planning, dynamic control, and effective communication, establishes the basis for the harmony, synchronization, and unity of effort on a continuing basis that constitutes effective coordination.

A WORD OF CAUTION

In this chapter there is a clear implication that certain aspects of the planning and control functions of management should be formalized. A comprehensive profit planning and control program provides for the essential degree of formalization. The primary reasons for a reasonable level of formalization are:

1. The management process cannot be carried out effectively in a completely random manner; planning and control should be logical, consistent, and systematic subprocesses.

2. Since a large number of individuals are involved in the managerial process (both the supervisors and the supervised) the environment must be characterized by a reasonable degree of stability and consistency upon which they can rely from day to day.

3. Objectives and goals, if not reduced to writing and expressed in terms of the probable financial future impacts on the enterprise, frequently turn out to be vague and uncommunicated "half-thoughts" of one or more individuals. Casual observation alone tells us that objectives, goals, policies, and procedures lack the necessary precision, consistency, understanding, and stability when "carried around in the head" of one individual or of diverse groups of managers and nonmanagers.

4. For effective communication—mutual understanding—formalization of certain objectives, goals, policies, and procedures is essential.

5. Formalization requires the establishment and observance of relevant deadlines for decision-making, planning, and control action.

6. Formalization provides a logical basis for rational, meaningful, and consistent flexibility in implementing the planning and controlling processes.

Alternatively, overformalization and inflexible administration involve serious hazards of perhaps greater import than a lack of formalization. An unfavorable aspect that frequently derives from formal approaches is that the "written words and figures" are viewed inflexibly, thereby precluding the dynamics that are essential in all human endeavors. One cannot manage by rules alone. Obviously, there are many aspects of the management process that cannot be implemented in a formal way. Informality has merit at all levels of management and the executive should strive to attain an appropriate degree of balance between the two extremes. The essence of the concept of comprehensive profit planning and control is that *specified* aspects of the management process can be formalized to advantage; however, application and implementation of written plans, policies, and procedures must be on a flexible basis, which takes into account the salient features of each situation. To put it more directly, a set of plans should not be allowed to "manage" the operation; rather the formal plans provide basic guidelines within which decisions are made, some of which necessarily will alter those particular plans.

SUMMARY

In conclusion, clearly profit planning and control cannot replace good management; nor can it correct the errors of an unenlightened management. It is the quality of the managers that makes the difference. Profit planning and control, although resting on important conceptual foundations, is basically only a managerial tool, and it is no better than the individual or group using it. It can make the task of managing more systematic, more effective, and more rewarding. It can be applied so as to impart a high degree of flexibility in the management process. It is a relatively complex and sophisticated tool, not in the procedural or mechanical sense but in the conceptual realm. In view of its conceptual subtleties it demands a reasonable degree of sophistication on the part of the user. Very seldom does the profit planning and control approach to managing break down because of mechanical failure; alternatively, there are many situations where it is ineffective or has actually failed because of conceptual errors. Even without profit planning and control, it is significant to know that it is the same such conceptual errors that cause the management process and the decision-making process to be ineffective in many instances. There is clear evidence that a management seriously committed to a comprehensive profit planning and control approach very rapidly raises its level of conceptual sophistication, and as a consequence there is a significant elevation of the long-range profit potentials of the enterprise. The basic conceptual perspectives of profit planning and control may be outlined as follows:

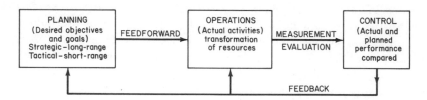

For the reader then, it is strongly suggested that, although attention should be given to the techniques and approaches discussed throughout this book, special attention is recommended in regard to the underlying concepts. Throughout the discussions that follow the focus will be upon the concepts, which will be reemphasized again and again.

DISCUSSION QUESTIONS

1.   Basically, why do all types of endeavors (business and nonbusiness) have essentially the same planning and control problems?

2.   Broadly define comprehensive profit planning and control.

3.   List the five functions of the manager provided by Koontz and O'Donnell, and briefly describe each.

4.   Continuing generation of profits by managerial manipulation of the inflows and outflows is the central task of management. Explain the meaning of the term manipulation as used in this context.

5.   There are a number of relevant variables that bear down on each enterprise; a task of the management is to cope with these relevant variables. Explain the nature of these variables and a classification approach that is useful for analytical and decision-making purposes.

6.   There are two opposite extremes in respect to a conceptual view of the real role of management; these two extremes have been labeled as the *market theory* and the *planning and control theory*. Explain the nature of these two opposing philosophies and indicate their significance.

7.   Define management planning and distinguish between strategic and tactical planning.

8.   Ackoff identified three types of projections that might be developed during the planning process. Identify and briefly explain each.

9.   Why is planning a continuous process?

10.   In respect to management planning briefly distinguish between objectives, goals, and strategies.

11.   What is a profit plan?

12.   Explain the essence of control, and indicate the principal activities that are involved.

13.   What is meant by the statement that, "Control cannot be *ex post facto*"?

14.   Explain the exception principle, and relate it to a profit planning and control program.

15.   From a control point of view, what are the implicit weaknesses of a comparison of actual results for the current month just ended with the same month in the preceding year?

16.   Broadly define *coordination*, and indicate generally how it may be attained in the management context.

17.   The planning function of management can be accomplished (1) with absolute formality at one extreme, or (2) with complete informality at the other extreme. Explain the essence of these two extremes, and indicate what you think would be a rational approach in the typical medium-size business.

18.   Elaborate on the statement, "A meandering management is sure to be an inefficient management."

19.   Someone has said in respect to business management that, "If you don't know where you are going, any old road will get you there." What are the implications of this statement?

CASE 1-1
Grass-Roots Manufacturers, Incorporated

Grass-Roots Manufacturers, Incorporated, is a small company that has grown very rapidly since its formation seven years ago. The president now is thirty-six years of age and was the "promoter" of the company at its formation. He is aggressive and innovative. He recently returned from a three-day conference conducted by the American Management Association. During the conference several sessions were devoted to the broad subject of "Management by Objectives." He felt that the broad ideas discussed in those particular sessions would have relevant applications for his company. In discussing certain ideas with his top managers, the president stated : "Now I believe we should design a planning and control system so that we will have a 'grass-roots approach.'"

Required :

Explain what the president meant by the "grass-roots approach." What are the primary advantages and disadvantages of this approach for a small firm such as this one ? Assuming Grass-Roots Manufacturers, Incorporated, has three sales districts and five departments in the factory, indicate in broad terms how this approach might be implemented in this particular company.

CASE 1-2
Maxwell Sales Company

Maxwell Sales Company is a wholesale distributor covering a two-state region. The company has been moderately successful and has been operating for ten years. During the past year the management has become particularly concerned about profits. As a result, initial steps are being taken to institute a profit planning and control program. The first profit plan is being developed and in the process a sales plan is being carefully considered. At a recent meeting of the sales supervisors, attended by the president and the vice president in charge of sales, a program of "aggressive sales efforts and expanded promotional programs" was worked out. The discussions of expenses were quite lively since considerable pressure was exerted by the president and the vice president to "minimize sales expenses." Near the end of the discussion one of the younger and more successful regional sales supervisors stated, "Well, we've squeezed a lot of money out of the regional sales expenses, but it seems to me, we have used all of the savings by increasing home office expenses, if I interpret correctly the reason for the increase to my district of the 'allocated home office expenses.'"

Required :

Assess the situation including its implications, and provide appropriate recommendations.

CASE 1-3
Krandall-Knox Company

Samuel Krandall for a number of years had sold a line of supplies used by hotels, motels, and similar establishments. He had managed to save a tidy amount, which he invested in common stocks. At the age of forty-four, Sam, with his brother-in-law Harry Knox, decided to open a small wholesale distribution firm in another state (where Knox resided). In 1964 the Krandall-Knox partnership was formed to distribute a line of supplies similar to that sold by Krandall over the years. Sam invested $25,000 and Harry invested $10,000. Two salesmen were employed initially. Sam was to sell and work directly with the salesmen in developing statewide distribution. Harry was to do the purchasing, shipping, and other administrative duties.

The company was successful, as a result principally of Sam's work with the sales force, as well as the fact that the chief competitor was an old "family" corporation operated by two men who had married the daughters of the founder. Harry believed the competitor still operated "in the horse and buggy days," and he was about right.

Within ten years Krandall-Knox had grown substantially. The data tabulated below are indicative of the growth at the end of the first, fifth, and tenth years:

	FIRST YEAR	FIFTH YEAR	TENTH YEAR
Home office employees	2	4	14
Sales force	3	8	18
General employees	0	1	2
Total assets	$27,500	$ 60,000	$240,000
Sales dollars	34,000	110,000	480,000
Partners' salaries	12,000	20,000	36,000
Income (after salaries)	($ 7,500)	4,200	14,500

In accordance with the partnership agreement, an annual audit was prepared by an independent C.P.A. After submission of the last audit report the C.P.A. handed Mr. Knox a separate memorandum. In it the C.P.A. noted the profit trend and other data that tended to indicate some developing internal inefficiencies. The memorandum suggested that, in view of the increasing size of the company, serious consideration be given to establishing a profit planning and control program. The memorandum stated that such a program could be particularly helpful in (1) setting prices, (2) increasing sales volume, (3) controlling expenses, and (4) managing inventory. The memorandum noted that inventory control appeared to be a growing problem in the firm.

Mr. Knox was impressed with the suggestions: "Sam, I believe the C.P.A. has something; why don't we get a program started right away? Our profit margin certainly is shrinking." "Well, I don't know, Harry; I'd have to oppose a budget if that is what they mean. The company I used to sell for had a budget and they were always hounding me on the expense budget and sales quota budget. I didn't need a budget. If I could have saved the time and worry, I could have sold even more," was Sam's reply.

Required:

Analyze the situation. Identify the primary problem or problems and provide recommendations and support for them.

CASE 1-4
Leon Manufacturers, Incorporated

Leon Manufacturers, Incorporated, produces and sells five products; sales efforts encompass a ten-state area. The company is considered medium in size in relation to other companies in the industry. The company employs approximately five hundred people and has thirty-two departments and sales districts combined. In the last three years the company has experienced a gradually decreasing profit. The company does not have a "profit planning and control program" although, as the executive vice president stated: "We do an awful lot of planning and controlling." Recently the president sent a letter to all departmental managers that included the following directive: "Each department is expected to effect a 10 percent across-the-board cut in total departmental expenses during the coming year. The quarterly financial statements will be evaluated to ascertain the effectiveness with which this directive is implemented."

Required:

Evaluate the approach taken by the president to enhance the profit of the company. Assuming some costs were in fact out of line, what suggestions would you make as to a general approach for improvement?

CASE 1-5
Lamar Sales Company

Lamar Sales Company sells residential and industrial air conditioning units in a twenty-county area in one of the midwest states. The units are purchased from three different manufacturers and are sold direct to contractors and users. Company salesmen call on potential buyers; the territory is divided into five sales districts. At the end of May 19B the following internal performance report, following the format used in prior years, was distributed:

Sales Report

| | ACTUAL SALES | | | | VARIANCES* | |
| | | | YEAR TO DATE | | | YEAR |
DISTRICT	MAY 19A	MAY 19B	19A	19B	MONTH	TO DATE
1	$43,000	$47,000	$130,000	$135,000	$4,000	$5,000
2	56,000	57,000	165,000	164,000	1,000	1,000*
3	37,000	35,000	113,000	110,000	2,000*	3,000*
4	76,000	79,000	220,000	227,000	3,000	7,000
5	62,000	60,000	190,000	191,000	2,000*	1,000

*Unfavorable

Sales Expense Report

| | ACTUAL EXPENSES | | | | VARIANCES | |
| | | | YEAR TO DATE | | | YEAR |
DISTRICT	MAY 19A	MAY 19B	19A	19B	MONTH	TO DATE
1	$ 4,500	$ 4,800	$ 15,000	$ 18,000	$ 300*	$3,000*
2	5,400	5,600	16,000	17,000	200*	1,000*
3	3,800	3,500	14,000	11,000	300	3,000
4	7,200	7,400	19,000	20,000	200*	1,000*
5	6,100	5,800	21,000	22,000	300	1,000*

*Unfavorable

Prior to the beginning of 19B a budget for the sales division was prepared. This was a first effort in the company. The budget developed was as follows:

| | BUDGETED SALES | | BUDGETED EXPENSES | |
| | | YEAR TO | | YEAR TO |
DISTRICT	MAY 19B	DATE	MAY 19B	DATE
1	$46,000	$133,000	$ 4,900	$ 17,000
2	60,000	170,000	5,700	18,000
3	32,000	105,000	3,200	10,000
4	82,000	230,000	7,000	18,000
5	60,000	190,000	5,700	23,000

Required:

Do you agree with the design of the performance report shown above for 19B? In what ways do you think it should be redesigned? Recast the report to reflect your recommendations. Also provide comments pointing up good and poor performances.

The Fundamentals
of Profit Planning
and Control

chapter two

Chapter 1 dealt with the broad role of management and focused primarily on planning and control. In a general way, accomplishment of the management functions was related to a comprehensive profit planning and control program. In Chapter 2 we will identify and briefly discuss some fundamental distinctions and other salient issues in order to continue building a broad foundation to understanding profit planning and control. Starting with Chapter 3 the material will progressively bring the concept of profit planning and control into sharper focus.

At the outset it is important that we adopt a broad view of comprehensive profit planning and control. In earlier years, the common view of budgeting was the notion that the accountants in a firm should be assigned the responsibility for developing a "financial evaluation of what the future year probably will hold." In recent years there has been a tendency to view profit planning and control primarily as a "mathematical model" for the entity. Obviously, these attitudes tend to overlook the single most relevant aspect of the concept, that is, budgeting is an integral aspect of the management process and it is basically a management decision-making activity with critical behavioral implications. Recently, noteworthy attention has been given to the behavioral implications of various management approaches, but even greater import has been recognition of the concept as a "way of managing."

In modern-day business, except in the very small company, it is virtually impossible for the manager to have firsthand knowledge of all the relevant factors operating throughout the firm; nor can a single individual be expected to have the range of experience and competence to make all the decisions for the firm. He or she must place more and more reliance on managers under their supervision, both as sources of reliable information and as participants in decision-making. The quality of the judgment of the combined management effort will continue to distinguish the better-managed and more successful companies. It is not likely that techniques, mathematical models, and simulations will substitute in major respects for human judgment in the management of complex endeavors. These important tools, on the other hand, can be used to increase significantly the sophistication of a management and to place managerial judgment on a more objective and efficient footing.

Basically comprehensive profit planning and control offers a systematic, practical and proven approach to the management process. Properly viewed, profit planning and control is a comprehensive system to coordinate all aspects of the management process, carefully knitting together the loose ends of management and operations. This all-inclusive concept of the profit planning and control process is frequently minimized or completely overlooked in much of the literature and discussions on the subject.

FUNDAMENTAL DISTINCTIONS

Careful analysis of a wide range of successful profit planning and control programs has indicated that there are certain common ingredients and basic distinctions that are crucial to sophisticated understanding and effective application of the concept. Failure to grasp an adequate perspective of these ingredients and distinctions leads to ineffective profit planning and control and to misunderstanding of the comprehensive budgetary process. Thus, careful distinction should be made between:

1. The *mechanics* of profit planning and control. Mechanics are such matters as design of budget schedules, clerical methods of completing such schedules, and routine computations. Throughout this book some attention (primarily by illustration) is given to the requisite mechanics.

2. The *techniques* of profit planning and control. Techniques are special approaches and methods of developing information for managerial use in the decision-making process. The techniques are many, varying from the simple to the sophisticated. For example, we may note some of the more commonly used techniques are: methods of forecasting sales volume; approaches in resolving the sales-production-inventory problem (a frequent application of operations research); breakeven analyses; resource determinations (such

as the discounted-cash-flow approach); cash flow analyses; and variable budget procedures.

3. The *fundamentals* of profit planning and control. The fundamentals concern effective implementation of the management process in reasonably complex endeavors. The fundamentals, as we define them at this point, represent desirable management orientations, activities, and approaches necessary for proficient and sophisticated application of comprehensive profit planning and control. These fundamentals need to be established on a sound foundation of managerial commitment. The more important fundamentals are:

a. Managerial involvement and commitment.

b. Organizational adaptation.

c. Responsibility accounting.

d. Full communication.

e. Realistic expectations.

f. Timeliness.

g. Flexible application.

h. Individual and group recognition.

i. Follow-up.

Each of these important fundamentals is discussed briefly in the following paragraphs. Elaboration and application are presented in subsequent chapters.

Managerial Involvement. Managerial involvement entails managerial support, confidence, participation, and performance orientation. In order to engage competently in comprehensive profit planning and control, all levels of management, especially top management, must (1) understand the nature and characteristics of profit planning and control; (2) be convinced that this particular approach to managing is preferable for their situation; (3) be willing to devote the effort required to make it operative; (4) support the program in all its ramifications; and (5) view the results of the planning process as performance commitments. For a comprehensive profit planning and control program to be successful, it must have the full support of each member of management, starting with the president; the impetus and direction must come from the very top.

A company is fortunate if the chief executive decides to initiate, implement, and foster a comprehensive profit planning and control program. Alternatively, one of the central and most difficult problems facing a financial executive, budget director, or other staff officers is to "sell" the program to the chief executive and other top managers.

Managerial involvement and commitment in a profit planning and control program is directly related to the *confidence* that top management has in its ability to influence the future course of certain events significantly and, hence, the success of the enterprise. In harmony with this confidence, the management must clearly perceive its duty to plan the future with reasonable precision. The management of the enterprise must be convinced that realistic objectives and goals can be developed in advance, and they must be willing to make a firm commitment to plan on a continuing basis. Management should recognize that individuals having administrative responsibilities tend to tie their own success to that of the firm; therefore, they will strive aggressively to attain *realistic* and *known* objectives, particularly if they are permitted to participate in a meaningful way in developing these objectives. Then, too, management must be firmly convinced that the objectives, goals, and plans thus established can be attained. This is the essence of management performance commitments. This commitment moves toward logical, organized, and aggressive efforts to attain the goals of the enterprise. The idea of participation in profit planning and control by all levels of management entails a behavioral sophistication that the better-managed companies now recognize. Each manager in the enterprise should expect to carry out assigned responsibilities in every respect, including participation in developing plans for his responsibility center, implementing those plans, and exercising direct control in their attainment.

Attaining meaningful involvement in the planning process is not easy. Lower levels of management react favorably to participation, yet certain checks and constraints are necessary. No plan, estimate, or objective suggested by subordinates should be accepted without careful analysis and evaluation. Upper echelon executives must make the final decisions; however, subordinates should be heard. Also there will always be some individuals who deliberately set budget allowances at a level that presents no challenge. This somewhat natural tendency to "protect one's self" can be controlled by making it clear that favorable as well as unfavorable variations between actual performance and the goals, as specified in the profit plans, will be carefully scrutinized. Further supervisor and executive ratings should include (as one factor) their competence in planning. Differences in respect to objectives, goals, and standards suggested by lower levels of supervisors and higher managers should be carefully analyzed and discussed and a definite decision made. In this way, realistic plans for each responsibility center and for the entire entity can be developed.

Token participation is likely to create negative motivation. Participation in the planning process by lower levels of management in a meaningful way imposes a prior responsibility on higher management to define and circumscribe clearly basic objectives, goals, and strategies well in advance. The role of participation was emphasized in an excellent research study as follows.

The participation of employee *and* boss in setting, reviewing, and revising objectives and standards is all-important. The relative influence either will have on the product of their engagement will depend on, among other factors: the supervisor's philosophy of management; the subordinate's experience and competence; and the economic health of the organization. The number of other managers to become involved at higher or lower levels in the organization or in other functions seems to depend on the company's sophistication in using the techniques and on its aggressiveness. The more sophisticated enlist the participation of more managers for each manager's job, and the more aggressive emphasize better-directed effort through better-shared knowledge.

The companies that participated in this research agreed that "Participation tends to increase commitment; commitment tends to heighten motivation; motivation which is job-oriented tends to make managers work harder and more productively; and harder and more productive work by managers tends to enhance the company's prosperity; therefore, participation is good."[1]

Neither the financial executive nor the director of profit planning and control (budget director) makes the budget; rather their role should be to supervise its compilation and to develop the system itself. Responsibility for providing the decisions encompassed by the planning process rests squarely on the line executives; in this manner the profit plans are viewed as their own and there will be no basis to say that objectives and budget allowances are not fair or realistic. Thus, it is crucial that those line executives who must achieve the plans and goals should be deeply involved in providing the *planning decisional inputs* for their respective responsibility centers. This procedure makes possible effective implementation of the participation principle in management.

In comprehensive profit planning and control, a central issue is that of developing work programs and *performance expectations* essential to attainment of enterprise objectives and goals. The primary emphasis in profit planning and control, therefore, must be on a *performance concept*, as opposed to a *fiscal concept*. The latter emphasizes dollar results. If exclusive emphasis is given to simply estimating the dollar effect of planned operations, without consideration of work programs and performance expectations by assigned responsibilities, the many indirect and important facets of comprehensive profit planning and control that *cannot be quantified* may not be realized. The fiscal concept of comprehensive budgeting appears to have preceded the performance concept because the early emphasis in budgeting was directed almost exclusively toward estimating dollar values for the various accounting classifications of revenue and expense. Unfortunately, many people today adopt this view of the budgetary process; hence, some firms continue this emphasis and thereby significantly limit the potentials of profit planning and control. Throughout the discussions and illustrations to follow, primary emphasis will be given to the performance concept, secondary emphasis to the fiscal concept. Yet it must be realized that a logical and practical blending of the two concepts is necessary for effective profit planning and control.

[1] Ernest C. Miller, *Objectives and Standards; An Approach to Planning and Control*, AMA Research Study 74 (New York: American Management Association, Inc., 1966), p. 38.

Organizational Adaptation. A profit planning and control program must rest upon sound organizational structure for the enterprise and a clear-cut designation of lines of authorities and responsibilities. The purpose of organizational structure and the assignment of authority is to establish a framework within which enterprise objectives may be attained in a coordinated and effective way on a continuing basis. The scope and interrelationship of the responsibilities of each individual manager are specified. One authority succinctly states the essence of this notion as follows:

> Viewed internally with respect to the enterprise, responsibility may be defined as the obligation of a subordinate to perform assigned and implied duties. The essence of responsibility is, then, *obligation*. Responsibility has no meaning except as applied to a person; a building, a machine, or an animal cannot be held responsible.
>
> Responsibility arises from the superior-subordinate relationship, from the fact that someone (in this case, a manager) has the authority to require specified services from another person. This authority in business normally results from a contractual arrangement by which the subordinate agrees to perform such services—perhaps using delegated authority—in return for monetary and other rewards. Thus, authority flows from the superior to the subordinate manager when duties are assigned; and responsibility is the obligation simultaneously exacted from the subordinate for the accomplishment of those duties.
>
> Responsibility may be a continuing obligation, or it may be discharged by a single action and not arise again. The relationship between a president and his sales manager is typical of a continuing obligation: on the other hand, the president may hire, for an organization study, a consulting management engineer whose obligation will cease when the assignment is completed.
>
> A problem in responsibility sometimes arises when informal leadership appears. For example, a sales manager may have as subordinates an advertising manager, a sales promotion manager, and three district sales managers. For many reasons—among them, perhaps, the powerful position of the production manager—some of the sales manager's subordinates may look to the production manager for guidance. This informal relationship may have the effect of reducing the influence but not the authority of the sales manager over his subordinates. Unless this shift is made with the approval of the president or the sales manager—thus constituting a change in the organization structure itself—the basic responsibility relationships would not be changed. The president would still hold the sales manager responsible for the department's performance, and the subordinates would still be responsible to the sales manager.
>
> Responsibility cannot be delegated. While a manager may delegate to a subordinate authority to accomplish a service and the subordinate, in turn, may delegate a portion of the authority received, neither delegates any of his responsibility. Responsibility, being an obligation to perform, is owed to one's superior, and no subordinate reduces his responsibility by delegating to another the authority to perform a duty.[2]

To increase management and operational efficiency, practically all enterprises, except perhaps the very smallest ones, should be structurally dis-

[2] Harold Koontz and Cyril O'Donnell, *Principles of Management and Analysis of Managerial Functions*, 5th ed. (New York: McGraw-Hill Book Co., Inc., 1972), pp. 62–63. This source is highly recommended for further study of these important issues.

aggregated into organizational subunits. The manager of each subunit would be assigned specific authority and responsibility for the operational activities of that subunit. These subunits are often referred to as *decision centers* or *responsibility centers*. Although the latter term is widely used, the former is more descriptive of the primary focus that is the most fundamental. A responsibility center (or decision center) may be defined as an organization unit (or subunit) headed by a manager with specified authorities and responsibilities. Thus the company as a whole is a responsiblility center, as is a division, a department, a sales district. Responsibility centers are further classified in respect to the extent of responsibility as follows:

1. Cost center—a responsibility center for which the manager is responsible for the controllable costs incurred in the subunit, but is not responsible, in a financial sense, for profit or investment in the center. The lower level, and smaller, responsibility centers tend to be cost centers.

2. Profit center—a responsibility center for which the manager is responsible for both revenue and costs, and hence profit, for the center. An important planning and control point focuses on the center's profit figure.

3. Investment center—a responsibility center that goes one step further than a profit center. In an investment center, the manager is responsible for revenue, costs (profit) and the amount of resources invested in the assets used by the center. An important planning and control point, therefore, focuses on the return on investment earned by the center.

Organizational subunits, whether cost, profit, or investment centers, are variously labeled, such as subsidiaries, divisions, departments, plants, districts, and functions. It is through these responsibility centers that plans are implemented, objectives attained, and control achieved. The subdivision of an enterprise in this manner is generally referred to as organizational structure. Organizational structure also includes the assignment of managerial authority relationships and responsibilities. Organizational structure must be viewed not as an end in itself, but as a managerial tool for accomplishing enterprise objectives. Consequently, a comprehensive profit planning and control program must be tailored to the organizational subunits and the related structural characteristics of the firm. Thus, in better-managed companies we observe that within the specified time dimensions the project plans, the strategic long-range plan, and the tactical short-range profit plan are structured first, by organizational authorities and responsibilities, and second, by product or service lines. In harmony with this frame of reference, the goals and plans of the several responsibility centers aggregate to the goals and plans for the enterprise as a whole. As a result, comprehensive profit plans normally are developed each year in the following broad pattern:

1. Top management specifies entity objectives, broad goals, planning assumptions (premises), and guidelines that are communicated to the managers of the respective subunits.

2. The manager of each subunit, conforming to the broad guidelines, develops his own segment of the comprehensive profit plans. Typically, the first segment of the profit plan that must be completed is the sales plan, since the activities of most firms must pivot on sales volume.

3. The manager of each subunit presents his segment of the profit plans to the top management for critical review, evaluation, and suggested revisions where appropriate.

4. The plans of each subunit, as approved by higher management, are consolidated into the comprehensive profit plans for the whole company.

Subsequent discussions will emphasize the essentiality of relating planning and control functions to the assigned authorities and responsibilities of the various subunits of the enterprise. From both the conceptual and procedural points of view, the primary structure or classification of profit plans must be by organizational subdivisions—responsibility centers—of the enterprise. Obviously, *control* is attained in an enterprise through people, not through things; therefore, this specific function of management also requires sound organizational structure and clear-cut delineation of authorities and responsibilities. As with the profit plans, the performance reports must be tailored precisely to the organizational structure.

In consequence of these compelling requirements, a firm in the process of initiating a profit planning and control program should first turn its attention to its organizational structure and the related assignment of authorities and responsibilities. In most cases, it will be found that organizational adaptation and greater precision are necessary to place the operation on a sound footing for proficient implementation of the planning and control processes through comprehensive budgeting. Careful delineation of such responsibility is a management task that is necessary to avoid overlapping effort and dilution of responsibility.

Responsibility Accounting. The above paragraph emphasized the relationship of both planning and controlling to assigned responsibilities. Planning, in some respects, is based upon historical data, which are largely generated by the accounting system, and control includes the measurement of actual results against objectives, goals, and plans. Consequently, the accounting system must be built around the responsibility structure of the enterprise. In order to set up profit planning and control on a sound basis there must be a *responsibility accounting system*—that is, one tailored first and foremost to the organizational responsibilities. Within this primary accounting structure, secondary classifications of costs, revenues, and other financial data that are relevant may be utilized in accordance with the needs of the enterprise. A responsibility accounting system can be designed and implemented on a relevant basis regardless of the other features of the accounting system—noncost systems, mercantile accounting systems, standard cost systems, direct costing systems, and so on. When the accounting system is established on a responsibility basis, the historical data generated become especially pertinent for planning and control purposes.

Historical cost accounting has two main objectives with respect to costs (1) to determine the cost of goods produced; and (2) to provide relevant data for planning and controlling costs. Traditionally, cost accounting has been focused more on determining the cost of the products than on cost planning and control; as a result, the emphasis in account classifications has been, and in many firms continues to be, on a product cost basis rather than on a responsibility basis. In responsibility accounting, this emphasis is reversed. Cost and revenue planning and control receive the primary emphasis. This concept does not imply that product costing will be less accurate. It is a fact that costs initially accumulated for control purposes can be accurately recast for product costing purposes; costs initially accumulated for product costing purposes; however, cannot generally be recast effectively for planning and control purposes. In sum, effective profit planning and control requires that the traditional accounting emphasis be reversed—the accounting system must be primarily oriented toward the planning and control needs of management. Most companies initiating a profit planning and control program find it necessary to analyze carefully all aspects of the accounting system with a consequent reorganization of the system on a responsibility accounting basis.

Comparisons between plans and actual results are meaningless if the classifications of costs and revenues used in the profit plans and in the accounting systems are not in harmony. A *chart of accounts* should be developed by responsibility centers and should be supplemented with standard instructions that prescribe in some detail the authorized charges and credits to each type of account. This is a requisite to successful profit planning and control because the recording of an actual value in the wrong account obviously would affect two or more accounts, resulting in erroneous budget variations in each account on the internal performance reports for the respective responsibility centers.

If predetermined (budgeted) factory overhead rates are used in the cost accounting system, these should normally coincide with those developed in the budget planning process. The author has observed cases where the cost accounting department developed budgets of overhead costs to compute overhead rates, and the profit plan reflected different overhead rates. Obviously, this lack of harmony is undesirable and also represents a duplication of effort. The same factory overhead rates should be used for both purposes, and it is a responsibility of the financial executive to see that such efforts are coordinated. The use of identical factory overhead rates for costing purposes and for profit planning and control purposes is illustrated in a later chapter.

Standard costs (see Chapter 17) provide a logical basis for profit planning and control. Where standard costs are available they should be completely integrated with the comprehensive budget program both in preparation of the profit plans and in the performance reports.

An accounting system tailored only to *external needs* and to "generally accepted accounting principles," although essential, is inadequate for internal management planning and control needs.

Full Communication.   *Communication* in the management and operation of an enterprise is a major managerial problem. Communication can be broadly defined as an interchange of thought or information to bring about a mutual understanding between two or more parties; it may be accomplished by a combination of words, symbols, messages, and subtleties of understanding that come from working together, day-in and day-out, by two or more individuals. Communication may be thought of as the link that brings together the human elements in an enterprise. We have stated that one primary responsibility of management is to develop objectives and plans for the enterprise and then to devise ways and means of accomplishing those objectives. This fact says that one of the crucial issues encountered by management, starting at the top, is to implement the concept of *feed forward*. To do this the management must communicate the objectives and modes of implementation throughout the organization so that there is a unity of effort directed toward attaining those goals.

Management is implemented through communication, the means by which behavior is affected, modified, and energized. Decision-making rests in large measure upon effective communication. Too often communication is taken for granted; consequently, information flow is inadequate. There must be three primary flows of information in an entity: downward, upward, and laterally in the organization. Koontz and O'Donnell list the following barriers to effective communication: badly expressed messages, faulty translations, loss by transmission and poor retention, inattention, unclarified assumptions, insufficient adjustment period, distrust of the communicator, premature evaluation, fear, and failure to communicate.[3] A mere listing of these barriers suggests the dimensions of the management communication problem. There are numerous approaches for improving communication in the management process. Comprehensive profit planning and control, rest-

[3] Ibid, Chapter 27.

ing upon a sound foundation of communication, provides important avenues to enhance effective communication. Fundamentally, these relate to the process of developing enterprise objectives, specification of goals, the development of profit plans, and the reporting and follow-up activities related to performance evaluation for each responsibility center.

Communication for effective planning and control requires that both the executive and subordinate have the same understanding of responsibilities and goals. Profit plans, if developed through full participation and in harmony with assigned responsibilities, assure a degree of understanding not otherwise possible. Full and open reporting in performance reports that focus on assigned responsibilities likewise enhances the degree of communication essential to sound management.

Throughout the remaining chapters of this book considerable emphasis will be given to the potential impact of a comprehensive profit planning and control program on the communication process.

Realistic Expectations. In profit planning and control, management must be realistic and avoid either undue conservation or irrational optimism. The care with which budget goals and objectives are set for such items as sales, production levels, costs, capital expenditures, cash flow, and productivity determines in large measure the future success of the profit planning and control program. For profit planning and control purposes, enterprise objectives and specific budget goals should represent *realistic expectations*. To be realistic, expectations must be related (1) to their specific time dimension and (2) to an assumed (projected) external and internal environment that will prevail during that time span. Within these two constraints, *realistic* expectations should assume a high level of overall efficiency; the objectives and goals should be capable of attainment. Goals set so high as to be practically impossible of attainment discourage serious efforts to achieve them; alternatively, goals set so low that they require no special effort will provide no motivation. Thus, enterprise objectives and specific budget goals, in order to constitute realistic expectations, must represent a real challenge to the manager and to the operational unit. As a practical matter, the top management of the enterprise has the direct responsibility to define, as a matter of broad policy, the degree of challenge that should be represented by *realistic expectations*. The definition is unique to each enterprise. It involves a wide range of psychological factors; the central objective is to provide maximum motivation to excel by the individual managers, the operational units, and the overall enterprise. The definition of realistic expectations in a given enterprise, therefore, should be related to many pervasive variables such as: size of the enterprise; characteristics of the managers; leadership characteristics; maturity of the enterprise; sophistication of the management (at all levels); nature of operations; and numerous psychological factors. Finally, in this discussion of the definition of realistic expectations, we have taken the firm stand that managers at all levels will be better motivated in the long run if they are provided realistic expectations as opposed to spurious expectations based on the premise that "high unattainable expectations are necessary for these kinds of people." Basically, the point goes directly to the philosophical question. "By nature, is man good or bad?" We have taken the former position that man, the manager in this case, prefers to excel—both individually and for the enterprise—and that, subject to positive leadership, he is competent to make the best decisions for both.

For profit planning and control purposes, then, objectives should represent "expected actual," under the assumption that operations will be efficient under the expected conditions during the planning period.

In developing planned objectives through managerial participation, a problem frequently arises commonly called *padding the budget*. This problem may be indicated by examples such as the following:

1. Sales budget estimates are understated "to protect ourselves and exceeding the sales budget certainly can't be criticized."
2. Overestimating expenses "so we will have plenty of money and spending less than the budget looks good to the management."
3. Requesting more cash than needed "so that we won't have to ask for more and if we turn some back it will look good."

Enlightened managements have developed effective approaches to minimize these somewhat natural tendencies. The solution lies in budget education aimed at developing positive attitudes toward planning and control. Management should emphasize that *both* favorable and unfavorable variations will be carefully considered. Whether favorable or unfavorable, variations due to improper planning should be identified and discussed with the responsible party; the broader problems created by poor planning should be emphasized. For example, a deliberately understated sales budget may have serious consequences in planning other functional activities; production and inventories may be inadequate; the advertising program and distribution expense budgets may be adversely affected; the cash flow plans will be inadequate; and so on. Each responsible executive and supervisor must be given guidance in evaluating the potential ramification of his own plans and estimates on other functions of the business. Overstated expense and cash estimates likewise may seriously affect other aspects of managerial policies and planning. An important facet in preventing overestimates of expense and cash requirements is a clear-cut policy relative to the approval of plans and estimates. Starting with the lower levels of management and moving up in the management hierarchy, requests for cash and expense allowances should stand the test of logic, realism, and identification of specific needs as anticipated. Then, too, management must convince lower echelons that *additional allowances* will be approved at any time, notwithstanding the budget as originally developed, should sufficient *business reasons* be evident. Lack of definite policies and failure by higher management to take sufficient time to evaluate such requests usually are prevalent where "padding" persists.

A related problem is the tendency of lower management to spend money unwisely near the end of the budget period when there is an excess since "our budget allowance for the next period will be cut if we turn some back now." Again, the resolution of this type of problem is to be found in the area of enlightened management policies, flexibility, and the attitudes of top management as perceived by the lower levels of management. Enterprise subunits should be strongly encouraged to save and turn back funds not needed, while at the same time being assured, both by policy and by action, that subsequent budget allowances for their activity will not be adversely affected by this prior favorable action. Subsequent budget approvals should be evaluated on the basis of proposed programs and demonstrated needs rather than upon the level of prior expenditures.

The author is firmly convinced that these problems exist because of insufficient attention to policy making, communication, the budget approval process, and the motivational aspects of managing. These problems often are identified with governmental budgeting, but there is no reason to assume that they do not exist in the profit-making segment of our economy. These problems are much more critical in the public sector because the approval bodies (legislatures) are not involved in the management process subsequent to approval.

All these problems basically can be resolved through effective and continuous budget education that focuses on enlightened management policies that exhibit sophistication in behavioral application and flexibility in implementing the planning and control program. The budget education program must have as its objectives: (1) communication of the policies and intentions of the top management relative to the planning and control program; (2) development of positive attitudes wherein the individual manager identifies the success of the firm with his own personal success; and (3) instruction in the ways that the profit planning and control program can contribute to the effective performance of the managerial tasks of each individual.

Time Dimensions.   Whether an individual or an entity is idle or busy, time passes at the same rate. We seldom, if ever, have time to do all of the things that we would like to do, nor do we have the time to do many things as well as we would like. This is the plight of the manager. As a result, the planning function often suffers. There are two important phases of time that require careful attention if the planning function is to be effectively car-

ried out; one relates to the concept of planning horizons and the other to the
timing of planning activities. We will consider each briefly.

Planning horizons refers to the period of time into the future for which
management should plan. At the outset, it should be understood that, in
practically all situations, there is a need for a number of planning horizons.
The continuum of managerial decisions is the total of managerial planning—
that is, that every managerial decision reflects a plan for a particular event
and that the aggregate of all decisions constitutes the overall policies and plans
for the operation. Decisions obviously can affect only the future—the next
minute, day, month, year, or series of years. No present decision can affect
or change the past; enterprise history cannot be changed, although it may be
incorrectly recorded, reported, and interpreted. Since all managerial decisions are futuristic, each management is faced with the basic question of
time dimension in planning and decision-making. The complexity of this
particular problem is compounded by the fact that the time dimension is
unique to the type of decision being made. For example, a sales manager,
because of procrastination, may decide upon his basic promotional strategy
on a last-minute basis just in time to meet a particular publication deadline.
Alternatively, a sophisticated sales manager will anticipate the major promotional decisions far in advance to permit adequate consideration and
consultation with others prior to the commitment deadline. This simple
example demonstrates the need for an integrated and systematic approach
to resolving the time dimension in planning and decision-making. Without
exception, major decisions made on a "last-minute" basis suffer from lack of
adequate supporting study, analysis, evaluation, and consultation. Profit
planning and control has evolved as a systematic approach to resolve many
aspects of this critical planning problem.

Effective implementation of the profit planning and control concept
requires that the management of the enterprise establish a definite time
dimension for certain types of decisions. Illustration 6 presents the time
dimensions established for planning purposes by a well-known firm as reflected in its comprehensive profit planning and control program. Illustration
6 focuses on several salient aspects of comprehensive profit planning and
control. To point up the important aspects, the next several paragraphs
discuss Illustration 6.

In viewing time-dimension perspectives in managerial planning, a clear-
cut distinction should be made between *historical* considerations and *futuristic*
considerations. Historical decisions and the results of operations in the past
often constitute, in effect, the launching platform for futuristic determinations. In regard to futuristic determinations in Illustration 6, there is a fundamental distinction between *project plans* and *periodic plans*. Classifying
managerial planning into these two categories focuses on the characteristics
of managerial planning and the differing related needs. Specifically, in each

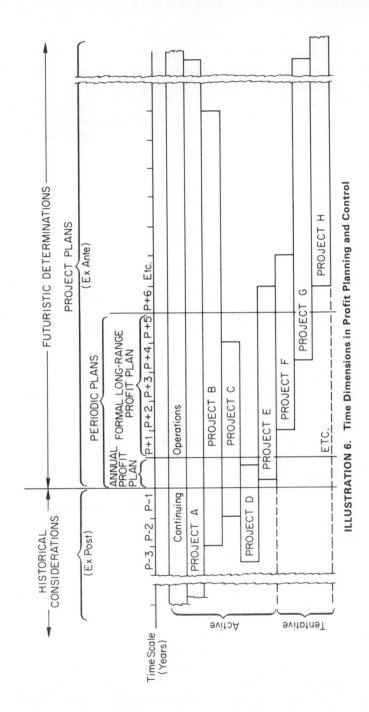

ILLUSTRATION 6.   Time Dimensions in Profit Planning and Control

42

enterprise there is a continuing necessity for the management to plan in respect to specific and identifiable projects (programs), each of which has a unique time dimension, because they entail commitments over a particular time span. The focus in *project planning* is on the project itself, which may represent either an operational or nonoperational commitment. Examples of projects are: the contemplated addition of a new machine; the construction of a new plant; the development and testing of a new product line; the acquisition of another going business; phasing out a current product; expansion of marketing to another geographical area; a research and development thrust; a government contract. Such activities and programs obviously should be planned over their life span and should be viewed as special commitments, although they necessarily must be integrated with other activities, programs, and operations of the enterprise. *Periodic planning* reflects the environmental necessity for management to plan, evaluate, and control operations within relatively short and consistent interim periods of time.

Periodic plans reflect the calendar constraints that have been self-imposed by mankind. Specifically, managers, owners, and other interested parties demand timetables; the result is *periodic* reports and evaluations of the progress of an enterprise. Thus, we usually observe plans and progress reports prepared by month, quarter, and year. In harmony with these environmental time constraints, the concept of periodic planning has evolved. Periodic planning directly represents a cross-sectional focus by time on income determination and periodic performance. In Illustration 6 observe that periodic plans are depicted as cutting vertically across all the projects and continuing operations for specific periods of time. It may be observed also that periodic plans encompass two subcategories, that is, the *tactical or short-range profit plan* and the *long-range or strategic profit plan*. There is exhibited what is commonly referred to as a "one-five" approach, that is, a one-year (short-range) profit plan and a five-year (long-range) profit plan. This arrangement is perhaps the one most commonly found in industry today, although the "one-three" and "one-four" arrangements also are common.

The concept of comprehensive profit planning and control encompasses a systematic and integrated approach to project planning, to tactical planning, and to strategic planning. Illustration 6 presents only one suggested time dimension; many variations are to be found in enterprises of various types. The time dimension should be unique to the enterprise and should be designed to fit the particular needs and characteristics of the enterprise. Ideally, every management that aspires to be successful in the long run should develop a similar time-dimension chart for decision-making and planning purposes. It is also appropriate to suggest that articulation and communication in a form similar to Illustration 6 would be quite effective in most situations. A similar time-dimension chart, if viewed as a matter of basic policy, literally forces early consideration of major decisions and focuses on timely planning. This latter point is relevant because planning is generally recognized as the one function on which management tends to procrastinate; it is so easy to "put off planning." In subsequent chapters of this book, application of these concepts of time dimension in profit planning and control will be considered in depth and illustrated.

Timing of planning activities suggests that there should be a definite management time schedule established for initiating and completing certain phases of the planning process. Managerial planning should be viewed as a *continuous* process at all levels of management. In day-to-day decision-making, as well as in long-range matters, all levels of management must be continually reassessing the future, replanning, and revising prior plans in the decision-making process. However, certain aspects of planning are best accomplished in a formal way and on a definite time schedule. For example, Illustration 6 depicted a "one-five plan" that entails the development of annual short- and long-range profit plans. This suggests that there should be a schedule of planning activities as a matter of management policy, frequently referred to as the *planning calendar* or planning cycle. Once management commits itself in this manner, procrastination in planning usually ends. Successful managers report this result to be an important indirect benefit accruing from a comprehensive profit planning and control program. Whereas it was previously almost impossible to assemble management groups intact for planning sessions, after the adoption of a planning calendar, the planning sessions generally assume a top priority. In many companies, executives absolutely refuse to make outside commitments during the critical phases of formal profit planning. Many companies that plan effectively report that for the first time both strategic and tactical planning are on a rational and timely basis. Nothing is more devastating to effective profit planning than for the management to issue a profit plan sometime after the beginning of the period involved.

Similarly, with respect to control, performance reports should be issued for interim time periods—that is, on a monthly, weekly, or, in some cases, certain reports on a daily basis. To be effective, performance reports must be in the hands of the responsible managers and supervisors shortly after the end of the interim period covered. Reports received weeks after the end of the period are of little value; by that time the supervisor is involved in too many new problems to be much concerned about a set of historical events that cannot be changed.

This fundamental also carries the implication that control action, to be potent, must be forthcoming immediately after identification of the causes of the problem; the longer control action is deferred, the greater the unfavorable financial effect. Follow-up activities are desirable (1) to determine the effectiveness of control action and (2) to establish the basis for improvement in efficiency. As with control action, follow-up activities must be timely and decisions based on the findings should be implemented as early as possible.

Flexible Application. This fundamental stresses that a profit planning and control program (or any other management technique) must not dominate the business, and that *flexibility* in applying the plans must be a forthright policy so that "strait jackets" are not imposed and all favorable opportunities are seized even though "they are not covered by the budget."

It is not uncommon for budgets to impose inflexibility on an endeavor and act as a severe constraint on the decision-making freedom of managers and supervisors. Contrary to this view, a profit planning and control program administered in a sophisticated manner permits greater freedom at all management levels. This effect is possible because all levels of management are brought into the decision-making process when plans are developed. When the basic profit plan has been approved, the higher level of management is then in a position to delegate more responsibility than otherwise would be possible. Also, the mere fact that an event or opportunity was not anticipated in the plans (and there will always be many) should have no bearing on whether the situation should be investigated and a decision made that seems most favorable to enterprise operations. In such situations the profit plans place management in the position of being able to assess, on a more objective basis, the soundness of a contemplated decision. Simply, the profit planning and control approach focuses on such exceptions and anticipates exceptions, adjustments, and replanning as situations evolve. The prior profit plan provides a basis for evaluating the broader impact on the total financial picture for the enterprise.

To cost control, the principle of flexibility is especially important. Expense and cost budgets must not be used and interpreted rigidly; the budget must not prevent the making of rational decisions in respect to expenses merely because an expenditure was not anticipated. Variable (flexible) expense budgets frequently are employed to meet one of the problems of cost control arising from a change in circumstances.[4] To illustrate, assume that the budget for Department X carries an expense allowance of $2,000 for labor and an expectation of 10,000 units of output (20 cents per unit). Now assume that unforeseen circumstances make it necessary for the department actually to produce 12,000 units of output and to incur direct labor costs of $2,350. Assuming further that direct labor is a cost that varies directly with output, a comparison of actual direct labor costs incurred in producing 12,000 units of output with a budget allowance for that cost based on 10,000 units of output would show an unfavorable, and more significantly, a meaningless variation of $350. Under variable budget procedures the budget

---

[4] Variable budgets are discussed in Chapter 9.

allowance would be adjusted to $2,400 that is, 12,000 × $.20, and a favorable variance of $50 would be reported (discussed in detail in Chapter 9).

Throughout the following chapters managerial flexibility to implement the results of the planning process is emphasized. Continuing emphasis is important to emphasize clearly that the budget not be viewed as a straight jacket and to emphasize that the planning and control approach to management does not constrain the management in seizing all opportunities, whether planned for or not, that will accrue to the economic well-being of the enterprise.

Behavorial Viewpoint.   The motivation of human resources through dynamic leadership is central to effective management. The behavioral aspects of the management process have been accorded extensive and intensive investigation by psychologists, educators, and businessmen. This attention is increasing in scope and intensity in recognition that there are many unknowns, misconceptions, and speculations concerning the responses of the individual and the group in varying situations. The comprehensive profit planning and control approach to managing brings many of these behavioral problems into sharp focus. A sophisticated view of profit planning and control focuses on a positive approach to resolve certain behavioral problems. Clearly, the approach cannot resolve behavioral problems, but in many respects it can provide one effective approach to their partial resolution.

Goal orientation is characteristic of ambitious and competent individuals who are normally involved in the management process. Such individuals have strong personal goal needs; their performance is enhanced through a hierarchy of realistic goals with which they can identify. For positive motivation there must be a harmony of goal orientation between the personal interests of the manager and his relationship with the enterprise. Monetary rewards, although goal satisfying in certain ways for most individuals, cannot satisfy all, or even most, goal needs of competent and intelligent people. The more subtle goal needs relate to the satisfactions that one gets from accomplishment and from being a participant in activities that appear relevant to him. Related to goal orientation is the recognition that managers at all levels are much more likely to understand, accept, and pursue those goals and plans that they help formulate in a meaningful way. Participation in the establishment of enterprise objectives, goals, and policies with which they will be directly involved has come to be recognized as one of the more effective approaches to managerial motivation at all organizational levels. Realistic goals, established through meaningful participation, tend to raise the aspiration level of the entire management in a firm.[5] The profit planning and con-

---

[5] See Andrew C. Stedry, *Budget Control and Cost Behavior* (Englewood Cliffs, N.J.: Prentice-Hall, Inc., 1960), Chapters 3–4.

trol concept provides a means to resolve largely the goal orientation problems in an enterprise, since effective participation by all levels of management is required in the development of those goals, the related policies, and their modes of implementation.

Industrial psychologists have conducted relevant studies of the behavioral effects of *pressure* in the management process. Consistent with these studies, casual observation indicates that most individuals and groups perform more effectively under certain amounts and types of pressure. Thus, it appears that some form of pressure is essential to effective managerial leadership. The significant problems posed in the managerial context concern the duration, extent, and types of pressure that tend to maximize continued motivation of the individual manager and the respective management teams. The effects of pressure are thought to be unique to the people involved and the prevailing environment. Pressure that is harsh, extensive, unrealistic, inconsistent, inflexible, and misunderstood very soon will push the individual or group to a critical, antagonistic point. Certain aspects of the profit planning and control approach have been used as extreme pressure devices to goad people toward greater efforts. Unbiased analyses of such situations clearly show that the central problem is an insecure and/or unsophisticated executive or management group. Even if the budget were not the available tool for exerting unreasonable pressure, such persons would still commit their managerial sins in other ways. Nevertheless, a potential behavioral problem with significant overtones does exist in respect to practically all of the so-called managerial techniques; they are susceptible to easy behavioral misuse by unenlightened managers. This point emphasizes the fact that the *concept* of profit planning and control is fundamental since it provides sophisticated guidance for effective management and, thereby, avoidance of many of the behavioral errors on the part of managers. In contrast to effective implementation of the concepts in a sophisticated manner, if management understands and implements only the *procedural and mechanical* aspects of profit planning and control, it will be an exercise in futility; and worse, negative results are the likely outcome.

Individual accomplishment, both outstanding and substandard performance, should be identified and recognized in the management process. The system of individual evaluation must be fair, understandable, and accurate. It should give recognition to the abilities and performances of each manager—his aspirations, his reactions—and to the group pressures that affect him. The dignity of the individual is important in the management process. Profit planning and control entails placing a high degree of responsibility on the individual manager. It entails a procedure for careful evaluation of the planning capabilities of the manager, and through the medium of performance reports and other observations, a careful reading of his performance as a manager. Thus, the profit planning and control approach establishes a basis for some precision in measuring the performance of the individual manager; in the process, it is likely that those with high competence will soon be noticed and those with low competence will be identified. This potential for capable evaluation of the management potentials of each individual, of course, poses behavioral implications of consequence. This fundamental focuses on this problem; it requires sophisticated attention and implies that superiors should give a high degree of recognition to outstanding performance as well as being concerned about low performance. By and large, the human element is the dominant feature of effective management planning and control.

A common problem encountered when *introducing* the profit planning and control approach is overt and subtle resistance from certain individuals and groups. There are a number of very human reasons why resistance at this point is generally encountered; among them are the following: resistance to change; lack of understanding of the program and how it is to operate; concern about the potential consequences and the manner in which these may affect their particular status; expectation of increased pressure; disagreement with the importance of planning; distaste for performance measurement; a general preference for less formal approaches in the management process. All these concerns have some rational basis, and they must be given serious attention in view of their potentially significant effect on the motivations of the individuals concerned.

At this point we have mentioned only a few of the important behavioral problems and their many dimensions, but, hopefully, enough to suggest some of the related potentials that may be derived from an enlightened approach to comprehensive profit planning and control. A prominent psychologist emphasized some of the behavioral implications as follows:

> The key problem facing a mature managerial group is to define a common purpose—a goal which excites the imagination of the rank and file and which is attainable if they go after it as a team. To be exciting, it must either be something new that will give them a distinction they can share or something hitherto considered too difficult or even impossible, so that they can feel that they are spearheading a breakthrough for the rest of their industry. Morale is, after all, a matter of feeling that one has a common cause with his organization. It is increasingly apparent today that what many people want most is a sense of accomplishment—a feeling that what they are getting paid to do helps to make the world better and isn't just a meaningless exercise for the sake of money.
>
> The standard against which mature management judges its performance is the ultimate potentialities of its own organization—not the performance of its competitors. The essential obligations of an enlightened management are to define the potentialities, to create a working atmosphere in which men will

want to strive toward them, and to attract the kind of man who can and will participate in such a growth process.[6]

Follow-up.   This fundamental holds that both good and substandard performance should be carefully investigated, the purpose being threefold: (1) in the case of substandard performance, to lead in a constructive manner to immediate corrective action; (2) in the case of outstanding performance, to recognize it and perhaps provide for a transfer of knowledge to similar operations; and (3) to provide a basis for better planning and control in the future.

MANAGERIAL EVALUATION OF ALTERNATIVES IN PLANNING

Essentially managerial planning entails an analysis of alternative courses of action and leads to a decision. The comprehensive profit planning and control approach is especially useful in the evaluation and selection of alternatives in many instances because of the implicit financial impacts normally encountered. The tactical short-range and strategic long-range profit plans, in effect, constitute simulation models that are quite useful to evaluate the financial effects of many different alternatives under considera- tion. In the process of profit plan construction, the use of procedures such as decision models, income summaries, cash flow analyses, break-even analyses, inventory models, differential cost analyses, and return on investment analy- ses provide critical information for assessing the impact of different alterna- tives.

The tentative choices made for profit plan purposes must be consistent with the overall return on investment objective, the growth objective of the firm, and other relevant overriding objectives. Throughout the process of developing a coordinated profit plan the management must tentatively approve definite courses of action relative to pricing policy, advertising pro- grams, capital-additions plans, financing arrangements, research programs, product development and expansion, and so on. The tactical profit plan buildup often involves building, reevaluating, tearing down, and rebuilding the plan until the best possible plan of operations is developed. Development of certain aspects of the plan of operations may indicate that previously

[6] Saul W. Gellerman, *People, Problems, and Profit—The Uses of Psychology in Management* (New York: McGraw-Hill Book Co., Inc., 1960), pp. 249–50. Additional reference, W. J. Bruns and D. T. DeCoster, *Accounting and Its Behavioral Implications* (New York: McGraw-Hill Book Co., Inc., 1969).

selected alternatives should be discarded and other courses of action reconsidered. Tentative, step-by-step approvals of planning decisions throughout the profit planning process are discussed in detail in subsequent chapters. Final approval of the profit plan, as opposed to tentative approval, represents the last step in construction of profit plans, because at this point planning decisions have been made on all alternatives, and their probable financial effects incorporated in the tactical short-range and strategic long-range profit plans.

APPLICATION OF PROFIT PLANNING AND CONTROL TO VARIOUS TYPES OF FIRMS

Occasionally it is said that comprehensive profit planning and control is applicable to only very large and complex organizations. A not unusual comment is that "comprehensive budgeting is a fine idea for most concerns, but ours is different," and so on. To the contrary, profit planning and control can be adapted to any organization (profit or nonprofit), except perhaps the smallest, regardless of special circumstances and conditions. The fact that a company has peculiar circumstances or critical problems frequently is good reason for the adoption of certain profit planning and control procedures. In respect to size, when operations are extensive enough to require more than one or two supervisory personnel, there may be a need for profit planning and control applications. The smallest concern certainly has different needs in this respect than a large one. As with accounting, no one system of profit planning and control can be designed for all operations; a profit planning and control system must be tailored to fit the particular environment, and it must be continually updated and adapted as that environment changes.

ADVANTAGES AND DISADVANTAGES OF PROFIT PLANNING AND CONTROL

The potentials of comprehensive profit planning and control have been emphasized in the preceding discussions; however, it should not be assumed that the concept is foolproof nor that it is free of problems. The principal problems in profit planning and control are: (1) developing management sophistication in its application; (2) developing a realistic sales plan (budget); (3) developing realistic objectives and standards; (4) adequate communication of the attitudes, policies, and guidelines by higher levels of managment; (5) attaining managerial flexibility in application of the system; and (6) updating the system to harmonize with the changing environment within which the management operates.

In developing and using a profit planning and control program, the following four additional limitations should be kept in mind:

1. The Profit Plan Is Based on Estimates.   The strength or weakness of a profit planning program depends to a large degree on the accuracy with which the basic estimates are made. For example, estimates must be based on all available facts and good managerial judgment. The estimating of sales and expenses cannot be an exact science; however, there are numerous statistical, mathematical, and other techniques that may be effectively applied to the problems that produce satisfactory results when tempered with sound reasoning and judgment. If there is conviction that such estimates can be made realistically, serious effort generally gives satisfactory results. Because the profit plan is based entirely on estimates and judgments, flexibility is essential in interpreting and utilizing the results.

2. A Profit Planning and Control Program Must Be Continually Adapted to Fit Changing Circumstances.   A comprehensive budget program cannot be installed and perfected in a short time. Profit planning and control techniques must continually be adapted, not only for each particular concern but for changing conditions within the concern. Various techniques must be tried, improved, or discarded and replaced with others. In other words, a profit planning and control program must be dynamic in every sense of the word. Normally, it will take more than one year to attain a reasonably good program, and management must not expect too much during this period. Continuous budget education is necessary, especially during the formative period.

3. Execution of a Profit Plan Will Not Occur Automatically.   Once the profit plans are complete, they will be effective only if all responsible executives exert continuous and aggressive effort toward their accomplishment. Department heads must feel responsibility to achieve or better department goals laid down in the profit plans. All levels of management must have a sophisticated understanding of the program, be convinced of its relevance to their function, and must participate in its operation in a meaningful way.

4. The Profit Plan Will Not Take the Place of Management and Administration.   Profit planning does not take the place of management; it is a tool that can aid in performing the management process in relevant ways. The budget manual of one prominent concern reads as follows on this point:

> The profit plan should be regarded, not as a master, but as a servant. It is one of the best tools yet devised for advancing the affairs of a company and the individuals in their various spheres of managerial activity. It is not assumed

that any profit plan is perfect. The most important consideration is to make sure, by intelligent use of the profit plans, that all possible attainable benefits are derived from the plans as rendered.

The broad advantages of profit planning and control have been enumerated in the preceding paragraphs. More specific advantages may be enumerated as follows:

1. It forces early consideration of basic policies.

2. It requires adequate and sound organization structure; that is, there must be a definite assignment of responsibility for each function of the enterprise.

3. It compels all members of management from the top down to participate in the establishment of goals and plans.

4. It compels departmental managers to make plans in harmony with the plans of other departments and of the entire firm.

5. It requires that the management put down in cold figures what is necessary for satisfactory performance.

6. It requires adequate and appropriate historical accounting data.

7. It compels management to plan for the most economical use of labor, material, facilities, and capital.

8. It instills at all levels of management the habit of timely, careful, and adequate consideration of all the relevant factors before reaching important decisions.

9. It reduces cost by increasing the span of control since fewer supervisors are needed.

10. It frees executives from many day-to-day internal problems through the media of predetermined policies and clear-cut authority relationships and thereby provides more executive time for planning and creative thinking.

11. It tends to remove the cloud of uncertainty that exists in many firms, especially among lower levels of management, relative to basic policies and enterprise objectives.

12. It pinpoints efficiency and inefficiency.

13. It promotes understanding among members of management of their coworkers' problems.

14. It forces the management to give time and adequate attention to the effect of the expected trend of general business conditions.

15. It forces a periodic self-analysis of the company.

16. It aids in obtaining bank credit.

17. It checks progress or lack of progress toward the objectives of the enterprise.

ESTABLISHING THE FOUNDATION FOR PROFIT PLANNING AND CONTROL

In Chapters 1 and 2 the discussions have been general, although specific references have been made to certain aspects of profit planning and control programs. At this point it seems appropriate to summarize the steps that an enterprise should take to establish a sound foundation for initiating a profit planning and control program. These steps may be summarized as follows: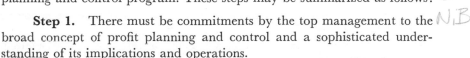

Step 1. There must be commitments by the top management to the broad concept of profit planning and control and a sophisticated understanding of its implications and operations.

Step 2. The characteristics of the firm and the environment in which it operates—including the controllable and noncontrollable variables—must be identified and evaluated so that relevant decisions may by made concerning the characteristics of a profit planning and control program that would be effective and practical.

Step 3. There should be an evaluation of the organizational structure and assignment of managerial responsibilities and implementation of changes deemed necessary for effective planning and control.

Step 4. There must be an evaluation and reorganization of the accounting system and where desirable to assure that it is tailored to the organizational responsibilities (responsibility accounting) so that it can provide historical data particularly useful for planning and control purposes.

Step 5. A policy determination must be made in respect to the time dimensions to be used for profit planning and control purposes.

Step 6. A program of budget education should be developed to acquaint management at all levels with (a) purposes of the program; (b) the manner in which it will operate, including the basic management policies and guidelines for its administration; (c) the responsibility of each level of management in the program; and (d) the ways in which the program can facilitate the performance of each manager's functions.

These six steps, if taken seriously at the outset, should pave the way for instituting a sound profit planning and control program.

In the following chapters we will look at the various components of a comprehensive profit planning and control program. Specific examples will be given of the major components to serve as a basis for much of the discussions. In this manner it is hoped that the presentations will be both conceptual and especially practical.

DISCUSSION QUESTIONS

1. It has been said that techniques, mathematical models, and simulations will not substitute for competent management. In light of this statement explain the role of these tools in the management process.

2. Distinguish between mechanics, techniques, and fundamentals of profit planning and control. Explain why these distinctions are important.

3. Managerial involvement in a profit planning and control program is especially important; explain the basic aspects of managerial involvement in the program.

4. Explain management participation in profit planning and control, and indicate some pitfalls to be avoided.

5. Basically, what managers in a company should provide the decisional inputs in planning process? Explain.

6. Why is sound organizational structure fundamental to effective profit planning and control?

7. Distinguish between (a) cost centers, (b) profit centers, and (c) investment centers.

8. Explain the underlying concept of responsibility accounting, and indicate why it is fundamental to effective profit planning and control.

9. Define communication. Why is it critical in the management process?

10. How does a profit planning and control program enhance communication?

11. Discuss the following statement with respect to profit planning: "Objectives should represent goals that are attainable and yet present a real challenge."

12. It has been said that, "Padding the budget serves to invalidate the budget concept and little can be done about it." Explain the implications of this statement.

13. Explain the essence and implications of the statement that "each management is faced with the basic question of *time dimension* in planning and decision-making."

14. What is meant by the term "planning horizon"?

15. Distinguish between periodic and project plans.

16. What is the purpose of a planning calendar? Why is it frequently essential?

17. Why is flexibility in application of the concept of profit planning and control critical?

18. Explain what is meant by the "behavioral" aspects of profit planning and control. Relate your explanation to goal orientation and pressure.

19. Why should management attention be devoted to favorable variances as well as unfavorable variances on performance reports?

20. In a general way explain how profit planning and control aids management in the evaluation of alternatives.

21. Can profit planning and control be applied in small enterprises?

22. Outline the broad steps that an enterprise should take in establishing a sound foundation for initiating a profit planning and control program.

CASE 2-1
Dowd Department Store

The president of the Dowd Department Store stated to the case writer that "my people do much, much better under a budget program if I give them budgets quite a bit in excess of what I really expect them to be able to do. Of course, they don't know what I really expect; therefore, the high budget goals that I give them for sales keep the pressure on." In implementing this concept, the sales budgets for each of the departments in the store are set at approximately 20 percent above what is "realistically expected." The president responded to the following question: Do you also give them expense budgets similarly overstated? "Of course not, I give them tight expense budgets, and for the same reason!"

Required:

Do you agree with the viewpoints of the president? Explain the basis for your agreements or disagreements.

CASE 2-2
Bowers, Incorporated

In an off-the-record discussion between the case writer and the assistant to the president of Bowers, Incorporated, a manufacturer of small parts for automobiles, the following statement was made: "Our budget system doesn't work too well for a number of reasons. For example, when the controller's department has prepared the annual budget we sometimes ask him for evaluation of the impact of some alternative plans, we have to wait for four or five weeks, and I have a feeling that all we get is the same set of figures as for the other alternatives, except that they are reshuffled projections based on historical trends and ratios. It is my view that management needs better and more timely financial analyses on budgets from the controller than this."

Required:

Indicate the relevant implications of this statement. Analyze the primary problem and provide some constructive suggestions.

CASE 2-3
Technical Equipment Corporation

Technical Equipment Corporation was organized in 1935 to conduct geophysical services for oil-producing companies in the southwest. Its expansion since that time, both in operations and revenues, has been phenomenal. It now also manufactures equipment in related fields and sells to the U.S. government as well as to private operators. Sales for the calendar year 1977 are expected to reach $65 million. The company has manufacturing plants located in two large southwestern cities and has subsidiaries in nine foreign countries.

The firm is alert to the latest management developments. Likewise, it is alert for new fields that it may enter profitably and for methods of improving present products and operations.

The attached chart (Exhibit 1) summarizes the organizational relationships within the firm. The company uses a responsibility accounting system and an effective comprehensive profit planning and control program. The management is considered to be both sophisticated and aggressive.

The activities included in the Control and Finance Division (a staff group) are centered in the five following departments: a Central Plant and Office Services department; the secretary treasurer, who has responsibility for matters concerning corporate affairs and financial policy; the Planning department, which coordinates preparation of the annual (short-term) profit plan; the Central Accounting department, where consolidation accounting is handled and where internal auditing is done; and the Management Services department, which prepares special reports and studies.

The six product divisions are decentralized as profit centers, and each division head reports directly to top management for the operations of his division. Staff department managers in the product divisions report to the division head and have only a functional relationship with their staff counterparts at the home-office level. TEC believes that the experience gained in specific product areas enables these staff individuals to develop their abilities to the fullest extent possible and thus justifies the possible extra cost resulting from some duplication of effort in performing staff functions.

There is no line of authority from the vice president of Control and Finance, Mr. Watson, to the six product division controllers; each product division controller reports directly to the manager of the product division in which he works. Informal communication results from regular monthly meetings held by the vice president of Control and Finance and attended by the seven controllers. At these meetings profit planning and control problems of concern to the majority are discussed. Each division controller can thus learn how the others are handling problems similar to his own, or he can receive suggestions from them. These meetings are viewed by the top management as especially useful.

In addition, each product division controller prepares a monthly performance report for the division manager, a copy of which goes directly to the vice president of Control and Finance. The latter officer reviews these performance reports and submits pertinent comments to the executive vice president, the Product Division head, or the Product Division controller, depending on the nature of the matter. The vice president of Control and Finance has been assigned overall responsibility for the reporting function (external financial reports and internal performance reports). A recent situation illustrates a problem that arose reflecting the line-staff relationships:

In examining the monthly performance reports from the Measurements Equipment Division, Mr. Watson observed that the inventory of manufactured parts had exceeded the planned level of $50,000 to $200,000 in a period of three months. Mr. Watson had missed the last two group meetings; apparently the inventory variance had not been raised by his assistant who conducted the meetings when Mr. Watson was absent. He questioned Mr. Nolan, the Measurements Equipment Division controller, who had no specific information relative to the variance, stating that "it was nothing to be alarmed about." In view of the large amount of funds involved, Mr. Watson pursued the subject, rather forcefully suggesting to Mr. Nolan that he should have investigated the reasons

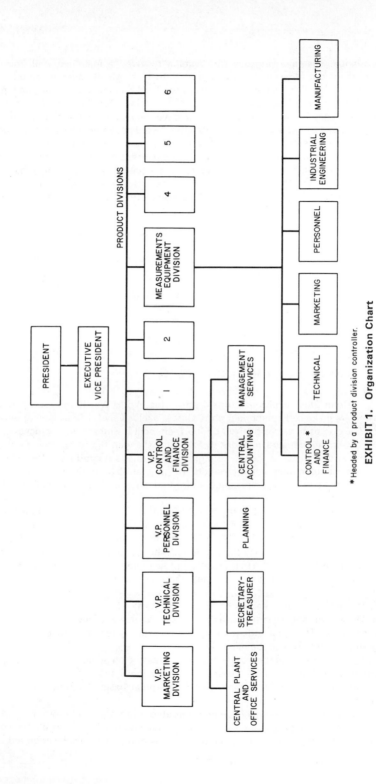

* Headed by a product division controller.

EXHIBIT 1. Organization Chart

for the variance. The following day Mr. Watson received a telephone call from Mr. Sumner, head of the Measurements Equipment Division. Mr. Sumner appeared to be annoyed, stating that "Nolan felt that you were too hard on him. Incidentally, he reports to me and the inventory is my responsibility." Nevertheless, Mr. Watson inquired about the unusual variance in inventory. Mr. Sumner gave the distinct impression that he had not been aware of the variance and flatly stated that he did not know why it had happened. The telephone conversation ended with neither party indicating any further action.

Mr. Watson was deeply concerned about the matter since it involved a significant impact on cash flow and other financial factors; consequently, he felt strongly that some action should be taken. Therefore, he discussed the situation in detail with Mr. Porter, the executive vice president, who requested a complete explanation of the inventory variance in writing from Mr. Sumner.

Required:

Be prepared to analyze the case and pinpoint the significant problems. How should the primary problems be resolved?

CASE 2-4
Colin Steel Works

Colin Steel Works was organized during World War II and for a period of about five years produced component parts almost exclusively for firms having defense contracts. The company was organized by fourteen local businessmen to process scrap. Due to the continuing demand immediately following the war, the company experienced a reasonably strong demand for the semifinished products it produced. By 1950 the company was manufacturing some products for general distribution. Because the firm was located in the southwest a substantial freight advantage existed, particularly on the heavier items manufactured.

As a result of increased competition and a falloff in the profit margin during the last several years, the management found it necessary to tighten up on operations. The management had devoted considerable efforts to improving supervisory skills and to upgrading hourly paid workers. During the period, there had been some layoffs; in such cases the management attempted to evaluate employees carefully so that the less efficient were laid off. The management felt that they had been fairly successful in keeping the better workers.

During the last several years, considerable efforts also have been devoted to reducing costs. The accounting system was revised in accordance with the concept of responsibility accounting. The independent CPA has consistently recommended that a profit planning and control program be initiated.

Although competition remained strong and pressure on prices heavy, the company has experienced a slight annual increase in gross business except for the last year. The company has approximately 225 employees on a regular basis. From time to time ten to fifty temporary employees are employed.

During the past year the management initiated a profit planning program for the company. The president of the firm was convinced that such a program would be worthwhile. He was strongly influenced by the discussions at a conference he attended conducted by the American Management Association. The president felt that the program would be of value in management planning and control. In addition, he felt that some effective approach was needed to control costs more effectively.

The profit planning and control program during the past year involved numerous problems; however, the president felt that this was to be expected during the first year. The budget supervisor was a long-time employee and, not having had previous experience with a budget program, he too was learning. Meetings were scheduled at the end of the year to review the procedures, progress, and related problems.

The factory manager and the budget supervisor recently had a meeting of the factory supervisors, excluding the foremen. The purpose of the meeting as described in the announcement was "to critically examine our budget experience during the past year with a view to improving procedures."

During the discussions, Sam Grant, one of the factory supervisors, commented: "I don't like this participation idea that we keep talking about. Last year I followed the instructions and let the foremen participate all over the place and it has given me nothing but trouble. I used to have firm control over these men, but after this year I'm about ready to throw in the sponge." "What's the problem?" replied Bill Winter, the budget supervisor. "Well, it's like this. First, I spend a lot of time telling these guys that they are to draw up their own expense budgets; they were not too happy about it and I had a heck of a time getting them in on time. Then they were all wrong and I had to change them. Then I had to spend a lot of time in cozy little chats trying to explain to them why they had to be changed. Finally, we got them in; then the performance reports began to arrive. Of course, the performance reports had all kinds of unfavorable variations and you should hear the excuses. After I get through with all the conferences, I don't have much time left to supervise. But more important, I feel that I have lost control over the foremen. They are giving me too much static and excuses now. I feel we should tell them what to do, how much to spend, and not encourage them to question everything. You need discipline and respect at this level and the only way to get it is to be firm and rule with an iron hand; otherwise we supervisors will lose our authority. Too much talk with the foremen is not good." "But Sam," replied Fred Matson, the factory manager, "we let you participate; don't you think that is working?" "Well, the management will have to decide on that; I think supervisors have enough sense to know how to get along with their superiors. They realize you can't run an operation by mob rule." After a few more comments the meeting was adjourned for lunch.

Required:

Analyze the situation, pinpoint the primary problem(s), and present recommendations.

Comprehensive Profit Planning and Control Outlined

chapter three

The broad foundation underlying comprehensive profit planning and control has been discussed; we now focus our attention more directly on its specific components. Although we are focusing more sharply on the characteristics of profit planning and control, we nevertheless will generalize in an attempt to keep the discussions appropriate to the problems of a wide variety of enterprises. Therefore, remember that all the points and issues discussed are not necessarily relevant to any one enterprise. Throughout these discussions, we will also focus on profit-making enterprises, although the general approach has wide application in other types of endeavors.

Regardless of the type of endeavor, the management task is essentially the same, that is, to create and maintain an internal environment in which individuals working together as groups attain efficient performance harmonious with the broad objectives of the enterprise. The environment must be conducive for individuals to make their maximum contribution to the efforts of the group. Since economic, political, social, and technological factors operating in the external environment have a significant internal impact, the manager must understand them and try to harmonize the internal environment with them. Thus, the basic tasks of managing, planning, organizing, directing, and controlling are the same in business and non-business enterprises.

Comprehensive profit planning and control entails a systematic approach to management, focusing on a quantitative evaluation of the results of managerial objectives and dynamic control through application of the management exception principle.[1] In harmony with this broad objective, the purpose of this chapter is to discuss briefly the system, procedures, and technical aspects of a comprehensive profit planning and control program that have general applicability. Most of the topics in this chapter will be treated in detail in subsequent chapters.

COMPONENTS OF A COMPREHENSIVE PROFIT PLANNING AND CONTROL PROGRAM

A comprehensive profit planning and control program encompasses much more than the traditional idea of a periodic budget. Rather, it encompasses the application of a number of management concepts through a variety of approaches, techniques, and sequential steps. The term *comprehensive* implies (1) application of the broad concept of profit planning and control to all phases of operations in an enterprise, and (2) the application of a total systems approach outlined below. The essential steps implicit in a comprehensive profit planning and control program may be outlined sequentially as follows:

1. Evaluation of the potential effect of all relevant variables on the enterprise.
2. Specification by executive management the broad objectives of the enterprise.
3. Establishment of specific goals for the enterprise.
4. Development and evaluation of enterprise strategies.
5. Preparation of planning premises.
6. Preparation and evaluation of project plans.
7. Development and approval of a strategic long-range profit plan.
8. Development and approval of a tactical short-range profit plan.
9. Development of supplementary analyses.
10. Implementation of plans.
11. Development, dissemination, and utilization of performance reports.
12. Implementation of follow-up actions.

[1] For an excellent discussion of the significance of objectives in managing see: *Managing by—and with—Objectives, Studies in Personnel Policy, No. 212* (New York: National Industrial Conference Board, Inc., 1968). Also see the following special research series: Subhash Jain and Surendra Sighvi, eds. *Essentials of Corporate Planning*, Research Series (Oxford, Ohio: Planning Executives Institute, 1973). George A. Steiner, *Comprehensive Managerial Planning*, Research Series (Oxford, Ohio: The Planning Executives Institute).

This list has been presented in a sequence that probably would be followed by a firm each year. Thus, the above list can be thought of as a series of steps in the planning and control processes performed on a continuing basis. For discussion purposes, we will assume that the strategic long-range profit plan covers a five-year time span and that the tactical short-range profit plan encompasses a twelve-month planning period. To visualize how the total systems approach as outlined might operate, let us also assume that the formal planning process—steps one through nine above—is *repeated on an annual basis*. Thus, all the basic steps in the planning phase would be reviewed and evaluated annually, the purpose being to update each component on a basis of managerial judgment and actual enterprise performance. In a particular year, some of the components, such as the broad objectives of the enterprise, may not be changed in any respect, whereas other components may be completely revised for the upcoming year. In every case, however, one must anticipate that steps five, six, seven, eight, and nine would involve complete restatement each year.[2]

In the paragraphs to follow we will discuss the relevant aspects of each of the twelve components. In Chapter 4 each will be illustrated in summary fashion, with detailed illustrations included in subsequent chapters.

Evaluation of Relevant Variables Affecting the Enterprise. Chapter 1 included a discussion on the identification and evaluation of the relevant variables affecting the destiny of an enterprise. It was recommended that the relevant environmental variables be classified as *controllable variables* and *noncontrollable variables* (see Illustration 2).

The cardinal points noted were: (1) managerial planning must be focused on the planning of the controllable variables; and (2) there must be managerial planning *for* the noncontrollable variables, that is, to take advantage of their potential favorable impacts and to minimize their potential unfavorable impacts on the enterprise. Illustration 2 provided an example of one step in the evaluation of relevant variables. By relevant variables we obviously imply those that will have a direct and significant impact on the enterprise. For a large firm with a national market, the relevant variables obviously would be broad in scope, whereas a small firm would be concerned primarily with regional and local variables operating within the narrow environment of the enterprise. Analysis and evaluation of the environmental variables are a matter of continual concern to the manager. However, in most enterprises there is a strong need for a periodic

---

[2] The planning process should involve periodic, consistent, and in-depth replanning so that all aspects of operations are carefully re-examined and re-evaluated. This prevents a budget planning approach that involves only justification of increases over the prior period. The concept of re-evaluation and the necessity to justify all aspects of the plans periodically finds its strongest support in what has been called "zero-base budgeting." For a detailed discussion see; Peter A. Pyhrr, *Zero-Base Budgeting* (John Wiley & Sons, New York, 1973).

evaluation of the relevant variables, usually on an annual basis. A comprehensive profit planning and control program uses such a periodic evaluation in depth. An evaluation of the relevant variables should involve all the members of executive management who in turn should expect various staff groups to provide analytical data and recommendations. It is not unusual for an enterprise to utilize specialized consultants from time to time to buttress the internal analysis and evaluations.

A particularly significant aspect of this step includes an analysis of the *present strength and weakness of the enterprise.*[3] Planning for the future necessarily must start with an objective and realistic comprehension of the present status of products, services, markets, profits, and returns on investments, cash flow, availability of capital productive capabilities, and the competence of both the management and nonmanagement personnel. Obviously, it is crucial to realistic planning and strategy that management develop a practical and objective evaluation of strengths and weaknesses of the enterprise. This particular aspect of the planning process is perhaps the more difficult for most managements since deficiencies and inefficiencies are frequently difficult to observe and evaluate objectively by those directly involved. The comprehensive profit planning and control approach is based upon the notion that these significant aspects of operations will be critically analyzed and evaluated periodically and in an orderly manner. In many companies, outside, independent assistance is almost essential to such an assessment. In this assessment and evaluation, present strengths and weaknesses should be classified between short-term and long-term potentials. For example, production capacity problems and the efficiency of certain groups of employees may be subject only to long-term resolution, whereas defective products may well respond to short-term efforts. The better-managed companies have found that periodic (generally on an annual basis) assessment of strengths and weaknesses is a much more effective policy than one that states: "We will assess our strengths and weaknesses on a day-to-day basis as things are happening."

Specification by Executive Management of the Broad Objectives of the Enterprise. On the basis of a realistic evaluation of the relevant variables and a practical assessment of the strengths and weaknesses of the company, executive management is in a position to specify the broad objectives of the enterprise or, alternatively, to restate the prior broad objectives, should this be suggested by the present situation. In view of the subsequent components, the statement of broad objectives simply can be viewed as a pervasive, although general, expression of the philosophical objectives of the enterprise. The broad objectives normally should avoid specific state-

[3] For an excellent discussion of related problems see: George Steiner, *Strategic Factors in Business Success* (New York: Financial Executives Research Foundation, 1969).

ments of quantitative goals; rather they should focus on such broad factors as long-range economic potentials, attitudes toward customers, product and service quality, employee relations, and attitudes toward owners. It is not unusual to read a simplified version of the broad objectives of the enterprise in the company "house organ" and other publications made available to interested parties.

The statement of broad objectives should express the mission, vision, and ethical tone of the enterprise. It tends to provide enterprise identity, continuity of purpose, and definition. One prominent writer lists the purposes of the statement as follows:

1. To define the purpose of the company (to state exactly why the company is in business).
2. To clarify the philosophy-character of the company (to state the moral and ethical principles guiding actions).
3. To create a particular "climate" within the business (to communicate the basic purposes and ethics of the company to all those in the company ranks so that they may communicate them to customers and others outside the firm through their actions).
4. To set down a guide for managers so that the decisions they make will reflect the best interests of the business with fairness and justness to those concerned (to provide an overall guide to those in decision-making positions so that they can act independently but within the framework of the firm's basic goals and principles).[4]

Thus, the statement of broad objectives has as its primary purpose to serve as the basic foundation or building block to develop respect in and pride for the company by management, other employees, owners, customers, and other firms who have commercial contacts with it. It should be designed for wide dissemination and should be "believable," which means that in the long run the company's actions must be in harmony with the statement itself. An example is provided in the case presented in the next chapter.

Establish Specific Goals for the Enterprise. The purpose of this step is to bring the statement of broad objectives into sharp focus and at the same time to move from the realm of general information to the confines of internal management. This component of a comprehensive profit planning and control program details specific short-range and long-range goals for the enterprise. This step provides *definite and measurable goals* for the whole enterprise and for each of the major subdivisions (the responsibility centers).

[4] Adapted from Stewart Thompson, *Management Creeds and Philosophies*, Research Study No. 32 (New York: American Management Association, 1958), p. 9. Also see, Alfred W. Schoennauer, *The Formulation & Implementation of Corporate Objecteves & Strategies*, Research Series (Oxford, Ohio: The Planning Executives Institute, 1972).

Executive management must exercise leadership in this respect so that there will be a realistic and articulated framework in which operations will be conducted toward common goals and there will be a basis for measurement of performance.

For both the strategic long-range profit plan (say, five years) and for the tactical short-run profit plan (annual), the statement of specific goals should define such operational goals as expansion and/or contraction of product and service lines, geographic areas, share of the market by major product service lines, growth trends, production goals, profit margins, and return on investment. These specific goals in large measure are quantified and specified for each major subdivision of the firm. Executive management develops measurable goals in areas of operation critical to long-run success of the enterprise. These goals must represent *realistic* potentials as opposed to mere guesses. An example of a statement of specific goals is illustrated in the case presented in the next chapter.

Development and Evaluation of Enterprise Strategies. Development of enterprise long-range and short-range strategies requires management to find the best available alternatives for attaining the broad and specific objectives already established. Strategies focus on the "how;" they represent the plan of action. In this step, as in all the other steps discussed in this chapter, the issues and determinations interrelate and overlap with the other components. Executive management continually must be involved in the development of new strategies and in the adaptation of currently ongoing strategies in harmony with the relevant variables with which management must cope. In the development of basic strategies for the enterprise, executive management must focus on identification of the *critical areas* that influence the long-range success of the enterprise. Critical areas should be pinpointed through evaluation of relevant variables. Although the critical areas are unique to each firm, they generally relate to the following:

1. Financial performance (profitability and return on investment).
2. Market effectiveness (market penetration and product and service leadership).
3. Product and service quality.
4. Productivity improvement and internal strengths (including organization, financing, people, and training).
5. Financial and physical resources.
6. Public acceptance (including responsibility to the public and the public's positive acceptance of the enterprise).

Although strategy formulation is of continual concern to executive management, better-managed companies have found that periodic reassessment of the strategies is essential in light of a careful analysis of all relevant variables and their future potential impacts. A specification of strategies is illustrated in the case in the next chapter.

Preparation of Planning Premises.   In the first four steps outlined above, executive management explicitly establishes a planning foundation that is *a condition precedent to the involvement of other levels of management in the planning process.* Top management leadership is fundamental to develop and articulate this planning foundation, including the formulation of relevant strategies. Consequently, at this point in the planning process, the foundation has been established to articulate and communicate the broad and specific objectives of the enterprise and the strategies that harmonize with them. Thus, the instructions and formal guidelines as communicated by the top management at this point in the planning process have come to be generally identified as the *statement of planning premises* (that is, the planning guidelines). The statement of planning premises is prepared as *executive management instructions* and is disseminated in order to initiate a sophisticated and potent move from broad corporate planning to the development of profit plans by each major responsibility center in the enterprise. It is simply a communication step from executive management to the lower levels of management. For example, the executive in charge of the sales department, as well as the manager of Plant 2, both receive the planning premises and supporting procedural instruction for formulating, say, a five-year and one-year sales plan in the one instance and profit plans for Plant 1 in the latter instance. Thus, we return to a fundamental principle stated in the preceding chapter; that is meaningful communication in the planning process. Illustration 10 in the next chapter shows a statement of planning premises.

Preparation and Evaluation of Project Plans.   In Chapter 1 and in Illustration 6 a careful distinction was made between *periodic plans* and *project plans.* It will be recalled that project plans encompass variable time horizons since each project has a unique time dimension. Also, recall that project plans encompass such items as plans for improvement of present products, new and expanded physical facilities, entrance into new industries, exit from products and industries, new technology utilizations, and other major activities that can be separately identified for specific planning purposes. The nature of projects is such that they must be planned as separate units. In planning for a project the time span to be considered normally must be the anticipated life span of the project. Projects approved then must be fitted into the strategic and tactical profit plans as diagrammed in Illustration 6.

The internal environment should be conducive to the submission of project proposals from any source within the enterprise on a continuing basis. As a result higher levels of management normally would expect to be involved in the development and evaluation of project plans at various intervals throughout the year. Consistent with this approach, during the formal planning cycle management must evaluate and decide upon the status to be planned for each project *in process* and to select those projects to be initiated during time dimensions covered by the strategic and tactical profit plans. Although this step has been shown sequentially in the above list, we do not intend to suggest in this instance—nor with respect to the other steps for that matter—that it is only a once-a-year management concern. Preparation and evaluation of current and future project plans, however, are essential on a formal basis as a part of the profit planning activities envisioned in the twelve components enumerated above. See Illustration 10 for an example of a project plan.

Development and Approval of Strategic and Tactical Profit Plans. These two steps suggest that the strategic long-range and the tactical short-range profit plans normally should be developed concurrently, for all practical purposes, and that the executives in charge of each of the responsibility centers throughout the firm should participate in their development in harmony with the planning premises. Of course, it is possible for a firm to develop these two profit plans for all aspects of the operation centrally; however, we have expressed the prevailing view that meaningful participation in the planning process generates positive behavioral effects. Therefore, these two steps envision that upon receipt of the planning premises and procedural instructions each manager in charge of a major responsibility center will immediately initiate activities within his own functional sphere to develop a strategic long-range profit plan (say, five years) and in harmony with the five-year plan, a tactical short-range profit plan (one year). Certain procedural instructions that should be received with the planning premises would provide instructions from a centralized source, normally the financial function, establishing the general format, amount of detail, and other relevant procedural and format requirements essential for aggregation of the plans of the subunits into the overall profit plans. After development of the two profit plans, a normal expectation would be that the head of each major responsibility center would be scheduled to present to the executive management his plans and their underlying justifications. Each member of the executive management group should have been provided a copy of the tentative plans to study before the formal presentation. The manager of each major responsibility center should be given the opportunity to make a complete presentation of his plans and to utilize members of his staff and line organization in this meeting. Following his presentation the conference should be devoted to an in-depth discussion on a give-and-take basis involving the members of the executive group and the manager of the responsibility center. The central purposes of the presentation and related discussions are (1) to provide the manager of the responsibility center with full opportunity to "sell" his plans to executive management; (2) to provide the members of the executive committee an opportunity to discuss among themselves, and with the responsible manager, all relevant implications and assumptions implicit in his plans; and (3) to develop the best possible plan that the combined talents of the entire group, including the manager of the responsibility center, can devise. From these discussions some revision of the plans may be forthcoming or, alternatively, the plans may be considered sound in every major respect. Significantly, this approach enhances communication, coordination, and mutual understanding. It is through this process that the basis for overall coordination and harmony of operational plans and efforts may be attained. After this process is completed for each major responsibility center and all relevant differences are resolved, the various plans and programs from the several major responsibility centers are then combined into the overall strategic and tactical profit plans for the enterprise as a whole. Bringing the separate plans together, each of which presumably is in harmony with the planning premises previously communicated by the executive management, is normally done by a centralized staff function under the supervision of the financial executive. Generally, this subfunction is managed by the budget officer or more appropriately the *Director of Planning and Control*. When the two profit plans for the overall enterprise are completed, executive management should subject it again to a careful analysis and evaluation to determine whether they are the most realistic overall plans that can be developed under the circumstances. When this point has been reached, then and only then, should the two profit plans be formally approved by the chief executive and released for duplication and distribution to the appropriate managers throughout the firm. At this point we may note that as a matter of security, only the top executives receive a complete copy of the two profit plans.

A strategic and a tactical profit plan are presented in the illustrative case in the next chapter and much of the chapters to follow is devoted to relevant aspects of these two profit plans.[5]

Development of Supplemental Analyses. A number of important analyses may be developed supplementary to the short- and long-range profit plans. These analyses apply many useful managerial techniques in the decision-making process. Specific important analyses are: planning model simulations; cost-volume-profit (break-even); marginal cost; return on investment; linear programming models; variable expense budgets; and accessory statistics both historical and prospective.

[5] Two excellent supplemental references are: Robert M. Fulmer and Leslie W. Rue, *The Practice and Profitability of Long-Range Planning, Research Series* (Oxford, Ohio: The Planning Executives Institute), and George A. Steiner, *Pitfalls in Comprehensive Long-Range Planning, Research Series* (Oxford, Ohio: The Planning Executives Institute, 1972).

To elaborate on one of them, the concept of the *variable expense budget* is important in the planning and control of costs. It is variously referred to as the variable budget, the flexible budget, sliding scale budget, expense control budget, and formula budget. The variable budget is concerned *only with expenses*. It is completely separate from profit plans but can be used to complement them. Many firms do not employ variable budget procedures, whereas other firms integrate profit planning and variable budget procedures. Whether or not both techniques should be employed in a particular situation depends upon circumstances.

Variable budgets provide projected data on expenses that make it possible to compute budget allowances for various volumes or rates of activity in each responsibility center. In effect the variable budget provides a *formula* for each expense classification in each center. The formula indicates the relationship of each expense to *output* (volume of work) in the center. Each formula includes a constant factor (fixed expense) and a variable rate (variable expense). In the case of a fixed cost, the variable rate is zero; in the case of variable cost, the constant factor is zero; and in the case of a semivariable expense, there will be a value for both the constant factor and the variable rate. To apply the concept in a department then each cost must be classified into one of three categories:

Fixed costs—those that remain essentially constant in the short-run regardless of changes in output.

Variable costs—those that vary directly (in proportion) with changes in output.

Semivariable costs—those that are neither fixed nor variable.

We may briefly illustrate each category by assuming there are three types of costs in Department 1. Supervisory salaries of $10,000 per month is a

DEPARTMENT 1. Variable Budget Formulas

COST	FIXED AMOUNT (PER MONTH)	VARIABLE RATE (PER 100 DIRECT LABOR HOURS)
Supervisory salaries	$10,000	$ .00
Indirect materials	0	1.50
Indirect labor	450	5.50

fixed cost; indirect materials used in the manufacturing process amounting to $1.50 per 100 direct labor hours of activity (that is, the measure of output) clearly is a variable cost; and let us assume an indirect labor cost that is semivariable; it is $450 per month fixed (the constant) plus $5.50 (the variable rate) per 100 direct labor hours. We will assume also that the output (work done or activity) of the department is measured in *direct labor hours worked*. The Department variable budget formulas would look like those shown above.

Now, assume January has just ended and that the *actual accounting data* for the month were as follows.

Output (departmental activity)	2 000 direct labor hours
Supervisory salaries	$10,000
Indirect materials	$ 40
Indirect labor	$ 540

The variable budget formulas would be used to develop a *performance report* at the end of January as follows.

DEPARTMENT 1. January Performance Report

COST	COMPUTATION OF BUDGET ALLOWANCE	BUDGET GOAL	ACTUAL COST	VARI-ANCE
Supervisory salaries	$10,000 fixed plus zero variable	$10,000	$10,000	$ 0
Indirect materials	Zero fixed plus variable ($1.50 × 20)	30	40	10*
Indirect labor	$450 fixed plus variable ($5.50 × 20)	560	540	20
Totals		$10,590	$10,580	$10

*Unfavorable variance

From this simple example the relevance of the variable budget approach in cost control should be obvious. To illustrate the relevance, assume the tactical *profit plan* anticipated 1,500 hours of output. The three budget goals included in the tactical profit plan would have been $10,000, $22.50, and $532.50. Comparison of the actual costs for January with these budget goals would have shown *unfavorable variances* of $17.50 and $7.50, neither of which would be meaningful nor fair to the supervisor of the department.

The concept just illustrated is referred to as *dynamic cost control*. It is significant in situations where it is impossible to plan accurately the volume or rate of activity in specific responsibility centers. From this example it is obvious that if variable expense budgets are available when the annual (tactical) profit plan is being prepared, determination of expense goals at the planned *volume* involves simple computations similar to those indicated above. On the other hand, if variable expense budgets are not available, considerable analyses of expenses would be necessary to determine the detailed expense goals.

The example indicates the complementary relationship, or integration, of profit planning and variable budget procedures. It is claimed occasionally that these two techniques represent a duplication. On the contrary, when they are properly understood and used, they complement each other. Variable budgets are usually constructed early in the budget planning period because, as indicated, they provide cost data for the tactical profit plan. Variable budgets and other supplementary analyses are discussed in detail in subsequent chapters.

Implementation of Plans.   Implementation of management plans that have been developed and approved in the planning process involves the management function of directing subordinates in the accomplishment of enterprise objectives and goals. Communication is an especially important aspect of direction. Thus, competent management at all levels requires that enterprise objectives, goals, strategies, and policies be keenly appreciated and understood by subordinates. There are many facets involved in management direction. However, a comprehensive profit planning and control program may aid substantially in the accomplishment of this function. Plans, strategies, and policies developed through meaningful participation along the lines described in the preceding steps establishes the foundation for effective communication. Preceding discussions emphasized that objectives and goals should be realistic and attainable, yet they should present a real challenge to the overall enterprise and to each responsibility center. The plans should have been developed with the managerial conviction that they are going to be met or exceeded in all major respects. If these principles are made effective in the developmental process, the various executives and supervisors certainly should have a clear understanding of their responsibilities and the expected level of performance.

The distribution of the profit plans within the firm was mentioned in a preceding paragraph. It is desirable for the top executive to distribute the profit plan accompanied by a covering *letter of instruction* that emphasizes performance, encouragement, and challenge. After distribution of the profit plans a series of *profit plan conferences* should be scheduled for each level of management. Usually the chief executive should meet initially with the other top executives to discuss implementation and action in conformance with the objectives and goals as specified in the profit plans. Similar conferences should be conducted until all levels of management are reached. These conferences serve to induce profit consciousness, performance orientation, and aggressive yet flexible application of the plans to attain the objectives. Ideally, these conferences also should deal with the broader spectrum of the management process, including motivational and other behavioral issues. The conferences also should emphasize aggressive action and flexibility in implementation of the plans and in the control process. Special emphasis should be devoted to the manner in which unanticipated events and problems will be handled at the several management levels. Keep in mind that profit plans cannot manage the business and that they must not serve to constrain management in taking advantage of opportunities, even those not anticipated in the profit plans. Application of the management exception principle and the principle of flexibility, both in respect to unforseen events and opportunities, and in the control process, are basic policy.

Development, Dissemination, and Use of Periodic Performance Reports. Implementation of plans necessitates continuous and dynamic control in harmony with the assigned managerial responsibilities in the enterprise. One salient feature of control is the utilization of periodic performance reports. Performance reports are considered in detail in a subsequent chapter; in that chapter a clear-cut distinction is made between *external* financial reports and *internal* reports. Internal reports are further classified as: (1) statistical reports that reflect the basic quantitative internal statistics with regard to the operations of the enterprise; (2) special managerial reports that are devoted to nonrecurring and special problems; and (3) periodic performance reports. The latter reports focus on dynamic and continuous control tailored to the assigned managerial responsibilities. These are repetitive reports *disaggregated by responsibility centers*, which compare actual performance with planned performance and thus provide *performance variations* (which may be favorable or unfavorable). Dynamic performance reports usually are prepared and distributed on a monthly basis, although special needs may justify weekly or even daily reports on specific problems.

Execution of the management plans is assured through dynamic and flexible control. Thus, performance must be measured and reported to each level of management. Procedures must be established for reporting on performance so timely action can be taken to correct or minimize undesirable situations. Thus, *short-term* performance reporting is absolutely essential. For example, one important sales control approach is the comparison of actual sales with planned sales by areas of responsibility. Such a comparison at the end of the year would be of little or no value, because it is then too late to take corrective action. On the other hand, daily, weekly, or even monthly sales reports may serve as a basis for effective and timely action. Actual performance statistics alone do not indicate high or low performance; they must be compared with a realistic goal or standard to be evaluated competently. Chapter 15 is devoted to an in-depth discussion of performance reporting for internal management purposes.

Implementation of Follow-up Actions. Follow-up action is an important facet of effective control and replanning. Performance reports, since they indicate the status of performance by responsibility, provide a basis for certain follow-up actions. It is important to distinguish between cause and effect. The performance variations are *effects* (the results); the management must determine the *underlying causes*. The identification of causes primarily is a responsibility of *line management*. Analysis to determine the underlying causes of both favorable and unfavorable performance should be given immediate priority. In the case of unfavorable performance, after identifying the basic causes, as opposed to the results, and having selected what appears to be the most fruitful alternative for corrective action, the manager must initiate its implementation. In addition, a special type of follow-up procedure should be implemented continuously; it should be designed (1) to determine the effectiveness of the prior corrective actions, and (2) to provide a basis to improve future planning and control procedures.

SUMMARY

In the preceding paragraphs, twelve components of a comprehensive profit planning and control program were discussed separately for pedagogical reasons. However, it is especially important to realize that each of these components interrelates and overlaps with others and that no single component can be viewed as a mutually exclusive activity. A comprehensive planning and control program as envisioned in the twelve components involves a broad range of managerial philosophy, concepts, and techniques. Collectively, these suggest a sophisticated approach to decision-making, continuous communication, and integration of actual historical data, projections, and managerial judgments. Although the components were listed and discussed in a potential chronological sequence, there must be a continuous feedback, reconsideration, and integration of the various components. Thus, although there is a typical cycle in developing objectives and plans and in communicating them, there must be an intermeshing of a series of circular flows of information and managerial discussions based upon meaningful participation of all members of the management. Thus, in both the management and control processes, communication, feedback, flexibility, and managerial judgment are key factors to effective performance of those managerial functions.

The central objective in presenting this discussion of the twelve components was to provide the reader with a "broad-brush picture" of a comprehensive profit planning and control program. It is essential to develop a broad perspective at this point so that the ensuing discussions of specific aspects of the program may be perceived in proper relationship to the whole. It is the conviction of this author that the full potentials of the many techniques, procedures, and approaches involved can be realized only when they are integrated into a coordinated and practical, yet comprehensive, system. All the concepts, techniques, and approaches described as parts of the system are widely discussed in the literature of management and accounting. Very few attempts have been made, however, to "package" them so that their interrelationships may be more clearly understood and their full potentials realized in an enterprise. In this book they are packaged in a way generally observed in better-managed entities.

FREQUENCY AND TIME DIMENSIONS IN PROFIT PLANNING AND CONTROL

When initiating or revising a comprehensive profit planning and control program, management of the enterprise must make policy decisions on two separate yet complementary issues involving time. Specifically, policy decisions must be made in respect to: the length of time to be covered by the strategic long-range and the tactical short-range profit plans and the frequency with which the formal planning process (cycle) should be repeated. It is obvious that these are related policy determinations; however, they are not identical issues. For example, an enterprise may decide to use a five-year time horizon for the strategic profit plan and may decide to revise it on a annual basis. In contrast, another firm using a five-year profit plan may decide to revise it once every two years.

The length of the planning period varies among enterprises because of several factors, some internal, others external. It will be recalled that in Chapter 2 (Illustration 6) it was assumed that the management had adopted as a matter of policy a five-year time dimension for the strategic plan and a one-year time dimension for the tactical profit plan (frequently referred to as the "one–five" approach). Some enterprises operate under conditions that make it relatively easy to develop realistic profit plans well in advance, whereas others experience considerable difficulty in planning very far in the future. These variable conditions have given rise to several approaches to the problem. The two principle approaches are frequently referred to as *periodic profit planning* and *continuous profit planning*.

Periodic profit planning involves the selection of a definite combination of periods for the strategic and the tactical profit plans. The periods usually selected are five years and one year, the one year choice being primarily on the basis of the fiscal year used by the enterprise for financial reporting purposes. In this approach the tactical short-range profit plan and the strategic long-range profit plan are prepared to cover these specific periods respectively with complete restudy and replanning expected *once each year*. Thus, under this approach the formal planning cycle for the enterprise normally would be the last two to four months of the current annual fiscal period.

Continuous profit planning frequently is used where it is felt that realistic plans cannot be made except for relatively short periods of time and where frequent replanning and reprojection are desired or necessitated by the dynamics of the situation. The procedure usually followed for tactical planning under this approach is that of preparing either a semiannual or even an annual profit plan, which is revised and reprojected each month (or quarter) by progressively dropping the month (or quarter) just completed and adding another similar period in the future. To illustrate the continuous approach, assume that prior to January a tactical profit plan is prepared extending, say, through June. At the end of January the semiannual profit plan is reprojected by dropping January and adding July, and at the same time the projections for February through June are revised where deemed appropriate. Thus, this approach results in a *continuous* semiannual profit plan for the concern. An example of an even more dynamic approach to profit planning and control is followed by a company widely recognized for its effective management. This particular company has used the concept of continuous profit planning and control for many years. An *annual* profit plan is prepared by each division of the firm; these individual divisional plans are then combined and summarized into the overall profit plan for the enterprise. The annual profit plan is prepared in detail by month for the upcoming quarter and by quarter for the remaining nine months. Near the end of each quarter the profit plan is extended another quarter by reprojection of the upcoming quarter by month and of the following nine months by quarter. Thus, under this approach management has monthly goals for the immediate quarter and goals for each of the three following quarters. In this particular concern, there is a strategic long range projection covering a period of ten years in the future. This ten-year plan normally is restudied and reprojected every two years. It is obvious that the continuous approach largely eliminates the need for interim revision of tactical profit plans occasioned by unusual events and circumstances not previously anticipated. The salient distinction of the continuous approach to profit planning is that the management has detailed and continuous plans for a fairly consistent period of time in the future, whereas under periodic profit planning the short-range planning period runs out at year's end.

Such factors as selling seasons, length of the process or manufacturing time (or merchandise turnovers), seasonal cycles, natural business cycles for the industry, financial considerations, and other operating conditions may influence the length of the profit planning period that should be used by the enterprise.

With respect to the frequency of profit plan preparation and revision, it should be noted that the better-managed companies who have had many years experience with profit planning and control programs have found that profit plan reprojection should be undertaken *formally and extensively at least on an annual basis*. Obviously, those companies who utilize a time period of less than one year for the short-range plan necessarily would follow the pattern of reprojection to correspond with the length of the period selected. Utilization of the continuous approach explicitly establishes the timing and frequency of the reprojection process. With respect to the strategic long-range profit plan, some companies do not follow a pattern of annual revision but rather the policy of "revising when circumstances have changed significantly." In the opinion of the author, this latter policy is not sound; rather, it appears logical and sound from the managerial point of view to adopt a policy of periodic revision of the long-range plan that normally should correspond with the formal reprojection utilized for the tactical short-range plan.

Another facet of revision of profit plans is posed in the situation where the periodic approach is used and the planning period is, say, twelve months. In this situation, it is not unusual for major events to occur during the year, such as strikes or casualty losses (fires, floods, earthquakes), that could not have been anticipated in the profit plan. When such events occur during the period covered by the short-range profit plan, the problem arises whether that plan should be revised for the remaining months to take into account the effect of the major event. In the case of a major event such as one of those enumerated, and assuming it occurs relatively early in the year, it would appear that complete revision of the tactical profit plan for the remainder of the year may be in order. In contrast, minor events and low performance normally should not give rise to revision of the basic profit plan. Frequent revision of profit plans to take into account minor events and inefficiencies tends to destroy the credibility of those plans and to decrease the seriousness with which the managers regard plans during their developmental and implementation stages.

LINE AND STAFF RESPONSIBILITIES

A profit planning and control program necessitates definite assignments of responsibility for each facet of it. Obviously, the chief executive of the enterprise has ultimate responsibility for profit planning and control; however, there must be a concomitant assignment of responsibilities to the line and staff executives.

Line executives basically must be assigned the responsibility for (1) providing the operational decision inputs into the planning system, (2) implementation, and (3) exercising control. Thus, the profit planning and control program must be established upon a firm foundation of line responsibility and commitment to develop, implement, and attain enterprise objectives and goals. We cannot overemphasize the fact that a profit planning and control program must be viewed as an approach to assist managers in line positions in carrying out their basic responsibilities. They must view the plans as their own, and they must assume full responsibility for them. This is in harmony with their responsibility for both the successes and failures in their particular functional spheres of operations.

In contrast, staff executives should be assigned responsibility for (1) designing and improving the system (as opposed to making operational decision inputs), (2) supervising and coordinating the operation of the system, (3) providing expert technical assistance, analyses, and advice to the line managers, and (4) developing and distributing performance reports.

The chief financial officer should be assigned overall staff responsibility for the profit planning and control program. Normally within the financial executive function there is a budget director or director of planning and control who should be assigned the staff supervisory responsibility. In view of the importance of an effective profit planning and control program the position of the individual on the staff responsible for the program should be such that it will command attention and respect throughout the firm. It is advisable that the individual responsible for the profit planning and control function report directly to the chief financial officer or in the absence of such a position, directly to the top executive. If there is a budget director as well as a chief financial officer, it seems preferable for the former to report to the latter, who in turn should report to the top executive. The positions implied for the chief financial officer and the budget director do not imply that they should have line authority in respect to the decision inputs and control. The staff executives should never be assigned the responsibility for "enforcing the budget." The budget director is properly charged with the staff responsibility for designing the budget program and for providing technical assistance and advice to line personnel in developing and implementing it. The budget director definitely should not attempt to prepare the profit plans, but he should be responsible for providing technical assistance and supervision to bring estimates together in final form once the decision inputs have been developed by the respective operating executives. The budget director should be responsible for technical analyses needed by the various responsibility centers and for the preparation of internal performance reports.

The duties of the budget director with regard to the profit planning and control program may be summarized as follows:

1. To advise the chief executive, appropriate top management committees, and others on all aspects of the profit planning and control program.

2. To recommend the profit planning and control procedures and technical requirements for each component of the program.

3. To assume responsibility for organization of the program and the necessary time schedules to make it operative.

4. To provide overall technical supervision of the profit planning and control program.

5. To design and recommend essential forms, schedules, and reports relevant to the profit planning and control program.

6. To supervise the preparation and revision of the profit planning and control manual and other related materials for approval by the chief executive.

7. To furnish analyses of past and future costs, revenues, and so on, to interested executives.

8. To translate certain preliminary policy decisions into their probable or alternative financial effect on future operations.

9. To prepare performance reports by responsibility and by other relevant classifications.

10. To analyze and interpret variances between actual and planned goals (staff basis only).

11. To perform specific clerical work associated with the profit planning and control program.

12. To supervise revision of both the profit plans and the profit planning and control program.

13. To perform various statistical analyses (upon request) that are related to the profit planning and control program.

14. To receive tentative plans and transmit them to appropriate executives for review and revision.

15. To organize, coordinate, and conduct appropriate training sessions and conferences related to the profit planning and control program.

16. To reproduce and distribute in accordance with instructions of the chief executive various components of the profit plans.

Recent trends have indicated that most of the better-managed companies extensively utilize an executive committee—or a comparable committee—in the profit planning and control process. This top-level committee should comprise the president and vice presidents (including the chief financial executive). The chief executive often serves as chairman of this committee for planning and control purposes. The primary role of this top-level committee with respect to the profit planning and control program is to fulfill both advisory and line functions. The members of this committee should provide an excellent source of advice to the various managers of the major responsibility centers in the development of their respective profit plans. Perhaps their most relevant function in the program is to fill the role of a competent and seasoned group to analyze, investigate, and probe in depth the profit plans presented by the managers. Fundamentally, this committee should have the responsibility for ascertaining that all aspects of the profit plans for the subunits are sound and, when combined into the overall comprehensive profit plans, that they represent the best plans that can be developed under the circumstances. In other words, all profit plans should pass muster with this committee, and having done so, the normal expectation is that the chief executive would then approve the plans for implementation. The direct responsibilities of this top-level committee with respect to the profit planning and control program may be outlined as follows:

1. Receive and review profit plans from the major responsibility centers and make appropriate recommendations for their improvement.
2. Recommend decisions on major items incorporated in the profit plans where there may be conflict or lack of coordination between the functional subdivisions of the enterprise.
3. Recommend changes to improve the planning and control processes related to the profit planning and control program.
4. Receive and analyze periodic performance reports from all responsibility centers in the enterprise.
5. Consider various alternatives and make recommendations and decisions for corrective action.
6. Make recommendations for revision of the profit plans when conditions warrant.
7. Make recommendations for changes in profit planning and control program policies and procedures for greater effectiveness.

A statement of relevant policies such as a *profit planning and control manual* is normally desirable to enhance communication and to provide a reasonable degree of stability in the operation of the system. The profit planning and control manual should include the following:

1. A statement of objectives and potentials of the program.
2. Procedures to be followed in developing profit plans.
   a. Instructions and forms to be used
   b. Responsibility for developing input data (decisions)
      —Operating executives
      —Staff executives
      —Top management executives committee
3. A profit planning and control calendar that specifies completion dates for each part of the profit plan and for the submission of reports.

4. Distribution instructions specifying to whom the various profit plan schedules are to be provided.

5. Instructions and policies with respect to managerial performance reports.
   a. Responsibility for preparation
      —Actual data
      —Budget data and variation
      —Analysis of variations
   b. Form and content of performance reports
   c. Distribution instructions for performance reports

6. Responsibility for taking corrective action on variances
   a. Unfavorable variances
   b. Favorable variances

7. Follow-up procedures and actions.

PLANNING PERSPECTIVES

The discussions thus far have concentrated on the planning and control functions of management and on approaches to accomplish them. At this point it is appropriate to place some of the relevant aspects of the broad planning function in perspective. In the past, the management of enterprises (both profit and nonprofit) seldom became involved in planning beyond one year. However, during the last decade there has been a noticeable trend toward strategic long-range planning, particularly by profit-making enterprises. One of the obstacles to long-range planning, in the opinion of this author, has been confusion of its real nature and a tendency to pursue long-range planning on an informal, *ad hoc*, basis. One perceptive writer has attributed this state of affairs to three misconceptions:

1. Confusion between long-range planning and one of its major parts or elements;

2. Confusion between long-range planning and one of the key areas in which it is required;

3. Confusion between long-range planning and one of its common characteristics.[6]

[6] E. Kirby Warren, *Long-Range Planning: The Executive Viewpoint* (Englewood Cliffs, N.J.: Prentice-Hall, Inc., 1966), p. 17. This is one of the more perceptive books on the topic and, in the opinion of this author, represents a distinct contribution to the literature; it is recommended for further study of this important topic.

The failure on the part of many people to make a distinction between strategic long-range planning and forecasting was given by Warren as an example of the first type of misconception. Forecasting is a technical activity, usually assigned to technically trained staff specialists, the purpose being to predict a probable outcome from a given set of circumstances for a specified period in the future. A forecast necessarily rests upon certain assumptions made by the forecaster. Forecasting is one of many elements of planning, and it provides some of the basic data for the planning process. In contrast, planning, as we have fundamentally outlined it in the prior discussions, is a managerial activity (as opposed to a technical staff activity) involving development of enterprise objectives and strategies and evaluation of the effectiveness of those decisions. It requires definite management commitments to attain those objectives. Warren has offered the following definition, which seems to capture the essence of the concept: "Planning is essentially a process of preparing for the commitment of resources in the most economical fashion and, by preparing, of allowing this commitment to be made faster and less disruptively."[7]

The second misconception listed above is very common. For example, many firms carry on long-range planning in a single key area such as capital additions. No attention is given to developing comprehensive plans that cover all facets of expected future operations. Concern with strategic planning for only one or a few of the key areas has tended to narrow the scope of the planning activity of management. The third type of confusion has to do with the definition of the term "long-range." Some companies refer to their annual profit plan as long-range planning. Other firms attempt to make inflexible definitions covering long periods of time. An interesting response from one manager was as follows: "Our long-range plan covers three years because one year was considered too short and four years was considered too long." Long-range planning, as with all planning, is characterized by uncertainty. The length of the strategic long-range planning period fundamentally should be related (aside from project plans) to the lead time that the management needs in the future to make sound decisions rapidly (1) to effect major strategies and (2) for major events that are apt to arise that would significantly affect the long-range financial health of the enterprise. "If planning is essentially preparation for decision-making on the commitment of resources, the length of the planning period must be determined by (1) the time it takes to prepare for the decision plus (2) the time it takes to implement it in the light of (3) the time when implementation must be completed."[8]

[7] Ibid., p. 21.
[8] Ibid., p. 17.

The approach to planning that we have suggested in the preceding discussions suggests that there are two fundamental aspects of comprehensive profit planning:

1. The substantive plan.
2. The financial plan.

The *substantive plan* is represented by the broad objectives of the enterprise, the strategies, the specific plans, the programs, and the concurrent commitment of management to their long-range accomplishment. Warren has characterized this as the "prose part" of the plan, and he states that: "It is supposed to put muscle and meat around the skeleton of the financial plan."[9]

Warren also characterized the substantive plan as formal, or verbal, statements on the following:

1. Key economic and environmental assumptions: generally these are supplied by corporate management and are repeated and/or modified by subunits to "show" they were reflected in the plan.
2. Basic objectives of the unit: what the unit expects to accomplish, stated in terms of products, markets, facilities, people and subgoals for effectively developing each.
3. Operating assumptions: the specific premises and constraints which underlie the unit's plans.
4. Major programs: what the unit expects to do to accomplish its objectives.[10]

In some situations it may not be feasible to reduce the substantive plan to formal statements, but rather, it may be represented by mutual understandings of the management groups involved. The essence of the substantive plan is the managerial commitment made by the respective managers.

In contrast, the *financial plan* is an attempt to quantify the probable financial results of the aggregation of managerial objectives, strategies, plans, and policies. More specifically, the financial plan is represented by the financial schedules encompassed by the strategic long-range plan and the tactical short-range plan as outlined in preceding and subsequent discussions in this book. The financial plan then represents a translation into financial terms of objectives, goals, and strategies of management for a specific period of time.

With respect to these two basic aspects, it is generally recognized that

[9] Ibid., p. 72.
[10] Ibid., p. 72.

the substantive plan has been given inadequate attention by most companies. Alternatively, many companies give perhaps undue attention to the financial plan. The discussions in the first four chapters of this book attempt to place the substantive plan in proper perspective.

SUMMARY

In summary, a comprehensive profit planning and control program may be broadly outlined as follows:

I.   The Substantive Plan
  1.   Broad objectives of the enterprise
  2.   Specific enterprise goals
  3.   Enterprise strategies
  4.   Statement of planning premises
II to V. The Financial Plan
II.   Strategic long-range profit plan
  1.   Sales, cost and profit projections
  2.   Major projects and capital additions
  3.   Cash flow and financing
  4.   Manpower requirements
III.   Tactical short-range (annual) profit plan
  1.   The operating plan
    a.   Planned income statement
      (1)   Sales plan
      (2)   Production plan
      (3)   Administrative expense budgets
      (4)   Distribution expense budget
      (5)   Appropriation-type budgets
  2.   The financial position plan
    a.   Budgeted balance sheet
      (1)   Cash flow and funds flow budgets
IV.   Variable Expense Budgets
 V.   Supplementary Statistics
  1.   Special analyses
  2.   Cost-volume-profit analyses
  3.   Historical growth and cost-volume-profit tables and charts
VI.   Internal Reports
  1.   Statistical reports

2.   Special reports

3.   Performance reports

DISCUSSION QUESTIONS

1.   Outline one useful approach that a management could take to evaluate the relevant variables affecting the enterprise.

2.   Explain the nature and purpose of a statement of broad objectives for an enterprise.

3.   What is the purpose of stating the specific goals of an enterprise and how should they relate to a statement of broad objectives?

4.   Distinguish between enterprise goals and enterprise strategies; why is the distinction necessary?

5.   What is a statement of planning premises? What purpose does it serve?

6.   In a general way outline a participative approach for developing profit plans for a responsibility center in a medium-size firm (assume the responsibility center to be Plant 2).

7.   Explain in general terms the concept of the variable expense budget.

8.   What should be the management policy with respect to significant events that occur and were not anticipated in the profit plans?

9.   Explain the concept of performance reports. What basic purpose do they serve?

10.   Explain the implications of the statement: "In using performance reports, it is important to distinguish between cause and effect."

11.   What are the basic decisions with respect to time dimensions that must be made by management of a company when initiating a profit planning and control program?

12.   Distinguish between the periodic budget approach and the continuous budget approach.

13.   Differentiate between line and staff responsibilities with respect to a profit planning and control program.

14.   What should be the role of the executive committee with respect to the profit planning and control program?

15.   Why is a profit planning and control manual usually desirable, and what should it primarily encompass?

16.   Distinguish between forecasting and planning.

17.   Distinguish between the two aspects of planning: (1) the substantive plan, and (2) the financial plan.

CASE 3-1

Patrick Company

The president of Patrick Company recently appointed a special committee to make recommendations to the executive committee with respect to starting a profit planning and control program in the company. The committee spent considerable time investigating the various facets of such a program. At this point the committee is focusing its attention on the major potential problem areas that might be encountered upon initiation of such a program. Primary concerns of the committee are the motivational and behavioral implications. In reviewing the literature, the committee was particularly interested in several studies that have reported on the effect of budgets upon lower-level managers and supervisors. One study emphasized that budgets were used by higher management in one company primarily as "pressure devices for continually increasing efficiency." The study in effect concluded that in certain situations budgets tend to generate negative motivations and decreasing efficiency. Another study stated that in one company the "success of the budget people was dependent upon their ability to find fault with the operating managers." Another study found that in most of the companies studied "participation in budget development was believed to be very imporant." Still another study reported that "budgeting is more concerned with the concepts of human behavior than with the rules of accounting and that, if good principles of human relationships are implemented, profit planning and control will be effective as a management tool."

Required:

Appraise the quotations from the several studies examined by the special committee.

CASE 3-2
Bronson Company

The controller of the Bronson Company reported to the case writer that the company had been "budgeting for the last three years." The case writer learned of a particular sequence of events relating to the current budget year. Near the middle of October of last year, the president of the company telephoned the controller and asked, "Isn't it timo to start thinking about the budget for next year?" Although there were many problems on the controller's desk, he agreed with the president. After hanging up the phone, the controller was thinking, "I wish I could figure some way to keep from being saddled with this forecasting job." On Monday, November 5, the controller assembled his key staff people to discuss the "budgets for next year," in anticipation of a telephone call from the president around the first of December. As anticipated, the president called on December 3 and asked the controller to come in with "the summary budget statements for next year incorporating your recommendations." The next day the controller spent the entire morning with the president discussing the projected statements (an income statement detailed by quarter, a balance sheet for the end of the budget year, and a quarterly cash budget). In response to a question from the president, the controller stated that "these forecasts are a compilation of the best judgments of my staff on the projections of the trends of the actual results for the past year." The president expressed some definite ideas about the increase in sales that he would like to see, an increase in profit, and the general business environment. In addition, he indicated that, although union negotiations would probably cause an increase in some of the labor costs, costs generally should be budgeted "tighter than last year." At lunch the same day, the president and the controller discussed these matters with the vice president of sales and the vice president of manufacturing. From these discussions the controller could see that some changes had to be made "to coincide with the tentative decisions of the president." The president indicated to the controller that he would like to "get together again on December 15 for a final wrapup of the budget for next year." The controller was expected to have the revised budget statements available for a discussion with the president at a luncheon meeting on that date with the two vice presidents. As was anticipated by the controller, that meeting resulted in approval of the revised budget statements. Copies of the budget were distributed to the vice presidents during the last week of December.

Bronson Company is a small company enjoying a sales volume of approximately six million dollars and employs approximately 250 individuals. The company sells its products in a three-state area.

Required:

Provide a constructive, yet critical, assessment of the approach to developing a profit plan in this company, including your suggestions for change.

CASE 3-3
X Company

Assume you have been engaged to make an independent evaluation of the operations of the X Company, which is experiencing certain difficulties. You have concluded that a comprehensive profit planning and control program is advisable. In an executive meeting the company controller, an elderly man, comments in your presence, "Oh, I realize that budgeting is perhaps all right in a few extremely large firms, but not ours. We have special problems, such as sales forecasting, because we have five different products distributed all over the U.S. In addition, you just can't tell what our expenses for the year are going to be. Besides, I don't have the time or help to prepare a budget. I probably couldn't make those sales people follow it anyway." The rest of the executives look at him with what you interpret to be possible agreement. Narrate your reply exactly as you would give it to the executive group in the presence of the controller.

CASE 3-4
Compte Sales Company

Compte Sales Company uses a continuous profit plan covering a six-month period. The plan is revised monthly. Summary profit plan data for one six-month period are shown below.

Compte Sales Company—Planned Income Statement (summary)
For the Period March–August, 19xx

	MARCH	APRIL	MAY	JUNE	JULY	AUGUST	TOTAL
Sales	$210,000	$216,000	$224,000	$208,000	$190,000	$180,000	$1,228,000
Cost of goods sold	84,000	86,000	90,000	83,000	76,000	72,000	491,000
Gross margin	126,000	130,000	134,000	125,000	114,000	108,000	737,000
Distribution expenses	52,000	53,000	55,000	51,000	49,000	47,000	307,000
Administrative expenses	26,000	27,000	27,000	25,000	24,000	24,000	153,000
Operating margin	48,000	50,000	52,000	49,000	41,000	37,000	277,000
Financial expenses	1,000	1,000	1,200	1,200	900	900	6,200
Income (before income tax)	47,000	49,000	50,800	47,800	40,100	36,100	270,800
Income taxes (40%)	18,800	19,600	20,320	19,120	16,040	14,440	108,320
Net income	$ 28,200	$ 29,400	$ 30,480	$ 28,680	$ 24,060	$21,660	$ 162,480

In accordance with company planning procedures the following decisional inputs were developed by the management and given to the budget director:

1. Sales department revised estimates: Sales—April $220,000; May $225,000; June $210,000; July $192,000; August $182,000; September $195,000. Distribution expense—a flat 2 percent increase; September estimate $50,100.
2. Executive vice president's estimates—administrative expenses for September $25,000; no changes in prior months.
3. Treasurer's estimates—financial expenses for July through September $1,100 per month.
4. Accounting department estimates—cost of goods sold will increase in proportion to the increase in sales for each month, September estimate $78,000.

Required:

a. Prepare a revised profit plan following the concept of continuous budgeting. Include appropriate comments concerning the estimates and an evaluation of the changes.
b. Prepare a separate narrative appraising the planning approach used by the company.

CASE 3-5

Contracts, Incorporated

Contracts, Incorporated, is a small company (approximately eighty employees) organized eight years ago to perform certain government contracts related to the space program. All the work done to date by this company has been under government contract. Recently the government contracts in process by the company were reduced by approximately one-half. The management of the company are Ph. D.'s who have had highly technical training and experience related to the type of production required by the government contracts. It did not require much management sophistication to make decisions relatively soon to reduce the number of people in the manufacturing operation and to cut back on the purchase of materials. Nevertheless, the company suffered severe financial strains, and there is the strong possibility that it may not survive. An outside consultant was called in at this point in order to "make recommendations for remedying the financial situation of the company." The management of the company, up to this time, had not shown much interest in the financial affairs of the firm other than in the reported profit figures. In view of the fact that the company had been working at full capacity under government contracts and primarily on a cost-plus basis, the profit situation had been favorable. There were situations in the past where profits had dipped substantially as a result of reduced contracts; however, the present instance is the first one that the company encountered where a major and perhaps permanent reduction was imminent.

The consultant analyzed the situation in depth and made three broad recommendations that may be summarized as follows:

1. The company should immediately explore all the potentials for developing products that can be sold to the general public and should not rely entirely on one customer—the government.
2. There should be a significant and immediate reduction of costs without severely damaging the production capacity needed for alternative products.
3. A management system should be developed to monitor the financial situation in the company on a continuing basis.

Required:

a. Assess the situation as it now stands and indicate any management oversights that are implicit in this situation.
b. Evaluate the recommendation of the consultant that costs be reduced in light of actions already taken by management to reduce employees and purchases of materials.
c. Recommend approaches to "monitor the financial situation."

CASE 3-6
Simplex Corporation

Simplex Corporation sells two similar products—Super and Super D. The company estimated that, aside from overall volume increases, an increase in sales of one product would, on a unit basis, proportionately decrease the sales of the other product. Management is considering two possible alternatives for profit planning purposes: (1) push Super sales or (2) push Super D sales. The following budget estimates have been prepared:

	SUPER	SUPER D
Unit sales price	$10.00	$13.00
Fixed overhead ($120,000 allocated on a 1 : 3 ratio)	1.00	3.00
Unit variable cost of sales	6.00	7.00
Sales commissions (20% of sales)	2.00	2.60
Net profit per unit	$ 1.00	$ .40

Required:

   a. How many units of Super and Super D were used in computing the above budget estimates?

   b. Compute the budgeted gain or loss in this case.

   c. Based on the data given, what alternative should management select? Support your decision with figures and appropriate comments.

CASE 3-7

Micro Corporation

Micro Corporation uses variable budget procedures to aid in the control of costs. The variable budget for Cost Center 23 is shown below.

Variable Expense Budget
for the Year 19xx Cost Center No. 23

EXPENSES	FIXED ALLOWANCE PER MONTH	VARIABLE RATE PER 100 DIRECT MACHINE HOURS
Supervisory salaries	$ 900	$ —
Indirect labor	200	.90
Maintenance parts	50	.05
Supplies used	—	.60
Power used	30	.10
Miscellaneous expenses	40	.12
Depreciation on machinery	100	—
Totals	$1,320	$1.77

Required:

   a. The annual profit plan is being developed. It includes an estimate of the planned output of work for Cost Center 23. What amount for each cost should be included in the plan for Cost Center 23: (1) for the January output estimate of 20,000 direct machine hours? (2) for the annual output estimate of 260,000 direct machine hours? Show your computations.

b. Assume the profit plan was approved and that January of the new year has now passed. The accounting department reported the following for Cost Center 23 for January: Actual machine hours 24,000; Actual expenses: Supervisory salaries $900, Indirect labor $415, Maintenance parts $65, Supplies used $140, Power used $50, Miscellaneous expenses $70, and Depreciation $100. Using these data and the planned allowances developed in requirement (1), prepare a performance report comparing actual expenses with planning budget allowances. Set up four amount columns: Actual expenses; Original profit plan allowances; Variations—amount; Variations—percent of budget.

c. Prepare another performance report comparing actual with variable budget allowances *adjusted to actual work done;* 24,000 DMH.

d. Which performance report should be used for Cost Center 23? Why?

CASE 3-8

Supreme Corporation

Supreme Corporation is a small firm manufacturing three different models of a simple household item. The product is sold through independent wholesale outlets in a three-state area. Recently, a competing device appears to have been dropped from the market. The management of Supreme is interested in an evaluation of the effect on operations and profits because they feel that an increase in volume may be anticipated.

The management of the company has never introduced profit planning and control. Planning has been on an informal and nonsystematic basis. In discussing the new development with the board of directors (who meet quarterly) the president raised both the volume and price aspects of the new situation. The board approved a resolution to have the company's independent C.P.A. help with some analyses.

Subsequently, in analyzing the situation (following certain procedures recommended by the C.P.A. firm), the management developed the following estimates for the coming year:

1. Physical volume of sales will increase by 20 percent.
2. Material prices will rise by 15 percent.
3. Administrative expenses will increase *in total* by 10 percent.
4. Direct labor wage rates will increase by 20 percent.
5. Selling expenses will increase *in total* by 30 percent of dollar sales if sales prices are increased. If sales prices are not increased these expenses will increase in total by 10 percent of dollar sales.
6. There will be a 10 percent reduction in the material content of each unit of finished goods.
7. Fixed manufacturing expenses of $20,000 will not change.

The income statement for the past year showed the following (simplified and rounded):

Sales		$500,000
Cost and expenses:		
Direct materials	$110,000	
Direct labor	80,000	
Manufacturing expenses—Fixed	20,000	
Manufacturing expenses—Variable	40,000	
Administrative expenses	30,000	
Selling expenses	120,000	
Total		400,000
Net income		$100,000

Among other considerations It Is desired to determino (1) the percent that selling prices (on the average) should be increased to bring a 20 percent return on $655,000, the amount of the total assets, and (2) the net income that might be expected for the coming year assuming no change in selling price.

Required:

    a.   Present computations showing the development of the desired information.

    b.   Re-evaluate (usefulness and limitations) the results.

    c.   What additional approaches and analyses would you suggest?

Comprehensive Profit Planning and Control Illustrated

chapter four

Since the subsequent chapters detail aspects of a comprehensive profit planning and control program, it is especially important at this point that the reader have an overall conception of such a program and its principal components. In order to provide this broad overview, the discussions in Chapter 3 are supplemented in this chapter with an actual case study that has been simplified for instructional purposes.

This case, the Superior Manufacturing Company, is used in most of the chapters for illustration. Generally, those aspects of the case relating to each chapter will be found at the end of that chapter. Since this is a comprehensive case, its continuity from chapter to chapter provides a learning vehicle. Therefore, the reader is urged to devote careful attention to the case and to follow the continuity so the broad view of comprehensive planning and control will be evident throughout the study of the detailed techniques, approaches, and procedures.

In this chapter we will illustrate each of the components of a comprehensive profit planning and control program listed in Chapter 3. They will be illustrated in the order listed there, and the same captions will be used.

CASE BACKGROUND

The Superior Manufacturing Company was organized during the late 1920s and has grown consistently so that it now conducts operations throughout the United States and in several foreign countries. There are approximately eighty responsibility centers in the parent company, and in addition, there are several small subsidiary companies. The case as illustrated will relate only to the U.S. operations of the parent company. Annual sales approximate $75,000,000, and twenty products are manufactured and distributed. During the depression, as was common in many companies, the Superior Manufacturing Company became involved in a number of management techniques including "standard costs and a budget program." At that time management interest in these and other techniques was occasioned primarily by the necessity to retrench operations and reduce costs radically. During World War II and immediately thereafter, the company did not continue the budget program; however, the standard cost system has continued in operation with certain revisions from time to time. Several years ago the management became interested in a comprehensive profit planning and control program. A special management committee of five members was appointed to "make an in-depth analysis of the applications and potentials of a comprehensive profit planning and control program."

The actual situation has been simplified in almost every respect, sufficient size and detail being retained only to the extent deemed adequate to provide an effective instructional approach and yet to avoid the excessive detail that would tend to obscure the important issues. For illustrative case purposes, it has been assumed that the Superior Manufacturing Company distributes only *two products*, in *three sales districts*, and that the manufacturing division includes *three service* and *three producing departments*.

Approximately one year after appointment, the special committee made a complete report to the executive committee. The committee strongly recommended early initiation of a comprehensive profit planning and control program. The committee also recommended that, prior to actual initiation, a careful study of the organizational structure of the firm and the related responsibilities be completed. This recommendation was implemented; the organization chart for the company shown in Illustration 7 indicates the current organizational and responsibility arrangements in the company. A detailed organizational manual that specified definite responsibilities for each executive and manager was prepared, approved by the management, and distributed to various levels of management. Pay particular attention to the various responsibility centers and the organization of the financial function, as well as the executive committee.

The special committee also recommended that "the accounting system be tailored to the organizational structure so that all costs, revenues, and other activities reported through the accounting system will be accumulated and reported on a responsibility basis." Thus, the committee recommended a responsibility accounting system. Accounting classifications were revised, and a formal accounting manual was prepared detailing the chart of accounts by responsibility. The manual also specified the type of entries to be made

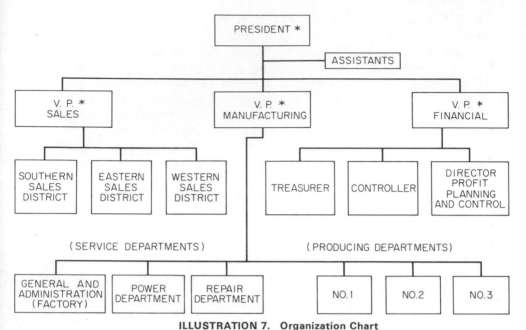

ILLUSTRATION 7. Organization Chart
Superior Manufacturing Company
*On the Executive Committee

in each account. In addition, the manual specified that standard costs for direct materials and labor should be used, and it stated the policies on cost allocations and on the application of overhead to products produced as well as many other details relative to standard accounting procedures.

Similarly, the *director of profit planning and control*, which was a new position, prepared a detailed profit planning and control manual coordinated with the accounting manual. These three manuals (statements of general policies) subsequently were considered by the executive committee; and after certain revisions, they were approved by the president and distributed as "standard company procedures." Following is a summary of certain pertinent information from the profit planning and control manual of the Superior Manufacturing Company as finally approved and updated to the present. It outlines the basic components of the comprehensive profit planning and control program in this company.

SUMMARY OF THE PROFIT PLANNING AND CONTROL MANUAL

1. Objectives of the profit planning and control program.
2. Responsibilities and procedures for annual evaluation of the

relevant environmental variables affecting the future success of the company.

3. Annual evaluation by the executive committee of the statement of broad objectives of the company.

4. Top management specification, on an annual basis, of the specific goals of the company:

    a. Growth objective,

    b. Return on investment objective,

    c. Social objectives.

5. Development of basic strategies by executive management.

6. Procedure for development of the profit plans:

    a. Distribution of planning premises

    b. Profit plans to be prepared:

        (1) Strategic long-range profit plan—five-year time span, detailed by year, to be revised annually.

        (2) Tactical short-range profit plan—one-year time span, consistent with the annual fiscal period used for financial reporting purposes; broken down by quarters. Each quarter to be further disaggregated by month during the month preceding the beginning of each quarter.

        (3) Variable expense budgets—to be prepared annually for factory costs, distribution expenses, and administrative expenses.

    c. Responsibilities for preparation of profit plans:

        (1) Overall responsibility—president (and executive committee).

        (2) Approval of planning premises—president (and executive committee).

        (3) Overall supervision of the budget program—financial executive and director of profit planning and control.

        (4) Sales plan—vice president in charge of sales.

        (5) Departmental expense budgets—manager of the respective departments (statistical analyses, cost analyses, and other services essential to the development of expense budgets, director profit planning and control).

        (6) Profit plan consolidations and summaries—director of profit planning and control.

        (7) Manufacturing budgets—vice president in charge of manufacturing.

(8)   Cash flow and capital addition budgets—treasurer.

d.   Initiation of departmental budgets—departmental manager:

(1)   Profit plans.

(2)   Variable budgets.

e.   Profit plan approvals:

(1)   Initial approval by responsible manager concerned.

(2)   Approval by next higher manager.

(3)   Presentation and discussion of profit plans with the executive committee.

(4)   Final approval—president.

7.   Profit planning calendar (the strategic and tactical profit plans will be prepared concurrently):

a.   September 30—distribution of statement of planning premises.

b.   October 1—start preparation of sales plan and departmental variable budgets.

c.   November 15—sales plan and variable budgets completed.

d.   December 1—production budget, materials budget, direct labor and factory overhead budgets completed.

e.   December 7—proposed project budgets and tentative profit plans presented to the executive committee for analysis, suggestions, and evaluation.

f.   December 12—final copy of revised profit plans and related proposals reviewed by the executive committee.

g.   December 14—final approval of the profit plans by the president.

h.   December 22—completion of reproduction of the profit plans.

i.   December 30—distribution of the profit plans with covering letter prepared by the president.

j.   Monthly budgets—by the end of March, June, and September, respectively, monthly breakdowns of quarterly budgets.

k.   Expense control budgets—by the 25th of each month, the director of profit planning and control will submit to the various departmental managers budget expense estimates based on planned production for the upcoming month.

l.   Monthly performance reports—the director of profit planning and control will distribute no later than the 7th of the following month the *performance reports* covering the preceding month. The *actual* data to be provided by the accounting department; budget allowances to be provided by the profit planning and control department.

For illustrative purposes, we will assume in the case for Superior that the current year is 1976 and the period planned is 1977 and beyond. Therefore, the tactical short-range profit plan will cover the year 1977 and the strategic long-range profit plan will cover the years 1978–82 inclusive.

EVALUATION OF RELEVANT VARIABLES AND STRENGTHS AND WEAKNESSES ILLUSTRATED

The president of Superior, during the early part of the current year, concluded that his management had not been considering adequately the controllable and noncontrollable variables affecting the company. Further, there was no in-depth analysis of the strengths and weaknesses of the company. To establish a basis for more emphasis on these factors in the planning process, and to gain some expert assistance, he engaged an outside consultant. The consultant's report was presented to the president on September 3. The report was comprehensive, and separate sections were devoted to two problems: (a) relevant variables and (b) strengths and weaknesses. With respect to the relevant variables, the consultant developed the matrix shown in Illustration 2, which was supplemented with analyses and recommendations. The consultant recommended that more attention be given to annual assessment of the noncontrollable variables and made specific recommendations with respect to planning for their impacts on the company.

The consultant's report listed the company's primary strengths as (a) quality of the employees, (b) financial soundness of the company, and (c) the participative attitudes fostered by the management. The primary weaknesses listed were (a) lack of innovative and aggressive marketing strategies, (b) excessive returns of products because of quality, and (c) insufficient involvement in long-term social problems. After discussing the report management decided to incorporate most of the recommendations into future planning.

STATEMENT OF BROAD OBJECTIVES ILLUSTRATED

The statement of broad objectives of the company was completely rewritten to emphasize some of the major recommendations of the consultant and to make it suitable for inclusion in the annual financial report to be distributed to shareholders. The final draft as revised by the executive committee and approved by the president is shown in Illustration 8.

**ILLUSTRATION 8.   Statement of Broad Objectives—Superior
Manufacturing Company**
January 1, 1977

The broad long-range objective of the Superior Manufacturing Company is to create and maintain an enterprise environment that maximizes the interest and motivations of all its employees. This climate must be characterized by recognition of the personal long-range goals of its employees. The environment must be characterized by high ethical tone, honest and forthright actions, high standards of performance, and realistic and fair rewards for that competence. To accomplish this goal there must be fair evaluation of the performance of individuals, particularly those in management positions. In addition, adequate attention to the welfare and working conditions of the employees and realistic compensation for performance require that the company operate on a profitable basis both in the short run and the long run, and that it earn a realistic rate of return on the funds invested in the business.

Another broad objective of the company is to grow in sales by expanding into new products and new geographical areas. The growth objective of the company, in turn, entails expansion of employees, facilities, and financial resources. Specifically, the growth objective of the company is to expand at a rate faster than that for the industry in which it operates.

Another broad objective is to develop an expanding number of customers who have high confidence in the products distributed by the company and a high trust in the fair dealings and basic honesty of all the company representatives and of the company overall. In order to accomplish this broad objective we aim to manufacture and distribute only quality products and to maintain a high level of excellence in the manufacture of those products. Our pricing policy will be competitive when related to quality and dependability. We want our customers to be proud of the products they acquire from us since we realize that our present customers should be our best salesmen.

Since the Superior Manufacturing Company is a corporation owned by approximately 3,000 shareholders, another broad objective is to earn for those owners a realistic rate of return on their investment and to build for them a larger and more dynamic company. We aim to speak candidly with our shareholders in matters of broad company policy and financial performance.

Another broad objective is to fill the role of a responsible citizen in the broader community. This role entails responsible participation in community affairs and in the promotion of broad programs aimed at improving the social and economic well-being of the broader citizenry. Consistent with our profit objectives, the company will engage in broad programs to train and utilize individuals from all walks of life with particular emphasis on the disadvantaged. In these matters the basic guidelines shall be the long-range impacts on the broader community and on the long-range affairs of the company itself.

A final broad objective of the Company is to operate with a positive and dynamic philosophy of management, which is vital to a competitive and growing company. In accomplishing this objective, long-range efforts shall be planned and implemented to continuously and consistently increase the sophistication of the management at all levels and to take full advantage of the latest techniques and innovations as they are developed. In carrying out this objective, the management is committed to give long-range priority over short-range results and to a management development program that will assure an adequate supply of competent young managers from within the company so that the long-range success of the company is assured. In fulfilling this role the management is committed to an enlightened approach to the behavioral problems in industry and to full managerial participation by those found competent.

The President

ILLUSTRATION 9. Statement of Specific Goals—Superior Manufacturing Company
January 1, 1977

a. Growth objective—a 4 per cent annual growth in sales volume for the next five years; the growth for the upcoming year should approximate 3 per cent and for the following year approximate 4 per cent, then exceeding 4 per cent in subsequent years of the five-year plan. The relevant factors influencing this growth plan are:
   (1) Product Z will be introduced at the beginning of future year two.
   (2) Two years hence entry into the market in foreign country "C" will be initiated.
   (3) An intensive market training program will be initiated during the coming year.
   (4) Product pricing policies shall remain unchanged.
   (5) Aggressive and sophisticated sales efforts will be appropriately funded.

b. Return on investment objective for the company—24 per cent pretax; the actual return on investment for the current year will be approximately 22 per cent. The return on investment objective should be realistic if:
   (1) The contemplated sales plan is accomplished.
   (2) Cost control objectives are competently planned and attained.
   (3) Investment in assets is realistically planned and controlled.

c. Profit margin objectives are as follows:
   (1) Company overall pretax 15 per cent.
   (2) Direct district operating profits margin: Southern 21 per cent; Eastern 23 per cent; Western 23 per cent.

d. Cash flow objective—to internally generate sufficient cash for company operation.

e. Research objective is to undertake and complete analysis and evaluation of Product X with a view to improving its applications; to experiment with and test the relevance of certain suggestions that have been received from customers in respect to Products X and Y; to continue active research in the development of new products. Plan an increase in the research budget of approximately 5 per cent over the preceding year (see actual data attached).

f. Factory productivity objective—to plan a realistic increase in productivity (efficiency in factory operations); this increase to be reflected in the plans through increased quality control, better cost control, and lower unit costs particularly for factory overhead and labor costs. Plans should also be incorporated for improving the technology of the plant and for expanding the application of our computer resources.

g. The profit plan shall include initiation of a formal executive development program and revitalization of the performance evaluation system with particular attention devoted to evaluation of managerial competence at all levels.

h. Cost control objective—plans should reflect a commitment to improve cost control at at all levels of management and to relate expenditures to output (productivity). Variable budgets will be used in the control of costs. The emphasis shall not be on reducing costs; rather the emphasis should be on improving the ratio between costs and output. Profit plans should include cost estimates based only on real needs justified by programs. The attention of all managers and supervisors is called to the company policy on cost control, that is, flexibility shall be the focus of management's attention so that when unanticipated events arise additional funds will be made available for essential costs even though not budgeted; similarly, when needs decrease, and excess budget allowances are imminent, such unused funds will be utilized for other needs in accordance with the judgment of the management concerned. Unspent funds of this nature shall not reflect unfavorably on future budget requests of the department concerned.

STATEMENT OF SPECIFIC GOALS ILLUSTRATED

Consistent with the statement of broad objectives the executive committee developed the statement of specific goals for the company shown in Illustration 9.

STATEMENT OF BASIC STRATEGIES ILLUSTRATED

In harmony with the evaluation of relevant variables, the broad enterprise objectives, and the specific goals, top management developed basic strategies for the coming year, as summarized in Illustration 10.

> **ILLUSTRATION 10.   Summary of Basic Strategies—Superior Manufacturing Company**
> January 1, 1977

1. To increase market penetration and to stay out in front of the competition in all the marketing areas. The following strategies to attain this goal will be aggressively pursued.
   a. Establish product research (new product development and improvement of present products) on a long-range budgetary basis. To this end we will commit to research an increasing share of funds available for the next five years.
   b. During future year two, introduce in all market areas the new product (Product Z) that has shown considerable promise in the three market tests completed to date. Special promotional efforts shall be planned and funded.
   c. To increase the quality of our products by:
      (1) Increasing technological efficiency in our plants;
      (2) Increased competence of selected factory employees (and factory supervisors); and
      (3) Improvement of quality control techniques.
   d. Revitalize the training program for our marketing specialists, giving a special emphasis to aggressive sales efforts on a sophisticated level in order to appeal to preferred customers.
2. Except for short-term needs, to finance all expansion of company operations from internally generated funds.
3. To increase our productive efficiency aggressively by:
   a. Upgrading productive personnel through:
      (1) Careful evaluation and improvement of quality control;
      (2) Identification of weaknesses in individual performance and to correct these through training and positive approaches on a sound psychological basis;
      (3) Improving selectivity in initial employment; and
      (4) Keeping machinery in top operating condition.
   b. Utilizing the latest technological advances for productive facilities including expansion of our computer applications in the factory.
4. To increase management sophistication of all levels by expanding our executive

ILLUSTRATION 10. Continued

development program. During the coming year we will develop a formal plan for raising the competence of our younger managers in order to provide a sufficient and ready supply of competent individuals for the higher management positions.

5. In order to increase our return on investment in accordance with the broad objectives, we will:

    a. Increase market penetration as specified in item 1 above;

    b. Improve cost control at all levels, and relate cost and other expenditures to output (productivity); and

    c. Continue our present pricing strategy.

PLANNING PREMISES ILLUSTRATED

Each year the formal planning activities at the lower levels of management are initiated by means of a "planning premises letter" distributed by the president to the manager of each major responsibility center. Attached to the letter are the relevant guidelines and instructions developed by the executive committee and approved by the president. The planning premises letter is shown in Illustration 11.

ILLUSTRATION 11. Planning Premises Letter—Superior Manufacturing Company
September 25, 1976

To all vice presidents and division managers:

    The purposes of this letter and the attachments are (a) to initiate the formal planning activities in each of your responsibility centers for the next planning period (1977 and beyond), and (b) to provide guidelines and planning premises that we will use in developing the new profit plans. There have been no changes in the policies explained in the profit planning and control manual. For your convenience our planning calendar is attached; you will note that it has been slightly revised to harmonize with the current calendar. In accordance with our standard procedure manuals and the related responsibilities, the project plans, the five-year strategic profit plan, and the annual tactical plan will be developed.

    I think all can take justifiable pride in the accomplishments of our company over its life span, particularly in recent years. The interest, enthusiasm, and understanding with respect to the new comprehensive profit planning and control program that have been exhibited by all levels of management are commendable. At the outset, I want to encourage each of you, collectively and individually, to continue making constructive suggestions to increase the operational efficiency of our company, the sophistication of our management, and the effectiveness of our management programs.

    Last year our annual sales volume reached record levels, and in my judgment our operational efficiencies also established new peaks. It is well to take satisfaction with our accomplishments in the past but it is more important that we focus our energies and attention on the future. In this light, then, the guidelines provided in this letter represent the collective judgments of your executive committee and of myself and are intended to provide a basis for greater accomplishments in the future, accomplishments that will, in the long-run, be reflected to the advantage of all competent employees individually and collectively.

ILLUSTRATION 11. Continued

The executive committee has just completed an in-depth assessment of the company in view of our long-term expectations. As a result of that assessment we have concluded that increased emphasis should be given to marketing strategies, consistent product quality, and certain programs that tend to serve broad societal needs. This increased emphasis has been incorporated into the guidelines attached to this letter. A copy of the statement of broad objectives of the company is attached; you will observe that it has been significantly revised from the one for this year.

Attached to this letter for your guidance are the following:

1. Statement of broad objectives.
2. Statement of specific goals.
3. Summary of basic strategies.
4. Historical data (relating to the industry and our company for the past 10 years). The data presented were selected by the financial vice president on the basis of their relevance to your planning problems. Additional data desired may be obtained readily from him upon request.
5. Economic statistics (including economic projections and relevant commentary that may be useful to you in making certain planning decisions for your responsibility center). These data were developed by the economic analysts and from selected sources. If additional data are required you should contact the financial vice president.
6. Planning calendar.
7. Instructions prepared by the director of profit planning and control with respect to schedule format and related matters essential to aggregating your planning results into the overall company plans. Please contact the director if there are any procedural questions.

In preparing plans for your responsibility center the following *underlying assumptions* should be observed:

a. The industry is expected to continue its expansion at about 3 percent per year. Our sales growth will continue to exceed the industry rate.
b. General business conditions are expected to continue at the present growth rate during the next five years. A slight decrease in business conditions is expected during the last half of next year (refer to economic analysis attached).
c. No major economic, social, or military catastrophe is anticipated.

To provide additional guidance and to discuss your specific problems, within the next two weeks I will schedule several meetings with the vice presidents and other senior members of the management group. Following these discussions, each vice president should schedule planning conferences with his key managers, at which time the policies with respect to the profit planning and control program should be discussed. In addition, these guidelines and their application should be discussed with the managers to establish a basis for meaningful participation the planning process.

It is essential that we adhere to the planning calendar and that we exert our best efforts to develop realistic programs and plans, then to evaluate them in dollars and cents so that we may have a firm projection of the probable financial results for the future.

ILLUSTRATION 11. Continued

We should remember that planning is one of our major managerial responsibilities; therefore, we should expect to spend the effort required to develop realistic plans. In the process each member of the executive committee, including myself, will be available for advice, suggestions, and tentative evaluations. Each member of management is urged to work closely with the financial executive who has staff responsibility for overall supervision of the operation of the profit planning and control program. However, in this connection, I want to make it clear, as does the financial vice president, that his division will serve in a strictly staff capacity to provide advice and assistance.

The line executives and managers are directly responsible for the decision inputs; the profit plan, when completed, must be viewed as the plans and commitments of operating management and not of the staff.

I am confident that we will develop an excellent profit plan and that we will meet or exceed its goals by the end of the planning period. Your cooperation and constructive efforts will assure the attainment of this objective.

The President

PROJECT PLANNING ILLUSTRATED

The company implements the project planning concept for practically all major efforts. For example, the new product (Z) is set up as a project plan. Project plans attempt to cover the estimated life-span of the effort. Ideas for new projects (including improvements in current operations) are encouraged at all levels of management. To this end the company has established a set of procedures to assure that all ideas and suggestions are given careful attention and evaluation. A project number is assigned, and if the project is approved, it is incorporated into the strategic and tactical profit plans (see Illustration 6, Chapter 2).

Illustration 12 shows a suggestion that has been processed through the various evaluations and has survived for inclusion in the five-year and one-year profit plans. The illustration clearly indicates the evaluation and approval processes as well as instructions for including the project in periodic profit plans. The capital-additions budget subsequently illustrated will reflect this project.

STRATEGIC AND TACTICAL PROFIT PLANS ILLUSTRATED

Recall that Superior Manufacturing Company annually prepares two periodic profit plans—a strategic long-range profit plan encompassing a time horizon of five years beyond the upcoming year (for the period 1978–82) and a tactical short-range profit plan encompassing twelve months that correspond with the upcoming fiscal period used by the company (calendar year 1977). First, we will illustrate some aspects of the long-range profit plan followed by illustrations from the short-range profit plan.

ILLUSTRATION 12.   Project Proposal Summary
Superior Manufacturing Company

THE SUPERIOR MANUFACTURING COMPANY

PROJECT PROPOSAL SUMMARY

PROJECT NO. _1-101_   DATE _10-1-74_

DIVISION OR DEPARTMENT _Company_

ORIGINATED BY _A.B. Commerce_   TITLE _Vice President_

EVALUATIONS: (File Code _20_)

	Date Completed	Supervisor	Recommendation
Policy	_8-1-69_	_Hudson_	_Proceed with technical and economic evaluations_
Technical	_7-1-70_	_Hammer_	_Favorable_
Economic	_9-1-70_	_Donley_	_Cost $120,000 (est.)_

APPROVALS:

Tentative Approval by Executive Committee _11-71_
Approval by President for Inclusion in Profit Plan Dated: _Include in 1977_
plans for construction to start in 1978.
Project Authorization (AFE) Date _____

REVIEWS subsequent to Approval for Inclusion in Profit Plan:

(1) _____
(2) _____
(3) _____

PROJECT SUMMARY:

DESIGNATION: _New building - for expansion of Mfg facilities_
(see file 20-1-101-9
ESTIMATED STARTING DATE _Jan.1978_ ESTIMATED COMPLETION DATE _Sept.1978_
PRIORITY _a-5_
COST ESTIMATES (Cash Flow): TOTAL $ _120,000_
       BY YEAR: Yr 1 _$120,000_ Yr 2 ____ Yr 3 ____ Yr 4 ____ Yr 5 ____
                Balance _____
RETURN ON INVESTMENT ANALYSIS _17% (DCF) See file 20-1-101-9_

COMMENTS _____
_____

Strategic Profit Plan Illustrated.   The strategic long-range plan for Superior Manufacturing Company is characterized by its harmony with the broad objectives of the enterprise, the more specific objectives laid down by the management, and the long-range strategies. The long-range plan is very broad and in general terms. A good portion of the long-range plan is more or less informal as represented by tentative commitments made by the executive committee in its planning sessions. The formal portion of the long-range plan includes the following basic components detailed by each year: income statement; cash flow projection; capital expenditures plan; manpower requirements; research plans; and a long-range market penetration plan. The strategic plan does not include a formal balance sheet; however, it is anticipated that important balance sheet items would be included. Thus, the long-range plan covers all the *key areas* of anticipated activity: sales; expenses; research and development; capital expenditures; cash; profits; and return on investment. The income-statement component of the long-range plan for Superior Manuacturing Company is shown in Illustration 13.

Several salient features may be observed in Illustration 13. In the first instance, although sales are shown as a total amount for each year, there is a supporting plan that provides more detail with respect to the various products, the distribution expenses, and the planned promotional efforts. Another important aspect of the illustration is the classification of costs into

ILLUSTRATION 13.   Strategic Long-Range Plan (Profits)

Superior Manufacturing Company
Five-Year Plan—Income Statement
(In Thousand Dollars)

	ACTUAL			PROJECTED					
	1974	1975	1976	1977	1978	1979	1980	1981	1982
Sales	$5,505	$5,691	$5,963	$6,100	$7,000	$7,400	$8,000	$8,800	$9,500
Variable costs	3,600	3,700	3,870	3,940	4,650	4,880	5,350	5,890	6,360
Marginal income	1,905	1,991	2,093	2,160	2,350	2,520	2,650	2,910	3,140
Fixed costs	1,220	1,100	1,160	1,310	1,400	1,430	1,470	1,580	1,680
Miscellaneous items	(30)	(15)	10	(20)	(50)	(20)	(30)	(16)	(20)
Net before taxes	715	906	923	870	1,000	1,110	1,210	1,346	1,480
Estimated taxes	290	270	325	260	490	540	590	650	700
Net income	$ 425	$ 636	$ 598	$ 610	$ 510	$ 570	$ 620	$ 696	$ 780
Ratios:									
Profit margin —pretax	13.0	15.9	15.5	14.3	14.3	15.0	15.1	15.3	15.6
Return on investment—pretax	21.0	28.0	27.6	17.4	29.6	30.0	30.0	31.0	31.0
Sales trend	90.2	93.3	97.8	100.0	114.7	121.3	131.1	144.3	155.7

two categories, variable costs and fixed costs (to be discussed in detail in subsequent chapters). The projection of three important ratios—that is, two profitability indices, profit margin and return on investment, and the growth trend as reflected in sales dollars—should be particularly noted.

Tactical Profit Plan Illustrated. In order to provide a broad general view of a complete short-range profit plan, certain summary profit plans for the Superior Manufacturing Company are presented in this section. The plans shown here deal primarily with *annual results;* detail classification by months, responsibility, and products will be discussed and illustrated at the end of subsequent chapters. The annual summaries and discussions presented in this chapter include only those essential (1) to impart the general understanding of the annual profit plan and (2) to provide an overall conception of the comprehensive short-range profit plan. The reader should review the organizational chart, the statement of broad objectives, the statement of goals, the statement of strategies, and the planning premises letter as background for study of these schedules. In addition, the reader should notice how the tactical profit plan dovetails with the strategic long-range profit plan.

The reader is urged to observe particularly the fact that various budgets and subbudgets illustrated below and in subsequent chapters are segmented as follows:

1. By organizational responsibility. We have said that there should be participation in the planning process and that control can be exercised effectively only through assigned responsibilities. Consequently, the profit planning and control program must be tailored, first and foremost, to the organizational structure and related responsibilities. This frame of reference is observable in almost all the schedules included in the short-range profit plan and also in the periodic performance reports prepared and distributed throughout the year to all levels of management.

2. By interim periods. With respect to the tactical profit plan, Superior Manufacturing Company segments the first quarter of the annual period on a monthly basis; estimates for subsequent quarters are subsequently categorized by monthly periods during the year. Segmentation on a time basis is especially significant, because to be meaningful, many goals must be immediate goals. For example, an annual sales quota would not motivate as much as a series of monthly, or even daily, sales quotas. The strategic profit plan is categorized by years.

3. By product-cost classifications. The tactical profit plan must be structured to meet the data needs for unit product cost, project

cost, and other cost constructions that are not necessarily based on organizational responsibilities nor uniform time periods.

Remember that some of the budget schedules illustrated in this and subsequent chapters are designed to illustrate the approach used in their development. This approach has been adopted for instructional purposes. For the final profit plans, many of the schedules should be redesigned to increase their readability and understanding, and some of them may well be omitted from the profit plan distributed to the management.

For ease in understanding we will refer to the various subbudgets by *schedule number* in contrast with other exhibits throughout the text that are designated as illustrations. The following discussions outline the subbudgets for the Superior Manufacturing Company. At this point, concentrate on (1) the decisional input sources for the information that are reflected in the various budgets (plans), (2) the flow of information from one phase to the next, and (3) the arrangement of the schedules themselves to reflect responsibility, time horizons, and product classifications.

Sales Plan Illustrated. After the planning premises have been received, the development of the sales plan is the next step in preparing the profit plans for the Superior Manufacturing Company. The strategic and tactical sales plans have three distinct parts: (1) the projected volume of sales at a projected sales price per unit for each product; (2) the sales promotional plan (advertising and other promotional costs); and (3) the sales expense plan (salesmen's remuneration and other order-getting and order-filling costs). Recall that Superior Manufacturing Company sells two products (designated X and Y) in three sales districts (designated Southern, Eastern, and Western). In all respects the sales plan is the direct *responsibility of the vice president in charge of sales*. A tentative sales plan is presented to the executive committee by the sales vice president at a planning meeting and is then tentatively approved by the president after revision in accordance with the judgments of the executive committee.

The annual *sales budget summary* (as approved) for the company for the planning year ending December 31, 1977 is shown in Schedule 1. Attention is called to the reference heading, Ref., which provides a line and a column to indicate sources of data when taken from prior schedules; when the data come from a basic input source—a decision-making authority—the work *input* is used for instructional purposes. You should note that the basic inputs in constructing this schedule were: (1) the planned unit sales price—a decision of top management, and (2) planned number of units to be sold (assuming the planned sales price and the planned promotional and other sales efforts). The other components of the sales plan will be illustrated in Chapter 5.

SCHEDULE 1.   Superior Manufacturing Company

Sales Plan Summary—Volume and Dollars
By District, By Product
For the Year Ending December 31, 1977

RESPONSIBILITY		TOTALS	PRODUCT X		PRODUCT Y	
			UNITS	AMOUNT	UNITS	AMOUNT
	Ref.		(Input)		(Input)	
Southern Sales District		$2,120,000	340,000	$1,700,000	210,000	$ 420,000
X—$5.00; Y—$2.00*	(Input)					
Eastern Sales District		2,907,000	500,000	2,550,000	170,000	357,000
X—$5.10; Y—$2.10*	(Input)					
Western Sales District		1,068,000	160,000	816,000	120,000	252,000
X—$5.10; Y—$2.10*	(Input)					
Totals		$6,095,000	1,000,000	$5,066,000	500,000	$1,029,000

*Average unit sales prices projected. (See Schedule 21 for detail.)

Production Plan Illustrated.   When the tentative sales plan is completed, the next step in building the short-range profit plan for Superior Manufacturing Company is development of a *production plan.* The production plan involves determination of the number of units of each product that must be manufactured to meet planned sales and to maintain the planned inventory levels of finished goods. Determination of production requirements necessitates another decisional input, that is, the management policy with respect to the inventory levels of finished goods that are to be maintained. Thus, the production budget summary shown in Schedule 2 was constructed by using the sales requirements from Schedule 1, the beginning inventories of finished goods and the ending inventory levels of finished goods. At this point we will not consider inventory policy except to assume that the final inventories shown in Schedule 2 are in harmony with inventory policy.

Since production planning and scheduling are factory functions involving determination of the amount of goods to produce and production timing, the production plan is the *primary responsibility of the manufacturing vice president* in Superior Manufacturing Company. Product X is processed through all three factory production departments, and product Y is processed through production departments 1 and 3 only.

In the next several paragraphs we will see that the production plan provides the basic foundation for planning the costs of direct material, direct labor, and manufacturing overhead.

Direct Materials Budget Illustrated.   Direct materials, as a manufacturing cost, is represented by the materials and parts utilized directly in the manufacture of finished goods. The direct materials budget reflects the estimated amount of materials required to produce the number of units of finished goods called for in the production budget. One basic input is

SCHEDULE 2. Superior Manufacturing Company
Production Budget Summary*
By Product Units
For the Year Ending December 31, 1977

		PRODUCTS (UNITS)	
		X	Y
	Ref.		
Units required to meet sales budget	1	1,000,000	500,000
Add desired finished goods final inventory, Dec. 31, 1977	(Input)	200,000	120,000
Total units required		1,200,000	620,000
Less finished goods initial inventory, Jan. 1, 1977	(Given)	240,000	100,000
Planned production for 1977		960,000	520,000

*(See Schedules 22 and 23 for detail.)

required to develop the direct materials budget, that is, the number of units of each type of material required to manufacture each unit of finished goods. Thus, preparation of the direct materials budget necessitates a careful study of the products in order to determine *unit material usage rates*. The unit material usage rates are multiplied by the number of units of finished goods to be produced in order to derive the total units of material required.

The direct materials budget summary *in units* for Superior Manufacturing Company is shown in Schedule 3. Observe that the company utilizes

SCHEDULE 3. Superior Manufacturing Company
Direct Materials Budget Summary in Units*
By Material, By Product, By Department
for the Year Ending December 31, 1977

RESPONSIBILITY		DIRECT MATERIAL (UNITS REQUIRED FOR PRODUCTION)		
		A	B	C
	Ref.			
By product:	24			
X	&	960,000	1,920,000	1,920,000
Y	25	520,000	520,000	
Totals		1,480,000	2,440,000	1,920,000
By department:				
No. 1		1,480,000		
No. 2			1,920,000	
No. 3			520,000	1,920,000
Totals		1,480,000	2,440,000	1,920,000

*(See Schedules 24 and 25 for details.)

three direct materials designated as A, B, and C. Computations underlying this schedule are shown in a later chapter in Schedules 24 and 25.

Purchases Budget Illustrated. The direct materials budget provides the *purchasing manager* with data essential to develop a plan of purchases. To do this, however, a decisional input is required, that is, the management policy with respect to the level of material inventories to be maintained. With these two sets of data the number of units of each type of material that must be *purchased* to support the production plans can be readily planned as illustrated in Schedule 4, the purchases budget summary.

SCHEDULE 4. Superior Manufacturing Company
Purchases Budget Summary
For the Year Ending December 31, 1977*

| | | DIRECT MATERIALS | | |
		A	B	C
	Ref.			
Units required for production	3	1,480,000	2,440,000	1,920,000
Add desired final inventory, Dec. 31, 1977	(Input)	245,000	370,000	450,000
Total units required		1,725,000	2,810,000	2,370,000
Less initial inventory, Jan. 1, 1977	(Given)	220,000	360,000	460,000
Units to be purchased		1,505,000	2,450,000	1,910,000
Planned unit purchase price	(Input)	$.30	$.20	$.25
Total cost of purchases		$ 451,500	$ 490,000	$ 477,500

*(See Schedules 26, 27, and 28 for detail.)

Another decisional input is required at this point—the planned unit purchase price for each type of material. With this additional input, computation of total cost of planned purchases for each material can be determined.

The purchases budget is a *direct responsibility of the purchasing manager* in Superior Manufacturing Company. This manager works under direct supervision of the manufacturing vice president. It is a direct responsibility of the purchasing manager to be knowledgeable in respect to the market for the materials that he must purchase; therefore, it is his responsibility to provide projected unit material costs for use in the purchases budget.

Regarding the purchases budget summary, observe that both units of material and dollar cost are specified; thus, this schedule represents one of the building blocks for the cash flow plan, which is discussed subsequently.

Direct Labor Budget Illustrated. Direct labor, as a manufacturing cost, is defined as those labor costs directly identifiable with the production of specific units of finished goods. The production plan (Schedule 2) provides the underlying data for planning the direct labor requirements. The direct labor budget requires two additional decisional inputs—standard direct labor hours per unit of each finished good and the average hourly wage rates expected. This subbudget must be organized in a manner similar to that for the direct materials budget; the direct labor requirements are planned both by organizational responsibility and by product. The manufacturing vice president is directly responsible for planning the direct labor budget. The three production department managers and the standards measurement group cooperatively develop the decisional inputs (that is, the standard times and wage rates) for this budget, which goes to the manufacturing vice president. The direct labor budget summary for Superior Manufacturing Company is shown in Schedule 5.

SCHEDULE 5. Superior Manufacturing Company
Direct Labor Budget Summary
By Product, By Department
For the Year Ending December 31, 1977

		UNITS TO BE PRODUCED	STANDARD LABOR HOURS	TOTAL STANDARD HOURS	AVERAGE WAGE RATE	DIRECT LABOR COST
	Ref.	2	(Input)		(Input)	
By product:						
X		960,000	1.0	960,000	$1.50	$1,440,000
Y		520,000	.4	208,000	1.50	312,000
Totals				1,168,000		$1,752,000
By department (responsibility):						
1*				488,000	$2.00	$ 976,000
2*				192,000	1.50	288,000
3*				488,000	1.00	488,000
Totals				1,168,000		$1,752,000

*Computation shown in Schedules 30 and 31.

Building Services Budget Illustrated. Prior to illustrating the planning of manufacturing overhead costs, we must consider the building services budget since Superior Manufacturing Company utilizes one building for the three major home-office functions of administration, production, and sales. The cost of operating the building are allocated to these three functions. Concurrent with the profit planning activities as illustrated for the sales vice president and the manufacturing vice president, the supervisor of the building must develop a building services budget. This budget, shown in Schedule 6, is a cost projection based upon expected building utilization. The *building supervisor is directly responsible for this budget* and must work in cooperation with a number of other managers with respect to certain estimates. For example, the salaries are based on top management decisions; depreciation expense basically is an accounting determination; and insurance and taxes would reflect managerial policies and externally determined rates. Superior Manufacturing Company allocates building costs to the three major functions on the basis of floor space occupied; the planned allocation is shown on Schedule 6.

SCHEDULE 6.   Superior Manufacturing Company
Building Services Budget Summary*
For the Year Ending December 31, 1977

	TOTAL YEAR
Supervisory salaries	$ 24,000
Repairs and maintenance	18,000
Depreciation	60,000
Insurance	3,600
Taxes	2,400
Wages	27,000
Heat	13,000
Water	2,000
Total	$150,000
Occupancy cost distribution: (on basis of floor space)	
Selling (20%)	$ 30,000
Administrative (20%)	30,000
Factory (60%)	90,000
Total	$150,000

*(See Schedule 34 for detail.)

Factory Overhead Budget Illustrated.   It will be recalled that Superior Manufacturing Company has three producing departments and three service departments in the factory. Accordingly, factory overhead (expense) budgets for *each* of these six departments must be prepared by the manufacturing vice president. In turn, he established a policy requiring each department supervisor to develop his own proposed factory overhead budget.

The production budget, since it indicates the planned production for each product manufactured, provides the basic foundation for planning factory overhead costs. The production budget provides a basis for projecting the *planned volume of work* or activity for each producing department. In turn, the planned activities of the producing departments provide a basis for estimation of the volume of work or activity that can be expected in each of the three factory *service departments*. With respect to the service departments, the General Factory Overhead Department is the administrative center for the factory; the Power Department manufactures electricity for use by the producing departments; and the Repair Department repairs machinery and other facilities utilized by the three producing departments.

The departmental factory overhead budgets for each of the six factory departments, as approved by the vice president of manufacturing, are summarized in Schedule 7. Observe that the expenses are planned by responsibility (that is, by department) and that the accounts listed for each department are those used in the responsibility accounting system. Observe also that the building service allocation is included in Schedule 7 as a total but is not reallocated to the six departments individually. This treatment reflects the fact the departmental supervisors do not exercise control over building services cost nor the allocation of its costs. Alternatively, control of building services cost is the direct responsibility of the building superintendent. In developing this schedule, the fundamental decisional inputs are the *dollar-cost estimates* account by account for each department. The building services allocation was taken from Schedule 6.

Inventory Budgets Illustrated.   At this point, the company executives have planned the costs for the factory function; now the information is available to develop the planned dollar values of the inventories for (1) raw materials, (2) work in process, and (3) finished goods. Production, direct materials, purchases, direct labor, and factory overhead budgets are submitted directly to the budget director. His staff utilizes these figures to compute and assemble data relative to the budgeted inventory levels (units and dollars) and cost of goods sold. To compute these two budgets *no additional decisional inputs* are necessary with the exception of the *inventory cost flow method* to be used. Superior Manufacturing Company management has adopted a first-in first-out cost flow policy for all inventories.

The budget of initial and final inventories is shown in Schedule 8 and the related cost of goods sold budget summary is shown in Schedule 9. The assembly details are illustrated in subsequent chapters. With the information included in the sales plan the director of profit planning and control now can prepare the planned income statement through gross margin.

Distribution and Promotional Expense Budgets Illustrated. Recall that the sales plan for Superior Manufacturing Company included three components: (1) planned sales volume; (2) planned promotional costs (plans); and (3) other planned distribution costs. Distribution and promotional costs in this company are combined into one budget, which reflects separate subbudgets for each of the three sales districts and for home office sales activities (by responsibility). The sales vice president, in conformity with basic planning policies of the company, requested each district sales supervisor to submit expense plans in harmony with the volume of sales planned for his district. Home office sales costs were planned by the assistant to the vice president. These four distribution expense budgets, as approved by the vice president of sales, are shown in Schedule 10. The building service allocation is reflected in Schedule 10, although it is unallocated to the four

SCHEDULE 7. Superior Manufacturing Company
Manufacturing Overhead—Budget Summary*
By Department for the Year Ending December 31, 1977

	Ref. (Inputs)	PRODUCING DEPARTMENTS			RESPONSIBILITY — SERVICE DEPARTMENTS			TOTAL ALL DEPTS.
		No. 1	No. 2	No. 3	GENERAL FACTORY OVERHEAD	POWER DEPT.	REPAIR DEPT.	
Supervisory salaries		$120,000	$22,440	$ 35,040	$ 96,000	$ 36,000	$ 3,600	$313,080
Indirect labor	"	145,800	3,648	44,248				193,696
Maintenance parts	"	10,920	624	4,240		6,800		22,584
Fuel	"					24,000		24,000
Supplies used	"	32,240	1,440	14,600			1,360	49,640
Travel and entertainment	"				7,040			7,040
Telephone and telegraph	"				7,856			7,856
Depreciation	"	7,320	768	4,392	1,560	5,400	120	19,560
Insurance	"	1,200	120	600	240	840	36	3,036
Taxes	"	1,800	240	720	360	960	84	4,164
Stationery and office supplies	"				3,744			3,744
Wages	"					36,000	4,800	40,800
Totals		$319,280	$29,280	$103,840	$116,800	$110,000	$10,000	$689,200
Building service allocation	6							90,000
Total factory overhead								$779,200

*(See Schedules 33 and 34 for detail.)

SCHEDULE 8. Superior Manufacturing Company
Budget of Initial and Final Inventories*
For the Year Ending December 31, 1977
(Input-FIFO Method)

INVENTORY	Ref.	UNITS 2 & 4	INITIAL INVENTORY UNITS PRICE	TOTAL VALUE	UNITS 2 & 4	FINAL INVENTORY UNITS PRICE	TOTAL VALUE
Raw materials:							
Material A		220,000	$ .30	$ 66,000	245,000	$.30	$ 73,500
Material B		360,000	.20	72,000	370,000	.20	74,000
Material C		460,000	.26	119,600	450,000	.25	112,500
Totals				$257,600			$260,000
Work in process		10,000	1.38	$ 13,800	10,000	1.38	$ 13,800
(Prod. Y—Dept. 3)							
Finished goods:							
Product X		240,000	3.36	$806,400	200,000	3.36	$672,000
Product Y		100,000	1.38	138,000	120,000	1.38	165,600
Totals				$944,400			$837,600

*(See Schedules 27 and 60.)

responsibility centers. It is obvious that the projection of each expense involved judgmental decisions on the part of sales supervisors. Historical data and planned sales efforts provided background for these judgmental inputs.

Administrative Expense Budget Illustrated. There are three general administrative departments designated as: administrative; accounting (including the director of profit planning); and treasurer. The head of each of these departments submitted an expense budget for consideration and approval by the financial vice president. These three expense budgets are shown in Schedule 11. The budget of other income and expense for the company was prepared by the financial vice president as shown in Schedule 12.

Statement of Planned Income. The sales, factory costs, and expense budgets are forwarded to the budget director; obviously they provide the information needed by the director's staff to complete the *planned income statement*. At this point his staff estimated the income taxes and completed the planned income statement as shown in Schedule 13. We may observe in particular that the resultant profit margin of 14.13 percent is close to the objective specified earlier in the statement of goals (Illustration 9). At this point, the budget director, by introducing the decisional input on planned

SCHEDULE 9. Superior Manufacturing Company
Cost of Goods Sold Budget Summary*
For the Year Ending December 31, 1977

		ANNUAL	
	Ref.		
Direct raw materials used:			
Inventory, Jan. 1, 1972	8	$ 257,600	
Purchases of raw materials	4	1,419,000	
Total		$1,676,600	
Less inventory, Dec. 31, 1972	8	260,000	
Cost of raw materials used			$1,416,600
Direct labor	5		1,752,000
Manufacturing expenses	7		779,200
Total charges to manufacturing			3,947,800
Add initial work in process inventory	8		13,800
			3,961,600
Less final work in process inventory	8		13,800
Total cost of goods manufactured			3,947,800
Add initial finished goods inventory	8		944,400
			4,892,200
Less final inventory of finished goods	8		837,600
Cost of goods sold			$4,054,600

*(See Schedule 61 for detail.)

dividends (to stockholders), prepared the planned statement of retained earnings as shown in Schedule 14.

Budget of Capital Additions Illustrated. The capital additions budget includes such items as planned extensions of plant, new buildings, extraordinary repairs that are to be capitalized, building programs, machinery acquisitions, and other capital additions. The budget of capital additions that is included in the tactical short-range profit plan presents that specific portion of the strategic long-range capital additions plan that will materialize during the upcoming year. The budget of capital additions included in the annual profit plan for Superior Manufacturing Company was assembled by the financial vice president and his staff. However, the *decisional inputs* to this budget were initiated and decided upon by the line executives and approved by the executive committee and the president. Note that each item in the capital additions budget represents a *project plan* such as was shown in Illustration 12. The capital additions budget summary for Superior Manufacturing Company is shown in Schedule 15. Observe, as in the preceding schedules, the basis for constructing a cash flow budget is being established, since cash requirements are pinpointed in the schedule.

SCHEDULE 10. Superior Manufacturing Company
Distribution Expense Budget Summary*
For the Year Ending December 31, 1977

ACCOUNT	Ref.	GENERAL SALES OVERHEAD	SALES DISTRICT			TOTAL
			SOUTHERN	EASTERN	WESTERN	
Supervisory salaries	(Input)	$144,000	$ 72,000	$ 96,000	$ 36,000	$348,000
Travel and entertainment	//	38,907	25,279	30,812	11,641	106,639
Telephone and telegraph	//	15,861	9,379	14,828	4,915	44,983
Depreciation—office equipment	//	600				600
Stationery and office supplies	//	11,049				11,049
Auto expense	//	25,913				25,913
Commissions	//		84,800	116,280	42,720	243,800
Freight and express	//		19,198	19,471	7,844	46,513
Advertising	//	60,000	24,000	36,000	12,000	132,000
Totals		$296,330	$234,656	$313,391	$115,120	$959,497
Building service allocation	6					30,000
Total distribution expense						$989,497

*(See Schedule 42 for detail.)

SCHEDULE 11. Superior Manufacturing Company
Administrative Expense Budget Summary*
For the Year Ending December 31, 1977

ACCOUNT	Ref.	DEPARTMENTS			TOTAL
		ADMINIS-TRATIVE	ACCOUNT-ING	TREAS-URER	
Supervisory salaries	(Input)	$60,000	$48,000	$36,000	$144,000
Travel and entertaining	//	9,000	1,200	1,200	11,400
Telephone and telegraph	//	9,114	1,210	3,158	13,482
Depreciation—office equipment	//	600	2,400	1,200	4,200
Insurance	//	240	240	480	960
Taxes	//	240	360	120	720
Stationery and office supplies	//	122	610	1,829	2,561
Lawyers' retainer fee	//	1,800			1,800
Loss on bad debts	//			12,190	12,190
Audit fees	//	2,400			2,400
Totals		$83,516	$54,020	$56,177	$193,713
Building service allocation					30,000
Total Administrative Expense					$223,713

*(See Schedule 44 for detail.)

SCHEDULE 12. Superior Manufacturing Company

Budget of Other Incomes and Expenses
For the Year Ending December 31, 1977

		ANNUAL
	Ref.	
Other incomes:		
Interest income (on building fund)	(Input)	$ 500
Miscellaneous incomes	″	37,120
Total		$37,620
Other expenses:		
Interest expense	″	3,750
Net (other income)		$33,870

SCHEDULE 13. Superior Manufacturing Company

Statement of Planned Income*
For the Year Ending December 31, 1977

	Ref.	AMOUNT	PER CENT OF SALES
Sales	1	$6,095,000	100.00
Cost of goods sold	9	4,054,600	66.52
Gross margin on sales		$2,040,400	33.48
Less:			
Distribution expenses	10	989,497	16.23
Administrative expenses	11	223,713	3.67
Totals		$1,213,210	19.90
Operating income		$ 827,190	13.57
Add net of other income and expense	12	33,870	.56
Net income before federal income taxes		$ 861,060	14.13
Federal income taxes	(Input)	258,318	4.24
Net income		$ 602,742	9.89

*(See Schedules 64, 65, and 66 for detail.)

SCHEDULE 14. Superior Manufacturing Company

Statement of Planned Retained Earnings
For the Year Ending December 31, 1977

	Ref.	
Balance, retained earnings, Jan. 1, 1977	(Given)	$ 522,770
Add net income budgeted	13	602,742
Total		$1,125,512
Less budgeted dividends	(Input)	12,000
Balance, retained earnings, Dec. 31, 1977		$1,113,512

SCHEDULE 15. Superior Manufacturing Company
Capital Additions Budget Summary*
For the Year Ending December 31, 1977

ITEMS	ESTIMATED STARTING DATE	ESTIMATED COMPLETION DATE	ESTIMATED COST	YEAR BUDGETED FOR 1977	YEAR BUDGETED FOR 1978
New building	Jan. 1978	Sept. 1978	$120,000		$120,000
Machinery—Dept. 1	July 1978	Sept. 1978	10,000		10,000
Repair tools	Jan. 1977	Jan. 31, 1977	200	$ 200	
Power motor	Dec. 1977	Dec. 31, 1977	8,500	8,500	
Total			$138,700	$ 8,700	$130,000
Assets funded:					
New building				20,000	
Total cash required in 1977 for capital additions				$28,700	

Depreciation data:
　　Repair tools—5-year life, no scrap value.
　　Power motor—10-year life, no scrap value.
　*(See Schedules 46 and 47 for detail.)

Cash Flow Budget Illustrated.   The cash flow budget reports the planned sources and dispositions of cash throughout the budgeted year. The profit plan schedules prepared and illustrated up to this point, with certain adjustments, provide the essential data to develop the cash flow budget. The financial vice president is directly responsible for developing the cash flow budget (illustrated in Schedule 16). It is obvious that cash disbursements for expenses do not coincide precisely with expense totals reflected in the expense budgets because there are certain noncash expense items such as depreciation, accrued expenses, and bad debt expense. Schedule 16, which is a summary for the year, does not indicate the adjustments and computations necessary to convert planned revenues and planned expenses on an accrual basis to a cash flow basis; these adjustments and computations are illustrated in a subsequent chapter.

Projected Balance Sheet Illustrated.   The projected balance sheet reports the effect of the plan of operations on the assets, liabilities, and capital of the company. The budgeted balance sheet is prepared by the budget director from plans shown in other components of the profit plan. The annual projected balance sheet for Superior Manufacturing Company is shown in Schedule 17. Detailed computations are shown in subsequent chapters.

Approval of the Profit Plans.   The strategic long-range profit plan and the tactical short-range profit plan for Superior Manufacturing Company, as illustrated, are assembled under the supervision of the budget director. When their consolidation is completed, the two plans are repro-

SCHEDULE 16. Superior Manufacturing Company
Cash Flow Budget Summary*
For the Year Ending December 31, 1977

	Ref.		
Beginning cash balance, Jan. 1, 1977	(Given)		$ 54,000
Budgeted cash receipts:			
Collections of accounts receivable†		$6,095,886	
Other income	12	37,120	
Proceeds of short-term notes payable	(Input)	100,000	
Total budgeted receipts			6,233,006
Total			$6,287,006
Budgeted cash disbursements:			
Raw material purchases—accounts payable†		$1,429,140	
Direct labor	5	1,752,000	
Factory overhead costs†		612,800	
Distribution expenses†		958,897	
Administrative expenses†		173,243	
Building services†		84,000	
Capital additions	15	28,700	
Notes payable	(Input)	250,000	
Dividends	14	12,000	
Accrued and deferred items	(Input)	359,710	
Total budgeted disbursements			5,660,490
Ending cash balance, Dec. 31, 1977			$ 626,516

*(See Schedules 50, 54, and 57 for detail.)
†Computations illustrated in subsequent chapters.

duced and distributed to the members of the executive committee about one week prior to the final planning session. When the executive committee and the president are satisfied that the best plans possible under the circumstances have been devised, the plans are approved by the president and returned to the financial vice president for distribution in accordance with company policy. Each vice president receives a complete copy of the profit plans; other managers receive components that are relevant to their particular functional responsibilities.

The next important step is implementation of the profit plans and control to assure the attainment of the broad objectives and specific goals explicitly included in the two profit plans. This step requires aggressive and continuous effort on the part of each manager to meet or surpass the planned goals in his particular responsibility center.

Variable Budgets of Expense Illustrated. Superior Manufacturing Company uses variable budgets for factory overhead, distribution expenses, and administrative expenses. These special budgets are used in a supplementary manner to:

SCHEDULE 17.   Superior Manufacturing Company
Projected Balance Sheet
As of December 31, 1977

ASSETS

	Ref.			
Current assets:				
Cash	16		$ 626,516	
Accounts receivable*		$ 156,114		
Less allowance for doubtful accounts*		$ 18,190	137,924	
Raw material inventory	8		260,000	
Work in process inventory	8		13,800	
Finished goods inventory	8		837,600	
Unexpired insurance*			17,724	
Supplies inventory*			5,200	
Total current assets				$1,898,764
Funds:				
Building fund*				40,500
Fixed assets:				
Land			25,000	
Building		1,800,000		
Less allowance for depreciation		420,000	1,380,000	
Machinery and equipment		288,700		
Less allowance for depreciation		107,740	180,960	
Total fixed assets				1,585,960
Total assets				$3,525,224

LIABILITIES AND CAPITAL

Current liabilities:				
Accounts payable*		$ 41,960		
Audit fee owed	(Input)	2,400		
Property taxes payable*		7,284		
Accrued interest payable*		1,750		
Federal income tax payable	(Input)	258,318		
Total current liabilities			$ 311,712	
Fixed liabilities:				
Long-term notes payable	(Input)		50,000	
Total liabilities				$ 361,712
Capital:				
Common stock	(Given)	2,000,000		
Premium on stock	(Given)	50,000	2,050,000	
Retained earnings	14		1,113,512	
Total capital				3,163,512
Total liabilities and capital				$3,525,224

*Computations explained in subsequent chapters.

1. Develop expense schedules for the annual profit plan. For example, refer to the profit plan summary for manufacturing overhead (Schedule 7); the planned expense allowances for Producing Department 1 were based on

Producing Department No. 1—1977

ACCOUNT	COMPUTATION BASED ON VARIABLE BUDGET (SCH. 18)	BUDGETED AMOUNT
Supervisory salaries	($10,000 × 12) plus ($0 × 4880)	$120,000
Indirect labor	($3,000 × 12) plus ($22.50 × 4880)	145,800
Maintenance parts	($300 × 12) plus ($1.50 × 4880)	10,920
Supplies used	($450 × 12) plus ($5.50 × 4880)	32,240
Depreciation	($0 × 12) plus ($1.50 × 4880)	7,320
Insurance	($100 × 12) plus ($0 × 4880)	1,200
Taxes	($150 × 12) plus ($0 × 4880)	1,800
Total	($14,000 × 12) plus ($31.00 × 4880)	$319,280

488,000 direct labor hours (taken from the direct labor budget, Schedule 5). The expense allowances for Schedule 7 were computed as follows using the information given in Schedule 18:

SCHEDULE 18. Superior Manufacturing Company
Variable Expense Budget—Manufacturing Division*
For the Year Ending December 31, 1977

	PRODUCING DEPARTMENTS			
	DEPT. 1		DEPT. 2	DEPT. 3
	FIXED ALLOWANCE PER MONTH REGARDLESS OF VOLUME OF WORK	VARIABLE AMOUNT PER 100 DIRECT LABOR HOURS WORKED		
Supervisory salaries	$10,000	—		
Indirect labor	3,000	$22.50		
Maintenance parts	300	1.50		
Supplies used	450	5.50		
Depreciation (output basis)	—	1.50		
Insurance	100	—		
Taxes	150	—		
Totals	$14,000	$31.00		

*Refer to Schedule 33.

2. Develop expense allowances on the monthly performance reports as explained in the section below on performance reports.

To derive the expense allowances shown in the variable budgets, the budget staff prepared an analysis of historical monthly costs. The results of the analysis are tempered to take into account expected conditions during the budget period. They are then presented to the respective divisional executives and departmental supervisors for consideration and recommended revisions. The variable budgets are finally approved by the president.

Only the variable budget for one department of Superior Manufacturing Company is illustrated because the procedure for other departments is similar. The variable budget for Producing Department 1 is shown in Schedule 18. The variable budget approach is discussed in detail and illustrated in Chapter 10.

Performance Reports Illustrated. The extent to which the planned objectives are being attained, exceeded, or not attained is reported to all levels of management by means of internal *performance reports*. Performance reports are prepared for each responsibility center and are distributed monthly to all levels of management. As with the profit plans, distribution of the total package of performance reports is limited to the vice presidents; other managers receive those parts of the performance reports that are relevant to their particular responsibility centers.

To illustrate the general approach used by Superior Manufacturing Company, two separate performance reports are shown in Schedules 19 and 20. Schedule 19 is a performance report on *sales effort*, whereas Schedule 20 is a performance report on *factory overhead*. In these performance reports, notice two distinct features: (1) reporting by responsibility centers; and (2) comparison of actual results with planned goals and the resultant variations, both in dollars and percentage of budget. The *variations column* calls attention to the exceptional items.

In Schedule 20 the "budget" column is headed Variable Budget Adjusted to Actual Volume. This heading suggests use of the variable budget approach to control expenses. This is a technique for providing budget allowances for expenses adjusted to the *actual output* of the department rather than to the output originally planned for that department. Thus, on Schedule 20 the amounts in the column, Variable Budget Adjusted to Actual Volume, were derived by applying 35,000 direct labor hours (actual output measured in terms of actual hours worked) to the variable budget allowances shown in the variable budget for Department 1 in Schedule 18.[1] For example, the indirect labor allowance of $10,875 was computed as follows;

$$(\$3,000) + (\$22.50 \times 350) = \$10,875$$

[1] Many firms adjust on the basis of *standard* productive hours rather than actual productive hours. Generally the former is preferable.

SCHEDULE 19. Superior Manufacturing Company
Sales Performance Report by District, by Product
January 1977

RESPONSIBILITY	Ref.	ACTUAL SALES JANUARY		PLANNED SALES		VARIATIONS FAVORABLE—UNFAVORABLE*		
		UNITS	AMOUNT	UNITS	AMOUNT	UNITS	AMOUNT	% OF BUDGET
Southern District:								
Product X		34,000	$170,000	30,000	$150,000	4,000	$20,000	13
Product Y		14,000	28,000	15,000	30,000	1,000*	2,000*	7*
Totals			$198,000		$180,000		$18,000	10
Eastern District:								
Product X[b]		38,000	$190,000	40,000	$204,000	2,000*	$14,000*	7*
Product Y		10,000	21,000	11,000	23,100	1,000*	2,100*	9*
Totals			$211,000		$227,100		$16,100*	7*
Western District:								
Product X		16,000	$ 81,600	15,000	$ 76,500	1,000	$ 5,100	7
Product Y		9,000	18,900	8,000	16,800	1,000	2,100	13
Totals			$100,500		$ 93,300		$ 7,200	8
Grand totals			$509,500		$500,400		$ 9,100[a]	2
Summary by product:								
Product X		88,000	$441,600	85,000	$430,500	3,000	$11,100	3
Product Y		33,000	67,900	34,000	69,900	1,000*	2,000*	3*
Totals			$509,500		$500,400		$ 9,100[a]	2

[a] Variation due to:
(1) Variation in Units $12,900
(2) Variation in Sales Price $ 3,800*
    Total $ 9,100

[b] Authorized price reduction in this district to $5.00 per unit, in effect for entire month.

Comments:
1. Southern District failure to meet forecast for product Y should be investigated.
2. Eastern District needs immediate attention.
3. Western District should be commended—investigate possibility of transfer of "know-how" to other districts.

SCHEDULE 20. Superior Manufacturing Company
Performance Report on Factory Overhead
January 1977
PART 1—Departmental Report of Manufacturing Expenses (Overhead)

	COST REPORT MONTH ACTUAL	VARIABLE BUDGET ADJUSTED TO ACTUAL VOLUME	BUDGET CONTROL REPORT	
			VARIATIONS INDICATING STATUS OF CONTROL: FAVORABLE —UNFAVORABLE*	
RESPONSIBILITY			AMOUNT	% OF BUDGET
Producing Dept. No. 1:				
(Actual Volume 35,000 DLH)				
Supervisory salaries†	$10,000	$10,000		
Indirect labor	10,550	10,875	$325	3
Maintenance parts	1,500	825	675*ᵃ	82*
Supplies used	2,200	2,375	175	7
Depreciation†	525	525		
Insurance†	100	100		
Taxes†	150	150		
Total	$25,025	$24,850	$175*	1*
Producing Dept. No. 2:				
(Actual Volume 13,800 DLH)				
Supervisory salaries†	$ 1,870	$ 1,870		
Indirect labor	240	262	$ 22	8
Maintenance parts	60	48	12*	25*
Supplies used	80	109	29	27
Depreciation†	55	55		
Insurance†	10	10		
Taxes†	20	20		
Total	$ 2,335	$ 2,374	$ 39	2
Producing Dept. No. 3:				
(Actual Volume 36,200 DLH)				
Supervisory salaries†	$ 2,920	$ 2,920		
Indirect labor	3,600	3,370	$230*	7*
Maintenance parts	370	331	39*	12*
Supplies used	1,170	1,105	65*	6*
Depreciation†	326	326		
Insurance†	50	50		
Taxes†	60	60		
Total	$ 8,496	$ 8,162	$334*	4*

†These items are noncontrollable within the department.
Comments:
a Due to breakdown of machine resulting from faulty adjustment.

In other respects the two performance reports are essentially self-explanatory.

DISCUSSION QUESTIONS

1. What do you consider to have been the significant steps taken by Superior Manufacturing Company preliminary to initiating the profit planning and control program?

2. Relate the "president's profit planning letter" to the statement of broad objectives, the evaluation of relevant variables, and strategy formulation.

3. Superior Manufacturing Company uses project planning and periodic planning. How do these two facets of planning interrelate in the examples given in the chapter?

4. Throughout the chapter various budgets and subbudgets for Superior Manufacturing Company are illustrated; what are the primary segments explicitly included in each one?

5. The production plan (budget) provides the foundation for certain other subbudgets. Identify each of them.

6. How does Superior Manufacturing Company use variable expense budgets?

CASE 4-1

Summary Manufacturing Company

Summary Manufacturing Company produces seat covers for automobiles. There are two models: Custom and Standard. The covers are sold in two states, Texas and Arizona. Three materials are used, designated as A, B, and C. There are two producing departments—Cutting and Finishing. The following profit plan estimates have been made for the coming year.

1. Sales plan—Custom 10,000 in Texas, 4,000 in Arizona; Standard 30,000 in Texas, 10,000 in Arizona. Sales prices to retailers—Custom $15; Standard $12.

2. Inventories (*fifo*):

	BEGINNING		ENDING	
	UNITS	UNIT COST	UNITS	UNIT COST
Raw material:				
A	500	$ 1.25	1,000	$ 1.25
B	2,000	.50	2,000	.50
C	3,000	.40	2,000	.40
Work in process	—		—	
Finished goods:				
Custom	200	$11.00	200	12.00
Standard	400	7.00	300	8.00

3. Raw material requirements—Each unit of Custom produced requires one unit of material A and two units of B. Standard requires two units of B and two units of C.

4. Estimated cost of material—Material A, $1.25; B, $.50, C, $.40.

5. Estimated unit direct labor cost—Custom $3.00 in Cutting and $4.50 in Finishing. Standard $2.50 in each department.

6. Overhead budgets have been prepared that show the following unit overhead rates:

	CUSTOM	STANDARD
Cutting	$1.00	$.50
Finishing	1.25	.70

7. Expenses:

Distribution	$70,000	(including noncash items $10,000)
Administrative	50,000	(including noncash items $5,000)

Net of other expenses
  over other incomes   2,825
Federal income tax average rate 30%

Other Data:

8. Beginning balance in retained earnings $125,000.

9. Planned dividends to be paid during year $30,000.

10. Planned cash receipts:

Cash sales	$475,000
Accounts receivable collections	225,000
Other incomes	175
Proceeds of bank loan	10,000
Sale of treasury stock	15,000

11. Planned cash disbursements (in addition to those previously indicated):

Accounts payable (assume all raw materials are purchased on account)	$105,000
Capital additions	40,000
Accrued and deferred items (assume no unpaid wages)	15,000
Other expenses	3,000
Estimated income taxes to be paid during the year	20,000
Payment on long-term note	50,000

12. Beginning cash balance $60,000.

13. Noncash items in the overhead budget amounted to $10,380.

Required:

Prepare the following budgets using the decisional inputs provided above. Design the budgets to provide the essential data in easily understood form. Use the schedule numbers and titles listed below.

BUDGET SCHEDULE NUMBER	TITLE
1	Sales plan summary—by product, by district
2	Production plan summary—by product units
3	Direct materials plan summary (in units)—by material, by product
4	Purchases budget summary—by material
5	Cost of raw materials required for production—by material, by product
6	Schedule of initial and final inventories
7	Direct labor plan summary—by product, by department
8	Overhead plan summary (overhead applied)—by product, by department
9	Cost of goods manufactured and sold summary
10	Profit and loss summary
11	Planned statement of retained earnings
12	Cash plan summary

CASE 4-2

Easter Company

Easter Company is a medium-size manufacturer whose products are sold throughout the Midwest. The company is organized into five separate divisions (as profit centers) along product lines; there are five major product lines. In an interview with the case writer, the financial vice president outlined company procedures used for developing profit plans each year.

During the last quarter of each calendar year the company prepares an annual profit plan and a three-year profit plan. The manager of each profit center is responsible for developing these two plans for his division. The controller outlined the planning procedures as follows: "On September 1, each division manager receives a brief statement of planning guidelines from top management; basically these guidelines specify that the division managers must follow the format for budget schedules designed by my people and that there must be a 6 percent increase in sales each year (we are rather inflexible on this from year to year) and that there must be an improvement in the profit situation. Also, major strategies are reviewed. These profit plans must be completed by October 15 and submitted to me for review. Around November 1, we schedule a meeting with the top management for each division manager at which time he presents his plans, and they are carefully evaluated by the top management group. Subsequent to that meeting, each manager has ten days to revise his plans and return them to my office for another review. We then send them to the president of the company, who approves them and returns them to me for distribution. The plans are distributed back to the divisions shortly after Christmas.

"The vice president of engineering is responsible for preparing a research and development plan and a capital-additions budget. He does this by working closely with the division managers. Although each division is responsible for preparing its own sales plan, each must work closely with the company sales vice president, and also with the company manufacturing vice president. The manufacturing division is set up as a cost center. Products are transferred to the sales divisions at actual cost. Of course, my people work directly with the division managers to help translate their programs into dollars. I work directly with the president and the other members of top management in analyzing the plans, developing possible alternatives, and in working out problems revealed by the plans of the divisional managers. It is not unusual for me to return a tentative profit plan to a divisional manager prior to its submission to the top management group for critical analysis. I do this to help the divisional manager prepare the best possible plan prior to his exposure to the other members of top management."

Required:

Evaluate this company's approach in developing its profit plans each year.

CASE 4-3
Dial Company

Dial Company is a wholesale grocer distributing in a ten-county area. It has six warehouses, each located in a different city and varying in size with the population of the immediately surrounding area. The company uses a budget system which was designed about twenty years ago by the company accountant. Practically all of the "budgetary work" has been done by this individual and his assistants in the accounting department. Annual budgets are prepared and distributed to eleven store managers in the company. Monthly reports have been provided to each of them wherein the budget revenues and costs were compared with actual revenues and costs on a monthly and cumulative basis. A separate budget report has been prepared for each of the six warehouses and for general administration. Recently the company accountant retired and a replacement was hired. The replacement has been given the title of financial vice president; he received a degree in accounting and finance from an excellent institution and has had three years of experience with a national accounting firm. At the time of his employment it was agreed that "the financial function will be reorganized and modernized so that the management will have access to the latest approaches and techniques for improving the profitability of the company."

The new financial vice president has made a list of a number of ideas that he is considering for implementation in the near future. His list includes the following: (1) management participation in planning; (2) emphasize financial data that are useful to management; (3) emphasize controllability; (4) introduce responsibility accounting; (5) do not include cost allocations on performance reports; (6) implement project planning; (7) implement periodic planning—time dimensions; and (8) responsibility for planning decisional inputs.

Required:

Evaluate the situation facing the new financial vice president. Briefly explain the essence of each item on the list prepared by the new financial vice president. Indicate generally how each might be applied in this particular company.

CASE 4-4

Consolidated Corporation

Consolidated Corporation had been operating for a period of eight years. During this period profits fluctuated considerably and were never particularly good. Within the last two years, two wholly-owned subsidiary corporations were formed.

The members of the board of directors were particularly disturbed by the profit situation and the evidence of inadequate planning and control. Accordingly they engaged a consultant to make a study of the company and to make specific recommendations for correcting these problems. The consultant submitted a comprehensive report to the board including specific recommendations. Included in the recommendations were specific proposals relating to organization structure and policy formulation. In addition, a revision of the accounting system was recommended to make possible accounting and reporting by responsibility.

Excerpts from the consultant's recommendations relative to a planning and control program follow:

PROFIT PLANNING AND CONTROL

General

Management planning and control are essential to the success of business operations. The more complex and decentralized operations become, the greater the need for a program designed to aid operating management in performing these functions.

Profit planning and control involve the development of a *plan of operations* by those directly responsible for the management of the major units of the company. This requires the formal expression of the plans in financial terms; formal approval of the plans by the policy-making body; and finally, dynamic control to assure conformance with the approved plans, except to the extent that the original plans are revised by the approving authority. Control requires monthly performance reports covering each major unit, showing (1) plans (budget), (2) actual, and (3) differences or variations. It is recommended that a copy of the monthly performance report be given to each member of the board of directors.

Application to Consolidated and Subsidiaries:

The concept of profit planning and control should be applied to the operations of Consolidated Corporation and the two subsidiary corporations:

1. Consolidated Corporation
   a. The board of directors initially should establish broad objectives and goals and lay down broad operational policies relative to the major units of the company.
   b. The president of Consolidated should develop a statement of planning guidelines for the company.
   c. The president should distribute the planning guidelines to the managers of the subunits with a time schedule for responses.

d. Each manager (c. above) should develop a plan of operations relating to his specific function. Each plan should specify:

   (1) Time covered (one year/5 years)

   (2) Planned revenues

   (3) Planned expenses

   (4) Planned expenditures for capital assets

   (5) Cash requirements

   (6) Other major items.

   Items (2) through (6) should be scheduled by month; the long-range plan should be scheduled by year.

   The plans thus developed should be presented to the president, whose responsibility it is to assure they are in conformance with his guidelines and those of the board of directors. The president is responsible for the soundness of the final plans.

e. The president should consolidate these several plans into an overall coordinated plan for presentation to the board of directors. This should be accomplished prior to the beginning of the budget year.

f. The board of directors should evaluate the plan and give final approval after making any changes deemed advisable.

g. The president should be allowed to assume full responsibility within the general framework of the approved plans. He should be assigned responsibility to assure that operations (including all expenditures) conform to the plan to the fullest extent possible. Major revisions in the plan during the year should be brought before the board for prior approval.

h. Records should be maintained so that monthly performance reports for each responsibility area can be developed for management. These reports should be as follows:

CONTROLLABLE ITEMS	MONTH			YEAR TO DATE		
	PLAN	ACTUAL	VARIATION	PLAN	ACTUAL	VARIATION
Wages, etc.	$2,000	$2,100	($100)	$6,000	$5,800	$200

The board should evaluate performance and keep in touch with operations through the president and by means of the performance reports.

2. Subsidiaries

   a. The president of Consolidated should prescribe broad policies, major operational decisions, and planning guidelines for the subsidiaries.

   b. The subsidiaries should follow the planning and control approach outlined above. Authority (and hence budget control) should be as follows: functional supervisors to general managers to Consolidated president to Consolidated board of directors.

At the next meeting of the board of directors the consultant's report was discussed. The members appeared to be favorable to the report. Near the end of the discussion the president made the following comments: "I'm afraid this budget will put me in a straight jacket. Conditions around this area are just too dynamic for such precision—every day new problems arise that could not possibly have been anticipated in the budget. We just can't plan ahead like this—there would be so many necessary changes that it would be a waste of time. We've got to meet these problems as they arise. Further, if I took all the time needed to develop a budget, I wouldn't have time to do much else. I know Bowers and Brown pretty well, and I don't think either of them would take to it at all; they like action—not paper work. Their operations are just starting and we have to feel our way along there too. If you ask them you will find that paper work will not solve any control problems that they may have."

Required:

    a. Be prepared to discuss and evaluate the recommendations relating to profit planning and control.

    b. Consider the points raised by the president. What would you suggest relative to them?

    c. What reasonable alternatives should the board consider? Comment on each.

CASE 4-5
G and M Company

      The G and M Company manufactures six lines of products that are variously processed through five production departments in the factory. There are three service departments in addition to the productive departments. The company has been budgeting for three years and is in the process of updating their system, including reorganization of the internal reporting.

      It has been decided that monthly performance reports for each responsibility center will be distributed wherein the data are reported by two dimensions: by the nature of the expenditure, and by the responsibility unit where the decision or action occurred. Dollar budget allowances are to be compared with actual performance and the resultant variances are to be expressed in dollars and as a percentage of budget for each item of expenditure. The controller has been busy developing account codes and formats for the performance reports.

      An issue yet to be resolved is whether to apply the concept of a fixed budget or the concept of a variable budget in the performance reports. Sales are highly seasonal for this company, and it is not economical to stock finished goods inventory in sufficient quantity to permit a stable level of production from month to month. To illustrate the problem, Producing Department 1 is used. The output (amount of work) of this department is measured in direct machine hours (each of the six products passes through this particular department). The short-range profit plan indicates an expected productive departmental output for January of the budget year of 20,000 direct machine hours. At this level of supervisory salaries were budgeted at $8,000; indirect materials at $3,000; and indirect labor at $10,000. There were a number of other items of expense incurred in this department; however, these three are sufficient for illustrative purposes.

      At the end of January the accounting department reported that Producing Department 1 actually operated at 22,000 direct machine hours and incurred the following costs: supervisory salaries, $8,000; indirect materials, $3,500; and indirect labor $11,200.

In considering the variable budget concept, it was tentatively decided that supervisory salaries represent a fixed cost that should be budgeted at $8,000 per month; indirect materials was considered to be a variable cost amounting to $.15 per direct machine hour; and direct labor a semivariable cost with a fixed monthly amount of $4,000 plus a variable rate of $.30 per direct machine hour.

Required:

a. Explain the concept of a fixed budget versus a variable budget as applied in controlling costs.

b. Explain why the output of the department was not measured in units of goods produced during the period.

c. Prepare a simplified performance report for Department 1 using the fixed budget concept.

d. Prepare a performance report using the variable budget concept.

c. For this particular department, which concept appears to you to be preferable from the control point of view? Explain the basis for your choice.

CASE 4-6
Quaker Oats Company

The Quaker Oats Company has a long reputation for quality products distributed internationally. The company is also widely recognized for management competence. The statement of *Principles and Objectives,* after being debated, drafted, and approved by the Executive Committee, was distributed to shareholders, employees, and other interested parties. This statement was as follows (with no changes or omissions by the case writer):

Introduction

The Principles and Objectives of The Quaker Oats Company, as set forth here, are the result of long study, analysis, and discussion by senior management. They are consistent with a Company history rich in change and successful response to opportunity. At the same time, they delineate the Company's goals for the future.

They are to guide all Quaker divisions, departments, and subsidiaries in two vital areas: planning for the near- and long-term future, and measuring the quality of corporate progress.

These basic Principles and Objectives do not vary significantly from the informal guidelines we have been following. They do, however, commit us formally and provide important direction for an increasingly diversified business.

We think it is appropriate to do this
in conjunction with a new corporate symbol
that was designed to represent both our
heritage and our contemporary thrust.

It is our hope that these basic Principles
and Objectives will frequently be read and
reflected on by our own people, and will help
them relate their roles to the Company's
overall purpose. It is also our hope that these
statements will prove informative and valuable
to customers, suppliers, community neighbors,
and others who may wish to know
more about Quaker's character and goals.

Robert D. Stuart, Jr.
President and Chief Executive Officer

September, 1970

Principles.   These basic principles guide The Quaker Oats Company in achieving its corporate objectives:

We apply the highest ethical and moral standards, and strive for excellence and leadership in everything we do.

We believe in a dual responsibility to sharcholders:

—To earn a return on their investment that compares favorably with the return for other leading companies in our industries;

—To apply our corporate resources wherever practical to the solution of public problems in which the interests of shareholders, employees, customers, and the general public are fundamentally inseparable.

We concentrate our efforts on products and services that are useful, of good quality, and of genuine value to consumers.

We conduct our operations with respect for the intelligence and good taste of consumers.

We seek to provide an environment for personal development and advancement that attracts, stimulates, and rewards outstanding employees, whose integrity, ability, and ambition are essential to the Company's progress.

We believe that a high degree of competitive aggressiveness, in the context of the above principles, is the best means of achieving our corporate objectives.

Objectives

1. Consumer Products and Services
    To create and provide an increasingly diversified line of consumer products and services that:
    —satisfy genuine consumer needs and desires,
    —have characteristics of distinctiveness and high quality that permit marketing under brand or proprietary names,
    —appeal to large and fast-growing market segments, and have the potential to become market leaders.

2. Industrial Products

   To create and provide an increasingly diversified line of industrial products that are unique because of Quaker patents, technology, or specialized application and service.

3. International Growth

   To grow internationally by providing products and services of high quality and value where we can realize a return on investment and a rate of growth at least equal to our corporate average.

4. Research and Development

   To achieve a level of technical excellence that will result in a continuing flow of new concepts, products, and services that are essential to corporate growth.

5. Financial

   To improve per-share earnings an average of at least 10 percent per year over any five-year period; to strive for an after-tax return on shareholders' investment that is above average for the industries in which we participate; to make aggressive use of capital, while maintaining a strong financial condition.

6. Personnel

   To provide equal employment opportunities for all persons; to encourage and help employees realize their full potential; to develop, primarily from within the Company, managers of exceptional ability; to reward employees fairly and in accord with objective standards; to maintain personnel relations that reflect the Company's belief in the importance of people.

7. Shareholders

   To provide shareholders an above-average return measured by market value and dividends combined; to communicate effectively on all significant developments that may affect investors.

8. Trade Customers and Suppliers

   To maintain excellent relations with trade customers and suppliers by working cooperatively to achieve mutual goals, and by following business practices that are mutually fair and responsible.

9. Communications

   To adhere strictly to high standards of integrity, responsibility, and quality in all our advertising, packaging, and other communications.

10. Social Progress

    To be leaders in developing programs by which Quaker, our personnel, and the industries in which we are involved can contribute to social justice and to solutions of major public problems.

Our New Symbol. Of the many trademarks used by companies over the years, none is more familiar to the public than the Quaker Man. As the symbol of Quaker Oats, he has stood for quality, dependability, honesty, and good value to four generations of customers and shareholders. The friendly face appearing on packages of Quaker Oats today is as effective now as it has been over the years. In a world where it seems that everything is changing, the Quaker Man on our oatmeal packages is not changing. That personal symbol will remain as our most valued trademark on hot cereals and some other products.

We have felt the need, however, for a *corporate* symbol that could represent the heritage and meaning of the Quaker Man but be appropriate for all areas of our modern and diverse business, of which hot cereals account for only 15%.

We wanted the symbol to be warm, friendly, distinctive, and representative of the values on which the Company is built. But we also wanted it to be dynamic and contemporary, a mark which could embrace the full scope of our current—and future—businesses. Already these involve a wide range of food products, pet foods, chemicals, and toys.

We believe this symbol will achieve our objectives. We think it captures well the essence of our tradition, our contemporary development, and our optimism about the future.

By way of elaboration the management stated that "internal management documents expand on our objectives and strategy for achieving them but these, obviously, are confidential."

The statement was approved and distributed in 1970. In 1974 management stated that: "We anticipated that the statement would be relatively durable. However, in the light of the extraordinary changes that have taken place in the environment around us, it is now being reviewed as an integral part of the long-range planning process."

Required:

Develop an outline suitable for a constructive discussion of this statement: its purpose, method of development, and its relationship to the comprehensive profit planning and control program. Also include consideration of the planned revision and the nature of the "extraordinary changes in the environment."

CASE 4-7

Blye Manufacturing Company

Blye Manufacturing Company produces quality batteries. To simplify the case assume there are two products: auto batteries and boat batteries. The batteries are sold in two regions—Southwest and Southeast. Assume the company is organized into the following responsibility centers:

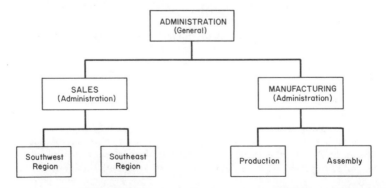

The company executives are developing the annual profit plan on a responsibility basis. The executives have assessed the relevant variables, agreed on the broad company objectives and basic strategies and completed the 5-year, long-range plan on a tentative basis. The following relevant data (such as decisional inputs) for the annual profit plan have been assembled:

(1) Sales prices: Auto $30; Boat $35

(2) Average raw material costs (per unit of raw material): Material A $1; Material B $2

(3) Average direct labor rates (per hour): Production $4; Assembly $3

(4) Product specification:

	UNITS OF RAW MATERIAL REQUIRED PER UNIT OF PRODUCT		DIRECT LABOR HOURS REQUIRED PER UNIT OF PRODUCT	
	PRODUCTION MAT.—A	ASSEMBLY MAT. B	PRODUCTION	ASSEMBLY
Auto	6	1	1½	1
Boat	7	1½	1½	1

(5) Planned sales (in units):

	SOUTHWEST	SOUTHEAST
Auto	20,000	19,500
Boat	4,200	5,000

(6) Inventory levels planned (in units):

	BEGINNING	ENDING
Auto	3,000	3,500
Boat	1,200	1,000
Raw Mat—A	2,100	1,100
Raw Mat—B	1,500	2,000

Note: Assume no change in work in process inventory. The company uses LIFO standard cost.

(7) Planned costs by responsibility center (excluding raw materials and direct labor):

		MANUFACTURING	
	ADMINISTRATION	PRODUCTION	ASSEMBLY
* Salaries (supervision)	$33,450	$ 62,415	$16,510
Indirect labor		7,350	4,900
Power		4,410	2,940
*#Insurance	300	900	600
*#Depreciation	600	15,000	3,000
*#Taxes	2,400	1,200	900
* Maintenance		30,000	3,000
Maintenance		3,675	2,450
Totals	$36,750	$124,950	$34,300

* Fixed costs; others are variable costs.
#Noncash items.

(8) Administration (general) and distribution costs are planned to be $265,900. This amount includes $30,000 noncash items.

(9) The beginning cash balance was $33,000; the company policy is to maintain a $30,000 minimum cash balance. Purchases of raw materials are on a strict cash basis because of favorable cash discounts. Assume a beginning accounts receivable balance of $60,000. At year-end accounts receivable is expected to be 5 percent of annual sales. Cash also will be expended for: capital expeditures $50,000; notes payable $75,000; and dividends $20,000. Money can be borrowed in multiples of $1,000 at 10 percent annual interest. Assume a minimum of 6-month loans and borrowings and repayments at the beginning of quarters only.

Required:

Prepare the following subbudgets for the annual profit plan using the decisional inputs given above. Design the budgets to provide the essential data needed for communication to the various managers. Use the schedule letters and titles below.

SCHEDULE	TITLE
(a)	Sales plan summary—by product, by responsibility.
(b)	Production plan summary—by product.
(c)	Direct materials planned usage (units)—by raw material, by product.
(d)	Purchases budget summary—by raw material.
(e)	Planned inventory levels (units & dollars)—by raw material, by finished goods.
(f)	Cost of raw material required for production (summary)—by responsibility, by product, by raw material.
(g)	Cost of direct labor required for production (summary)—by responsibility, by product, by material.
(h)	Manufacturing overhead costs applied to products (summary)—by product, by department. The manufacturing overhead rates, based on direct labor hours, are: production $2.00; assembly $1.00.
(i)	Show how the two manufacturing overhead rates were computed assuming manufacturing administrative costs are allocated to the production and assembly departments on the basis of relative planned direct labor hours.
(j)	Planned cost of goods manufactured (summary)—by product.
(k)	Planned income statement (summary)—by product and total. To compute cost of goods sold use unit costs computed in (j) above. Assume a flat 50 percent income tax rate.
(l)	Planned cash inflows and outflows. Comment on the indicated cash position at year end.

Sales Planning and
Control

chapter five

This chapter places sales planning and control in perspective, reviews the basic features of a sales plan, and suggests practical approaches for developing and utilizing a sales plan. A plan of operations must necessarily be built around the activity or volume of business that can reasonably be expected during the specific period covered by the profit plans. Unless there is a realistic sales plan, practically all other elements of a profit plan will be out of kilter with reality. The sales plan is the foundation for periodic planning in the firm, because practically all other enterprise planning is built on it. The primary source of cash is sales; the capital-additions needed, the amount of expenses to be planned, the manpower requirements, the production level, and other important operational aspects depend on the volume of sales.

Obviously, there are many technical and practical difficulties in planning sales quantities and revenue. Despite these difficulties, it is not unusual today for enterprises operating in extremely complex environments to attain a relatively high degree of accuracy in sales planning. In those enterprises two crucial factors are operating: (1) top management commits serious attention and resources planning; (2) top management views the resultant sales plans as objectives to be attained and develops strategies and commits necessary resources to attain them. With respect to the first factor, if it were impossible to appraise the hazards of a business with respect to sales potentials, then there would be little incentive for investment in the business initially or for continuation of the enterprise, except for highly speculative ventures that many managers and investors prefer to avoid.

LONG-RANGE AND SHORT-RANGE SALES PLANNING COMPARED

In harmony with the comprehensive profit plan, both strategic long-term and tactical short-term sales plans must be developed. Thus, one commonly observes a five-year strategic sales plan and a one-year tactical sales plan. Many management decisions commit a large amount of resources involving a life-span of many years. Basic strategies and major moves often involve irreversible commitments of resources and long life-spans.

Sometimes it may be desirable to view the development of the long-range and short-range sales plans as separate activities. However, they must be integrated because the short-range profit plan brings into sharp focus the plans for the year immediately preceding the beginning of the long-range profit plan. Thus, the short-range sales plan dovetails with the *strategic long-range sales plan* in all major respects. As a practical approach, many firms schedule completion of the long-range sales plan as one of the first steps in the overall planning cycle. For example, a company operating on a calendar year normally will complete the long-range sales plan, at least in tentative form, by the end of July since this gives sufficient lead time for interim considerations essential to development of the comprehensive short-range profit plan during the latter part of the calendar year. Long-term sales plans normally are developed as annual amounts, whereas the short-term sales plans normally are developed for the year by quarter or by monthly breakdown. The long-range sales plan utilizes broad groupings of products (product lines). Long-term sales plans usually rest very heavily upon sophisticated analyses of future market potentials, which may be built up from a basic foundation such as population changes, industry projections, and finally company projections. The company projections are tempered by management's major long-range strategy decisions (see Chapters 3 and 4). Managerial strategies for the long range would affect such areas as long-range pricing policy, development of new products and innovations of present products, new directions in marketing efforts, expansion of productive capacity, entering new industries, expansion or changes in distribution channels, and cost patterns. The influence of managerial strategy decisions is explicitly brought to bear on the long-range sales plan primarily on a judgmental basis. Thus, we often see in long-range sales planning, at least from the forecasting point of view, the general application of a three-stage model: (1) a forecasting model for the general economy; (2) a forecasting model for determining total industry sales; and (3) finally a unique model for assessing the company's market potential. Some of the characteristics of a long-range sales plan are shown in Illustration 14.

ILLUSTRATION 14.   Summary of Tactical and Strategic Sales Plan

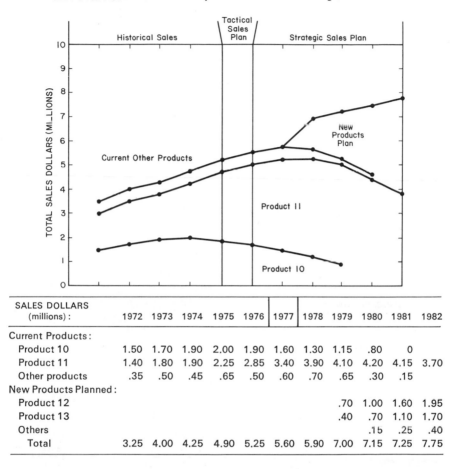

SALES DOLLARS (millions):	1972	1973	1974	1975	1976	1977	1978	1979	1980	1981	1982
Current Products:											
Product 10	1.50	1.70	1.90	2.00	1.90	1.60	1.30	1.15	.80	0	
Product 11	1.40	1.80	1.90	2.25	2.85	3.40	3.90	4.10	4.20	4.15	3.70
Other products	.35	.50	.45	.65	.50	.60	.70	.65	.30	.15	
New Products Planned:											
Product 12								.70	1.00	1.60	1.95
Product 13								.40	.70	1.10	1.70
Others									.15	.25	.40
Total	3.25	4.00	4.25	4.90	5.25	5.60	5.90	7.00	7.15	7.25	7.75

Now consider the *tactical short-term sales plan.* A common approach used with respect to time horizons is for a company to plan sales for twelve months into the future, detailing the plan initially by quarters and by months for the first quarter. At the end of each month or quarter, the sales plan is restudied and revised by adding a period in the future and by dropping the period just ended. Thus, the tactical sales plans are generally subject to review and revision on a quarterly basis. The short-term sales plan normally comprises a detailed plan for each major product and for groupings of minor products. Short-term plans usually are developed in terms of physical units and in sales dollars. Short-term sales plans must be structured by *marketing responsibility* for control purposes. Price changes anticipated during the year should be incorporated in the sales plan. Short-term sales plans may involve the application of sophisticated statistical and mathematical analyses; however, managerial judgment plays a large part in their determination.

The amount of detail in a tactical sales plan, particularly the marketing plan, is a function of the environment and the characteristics of the company. Of course, the short-range sales plan should include considerable detail, whereas the long-range plan should be only in broad terms. In establishing policy with regard to detail in the short-range sales plan, there is first and foremost the basic question of utilization of the results. The primary consideration is to provide detail by *responsibility* for control purposes. Secondarily, the short-range sales plan must provide detail needed for completing the profit plan components by other functional managers—that is, the production managers will need sufficient detail for planning production levels and plant capacity needs; the financial executive will need sufficient detail for assessing and planning cash flows, unit product costs, and inventory needs, and so on. The amount of detail also depends upon the type of industry, the size of the firm, the availability of resources, and the utilization of the results by management. In view of the wide range of criteria, we can only suggest the more common basic segmentations of the sales plan as follows: responsibility for marketing effort; product detail; customer classification; geographical breakdown; and market breakdowns (types of markets) by distribution channels.

COMPREHENSIVE SALES PLANNING

A comprehensive sales plan, sometimes referred to as a market penetration plan, comprises all sales activities. A common misconception is that sales planning involves developing only a projection of the amount of expected sales volume and dollars. Since there are many variables that influence sales, a comprehensive approach to sales planning is necessary. For example, such factors as planned size of the sales force, resources committed to promotion and advertising, and the planned amounts of other selling expenses have a direct impact on the volume of sales that can be expected realistically. Therefore, a comprehensive sales plan encompasses both *revenue* (that is, sales volume) and selling cost components. For profit planning and control purposes it is useful to view sales planning as encompassing a series of *components* or parts that can be generalized as follows:

Establish the foundation by developing:
   1.   Enterprise objectives.

2. Enterprise strategies.
3. Sales forecasts.

Build the sales plan by developing goals specified in:

4. A promotion and advertising plan.
5. A selling expense plan.
6. A marketing plan.

Before discussing each of these components, it is appropriate to comment upon the primary interrelationships between them. The primary objective of a sales plan is to express the best judgment of the management on potential future sales revenues based upon: (1) present knowledge of the company; (2) the environment; (3) the impact on the firm of enterprise objectives; and (4) managerial strategies, both in the long run and the short run. This purpose is then served by a definite managerial commitment to pursue aggressive actions throughout the time horizon involved to attain the specific objectives in the sales plan. Enterprise objectives provide the broad goals around which the sales plan is developed; managerial strategies provide a basis for judgments of the impact of aggressive company actions: the *sales forecast* provides technical projections of customer demand under certain assumptions; and the promotion, advertising, and selling expense plans express planned commitments of resources necessary to attain the volume of business included in the final *marketing plan*. The marketing plan then represents sales volume and sales revenue *expectations* to be generated by the planned commitment of company resources in the sales effort. To summarize, the overall *sales plan* basically represents the revenue generating portion of the comprehensive profit plan. The sales plan includes three subbudgets: the marketing plan, the promotion and advertising plan, and the selling expense plan.

The above listing of components is not intended to suggest that they should be developed in any particular chronological sequence. Nevertheless, depending upon circumstances, some aspects of sales planning must be sequential, and others must be concurrent. For example, the development of broad enterprise objectives and strategies normally should occur early in the planning process, as outlined in the preceding chapters. Development of the *sales forecasts* should occur early in the planning cycle. Concurrent development of promotion and advertising plans, selling expense plans, and marketing plans logically follow, for each of these subplans influences the others. It is only when these three subplans are developed and are in harmony with one another that we can say that the *sales plan* is complete and ready for managerial approval. Upon approval of the sales plan by the top management, it is distributed to the other functional and divisional units of the enterprise so that their particular components of the profit plan can be built upon this foundation.

Enterprise Objectives and Strategies.   The top management of an enterprise exercises an important element of leadership in developing the broad objectives and strategies for the future. The broad objectives and strategies must include careful attention to the marketing function. In the two preceding chapters, these two steps in the planning process were discussed in detail, and it was suggested that top management should distribute a *planning premises* letter, with certain attachments (see Illustration 11) to the appropriate responsibility center managers as the initial step in the formal planning process.

The Sales Forecast.   A sales forecast, as distinguished from a sales plan, is a technical projection of the potential customer demand for a specified time horizon and with specified underlying assumptions. A sales *forecast is converted to a sales plan when management has brought to bear on it judgment, planned strategies, commitments of resources, and the managerial commitment to aggressive actions to attain the sales goals.* Thus, a sales forecast and a sales plan may or may not project the same volume of business. When this distinction is made, the sales forecast represents one of the important analytical steps or activities to be taken in developing a sales plan. Typically, sales forecasts are prepared at the staff level by technically trained individuals employing numerous sophisticated analyses, such as trend fitting, correlation analysis, mathematical models, exponential smoothing, and operations research techniques. One of the most important recent developments in sales forecasting is wide application of the computer to provide complex and sophisticated analyses; the substantial amount of research in this area has served to reduce significantly the risks and pitfalls in forecasting. One central problem in sophisticated sales forecasting is the accumulation, classification, and availability of relevant historical data for analytical purposes. For a thorough discussion of sales forecasting techniques the reader is referred to the several excellent books specifically devoted to this subject.[1]

The sales forecast represents the primary contribution of the technical staff to the important managerial activity of developing a sales plan. The sales forecast is fed into the planning process so that the imprint of management judgment and strategy is brought to bear. The forecast is *revised* in the planning process to take into account management objectives, strategies, and resource commitments (advertising, promotion, and other sales

[1] The following books are representative: Vernon G. Lippitt, *Statistical Sales Forecasting* (New York: Financial Executives Research Foundation, 1969); Robert S. Reichard, *Practical Techniques of Sales Forecasting* (New York: McGraw-Hill Book Co. Inc., 1969); and W. F. Butler, R. A. Kavesh, and R. B. Platt, eds., *Methods and Techniques of Business Forecasting* (Englewood Cliffs, N.J.: Prentice-Hall, Inc., 1974).

efforts) so that a realistic sales plan results. We should note that a sales forecast necessarily is based upon certain assumptions regarding enterprise objectives, the level of advertising and promotion expenses, and other sales efforts; however, these assumptions normally project existing levels for the immediate future. It is important to make a distinction between the sales forecast and the sales plan primarily because the technical staff should not be expected—or permitted—to make the fundamental management decisions and judgments implicit in every sales plan. More directly, the influence of management actions on sales potentials is very difficult to quantify for sales forecasting; therefore, the elements of experienced management judgment must mold the sales plan. Another reason for identifying sales forecasting as a step in sales planning is that the sales forecasts are conditional. They normally must be prepared prior to management decisions or plans in such areas as plant expansion, price changes, promotional programs, production scheduling, expansion or contraction of marketing activities, and other resource commitments. Thus, the initial forecasts—and there should be more than one to indicate probable sales under various alternative assumptions—can be an important source of information in the development of strategy and resources commitments. This view is consistent with the following statement:

> This two-fold contribution of sales forecasting, in decision-making and in follow-up control, suggests the need for a two-stage preparation of forecasts. The first stage can be based on the assumption that the company products and marketing efforts will continue as in the recent past, or else indicate what changes in sales would arise from assuming changes in company actions. A review of this forecast by the management would lead to the setting of company objectives and strategies for the planning period. The sales forecast could then be recycled and adjusted to conform with the chosen actions.[2]

Developing the Sales Plan.   The sales plan includes the promotion and advertising plan, the selling expense plan, and the marketing plan. The marketing plan, frequently referred to as the sales budget, quantifies sales in units and dollars for each major subdivision of sales. At this point in our discussion we are considering primarily the tactical short-term sales plan, which usually covers one year and focuses on the *current portion* of the long-range sales plan. The central purpose of the short-range sales plan is not to attempt to guess what sales will be, but, rather, to plan with clearly defined objectives toward which operational effort will be directed. Developing a realistic short-term sales plan involves serious and sophisticated effort on the part of top management—and the sales executives in particular. Having approved the sales plan, the top management should expect the sales depart-

[2] Lippitt, *Forecasting,* p. 10.

ment to take the necessary steps to reach the sales and cost goals stated in the sales plan. Development of the short-term sales plan involves detail with respect to organizational responsibility, product, and time. A completed marketing plan should indicate in addition to annual unit volume and dollar revenue, sales by organizational subdivision—sales territories, sales by month and/or quarter, and sales by product. A complete market plan for a medium to large size concern mechanically involves numerous detailed subsidiary schedules in addition to a summary. The illustrative case continued at the end of this chapter indicates the possibilities to some extent.

Starting with the foundation of enterprise objectives, enterprise strategies, and appropriate sales forecasts, the manager responsible for the sales function is in a position to develop the sales plan with the assistance of his managers. The manager of the sales function is responsible for developing a promotion and advertising program and costing it out in detail since it will form the basis for these specific budget allowances. In a similar manner he must develop a distribution expense plan, which involves planning the order-getting and order-filling costs required to support the marketing effort. Thus, in harmony with the planning process described in the preceding chapters, the manager in charge of the marketing function would present to the executive committee his sales plan as a complete unit including the three subplans enumerated above. Subject to the decisions of the executive committee, it is anticipated that the complete sales plan would be given tentative approval. Relevant portions then would be distributed to managers of other functions as a cornerstone for their planning efforts. An important complement to the sales plan proposed to the executive committee could be a "flash report" prepared by the financial executive (or budget director), which would reflect broadly the approximate profit potential of the proposed sales plan. The flash report would involve a broad projection, by the financial executive of the other costs that would be generated in meeting the sales volume projected. Normally, it should take the form of a broad cost-volume-profit analysis (Chapter 14). This tentative profit projection by the financial executive would represent a "first cut" and would be replaced later by the detailed profit plans from the other functional managers.

CONSIDERATION OF ALTERNATIVES

Developing a sales plan involves consideration of numerous policies and related alternatives and a final choice by executive management from among many possible courses of action. Decisions must be made about new products, discontinuance of present products, pricing, expansion or contraction of sales areas, size of sales force, distribution cost limitations, and advertising and other promotional policies. A sound sales plan embodies a whole complex of management decisions. In addition to the advertising expense, selling expense, and marketing plans, a completed sales plan encompasses work programs and organization for sales effort and a host of other coordinative understandings necessary for efficient and aggressive efforts to maximize sales potentials at minimum cost. Obviously, many possible combinations of emphasis are possible. This suggests the importance in sales planning of applying sophisticated approaches to the fullest extent possible and utilization of the computer for data processing and analyses. It also implies numerous subjective judgments on the part of management. The sophisticated analyses, techniques, and approaches serve to provide more relevant information upon which these managerial judgments are made under conditions of uncertainty. To the extent that the sophisticated approaches shed additional light on the probable outcomes of different alternatives, they make a contribution to decision-making by reducing the element of uncertainty.

PRICING POLICY IN SALES PLANNING

Pricing strategy is a vital part of sales planning. Obviously, planned sales price and expected sales volume are mutually interdependent. Since sales volume and price are so closely tied together, a complicated problem is posed for the management of practically every firm. Thus, two related basic relationships involving the sales plan must be considered: (1) estimation of the demand curve, that is, the extent to which sales volume varies at different offering prices; and (2) the unit cost curve, which varies with the level of productive output. Thus, price-cost-volume relationships have a significant impact on the managerial strategy that should be adopted.

There is an obvious, but frequently overlooked, contrasting relationship that should be analyzed in depth in the development of pricing strategy. An increase in sales price with no resultant change in volume is reflected dollar for dollar in pretax profits; alternatively, an increase in sales volume with no increase in sales price is reflected in pretax profit only by the difference between sales dollars and variable cost per unit of product. To illustrate simply, assume that a firm is considering their price-volume strategy for one of its products. The initial sales plan indicated a potential volume of 5,000 units at $2 per unit with related costs amounting to $3,000 fixed and $4,000 variable. Management tentatively concluded that the sales plan was inadequate to meet enterprise objectives, and consequently, they are considering either (1) increasing price 10 percent, or (2) increasing volume 10 percent with no change in the price. For illustrative purposes, assume that either strategy can be pursued realistically. One simple and direct analysis of the three alternatives could be as follows:

	ALTERNATIVE 1 (INITIAL PROPOSAL)	ALTERNATIVE 2 (10% PRICE INCREASE)	ALTERNATIVE 3 (10% VOLUME INCREASE)
Units	5,000	5,000	5,500
Unit sales price	$ 2.00	$ 2.20	$ 2.00
Sales revenue	$10,000	$11,000	$11,000
Costs:			
Fixed	$ 3,000	$ 3,000	$ 3,000
Variable	4,000	4,000	4,400
Total costs	7,000	7,000	7,400
Pretax profit	$ 3,000	$ 4,000	$ 3,600

Although Alternatives 2 and 3 produced the same amount of sales revenue, Alternative 2, the price-increase strategy, produced $400 more pretax profit than Alternative 3, the volume-increase strategy. It is not difficult to perceive why a manager, when facing a profit squeeze, first considers a price increase. On the other hand, although its effect may be dramatic, the volume assumption may not hold. As ignificant drop in volume resulting from a price increase often more than offsets the price-increase effect. An alternative that always should be considered is to pursue a strategy of cost control and not disturb the price-volume relationship; this strategy keeps it "internal" to the enterprise. Experienced managers know that a price strategy that is significantly below the competitive industry price may create havoc for the firm and to some extent for the industry. The best safeguard in pricing strategy is for management to become deeply involved and committed to the development of a realistic sales plan of the type described in these discussions. Prices must be analyzed not only in relation to costs but in relation to direct competition, the industry, and geographical areas. Generally, prices must be in line with the market with respect to product quality. In addition to sophisticated price analyses, the opinions of the sales force should be taken into consideration in many instances. Sales supervisors and even salesmen may be in a good position to appraise the effect on physical volume of a contemplated price change.

A topic favored by some is the utilization of a pricing strategy based upon the variable costs of the product rather than upon the total cost characteristics of the enterprise. Academic economists are prone to suggest this type of pricing strategy; however, the practical businessman has long since found that a pricing strategy developed along these lines soon creates a sick industry and spells long-range doom for his particular enterprise. It can be demonstrated under certain circumstances that revenue received for a product above the variable cost of producing and distributing that product will increase the total profits of the enterprise. However, the argument generally overlooks the long-range impacts of such a strategy on the market and the industry. To illustrate the point very simply, let us assume that a company is selling a single product at $50 per unit. Let us assume further that the company is selling 1,000 units per period; at 1,000 units the fixed costs amount to $25 per unit, and the variable costs amount to $20 per unit. Thus, the company would earn $5,000 for the period. Now let us assume that a pricing strategy has been proposed to accommodate a *new customer* who will pay $30 per unit for 500 units. We will assume also that the plant capacity is sufficient to produce the 1,500 units of product required. The proposal states that the total net profit, assuming the new customer is granted the contract, will be $10,000. The proposal may be summarized as follows:

	PRESENT MARKET	NEW CUSTOMER	TOTAL MARKET
Sales price per unit	$ 50	$ 30	
Sales volume	1,000	500	1,500
Total sales revenue	$50,000	$15,000	$65,000
Costs:			
Fixed	$25,000		$25,000
Variable	20,000	10,000	30,000
Total costs	45,000	10,000	55,000
Net pretax profit	$ 5,000	$ 5,000	$10,000

Obviously, the proposal and the related analysis are based on the premise that (1) the present market will carry all the fixed costs, and (2) the new contract will have no impact on volume and price in the present market. Clearly, if the assumptions were valid, both in the short run and long run, the pricing strategy suggested would be appropriate; otherwise, it would be a very undesirable strategy.

PRODUCT LINE CONSIDERATIONS

Determination of the number and variety of products that the company will offer is crucial in the development of a sales plan. Both the long- and short-range sales plans must include tentative decisions relative to new product lines to be introduced, old product lines to be dropped, innovations, and product mix. Product mix refers to the volume relationship as between two or more products. For example, assume 1,000 units of product R and 2,000 units of product S were sold, and that the sales plan for the coming year calls for 1,200 units of product R and 1,800 of S. The overall volume in both instances is 3,000 units, but we would say that a change in sales mix is planned.

Assuming the long-range sales plan includes changes in product lines, with broad specification as to the timing of such changes, those changes anticipated for the coming year (the period for which the short-range sales plan is being developed) must be brought into sharp focus through management decisions and be included in the short-range plan. Thus, to develop the annual sales plan, top management must lay down specific policies concerning product line development and marketing activities. Policies must be firmed up relative to such matters as: What products will be pushed? When will the new product be available for shipment? What products will be dropped and when? What quality and style changes will be made? What about "loss leaders"? In these policy decisions concerning both the long-range and short-term sales plans, the effect on plans in other areas of the company, such as plant capacity, financing, territorial expansion, and research, must be taken into account; the crucial problem is coordination.

It is appropriate to emphasize that a primary objective in sales planning should be to maximize profits in the long run rather than the short run. For example, it is obvious that certain short-run decisions may increase immediate profits, but adversely affect profits in the long run. We see then that short-run decisions may, if care is not exercised, be in conflict with long-range objectives.

As an indication of the importance of product line decisions, several recent surveys seeking to determine why businesses failed have revealed that one primary cause is failure of management to keep up with competitors in product development, improvement, and design.

MANAGING SALES PLANNING

Managing the sales planning function primarily involves: (1) assignment of definite responsibilities for each major aspect of sales planning, (2) establishment of an overall timetable to provide for an orderly flow of work, and (3) establishment of orderly procedures for evaluating and approving the sales plan on a step basis as it is developed.

We already have implied the major responsibilities in developing a sales plan. To be more specific, careful distinction must be made between line responsibilities and staff responsibilities. Decisional inputs for the sales plan should be the responsibility of line management. Thus, executive management would be responsible for providing broad objectives and basic strategies as well as related policy guidelines. The marketing executive should develop and present a comprehensive sales plan encompassing the three subplans enumerated in the preceding section. Thus, decisional inputs with respect to promotion and advertising programs, cost estimates for sales order-getting and order-filling costs, and the sales volumes and revenues included in the marketing plan are the direct responsibility of the marketing executive.

Staff responsibility related to the marketing plan involves system design, analytical assistance, and staff advice. Specifically, the executive in charge of the financial function (or budget director) working with the marketing manager should develop the *mechanical design* (format) and the related procedures essential to developing a realistic sales plan. The design and the procedures must be in harmony with the broader design and procedures utilized in a comprehensive profit planning and control program. The development of sales forecasts, market analyses, and economic projections should be viewed as a staff responsibility. The staff performing these functions generally should report to executive management. In addition to the design and procedural responsibilities, the manager of the financial function should be responsible for providing historical accounting data and other data relevant to the analyses and decisions to be made in developing the sales plan. The executive committee and the president should perform the appraisal and approval functions.

CONSIDERATIONS IN SELECTING APPROACHES FOR PLANNING SALES

Numerous approaches have been devised for forecasting sales and developing a sales plan. These approaches range from highly refined statistical approaches to rather crude rules of thumb. Quite obviously there is no one best method for all enterprises. The approaches used must be consistent with the characteristics of the total environment and constantly revised and improved consistent with the growth and needs of the enterprise. The selection and adaptation of particular approaches in developing a sales plan must take into account:

1. **Characteristics of the Company**—Some enterprises operate at the local level while others operate on a regional, national, or international scope. The size of the firm, type and variety of products, and methods of manufacturing are influencing factors. In addition, the channels and methods of distribution should be taken into account. Obviously, other characteristics peculiar to the individual enterprise should influence the selection of methods of planning sales, but these would be too diverse to catalog here.

2. **Costs**—The cost of developing a sales plan will vary with individual entities and with different approaches. In selecting approaches the costs involved in relation to the accuracy desired and the extent of utilization of the sales plan must be considered.

3. Available Personnel—The availability of personnel is frequently a determining factor. Technically trained personnel are required for the sophisticated approaches, and a good measure of executive time is required regardless of the approach. A frequently critical area is employing and training sufficient technical staff to perform certain analytical functions.

4. Status of Managerial Sophistication—At the initiation of a comprehensive profit planning and control program, it is frequently desirable to utilize simplified approaches in planning sales and to move to a more sophisticated level as the executives and staff become more experienced. Experience has demonstrated that unless the executives involved in developing and utilizing the sales plan understand the approaches used and broadly comprehend the sophisticated analyses, they will not have confidence in the results and the plans may suffer from low quality and nonutilization.

5. Time Dimensions—Approaches for developing a short-range sales plan are somewhat different from those generally appropriate for a long-range projection. Although many approaches are common, they may be applied differently, and the role of judgment assumes different proportions as between the long term and the short term.

STEPS IN PLANNING SALES

The steps that should be taken to develop a sales plan in a particular company must be contingent upon the characteristics of that particular company and the environment in which it operates. We can generalize by presenting the following major steps in sales planning:

Establish the foundation (discussed in Chapters 3 and 4):
1. Evaluation of relevant variables affecting the enterprise.
2. Establishment of broad objectives and specific enterprise goals.
3. Development of enterprise strategies.

Sales forecasting activities:
4. Economic analysis and appraisal of the future economic conditions on a national and even international basis. In general there are three approaches used by enterprises in assessing and forecasting general business conditions. One approach used by many firms is to establish a special staff group for economic analysis. The personnel in such a group are primarily economists and statisticians specially trained and experienced in this type of work. Another approach involves primary dependence on outside professional assistance for guidance and help in appraising the general

economic picture as it affects the entity. A third approach revolves around the "considered judgment" of the top executives, little or no formal statistical and economic analyses being made in the company.

5. Industry forecasts and analyses to determine the future potentials. These types of analyses may follow a general pattern outlined immediately above for the broader economic analyses.

6. Analysis of past sales performance of the enterprise by interim periods, products, sales territories, customers, size of orders, salesmen, and so forth. It is not uncommon to conduct a survey of the primary customers of the company in order to evaluate total demand for a specific period in the future.

7. Development of sales forecasts based upon preceding analyses, usually by staff specialists.

Managerial judgments applied:

8. Managerial evaluation of the limitations of the company, such as plant capacity, personnel limitations, capital resources, and procurement of supplies and materials.

9. Establishment of enterprise policies relating to strategies that will affect sales expectations. Examples of such policies are decisions concerning advertising and promotion programs, development of the sales force, product expansion, territory expansion, research, pricing policy, and expenditures for order-getting and order-filling activities.

10. Application of managerial judgments and decisions to the sales forecast (step 7 above) to develop a tentative sales plan that encompasses the promotion plan, the sales expense plan and the marketing plan.

11. Financial testing (usually by the budget director) of the probable profit effects of tentative sales plans and the resultant adjustments.

12. Development of a final sales plan approved by executive management.

13. Distribution of the approved sales plan to other appropriate functions in the business. This approved plan will be used as a foundation for additional planning.

In the next section an outline of the principal *methods* utilized in planning sales are discussed. The selection of the method or combination of methods to be used in a particular firm necessarily will significantly influence the above list of steps. The method or methods selected also will condition the relative importance of certain steps.

In the larger enterprises generally there is a market research group that is primarily responsible for the broad and specialized activities involved in sales forecasting. Both qualitative and quantitative market analyses may be performed. Although a market research or economic analysis group is utilized, management still must translate their outputs (forecasts) into sales programs and commitments. In smaller businesses, it is usually not possible to have a separate market research group; in such a case, sales and other executives must assume direct responsibility for this analytical function.

Fundamentally, sales estimates may originate (1) in the field (from the sales force), or (2) in the home office (sales executives and market research groups). Surveys show that in large enterprises the estimates generally originate in the home office, whereas in smaller concerns they tend to originate in the field. In either event, both the field force and the home office should have a definite responsibility in shaping the final sales plans.

One of the most important factors in forecasting sales is analysis of historical sales of the enterprise by time periods, products, geographical sales territories, sales areas, salesmen, and so forth. Therefore, it is essential that accounting records be maintained to provide both unit and dollar sales for these and other relevant classifications. If such information is readily available, a primary basis for meaningful sales forecasting and planning is provided, because past performance generally is the best indicator of what can be done in the immediate future. Analysis of historical sales, however, is only one step in developing a realistic sales plan. Computer applications in the area of sales analyses are particularly useful.

METHODS OF PROJECTING SALES

Methods commonly used in developing a sales projection may be classified in several ways. One classification involves two approaches. One is the *causal* approach; under this approach the underlying variables that have a causal influence on future sales are identified. The underlying causes (variables) are analyzed in depth and then projected into the future; on the basis of the projections and estimates of the causal variables, a sales projection is derived. Causal variables in turn are of two types: (1) causal variables over which the company has no control, such as population, gross national product, and general economic conditions; (2) causal variables over which the company has control, such as product lines, price, advertising and promotion expenditures, size of the sales force, and sales areas.

The second category may be designated as the *noncausal* approach; under this approach historical sales of the company are analyzed in depth and an expression of the past pattern is plotted in order to project future sales.

Under this approach no serious attempt is made to identify and evaluate the underlying causal variables. The method assumes that the underlying causal variables will continue to influence future sales in the same manner that they have in the past. The noncausal approach has many variants, frequently referred to as "naive" approaches, although certain statistical techniques frequently are utilized to extrapolate past sales trends into the future.

Another useful classification of methods also involves two approaches—*direct* and *indirect*. Under the *indirect* method of projecting future sales, industry sales are projected, followed by a projection of the company's share of the industry total. In contrast, the *direct* method involves straightforward approaches to develop company sales estimates without a prior projection for the industry as a whole. Both the direct and indirect methods may utilize the causal or noncausal approaches.

A third classification of methods of projecting sales may be generally outlined as follows:

1. Judgmental methods (nonstatistical)
   a. Sales force composite.
   b. Sales division supervisors composite.
   c. Executive opinion method.
2. Statistical methods
   a. Economic rhythm method (trend analysis).
   b. Cyclical sequence method (correlation analysis).
   c. Special historical analogy.
   d, Cross-cut method.
3. Specific purpose methods
   a. Industry analysis.
   b. Product-line analysis.
   c. End-use analysis.
4. Combination of methods.

This classification encompasses the others. In considering these various approaches observe that: (1) in many respects they overlap; (2) certain approaches are useful only for specific purposes; (3) some have application for short-term sales planning, others for long-term planning; and (4) very rarely would a single firm use only one approach. In the paragraphs to follow we will consider each of these methods briefly.

Sales Force Composite. This method places a heavy responsibility on the judgments and expertise of the sales force and provides for a series of screenings and approvals. A high degree of participation, from the bottom up, is emphasized. This approach is limited primarily to short-term sales planning. It may be outlined as follows:

1. The home sales office provides district sales offices with (1) a record of previous sales, (2) any new or revised managerial policies relative to sales, and (3) any other data that may be of value to the sales districts in making a sales estimate for the planning period. Usually the historical sales data are listed on a standard form that provides space to record the sales projections.

2. Salesmen are requested to fill in their estimates based on the historical data and their knowledge of the particular territory and customers. Salesmen usually are asked to make their estimates on the basis of current economic conditions in the area, because it is generally undesirable to have each salesman make his own appraisal of future economic conditions. When the salesmen provide dollar estimates as well as units, they are generally requested to assume current selling prices.

3. Salesmen's estimates are reviewed by the district sales manager. The form previously mentioned provides space for revision of the salesmen's estimates by the district sales manager. The completed estimates are transmitted by each district sales manager to the home office by a specified date.

4. The various district estimates are reviewed and revised by the general sales executives. Significant revisions should be discussed thoroughly with the district sales managers concerned. The home office sales executives also may convert the quantity estimates to dollar estimates by applying unit selling prices consistent with revised managerial pricing policies. The general sales executives, working in cooperation with the company economist or with others who have responsibility for appraising the general economic outlook, adjust the sales estimate for this factor. Because general economic conditions can affect the sales potential markedly, serious consideration must be given to this important factor in developing the sales plan.

5. The sales estimates then are presented to the executive committee and to the president for consideration and tentative approval. The deliberations at this level should be concerned with the soundness of the unit and dollar estimates and may well result in (1) tentative approval, (2) tentative approval with certain changes, or (3) instructions for a complete or partial reconsideration of the sales potential. The sales estimate is judged also by whether it is within the capacities of the firm.

6. After tentative approval, copies of the tentative sales plan are distributed to the heads of other functional subdivisions so that the work of developing departmental plans may be started. As the overall profit plan begins to take form, it may be necessary to reconsider the sales program in some respects. This balancing of considerations, and the resulting adjust-

ments in the profit plan as it develops, should provide a satisfactory plan of operations for the firm.

7. The approved sales plan is distributed through the sales organization and becomes the basis for sales quotas and day-to-day planning in sales activities.

8. In this approach, the promotion, advertising, and distribution expense components are developed concurrently through the same process, as outlined above for the marketing plan (estimates of sales volume).

Obviously, the above method can have numerous variants, and it makes no distinction between sales forecasting and sales planning. It is used more frequently by small companies and by those having a small number of products. The principal advantages are that estimates are made by the individuals closest to the customer and approved initially by those who have the responsibility for achieving the sales goals. On the other hand, salesmen may be too optimistic or, conversely, turn in low estimates as a matter of self-protection. Also, inadequate attention may be accorded the broad causal variables. They may not give sufficient attention to the problem and thus improperly evaluate the general market potential. These tendencies can be largely overcome through a program of budget education and motivation.

Sales Division Supervisors Composite. This method emphasizes the responsibilities of the sales supervisors rather than the individual salesmen. The method is commonly used for short-term sales planning. It operates in a manner almost identical with that outlined above for the sales force composite method except that the estimates *originate* with the sales supervisors rather than with the salesmen. The method is widely used by firms of all sizes.

A variation of this approach is based on an informal survey of the principal customers of the firm. Under this approach, sales are estimated on the basis of reports rendered by special company representatives who contact customers for the primary purpose of evaluating their future needs. From the information gathered by the special representatives and interpreted through their personal observation and judgments, an estimate for each geographical sales division (or product) is developed. These estimates are then adjusted to take into account basic information the company has concerning such factors as expected economic conditions, population trends, purchasing power, and other conditions likely to affect the market. In addition, consideration must be given to sales of the last year or two and to stock holdover on the part of customer outlets. This method is useful in situations where there are a limited number of customers.

Executive Opinion Method. Some companies find it inappropriate to send representatives into the field or to ask the sales force to make estimates. This is especially true where salesmen are not trained to perform this function or when the market situation is somewhat complex. Therefore, it is not uncommon to see sales planning initiated, and essentially completed, in the central offices of such companies. This method, too, has numerous procedural variants.

Perhaps the simplest method, often used by medium to small concerns, is known as the *jury of executive opinion method*. In its simplest form, it represents the combined judgments, or opinions, of the top executives within the firm. Although it may represent a wide range of specialized experience and knowledge, unless supplemented with facts concerning historical sales and the effect of causal variables, the resulting estimates must be viewed as guesses, more or less educated.

Smaller concerns are inclined to use simple procedures, starting with an analysis of historical sales data by product, territory, and salesmen, thereby developing a basis for an informed sales projection by the executives. The projection then is adjusted for such factors as expected economic conditions, management sales policies, and desired growth objectives. Next, the tentative estimates are transmitted to the respective district sales offices for consideration, review, and suggested revision. Using this procedure many companies have been able to develop realistic sales estimates.

The executive opinion method is used frequently because it is simple, direct, and economical. It may be buttressed by a technical sales forecast.

Statistical Methods. A well-known source suggests four statistical methods of forecasting sales.[3] These methods are similar to those suggested by other authors. They are:

1. Economic rhythm method.
2. Cyclical sequence method.
3. Specific historical analogy method.
4. Cross-cut analysis.

Earlier in this chapter a distinction was made between a sales *forecast* and a sales *plan*. We should observe that regardless of method, these approaches serve to develop a sales forecast for the enterprise. To convert the resultant forecast to a sales plan, management judgment, decisions, and commitments must be applied. A discussion of the technical aspects of the statistical methods is beyond the scope of this book. Consequently, we will

[3] Frederick E. Croxton, Dudley J. Cowden, and Sidney Klein, *Statistics,* 3rd ed. (Englewood Cliffs, N.J., Prentice-Hall, Inc., 1967); Carl A. Dauten, *Business Cycles and Forecasting,* 2nd ed. (Cincinnati, Ohio: Southwestern Publishing Company, 1961), Chapter 22; Vernon G. Lippitt, *Statistical Sales Forecasting* (New York: Financial Executives Research Foundation, 1969); Robert S. Reichard, *Practical Techniques of Sales Forecasting* (New York: McGraw-Hill Book Co., Inc., 1969).

merely indicate the general characteristics of each and suggest that those who are interested in pursuing the subject further consult the selected references listed in the footnotes.

Use of the statistical methods requires the services of technically trained individuals. Most companies relying on these sophisticated approaches have organized an economic or marketing research group variously staffed by statisticians, economists, and mathematicians. In some firms the economic research group develops a detailed sales forecast for the firm, which is then transmitted to the sales executives and the executive committee for evaluation and recommendations. In other cases the research group deals primarily with analysis of trends in the general economy and the industry. Data concerning trends (usually expressed as indexes) are then made available to the various executives in the firm who are involved in developing the long-range and short-range sales plans. To illustrate, in one well-known, highly decentralized company, each plant manager is required to develop (1) a five-year profit plan for his plant and (2) a one-year profit plan. The economic research staff (at the home office) develops projections of approximately fifteen different indexes relating to various economic indicators (causal variables) such as gross national product, housing starts, and regional bank deposits. These fifteen or more projections are furnished to each plant manager. He may choose to use one or more of them (or none) in developing his operation plans.[4]

The *economic rhythm* method projects historical trends into the future. Projecting sales this way generally requires the following steps:[5]

1. Obtain *historical sales data* as far back as it is thought to be representative of current trends.

2. Compute *adjusted sales values* by dividing actual sales data by an index (such as the wholesale price index).

3. Use the adjusted sales values (item "2") to compute an *adjusted sales value trend* (item "a" in Illustration 15), preferably by utilizing the method of least squares. If annual values are computed, the annual values are then used to develop monthly trend values.

---

[4] Companies who have need for similar data but who do not have an economic analysis group may obtain some assistance from the following sources: National Industrial Conference Board, Economic Institute, Barron's, F. W. Dodge Corporation, Business Week, Kiplinger Washington Agency, U.S. News and World Report, Fortune, "Business Roundup," and governmental aids (*Survey of Current Business, Federal Reserve Bulletin, Economic Almanac,* and *Business Statistics,* U.S. Dept. of Commerce, Bureau of the Census, Business Cycle Developments, U.S.G. Printing Office, Washington, 25 D.C.). Also for a complete list of sources of data for sales forecasting see: Vernon G. Lippitt, *Statistical Sales Forecasting* (New York: Financial Executives Research Foundation, 1969), Appendix H.

[5] M. Whitney Greene, "Combining the Statistical Approach with Other Forecasting Methods," *Methods of Sales Forecasting, Report No. 27* (New York: American Management Association).

4. Develop or obtain a *cyclical forecast* (example, the index of industrial production).

5. Develop an index of *seasonal variation* based upon the monthly historical data for the firm.

6. The sales forecast is then developed by using each of the values indicated above in (1) through (5). These values may be inserted in a work sheet similar to that shown in Illustration 15.

From the brief outline above and the information shown in Illustration 15 it is clear that the method is rigorous and subjective. Those using this method should be aware of its rigidity and underlying assumptions. Basically it assumes that future data will essentially follow the patterns of historical data. All this suggests that the results should be tempered by the sound judgment, knowledge of the company, and long experience of the top executives.

The *cyclical sequence* or correlation method is widely used. It is based upon the selection of a basic series of economic or business data that the product sales of the company tend to follow. A statistical analysis is used to measure the correlation between the basic series and the company sales. A central problem is to locate a basic series (such as an index of bank deposits or the index of industrial production) with which company sales correlate. The basic series selected, in addition to having a high degree of correlation, should be one that is (1) available and reliable (or computable) and (2) ideally, one that is known to lead company products in movement. The aim is to discover a series that either:

1. Changes consistently with the values to be forecast, but sufficiently in advance so that the correlated forecast data will be of value, or

2. Changes consistently with a series of data that can be more accurately predicted than the desired series.

Once the basic economic series is selected its past correlation with company sales is measured, and the company must either obtain a projection of the basic series from an outside source or make one of its own. The next step is to extrapolate the company sales potential related to the projection of the basic series.

As with the economic rhythm method, in order to convert it to a sales plan, careful evaluation of the rigid results and application of sound judgment on the part of the company executives are essential.

The *special historical analogy* method is based upon the idea of selecting some previous situation or period in the past that appears to have most of the earmarks of the present situation; the implied rationale is that what

ILLUSTRATION 15. Worksheet—Economic Rhythm Method

Buildup of Monthly Sales Forecast Based on Past Sales Trends, Cyclical
Movements, Seasonal Variations, and Price Changes

YEAR AND MONTH	(a) MONTHLY ADJUSTED SALES VALUE TREND	(B) CYCLICAL FORECAST (INDEX)	(c) SALES ADJUSTED FOR CYCLICAL VARIATION	(d) SEASONAL VARIATION (INDEX)	(e) SALES ADJUSTED FOR CYCLICAL AND SEASONAL VARIATION	(f) WHOLESALE PRICE INDEX	(g) FORECASTED SALES
	Source: Company records; data adjusted	Source: Based on index such as industrial production	Source: Col. (a) times Col. (b)	Source: Based on experience of firm	Source: Col. (c) times Col. (d)	Source: Selected	Source: Col. (e) times Col. (f)
Example: 1970: January	$100,000	95.0	$95,000	103.0	$97,850	120.0	$117,300

happened in the past is very likely to happen again.[6] This method has found limited use and cannot be strictly considered as a statistical method. It does have some of the characteristics of the executive opinion method.

The *cross-cut method* of forecasting sales is based on the concept that no two cycles are alike but like causes always produce like results.[7] The facts about a given situation are assembled, and relying on knowledge of economic processes, the forecaster makes some judgments as to future trends. This method has very limited use. It does not attempt to forecast the extent of sales trends. Rather it tries to determine the direction of the movement of economic activity and suggests that sales will move in the same direction and generally to the same extent. As a method of forecasting sales for a specific company, this method is not suitable; however, the concepts implied may be useful in buttressing the development of data using another method.

Industry Analysis Method.   In general terms, this method may be characterized in the following manner. A forecast of the total volume of business for the industry is developed. Once this forecast is completed, a projection is made of the *share of the market* that the individual company can reasonably expect. This approach is commonly used in the automotive industry. The first step in this method is to analyze industry statistics to determine historical growth rates. Next, the causal variables underlying industry sales are identified, evaluated, and projected. Then a projection of the industry volume is developed. Next, the company's growth patterns are analyzed and compared with the industry patterns. From these analyses it can be determined whether the company's share of the market has been increasing, decreasing, or remaining about the same. The final step, and the most critical one, is to develop a projection of the share of the market the company should adopt as its objective for the period. In this final step, all identifiable factors affecting the sales of the company must be analyzed. Hopeful projections of shares of the market of some firms, without adequate analysis and without sound plans to attain the projected shares, have been rather common. Making such managerial choices lightly has proved nearly disastrous for several well-known firms in the last few years. On the other hand, the method is particularly sound assuming (1) industry statistics are available, (2) appropriate statistical approaches are used in the analyses, (3) industry sales can be projected realistically, and (4) sound managerial judgments are brought to bear throughout the development of the sales projection.

The Product Line Method.   This approach requires a separate analysis and a sales projection for each product. The sum of the product line projections constitutes the sales projection for the company overall.

[6] Frederick E. Croxton and Dudley J. Cowden, *Practical Business Statistics,* 3rd ed. (Englewood Cliffs, N.J.: Prentice-Hall, Inc., 1960).
[7] Ibid.

This approach is used by firms that distribute lines of major items and use a different channel to distribute each item. In other words, the distribution system is organized by product rather than by geographical area or by customers. The method may vary from the more sophisticated procedures discussed above to rather simple approaches. Obviously, its effectiveness depends upon the adequacy of the analyses, evaluations, and judgments used in its application.

End-Use Method. This method involves, in general, a detailed breakdown into *use* categories for the products sold and a careful analysis of the end-use of each product. Essentially this approach requires a careful analysis (and direct communication with) the major consuming industries or segments of an industry. For example, assume certain automobile manufacturers purchase, rather than manufacture, the batteries that are placed in new vehicles. Assume further that the company in question manufactures batteries and sells practically all of its output to automobile manufacturers. In projecting sales, this particular company would have to depend on one or two customers for estimates of demand. If these customers prove to be of little help, it is not unreasonable to assume that the battery manufacturer would be forced to make a projection of the market for the customers' products. Parenthetically, the battery company in this assumed example is obviously in a very untenable position in the long run. In end-use analysis, the company should take into account possible new uses and plans to promote such new uses. To use the battery illustration again, assume an unprecedented demand for small boats increases significantly the demand for batteries. Several battery companies, by aggressive planning, gained a considerable advantage by developing a battery that meets the peculiar use-conditions in pleasure boats. Thus, you see, the end-use method may well require use of certain nonstatistical, as well as statistical, techniques.

Combination of Methods. The fact that no two companies have the same situation when developing a sales plan suggests that an approach used successfully in one situation will seldom be effective in another company. Then too, methods of developing a sales plan (or sales forecast as the case may be) are not, by any stretch of the imagination, standard. Differences in the characteristics of the firm, the environment in which it operates, the type of industry, size of the company, and even the state of the general economy, may significantly affect the approach that should be used. Sales budgeting can never be static; the individual company must continually strive to improve the various techniques, approaches, and concepts underlying its particular method of predicting sales.

Most companies that have developed an effective approach to planning sales have found that a combination of approaches is essential. The small firm, by the very nature of certain unavoidable constraints, generally must utilize the judgmental (less refined) approaches and rely on data and assistance from external sources. In contrast, the large firm can afford to employ sufficient specialists to apply the refined and sophisticated approaches. Alternatively, all enterprises must rely heavily on the business judgment of their management in developing a sales plan whether for the long run or short run. The refined statistical approaches provide precise but rigid results, and the underlying assumptions are essentially judgmental. It is not realistic to expect, or allow, the fundamental managerial judgments to be made by forecasting specialists, however competent. Their recommendations should be accorded consideration commensurate with their competences (including a broad understanding of the enterprise); however, the final judgments (decisional inputs) must be made by the executive management. This viewpoint rests upon the fundamental proposition that the sales plan represents enterprise *goals*; that the management is making a *commitment* to accomplish them; and, finally, that the goals are identified with those having responsibility for accomplishing them (as opposed to being identified with some specialized staff group).

Consistent with this viewpoint we can generalize on the common pattern that is followed by better-managed companies to develop realistic sales plans. The pattern involves a two-pronged attack.

1. The central forecasting group, utilizing numerous statistical techniques and approaches, develops a series of sales forecasts for the company. Their forecasts include precise statements of the underlying assumptions including those relating to company actions (promotion and advertising programs, expansion or contraction of sales efforts, pricing policies, inventory policies, product quality, etc.). Fundamentally, the central forecasting group attempts to estimate market potentials under stated assumptions. The forecasting effort is conducted on a continuing basis at the staff level.

2. The management of the marketing function, utilizing historical data, economic analyses (from varying sources including the central forecasting group), and judgment (of sales executives, sales supervisors, sales force), develop a sales plan independently.

At the higher management level the two results (central forecast and the management sales plan) are critically compared and evaluated. The assumptions of each are judgmentally tested and evaluated in the light of the broad company objectives and enterprise strategies.

On the basis of the evaluations in the preceding step, definite management *decisions* are made with respect to basic assumptions (pricing policies, marketing strategies, promotion plans) and a *final sales plan* is developed. The final sales plan is viewed as the enterprise goal and managerial commitments are explicit to pursue aggressively and attain the approved objectives.

THE CONCERN'S CAPABILITIES AND ITS SALES PLAN

The immediately preceding discussion was concerned principally with the sales potential of the enterprise. Another important factor that must be considered before the sales plan is approved is the internal capabilities of the company during the period covered by the sales plan. There are four principal factors concerning internal capabilities that may constrain the sales plan:

1. Capacity of the plant.
2. Availability of personnel.
3. Adequacy of raw materials and supplies.
4. Availability of capital.

These four factors suggest the importance of coordination among the heads of the various functional areas in developing a realistic sales plan.

Capacity to produce is critical; its evaluation involves the plant superintendent and others concerned with capital additions. There is no point in planning a greater quantity of sales than can be produced, nor is it advisable generally to operate the plant above economical capacity. Alternatively, there may be excess productive capacity. Idle facilities usually are costly. The capital additions budget thus becomes involved with the sales plan because new capacity, rearrangement, extraordinary repairs, and expansion frequently need special consideration. The sales plan frequently necessitates a complete study of plant capacity.

Availability of personnel can be a very critical factor in determining the amount of goods that can be produced and, hence, sold. This factor may apply to all classes of personnel but is more likely to be crucial with respect to supervisory personnel and highly skilled employees. This situation poses a problem for the director of personnel with respect to recruitment and training programs, especially if there is to be a significant increase in sales and production. The cost of training personnel is often a decisive factor. Obviously, a significantly reduced sales volume can likewise create serious personnel problems.

The adequacy of funds for capital additions and working capital is also of great consequence in planning. This consideration involves the company treasurer in sales planning because it entails the problem of financing the production, capital additions, and sales effort implicit in the sales plan. In addition to the adequacy of capital, there is also the question of liquidity. Cash is required for capital additions, payrolls, raw materials, inventories, expenses, liabilities, and dividends, yet sales may not provide sufficient ready cash if credit sales are high and collections slow. This related problem is discussed later in connection with the cash budget.

Unless these internal capabilities and the timing related to them are recognized and taken into account, the sales plan may not be realistic with respect to both market potentials and enterprise efficiency.

CONTROL OF SALES AND RELATED COSTS

The development of a realistic sales plan provides the foundation for effective control of sales and distribution costs. We have emphasized that the several components of the sales plan should be developed in terms of assigned *management responsibilities*; it is on this basis that effective control may be attained. Control in the sales function should be viewed as a comprehensive activity encompassing sales volume, sales revenue, promotion costs, and other distribution costs. *Effective control requires that both sales volume and distribution costs be viewed as one problem rather than as two separate and diverse concerns.* The sales plan reflects the goals that are to be attained by the sales division. The marketing executive has overall responsibility for control of all facets of the distribution effort. Normally, sales quotas for salesmen should be consistent with the sales plan, although in some situations there may be temporary reasons for developing quotas for individual salesmen that are somewhat in excess of or, in other cases, somewhat below realistic expectations. However, in such cases the sales goals, cost standards, and other distribution objectives included in the sales plan must represent realistic expectations. Those expectations should be communicated to all levels of management without change. Control in the distribution function, as in all other functions, is attained through many facets of management action.

The sales goals (volume and dollar revenue), promotion plans (planned expenditures), and distribution activities (distribution costs) represent basic goals. These are relatively broad goals, which suggest the need for numerous short-term and specific standards as a part of the total control effort of the management. Examples of specific standards that may be used for control purposes are:

1. Number of calls per period per salesman.
2. Number of new customers to be obtained.
3. Dollars of direct selling expense per salesman.
4. Selling costs as a percent of sales dollars.
5. Average size of order to be obtained.
6. Number of orders to be secured per call made.
7. Dollar sales quotas per salesman per period.

Effective control of distribution efforts also requires *periodic performance reports by responsibility* that cover all facets of performance. Performance reports normally should be prepared and distributed on a monthly basis; however, certain critical aspects of the sales effort and the related problem areas may require weekly or even daily performance reports. Performance reports for the marketing function should be prepared by the financial executive's staff and distributed as soon as possible after the end of the period.

The report should be comprehensive for each responsibility center. For example, a sales district performance report should report (1) performance in generating sales revenue, (2) performance in controlling district distribution expenses, and (3) performance of other related activities under the direct control of the district sales manager. The performance report should compare actual with planned and report the exceptions or variances. Normally, the report should be for the period just ended and *cumulative* to date. Performance reports should be consistent with the pyramiding principle; that is, the performance reports for the lowest level of management should report specific revenues and costs by detailed classifications (products in the case of sales and nature of the costs in the case of expenses). For each higher level of management, the pyramiding effect requires summary performance reports that show totals by *responsibility centers*. This type of report is illustrated in Case 5-9, Brown Wholesale Company, and in the Superior Manufacturing Company case illustrated throughout this text. Interpretation, utilization, and adaptation of performance reports are considered in detail in Chapter 15.

THE SALES PLAN ILLUSTRATED

Superior Manufacturing Company develops two sales estimates: (1) a small central forecasting group develops a sales forecast by product and by sales district both for the short run and for the long run; (2) a sales plan is initiated in each sales district, primarily on a judgmental basis.

During September of the current year, the director of profit planning and control obtains from the accounting department historical sales data for each district for the past twelve months. The historical sales data are broken down by month, by quarters, and by product. These data are entered on *special forms*, which are sent to the sales district supervisors by September 15; these forms are returned to the vice president in charge of sales by October 15 with the recommended sales plans entered by the sales district supervisors. The plans include the district supervisors' recommendations with respect to sales volume, sales price, district advertising and promotion programs and costs, number of salesmen, and other distribution costs. The marketing executive reviews the district estimates in depth and compares them with the sales forecast developed by the forecasting group. The marketing executive working directly with the various district supervisors and the central forecasting group develops a *tentative* sales plan for the company. The tentative sales plan is then presented to the executive committee by November 1.

Since the company prepares a detailed projected income statement, the sales plan is developed in harmony with it—that is, by time periods, by district, and by product. The time periods during the year consist of a break-down by month for the first quarters and by quarters for the rest of the year. Quarters other than the first are broken down (reprojected) during the last month of the preceding quarter. The summary *marketing plan* for Superior Manufacturing Company was illustrated in Chapter 4, Schedule 1. The detailed marketing plan is given in Schedule 21. The detailed promotion and advertising program is not illustrated; however, the funds budgeted for this purpose are included in the budget of distribution expense (Schedule 39). It may be observed that the detailed marketing plan includes a three-way classification of sales—by district, by product, and by time period. Because of the simplification of the illustration, one detailed marketing plan schedule is sufficient; however, in more complex situations there would obviously be a need for several budget schedules in the sales plan.[8]

The reader is reminded that it may be desirable to recast certain of the budget schedules illustrated throughout this text. It is not desirable to incorporate budget schedules (prepared in worksheet form) into the formal profit plan without some recasting. In order to conserve space, the schedules in this book have been designed to indicate computation and buildup. Notice that the summary schedule is frequently presented after the detailed schedules. This presentation suggests that it is frequently necessary to complete the detailed schedule prior to the summary. The design of profit plan schedules is an important responsibility of the director of profit planning and control. There is no standard design suited to all purposes; the schedules must be especially designed to fit the needs and characteristics of each concern. The schedules illustrated for Superior Manufacturing Company are merely suggestive.

Because of the critical importance of sales planning, the following brief bibliography is presented to aid those who need to pursue the subject in greater depth.

Beidleman, Carl R., "Some Moderation to Rigors of Financial Forecasting," *Managerial Planning* (July-August 1973), pp. 29–36.

Benton, William K., *Forecasting for Management.* Reading, Mass: Addison-Wesley Publishing Company, 1972.

Butler, W. F., R. A. Kavesh, and R. B. Platt, eds., *Methods and Techniques*

---

[8] Throughout the illustrative problem, 1976 will be referred to as the *current year* and 1977 as the *budget year*.

SCHEDULE 21. Superior Manufacturing Company
Marketing Plan
(Detailed)
By Product, Time, and District
For the Year Ending December 31, 1977

	TOTALS		SOUTHERN DISTRICT		EASTERN DISTRICT		WESTERN DISTRICT	
PRODUCT X:	Ref. (INPUT) UNITS (INPUT)	AMOUNT	UNITS (INPUT) $5.00 PER UNIT	AMOUNT	UNITS (INPUT) $5.10 PER UNIT	AMOUNT	UNITS (INPUT) $5.10 PER UNIT	AMOUNT
January	85,000	$ 430,500	30,000	$ 150,000	40,000	$ 204,000	15,000	$ 76,500
February	90,000	455,500	35,000	175,000	45,000	229,500	10,000	51,000
March	95,000	481,500	30,000	150,000	50,000	255,000	15,000	76,500
Total 1st Quarter	270,000	$1,367,500	95,000	$ 475,000	135,000	$ 688,500	40,000	$ 204,000
2nd Quarter	260,000	1,317,000	90,000	450,000	135,000	688,500	35,000	178,500
3rd Quarter	190,000	962,500	65,000	325,000	90,000	459,000	35,000	178,500
4th Quarter	280,000	1,419,000	90,000	450,000	140,000	714,000	50,000	255,000
Total X	1,000,000	$5,066,000	340,000	$1,700,000	500,000	$2,550,000	160,000	$ 816,000
Product Y: (INPUT)			$2.00 PER UNIT		$2.10 PER UNIT		$2.10 PER UNIT	
January	34,000	$ 69,900	15,000	$ 30,000	11,000	$ 23,100	8,000	$ 16,800
February	41,000	84,500	16,000	32,000	14,000	29,400	11,000	23,100
March	45,000	92,600	19,000	38,000	15,000	31,500	11,000	23,100
Total 1st Quarter	120,000	$ 247,000	50,000	$ 100,000	40,000	$ 84,000	30,000	$ 63,000
2nd Quarter	135,000	278,000	55,000	110,000	45,000	94,500	35,000	73,500
3rd Quarter	95,000	195,500	40,000	80,000	35,000	73,500	20,000	42,000
4th Quarter	150,000	308,500	65,000	130,000	50,000	105,000	35,000	73,500
Total Y	500,000	$1,029,000	210,000	$ 420,000	170,000	$ 357,000	120,000	$ 252,000
Total X and Y		$6,095,000		$2,120,000		$2,907,000		$1,068,000

of Business Forecasting. Englewood Cliffs, N. J.: Prentice-Hall, Inc., 1974.

Carroll, Archie B., "An Organizational Need: Forecasting and Planning for the Social Environment," *Managerial Planning* (May-June 1973), pp. 11–13.

Chambers, John C., Satinder K. Mullick, and Donald D. Smith, "How to Choose the Right Forecasting Technique," *Harvard Business Review* (July-August 1971), pp. 45–74.

Clark, John J., ed., *The Management of Forecasting.* New York: St. John's University Press, 1969.

Courtney, Harley M., and Frederick V. Brooks, "Cumulative Probabilistic Sales Forecasting," *Management Accounting* (May 1972), pp. 44–47.

Fosberg, J. Marvin, "Forecasting and Trend Analysis," *Financial Executives Handbook,* ed. Richard F. Vancil. Homewood, Ill.: Dow Jones-Irwin, Inc., 1970.

Lippitt, Vernon G., *Statistical Sales Forecasting.* New York: Financial Executives Research Foundation, 1969.

Mobert, V. A., and R. C. Radcliffe, "A Forecasting Methodology as Applied to Financial Time Series," *The Accounting Review* (January 1974), pp. 61–75.

Parker, George G. C., and Edilberto L. Segura, "How to Get a Better Forecast," *Harvard Business Review* (March-April 1971), pp. 99–109.

Reichard, Robert S., *Practical Techniques of Sales Forecasting.* New York: McGraw-Hill Book Co., Inc., 1969.

Sobek, Robert S., "A Manager's Primer on Forecasting," *Harvard Business Review* (May-June 1973), p.6.

Wheelwright, Steven C., and Spyros Makridakis, *Forecasting Methods for Management.* New York: John Wiley & Sons, 1973.

Wolfe, Harry Deane, *Business Forecasting Methods.* New York: Holt, Rinehart, and Winston, 1966.

DISCUSSION QUESTIONS

1. Explain two crucial factors that generally are present in companies that attain a high degree of realism in sales planning.

2. Define a sales plan, and relate its importance to the overall profit planning and control program.

3. What is the relationship of the long-range sales plan to the sales plan included in the annual profit plan?

4. With which of the following statements do you agree? Why?

    a. The objective in sales planning is to guess what actual sales will be and then to compare actual sales with planned sales to determine whether or not the plan was realistic.

b.   The objective in sales planning is to establish sales goals, to make a commitment to accomplish them, and then to compare actual sales with planned sales to determine whether or not the sales effort was adequate.

5.   Distinguish between a sales forecast and a sales plan.

6.   Why is it important that a clear-cut distinction be made between a sales forecast and a sales plan?

7.   Relate the concept of a "flash report" to the sales plan.

8.   Define sales mix, and indicate why it is an important consideration in planning sales.

9.   What are the six components in sales planning?

10.   List five important factors that should be taken into account by a company in selecting the particular approach to be used for developing a sales plan.

11.   What is the relationship between the marketing plan and the sales quotas for salesmen?

12.   How should the sales plan be broken down with respect to detail?

13.   What internal limitations of the company may affect the sales plan?

14.   What are the principal facets of control in using a sales plan?

CASE 5-1
Pinkerton, Inc.

Pinkerton, Inc., is a medium-size firm that manufactures approximately twenty products that are widely distributed. For approximately eight years the company has been using an annual profit plan and monthly performance reports. The profit plan is developed each year during the last three months of the fiscal year and is detailed by month. The short-range profit plans focus on standard profit margin, return on investment, and percentage growth in sales as specified by the top management. The important segments of the short-range plans have been the following: (1) an annual sales projection detailed by month; (2) an annual income statement detailed by month; (3) an annual cash flow plan detailed by months; and (4) a capital-additions budget. The company management has never undertaken a comprehensive assessment of the variables that influence the long-range growth of the company nor have they been involved in longrange planning. The company is divided into three profit centers.

Recently, the management made a decision to "evaluate our long-range potentials on an annual basis and to develop concurrently with the annual profit plan a five-year plan. In our considerations each year we must be concerned with the following basic issues:

1.   Establish long-range return on investment and growth goals;

2.   Determine the needs for long-range expansion of company facilities;

3.   Develop plans for new markets (new products and expanded market areas);

4.   Development of new sources of raw materials."

The above quotation was taken from a memorandum written by the president and distributed to top management. The list represents the only steps considered thus far.

Required :

a. If you had drafted the memorandum what would you have listed as the "basic issues" (or phases) ?

b. What would you recommend as the role of the managers of the three profit centers with respect to developing the long-range sales plan ?

CASE 5-2
Bryan Company

Bryan Company is a manufacturer of pleasure boats. The boats are sold on a nationwide basis and have enjoyed excellent acceptance. Bryan Boats are noted for their style and durability. Annual sales approximate $50,000,000. The company has been budgeting, in a traditional way, for about seven years. The president is concerned about the approaches used in developing the annual sales plan. A dual approach has been used. Around September 1, the eight area sales managers are asked to submit a "judgmental" twelve-month sales plan for the upcoming year, detailed by month. The area managers are told that they are "on their own" in developing the judgmental sales plan. The home office sales executives carefully review the area plans and compile a company sales plan. Concurrent with these activities, an "economist" in the financial function prepares a statistical analysis of the industry and makes a "nonjudgmental projection" of the sales for each sales area. These two projections are "averaged" by the home office in order to develop a company sales plan that is then *tentatively* approved by the president. Typically the plans developed by the area managers are much more conservative than those developed by the economist.

Generally the sales plan as tentatively approved has had to be reconsidered by the top management "because the resultant profit projection was unsatisfactory." In each case, reconsideration of the sales plan and other components of the profit plan resulted in an improved plan, which generally was attained each year. The president has stated that "I am interested in reducing the time devoted to developing the annual profit plan ; I believe the key in saving time for the top managers is to do a better job on the tentative sales plan. If we could somehow get a better feel of the profit potentials of a given sales plan, we might be able to resolve most of the questions concerning the sales plan prior to the first tentative approval."

The budget for the past year for sales area No. 1 reflected the following :

Sales	$300,000
Cost of goods sold :	
Fixed	(90,000)
Variable	(66,000)
Fixed expenses	(36,000)
Variable expenses	(42,000)
District contribution	$66,000

Required:

    a. Explain any weaknesses that appear to exist in the procedures for planning sales. Present your recommended changes.

    b. What would you recommend relative to the problem of having to reconsider the sales plan each year? Illustrate your recommendations if feasible. Assume the tentative sales plan for Area No. 1 reflects $330,000 sales for the coming year.

CASE 5-3
Mite Manufacturing Company

      Mite Manufacturing Company makes two products, S and T, which are distributed in two sales districts. The sales executives developed the following decisional inputs for the coming year:

    1. Gross Sales:

	PRODUCT S (UNITS)		PRODUCT T (UNITS)	
	COMAL DISTRICT	DIBOL DISTRICT	COMAL DISTRICT	DIBOL DISTRICT
January	2,000	3,000	3,000	4,000
February	2,200	3,400	3,300	4,500
March	2,300	3,400	3,500	4,600
2nd Quarter	6,600	9,000	8,000	10,000
3rd Quarter	7,000	9,900	8,500	10,300
4th Quarter	5,000	7,000	6,000	8,000

    2. Sales prices planned:
        Product S—Comal District $3.30, Dibol District $3.40.
        Product T—Comal District $4.30, Dibol District $4.40.
    3. It is estimated that sales returns and allowances will be as follows:
        Product S—One percent of gross sales.
        Product T—One and one-half percent of gross sales.
    4. District expenses planned (summarized for case purposes):

	FIXED PER MONTH		VARIABLE PER $100 GROSS SALES DOLLARS	
EXPENSE	COMAL	DIBOL	COMAL	DIBOL
Distribution	$1,000	$1,500	$4.00	$4.00
Promotion	2,000	2,200	0	0

Required:

     a. The sales plan is to be completed using the above inputs. List and briefly explain the three basic components of the sales plan.

     b. Prepare budget schedules for the sales plan for each component. Design them to reflect relevant classifications such as responsibility, products, and time.

CASE 5-4
OK Manufacturing Company

OK Manufacturing Company has for many years manufactured a line of stoves. The line is fairly broad, varying from simple heating stoves to large combination heating and air conditioning units up to a seven-ton capacity. The firm also distributes an external condensing unit to complete the heating-air conditioning package. The condensing units are purchased from another manufacturer and the OK trade name is placed upon them prior to sale. In addition to selling the line to various trade outlets in a three-state area, the company manufactures the combination unit for another company that operates on a national basis. These units are sold under the trade name used by the other company. The combination unit manufactured by the company is recognized as one of the better units produced anywhere. On units sold in the three-state area OK has a definite freight advantage.

The OK company has been moderately successful—that is, the sales have been steady with a gradual and consistent increase in the three-state area. Orders from the national firm have increased from year to year during the past ten years at a rate approximately twice that of the distribution through trade outlets under the OK trademark; for 1974, sales of OK to the national outlet amounted to 26 percent of the total volume produced. The OK company realizes about 30 percent more profit per unit, after allocation of all overhead to regular sales, on the trade business than on the business from the national outlet. Profits for the OK Company overall have been good when related to investment.

The OK company executives have decided to expand into three additional states starting in 1975. The company has an effective profit planning and control program. The sales plan has been quite accurate for the past six years except for 1974 when sales were approximately 15 percent below budget.

A preliminary study by the controller of the OK company provided the following sales potentials for the new territory: 1975, $150,000; 1976, $200,000; and 1977, $500,000. A representative of the sales department worked with the controller in developing these preliminary estimates.

Required:

You have been engaged as an outside consultant to advise with respect to preparing a realistic sales plan for the new territory covering the period indicated above. The company has been using the *field approach* in developing the annual sales estimates. It is expected that the 1975 estimate in the new territory will be considered with particular care because purchases of component parts, materials, employment of additional personnel, etc., will be based upon this projection. Specifically, you are to respond to whether the company should enter the new market. Justify your recommendation.

CASE 5-5
Richard Sales Company

The executives of the Richard Sales Company are considering pricing policies in connection with the sales projection currently being developed. One particular problem concerns the price of the principal product. The current selling price is $10.50 per unit.

The Sales department manager generally feels that the price should be reduced to $10; the other executives feel that this decrease in price would not be offset by increased volume as is claimed. As a result of the discussions concerning the various alternatives that exist, a rather complete study has been made. The following data were developed:

1. Sales price-volume data:

ASSUMED SELLING PRICE	ESTIMATED MARKET AT GIVEN PRICE (UNITS)
$10.00	12,000
10.20	11,500
10.40	11,300
10.50	11,000
10.60	10,600
10.80	9,500
11.00	9,000

2. Total fixed costs, $35,000. (It is assumed this cost will be constant at all the volumes listed above.)
3. Estimated variable cost per unit of product, $6.00.

Required:

a. Assume you are the staff representative that developed the above data. You are to present it to the executive committee. Prepare a volume-price analysis that suggests the alternative that should be selected. Prepare the analysis in a form suitable for submission to the executive committee, supplementing it with comments or graphs, if these would add to the effectiveness of the presentation.

b. Indicate some approaches you may have used in developing the sales price-volume data.

CASE 5-6
Dement Company

The Dement Company is one of approximately twenty known companies in its industry. It is significantly below the average-size company in the industry, and the sales volume last year was approximately $15,000,000. The company has never been involved in comprehensive profit planning and control, although the sales division for many years has developed weekly sales quotas for each salesman and for each sales district. The weekly sales quotas in the past have been developed for four weeks in advance. For example, by the middle of January the home sales office would have completed and mailed to the various sales districts the weekly sales quotas by salesmen for the first week starting around February 1. At the end of each four-week period, sales quota performance reports were prepared and distributed to each sales district. These performance reports compare actual sales for each week with the planned sales quotas by salesmen.

In the last few years the company has been "losing ground" with the other medium-size competitors in the industry. Percentage increases in sales and profit margin have been gradual but small in the company. The top management of the company has become concerned about the trends and has decided "to make a determined effort to reverse the situation." As a consequence, a number of changes in operations have been initiated. Additionally, the president has been looking at some of the management approaches utilized in the company. A consultant was engaged to "provide a broad survey of management practices and to make recommendations." Among the consultants' recommendations was one advising company management to initiate a planning program. The consultant questioned the value of the sales quota approach as utilized by the company. His report stated that "serious management attention should be given to developing a long-range and short-range sales plan as a foundation for similar planning in other functional areas of the company." In harmony with the terms of the initial engagement, the report of the consultant was general and covered many areas of operation and managerial approaches.

Based upon the report of the consultant, the president decided to establish an "economic analysis and sales forecasting group." Through a mutual friend the president learned of a "very bright young man who had just completed a master's degree at a large university." His areas of concentration at the university were economics and quantitative methods. Shortly after his employment and upon his recommendation, another individual was hired who had received a bachelor's degree with a concentration in marketing from the same university. These two individuals and a secretary comprised the new group. Upon instructions from the president, the group immediately plunged into the process of developing "a five-year, long-range sales forecast and a one-year sales forecast; the latter to be developed in detail." The two experts started to work on this charge with considerable zeal. The first step taken was to obtain from the accounting department sales by product for the last five years, detailed by month. Since the company sold approximately twenty different products over that time, a significant amount of historical data was at hand. The data reflected only dollar sales by product each month. After some experimentation with statistical techniques, it was decided to use total company sales for extrapolation purposes. Well-known statistical techniques were utilized to isolate the seasonal effect in the series. Next the cyclical component was isolated by using an economic indicator with business cycle movements that seemed "relevant to the company situation." Next a trend was fitted to the data. The trend was projected for the five-year period and the seasonal for the next twelve months. The cyclical component was likewise projected for the five-year period, and on this basis a one-year monthly and a five-year, long-range forecast were developed. Next the forecasting group decided to develop a sales forecast in a different way and to compare the results. Population estimates for the area covered by the sales efforts were developed for the five-year period. A projection of the general economic conditions was developed next. In turn, a projection of total industry sales was developed. The industry projection was based in large measure on industry statistics and projected data that were obtained from the industry association. Next, percentages of the industry sales were projected by year so that application of these percentages to the industry forecast would provide the company sales forecast. The two approaches provided substantially different results. However, the forecasters felt that the background that they had gained put them in a position to make reasonable judgments so that a realistic sales forecast might be developed. At the end of approximately three months, the forecasters informed the president that they had completed a one-year sales forecast by month and a five-year, long-range sales forecast. A copy of their forecasts was given to the president. The next day he called their secretary and indicated that he had scheduled a meeting of the vice presidents at which time he wanted "the sales forecasts presented, explained, and all questions resolved." Since the meeting was scheduled within one week, the forecasters were quite concerned about the best approach for presenting it.

Required:

What are the primary problems? Present your recommendations for resolving them.

CASE 5-7
Economy Manufacturing Company

The executives of the Economy Manufacturing Company are in the process of developing the sales plan (and planning budget as well) for the coming year 19B. A meeting of the executive committee is scheduled for next Monday at 9:00 A.M. This is the third meeting concerned with the sales plan. Data developed to date are as follows:

1. The Sales division has prepared the following sales plan: Product X, $200,000; Product Y, $315,000. The long-range plan calls for a 12 percent increase in sales in 19C and a 7 percent increase in 19D. The top management believes these plans are realistic assuming the "other problems can be ironed out."

2. The treasurer has prepared a tentative cash budget at the budgeted sales volume (excluding capital additions requirements), which indicates a cash deficit during the third and fourth quarters. The deficit is approximately $60,000 in September.

3. The Manufacturing division has estimated the present plant capacity for economical operation to be 450,000 direct machine hours (DMH).

4. The personnel supervisor is concerned about the estimate of the vice president in charge of manufacturing that additional highly skilled workers would be required to meet the production requirements of the sales plan. It is believed that the workers can be hired, but that the wage demands likely will be above what is currently paid the skilled workers in the same category.

5. The purchasing officer anticipated no difficulty in obtaining the required quantity and quality of raw materials and supplies. In fact, there may be a slight cost saving due to increased volume.

6. The Sales division recommended the following budgeted sales prices: Product X, $2.00; Product Y, $2.25.

7. The company had established a line of credit for $100,000. The treasurer felt it would be difficult to increase this amount materially. The company has 10,000 shares of unissued common stock; the current market price is $9.50 per share. Two years ago the board of directors voted not to sell the shares.

8. The industrial engineers have developed the following standard direct machine hours per unit of product: Product X, $1\frac{1}{4}$; Product Y, $2\frac{1}{2}$.

9. A survey of plant capacity indicated additions to plant and machinery could be made as follows at the cost indicated:

INCREASE IN CAPACITY DMH	ESTIMATED COST
25,000	$ 40,000
50,000	70,000
100,000	110,000
150,000	150,000

Required:

Assume the sales plan as presented by the sales division is approved. Identify and present an analysis of the "other problems to be ironed out."

CASE 5-8
Dora, Inc.

Dora, Inc., is a medium-size manufacturing enterprise that has been in operation for over forty years. The company has an important advantage in that its plant is in a geographical location that posed serious transportation problems for other and larger companies in the industry. As a consequence, for many years the company has been the primary supplier in the area and has always faced the problem of inadequate capacity. The company is family owned, and they have been reluctant to increase capacity over the years. Consequently, the sales function was primarily an order-taking activity, and no real sales competence was required. The burden was always on the manufacturing people to "get out more production to meet the needs of the market." About five years ago another company constructed a plant in the area and exhibited an aggressive managing and marketing effort. During the past year, and for the first time in the history of the company, Dora, Inc., operated its plant at approximately 80 percent capacity due to a decrease in sales. Profits dropped significantly. During the year additional people were added to the sales function. However, the downward sales trend was not reversed. Recently, the president called a meeting of the top managers to discuss the situation. During that meeting the manufacturing executive said, "Over the years we in manufacturing have been doing everything humanly possible to satisfy the sales people, even to the extent of operating above capacity to meet the market demand. Our problem now, as I see it, is that sales people have not come through, and they want us to cut back on production. I take a firm stand that we should not do this next year because that action would increase our unit costs; we would not be able to make a profit even on the products that the sales people are selling. I think the sales people ought to get at the job like we have over the years so that we can continue operating at or near full capacity. It is their responsibility to develop markets to take care of our capacity." To this the sales vice president responded: "It seems to me in situations like this that sales has got to call the shots because we can't eat the goods that can't be sold. We're going to sell all that is humanly possible, and it seems to me that production is going to have to get in line with sales; otherwise, we will have a serious inventory problem." The president smoothed over the conversation and went to other matters. As the group was walking out of the room, the financial vice president remarked: "Now we're going to see whether sales, production, or someone else is boss around here; it's sure to come up again in the next meeting."

Required:

Analyze the situation, and present recommendations for resolving the problems.

CASE 5-9
Brown Wholesale Company

The Brown Wholesale Company distributes products on a national scale. The company has been in operation for approximately twenty years and has been quite successful. The management has operated a comprehensive budget program for a number of years. At the present time, the budget program is being revised to include "the latest approaches and techniques; increased utilization of our computer facilities; and attainment of a higher level of management sophistication." The financial and sales executives have been working to develop an improved system of performance reporting for the sales division.

The present approaches used for performance reporting have been unchanged for a number of years. Essentially, the approach involves a monthly performance report wherein actual sales and actual costs by sales district are compared with the budgeted sales goals and cost objectives included in the annual profit plan. The emphasis in the performance reports has been on product lines. In discussing these matters the sales executive stated: "My people sometimes get quite concerned about the variances in costs on their performance reports, particularly when their sales are above quotas for the period. At the same time, I have been concerned about the fact that unfavorable cost variances tend to show up when a sales force fails to meet its sales goals. Do you think we can do something about these problems?" The financial executive indicated that he would work on the problem and within the next few days "would have a definite approach to suggest."

On the following Monday the financial executive sent Schedules 1 and 2 to the marketing executive with a handwritten note stating: "Bob, let's get together tomorrow and discuss the ideas explicitly illustrated in the two schedules attached. I have roughed these out to suggest a flexible approach in developing the expense allowances in the sales division. I have used the Western Sales district as an example and have used hypothetical figures (simplified) to illustrate the concepts. You will note the fixed and variable expense classifications and the manning requirements; these are essentially new concepts for us that I think we should discuss with a view to their potential application to your problems. In Schedule 2, I have sketched out a revised summary performance report for your division and have carried forward the hypothetical figures from the Western Sales district. I will be interested in your reaction to these suggestions and your judgment as to whether or not the concepts can be applied on a practical basis in your division. Incidentally, these are similar to the approach that I suggested earlier for the purchasing department, and they have reacted favorably. How about 10 o'clock tomorrow in your office? Sam."

Required:

a.   Explain the basic concepts implicit in Schedule 1 as recommended by the financial executive.

SCHEDULE 1.   Brown Wholesale Company

Sales Plan—Budget of District Costs

Direct: Western Sales   Period: 1976
Supervisor: A.B. Combs   Approvals:

EXPENSE CLASSIFICATION	CONSTANT (PER MONTH)	VARIABLE RATE (PER $100 SALES)
Variable expenses:		
Salesmen's commissions		$5.00
Travel and entertainment		3.00
Telephone and telegraph		.40
Miscellaneous		.10
Fixed expenses:		
Supervisory salaries	$24,000	
Utilities	300	
Rent	800	
Miscellaneous	200	
TOTAL EXPENSES	$25,300	$8.50

Manning Requirements	
Supervisors	3
Salesmen	12
Secretaries	2
Total	17

b.   Explain the fundamental aspects of Schedule 2 with particular reference to the underlying concepts.

c.   Present computations to indicate how the budget variances were developed for the current month and the year to date for the Western Sales district.

SCHEDULE 2. Brown Wholesale Company

Performance Report—By Responsibility Center
Responsibility Center: Sales Division (Summary)   Period: Feb. 1976
Supervisor: R.M. Bacon   Reviews:

CURRENT MONTH		RESPONSIBILITY (SEE DISTRICT REPORTS FOR DETAIL)	YEAR TO DATE	
ACTUAL	PERFORMANCE VARIANCE*		ACTUAL	PERFORMANCE VARIANCE*
		Sales Revenue:		
		Eastern District		
		Mid District		
$310,000	$10,000	Western District	$640,000	$8,000
		Totals		
		District Expenses:		
		Eastern District		
		Mid District		
53,850	2,200*	Western District	107,050	2,050*
		Home Office Costs		
		Manning:		
		Eastern District		
		Mid District		
17	0	Western District	17	0
		Home Office		

*Unfavorable.

Planning Production:
Finished Goods
and Work in Process
Inventory Requirements

chapter six

In developing a comprehensive profit plan, the requirements of the sales plan must be translated into the supporting activities of the other major functions. In the case of a service company, the sales plan must be converted to service capability requirements; for a retail or wholesale enterprise, the sales plan must be translated into merchandise purchases requirements; and in the case of a manufacturing enterprise, the sales plan must be converted to production (manufacturing) requirements. Several later chapters focus on a manufacturing enterprise, hence, they discuss the *manufacturing executive's plan* (or budget). This plan comprises subbudgets (or subplans) for the following: production; finished goods and work in process inventories; direct material requirements; purchases; direct labor requirements; and manufacturing, or factory, overhead.

The marketing plan specifies the planned volume of each product (or groups of similar products) by time period throughout the planning period. The next step in a manufacturing enterprise is to develop a *production plan* (budget). This entails the development of policies with respect to desirable production levels, use of productive facilities, and inventory levels (finished goods and work in process inventory). The quantities specified in the marketing plan, adjusted to conform to production and inventory policies, give the volume of goods that must be manufactured by product, by interim time period. Thus, the production budget may be represented this way: SALES

VOLUME $\pm$ INVENTORY CHANGE = PRODUCTION REQUIREMENTS. The inventory change may be plus or minus. Illustration 16 presents graphically the flow of planning activities from sales through the manufacturing executive's plan.

Planning Production

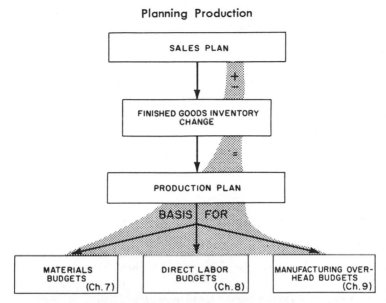

ILLUSTRATION 16.   Planning Manufacturing Operations

RESPONSIBILITY FOR PRODUCTION PLANNING

The completed marketing plan should be given to the manufacturing executive who is responsible for translating it into a balanced production program consistent with managerial policies and subject to certain internal limitations. Planning, scheduling, and dispatching of the actual production throughout the year are functions of the production department; so it is essential that responsibility for the planning and control of these functions be performed by production executives. These executives have firsthand knowledge of plant and personnel capacities, availability of materials, and the production situation. Although responsibility rests directly upon the production executives, top-management policies must be considered in such matters as inventory levels, stability of production, and capital additions (plant capacity). A balanced and coordinated production program generally requires the careful attention of top management, particularly where there is multiplant production requiring the determination of both time and place of production.

With respect to production planning, the planners must determine an *optimum balance* between sales, inventory, and production levels. The problem is complex; because of the three variables, only planned sales volume is known. If optimum balance is not achieved in planning this triangle of operations, many other aspects of the profit plan will be adversely affected. A well-balanced production program is necessary for economical manufacturing. Lower production costs usually result from standardization of products and from stable production levels. Sales managers generally are aggressive in requesting new products and changes in the old products. There may be pressure from both sales and manufacturing for high inventory levels. Therefore, there must be coordination between sales plans, production plans, and inventory policies. The production budget and the inventory policies provide the basis for obtaining this coordination.

The *production budget is an estimate of the quantity of goods to be manufactured during the budget period*. In developing the production budget, the first step is to establish policies relative to inventory levels. The next step is to determine the *total* quantity of each product that is to be manufactured during the budget period. The third step is to schedule or prorate this production to interim periods.[1]

The production budget is the initial step in budgeting manufacturing operations. In addition to the production budget, there are three other principal budgets relevant to manufacturing: (1) the *material budget*, which specifies estimates of raw material requirements; (2) the *labor budget*, which indicates the quantity and cost of direct labor; and (3) the *manufacturing expense or factory overhead budget*, which includes estimates of all factory costs other than direct material and direct labor. These three budgets are discussed in subsequent chapters.

To plan production effectively, the manufacturing executives must have, or develop, information relative to the manufacturing operations necessary for each product. They must have at hand information relative to the uses and capacities of each manufacturing department. The company cost accountants should provide certain historical data essential in planning production quantities and costs. The director of profit planning and control should provide staff assistance when needed.

When the recommended production plan (budget) is completed by the production department, it should be submitted to the executive committee for appraisal and then to the president for tentative approval prior to its use as a basis for developing the materials, labor, and factory overhead budgets.

---

[1] This chapter presumes a manufacturing situation. The production budget is the manufacturing equivalent of the merchandise budget in wholesale and retail establishments. Retail budgeting is discussed in a subsequent chapter.

GENERAL CONSIDERATIONS IN PLANNING PRODUCTION
AND INVENTORY LEVELS

The production plan does not aim to set the precise amounts and timing of actual production during the budget period. Rather, the production budget represents the conversion of planned sales volume to planned production volume as a basis for planning (and budgeting) the various aspects of the manufacturing function—plant capacity requirements, raw material requirements, timing of purchases, labor requirements and costs, and factory overhead. These latter items can be effectively planned only on the basis of a realistic estimate of production volume.

Generally speaking, production in manufacturing situations is: (1) for direct delivery; (2) for stock; or (3) partially for direct delivery and partially for stock. The latter situation is desirable from a production standpoint, because an inventory of finished goods provides a cushion for balancing sales requirements and desirable production levels.

Whenever possible the production budget should be developed in terms of quantities of *physical units* of finished goods. Therefore, when it is possible to plan sales volume by units as well as by values, production budgeting is simplified.

In developing the production plan, the manufacturing executives are faced with the problem of balancing sales, inventories, and production so that the lowest possible overall cost results. Careful consideration of a number of subsidiary, yet significant, matters is essential. The importance of this aspect of production planning cannot be overemphasized because it affects so many decisions relating to cost, capital commitments, employees, and so on. Decisions required in developing the production plan include the following:

1. Total production requirements (by product) for the budget period.
2. Inventory policies relative to levels of finished goods and work in process.
3. Plant capacity policies such as the limits of permissable departures from a stable production level throughout the year.
4. Adequacy of manufacturing facilities (expansion or contraction of plant capacity).
5. Availability of raw materials, purchased components, and labor.
6. The effect of the length of the processing time.
7. Economical lots or runs.
8. Timing of production throughout the budget period.

The approach used by a particular firm should depend upon its size and, more importantly, the characteristics of its manufacturing processes.

This chapter focuses on two rather complex issues—planning and controlling inventories, and planning and controlling production. It is outside the scope of this book to present or illustrate the many approaches that have been discussed in books devoted entirely to these problems. Those approaches vary from crude rule-of-thumb methods to very sophisticated approaches involving operations research, linear programming, other mathematical models, and computer techniques.[2] Thus, the remainder of this chapter will discuss some of the principal budgetary issues posed by these problems.

TIME DIMENSIONS OF PRODUCTION PLANNING

Planned levels of production are important from long-range and short-range points of view. In developing a long-range plan (say, five years in the future), broad estimates of production levels are necessary to project plant capacity requirements (involving capital additions), factory cost structures, manpower requirements, and cash flow. In long-range planning, only major increases or decreases in inventories need be taken into account.

Development of the tactical short-range profit plan requires an essentially different approach in view of the need for greater precision and detail. The short-range production plan should be in harmony with the time dimensions utilized in the short-range profit plan. Thus, the common pattern should be an annual production plan divided by months or quarters. To the fullest extent possible the production budget also should be detailed by product (units).

DEVELOPING THE PRODUCTION PLAN

The production executives must translate quantities called for in the sales budget into unit production requirements for the budget period for each product while considering management inventory policies. For example, assume that the inventory policies have been determined and that they spec-

---

[2] John F. Magee and David M. Boodman, *Production Planning and Inventory Control*, 2nd ed. (New York: McGraw-Hill Book Co., Inc.); Elwood S. Buffa, *Production-Inventory Systems, Planning and Control* (Homewood, Ill.: Richard D. Irwin, Inc., 1968); Franklin G. Moore and Ronald Jablonski, *Production Control*, 3rd ed. (New York: McGraw-Hill Book Co., Inc., 1969).

ify an ending inventory of finished goods of 1,500 units. The annual production requirements for the Baker Manufacturing Company for Product K may be computed as follows:

	UNITS OF PRODUCT K
Required for sales (from sales plan)	14,200
Add desired final inventory level of finished goods (per management policy)	1,500
Total required	15,700
Less beginning inventory of finished goods	2,000
Planned production for year	13,700

Because the production plan is developed prior to the end of the current year, the beginning inventory for the budget period has to be estimated. The estimate is based on the status of the inventory at the date the budget is being prepared and is adjusted for planned operations for the balance of the current year. Normally, there will be little difficulty in estimating this inventory with reasonable accuracy.

The budgeted production by product having been developed for the budget period, the next problem is one of prorating this production by interim periods during the year (item eight in the previous section). Prior to discussing this basic problem, we will focus on the major factors to be considered in making the proration; specifically, we must consider the listed items two through seven since it is the responsibility of the manufacturing executives to bring all these factors into optimum balance (see list, p. 185).

Interim production must be planned so as to: (1) have sufficient goods to meet interim sales requirements; (2) keep interim inventory levels within reasonable limits; and (3) manufacture the goods as economically as possible. These three objectives may not be in complete harmony. For example, assuming seasonal sales, it is possible to maintain a stable production level only if inventories are allowed to fluctuate inversely with sales. On the other hand, a stable inventory level is possible only if production is allowed to fluctuate directly with sales. From the point of view of economical operations, it is generally desirable to keep both inventories and production stable, a situation that is obviously impossible given seasonal sales. Thus the production plan should represent the optimum balance between sales, essential inventory levels, and stable production levels.

To illustrate the problem of achieving an optimum balance among planned sales, planned inventory policies, and planned production, we will continue the above illustration for the Baker Manufacturing Company. Assume that the marketing plan specifies the following:

	SALES PLAN (UNITS)		SALES PLAN (UNITS)
January	1,500	July	700
February	1,600	August	600
March	1,600	September	900
April	1,400	October	1,100
May	1,200	November	1,200
June	1,000	December	1,400
		Annual Total	14,200

Assume the following additional budget data:

1. Inventory at beginning of year (January 1), 2,000 units.
2. Inventory planned for end of budget year (December 31), 1,500 units.

Query. How should the annual production volume of the 13,700 units be planned or scheduled throughout the year? Note the problem of reducing inventory by 500 units.

With a highly seasonal sales volume planned, one of three basic patterns of production-inventory levels may be budgeted:

1. Give precedence to production stability. Establish an inflexible production policy (such as a stable level throughout the year) and thereby cause inventory to fluctuate *inversely* with the seasonal sales pattern. This alternative is shown in Illustration 17 as Proposal A and graphed in Illustration 18.
2. Give precedence to inventory stability. Establish an inflexible inventory policy (such as a stable level throughout the year) and thereby cause production levels to fluctuate directly with the seasonal sales pattern. This alternative is shown in Illustration 17 as Proposal B and graphed in Illustration 19.
3. Give neither inventory nor production precedence. Establish inventory and production policies with due consideration to the several factors discussed in the subsequent sections of this chapter so that reasonable flexibility is allowed in both inventory and production. In other words, try to develop the optimum balance (in terms of the effect on profits) among sales, inventory, and production. One possible alternative is shown in Illustration 17 as Proposal C and graphed in Illustration 20. In this case, it is assumed that the management specified the following policies: (1) production should not vary more than 15 percent above or below the yearly average, (2) observe a maximum inventory of

ILLUSTRATION 17. Production and Finished Goods Inventory Budgets

PROPOSAL A—Policy, Stable Production Level

	Year.	Jan.	Feb.	Mar.	Apr.	May	June	July	Aug.	Sept.	Oct.	Nov.	Dec.
Planned sales	14,200	1,500	1,600	1,600	1,400	1,200	1,000	700	600	900	1,100	1,200	1,400
Add—final inventory	1,500	1,700	1,300	900	600	500	600	1,000	1,500	1,700	1,700	1,700	1,500
Total	15,700	3,200	2,900	2,500	2,000	1,700	1,600	1,700	2,100	2,600	2,800	2,900	2,900
Less initial inventory	2,000	2,000	1,700	1,300	900	600	500	600	1,000	1,500	1,700	1,700	1,700
Planned production	13,700	1,200	1,200	1,200	1,100	1,100	1,100	1,100	1,100	1,100	1,100	1,200	1,200

PROPOSAL B—Policy, Stable Inventory Level

	Year.	Jan.	Feb.	Mar.	Apr.	May	June	July	Aug.	Sept.	Oct.	Nov.	Dec.
Planned sales	14,200	1,500	1,600	1,600	1,400	1,200	1,000	700	600	900	1,100	1,200	1,400
Add—final inventory	1,500	1,900	1,800	1,700	1,600	1,500	1,500	1,500	1,500	1,500	1,500	1,500	1,500
Total	15,700	3,400	3,400	3,300	3,000	2,700	2,500	2,200	2,100	2,400	2,600	2,600	2,900
Less initial inventory	2,000	2,000	1,900	1,800	1,700	1,600	1,500	1,500	1,500	1,500	1,500	1,500	1,500
Planned production	13,700	1,400	1,500	1,500	1,300	1,100	1,000	700	600	900	1,100	1,200	1,400

PROPOSAL C—Policy, Flexible Production and Inventory Levels

	Year.	Jan.	Feb.	Mar.	Apr.	May	June	July	Aug.	Sept.	Oct.	Nov.	Dec.
Planned sales	14,200	1,500	1,600	1,600	1,400	1,200	1,000	700	600	900	1,100	1,200	1,400
Add—final inventory	1,500	1,700	1,300	1,100	1,100	1,300	1,500	1,500	1,600	1,600	1,700	1,700	1,500
Total	15,700	3,200	2,900	2,700	2,500	2,500	2,500	2,200	2,200	2,500	2,800	2,900	2,900
Less initial inventory	2,000	2,000	1,700	1,300	1,100	1,100	1,300	1,500	1,500	1,600	1,600	1,700	1,700
Planned production	13,700	1,200	1,200	1,400	1,400	1,400	1,200	700	700	900	1,200	1,200	1,200

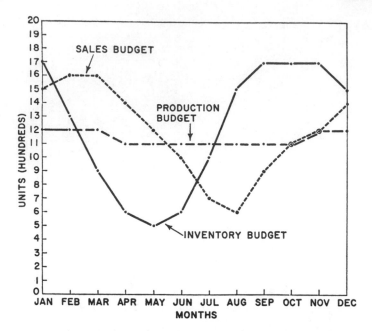

ILLUSTRATION 18.   Sales, Production, and Inventory
Budgets—Proposal A—Policy, Stable Production Level

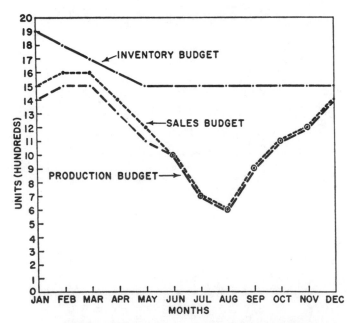

ILLUSTRATION 19.   Sales, Production, and Inventory
Budgets—Proposal B—Policy, Stable Inventory Level

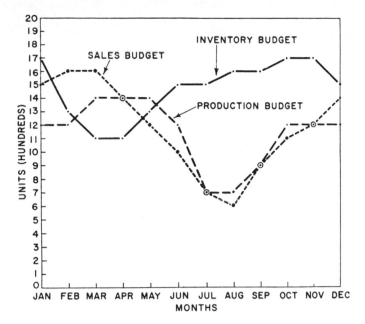

ILLUSTRATION 20. Sales, Production, and Inventory Budgets—Proposal C, Policy, Flexible Production and Inventory Levels

1,600 and a minimum inventory of 1,400 units, and (3) plan for vacations during July–September

In Illustration 17 there are two principal factors that complicate production timing: (1) highly seasonal sales and (2) a 25 percent reduction during the year in physical inventory. Proposal A causes the inventory to fluctuate from a low of 500 units to a high of 1,700 units and provides a relatively stable production level. On the other hand, Proposal B causes a stable inventory level of 1,500 units. Proposal B calls for an immediate reduction to a standard inventory level of 1,500 units; however, this procedure causes production to fluctuate with sales from a low of 600 units to a high of 1,500 units. Considering both inventory and production policies as stated, and the additional factor of vacations during July, August, and the first part of September, a workable balance is suggested in Proposal C, although management policies need to be slightly altered.

It is obvious from this simplified illustration that careful analysis is necessary to achieve the optimum balance between sales, production, and inventory. Graphs represent one means of analyzing and presenting the related aspects of the problem. In view of the significance and complexity of these types of problems, sophisticated approaches utilizing mathematical models, linear programming, and computers are especially useful.

SETTING INVENTORY POLICIES

In most businesses, inventories represent a relatively high investment and may exert significant influence on the major functions of the enterprise. Each function tends to generate different, and frequently inconsistent, inventory demands, such as:

> Sales—large inventories of finished goods are needed to meet market needs readily.
>
> Production—large inventories of raw materials are needed to assure availability for manufacturing activities, and a flexible inventory policy with respect to finished goods is needed to facilitate the attainment of stable production levels.
>
> Purchasing—large purchases minimize unit cost and overall purchasing expenses; therefore, a flexible inventory policy for raw materials is desirable.
>
> Finance—low inventory levels minimize investment requirements (cash) and reduce inventory carrying costs (storage, obsolescence, risks, and others).

The objectives of inventory policies should be (1) to plan the optimum level of inventory investment, and (2) through control, to maintain as near as feasible these optimum levels. Inventory levels must be maintained between two extremes: an excessive level causing unbearable carrying costs, risks, and investment, and an inadequate level resulting in failure to meet sales and production demands promptly (high stockout cost). An important consideration when planning and controlling inventories is that they serve to absorb the difference in stock between sales volume and production (or purchase) levels.

Management often neglects inventory planning and control. The neglect frequently results in a critical shortage of goods, excess inventory costs, and a consequent failure to meet sales delivery dates, or conversely, often large amounts of cash become tied up in excessive inventories. As a result, to compensate for this excess, management suddenly may have to reduce selling prices of the goods to an uneconomic level. This becomes necessary in order to liquidate the inventory rapidly to generate cash to meet immediate cash demands by creditors. Often this action also is accompanied by drastic reduction in production and other operational levels.

In an actual case, a firm applied for a sizable bank loan to obtain cash for current operations. The bank's investigations revealed that the company had no inventory control policies. The management had said that "no one in the firm would allow any appreciable overstocking." Yet an analysis of average withdrawals from inventory showed significant overstocking on many items; in fact, there was about an eighteen years' supply of several slow-moving items. With respect to these items, the manufacturing department, thinking only of the trouble and cost of setup time, had produced large quantities without considering the relative turnover of the items. It was simply a case of not having definite policies and controls on inventories.

The problem extends to inventories of supplies, raw materials, work in process, and finished goods. In developing production requirements, consideration must be given to the finished goods and work in process inventories. It is impossible to develop a satisfactory production program without definite inventory policies, and one of the principal advantages of production budgeting is that it forces advance consideration of the inventory problem.

Inventory policies should include (1) the establishment of inventory standards, such as maximum and minimum levels or turnovers, and (2) the application of techniques and methods that will assure conformity to selected inventory standards. Budgeting requires that inventory standards be established and provides for reporting variations of actual inventory levels from standard levels from month to month.

In determining inventory policies for finished goods, management should consider these important factors:

1. Quantities needed to meet sales requirements. Solving this problem entails consideration of the sales budget and the related seasonality of demand. The sales department executives should be directly involved in this consideration.
2. Perishability of items.
3. Length of the production period.
4. Storage facilities.
5. Adequacy of capital to finance inventory production some time in advance of sales.
6. Cost of holding the inventory. There are frequently numerous and significant costs connected with stocking large quantities of goods. The principal holding costs involved are labor, insurance, taxes, rents, depreciation, transportation, and extra handling.
7. Protection against raw material shortages.
8. Protection against labor shortages.
9. Protection against price increases.
10. Risks involved in inventory:
    a. Price declines.
    b. Obsolescence of stock.
    c. Casualty loss and theft.
    d. Lack of demand.

Some of these factors counteract one another; the point is that a good inventory policy must reflect an optimum cost balance between these factors. The author of a cost accounting text succinctly stated the problem as follows:[3]

Inventories comprise two types of associated costs: those of carrying and those of not carrying enough. The optimum solution minimizes the *total* of these two classes of costs:

COST OF CARRYING PLUS	COSTS OF NOT CARRYING ENOUGH
1. Risk of obsolescence.	1. Foregone quantity discounts.*
2. Desired rate of return on investment.*	2. Disruptions of production with extra costs of expediting, overtime, setups, hiring, and training.
3. Handling and transfer.	3. Contribution margins on lost sales.*
4. Space for storage.	4. Extra costs of uneconomic production runs.
5. Personal property taxes.	5. Loss of customer goodwill.*
6. Insurance.	6. Extra purchasing and transportation costs.
7. Clerical costs.	7. Foregone fortuitous purchases.*

*Costs that often do not explicitly appear on formal accounting records.

It is desirable to express the inventory policies relative to finished goods in as precise a manner as possible. To state inventory policy as "our plans are to keep inventory at the minimum," is obviously inadequate. In contrast, inventory standards should be expressed—*by product or by lines*—in terms such as the following:

METHOD	EXAMPLE OF POLICY EXPRESSION
1. Months' supply	For Product X—Three months' supply based on moving three months average of budgeted requirements. For Product Y—Two months' supply based on average annual issues budgeted for the year.
2. Maximum limit	For Product X—Inventory not to exceed 5,000 units.
3. Maximum and minimum limits	For Product X—Maximum 5,000 units; minimum 3,000 units.
4. Specific amount	For Product X—Double the sales of the past month. For Product Y—Equal to the sales budgeted for the following month.
5. Inventory turnover rates	For Product X—Turnover rate to be six annualized (six turnovers per year). For Product Y—Turnover rate to be two on a monthly basis (two turnovers per month).

[3] Charles T. Horngren, *Cost Accounting, A Managerial Emphasis,* 3rd ed. (Englewood Cliffs, N.J.: Prentice-Hall, Inc., 1972), p. 540.

More sophisticated approaches have been developed for computer application; experimentation along these lines is continuing. The method of developing and expressing a specific inventory policy must vary with the characteristics of each company and the nature of the inventory problems.

To illustrate some further inventory policy expressions, several simplified examples are presented in the next few paragraphs.

Assume the sales budget calls for 1,200,000 units of product K. Assume further that after careful consideration of the significant factors affecting inventory requirements, management has specified a standard inventory level of two months' supply based on an annual average. The two months' supply would be 200,000 units (1,200,000 $\times$ 2/12). Although simple and direct, such a policy would be rigid; consequently, it might be quite unrealistic if sales are highly seasonal.

To illustrate a less rigid approach, assume the inventory policy to be a two months' supply for the beginning inventory based on a three-month moving average of issues. This approach provides a fluctuating inventory level consistent with seasonal sales demands as is demonstrated below:

		BUDGETED UNITS TO BE SOLD	THREE MONTHS' MOVING AVERAGE	BEGINNING INVENTORY (TWO MONTHS' SUPPLY)
December (actual preceding year)		82,000		
January	budget year	85,000	85,667	171,334
February	budget year	90,000	90,000	180,000
March	budget year	95,000		
Etc.	budget year			

Some firms employ a standard inventory turnover as a basis for establishing inventory levels. Inventory turnover is computed by dividing units withdrawn by units in inventory. To illustrate the procedure, assume that 150,000 units of a certain product were budgeted to be sold during the year and that the average inventory on hand during the year was budgeted at 50,000. The inventory turnover would be computed as follows:

$$\frac{150{,}000}{50{,}000} = 3 \text{ turnovers during the year.}$$

Let us assume further that management decided that a turnover of four annualized (that is, a three months' supply) is a desirable standard for the budget year for this particular product. Assuming the sales budget for the first three months was as indicated in column one below, a standard inventory in units related to sales trend could be readily computed as illustrated. It will be noted that the inventory level parallels the variation in sales volume.

	BUDGETED SALES (UNITS)	COMPUTATION	INDICATED INITIAL INVENTORY (UNITS)
January	12,000	(× 12 ÷ 4)	36,000
February	11,000	"	33,000
March	14,500	"	43,500

If the standard turnover figure is applied to total annual sales rather than to monthly sales, a stable inventory standard results.

Regardless of the approach used in specifying inventory standards, it is essential that: (1) definite inventory policies be established and kept current; (2) responsibility for inventory planning and control be assigned to specified individuals; (3) procedures be developed for accounting for inventories; and (4) a reporting system be designed to inform management of the status of inventory control.

SETTING PRODUCTION POLICIES

Seasonal sales are typical in most companies; yet production efficiency usually is enhanced by relatively stable production levels. In many companies where sales of the primary product are seasonal, production levels have been stabilized by developing new products that can be stored or that have opposite seasonal patterns. The inventory provides a rather tempting method of leveling production, yet as previously pointed out, there are certain pitfalls to be considered. Stabilization of production is desirable for a number of compelling reasons and generally results in significant reductions of costs and improvements in operations. The advantages or relatively stable production levels may be outlined as follows:

1. Stability of employment, resulting in:
    a. Improved morale and hence greater worker efficiency.
    b. Less labor turnover.
    c. Attraction of better workers.
    d. Reduction of expense for training new workers.
2. Economies in purchasing raw materials as a result of:
    a. Availability.
    b. Volume discounts.
    c. Simplified storage problems.
    d. Smaller capital requirements.
    e. Reduced inventory risk.
3. Better utilization of plant facilities, which tends to:
    a. Reduce the capacity required to meet peak seasons.
    b. Avoid idle capacity.

Undoubtedly the greatest hazard of significant ups and downs in production is the effect on personnel. Periodic layoffs and subsequent efforts to hire employees destroys morale, discourages the ambitious employee, and tends to attract unstable employees. One of the objectives of modern management should be to offer job security. The introduction of profit planning and control, with the consequent *planning of production and inventories*, has changed the pattern of operations in many companies.

ADEQUACY OF MANUFACTURING FACILITIES

Planning the production program requires consideration of the adequacy of manufacturing facilities. There must be sufficient capacity to produce the planned total volume of goods and to meet the peak loads called for in the detailed production budget. The production capabilities of individual departments, processes, and machines must be assessed and carefully planned and coordinated in the production budget so as to avoid production bottlenecks and idle capacity.

Plant and department capacities should be analyzed by the production executives in terms of potential or maximum plant capacity and normal or practical capacity. *Maximum capacity* may be thought of as the "theoretical" engineering capacity, whereas *practical capacity* is somewhat less, representing the level at which the plant or department can operate most efficiently. Practical capacity is usually thought to be about 85 to 90 percent of maximum capacity. Idle or excess plant capacity is the difference between the actual operating rate of activity and practical capacity. *Breakeven capacity* is the rate of activity at which the sales value of the goods produced is equal to the cost of producing and selling those goods. It is important that top management be informed on maximum capacity, practical capacity, operating capacity, and breakeven capacity of the plant. Usually capacities are expressed as percentages of maximum capacity.

Plant and department capacities may be expressed in one of several ways. Of course, if there is only one product or several almost identical products, capacity should be expressed in physical units of output. In other circumstances, capacity must be measured in terms of some common measure of output, such as direct labor hours, machine hours, dollar sales of goods produced, dollar cost of goods produced, total tonnage, or some other measure of output.

Production budgeting is directly related to the capital additions budget with respect to (1) plant additions required, (2) extraordinary repairs and rearrangements, and (3) retirement or disposal of excess plant capacity. If plant equipment appears to be inadequate, management must make plans to obtain the additional capacity or revise the production and sales requirements. In planning capital additions, management must keep in mind the time that is required to obtain and ready the additions for production. There is also the related problem of financing. Care must be exercised lest expensive plant additions are planned to meet short-term peak demands only to remain idle for considerable periods of time thereafter. The capital additions budget is discussed in a subsequent chapter.

AVAILABILITY OF RAW MATERIALS AND LABOR

In some cases, the production program may be influenced by the availability of the required raw materials and labor. This situation is especially prevalent during periods of scarcity. Raw material availability may also be affected by such factors as prices, perishability, economies in purchasing, quality considerations, and quantities available. For example, canning plants obviously have to schedule production when the raw materials are in season. Even in cases where the raw materials can be stored, there is the problem of weighing the advantages of stable production against the problems and costs incident to warehousing large inventories. The availability of skilled labor and the time required to train workers are factors that may affect production planning.

LENGTH OF THE PRODUCTION PERIOD

The production budget illustrated on page 187 indicates the *units to be completed* to meet the sales plan and inventory requirements. A direct conversion from the sales budget to the production budget, as illustrated there, assumes that the manufacturing time is relatively short. In situations where production requires several weeks or months, it is necessary to prepare additional plans indicating the timing of the *units to be started*. For example, if processing requires approximately four months, the plan of units to be started must be moved forward at least four months ahead of the dates shown in the production budget for *units to be completed*. In addition, if the product consists of many parts that are manufactured by the firm, it is necessary to prepare a separate *parts production budget*, indicating the timing of (1) parts to be completed and (2) parts to be started. The schedules indicating *starting* dates provide essential data for the *purchasing department* in planning raw materials purchases.

Another factor influencing the production planning is the work in process inventory. If there is no significant fluctuation planned in this inventory during the year, obviously there is no significant effect on production; hence, inventory fluctuation can be ignored in production planning. However, should there be a significant change planned in the work in process inventory, this change must be taken into account in the planning. There are two approaches to the problem, depending on the circumstances. In cases where the processing time is short, a change in work in process inventory can be incorporated into the usual production budget format along the following lines:

Units required for sales	100,000
Add final inventory of finished goods	20,000
Total	120,000
Less initial inventory of finished goods	15,000
Units to be completed for finished goods	105,000
Add *equivalent units* in final work in process inventory*	5,000
Total	110,000
Less *equivalent units* in initial work in process inventory	6,000
Equivalent units to be manufactured	104,000

*Equivalent units represent the units produced, both completed and partially completed, in a given period. For example, if a department having no beginning inventory completed 1,000 units and had on hand an ending inventory of 200 units estimated to be one-half completed, the equivalent units produced would be [1,000 + (200 × 1/2)] = 1,100.

Where the manufacturing time is long enough to require the preparation of schedules of units to be started in addition to schedules of units to be completed, the adjustment for changes in work in process inventories can be made in these schedules rather than in the schedule of units to be completed, as illustrated above. The reasons for this procedure are obvious. In situations where processing time is not too long, it may be more practical to adjust production starting times to delivery times through flexibility in the work in process and finished goods inventories. The principal difficulty involved in using inventories for this purpose is that a large amount of working capital could inadvertently become tied up in such inventories.

THE PRODUCTION BUDGET AS A PLANNING, COORDINATING, AND CONTROL TOOL

The production budget contributes to planning, coordination, and control. The fact that a detailed production plan is developed, based on a realistic sales plan, means that several executives have given thought and effort to the production planning function and related problems. Developing a detailed production budget requires, in addition to production plans, specific planning with respect to material requirements, labor requirements, plant capacity, capital additions, and inventory policies. Production planning tends to divulge weaknesses and sources of potential trouble that can then be avoided by timely executive action.

Even more significant perhaps is the coordination that can result from effective production planning. The production plan must be coordinated with plans related to financing, capital additions, product development, and sales. A critical problem in all manufacturing situations comprises procedures established to coordinate effectively the operations of the sales and production departments. The sales executive must be as acutely aware of production problems as the production executive is aware of sales developments. It may be desirable to revise the sales plan to emphasize those products that the factory can readily and efficiently produce. The translation of sales demands into production effort can be quite complex and, if not resolved on a sound basis, may be the cause of considerable inefficiency in the firm. Such inefficiencies can generally be attributed to a lack of timely planning and to an indefinite assignment of responsibilities.

The production plan as finally approved should be viewed as a master production plan to be executed by the producing department. It should not be used inflexibly but rather as a guide to the actual, detailed production planning and scheduling carried on by the production department on a day-to-day or week-to-week basis. It should not be viewed ordinarily as an order to proceed with production; actual production should be ordered by the production planning and scheduling department on a current basis that reflects the actual sales trends as they evolve during the period. The production plan may be considered the framework within which current production orders are issued. Variations in actual sales and in other conditions call for departures from the original production plan.

The production budget is the primary basis for planning raw material requirements, labor needs, capital additions, factory cash requirements, and factory costs. Therefore, the production plan becomes the foundation for factory planning in general. It gives the factory executives something tangible upon which to base operational decisions.

An adequate production control system is essential to managerial control of costs, quality, and quantities. The principal procedures involved in production control are:

1. Materials control.
2. Process analysis.
3. Routing production.
4. Scheduling production.
5. Dispatching production.
6. Follow-up.

In addition to daily and weekly controls of production volume and the levels of the finished goods inventory, the status of these two factors should be reported on the *monthly performance report* wherein actual results are compared with plans and standards.

In summary, the production plan serves as an important tool of planning, coordination, and control. In expressing the manufacturing volume as a planning tool, it establishes the foundation for planning all aspects of factory operations: raw materials needs; factory labor needs; supervisory needs; factory overhead; plant capacity; factory service activities; and others. The coordination between sales plans, inventory policies, and production requirements comes into focus and is resolved in the production plan. It also is an important factor in overall coordination of such functional activities as cash flow, financing, production research and development, engineering, and capital additions. It establishes the basis for control of production, inventories, production costs, and manpower in the factory.

In planning and controlling production (and the related inventories), linear programming and inventory models have a broad application, which should be fully integrated with a comprehensive profit planning and control program. Some of these mathematical approaches are relatively simple— not requiring computer facilities—whereas others are highly sophisticated involving complex mathematical models and require a wide range of computer capability. The inventory models quantify the effects of relevant variables underlying policy decisions. They may be designed for cost minimization or other specified managerial objectives. Production models likewise vary from relatively simple to highly sophisticated mathematical and computer approaches. Models have been developed for resolving such production problems as: attaining optimum balance in production between sales and inventories; determination of economic production runs; allocation of productive capacity to products, product mix, and cost minimization in the manufacturing processes. Obviously, this book cannot treat these in a technical way; therefore, the reader is referred to other sources for more detailed discussion of them.

THE PRODUCTION PLAN ILLUSTRATED

It is impracticable to illustrate herein all the factors affecting the production budget. It is assumed that Superior Manufacturing Company inventory policy calls for a *three months' supply* of finished goods and that production will be kept essentially stable. Manufacturing conditions are such that variations of approximately 15 percent in production levels are possible without seriously affecting the number of permanent employees.

The manufacturing executive, in consultation with the other manufacturing managers and, in particular, with the production manager, prepared the production plan to meet the sales requirement. This production plan and the resulting inventory plans were submitted to the executive committee and tentatively approved by the president. The annual production plan for Superior Manufacturing Company was shown in Chapter 4 (Schedule 2).

The detailed production plan, by product, for Superior Manufacturing Company (Schedule 22) is shown below. Observe that production is budgeted by month for the first quarter and by quarter for the remainder of the year as was illustrated for the sales plan.

SCHEDULE 22. Superior Manufacturing Company
Production Plan (Detailed)
By Product, by Time
For the Year Ending December 31, 1977

REF.	REQUIRED FOR SALES 21	ADD FINAL INVENTORY OF FINISHED GOODS	TOTAL REQUIRED	LESS INITIAL INVENTORY OF FINISHED GOODS	UNITS TO BE COMPLETED
Product X					
January	85,000	225,000	310,000	240,000	70,000
February	90,000	215,000	305,000	225,000	80,000
March	95,000	200,000	295,000	215,000	80,000
Total 1st Quarter	270,000	200,000	470,000	240,000	230,000
2nd Quarter	260,000	180,000	440,000	200,000	240,000
3rd Quarter	190,000	220,000	410,000	180,000	230,000
4th Quarter	280,000	200,000	480,000	220,000	260,000
Total	1,000,000	200,000	1,200,000	240,000	960,000
Product Y					
January	34,000	100,000	134,000	100,000	34,000
February	41,000	95,000	136,000	100,000	36,000
March	45,000	88,000	133,000	95,000	38,000
Total 1st Quarter	120,000	88,000	208,000	100,000	108,000
2nd Quarter	135,000	93,000	228,000	88,000	140,000
3rd Quarter	95,000	125,000	220,000	93,000	127,000
4th Quarter	150,000	120,000	270,000	125,000	145,000
Total	500,000	120,000	620,000	100,000	520,000

(See Sch. 2 for Summary.)

In Schedule 22 note that the work in process inventory has been ignored. This omission was possible because it was assumed that this inventory level will remain unchanged during the budget year. Assume work in process inventories to be: Product X None; Product Y 10,000 units throughout the year.

In view of the fact that the finished goods inventory, *in units*, is developed concurrently with the production plan, it is appropriate at this time to prepare a budget of finished goods inventories similar to that illustrated in Schedule 23. Observe that provision is made for unit costs and total costs that can be entered later when the budgeted cost of manufacturing is determined. (See Schedule 63, Chapter 12.)

SCHEDULE 23.   Superior Manufacturing Company
Finished Goods Inventory Budget
For the Year Ending December 31, 1977

	TOTAL COST	PRODUCT X			PRODUCT Y		
1972: REF.	ALL PRODUCTS	UNITS	UNIT COST	TOTAL COST	UNITS	UNIT COST	TOTAL COST
January 1	$	240,000	$	$	100,000	$	$
January 31		225,000			100,000		
February 29		215,000			95,000		
March 31		200,000			88,000		
End of 2nd Qtr.		180,000			93,000		
End of 3rd Qtr.		220,000			125,000		
End of 4th Qtr.		200,000			120,000		

DISCUSSION QUESTIONS

1.   Define the production budget, and explain why it is a necessary step in developing the profit plan.

2.   What other budgets are closely related to the production budget?

3.   Who should be responsible for development of the production plan? Explain.

4.   What is the relationship of the work in process and finished goods inventories to the production plan?

5.   What is the central problem in developing the production plan?

6.   What is meant by "inventory policies"? What are the principal issues to be considered in developing realistic inventory policies as they affect the production plan?

7.   Why is it generally desirable to maintain a stable production level?

8.   In what ways are manufacturing facilities related to the production plan?

9.   Discuss the relationship between the production budget and the availability of raw materials and labor.

10.   What basis should be used in determining the detailed breakdown (disaggregation) of the production plan?

11.   Outline the planning, coordination, and control aspects of the production plan.

CASE 6-1
Corona Manufacturers

Corona Manufacturers has been in operation for approximately twenty years; it manufactures two primary products that are distributed in five geographical sales regions covering the entire United States. Manufacturing operations are conducted in three producing departments and there are two service departments in the factory. Top management is represented by the chief exectutive officer, an executive vice president, and vice presidents for each function—sales, manufacturing, and finance. The company employs approximately two hundred individuals, and annual sales last year were approximately $30 million.

In manufacturing the two products, three raw materials are used; the products are processed through each of the producing departments. Product A requires a relatively high proportion of direct labor cost and a lower proportion of raw material cost; in contrast, Product B requires a high number of machine hours and large amounts of raw materials. Production time for Product A is approximately twice that for Product B. Since raw materials are relatively cheap and there is high machine utilization, Product B is less costly per unit and more profitable per unit than Product A. However, the sales mix ratio is approximately three to one in favor of Product A. The two products are not substitutable since they generally are purchased by different customers and are used for different purposes.

Although the company has been reasonably successful and has grown steadily, profits and return on investment for the last three years have leveled off. Consequently, and as a result of the recent retirement of some long-term managers (including the chief executive officer), changes in certain management approaches have been undertaken during the past year. The new chief executive officer had been the financial vice president and had eight years experience with the company. The changes involved manufacturing operations, and approaches in hiring and training personnel. The new chief executive formed an executive committee comprised of himself and all the vice presidents (a first for the company). In addition, during the past year it was decided to implement a profit planning and control program that includes a five-year long-range plan and a one-year short-range profit plan. The first long-range plan has been completed, and the executives are now involved in establishing procedures for developing the short-range profit plan. The long-range plan is disaggregated for each year for the five-year span. It has been decided that the annual profit plan will be developed by quarter with the first quarter detailed by month; subsequent quarters will be detailed prior to the beginning of each quarter. Consistent with decisions already made, the marketing executive has completed a sales plan, and it has been tentatively approved by the executive committee. The sales plan encompasses the promotion plan, a distribution plan, and a marketing plan; the latter specifies the planned quantities and dollars of revenue by product.

The manufacturing executive currently (1) is developing approaches to set up the production plan and (2) subsequently will develop the production plan for inclusion in the annual profit plan.

Required:

You are requested to respond to the following factors being considered by the manufacturing executive.

a. Classifications of planned results that should be incorporated in the annual production plan.
b. Responsibilities for developing the annual production plan including the necessary procedures.
c. Underlying data and basic policies essential for developing the annual production plan.
d. Use of the completed production plan.

CASE 6-2
XY Company

XY Company has been engaged in profit planning for several years. The president stated (with justification) that inventory control and production planning in the budget program had not been satisfactory. This had been due primarily to poorly planned production and inventory budgets.

Accordingly, you are directed to make a detailed analysis and recommendation on the matter for the 19B profit plan currently in preparation. Your analysis and recommendations are to be presented to the executive committee.

Despite seasonality, the Sales department has been successful in developing a realistic sales plan on a monthly basis for each year. The following data are available for the profit plan currently being developed:

1. From the sales plan for 19B:

	UNITS		UNITS		UNITS
January	36,000	May	32,000	September	26,000
February	38,000	June	26,000	October	30,000
March	38,000	July	22,000	November	36,000
April	36,000	August	20,000	December	40,000

2. The January 1, 19B finished goods inventory is estimated at 96,000 units.
3. Work in process inventory will remain constant.
4. Actual annual sales for 19A, including the December estimate, were 350,000 units.
5. Average finished goods inventory for 19A was 70,000 units.

Required:

a. Prepare the *annual* production budget, assuming the policy of management is to budget the finished goods final inventory at a standard amount based on the 19A historical sales to inventory turnover ratio.
b. Prepare a table showing monthly sales, production and inventory levels assuming (1) a stable inventory, (2) stable production, and (3) *your* recommended inventory-production levels. In developing your recommendations assume the following policies have been established:

   a. The president has established a policy that a maximum inventory of 85,000 units and a minimum of 75,000 units should be observed except in unusual circumstances.

   b. A stable level of production is highly desirable, except that during vacation season (July and August) production can be reduced by 25 percent; also, a 7.5 percent variation in production is acceptable.

  c. What are the primary problems facing the company in planning production? What broad recommendations would you make?

CASE 6-3

Thomas Manufacturing Company

Thomas Manufacturing Company produces soil pipe, sewer pipe, fittings, joints, and numerous related items in many sizes and of several different materials. Most of the finished goods are stored outside between date of completion and date of shipment to customers.

Production problems are critical, particularly in view of high setup costs. In order to produce soil pipe, for example, considerable rearrangement in the factory is necessary and special forms must be taken out of storage and prepared for use. As a result of the high setup costs big runs are usually made in order to keep unit costs within reason.

Inventory storage costs are low (roughly estimated by the management to be about $.10 per unit per year), and deterioration is not a problem. Obsolescence is considered to be a relatively minor factor in terms of two or three years. The company finances the inventory locally.

Other than fixed factory overhead, production costs for material and labor tend to vary directly with the number of units produced.

The company has just started a budget program. A tentative sales plan has just been developed as shown on Exhibit 1. Other pertinent data available are:

		PROJECTED FOR 19E		
	INVENTORY ON HAND JAN. 1, 19E (UNITS)	AVERAGE UNIT COST[a]	AVERAGE (LOT) PRODUCTION[b] (UNITS)	AVERAGE SETUP COST	AVERAGE PRODUCTION AND SETUP TIME PER LOT (DAYS)[c]
Soil pipe	21,000	$8.50	30,000	$15,000	70
Sewer pipe	34,000	6.00	40,000	20,000	90
Fittings	22,000	1.50	25,000	10,000	70
Joints	4,000	4.50	10,000	8,000	20
Etc.					

[a] Includes setup costs based on average (lot) production.
[b] Estimated to be the economic production lot.
[c] Based on 250 working days per year.

EXHIBIT 1   Thomas Manufacturing Company

Sales Data and Budget for 19E

	19A	19B	19C	1ST JAN.	FEB.	MAR.	2ND	3RD	4TH
Soil pipe									
Actual (19D)	11,000	12,000	15,000	1,500	1,200	1,000	3,000	4,000	4,500
Budget, next year (19E)				1,500	1,500	1,200	3,500	4,000	4,500
Sewer pipe									
Actual (19D)	8,000	8,000	9,000	1,000	1,100	1,100	4,000	2,500	1,500
Budget, next year (19E)				1,200	1,200	1,200	4,800	3,000	1,500
Fittings									
Actual (19D)	15,000	16,000	23,000	2,400	2,200	2,000	6,500	6,500	6,000
Budget, next year (19E)				2,600	2,600	2,200	7,500	7,000	5,500
Joints									
Actual (19D)	4,000	4,500	4,800	700	700	800	2,200	2,300	1,900
Budget, next year (19E)				800	800	800	2,300	2,400	2,000
Etc.									

The header above the year columns reads: CURRENT YEAR 19D AND BUDGET 19E (spanning 1ST JAN./FEB./MAR., 2ND, 3RD, 4TH).

Required:

1. Evaluate the inventory position on Jan. 1, 19E to determine whether it is excessive.
2. Evaluate the production plans to determine whether planned production is adequate.
3. Evaluate the planned ending inventory position to determine whether it is excessive.
4. Evaluate the overall plans as reflected in your responses to 1, 2, and 3.
5. Indicate relevant approaches and factors that management should consider in resolving their production and inventory planning problems.

CASE 6-4
Lax Metal Works

For some time Lax Metal Works has been experiencing a critical shortage of cash to meet payrolls and to pay for raw materials. During July of the current year (19D) the situation became extremely critical. A request was made to the bank for a $200,000 loan. The company was unable to furnish the bank with an audited financial statement. The bank refused to consider the loan further until a C.P.A. was called in to conduct an examination of the present financial condition of the company and to report to them. The company agreed to these conditions. The C.P.A. developed the data shown below (as well as other pertinent data) concerning the finished goods inventory:

There are unusually high *setup costs* on items E and G. Item C has a relatively long processing period—(twenty-three days). The inventory condition was due to the fact that the *production manager* consistently overproduced on each order received from sales *to save setup costs*. He had no knowledge of any inventory policies or levels; also, the Sales Division maintained no formal record of inventory levels. Most of the items were stored outside in the yard.

ITEM	UNITS ON HAND	CURRENT AVERAGE UNIT COST	NUMBER OF UNITS SOLD 19A	19B	19C
A	12	$18	15	12	8
B	100	9	150	170	180
C	21,000	4	2,000	1,900	1,600
D	6,000	7	8,000	8,000	8,000
E	79,000	5	4,000	4,200	4,500
F	48,000	6	8,000	7,800	7,500
G	34,000	8	2,000	1,800	1,500
H	—	32	100	150	175
I	900	21	1,500	1,700	2,000
J	10,000	10	14,000	16,000	18,000

Required:

a. Estimate the overinvestment in inventory. In the process of examination of the company assume the C.P.A. came to the conclusion that there is no good reason why any item should be stocked in excess of a two years' supply.

b. Set forth your recommendations relative to inventory and production. Explain your recommendations.

CASE 6-5

Producto Company

Producto Company manufactures three principal products. The planning budget is being developed for the coming year. The tentative annual sales plan prepared by the Sales Division showed the following:

PRODUCT	UNITS PROJECTED
1	100,000
2	150,000
3	80,000

Sales are highly seasonal—for example, the sales plan showed the following for Product 1:

Jan.	10,500	July	5,200
Feb.	10,300	Aug.	5,000
Mar.	9,400	Sept.	7,500
Apr.	8,500	Oct.	8,800
May	8,000	Nov.	9,500
June	7,000	Dec.	10,300

The following inventory levels have been tentatively planned:

| | FINISHED GOODS | | WORK IN PROCESS | | | |
| | INITIAL | FINAL | INITIAL | | FINAL | |
PRODUCT			UNITS	PERCENT COMPLETE	UNITS	PERCENT COMPLETE
1	1,000	12,000	0	—	0	—
2	10,000	8,000	2,000	100	2,000	100
3	5,000	5,000	2,000	50	6,000	50

Required:

a. Prepare the annual production budget summary for the company; show each product separately.

b. What policies would you suggest relative to monthly inventory and production levels for the company for Product 1 ? Give support for your recommendations.

c. Prepare a production budget by month for Product 1 in conformance with your recommendations.

CASE 6-6
Staley Company

Staley Company executives presently are trying to establish inventory policies as a part of the development of a budget program. Several alternatives have been discussed concerning inventory levels, among them the moving average method and an average withdrawal method. The sales plan shows the following data for the main product:

DATE	UNITS
December (preceding year)	800,000
January	780,000
February	780,000
March	810,000
April	830,000
May	820,000
June	800,000
July	700,000
August	600,000
September	650,000
October	700,000
November	780,000
December	820,000
January (following year)	810,000

Required:

    a.   Use a three-month moving average to compute the inventory level by month assuming a one and one-half month's supply is specified by the inventory policy.

    b.   Compute the inventory level by month assuming inventory policy requires that average withdrawals for the fourteen periods be determined and that a one and one-half month's average be planned.

    c.   Compute the inventory level by month assuming the inventory policy is to start each month with an inventory equivalent to one-fourth of the sales planned for that month.

    d.   Evaluate each approach.

Planning and Controlling Materials Usage and Purchases

chapter seven

A comprehensive profit planning and control program encompasses a system for planning and controlling the various aspects of materials used in the manufacturing process. Here we have another optimum balance problem similar to the one discussed in the previous chapter; in this case, the *balance* to be planned and controlled is between (1) factory requirements for raw materials, (2) raw material inventory levels, and (3) purchases of raw materials. As soon as the quantities of each product to be manufactured are specified in the production plan, the next step in planning the manufacturing program involves consideration of the various production requirements and costs—direct materials, direct labor, and factory overhead. This chapter focuses on planning and controlling direct material costs.

To assure that right amounts of raw materials will be on hand at the time required and to plan for the costs of such materials, it is essential that the tactical short-term profit plan include (1) detailed budgets specifying quantity and cost of materials required, and (2) a related budget of raw material purchases. Thus, planning raw materials usually requires the following four subbudgets:

1. **Materials Budget.** This budget specifies the planned *quantities* of each raw material required for planned production. It should specify quantities of each raw material, by time, by product, and by using responsibility.

2. Purchases Budget. The materials budget specifies the quantities and timing of each raw material needed; therefore a plan for material purchases must be developed. The purchases budget specifies the estimated *quantities* to be purchased, and the estimated *cost* for each raw material and the required delivery dates.

3. Materials Inventory Budget. This budget reports the planned levels of raw material inventory in terms of *quantities* and *cost*. The difference in units between materials requirements as specified in the *materials budget* (1 above) and the *purchases budget* (2 above) is reflected as increases or decreases in the inventory budget.

4. Cost of Materials Used Budget. This budget reports the estimated *cost* of the materials planned for in the materials budget (1 above). Observe that the materials budget cannot be *costed* until the planned cost of purchases (3 above) is developed.

The four separate subbudgets listed above are directly related; collectively, they may be viewed as the *materials and purchases budget*. In simple situations, the four may well be combined; one and four are frequently combined. In more complex situations, a separation as indicated above is almost essential—especially when the data must be developed sequentially.

In designing each of these materials budgets, two basic objectives are overriding:

1. Control. Raw material costs are subject to direct control at the point of usage; therefore, the related activities and costs should be budgeted in terms of user responsibility, and by short, interim periods.

2. Product Costing. Raw material costs are included in manufacturing costs (product costs); therefore, they must be identified with the cost of finished goods (by product).

Because of these basic objectives, normally the planner must cope with a four-way classification of material costs: by type of raw material; by user responsibility; by interim periods; and by type of finished goods. These multiple classifications tend to complicate the mechanics of budgeting raw materials.

In the paragraphs to follow, we consider separately each of the four subbudgets indicated above. We will reemphasize the basic considerations, techniques, approaches, and decisions discussed in the preceding chapter that related to planning and controlling an optimum balance between (1) sales, (2) inventory levels, and (3) production. In general, the same factors must be considered; the same approaches and techniques are applicable; and essentially the same types of decisions are involved.

THE MATERIALS BUDGET

Materials used in a factory are traditionally classified as *direct* and *indirect*. *Direct* material is generally defined to include all material that constitutes an integral part of the finished product and can be directly identified with (directly traced to) the cost of the finished products. Direct material cost is usually viewed as a *variable* cost—that is, a cost that varies in *proportion* to changes in output or volume. *Iudirect* material is generally defined as material used in the manufacturing process but not directly traceable to each product. A related indirect cost, frequently referred to as factory supplies, consists of such items as grease, lubricating oils, and other maintenance supplies. *The materials budget deals only with quantities (not cost) of direct materials; supplies and indirect materials generally should be included in the manufacturing overhead budget.* In some cases, however, it may be desirable to include certain indirect materials and supplies in the materials budget.

The quantities of each raw material needed for each finished product must be estimated in total for the planning period and specified by *interim periods* (months and quarters) and by user responsibility in the materials budget. The product and interim period breakdown should follow the pattern used in sales and production budgets. Executives of the manufacturing division should be responsible for developing the basic input data for the raw materials budget.

The principal purposes in developing detailed raw material *quantity* requirements to meet planned production are as follows:

1. To provide quantity data for the purchasing department so that raw material *purchases* can be properly planned and controlled.
2. To provide quantity data so that the raw material *costs* of production can be budgeted by product.
3. To establish policy for *inventory levels* for effective planning and control of such levels.
4. To determine *cash requirements* (cash budget) for raw material purchases.
5. To control raw material *usage.*

The basic (estimated) inputs required to develop the direct materials budget are: (1) *volume of output* planned (from the production budget); and (2) *standard usage rates* by type of raw material for each product. Material usage rates are applied to the production data (from the production budget) to develop the materials budget. In many manufacturing situations it is not difficult to determine standard unit usage rates for unit raw materials used in each department per unit of finished product. For example, in the manufacture of such items as furniture, clothing, mechanical equipment, appliances, and liquids such as paint, there are definite and easily determinable quantities of raw material required. Indeed, in many cases precise measurement of the quantities of raw material is essential to the desired quality of the resulting output. Unit usage rates may be derived (1) during initial development of the product, (2) from engineering studies, or (3) from past consumption records and bills of materials.

Where specific unit usage rates cannot be derived along the lines indicated above, determination of raw material requirements may become a critical budget problem.

Two principal indirect approaches to developing usage requirements are available. One indirect approach is to develop some method of estimating total raw material *quantities* required for production through the use of adjusted historical ratios such as the ratio of material quantity usage to direct machine hours. The other indirect approach involves the development of a relationship (usually expressed as a ratio or percent) between material cost *in dollars* and some other series that can be projected with some degree of confidence. For example, some firms plan raw material cost as a percentage of direct labor cost. For obvious reasons the latter approach is the less desirable. In either indirect approach the individual responsible for preparing the raw material budget must usually resort to some form of ratio. The following relationships have been used:

1. The ratio of the quantity of each kind of raw material to the physical volume of production. This ratio, for the past few months or year, can be calculated from historical records and adjusted for new or changed conditions.

2. The ratio of the raw material used to some measure of production such as direct labor hours or direct machine hours.

3. The ratio of material cost to direct labor cost.

4. The ratio of material cost to some measure of productive output, such as direct labor or machine hours.

When a *standard cost system* is utilized in the accounting process, standard material usage rates are already available and should be used for profit planning and control purposes. However, should the standard-cost usage rates be viewed as unrealistic (that is, too tight or too loose), it is desirable to budget material usage variances from the standard cost. In planning the materials budget, realistic allowance must be made for *normal* spoilage, waste, and scrap.

The materials budget for Superior Manufacturing Company is shown in Schedules 24 and 25; the reader is urged to trace the sources of the basic inputs.

THE PURCHASES AND MATERIALS INVENTORY BUDGETS

Careful planning of purchases may offer an area of significant cost saving in many concerns. If realistic estimates of raw material requirements are specified in the materials budget for interim periods the purchasing manager can effectively plan his purchasing responsibilities. The purchasing manager should be assigned the direct responsibility for preparing a detailed plan of purchases and for submitting the plan in the form of a purchases budget.

The purchases budget specifies (1) the quantities of each type of raw material to be purchased, (2) the timing of the purchases, and (3) the estimated *cost* of raw material purchases (per unit and in total). Thus, the purchases budget differs from the materials budget in two principal respects. First, the budgets usually specify *different* quantities of each type of raw material; a difference in quantities is specified due to the *effect of planned changes in raw material inventory levels*. Second, the materials budget specifies *only quantities*, whereas the purchases budget specifies both quantities and *dollar costs*. The purchases budget is directly concerned with the timing of actual receipt of raw materials rather than with the timing of usage or purchase orders. The purchasing manager must order materials so that delivery dates will correspond to the materials inventory and usage requirements.

In developing the purchases budget the purchasing manager is responsible for three basic inputs:

1. Establishment of management policies with respect to raw material inventory levels.
2. Determination of the number of units and the timing of each type of raw material to be purchased.
3. Estimating the unit cost of each type of material to be purchased.

Raw Material Inventory Policies. The quantity differential planned between the materials budget and the purchases budget is accounted for by the change in raw material inventory levels. Thus, as with the finished goods inventory budget with respect to sales and production, the raw materials inventory budget provides a cushion between raw material requirements and purchases. If raw material requirements are seasonal, a stable raw material inventory level means that purchases must exactly parallel factory material requirements. Yet in the same case purchases could be at a uniform level only if inventory were allowed to absorb variations in factory raw material requirements. The optimum inventory purchasing program will generally range somewhere between these two extremes. The timing of purchases will depend on *inventory policies* established by management. The principal factors in setting inventory policies are:

1. Timing and quantity of needs by the factory.
2. Economies in purchasing through quantity discounts.
3. Availability of raw materials.
4. Perishability of raw materials.
5. Storage facilities involved.
6. Capital requirements to finance inventory.
7. Costs of storage.
8. Expected changes in the cost of raw materials.
9. Protection against shortages.
10. Risks involved in inventories.
11. Opportunity costs.

Like finished goods inventory policies, raw material inventory policies are intended to minimize the sum of two classes of costs: costs of carrying the inventory plus the cost of not carrying enough. Reference to the inventory discussions in the preceding chapter will indicate that some of the costs influencing inventory policy determinations are not reflected directly in the accounting reports. For example, interest on the money invested in raw materials inventory normally must be measured separately; yet it is a real cost. Management policy with respect to inventory must be specified to determine realistic inventory levels. The two basic factors are (1) how much to purchase at a time (economic order quantity) and (2) when to purchase.

One well-known approach to computing economic order quantity (EOQ) utilizes the following formula:

$$EOQ = \sqrt{\frac{2AO}{C}}$$

where: A = Annual quantity used in units.
O = Average annual cost of placing an order.
C = Annual carrying cost of carrying one unit in inventory for one year (storage, insurance, return on investment in inventory, and such).

To illustrate, assume the following data:

Annual usage planned (in units)	5,400
Cost to place an order	$10.00
Annual carrying cost per unit in inventory	$ 1.20

Computation:

$$EOQ = \sqrt{\frac{(2)(5,400)(\$10)}{(\$1.20)}} = \sqrt{\frac{\$108,000}{\$1.20}} = \sqrt{90,000} = 300 \text{ units}$$

Based on the data utilized, the economic order quantity is 300 units; at this value, cost is minimized. Observe that as A or O gets larger or as C gets smaller, EOQ increases. This item would be ordered eighteen times per year $(5,400 \div 300 = 18)$.

When to purchase is defined as the *reorder point*. The reorder point is reached when the inventory level is equal to the quantity needed to sustain production for a period equal to the time to reorder and receive the replenishments. Generally, it is also desirable to include a safety stock to accommodate unusual fluctuations in usage and replenishment time. To illustrate, assume a two-week replenishment time and a 15-day provision for unusual fluctuations. Using the above data the reorder point would be determined as follows:

	units
Average monthly usage planned (4,500 ÷ 12)	450
Two-week replenishment provision (450 ÷ 2)	225
Add safety stock provision	15
Reorder point (reorder when inventory level reaches this point)	240

Other approaches to this problem require turnover ratios, monthly supply, and specification of minimum and maximum limitations. The approaches suggested in the preceding chapter for planning and controlling finished goods inventories are also appropriate.

ESTIMATING RAW MATERIAL UNIT COSTS

The purchasing manager is responsible for projecting the unit cost of each raw material. Purchasing executives may hesitate to make such cost estimates, because they recognize that there may be many significant factors, external to the concern, that will affect raw material prices. Nevertheless, failure to develop realistic estimates may have far-reaching effects throughout the concern. For example, in situations where raw material is a significant part of the cost of the finished product, raw material costs are important in developing sales pricing policies, financing policies, and cost control, all which must be concerned with *future* rather than historical raw material costs. Top management should insist that planners chart the expected trends in raw material costs, involving detailed price studies based on such factors as the expected general economic conditions, industry prospects, demand for the raw materials, and market conditions. In short, the purchasing manager has a planning responsibility not too different from that faced by the sales executive, when the latter plans sales. A comprehensive approach is suggested.

The planned cost of material should be the invoice price, less any purchase discounts, plus freight, drayage, and handling charges incident to delivery of the goods. It is frequently impracticable, however, to identify transportation costs with specific raw materials; therefore, the planned purchase price is often the net cost of raw materials and transportation and handling costs are planned as separate items. From a planning point of view, unit material costs should be estimated in the light of cost accounting practices employed by the firm for recording actual costs.

Purchase contracts in existence may provide unit cost data. Historical costs, as indicated by the cost records, may provide a basis for estimating unit costs.

In many cases, fluctuating raw material unit prices must be budgeted for the budget period. Many raw materials have prices that tend to vary seasonally, thereby necessitating the budgeting of varying unit purchasing costs.

COST OF MATERIALS USED BUDGET

The quantity of materials required for planned production is specified in the materials budget, and unit raw material costs are specified in the purchases budget. Thus, quantity and unit cost data are available to develop the budgeted *cost* of materials to be used. If the purchases budget anticipates a constant unit cost during the planning period, multiplication of units by the unit cost provides budgeted material cost. Alternatively, when a changing unit price is planned for raw material, the budget of the cost of materials used and the related budget of raw material inventory must be developed utilizing a selected inventory flow such as fifo, lifo, moving average, and weighted average. Utilization of a worksheet specially designed to facilitate the computation is normally desirable. Development of the *four* materials budgets are illustrated at the end of the chapter for Superior Manufacturing Company.

PLANNING, COORDINATION AND CONTROL ASPECTS
OF RAW MATERIALS BUDGETING

Formulation of detailed plans for raw material requirements, inventories, and purchases is an important part of the planning function of top management. Planning and control of raw material costs frequently are critical, because the cost of production and the efficiency with which operation can be conducted on a day-to-day basis depend to a large degree on the smooth flow of raw materials (at reasonable cost) to the various subdivisions of the factory. Materials planning improves coordination of effort by pinpointing responsibilities; careful thought is required to anticipate and iron out difficulties that otherwise might not become apparent until after actual operations start, resulting in delays, mixups, and consequent high costs. Raw materials planning prevents the accumulation of excess inventories and inventory shortages, both of which can be extremely costly. Materials budgeting forces the manufacturing and purchasing executives to anticipate significant problems and to make decisions when they *should* be made rather than when they *have* to be made. Temporizing with managerial problems and decisions is inevitably costly. With purchases planning achieved, the purchasing department has definite objectives rather than the generalized goal "to buy what is needed." Definite purchasing plans should make possible better organization and more efficiency in purchasing department operations, with consequent cost reduction, and improved cash-flow planning.

Coordination of raw material requirements, inventory levels, and purchasing are important factors in efficient operations. Material costs and inventories may have an important effect on profits, working capital, and the cash position. Buying on the spur of the moment almost always results in excess costs—if the invoiced cost is not excessive, related clerical, handling, freight, and administrative costs are certain to be. Quality is also frequently sacrificed when hasty purchases become necessary to prevent production stoppages. Planned purchasing results in better coordinated efforts in the purchasing and warehousing functions, with consequent reductions in these overhead costs. Perhaps the most important results are greater coordination and control of inventory levels.

In carrying out his responsibilities, the purchasing manager must continuously develop and maintain dependable sources of supply. He should be knowledgeable concerning the various suppliers' potentials and limitations. Alternative sources of supply must be encouraged and developed in order to cope with such problems as new sources when other suppliers fail to deliver, securing improved quality, and obtaining reduced prices. The purchasing manager has the direct responsibility for knowing the current price situation and the probable future changes. All these responsibilities are best met when he can operate with definite policies and with realistic projections of future needs.

Control of raw materials is facilitated in many ways by effective budgeting. Having set definitive inventory policies and standards, management has taken the first step in inventory control. Reports comparing actual inventory levels to standard inventory levels, and actual unit raw material prices with the budgeted unit prices, facilitate *management by exception*. The purchases budget, having the approval of top management, constitutes approval for purchasing certain qualities and quantities of raw materials at the planned cost. Taking into account significant variations of actual production requirements from the budget, the purchasing executive should proceed with his primary responsibility of purchasing raw materials as planned. He will need to go to his superiors only when unusual circumstances arise. For example, should an opportunity arise to purchase an unusually large quantity of material at a favorable price, the proposal would be submitted to his superiors. The question, having been placed before top management, would also be considered by others, such as the finance executive and storage personnel, since their operations would be affected by the decision. Careful consideration of all factors affected by the purchase action, rather than one based on the single factor of a lower unit price, generally would result in a better decision. It might well be that problems in financing, warehousing, or other inventory risk factors offset the single advantage of a lower unit price. If raw material requirements are not known, as in cases where there is no profit plan, control of this type would be lacking and a large purchase at low prices might prove costly because of warehousing, deterioration, and inventory overstocking.

Internal performance reports on at least a monthly basis should show by responsibility (1) material price variances, (2) material usage variances (including spoilage, waste, and abnormal scrap), and (3) inventory level variances from standards. To illustrate, the *two basic responsibilities* for raw materials may be included in the monthly internal performance reports.

1. Purchasing Function—the Purchasing Officer's Responsibility for Prices, Quantities Purchased, and for Inventory Levels. The internal report structure may vary considerably. The following simplified example suggests, however, the key features.

Assume the purchases budget for raw material A showed the following for January:

Units to be purchased	12,000
Planned unit cost	$1.20

Assume further that actual purchases during January were:

Units	11,500
Actual unit cost	$1.26

The January performance report on the *purchasing function* should include the following:

Performance Report

DEPARTMENT	PURCHASING		MANAGER	B. M. KING	
			MONTH OF JANUARY, 19A		
				VARIANCE	
CONTROLLABLE ITEMS	MONTH ACTUAL	MONTH PLANNED		AMOUNT	PER CENT
Raw Material A:					
Units purchased	11,500	12,000		500*	4*
Unit price	$1.26	$1.20		$ .06*	5*
Cost	$14,490	$13,800**		$690.00	5*
Inventory turnover ratio	2.7	2.5		0.2	8
Raw Material B: (Etc.)					
Departmental Expenses:					
(Detailed)					
Etc.					

*Unfavorable variance.
**Planned cost is represented by actual units times the standard price (11,500 × $1.20 = $13,800).

This report reflects the responsibility only of the purchasing manager with respect to (1) quantities purchased against plan, and (2) purchase price variance, (3) the status of inventory turnover, and (4) control of purchasing department expenses.

2. User Function—the Departmental Supervisor's Responsibility for Material Usage. Actual material usage compared with standard material usage for the month and cumulative to date should be reported in the *performance reports* for user responsibility as shown below.

Assume the profit plan specified the following for Producing Department X:

Units of product to be manufactured in January	2,200
Units of raw material A required for each unit of product	2
Unit cost planned for raw material A (per prior example)	$1.20

Assume further that actual results in Producing Department X for January were:

Units of product manufactured	2,000
Units of raw material A used	4,300
Price paid during January for each unit of raw material A (per prior example)	$1.26

The January performance report on Producing Department X should look like this:

Performance Report

DEPT.	PRODUCING DEPT. X		DEPT. MANAGER	T. M. MOORE	

MONTH OF JANUARY, 19A

DEPARTMENTAL CONTROLLABLE COSTS	MONTH ACTUAL	MONTH PLANNED	VARIANCE	
			AMOUNT	PER CENT
Departmental Output	2,000	2,200	200*	9*
Raw Material A:				
Units	4,300	4,000	300*	8*
Cost	$5,160	$4,800	$360*	8*
Etc.				
Direct labor				
Etc.				
Departmental overhead				
Etc.				

*Unfavorable

Observe that "actual" cost ($5,160) is based on the standard price per unit of $1.20 (as opposed to $1.26) so that the departmental manager will not be accountable for the *price variance* since it is a responsibility of the purchasing manager. Observe also that the "planned" column is adjusted to actual output, that is 2,000 units (2,000 × 2 × $1.20 = $4,800). We must not compare an actual expenditure ($5,160 in this case) incurred in manufacturing 2,000 units with a budget amount based on the original planned volume of 2,200 units; the comparison would involve unlike items, and the resultant performance variance would not be meaningful.

THE MATERIALS BUDGETS ILLUSTRATED

We will illustrate the four budgets necessary in planning raw materials for Superior Manufacturing Company. Please refer to the sales plan illustrated at the end of Chapter 5 and the production plan illustrated at the end of Chapter 6 in order to observe the continuity in planning.

Superior Manufacturing Company uses three raw materials—A, B, and C—in producing the two products X and Y. The flow of these two products through the factory is indicated in Illustration 21. Note that Product X passes through the three producing departments, whereas Product Y passes through producing departments one and three only.

As shown in Illustration 21 the standard material usage rates per unit of finished goods are:

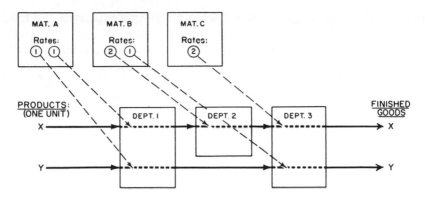

ILLUSTRATION 21. Raw Material and Product Flow
Superior Manufacturing Company

UNITS OF RAW MATERIAL REQUIRED FOR EACH UNIT OF PRODUCT

PRODUCT:	MATERIAL A	MATERIAL B	MATERIAL C
X	1 (in Dept. 1)	2 (in Dept. 2)	2 (in Dept. 3)
Y	1 (in Dept. 1)	1 (in Dept. 3)	

Materials planning by Superior Manufacturing Company comprises *four* subbudgets that encompass the following budget schedules:

1. **Materials Budget:**
   Sch. 24—*Units* of raw material required by product and by time periods
   Sch. 25—Units of raw material required by product and department.
   Sch.   3—Materials budget summary.

2. **Purchases Budget:**
   Sch. 26—Purchases budget, detailed.
   Sch.   4—Purchases budget, summary.

3. **Raw Materials Inventory Budget:**
   Sch. 27—Raw materials inventory budget.
   Sch.   8—Schedule of initial and final inventories.

4. **Cost of Materials Used Budget:**
   Sch. 28—Cost of materials used for production, detailed.
   Sch. 29—Cost of materials used for production, summary.

Materials Budget. The quantities (units) shown in the three schedules (24, 25, and 3) were derived by multiplying the production requirements from the production budget by the raw material usage rates given above.

The units usage rates have been included in these schedules for clarity of exposition. The classification of raw material by department in Schedule 25 is significant because control of raw material usage is the responsibility of operational supervisors. Classification by product in Schedule 24 is important principally for product costing purposes.

It is important to note that the materials budget shows quantities and timing of raw materials needed by the factory for specific production. The timing of raw material needs is an important factor in developing the purchases budget and in actual purchasing activities.

Purchases and Inventory Budgets. The purchasing manager provided the following decisional inputs:

Superior Manufacturing Company

Unit Raw Material Price (Net of Purchase Discount)

FOR THE YEAR ENDING DECEMBER 31, 1977	
RAW MATERIAL	UNIT PRICE
A	$.30
B	.20
C	.25

Beginning Inventories (January 1, 1977)

RAW MATERIAL	UNITS	UNIT PRICE
A	220,000	$.30
B	360,000	.20
C	460,000	.26

It may be observed that for Material C there is a different unit price for the initial inventory and purchases; therefore, it is necessary to know the *method of pricing issues* used by the cost accounting department. For raw materials Superior Manufacturing Company uses first-in, first-out (*fifo*). Obviously, the exact initial inventory of raw materials will not be known when the budget is being prepared. The inventory given above represents either (1) values taken from the prior budget or (2) estimates of actual final inventory levels (for December 31, 1976), based on actual levels and prices at budget preparation date, adjusted for changes expected during the remainder of the current year.

Based on the input data above, and additional quantity data from the materials budget, the purchases budget was constructed as illustrated in Schedule 26. Purchases are indicated in units and dollars by type of raw material by interim periods.

The purchases budget illustrated is more in the nature of a worksheet than an appropriate schedule for inclusion in the formal profit plan. Note that computation of the purchases budget *requires* that interim raw material inventory levels be determined. The purchases budget as illustrated does not indicate inventory *valuations*. Although the schedule could be designed to show this information, it is generally desirable to set up separate inventory valuation schedules. The raw material inventory budget for Superior Manufacturing Company, indicating inventory quantities and valuations by type of raw material by component time periods, is shown in Schedule 27.

Cost of Materials Used Budget. The final step with respect to planning raw materials is to prepare a budget schedule indicating the *cost of raw materials used for production*. This procedure is detailed for Superior Manufacturing Company in Schedule 28. The units agree with the materials budget and with the additional factor of dollar unit cost from the purchases budget. The schedule is designed primarily to show cost of raw materials used by time period for each type of *finished product*. This presentation is made so that the budgeted cost of manufacturing each product can be determined for each time period throughout the budget year. The estimated cost of materials used is summarized in Schedule 29.

DISCUSSION QUESTIONS

1. What are the principal budgets usually required in planning for raw materials? Briefly explain each.

2. Identify who should be responsible for developing each of the several budgets related to planning raw materials.

3. Distinguish between direct materials, indirect materials, and supplies. How does this classification affect profit planning and control?

4. Why is it important to plan raw material quantity requirements?

5. What are the principal approaches used in developing material usage rates?

6. What is the relationship between the materials budget, the purchases budget, and materials inventory budget?

7. In establishing inventory policies, what overriding factors should the management consider?

8. Explain the concepts of economic order quantity and the reorder point.

9. Who has the responsibility for providing the data input on estimated raw material unit costs, and how should these estimates generally be derived?

10. In controlling raw materials there are two basic responsibilities. Indicate the two responsibilities, and explain the profit planning and control approach to resolving them.

SCHEDULE 24. Superior Manufacturing Company
Materials Budget—Unit Requirements for Raw Materials
By Material, Product, and Time for the Year Ending December 31, 1977
The Materials Budget Illustrated

REF.	PRODUCT X PRODUCTION PLANNED 22	UNIT USAGE (GIVEN)	RAW MATERIAL REQUIRED (UNITS)	PRODUCT Y PRODUCTION PLANNED 22	UNIT USAGE (GIVEN)	RAW MATERIAL REQUIRED (UNITS)	TOTAL RAW MATERIAL REQUIRED (UNITS)
Material A							
January	70,000	1	70,000	34,000	1	34,000	104,000
February	80,000	1	80,000	36,000	1	36,000	116,000
March	80,000	1	80,000	38,000	1	38,000	118,000
Total First Quarter	230,000	1	230,000	108,000	1	108,000	338,000
Second Quarter	240,000	1	240,000	140,000	1	140,000	380,000
Third Quarter	230,000	1	230,000	127,000	1	127,000	357,000
Fourth Quarter	260,000	1	260,000	145,000	1	145,000	405,000
Total	960,000	1	960,000	520,000	1	520,000	1,480,000
Material B							
January	70,000	2	140,000	34,000	1	34,000	174,000
February	80,000	2	160,000	36,000	1	36,000	196,000
March	80,000	2	160,000	38,000	1	38,000	198,000
Total First Quarter	230,000	2	460,000	108,000	1	108,000	568,000
Second Quarter	240,000	2	480,000	140,000	1	140,000	620,000
Third Quarter	230,000	2	460,000	127,000	1	127,000	587,000
Fourth Quarter	260,000	2	520,000	145,000	1	145,000	665,000
Total	960,000	2	1,920,000	520,000	1	520,000	2,440,000
Material C							
January	70,000	2	140,000				140,000
February	80,000	2	160,000				160,000
March	80,000	2	160,000				160,000
Total First Quarter	230,000	2	460,000				460,000
Second Quarter	240,000	2	480,000				480,000
Third Quarter	230,000	2	460,000				460,000
Fourth Quarter	260,000	2	520,000				520,000
							1,920,000

SCHEDULE 25. Superior Manufacturing Company

Materials Budget—Unit Requirements for Raw Materials*

By Product, Department and Time, for the Year Ending December 31, 1977

	STANDARD MATERIAL RATES REF. (GIVEN)	RAW MATERIAL UNIT REQUIREMENTS							
		JAN.	FEB.	MARCH	1ST QTR.	2ND QTR.	3RD QTR.	4TH QTR.	TOTALS
Product X									
Scheduled Production in Units	22	70,000	80,000	80,000	230,000	240,000	230,000	260,000	960,000
Raw Material Requirements									
A used in Department 1	1	70,000	80,000	80,000	230,000	240,000	230,000	260,000	960,000
B used in Department 2	2	140,000	160,000	160,000	460,000	480,000	460,000	520,000	1,920,000
C used in Department 3	2	140,000	160,000	160,000	460,000	480,000	460,000	520,000	1,920,000
Product Y									
Scheduled Production in Units	22	34,000	36,000	38,000	108,000	140,000	127,000	145,000	520,000
Raw Material Requirements									
A used in Department 1	1	34,000	36,000	38,000	108,000	140,000	127,000	145,000	520,000
B used in Department 3	1	34,000	36,000	38,000	108,000	140,000	127,000	145,000	520,000
Total Material Requirements									
Department 1 Material A		104,000	116,000	118,000	338,000	380,000	357,000	405,000	1,480,000
Department 2 Material B		140,000	160,000	160,000	460,000	480,000	460,000	520,000	1,920,000
Department 3 Material B		34,000	36,000	38,000	108,000	140,000	127,000	145,000	520,000
Department 3 Material C		140,000	160,000	160,000	460,000	480,000	460,000	520,000	1,920,000

*See Schedule 3 for summary.

SCHEDULE 26. Superior Manufacturing Company
Purchases Budget
For the Year Ending December 31, 1977

REF.	UNITS REQUIRED FOR PROD. 24	ADD FINAL INVENTORY (GIVEN)	TOTAL UNITS REQUIRED	LESS INITIAL INVENTORY (GIVEN)	PURCHASES UNITS	PURCHASES UNIT COST (GIVEN)	TOTAL COST
Raw Material A							
January	104,000	208,000	312,000	220,000	92,000	$0.30	$ 27,600
February	116,000	232,000	348,000	208,000	140,000		42,000
March	118,000	240,000	358,000	232,000	126,000		37,800
1st Quarter	338,000	240,000	578,000	220,000	358,000		107,400
2nd Quarter	380,000	260,000	640,000	240,000	400,000		120,000
3rd Quarter	357,000	227,000	584,000	260,000	324,000		97,200
4th Quarter	405,000	245,000	650,000	227,000	423,000		126,900
Total	1,480,000	245,000	1,725,000	220,000	1,505,000		$ 451,500
Raw Material B							
January	174,000	350,000	524,000	360,000	164,000	$0.20	$ 32,800
February	196,000	380,000	576,000	350,000	226,000		45,200
March	198,000	400,000	598,000	380,000	218,000		43,600
1st Quarter	568,000	400,000	968,000	360,000	608,000		121,600
2nd Quarter	620,000	420,000	1,040,000	400,000	640,000		128,000
3rd Quarter	587,000	400,000	987,000	420,000	567,000		113,400
4th Quarter	665,000	370,000	1,035,000	400,000	635,000		127,000
Total	2,440,000	370,000	2,810,000	360,000	2,450,000		$ 490,000
Raw Material C							
January	140,000	470,000	610,000	460,000	150,000	$0.25	$ 37,500
February	160,000	480,000	640,000	470,000	170,000		42,500
March	160,000	470,000	630,000	480,000	150,000		37,500
1st Quarter	460,000	470,000	930,000	460,000	470,000		117,500
2nd Quarter	480,000	490,000	970,000	470,000	500,000		125,000
3rd Quarter	460,000	475,000	935,000	490,000	445,000		111,250
4th Quarter	520,000	450,000	970,000	475,000	495,000		123,750
Total		450,000	2,370,000	460,000	1,910,000		$ 477,500

SCHEDULE 27. Superior Manufacturing Company
Raw Material Inventory Budget
In Units and Dollars for the Year Ending December 31, 1977

	MATERIAL A ($.30 PER UNIT)		MATERIAL B ($.20 PER UNIT)		MATERIAL C (SEE FOOTNOTES)		TOTAL MATERIALS INVENTORY
REF.	UNITS 26	AMOUNT	UNITS 26	AMOUNT	UNITS 26	AMOUNT	
Beginning Inventories							
January	220,000	$66,000	360,000	$72,000	460,000	$119,600a	$257,600
February	208,000	62,400	350,000	70,000	470,000	120,700b	253,100
March	232,000	69,600	380,000	76,000	480,000	121,600c	267,200
2nd Quarter	240,000	72,000	400,000	80,000	470,000	117,500d	269,500
3rd Quarter	260,000	78,000	420,000	84,000	490,000	122,500	284,500
4th Quarter	227,000	68,100	400,000	80,000	475,000	118,750	266,850
Final Inventory	245,000	73,500	370,000	74,000	450,000	112,500	260,000

a $.26 per unit.
b 320,000 units at $.26; 150,000 units at $.25.
c 160,000 units at $.26; 320,000 units at $.25.
d All other units at $.25.

SCHEDULE 28. Superior Manufacturing Company
Estimated Cost of Materials Used for Production
For the Year Ending December 31, 1977

PERIOD AND MATERIAL	REF.	PRODUCT X			PRODUCT Y			TOTALS	
		UNITS REQUIRED 25	UNIT PRICE (GIVEN)	AMOUNT	UNITS REQUIRED 25	UNIT PRICE (GIVEN)	AMOUNT	UNITS 25	AMOUNT
January									
A		70,000	$.30	$ 21,000	34,000	$.30	$ 10,200	104,000	$ 31,200
B		140,000	.20	28,000	34,000	.20	6,800	174,000	34,800
C		140,000	.26	36,400				140,000	36,400
Total				$ 85,400			$ 17,000		$ 102,400
February									
A		80,000	$.30	$ 24,000	36,000	$.30	$ 10,800	116,000	$ 34,800
B		160,000	.20	32,000	36,000	.20	7,200	196,000	39,200
C		160,000	.26	41,600				160,000	41,600
Total				$ 97,600			$ 18,000		$ 115,600
March									
A		80,000	$.30	$ 24,000	38,000	$.30	$ 11,400	118,000	$ 35,400
B		160,000	.20	32,000	38,000	.20	7,600	198,000	39,600
C		160,000	.26	41,600				160,000	41,600
Total				$ 97,600			$ 19,000		$ 116,600
1st Quarter									
A		230,000	$.30	$ 69,000	108,000	$.30	$ 32,400	338,000	$ 101,400
B		460,000	.20	92,000	108,000	.20	21,600	568,000	113,600
C		460,000	.26	119,600				460,000	119,600
Total				$ 280,600			$ 54,000		$ 334,600

SCHEDULE 28 / (CONT'D)

PERIOD AND MATERIAL	REF.	PRODUCT X			PRODUCT Y			TOTALS	
		UNITS REQUIRED	UNIT PRICE (GIVEN)	AMOUNT	UNIT REQUIRED	UNIT PRICE (GIVEN)	AMOUNT	UNITS	AMOUNT
	25	25			25			25	
2nd Quarter									
A		240,000	$.30	$ 72,000	140,000	$.30	$ 42,000	380,000	$ 114,000
B		480,000	.20	96,000	140,000	.20	28,000	620,000	124,000
C		480,000	.25	120,000				480,000	120,000
Total				$ 288,000			$ 70,000		$ 358,000
3rd Quarter									
A		230,000	$.30	$ 69,000	127,000	$.30	$ 38,100	357,000	$ 107,100
B		460,000	.20	92,000	127,000	.20	25,400	587,000	117,400
C		460,000	.25	115,000				460,000	115,000
Total				$ 276,000			$ 63,500		$ 339,500
4th Quarter									
A		260,000	$.30	$ 78,000	145,000	$.30	$ 43,500	405,000	$ 121,500
B		520,000	.20	104,000	145,000	.20	29,000	665,000	133,000
C		520,000	.25	130,000				520,000	130,000
Total				$ 312,000			$ 72,500		$ 384,500
Total for Year				$1,156,600			$260,000		$1,416,600

SCHEDULE 29. Superior Manufacturing Company
Estimated Cost of Materials Used for Production—Summary
For the Year Ending December 31, 1977

		TOTALS		PRODUCT X			PRODUCT Y		
	REF.	UNITS 3	AMOUNT	UNITS 3	PRICE (GIVEN)	AMOUNT	UNITS 3	PRICE (GIVEN)	AMOUNT
Materials									
A		1,480,000	$ 444,000	960,000	$.30	$ 288,000	520,000	$.30	$156,000
B		2,440,000	$ 488,000	1,920,000	.20	384,000	520,000	.20	104,000
C		1,920,000	484,600	1,920,000	*	484,600			
	28		$1,416,600			$1,156,600			$260,000

*460,000 units @ $.26; balance @ $.25.

CASE 7-1
Smith Processors, Inc.

Smith Processors, Inc., is a medium-size manufacturer that distributes its products on a nationwide basis. The company produces three main products that are sold through wholesale channels to other manufacturers. The products sold reflect a moderate seasonality; however, the seasons tend to offset so that company production is fairly stable throughout the year. The company is in the process of developing a profit planning and control program. The management has decided to initiate a long-range plan extending four years into the future beyond the upcoming year and to reevaluate the plan on an annual basis. An annual profit plan is being developed, and in view of the relative stability of production, the plan will be disaggregated by month for the entire year during its initial preparation.

In analyzing the use of each raw material and the purchasing activities of the past year, the case writer noted the following:

a.   Manufacturing operations are carried on in seven processing departments; there are three service departments in the factory. In manufacturing the three products, twelve different raw materials are used in varying quantities; however, no single product requires all twelve of the raw materials. One raw material that is used primarily in one of the products is also used as "indirect materials" in four of the processes. Indirect material usage of this raw material approximates one-third of the total volume purchased. It is unrealistic to try to identify the usage of this particular raw material with the several products, hence it is classified as an indirect material (with the exception of the one product mentioned).

b.   Several of the raw materials involve quantity discounts; that is, when a purchase order exceeds a certain stated level, a quantity discount, say five percent, is granted to the purchaser. During the past year approximately two-thirds of the purchases of these particular raw materials involved orders large enough to qualify for the quantity discount.

c.   Some of the raw materials are purchased at a relatively uniform level throughout the year; however, some of the other raw materials are purchased on a highly seasonal basis. The seasonality is primarily a result of availability of those raw materials. They tend to have a lower unit cost when the supply is high. In some cases, perishability creates high storage costs.

d.   One raw material, purchased in large quantities, is obtained from one supplier only. Other suppliers in the market are at some distance, which poses a relatively high freight differential cost.

e.   The length of time between the date of an order and delivery date of the raw material varies widely across the twelve raw materials. For example, the shortest delivery time on a single raw material is approximately five days and the longest time is thirty-eight days. The average time for all raw materials is approximately fifteen days.

f.   Some of the raw materials have a high unit cost (the highest, $21), whereas others have a relatively low unit cost (the lowest, $1.20).

g.   Usage rates vary widely for the twelve raw materials. For example, the raw material that has the highest utilization requires approximately twelve times the amount of raw material that has the lowest utilization.

Procedures for planning raw materials are under consideration by the management. The sales plan and the production plan have been tentatively agreed upon with respect to procedures. The production plan will specify quantity of each of the three products to be produced each month throughout the year.

Required:

1. Briefly describe the system that you would recommend for planning raw materials in this company. You should include recommendations with respect to the subbudgets required, basic classifications of data, and responsibilities for decisional inputs required by the system.

2. Present recommendations, with support, for the planning approach that should be used for each of the peculiarities of the raw materials activity as enumerated above.

CASE 7-2
Hutton Company

Hutton Company is a medium-size manufacturer of several lines of products that are sold to other manufacturers. The company uses three principal raw materials, designated materials X, Y, and Z. Raw materials constitute the largest item of cost in the manufacturing process. The profit planning and control program has been in operation one year and is constantly being improved and adapted to new problems as they arise. An annual profit plan is developed and disaggregated by months for the year, and the long-range plan has a three-year time horizon. The manufacturing activities are conducted in five producing departments and there are four service departments. Production is under the general supervision of the factory manager; the purchasing manager reports to the factory manager as do the supervisors of the nine departments in the factory.

The factory manager stated that the control of raw materials is a problem in this company that has not been well fitted into the profit planning and control program. In order to concentrate on this problem, this case is limited to one producing department (Department 1), one raw material (raw material X), and one finished product (product B). The following standards have been tentatively established for the annual profit plan:
Planned production of product B:

TIME PERIODS	UNITS
January	10,000
February	12,000
March	14,000
2nd Quarter	42,000
3rd Quarter	35,000
4th Quarter	30,000

Usage rates for raw materials:

PRODUCT AND RAW MATERIAL	STANDARD USAGE RATE
Product B:	
Material X	3
Etc.	

Planned purchase price per unit of raw material:

PERIOD	UNIT COST FOR MATERIAL X
January	$5.00
February	5.50
March	5.50
2nd Quarter	6.00
3rd Quarter	6.00
4th Quarter	5.00

The inventory policy specifies that the beginning inventory for raw material X for each month shall be equal to one-half the planned monthly withdrawals for that period. Economic lot quantities and reorder points have been computed. The first month of the year covered by the annual profit plan (January) has just ended, and the performance reports covering January are being prepared. The budget manager and the factory manager are redesigning the performance report structure as it relates to the raw materials since this particular item has not been effectively reported in the past from the control point of view.

Actual results for January are:

a. Production of product B—10,500 units.
b. Units of raw material X purchased—30,000.
c. Unit price paid for raw material X—$5.20.
d. Units of raw material X used—31,610.

Required:

1. Prepare a planning schedule that reflects the "required units of raw material X for product B." This planning schedule should be viewed as one part of the overall profit plan that was developed before the year started; specifically, it would be a part of the materials budget.
2. Prepare the purchases budget through March for raw material X.
3. Design appropriate performance reports that will reflect the effectiveness with which raw materials were controlled during January. Utilizing the data in the case, present appropriate amounts in your suggested performance reports.
4. Explain and justify your recommendations with respect to the performance reports presented in requirement three.

CASE 7-3
Bacon Manufacturing Company

Bacon Manufacturing Company uses a special dry cell battery in its manufacturing process. Four batteries are used for each unit of finished product. The annual profit plan is disaggregated by quarters; the production plan specified the following output: 1st Quarter 31,500; 2nd Quarter 32,750; 3rd Quarter 16,750; and 4th Quarter 19,000.

The replenishment time averages seven days, and unusual demands from the factory and variations in replenishment time suggest the need for a three-day safety stock. Average cost to place an order is $11.00, and the carrying cost is estimated to be $.03 per unit in inventory. Throughout each quarter production is relatively stable. Unit purchase price planned is $.30.

Required:

1. Prepare a materials budget.
2. Calculate the reorder point and safety stock.
3. Calculate the economic lot size.

CASE 7-4
Stoner Company

Stoner Company uses three different components (materials) in manufacturing its primary product. Stoner manufactures two of the components and purchases one (designated as component 1) from outside suppliers. The company currently is developing the annual profit plan. Sales are highly seasonal. Component 2 cannot be acquired from outsiders; however, component 3 can be purchased. The three components have critical specifications. The annual profit plan provided data for the following computations:

	COMPONENT 3 UNIT COST (AT 12,000 UNITS)
Material (direct)	$1.40
Labor (direct)	2.20
Fixed overhead allocated	.40
Annual machinery rental (special machines used only for component 3)	.50
Variable factory overhead	1.00
Average storage cost per year	.40
Total	$5.90
Average inventory level 500 units.	

In view of the $5.90 unit cost, the purchasing manager investigated outside suppliers and found one that would sign a one-year contract to deliver "12,000 top-quality units as needed during the year at $5.20 per unit." Serious consideration is being given to this alternative.

Required:

Should Stoner make or buy component 3? Explain the relevant factors influencing your decision.

CASE 7-5
Barker Company

Barker Company uses two major raw materials in manufacturing one primary product. The company is in the process of developing the purchases and materials budgets. For the past three years the company developed a sales plan and has recently decided to extend budgeting to all phases of operation. In working on the problem the following data relating to raw materials was assembled:

	MATERIAL T			MATERIAL U		
	UNITS REQUIRED (BUDGETED)	DAYS RE-QUIRED FOR DELIVERY (AVER-AGE)	UNIT PRICE LAST YEAR	UNITS REQUIRED (BUDGETED)	DAYS RE-QUIRED FOR DELIVERY (AVER-AGE)	UNIT PRICE LAST YEAR
19A						
January	3,500	14	$8.50	12,250	8	$3.00
February	4,000	14	8.50	14,000	7	3.10
March	4,500	18	9.20	15,750	6	3.10
2nd Quarter	14,000	18	9.30	49,000	6	3.20
3rd Quarter	11,000	10	8.60	38,500	5	3.30
4th Quarter	8,000	7	8.10	28,000	5	3.50
19B						
January	3,300	14	—	12,000	8	—

The management is confronted with five problems about which they have requested assistance:

1. In view of the increasing price of material U, it has been proposed that a lower quality of material be used. This step, it is estimated, would reduce the unit cost for such material by 15 per cent.

2. The purchasing manager feels that an average price for the year should be used for planning purposes because, "It is only a guess anyway; I have no control over the price." The chief accountant feels that the price for each interim period should be used since, "We use fifo in accounting for raw materials, and an average price would produce meaningless variations particularly in view of the typical fluctuating price of our raw materials."

3. The third problem has to do with freight charges—that is, should the unit price be budgeted *before or after freight charges*? Experience has shown that freight charges on T average about 5 per cent of the cost, whereas freight charges on U average about 10 per cent. The problem is complicated by the fact that the freight charges are paid upon delivery of the materials, whereas the materials are paid for at the end of the discount period.

4. The cash discounts allowed on material T average 3 per cent whereas there are no cash discounts allowed on material U. During the past year Barker took advantage of discounts on approximately one-half of the purchases of T. The management is concerned about the best approach for planning cash discounts.

5. The management has determined that the beginning inventory of raw material T each period should be equal to the projected usage for that period, and for raw material U, one-half projected usage. They are now concerned about the safety stock level for each raw material.

Required:

    a. What are your recommendations with respect to each of these problems? Justify your recommendations.

    b. Apply the inventory policy already established and your recommended safety stock levels, and other data to develop a plan for Product T, only including for each period the following: (1) units to be purchased, and (2) order date.

CASE 7-6
Simple Products Company

Simple Products Company manufactures two products, S and P, processing them through two departments. Product P is processed through both departments, whereas product S is processed through Department 1 only. Raw material A is used in Department 1 for both products, and raw material B is used in Department 2 only. A profit plan is prepared on an annual basis. However, to simplify the case data are given for only one quarter. Budget estimates developed to date include the following:

1. Production budget (Units)

PRODUCT	JANUARY	FEBRUARY	MARCH
S	5,000	6,000	7,000
P	8,000	9,000	10,000

2. Estimated beginning inventories:
    Material A— 70,000 units @ $3.00.
    Material B—120,000 units @ $2.20.

3. Budgeted material prices (for purchases):
    Material A—$3.00.
    Material B—$2.00.

4. Raw material requirements for finished goods:

PRODUCT	MATERIAL A	MATERIAL B
S	5	0
P	6	7

5. Ending raw material inventories planned:
   Material A—January and February 70,000, March 80,000.
   Material B—To remain constant at 120,000.

Required:

Prepare appropriate profit plan schedules for the quarter relative to:

a. Materials.
b. Purchases.
c. Raw materials inventory (use fifo).
d. Cost of raw materials used (by department, product, material, and time period).

Be prepared to justify your particular approach.

Planning and Controlling
Direct Labor Costs

chapter eight

Labor costs are greater than all other costs combined in many companies. Even where this is not the case, careful planning and systematic control of labor costs are essential. Planning and controlling labor costs involve major and complex areas: (1) manpower needs, (2) recruitment, (3) training, (4) job evaluation and specification, (5) performance evaluation, (6), union negotiations, and (7) wage and salary administration. Each of these problems may be paramount in various situations. A comprehensive profit planning and control program should incorporate appropriate techniques and approaches applicable to each problem area. A profit planning and control program does not satisfy the specific needs with respect to these special personnel problems, but it directs careful consideration to them and aids in placing them in proper perspective. Careful planning and realistic control of long-term and short-term labor costs will benefit both the company and its employees.

Labor costs, in the broad sense, are composed of all expenditures for those employed by the firm: top executives; middle management personnel; staff officers; supervisors; foremen; skilled workers, and manual laborers. To plan and control these costs effectively, it is necessary to consider separately the different types of labor cost. This chapter is concerned with only one type of labor cost, *direct labor*.

Labor is generally classified as *direct* and *indirect*. Direct labor costs consist of the wages paid to employees who are engaged directly in specific productive output. As with direct material costs, labor costs that can be directly traced to specific production are defined as *direct*. Indirect labor involves all other labor costs, such as supervisory salaries, wages paid tool-makers, repairmen, storekeepers, custodians, and so forth. Direct material and direct labor costs are frequently referred to collectively as the *prime cost* of a product.

The direct labor budget comprises the estimates of direct labor requirements necessary to produce the types and quantities of outputs planned in the production budget. Although some companies prepare a labor budget that includes both direct and indirect labor, it is generally preferable to prepare a separate direct labor budget and to include indirect labor in the expense budgets. This procedure is consistent with the usual cost accounting treatment of labor costs in the manufacturing expense category.[1] Overtime and premium pay related to direct labor should be budgeted as separate items.

The principal reasons for developing a separate direct labor budget are to provide planning data with respect to the amount of direct labor required, number of direct labor employees needed, unit labor for cost of each product, cash flow requirements, and to establish a basis for control of direct labor.

The responsibility for preparing the direct labor budget should be assigned to the executive in charge of manufacturing. The cost accounting and personnel departments may well be called on for assistance and supplementary information. Once the direct labor budget is completed by the manufacturing executives, it should be submitted to the budget manager to be reviewed and then submitted to the executive committee at the appropriate stage in the construction of the planning budget. When the direct labor budget is tentatively approved, it becomes part of the period profit plan.

Technically, the direct labor budget may take several forms. Separate subbudgets generally are developed for (1) direct labor hours and (2) direct labor costs similar to those illustrated at the end of this chapter. Direct labor control is achieved best in terms of direct labor hours rather than in dollars.

APPROACHES IN PLANNING DIRECT LABOR COSTS

For the annual profit plan the direct labor budget should be developed in terms of both *direct labor hours and direct labor costs*. The budget also should

---

[1] Overtime and premium costs are those costs above the regular direct labor hour rate. For example, if one direct labor employee whose hourly rate was $6.00 worked one hour overtime at time and one-half, the overtime cost would be $3.00; the $6.00 is still considered as direct labor cost.

be developed by responsibilities, by interim periods, and by product. Classification by organizational responsibility and by interim periods is essential for control purposes; classification by product is essential for estimating the cost of producing each product.

The approach that should be used to develop the direct labor budget depends principally upon (1) the method of wage payment; (2) the type of production processes involved; (3) the availability of standard labor times; and (4) the adequacy of the cost accounting records relating to direct labor costs.

Basically, there are three approaches to the development of the direct labor budget:

1. Estimate the standard direct labor hours required for each unit of each product, then estimate the *average wage rates* by department, cost center, or operation. Multiplication of the standard time per unit of product by the average wage rates gives the labor cost per unit of production for the department, cost center, or operation. Multiplication of the units of goods to be produced in the department, cost center, or operation by the unit labor cost rate gives the total direct labor cost for each product.

2. Estimate direct *ratios* of labor cost to some measure of output that can be projected realistically.

3. Develop *manning tables* by enumerating manpower requirements for direct labor in each responsibility center.

Some companies develop *manning tables* to aid in planning and controlling overall labor costs. Under this approach each responsibility center must prepare a detailed manning table listing each position classified by type of job. One such classification is *direct labor*. Under this classification the exact number of employees (man days) for each type of work planned would be listed in the responsibility center.

PLANNING DIRECT LABOR HOURS

Internal conditions will determine whether it is feasible to relate planned production in a producing department to direct labor hours (productive hours) as well as to direct labor cost. Similarly, internal factors will determine the most practicable approach for planning direct labor hours.

Many firms have developed cost accounting systems that utilize direct labor hours in each department as the basis for applying manufacturing overhead to production (see Chapter 9). In such cases, generally sound approaches have been developed for estimating the level of direct labor hours at a given amount of production.

One important phase of *industrial engineering* is development of *standard labor times* for various operations and products. In some producing departments the development of reliable labor time standards is possible; in other situations, it may be impractical except in terms of averages based on experience. Four commonly used approaches in planning standard labor *times* may be outlined as follows:

1. Time and Motion Studies. These studies generally are made by industrial engineers. They analyze the work required on a product (or in a department) specifying a series of operations. By observation (and by actually timing with a stopwatch), a standard time for each specific operation is determined. Obviously, the industrial engineer has to decide (and frequently along with the union) whether the fastest, slowest, or an average employee time should be used. Nevertheless, time and motion studies may provide reliable information concerning the labor time necessary to perform specific operations. The result of time and motion studies can provide basic input data for developing the direct labor hour requirements to meet planned production. Under the supervision of competent industrial engineers, time and motion studies generally represent the best approach to the establishment of standard labor time.

2. Standard Costs. If a *standard cost accounting system* is used in the accounting records, careful studies of direct labor hour requirements per unit of production generally will have been made. In such cases, the standard labor time per unit of product used in the cost system can be multiplied by the planned production to derive labor hour requirements. Frequently such standards are rather exacting which would require that *budgeted* variations from standard hours be incorporated in the annual profit plan.

3. Direct Estimate by Supervisors. Some companies ask the supervisor of each productive department to estimate the direct labor hours required for the planned output of the department. In making such estimates, the supervisor must rely on (1) judgment, (2) performance of the department reported over the recent past, and (3) assistance from his supervisor and perhaps one or more staff officers.

4. Statistical Estimates by a Staff Group. Cost accounting records of past performance usually provide valuable information for converting production requirements to direct labor hours. This approach is frequently used for productive departments that process several products simultaneously. The historical ratio of direct labor hours to some measure of physical output is computed and then adjusted for planned changes in the responsibility center. Obviously the accuracy of this method depends upon the reliability of the cost records and the uniformity of the production process from period to period. However, it suffers from the weakness that past inefficiencies will be projected into the future. Even though some other method of estimating direct labor hours is used, historical ratios of direct labor hours to physical output are frequently good checks on the accuracy of other methods used.

Some companies find it desirable to use several approaches in estimating direct labor hours. A particular method applicable in one productive department or cost center may not be equally applicable in another. There should be continuous effort to improve existing procedures and to adopt new ones that are more appropriate.

To illustrate, assume two primary products are processed through four producing departments. However, we will concentrate on one product and one department for illustrative purposes. Assume the production budget specified 1,000 completed units of Product A in the first month of the planning period (January). In Department 1 this product undergoes four distinct operations (designated 2, 3, 5, and 6), each one involving direct labor time. The industrial engineers, through time and motion studies, developed the following standard times for each operation in the department:

	DEPARTMENT 1 STANDARD DIRECT LABOR HOURS PER OPERATION					
OPERATION	1	2	3	4	5	6
Time (Hours)	1.00	1.50	0.60	0.40	1.75	2.25

The planned direct labor hours would be 6,100 computed as follows:

JANUARY, 19A PRODUCT A:	OPERATION	COMPUTATION	DIRECT LABOR HOURS
	2	1,000 × 1.50 =	1,500
	3	1,000 × 0.60 =	600
	5	1,000 × 1.75 =	1,750
	6	1,000 × 2.25 =	2,250
	Total	1,000 × 6.10 =	6,100

PLANNING WAGE RATES

If it is possible to relate planned production to direct labor hours and to plan wage rates realistically for each productive department, computation of planned direct labor cost is merely a matter of multiplying the one by the other. Within a particular concern there may be one or more productive departments where this direct approach is feasible.

Determination of *average* direct labor wage rates in a particular productive department or cost center frequently may not present a serious problem. The preferred approach is to estimate such rates by counting the direct workers in the department and their expected wage rate, then to compute an average. For example, a company may develop the analysis as follows:

	PLANNED WAGE RATE	NUMBER OF DIRECT LABOR EMPLOYEES*	WEIGHTED AMOUNT	AVERAGE WAGE RATE
Operation 1:				
Group A	$4.00	4	$ 16.00	
Group B	6.00	16	96.00	
		20	$112.00	$5.60
Operation 2:				
Etc.				

*Full-time equivalents.

A less precise approach involves determination of the historical ratio between wages paid and direct labor hours worked in the department. The historical ratio is then adjusted for conditions that have changed or are expected to change.

It is important to realize that average wage rates based on historical data are useful for future planning only to the extent that there is consistency in operations and in the hours worked at different wage rates. For example, assume the following historical data:

WORKER GROUP	HOURS	RATE	LABOR COST
A	2,000	$4.00	$ 8,000
B	3,000	6.00	18,000
Totals	5,000	$5.20	$26,000

An average wage rate based on the data above would be $5.20; however, should the budgeted hours for each worker be 2,500, with no changes in wage rates, the average rate would be $5.00 rather than $5.20. The difference indicates the distortion that can occur in average rates if the ratio of hours worked to different individual wage rates changes.

In some cases the size of the department, the diversity of its work, and variations in hourly wages may be of such significance that the department, that is, the responsibility center, should be subdivided into *cost centers*. Separate direct labor estimates and average wage rates would then be planned for each cost center.

If a standard cost system is used in the cost accounting department the standard wage rates developed for that purpose may be used for budgeting purposes; however, it may be desirable to budget certain wage rate variances between standard allowances and planning budget allowances.

The preceding discussion sets forth two estimates—hours and wage rates—necessary to derive direct labor costs. This approach has definite advantages; however, practical considerations frequently may make this approach inadvisable if not impossible. The alternative approach is to estimate direct labor *cost*. This method involves making an estimate of direct cost (1) per unit of production or (2) in terms of some measure of output, such as direct machine hours or direct material cost.

If a straight piece-rate system of compensating labor is used, the labor cost per unit of production is known. The piece-rate system bases the compensation upon the quantity produced. Various bonus systems of wage payments complicate the estimation of direct labor costs. In such cases, ratios are generally used.

The ratio approach relates past direct labor cost to some measure of output for the same period. The cost ratio thus derived represents the historical labor cost relationships and therefore must be adjusted for planned changes affecting such relationships. In the case of new products a rough estimate may be necessary. If historical cost and production data are available and are carefully analyzed, accurate estimates of direct labor costs usually are possible.

ORGANIZING THE DIRECT LABOR BUDGET

The direct labor budget structurally must be in harmony with the structure of the annual profit plan; therefore, it should specify planned direct labor *hours* and *cost* by responsibility by time (month and/or quarter), and by product. When standard labor times and average wage rates are developed on the sound foundations discussed in the preceding two sections, construction of the direct labor budget is relatively simple. In complex situations it is usually desirable to develop a separate direct labor budget for each department encompassing two subbudgets, one specifying hours only and the other specifying direct labor cost. These aspects of the direct labor budget are illustrated for Superior Manufacturing Company at the end of this chapter.

PLANNING AND CONTROL FEATURES OF THE DIRECT LABOR BUDGET

Careful planning of direct labor requirements can benefit a firm in a number of ways:

1. The personnel function can be more efficiently performed because there is a basis for effective planning, recruitment, training, and

utilization of manpower. The personnel department can be better organized as a result of knowing the volume of activities expected of it.

2. The finance function can be more efficiently planned and carried out because labor may represent one of the largest demands on cash during the year. Knowing the direct labor cost enables the finance officer to estimate by interim periods the cash requirements for labor.

3. The budgeted cost of manufacturing each product (unit costs and total cost) can be developed. This cost may be an important factor in several areas of decision-making such as pricing policy and union negotiations.

4. Control and reduction of direct labor costs.

Control of direct labor costs may be a major problem facing the management. Effective labor cost control depends on consistently competent supervision, direct observation, and individual contact with the workers by foremen and supervisors. However, there is a definite need for standards by which the supervisor may gauge performance. Planning the work flow and arrangement of supplies and equipment may have a definite effect on direct labor costs. From these brief observations, we see the two primary aspects of the control of direct labor costs: (1) the day-to-day concern with such costs; and (2) the longer-run reporting and evaluation of results.

Considering the day-to-day concern with direct labor costs, aside from the direct supervision mentioned above, many firms have developed realistic labor standards for many operations. These standards are compared with actual results and frequently are reported daily. For example, one firm, where direct labor costs were particularly significant, instituted a daily report on direct labor costs for each foreman. By 9 a.m. daily, each foreman had a report on direct labor performance for the preceding day. Basically, the report showed (1) actual hours worked, (2) standard hours for the actual output, and (3) time variations. Such reports may be expressed in terms of time only or in terms of both time and dollar costs, depending upon the control elements that are vested in the foremen.

With respect to monthly reporting and evaluation of direct labor, the internal *monthly performance report* should include actual information, by responsibility, on direct labor as compared with the labor standards. These reports are essential for management evaluation of the status of control. They spur management actions directed toward higher operational efficiency. The performance reports on direct labor may be (1) separate reports or (2) incorporated in the departmental performance report. To illustrate, return to the example in Chapter 7 for Department X. Assume the annual profit plan specified the following for the department:

Units of product to be manufactured in January	2,200
Standard labor hours per unit required in Department X	2
Average direct labor wage rate per hour in Department X	$5.00

Assume further that actual results for Department X for January were:

Units of product manufactured in January	2,000
Actual direct labor hours incurred during January	4,250
Actual direct labor cost incurred during January	$21,800

The January performance report for Department X should reflect the following with respect to direct labor:

Performance Report

DEPT. PRODUCING DEPT. X		DEPT. MANAGER	T. M. MOORE	
		MONTH OF JANUARY, 19A		
DEPARTMENTAL CONTROLLABLE COSTS	MONTH ACTUAL	MONTH PLANNED	VARIANCE AMOUNT	PER CENT
Departmental output	2,000	2,200	200*	9*
Raw material:				
(as illustrated in Chapter 7)				
Direct labor:				
Hours	4,250	4,000	250*	6*
Average wage rate	$5.13	$5.00	$.13*	3*
Cost	$21,800.00	$20,000.00	$1,800.00*	9*
Departmental overhead:				
Etc.				

*Unfavorable.

Variations derived by comparing actual direct labor costs with the standard allowance may be due to (1) labor usage (labor efficiency variation) or (2) labor wage rates (wage rate variation) (see Chapter 16). Labor usage is controllable at the foreman's level by means described above. On the other hand, the wage rates often are determined in management-union negotiations. However, the wage rate variation frequently is controllable at the foreman's level. To illustrate, a foreman may cause a wage rate variation by using workers with higher wage rates than the rate standard called for in a particular operation.

THE DIRECT LABOR BUDGET ILLUSTRATED

Superior Manufacturing Company uses direct labor in each producing department. Since product X is processed through all producing departments, direct labor is used in each of the three departments; in contrast, since product Y is processed only through Producing Departments 1 and 3 direct labor is used at only two points. The standard labor times planned for each product for each department are:

| | DIRECT LABOR HOURS PER UNIT OF PRODUCT | |
DEPARTMENT	PRODUCT X	PRODUCT Y
1	.4	.2
2	.2	—
3	.4	.2

The following average wage rates have been tentatively approved for planning purposes:

DEPARTMENT	AVERAGE HOURLY WAGE RATES*
1	$2.00
2	1.50
3	1.00

*Simplified for illustrative purposes.

Superior Manufacturing Company develops two subbudgets for direct labor: one that specifies labor *cost* and one that specifies labor *hours* only. The first one is shown in Schedule 30. In developing this budget schedule, "units to be produced" were taken from the production budget and extended, using the *divisional input data* above. For clarity, computations are indicated on the schedule. It may be observed that the classification of labor cost is by product, time period, and organizational responsibility (department). This classification is consistent with that used for the overall profit plan, as indicated in all prior budget schedules prepared for Superior Manufacturing Company.

The direct labor budget *in hours only* is shown in Schedule 31. Obviously these hours agree with those shown in Schedule 30; however, the company has found it desirable to prepare a separate schedule that specifies hours only. These data are needed in subsequent budget schedules of manufacturing overhead. For purposes of simplicity in this illustration, payroll deductions have been disregarded.

DISCUSSION QUESTIONS

1. Define the direct labor budget, and place it in perspective with respect to the annual profit plan.
2. Who should be responsible for developing the direct labor budget?
3. What are the principal purposes of the direct labor budget?

SCHEDULE 30. Superior Manufacturing Company
Direct Labor Budget—Cost
For the Year Ending December 31, 1977

	REF.	TOTAL LABOR COST	PRODUCT X					PRODUCT Y				
			UNITS TO BE PRODUCED 22	STANDARD HOURS (INPUT)	TOTAL STANDARD PRODUCTIVE HOURS	RATE PER HOUR (INPUT)	AMOUNT	UNITS TO BE PRODUCED 22	STANDARD HOURS (INPUT)	TOTAL STANDARD PRODUCTIVE HOURS	RATE PER HOUR (INPUT)	AMOUNT
January												
Dept. 1		$ 69,600	70,000	.4	28,000	$2.00	$ 56,000	34,000	.2	6,800	$2.00	$ 13,600
Dept. 2		21,000	70,000	.2	14,000	1.50	21,000					
Dept. 3		34,800	70,000	.4	28,000	1.00	28,000	34,000	.2	6,800	1.00	6,800
Totals		$ 125,400	70,000		70,000		$ 105,000	34,000		13,600		$ 20,400
February												
Dept. 1		$ 78,400	80,000	.4	32,000	$2.00	$ 64,000	36,000	.2	7,200	$2.00	$ 14,400
Dept. 2		24,000	80,000	.2	16,000	1.50	24,000					
Dept. 3		39,200	80,000	.4	32,000	1.00	32,000	36,000	.2	7,200	1.00	7,200
Totals		$ 141,600	80,000		80,000		$ 120,000	36,000		14,400		$ 21,600
March												
Dept. 1		$ 79,200	80,000	.4	32,000	$2.00	$ 64,000	38,000	.2	7,600	$2.00	$ 15,200
Dept. 2		24,000	80,000	.2	16,000	1.50	24,000					
Dept. 3		39,600	80,000	.4	32,000	1.00	32,000	38,000	.2	7,600	1.00	7,600
Totals		$ 142,800	80,000		80,000		$ 120,000	38,000		15,200		$ 22,800
1st Quarter												
Dept. 1		$ 227,200	230,000	.4	92,000	$2.00	$ 184,000	108,000	.2	21,600	$2.00	$ 43,200
Dept. 2		69,000	230,000	.2	46,000	1.50	69,000					
Dept. 3		113,600	230,000	.4	92,000	1.00	92,000	108,000	.2	21,600	1.00	21,600
Totals		$ 409,800	230,000		230,000		$ 345,000	108,000		43,200		$ 64,800

SCHEDULE 30 (Cont'd)

REF.	TOTAL LABOR COST	PRODUCT X					PRODUCT Y				
		UNITS TO BE PRODUCED 22	STANDARD HOURS (INPUT)	TOTAL STANDARD PRODUCTIVE HOURS	RATE PER HOUR (INPUT)	AMOUNT	UNITS TO BE PRODUCED 22	STANDARD HOURS (INPUT)	TOTAL STANDARD PRODUCTIVE HOURS	RATE PER HOUR (INPUT)	AMOUNT
2nd Quarter											
Dept. 1	$ 248,000	240,000	.4	96,000	$2.00	$ 192,000	140,000	.2	28,000	$2.00	$ 56,000
Dept. 2	72,000	240,000	.2	48,000	1.50	72,000					
Dept. 3	124,000	240,000	.4	96,000	1.00	96,000	140,000	.2	28,000	1.00	28,000
Totals	$ 444,000			240,000		$ 360,000			56,000		$ 84,000
3rd Quarter											
Dept. 1	$ 234,800	230,000	.4	92,000	$2.00	$ 184,000	127,000	.2	25,400	$2.00	$ 50,800
Dept. 2	69,000	230,000	.2	46,000	1.50	69,000					
Dept. 3	117,400	230,000	.4	92,000	1.00	92,000	127,000	.2	25,400	1.00	25,400
Totals	$ 421,200			230,000		$ 345,000			50,800		$ 76,200
4th Quarter											
Dept. 1	$ 266,000	260,000	.4	104,000	$2.00	$ 208,000	145,000	.2	29,000	$2.00	$ 58,000
Dept. 2	78,000	260,000	.2	52,000	1.50	78,000					
Dept. 3	133,000	260,000	.4	104,000	1.00	104,000	145,000	.2	29,000	1.00	29,000
Totals	$ 477,000			260,000		$ 390,000			58,800		$ 87,000
Totals for Year	$1,752,000			960,000		$1,440,000			208,000		$312,000

SCHEDULE 31. Superior Manufacturing Company
BUDGETED DIRECT LABOR HOURS
For the Year Ending December 31, 1977

	REF.	TOTAL	DEPARTMENT 1			DEPARTMENT 2			DEPARTMENT 3		
			PRODUCT X 30	PRODUCT Y 30	TOTAL	PRODUCT X 30	PRODUCT Y	TOTAL	PRODUCT X 30	PRODUCT Y 30	TOTAL
January		83,600	28,000	6,800	34,800	14,000	—	14,000	28,000	6,800	34,800
February		94,400	32,000	7,200	39,200	16,000	—	16,000	32,000	7,200	39,200
March		95,200	32,000	7,600	39,600	16,000	—	16,000	32,000	7,600	39,600
Total 1st Quarter		273,200	92,000	21,600	113,600	46,000	—	46,000	92,000	21,600	113,600
2nd Quarter		296,000	96,000	28,000	124,000	48,000	—	48,000	96,000	28,000	124,000
3rd Quarter		280,800	92,000	25,400	117,400	46,000	—	46,000	92,000	25,400	117,400
4th Quarter		318,000	104,000	29,000	133,000	52,000	—	52,000	104,000	29,000	133,000
Total Year		1,168,000	384,000	104,000	488,000	192,000	—	192,000	384,000	104,000	488,000

4. What are the principal approaches that may be used in developing the direct labor budget?

5. Generally, how should direct labor hours be estimated?

6. Generally, how should estimated average wage rates be developed?

7. Is direct labor normally a fixed cost, a variable cost, or a semivariable cost? Explain.

8. How should direct labor be classified in the direct labor budget? Explain.

9. How can budgeting direct labor contribute to managerial planning?

10. What are the basic approaches that can be used to control direct labor?

CASE 8-1
Jacobs Company

Jacobs Company is a manufacturer of special metal parts that are sold in a seven-state region. There are two regular products, A and B, that are produced throughout the year; a small constant inventory of these two products is maintained at all times. In addition, the company performs special jobs (contracts) for regular customers. These special jobs are limited to the manufacturing capabilities of the company and are accepted principally as a service to the regular customers although the work is quite profitable. Generally, these jobs have a flexible delivery date and can be used as fill-in work. The principal problem posed by the special jobs is storage space "on the floor" since regular production moves around them. The company manufactures to the "highest quality obtainable"; therefore, regular customers remain over the years and have a close relationship with Jacobs.

There are three service departments and six production departments in the factory. One production department, No. 3, is subdivided into two cost centers. The company uses standards in accounting for direct materials and direct labor. The manufacturing manager has a two-man standards group that keeps the standards up to date. Operations are planned on a six-month cycle detailed by month. Certain planned inputs for the upcoming six-month period are summarized in Exhibit 1.

Product A passes through all six of the producing departments; product B passes through all producing departments except cost center 3B. Special jobs normally require the equivalent of 10 percent of the total work scheduled in each department on products A and B combined, except in Milling and Grinding where it amounts to 5 percent.

EXHIBIT 1. Departmental Operational Data Summarized (Planned)

DEPARTMENT	MINUTES TO PERFORM THE OPERATION	AVERAGE WAGE RATES PER HOUR
1 Preparation	30	$3.00
2 Cutting and Shipping	40	3.30
3 Cost center A—Drilling	10	2.00
3 Cost center B—Tapping	20	2.20
4 Milling and Grinding	50	4.00
5 Assembly	30	3.00
6 Inspection	15	Two salaries of $700 per month each

Required:

   a. Design suitable schedules for the direct labor budget; assume there is a need
       for separate schedules for (a) hours only and (b) cost.
   b. Develop the direct labor estimates for the first month (January) assuming the
       sales plan calls for 900 units of product A, 600 units of product B, and the
       "normal" quantity of special jobs. Also indicate unit cost.

CASE 8-2
Benson Machine Works

Benson Machine Works is a small company with approximately 145
employees. The corporation operates a machine-shop type of manufacture. Two regular
products are manufactured that are sold to distributors. In addition, the company accepts
jobs to manufacture items according to specifications furnished by the customer. These
items vary from small, simply constructed bearings to complex subassemblies. Orders may
vary from ten units to several thousand, with frequent repeat orders.

The company has been budgeting for the past two years. The budget year starts
each January 1. It is now December 16 and the budget for the upcoming year is being
completed. Although direct labor is controlled primarily through labor standards and by
close supervision at all times, a direct labor budget is prepared so that *income, cash, and
certain other budgets* may be realistically developed.

The direct labor budget is developed simply by relating labor costs to sales dollars.
The computations for the profit plan being developed were as follows:

DEPARTMENT	DIRECT LABOR COST DURING PAST 12 MONTHS	DOLLAR SALES PAST 12 MONTHS	HISTORICAL RATIO	PROJECTED RATIO
1	$13,500	$200,000	6.75	6
2	4,500	200,000	2.25	2
3	8,400	200,000	4.20	4
4	11,600	200,000	5.80	5
5	15,700	200,000	7.85	7
6	17,800	200,000	8.90	8
	$71,500		35.75	32

DIRECT LABOR BUDGET

QUARTER	PLANNED SALES	DEPT. 1 RATIO 6	DEPT. 2 RATIO 2	DEPT. 3 RATIO 4	DEPT. 4 RATIO 5	DEPT. 5 RATIO 7	DEPT. 6 RATIO 8	TOTAL RATIO 32
1	$ 50,000	$ 3,000	$1,000	$2,000	$2,500	$ 3,500	$ 4,000	$16,000
2	56,000							17,920
3	60,000	Etc.	Etc.	Etc.	Etc.	Etc.	Etc.	19,200
4	59,000							18,880
Year	$225,000	$13,500	$4,500	$9,000	$11,250	$15,750	$18,000	$72,000

Some producing departments are forced to work overtime during certain periods. Although there is some seasonality in the overtime, unusually large orders with tight delivery dates may come in at any time. The union contract requires that time and one-half be paid for overtime up to ten hours per week; above this the pay is double-time. During the past two years considerable discussions have taken place in the budget meetings as to how the overtime should be treated in the budget. The practice so far has been to "sort of average it in by increasing the average wage rates." The executive in charge of operations feels that the "inaccuracy of the direct labor budget has been due primarily to this approach; if we didn't have this problem we could budget direct labor with some assurance."

The management is also concerned about the upcoming union contract negotiations. Because the company has not had to consider this problem since the adoption of the budget program, no procedures have been established. The union contract expires at the end of February of the coming year. Preliminary discussions have been held with the union representatives. The union has presented a proposal that calls for a 15 percent increase in average hourly pay. The management has taken the position that the outlook does not justify a wage increase. It is felt that competition is stronger than ever; price resistance is very stiff; and any attempt to raise prices, as would be necessary in the face of a wage increase, would cause serious loss of business. The company would have to lay off workers. In a closed meeting on December 10 of the current year, top management tentatively decided that it would be willing to sign a new contract with a wage rate increase of 5 percent.

There is disagreement in the executive committee whether a wage increase should be included in the direct labor budget as constructed for the upcoming year. Several feel that "we don't want to develop another budget at the end of February."

Required:

Evaluate the approach used by the company to develop the direct labor budget. Present recommendations that appear appropriate (including overtime and the union demands).

CASE 8-3

Pocono Corporation

Pocono Corporation produces products X, Y, and Z. All three products are processed through process 1; Y and Z through process 2; and Z through process 3. The company prepares a semiannual profit plan. Profit plan data developed to date are:

1. Production budget (units):

	X	Y	Z
July	5,000	3,000	21,000
August	7,000	6,000	26,000
September	10,000	8,000	30,000
4th Quarter	25,000	18,000	75,000

2. Indirect labor cost estimates:

	PROCESS 1	PROCESS 2	PROCESS 3
July	$35,000	$20,000	$15,000
August	37,000	21,000	16,000
September	38,000	24,000	18,000
4th Quarter	98,000	62,000	48,000

3. Direct labor standard hours per unit of product:

	PROCESS 1	PROCESS 2	PROCESS 3
X	$1\frac{1}{2}$	—	—
Y	$1\frac{1}{2}$	3	—
Z	$1\frac{1}{2}$	2	5

4. Average wage rates budgeted:

Process 1	$2.00
Process 2	2.20
Process 3	1.80

Required:

Pocono develops two budgets related to direct labor designated as follows: (1) budgeted direct labor hours, and (2) budgeted direct labor cost.

a. Compute the following amounts that would be shown on the schedule for "budgeted direct labor hours."
   1. Direct labor hours during July for process 2, by product.
   2. Total direct labor hours for the six-month period for process 2, by product.
b. Compute the following amounts that would be shown on the schedule for "budgeted direct labor cost."
   1. Direct labor cost during July for process 2, by product.
   2. Direct labor cost for the six-month period, by product.

CASE 8-4
Bostrand Company

Bostrand Company produces two products, AX and BX. The products are processed through two departments, 1 and 2. Planning budget data developed are:

1. From the production plan (units):

	AX	BX
January	5,000	14,000
February	4,000	12,000
March	6,000	15,000
2nd Quarter	18,000	50,000
3rd Quarter	22,000	60,000
4th Quarter	16,000	45,000

2. Standard labor times developed by the industrial engineers (hours per unit of finished product):

PRODUCT	DEPARTMENT 1	DEPARTMENT 2
AX	4	3
BX	2	5

3. Average wage rates to be budgeted (simplified):

Department 1	$2.10
Department 2	1.90

Required:

Prepare the following direct labor budgets (by time, department, and product):

a. Direct labor hours.
b. Direct labor cost.

CASE 8-5
Roth Company

Roth Company manufactures four different products that are variously processed through seven producing departments. Direct labor is used in each of the departments. A comprehensive profit planning and control program is currently being developed. The first annual profit plan was recently completed; the following has been extracted from the direct labor budget:

	JANUARY			FEBRUARY
	PRODUCTION PLAN UNITS	PLANNED DIRECT LABOR HOURS	PLANNED DIRECT LABOR COST	ETC.
Department 1:				
Product X	5,000	9,000	$36,000	
Product Y	8,000	17,600	52,800	
Department 2:				
Etc.				

The first month (January) of operations under the annual profit plan has just ended; the controller's department has just developed the following actual data for January:

	UNITS PRODUCED	DIRECT LABOR HOURS	DIRECT LABOR COST
Department 1			
Product X	5,400	10,000	$41,500
Product Y	7,800	17,000	49,300

The format of the departmental performance reports is under consideration. Tom Collins, the manager of Department 1, has expressed a keen interest in both the format and "figures" that will be reflected in the reports.

Required:

Design a departmental performance report that incorporates all features that you consider relevant and useful in this situation. Present a sample report for Department 1. Use the above data on direct labor to illustrate your recommendations. Be prepared to justify your recommendations.

CASE 8-6
Doran Company

Doran Company prepares an annual profit plan broken down by months. At the end of each month, control reports are prepared for management that compare actual costs with budget allowances. At the end of March the following data are available:

1.   Actual direct labor costs:

	DEPT. A	DEPT. B	DEPT. C
January	$53,000	$53,000	$67,000
February	44,000	47,000	62,200
March	40,000	44,000	48,800

2.   Direct labor allowances in the profit plan:

	DEPT. A HOURS	DEPT. A AMOUNT	DEPT. B HOURS	DEPT. B AMOUNT	DEPT. C HOURS	DEPT. C AMOUNT
January	30,000	$60,000	27,000	$56,700	28,000	$61,600
February	24,000	48,000	23,000	48,300	27,000	59,400
March	23,000	46,000	23,000	48,300	20,000	44,000

3. Actual units produced:

	DEPT. A	DEPT. B	DEPT. C
January	13,000	8,500	30,000
February	11,000	7,500	28,000
March	10,000	7,000	22,000

4. Standard labor hours per unit of product:

Dept. A	2
Dept. B	3
Dept. C	1

5. Average wage rates budgeted:

Dept. A	$2.00
Dept. B	2.10
Dept. C	2.20

6. Actual direct labor hours:

	DEPT. A	DEPT. B	DEPT. C
January	28,000	29,500	39,500
February	19,000	20,000	19,500
March	20,000	20,500	21,000

Required:

Prepare a performance report showing the status of direct labor control for March and year to date. Be prepared to justify your approach.

Planning Expenses—
Manufacturing Overhead,
Distribution and Administrative
Expenses

chapter nine

In developing a profit plan, expenses must be planned carefully. Planning expenses should focus on (1) projecting cash outflows, and (2) effective cost control. Managers should view expense planning and control as necessary to maintain realistic expense levels essential to support the objectives and planned programs of the enterprise. Thus, expense planning should not focus on decreasing expenses but rather on better utilization of limited resources. Viewed in this light, realistic expense planning and control may prompt either decreased or increased expenditures. In the case of increased expenditures, the gain to the enterprise (such as profits, return on investment, cash flow) accrues as a result of better operational programs, increasing scope of activities, improved quality, and higher employee performance. Expense planning and control must focus on the relationship between expenditures and benefits derived from those expenditures. The essential benefits must be developed as *planned* goals, and sufficient resources must be planned to support the programs essential for their accomplishment. To illustrate, some companies, attempting to cut expenses without adequately planning benefits, fail to commit sufficient resources to maintenance of assets such as equipment and buildings. Inevitably, this short-range policy, although temporarily reducing expenses, soon generates even greater costs because of breakdowns, inefficient machines, frustrated employees, faulty machine tolerances, major repair costs, and shortened asset life.

Cost control must be tied firmly to (1) future goals and planned operations and (2) organizational responsibilities. The essence of expense control, aside from direct supervision, is the concept of a standard; that is, what each expense should be under a given set of conditions (for instance, work programs, products, management policies, and environmental variables).

This and the following chapters are devoted primarily to the problems of planning and controlling the three broad categories of expenses: manufacturing overhead; distribution expenses; and general adminstrative expenses. This chapter emphasizes cost planning for the tactical short-range profit plan. The next chapter focuses on the analysis and control of expenses.[1]

Up to this point planning and control of direct material and direct labor costs have been discussed and illustrated. It is logical to consider next other categories of business expense. Therefore, after a general discussion of certain cost concepts, this chapter will be subdivided as follows:

1. Manufacturing expense (factory overhead).
2. Distribution or selling expenses.
3. General administrative expenses.
4. Financial and other expenses.

SOME RELEVANT DISTINCTIONS

Because we are concerned primarily with cost planning and control it is appropriate to call attention to the prior discussions of the fundamentals of planning and control (Chapters 1–3). In this and the next chapter, the discussions will explain specific concepts and procedures useful in applying those fundamentals. In all discussions of costs, remember that cost constructions, to be useful, must be appropriate for the problem at hand; what is termed *cost* for one purpose or use may be an inappropriate cost construction for another purpose even though essentially the same *underlying data* may be relevant.

Classification of Costs by Responsibility. Because control is exercised through responsibilities, it is necessary that costs be planned according to organizational responsibilities; that is, separately for each cost center. The chart of accounts used by the accounting department and the design of the expense budgets must be tailored to organizational responsibilities.

Considering *costs by responsibility*, cost allocations essential for *financial accounting purposes* (such as for product costing) are inappropriate for control purposes; the basis used for the allocation of an expense generally is arbitrary

---

[1] Throughout these discussions the two terms "cost" and "expense" are used interchangeably.

and the resultant amount allocated is not controllable by the organizational unit in question. In principle, then, we emphasize that *cost allocation generally is inconsistent* with control objectives.

Cost Behavior. Knowledge of cost behavior—that is, the response of a cost to different volumes of output—is essential in cost planning and controlling. Cost behavior can be viewed from the vantage point of the entire enterprise (as in cost-volume-profit analysis) or in the context of a specific responsibility center (as is necessary in planning and controlling costs). Cost behavior may be expressed rather pragmatically. As the output (volume of work) in a responsibility center increases and decreases, what happens (or should happen) to each item of expense incurred in that center? When expenses are viewed in relationship to changes in output, three distinct cost categories emerge:

1. *Fixed costs*—Those items of cost that tend to remain constant, in total from month to month regardless of fluctuations in output or volume of work done. Because any cost can change, this concept must be applied (1) to a realistic or *relevant range of output* and (2) in relation to a given set of conditions (management policies, time constraints, and characteristics of the operation). Examples of fixed costs are salaries, property taxes, insurance, and depreciation (straight-line).

2. *Variable costs*—Those items of cost that change in total directly with changes in output or volume of work done. The work must be measured in terms of some *activity base*, such as units completed, direct labor hours worked, sales dollars, and number of service calls, depending upon the work of the organizational unit. Examples of variable costs in a factory are direct materials, direct labor, and power usage.

3. *Semivariable costs*—Those items of cost that are neither fixed nor variable —that is, they possess some characteristics of both. As output changes, semivariable costs change in the same direction but not in *proportion* thereto.

Determination of the relationship of costs to volume or output is fundamental to a number of important techniques such as variable expense budgets, cost-volume-profit analyses, marginal cost analyses, direct costing, and differential cost analyses. Each of these concepts is discussed in subsequent chapters; the next chapter is devoted exclusively to fixed and variable cost analyses and certain applications in cost planning and control.

Controllable and Noncontrollable Costs. Closely related to the expense classification by responsibility is the differentiation between controllable and noncontrollable expenses. *Controllable expenses* are those that are subject to the authority and responsibility of a specific manager. Care must be exercised because the classification of an expense item as controllable or noncontrollable must be made within a specific framework of *responsibility* and *time*. For example, the expenses of a particular responsibility center normally include some items, such as supervisory salaries, which are not ordinarily controllable within the center but rather at higher levels of management. Thus within the framework of the responsibility center such an expense may be classified as noncontrollable; yet when viewed in terms of larger organizational segments, or for the firm as a whole, it is controllable. Similarily, expenses such as depreciation generally are not controllable within the short run but are controllable in the long run because management decisions concerning capital additions determine subsequent depreciation charges. In the final analysis, all costs and expenses are controllable depending upon the responsibility and timing. Thus the concept of controllability is useful for cost control if cost classification is based upon a sound structure of authority and responsibility. The individual items of expense in each department, or other subdivisions of the business, should be clearly identified as controllable or noncontrollable within that particular area of responsibility. This designation is especially important in cost control and in the reporting of comparisons between actual and budget, which measure the performance of specific managers or supervisors. To apply this concept, occasionally it may be advisable to establish two accounts for a particular type of expense in a department. For example, departmental salaries may be carried in two accounts, Salaries—Controllable and Salaries—Noncontrollable, and budgeted in this context.

Some firms include in the monthly *performance report* for each responsibility center only those items of cost that are controllable within the center. Other firms include all of the costs and expenses of the center, clearly identifying the noncontrollable items. For either method, however, it is important that every cost and expense be included on some report and identified as the responsibility of a specified manager. An item classified as noncontrollable on a responsibility center performance report should be included as controllable on some other performance report relating to a higher level of responsibility.

Note that the classifications—controllable and fixed, and noncontrollable and variable—are not synonymous. It is generally true that in the short run, fixed costs are not subject to the same degree of control as are variable costs. Practically all variable costs, by their nature, are controllable in the short run. On the other hand, it is obvious that depreciation on an output basis, for example, is a variable cost noncontrollable in the short run; conversely, certain salaries are controllable in the short run yet are fixed costs.

Cost Reduction and Cost Control. In view of the imprecision of cost terminology, it is useful to keep in mind a distinction between two related concepts, *cost reduction* and *cost control*. Cost reduction programs are directed toward specific efforts to reduce costs by improving methods, approaches, work arrangements, and products. To illustrate, one company reported a significant reduction in the manufacturing costs of a small screen designed to cover an air intake by simply reducing the number of cross wires (without reducing the utility) that needed to be "turned" as shown below. Another firm, as a result of a cost reduction program, replaced all old-style water faucets with others that automatically turned off when released; the consequent cost reduction was substantial.

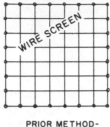   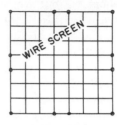

PRIOR METHOD–   NEW METHOD–
ALL 28 ENDS TURNED   ONLY 12 ENDS TURNED

Cost Reduction Example

In the broad sense, cost control includes *cost reduction*; in a narrower sense, cost control may be thought of as managerial efforts to attain cost goals within a particular operational environment. Obviously, management should attack costs from all directions—through cost reduction programs, cost planning, and continuous attention to the cost-incurring decisions. Separate attention to the concepts of cost reduction and cost control frequently is advisable.

PLANNING EXPENSES

In developing the tactical profit plan, the expenses for each responsibility center must be carefully planned. In harmony with the principle of participation, expense planning should involve all levels of management so that realistic expense budgets can be developed for each department, division, and other higher organizational units. In planning expenses for a responsibility center, it is necessary *first* that the *volume* of work, output, or activity for that center be planned. For example, in order to develop an expense plan for the power department, the expected demands for power must be estimated; an expenditure plan for research and development must be related to the type and extent of research activities planned. Thus, we see that all expense planning should be directly keyed to planned outputs.

With respect to formal development of the tactical short-term *profit plan*, we should expect to develop a separate *expense budget* for each responsibility center. We have already considered the development of direct material and direct labor budgets on this basis. To develop the manufacturing plans to be incorporated in the short-term profit plan, the following sequence is typical:

1. Direct Material and Labor Cost Budgets—Developed immediately after the production budget is completed and tentatively approved.

2. Factory Overhead Budgets—Developed immediately after the production budget, as tentatively approved, has been *converted* to expected output (however measured) for each producing and each service department in the factory.

3. Distribution Cost Budgets—Developed *concurrently* with the sales plan, because they are mutually dependent.

4. Administrative Cost Budgets—Developed immediately after the approved sales plan (and perhaps the production budget) has been *converted* to expected *activity* for each administrative department involved.

Detailed expense budgets for each responsibility center should be included in the short-term profit plan for a number of reasons, principally these:

1. So that the effects of various planned revenues and related expenses may be aggregated in a planned income statement.
2. So that the cash outflow required for costs and expenses can be realistically planned.
3. To provide an initial expense objective for each responsibility center.
4. To provide a standard to be used during the period covered by the profit plan for each item of expense in each responsibility center for comparison with actual costs on the performance reports.

These four reasons suggest the importance of the careful planning of expenses and use of the resultant projections for further planning, control, and evaluation.

PLANNING MANUFACTURING OVERHEAD

In building the overall manufacturing plans and after developing the production plan, expense budgets must be established for each responsibility center in the factory. These expense budgets must be detailed by interim time periods (months and/or quarters) and by the three categories of cost: direct materials; direct labor; and manufacturing overhead. After the production plan is completed, these cost budgets normally are developed simultaneously and are then consolidated into a budget appropriately labeled the *planned cost of goods manufactured*. The latter budget requires that all factory costs be identified, *either directly or by allocation*, for each product.

Manufacturing overhead is that part of total factory cost not directly identifiable (traceable to) with specific products or jobs. Manufacturing overhead consists of (1) indirect material, (2) indirect labor (including salaries), and (3) all other miscellaneous factory expense items such as taxes, insurance, depreciation, supplies, utilities, and repairs. Each of these costs present major problems in themselves. In highly mechanized manufacturing situations, overhead costs typically are considerably higher than in less mechanized situations.

The fact that manufacturing overhead includes many dissimilar expenses creates problems for management, especially in the *allocation* of these costs to products, and in *cost control*. Since there are many different types of expenses, control responsibility is often widely diffused. For example, such items as depreciation, taxes, and insurance are not generally subject to the direct control of factory management but to that of higher level management.

There are two distinct types of responsibility centers in practically all manufacturing situations, each involving complex cost accounting and budgeting: (1) producing departments and (2) service departments. *Producing departments* are those manufacturing departments that work directly on the products manufactured. *Service departments* do not work on the products directly but rather furnish service to the producing departments and to other service departments. Typical service departments in a factory are: maintenance or repair department, power department, purchases department, production planning department, time and motion study department and general factory administration. Remember that responsibility for the operation of each department should be assigned to a single manager; the expenses for each department should be classified separately in the chart of accounts used by the cost accounting department: and, finally, the expenses of each department should be planned and controlled separately.

The Dual Problem of Manufacturing Expense.   Relative to both budgeting and cost accounting, manufacturing overhead presents a unique challenge because the problem is twofold:

1. The control of manufacturing overhead.
2. The allocation of manufacturing overhead to products manufactured (product costing).

These two problems require different solutions. Frequently they are viewed as one problem, with a consequent limitation on the usefulness of the solution. *The difference between the two problems is critical with respect to the distribution of service department and other indirect factory overhead costs to the producing departments.*

Control of Manufacturing Overhead. We have emphasized that expense control necessitates identification of expense controllability with the specific responsibility center manager. This means that noncontrollable costs that have some relationship with the center must also be carefully identified and not reported as a responsibility of the manager of the center. Thus, to control manufacturing overhead, "clean" expenses must be used; that is, direct expenses only, exclusive of any allocated expenses. For example, let us assume that Producing Department 1 uses a considerable amount of power produced by the Power Department. In accumulating actual costs, budgeting expenses, and in reporting for *control purposes*, the expenses of the Power Department must be identified with the supervisor of the Power Department only, whereas the expenses of Producing Department 1 must be identified with the supervisor of Producing Department 1, exclusive of allocations of actual power cost. The supervisor of the Power Department is responsible for the costs of the services rendered; the supervisor of the using department has no control over those costs. What he *does* control is the *amount of the services (power) used*, rather than the cost of the service. Therefore the performance report of Producing Department 1 should reflect the quantity of power used compared with the quantity of power that should have been used in producing the goods completed. In summary, it is preferable that service usage be controlled on the basis of *units of service*, when possible, rather than on the basis of dollar cost of service. If it is desirable to use dollar cost, then the using department should be charged at *standard rates* rather than at actual rates. It is obvious that *cost allocation generally is inconsistent with effective cost control.*

Product Costing. To plan the *cost of goods manufactured* by product, it is necessary that indirect costs be allocated. In the example just cited, it is necessary that the costs of power used by Producing Department 1 be loaded on the output of the latter department to determine realistically the total cost of production in Producing Department 1. Thus, it is obvious that *cost allocation is consistent with product costing.* The two objectives, cost control and product costing, are brought into harmony by utilizing a separate approach for each. Costs are accumulated and reported for control purposes *prior* to allocation; product costing then follows through allocation procedures.

For the short-term profit plan the overall manufacturing expense budget includes a budget of expense for each department of the factory following the expense classifications used in the cost accounting department. The reliability with which the expense estimates can be made depends upon (1) the quality of the accounting records and (2) the seriousness of management's attitude toward expense planning. Where objectives and the work program are planned and there are adequate accounting records, the important sources for expense estimates are available.

As is the case with most of the subbudgets discussed up to this point, it is desirable to have estimates of manufacturing expense prepared by manufacturing managers. Thus, the manager of each responsibility center should assist in preparing the expense budgets. In some cases it may be impracticable for some managers to prepare their expense budgets. In such cases the next higher manager should prepare the estimates. In those situations it is highly desirable that they be transmitted to the managers concerned for study, appraisal, and recommendations. In all cases the budget and accounting departments should provide any essential data, technical analyses, and staff assistance that may be needed.

Selecting the Activity Base. A central problem in planning and controlling expenses is the selection of a meaningful measure of volume, output, or activity for each responsibility center. The measure of output or activity selected generally is referred to as the *activity base*, volume factor, output factor, or simply as the "output." Obviously, if a department produces only one product or renders only one service, the output of that department is best measured in terms of the particular product or service. Alternatively, in the case of a department that simultaneously produces multiple products or renders multiple services, the measurement of output becomes complex. The outputs of different products or services cannot be combined into a single sum; therefore, one is faced with the problem of selecting a common or equivalent measure that can be identified with each product or service so that aggregate output can be expressed as a single amount for certain purposes. For example, a producing department manufacturing several products simultaneously might accumulate the *direct machine hours* (the activity base) and use the total hours for the particular period to measure the total output or activity of the department. The following measures of activity for the two basic types of factory departments indicate some possibilities:

1. Producing departments:
   a. Units of output (if only one product).
   b. Direct labor hours.
   c. Direct machine hours.
   d. Direct labor dollars.
   e. Raw material consumed.

2. Service departments:
   a. Repair and maintenance—direct repair hours.
   b. Power departments—kilowatt hours delivered.
   c. Purchases department—net purchase dollars.
   d. General factory administration—total direct labor hours in plant or number of employees in plant.

The selection of an appropriate activity base for each department is a responsibility of the factory manager, in cooperation with the controller and the budget manager.

Developing Factory Overhead Budgets. The development of the various components of the factory overhead budget involves several steps that may best be communicated by illustration. Therefore, the next few paragraphs focus on a hypothetical illustration (1) to develop departmental overhead budgets and (2) to compute the *planned cost of goods manufactured*. Assume that the production plan, materials, and direct labor budgets have been completed for our hypothetical company and that the approved *production plan* specifies the following annual data:

PRODUCT	UNITS TO BE PRODUCED
A	7,000 gallons
B	4,000 pounds

Now we are faced with the problem of developing factory overhead enpense budgets for *each department*. There are one service department (repair and maintenance) and two producing departments. Department 1 works only on product A; Department 2 works on both products. The *activity bases* indicated below have been selected and approved:

DEPARTMENT	ACTIVITY BASE
1	Units of product A
2	Direct machine hours (DMH)
Repair and Maintenance	Direct repair hours (DRH)

The first step in developing the departmental overhead expense budgets is to translate the requirements specified in the production plan into output or activity in each department. Two decisional inputs have been developed for this purpose; they are:

1. Standard direct machine hours in Department 2: for product A—4; for product B—3.

2. Standard repair hours: for Department 1—.20 DRH (direct repair hours) for each unit of product A; for Department 2—.07 DRH for each direct machine hour.

These data make it possible to compute the volume of work or activity planned for each department as follows:

		PLANNED DEPARTMENTAL ACTIVITY	
DEPARTMENT	COMPUTATIONS	ACTIVITY BASE	QUANTITY
1	Taken directly from the production plan	Units of product A	7,000
2	Product A: 7,000 × 4 DMH = 28,000		
	Product B: 4,000 × 3 DMH = 12,000	DMH	40,000
Repair and	Dept. 1: 7,000 × .20 = 1,400		
Maintenance	Dept. 2: 40,000 × .07 = 2,800	DRH	4,200

Now that each department manager knows the planned volume of work for his department, he is in a position to plan the departmental overhead expenses. The expense budgets were detailed by month and by expense account; however, for our illustration we will utilize only the annual totals as follows:

DEPARTMENT	PLANNED VOLUME OF WORK	INPUTS BY DEPT. MANAGER PLANNED OVERHEAD—TOTAL
1	7,000 units of A	$26,000
2	40,000 DMH	16,000
Repair and Maintenance	4,200 DRH	6,000

The three departmental overhead budgets summarized immediately above were developed by the departmental managers on the basis of past experience and were approved by higher management. They will be utilized for three primary purposes: (1) to develop the planned cost of goods manufactured; (2) to estimate cash outflows and (3) for control during the upcoming year (that is, for cost goals and performance reports). Only the first use will be illustrated at this point; the others will be deferred to later chapters.

To develop the planned cost of goods manufactured, the total factory overhead must be allocated on a rational basis to the two products being manufactured. *Predetermined overhead rates* are developed for each of the two *producing* departments to accomplish this purpose. To do this the planned service department expenses must be allocated to the two producing departments. Thus the overhead rates for the two producing departments may be computed as follows:

	PRODUCING	DEPARTMENTS
	1	2
Producing department overhead planned (per above)	$26,000	$16,000
Allocation of repair and maintenance cost on the basis of planned service usage (DRH):		
$\frac{1,400}{4,200} \times \$6,000$	2,000	
$\frac{2,800}{4,200} \times \$6,000$		4,000
Total overhead to be allocated to products	$28,000	$20,000
Planned output (activity base):		
Dept. 1—Units of A	7,000	
Dept. 2—Direct machine hours		40,000
Overhead rates:		
Dept. 1—Per unit of A	$4.00	
Dept. 2—Per direct machine hour		$.50

Now we can develop the *planned cost of goods manufactured* by *application of factory overhead*; the planned volume of each product (translated to the activity base) is multiplied by the predetermined overhead rates. The computations are:

		PRODUCT A—7,000 UNITS		PRODUCT B—4,000 UNITS	
COMPUTATIONS		TOTAL COST	UNIT COST	TOTAL COST	UNIT COST
Direct material costs (planned)		$ 70,000	$10.00	$60,000	$15.00
Direct labor costs (planned)		35,000	5.00	14,000	3.50
Factory Overhead Costs Applied:					
Product A:					
Dept. 1 7,000 × $4.00	= $28,000				
Dept. 2 7,000 × 4 DMH × $.50	= $14,000	42,000	6.00		
Product B.					
Dept. 2 4,000 × 3 DMH × $.50				6,000	1.50
Totals		$147,000	$21.00	$80,000	$20.00

Since we have developed expense budgets for each department in the factory and have computed the planned cost of goods manufactured, the planning for this particular class of costs is completed. This is an area where profit planning and cost accounting merge directly because the predetermined overhead rates should also be used by the cost accounting department for application of factory overhead to products in the actual accounts during the year. The application of the above procedures in a more complex situation is illustrated for Superior Manufacturing Company at the end of this chapter.

PLANNING DISTRIBUTION EXPENSES

In the discussions in Chapter 5 on *sales planning*, we indicated that *three* steps were involved: (1) development of a promotion and advertising plan; (2) development of a selling expense plan; and (3) development of a marketing plan. The marketing plan represents the planned sales (volume and dollars) upon which the profit plan is built. This section focuses on the first two components, collectively referred to as the planned distribution expenses. Distribution expenses include all costs related to selling, distribution, and delivery of products to customers. In many companies this element of cost comprises a significant percentage of total costs. Careful planning of such costs coupled with effective control vitally affects the profit potential of the firm.[2]

There are two principal aspects of distribution expense budgeting:

1. Planning and Coordination—In the development of the overall plan of operations as expressed in the profit plan, it is essential that balance be achieved between sales effort (expense) and sales results (revenue).

2. Control of Distribution Costs—Aside from planning considerations, it is important that serious effort be devoted to controlling distribution costs. Control is especially important since (1) distribution costs are frequently a significant portion of total cost, and (2) both sales management and sales personnel tend to view such costs lightly, in some cases almost extravagantly. Take, for example, extravagant entertainment costs. Distribution cost control involves the same principles of control as manufacturing overhead. Control must be built around the concepts of (1) functional responsibility and (2) cost objectives.

Fundamentally, the sales management has the direct responsibility to plan the *optimum balance* (for profit potential) between the (1) sales budget, (2) advertising budget, and (3) the distribution expense budget. As a result profit planning and control views *sales, advertising,* and *distribution expenses* as one basic problem rather than as three separate problems. The logic of this view is obvious when we note the interrelationships between them. The sales budget rests solidly upon the promotional program; the amount of costs that can be expended for a given volume of sales is limited. The practice of some companies of starting with a sales projection, then budgeting a fixed percent of those sales for sales overhead, another fixed percent for field

[2] For comprehensive treatment of distribution costs see: Michael Schiff and Martin Mellman, *Financial Management of the Marketing Function* (New York: Financial Executives Research Foundation, Inc., 1962). Also, note the bibliography contained therein, pp. 251–56.

expenses, and still another fixed percent for advertising, represents a negative management approach to a serious planning problem. In contrast, the sales executives in the better-managed companies tentatively develop the marketing, promotional, and distribution expense plans simultaneously. Next, the dollars of costs essential to carry out the promotional, marketing, and distribution phases are planned with some precision. These cost estimates then become an important part of the input data for the profit plan. Although practice varies, these decisional inputs are given expression separately in (1) the promotion and advertising plan and (2) the budget of selling expenses.

Distribution expenses basically include two major types: (1) home office expenses and (2) field expenses. From the planning and control points of view these costs must be planned by responsibility centers. In some cases this might be by sales district, in other cases by products; in all cases the planning structure should follow the basis upon which the sales efforts are organized. As noted in the first part of this chapter, the concepts of controllable versus noncontrollable costs, fixed versus variable costs, and itemization by types of expenditure generally are applicable to planning and controlling such costs.

CONSTRUCTION OF DISTRIBUTION EXPENSE BUDGETS

Distribution costs are not considered to be a part of cost of goods manufactured (they are not product costs); therefore, *allocating* such costs to specific products is not done in contrast to manufacturing overhead. Thus we can concentrate more directly on the problems of planning and control. In many situations, however, it is desirable to compute the profit for each product, thereby necessitating an allocation of some or all the distribution costs. Such allocations when made are on a more or less arbitrary basis. Such allocations and related analyses are more meaningful if distribution costs can be classified as fixed and variable.

A separate distribution expense budget should be developed for each responsibility center in the distribution function; typically, this would encompass "home office" subunits and "field" subunits. The marketing executive has the direct responsibility for developing the distribution expense budgets; following the principle of participation, the manager of each responsibility center should be assigned direct responsibility for his particular distribution budget. Thus the promotion manager would be responsible for developing the promotion plan, and the field sales supervisors should be responsible for developing both their marketing plans (see Chapter 5) and their selling expense budgets. The selling expense budgets should separately identify the *controllable* expenses, and it should be detailed by interim time period, in harmony with the profit plan time dimensions, and by other relevant classifications. The selling expense budgets developed by the respective sales managers should be based upon a *planned volume of activity or output*. Generally, the *activity* base (that is, the method of measuring output or activity) for the various responsibility centers in the distribution function is *sales dollars*.

When developing the budgets for each responsibility center, the managers must conform to the broad guidelines (planning premises) established by higher management, planned programs of work, and their own judgment. The selling expense budgets should be submitted by the managers of the responsibility centers to the next level of management for evalution, approval, and consolidation. The approval of expense plans is the responsibility of the top management. The selling expense budgets, as finally approved, are utilized subsequently as a basis for: (1) evaluating the cash outflows generated (a function of the treasurer); (2) as a guide (expense objectives) to the manager in controlling expenditures during the period; and (3) for inclusion on the monthly performance reports against which "actual" expenditures are compared.

As in planning and controlling costs in other functional areas, there are a number of special problems in budgeting selling expenses. It would be impractical to attempt to treat comprehensively, or even list, all these problem areas. A good example of a problem that does not fit neatly into *general budget procedures* relates to travel expense incurred by salesmen. Many companies report that they plan and control these particular costs by computing them as a function of sales (either quantity or dollar sales); that is, they assume this particular cost should increase as sales increase and vice versa. Conversely, some sales executives say certain costs should be made to vary inversely with sales—as sales fall off *more* effort and travel may be essential to reverse the sales trend. Obviously, this particular problem, as with other special problems, must be analyzed, planned, and controlled separately. Such problems take on an entirely different complexion when encountered in new situations. Other special problems in planning distribution costs relate to freight, entertainment, warehousing, returned goods, and special allowances.

Development of the *promotion and advertising plan* in the typical company is a complex endeavor that should involve most of the marketing managers. For this reason, among others, companies commonly establish the position of advertising manager. The advertising may vary from international programs to local advertising on a small scale. Although a comprehensive treatment of this subject is clearly outside the scope of this book, we might note some aspects of the problem.[3] There are certain types of

[3] For comprehensive treatments of this subject see: Albert W. Frey, *Advertising*, 3rd ed. (New York: The Ronald Press Company, 1961).

expenditures in a business that are best planned and controlled on the basis of definite *appropriations* for specific time periods. Research costs and advertising costs are of such a nature that some justification for unlimited expenditures might be forthcoming. Therefore, top management should require that such activities be specifically programmed and planned and that the attendant costs be carefully estimated. Once such plans and related expenditures are approved by top management, they may constitute, in effect, an appropriation of a specific amount necessary for their execution. Control is achieved through continuous reporting of progress and expenditures.

Various methods are used to determine the promotion and advertising appropriation. The more commonly used methods may be characterized as follows:

1. Arbitrary appropriation.
2. All available funds.
3. Competitive parity.
4. Percentage of sales.
5. Fixed sum per unit.
6. Previous year's profits.
7. Return on investment.
8. The task method.

Under the task method, certain practical objectives to be achieved by promotion and advertising are established and then a program consistent with these objectives is set up. Recognized authorities in the advertising field generally agree that the task method is preferable.

It goes without saying that the expenditures for promotion and advertising must be within the reasonable capabilities of the firm. Accordingly, from the planning viewpoint, a detailed advertising budget must be prepared.

The promotion and advertising budget should be the direct responsibility of the marketing executives—specifically, the advertising manager—for it is inconceivable that an accurate sales budget could be developed without at the same time developing detailed promotion plans. The detailed promotion budget should be presented to the budget committee in conjunction with the sales budget. Certainly the two budgets should be approved or disapproved as a unit. Thus the budget department receives the detailed and approved promotion budget for incorporation in the overall profit plan. Control, in large measure, is achieved through reports of activities and actual expenditures to date compared with advertising appropriations to date as indicated in the advertising budget.

From a practical standpoint, costs or expenses set forth in an *appropriation* budget may be thought of as *fixed costs* for analytical purposes. The total amount of the cost for the period is determined by management policy. Note in the illustrative case at the end of the chapter that such costs are treated as fixed costs.

In the accounting department, promotion and advertising costs, after having been budgeted for the year, may be *accrued* on a monthly basis by a debit to advertising expense and a credit to an advertising clearing account; actual expenditures are then debited to the latter account. In such cases the related budget procedures should be consistent. Distribution expense budgets are illustrated at the end of the chapter for Superior Manufacturing Company.

PLANNING ADMINISTRATIVE EXPENSES

Administrative expenses include operational costs other than manufacturing and distribution. In general, they are incurred in the supervision of and service to all major functions of the business rather than in the performance of any one function. Because a large portion of adminstrative expenses are fixed rather than variable, the notion persists that they cannot be controlled. Outside of certain top-management salaries, which, in the case of a corporation, may be set by the board of directors, most administrative expenses are determined by management policies and decisions. It is common to find administrative costs top-heavy when measured by the volume of business done. In recent years a number of informed observers have expressed the opinion that a developing characteristic of industry in the United States is the high cost of administration. These costs, along with labor costs, frequently have made it difficult to price products competitively in the international market. As general administrative costs are close to top management, there is a strong tendency to overlook their magnitude and effect on profit potential. Each administrative cost should be directly identified with a reponsibility center, and the manager would be responsible for planning and controlling it. This fundamental of cost control is especially important for administrative costs because there is a strong tendency not to pinpoint responsibility for costs of a general nature or those incurred in large part by top management. For these and other reasons, many companies have found it helpful to use the fixed-variable classification for administrative costs. In such cases the variable costs are related (correlated) with total sales dollars. This approach tends to emphasize that when volume drops, these costs should decrease also, or else the profit potential is lowered.

Central administration in any company, except the very small ones, is carried on in a number of special responsibility centers, such as central administration, controller's department, treasurer's department, profit planning and control department, and central staff. Thus, the overall administrative expense budget comprises a number of departmental budgets. The manager of each of these departments should be assigned the primary responsibility for planning and controlling his operations, including the requisite expenses that are subject to his control. The administrative expense budgets for each responsibility center, after preparation by the respective managers, should be subject to approval by higher management in the same manner as discussed for all other budgets.

Generally, it is best to base budgeted administrative expenses on specific plans and programs. Past experience, adjusted for anticipated changes in management policy and general economic conditions, is helpful. Because most administrative expenses are fixed, an analysis of the historical record will generally provide a sound basis for budgeting them.

The principle of variable budgets (see Chapter 10) has been widely accepted to control manufacturing expenses, but there is seldom any practical reason for not applying the concept to administrative expense. The fact that most of the administrative expenses are fixed simplifies the application of variable budgets.

EXPENSE BUDGETS ILLUSTRATED

Recall that the factory division of Superior Manufacturing Company (Illustration 7, Chapter 4) has three service departments (General and Administrative, Power, and Repair) and three producing departments (designated 1, 2, and 3). There are three sales districts and the home office in the marketing function. There are four central departments (Administrative, Accounting, Treasurer, and Building Services). Since there are fourteen different departments, that number of expense budgets must be prepared. First we will illustrate the building services and factory expense budgets.

The management selected the following *activity bases* (measures of output or volume of work) for the factory departments:

DEPARTMENT	ACTIVITY BASE (OUTPUT)
Producing	Departmental direct labor hours (DLH)
General and administrative—factory	Total direct labor hours
Power	Kilowatt hours
Repair	Direct repair hours

The Company owns a building that houses all divisions of the company. The building is occupied by the three divisions as follows: factory division, 60 percent of the floor space; sales division, 20 percent; and general office, 20 percent. The occupancy costs are allocated to the three divisions on this basis. The building superintendent provided the building services budget shown in Schedule 32.

The next step was to translate the production budget (Schedule 22 Chapter 6) into volume of work, output, or activity generated for each department. Since direct labor hours constitute the activity base for the three producing deparments and General and Administrative, the direct labor budget (Schedule 31, Chapter 8) provides the requisite volume of work data. The managers of the power and repair departments, on the basis of past experience as reflected in the past reports, translated the production budget into the following *planned* outputs for their respective departments:

Planned Outputs

POWER DEPARTMENT		REPAIR DEPARTMENT	
	KILOWATT HOURS (000)		DIRECT REPAIR HOURS
January	1,450	January	290
February	1,600	February	330
March	1,600	March	320
Second Quarter	5,100	Second Quarter	1,000
Third Quarter	4,800	Third Quarter	970
Fourth Quarter	5,450	Fourth Quarter	1,090
Total	20,000	Total	4,000

The manager of each of the six factory departments, on the basis of the planned volume of work as translated from the production plan and past experience, developed tentative expense budgets for their respective departments. In developing these expense budgets, they were assisted by their immediate supervisor, staff from the manufacturing manager's office, and personnel from the office of the director of profit planning and control. The tentative expense budgets were carefully reviewed by higher management; after all agreed-upon changes were made, the budgets were approved as reflected in Schedules 33 and 34. Note that the expense budgets reflect (1) planned volume of work and (2) expense goals for each item of expense within the department. You should also observe that noncontrollable expenses are identified.

The next step in completing the overall manufacturing budget involves the allocation of planned factory overhead to each of the products being manufactured (X and Y). You should recall that direct material and direct labor costs were identified with each product in Schedules 28 and 31, Chapters 7 and 8. The Company utilizes predetermined overhead rates to apportion factory expenses to products. The computation of an overhead rate for each of the three producing departments is shown in Schedule 35. Observe that the total annual expense was taken from the six factory overhead expense budgets and entered on this schedule as *direct department costs*; next the build-

SCHEDULE 32. Superior Manufacturing Company
Expense Budget—Building Services
For the Year Ending December 31, 1977

| | ANNUAL | 1ST QUARTER | | | QUARTERS | | | |
	TOTAL (INPUT)	JANUARY (INPUT)	FEBRUARY (INPUT)	MARCH (INPUT)	1ST (INPUT)	2ND (INPUT)	3RD (INPUT)	4TH (INPUT)
*Supervisory salaries	$ 24,000	$ 2,000	$ 2,000	$ 2,000	$ 6,000	$ 6,000	$ 6,000	$ 6,000
Repairs and maintenance	18,000	1,500	1,500	1,500	4,500	4,500	4,500	4,500
*Depreciation	60,000	5,000	5,000	5,000	15,000	15,000	15,000	15,000
*Insurance	3,600	300	300	300	900	900	900	900
*Taxes	2,400	200	200	200	600	600	600	600
Wages	26,800	2,250	2,150	2,150	6,550	6,750	6,750	6,750
Heat and light	13,200	1,800	1,000	900	3,700	2,000	2,750	4,750
Water	2,000	150	150	170	470	630	500	400
Totals	$150,000	$13,200	$12,300	$12,220	$37,720	$36,380	$37,000	$38,900
Distribution of occupancy cost:								
Factory 60%	$ 90,000	$ 7,920	$ 7,380	$ 7,332	$22,632	$21,828	$22,200	$23,340
Sales 20%	30,000	2,640	2,460	2,444	7,544	7,276	7,400	7,780
Administrative 20%	30,000	2,640	2,460	2,444	7,544	7,276	7,400	7,780
Total 100%	$150,000	$13,200	$12,300	$12,220	$37,720	$36,380	$37,000	$38,900

*Not controllable in this department.

SCHEDULE 33. Superior Manufacturing Company
Factory Expense Budgets
(Service Departments)
For the Year Ending December 31, 1977

	REF.	ANNUAL TOTAL	FIRST QUARTER			QUARTERS		
			JANUARY	FEBRUARY	MARCH	SECOND	THIRD	FOURTH
General and administrative								
Factory Overhead								
Volume—Total DLH	31	1,168,000	83,600	94,400	95,200	296,000	280,800	318,000
*Supervisory Salaries	(Input)	$ 96,000	$ 8,000	$ 8,000	$ 8,000	$ 24,000	$ 24,000	$ 24,000
Travel and entertainment	"	7,040	518	572	576	1,780	1,704	1,890
Telephone and telegraph	"	7,586	627	649	650	1,972	1,942	2,016
*Depreciation	"	1,560	130	130	130	390	390	390
*Insurance	"	240	20	20	20	60	60	60
*Taxes	"	360	30	30	30	90	90	90
Stationery and office supplies	"	3,744	271	303	306	948	902	1,014
Totals		$ 116,800	$ 9,596	$ 9,704	$ 9,712	$ 29,240	$ 29,088	$ 29,460
Power Department:								
Volume—Kilowatt Hours (000's)	"	20,000	1,450	1,600	1,600	5,100	4,800	5,450
*Supervisory salaries	"	$ 36,000	$ 3,000	$ 3,000	$ 3,000	$ 9,000	$ 9,000	$ 9,000
Maintenance	"	6,800	506	548	548	1,728	1,644	1,826
Fuel	"	24,000	1,740	1,920	1,920	6,120	5,760	6,540
*Depreciation	"	5,400	450	450	450	1,350	1,350	1,350
*Insurance	"	840	70	70	70	210	210	210
*Taxes	"	960	80	80	80	240	240	240
Wages	"	36,000	3,000	3,000	3,000	9,000	9,000	9,000
Totals		$ 110,000	$ 8,846	$ 9,068	$ 9,068	$ 27,648	$ 27,204	$ 28,166

SCHEDULE 33. (Continued)

	REF.	ANNUAL TOTAL	FIRST QUARTER			QUARTERS		
			JANUARY	FEBRUARY	MARCH	SECOND	THIRD	FOURTH
Repair Department:								
Volume—Repair Hours	(Input)	4,000	290	330	320	1,000	970	1,090
*Supervisory salaries	"	$ 3,600	$ 300	$ 300	$ 300	$ 900	$ 900	$ 900
Supplies used	"	1,360	99	112	109	340	330	370
*Depreciation	"	120	10	10	10	30	30	30
*Insurance	"	36	3	3	3	9	9	9
*Taxes	"	84	7	7	7	21	21	21
Wages	"	4,800	400	400	400	1,200	1,200	1,200
Totals		$ 10,000	$ 819	$ 832	$ 829	$ 2,500	$ 2,490	$ 2,530

*Not controllable in this department.

SCHEDULE 34. Superior Manufacturing Company
Factory Expense Budgets
(Producing Departments)
For the Year Ending December 31, 1977

	REF.	ANNUAL TOTAL	FIRST QUARTER			QUARTERS		
			JANUARY	FEBRUARY	MARCH	SECOND	THIRD	FOURTH
Producing Department 1								
Volume—DLH	31	488,000	34,800	39,200	39,600	124,000	117,400	133,000
*Supervisory salaries	(Input)	$120,000	$10,000	$10,000	$10,000	$30,000	$30,000	$30,000
Indirect labor	"	145,800	10,830	11,820	11,910	36,900	35,415	38,925
Maintenance parts	"	10,920	822	888	894	2,760	2,661	2,895
Supplies used	"	32,240	2,364	2,606	2,628	8,170	7,807	8,665
*Depreciation	"	7,320	522	588	594	1,860	1,761	1,995
*Insurance	"	1,200	100	100	100	300	300	300
*Taxes	"	1,800	150	150	150	450	450	450
Totals		$319,280	$24,788	$26,152	$26,276	$80,440	$78,394	$83,230
Producing Department 2								
Volume—DLH	31	192,000	14,000	16,000	16,000	48,000	46,000	52,000
*Supervisory salaries	(Input)	$22,440	$1,870	$1,870	$1,870	$5,610	$5,610	$5,610
Indirect labor	"	3,648	266	304	304	912	874	988
Maintenance parts	"	624	48	52	52	156	152	164
Supplies used	"	1,440	110	120	120	360	350	380
*Depreciation	"	768	56	64	64	192	184	208
*Insurance	"	120	10	10	10	30	30	30
*Taxes	"	240	20	20	20	60	60	60
Totals		$29,280	$2,380	$2,440	$2,440	$7,320	$7,260	$7,440

SCHEDULE 34. (Continued)

	REF.	ANNUAL TOTAL	FIRST QUARTER			QUARTERS		
			JANUARY	FEBRUARY	MARCH	SECOND	THIRD	FOURTH
Producing Department 3								
Volume—DLH	31	488,000	34,800	39,200	39,600	124,000	117,400	133,000
*Supervisory salaries	(Input)	$ 35,040	$ 2,920	$ 2,920	$ 2,920	$ 8,760	$ 8,760	$ 8,760
Indirect labor	"	44,248	3,271	3,583	3,612	11,204	10,735	11,843
Maintenance parts	"	4,240	324	346	348	1,070	1,037	1,115
Supplies used	"	14,600	1,070	1,180	1,190	3,700	3,535	3,925
*Depreciation	"	4,392	313	353	356	1,116	1,057	1,197
*Insurance	"	600	50	50	50	150	150	150
*Taxes	"	720	60	60	60	180	180	180
Totals		$103,840	$ 8,008	$ 8,492	$ 8,536	$ 26,180	$ 25,454	$ 27,170
Summary:								
*Building services		$ 90,000	$ 7,920	$ 7,380	$ 7,332	$ 21,828	$ 22,200	$ 23,340
Service departments		236,800	19,261	19,604	19,609	59,388	58,782	60,156
Producing departments		452,400	35,176	37,084	37,252	113,940	111,108	117,840
Totals		$779,200	$62,357	$64,068	$64,193	$195,156	$192,090	$201,336

*Not controllable in this department.

SCHEDULE 35. Superior Manufacturing Company
Computation of Planned Overhead Rates
For the Year Ending December 31, 1977

	TOTAL	SERVICE DEPARTMENTS			PRODUCING DEPARTMENTS		
		GEN. ADM.	POWER	REPAIR	1	2	3
Direct Dept. Costs (Schedules 33 and 34)	$689,200	$116,800	$110,000	$10,000	$319,280	$ 29,280	$103,840
*Allocations:							
1. Building Services (Schedule 32)	90,000		9,000	4,500	33,201	16,481	26,818
2. General and Administrative		$116,800	11,680	11,680	58,400	11,680	23,360
3. Power Department			$130,680	3,267	65,340	32,670	29,403
4. Repair Department				$29,447	11,779	5,889	11,779
Totals	$779,200				$488,000	$ 96,000	$195,200
Direct labor hours (Schedule 31)					488,000	192,000	488,000
Overhead rates (per DLH)					$1.00	$ .50	$ .40

Standard service charges:

Power: $\dfrac{\$130,680}{20,000}$ = $6.53 per 1,000 kilowatt hours

Repair: $\dfrac{\$29,447}{4,000}$ = $7.36 per direct repair hour

*Distribution basis:
1. Relative floor space.
2. Selected percentages.
3. Planned kilowatt hours.
4. Planned direct repair hours.

ing services and the three service department costs were allocated to the three producing departments so that these three rates "carry" all the overhead. Allocations were based on the following data:

1. Building Service—The 60 percent allocated to the factory is further allocated to the factory departments on the basis of relative floor space occupied (note: treated as a fixed cost):

DEPARTMENTS	PERCENT
Power	10
Repair	5
Producing 1	36.890*
Producing 2	18.312
Producing 3	29.798

*Carrying percents to decimal places in situations such as this is ordinarily impracticable. It is done here to make the overhead rates come out even for illustrative purposes only.

2. General and Administrative Factory Overhead—The following percentages, agreed upon by factory management:

DEPARTMENTS	PERCENT
Power	10
Repair	10
Producing 1	50
Producing 2	10
Producing 3	20

3. Power Department—The budgeted usage of kilowatt hours by department:

DEPARTMENTS	KILOWATT HOURS (000)
Repair	500
Producing 1	10,000
Producing 2	5,000
Producing 3	4,500
	20,000

4. Repair Department—The budgeted usage of direct repair hours by department:

DEPARTMENTS	DIRECT REPAIR HOURS
Producing 1	1,600
Producing 2	800
Producing 3	1,600
	4,000

The total costs of each producing department (direct plus service department allocations) were divided by the planned direct labor hours (volume of work) to derive the three *planned overhead rates* (per DLH).[5]

The next step is to utilize the overhead rates to apply planned overhead to each product. Since the overhead rates were based on direct labor hours (that is, activity base) and the direct labor budget (Schedule 31, Chapter 8) specifies direct labor hours by product, we can apportion overhead to the two products by multiplying the respective rates by the planned hours. Schedule 36, Manufacturing Expenses Applied by Product, shows the computations. Note that the total overhead expenses planned ($779,200 in Schedule 34) agrees with the total applied in Schedule 36.

The use of predetermined overhead rates to allocate factory overhead, which includes both fixed and variable costs, results in a stable charge during the year to each unit of product for this particular element of cost. Because the departmental expense budgets show costs as they are expected to *accrue* and the application of overhead through the rates follows the seasonal pattern of production, one can expect a *budgeted over/under-applied* factory overhead for interim periods during the year. This effect may be observed in Schedule 37, *Budgeted Overhead Over/under-Applied*. It should be noted, however, that at year-end the total expenses planned and the total applied are equal; that is, the over/under-applied balances for the year as a whole (except for the possibility of a rounding error).

All budgeted factory costs for Superior Manufacturing Company have been identified with the various types of finished goods, viz:

ITEM OF COST	SCHEDULE
Direct materials	28
Direct labor	30
Manufacturing expenses	36

The planned cost of goods manufactured can now be developed. This schedule is illustrated in Chapter 12.

[5] When it is possible to identify separately the fixed and variable components of cost in each departmental overhead budget, overhead rates can be computed separately for the fixed and variable components in each department. This feature is particularly relevant for (1) variation analyses, (2) direct costing, and (3) breakeven analyses. (These topics are discussed in Chapters 14, 16, and 17.) Additionally, it is generally agreed that a more theoretically correct and useful allocation is possible if fixed and variable costs are treated differently. Generally, fixed service department costs should be allocated on the basis of *capacity to use* services, whereas variable costs should be allocated on the basis of expected actual use of service.

Observe also that the overhead rates are based on *expected actual volume* for the year. Generally speaking, there are three levels at which overhead rates may be set. Authorities are not in agreement about the preferable rate. The reader is referred to books on cost accounting for further study. The three levels are:

1. Budgeted volume for the year.
2. Practical plant capacity.
3. The average or normal volume over several years.

SCHEDULE 36. Superior Manufacturing Company
Manufacturing Expenses Applied by Product
For the Year Ending December 31, 1977

	REF.	TOTALS	FIRST QUARTER			QUARTERS			
			JANUARY	FEBRUARY	MARCH	FIRST	SECOND	THIRD	FOURTH
Product X									
Department 1									
Direct labor hours	31	384,000	28,000	32,000	32,000	92,000	96,000	92,000	104,000
Rate	35	$1.00	$1.00	$1.00	$1.00	$1.00	$1.00	$1.00	$1.00
Amount		$384,000	$28,000	$32,000	$32,000	$ 92,000	$ 96,000	$ 92,000	$104,000
Department 2									
Direct labor hours	31	192,000	14,000	16,000	16,000	46,000	48,000	46,000	52,000
Rate	35	$ .50	$ .50	$ .50	$ .50	$ .50	$ .50	$ .50	$ .50
Amount		$ 96,000	$ 7,000	$ 8,000	$ 8,000	$ 23,000	$ 24,000	$ 23,000	$ 26,000
Department 3									
Direct labor hours	31	384,000	28,000	32,000	32,000	92,000	96,000	92,000	104,000
Rate	35	$ .40	$ .40	$ .40	$ .40	$ .40	$ .40	$ .40	$ .40
Amount		$153,600	$11,200	$12,800	$12,800	$ 36,800	$ 38,400	$ 36,800	$ 41,600
Total product X		$633,600	$46,200	$52,800	$52,800	$151,800	$158,400	$151,800	$171,600

SCHEDULE 36 (continued)

	REF.	TOTALS	FIRST QUARTER			QUARTERS			
			JANUARY	FEBRUARY	MARCH	FIRST	SECOND	THIRD	FOURTH
Product Y									
Department 1									
Direct labor hours	31	104,000	6,800	7,200	7,600	21,600	28,000	25,400	29,000
Rate	35	$1.00	$1.00	$1.00	$1.00	$1.00	$1.00	$1.00	$1.00
Amount		$104,000	$ 6,800	$ 7,200	$ 7,600	$ 21,600	$ 28,000	$ 25,400	$ 29,000
Department 3									
Direct labor hours	31	104,000	6,800	7,200	7,600	21,600	28,000	25,400	29,000
Rate	35	$ .40	$ .40	$ .40	$ .40	$ .40	$ .40	$ .40	$ .40
Amount		$ 41,600	$ 2,720	$ 2,880	$ 3,040	$ 8,640	$ 11,200	$ 10,160	$ 11,600
Total Product Y		$145,600	$ 9,520	$10,080	$10,640	$ 30,240	$ 39,200	$ 35,560	$ 40,600
Total all products		$779,200	$55,720	$62,880	$63,440	$182,040	$197,600	$187,360	$212,200

SCHEDULE 37. Superior Manufacturing Company

Budgeted Overhead Over/Under-Applied*

For the Year Ending December 31, 1977

		ALL DEPARTMENTS			
	PLANNED ACCRUALS	TOTAL APPLIED	OVER	UNDER	CUMULATIVE
REF.	33 & 34	36			
Time Periods:					
January	$ 62,357	$ 55,720		$ 6,637	$ 6,637
February	64,068	62,880		1,188	7,825
March	64,193	63,440		753	8,578
First Quarter	190,618	182,040		8,578	8,578
Second Quarter	195,156	197,600	$ 2,444		6,134
Third Quarter	192,090	187,360		4,730	10,864
Fourth Quarter	201,336	212,200	10,864		
Annual totals	$779,200	$779,200	$13,308	$13,308	

*Although not illustrated here, it is frequently advisable to compute the application of fixed and variable overhead separately, thereby maintaining such segregation in cost of goods manufactured, sold, and in inventories. This segregation may be accomplished in the accounts or as a separate analysis and is useful as a basis for certain types of managerial decisions.

Selling Expense Budgets Illustrated. Recall that the sales division of Superior Manufacturing Company (Illustration 7, Chapter 4) has three sales districts (Southern, Eastern, and Western) and one general department (General Sales Overhead, that is, home sales office).

The promotion plan developed by the advertising manager is summarized in Schedule 38. Note that one-twelfth of the annual allowance is shown in the expense budgets as a monthly fixed cost since it represents an annual appropriation.

SCHEDULE 38. Superior Manufacturing Company

Promotion Plan Summary

For the Year Ending December 31, 1977

DEPARTMENT	ANNUAL APPROPRIATION
Home Office	$ 60,000
Southern District	24,000
Eastern District	36,000
Western District	12,000
Total	$132,000

The supervisor of each sales district and the home sales office developed a tentative expense budget, which was submitted to higher management for evaluation and approval. You should observe that the *activity base* (measure

SCHEDULE 39. Superior Manufacturing Company
Selling Expense Budgets
For the Year Ending December 31, 1977
Activity Base—Sales Dollars

			FIRST QUARTER				QUARTERS		
	REF.	ANNUAL TOTAL	JANUARY	FEBRUARY	MARCH	FIRST	SECOND	THIRD	FOURTH
General Sales Overhead									
*Supervisory salaries	(Input)	$144,000	$12,000	$12,000	$12,000	$ 36,000	$ 36,000	$36,000	$ 36,000
Travel and entertainment	"	38,907	3,208	3,389	3,545	10,142	10,053	8,052	10,660
Telephone and telegraph	"	15,861	1,314	1,353	1,387	4,054	4,035	3,607	4,165
*Depreciation—office equipment	"	600	50	50	50	150	150	150	150
Stationery and office supplies	"	11,049	909	968	1,019	2,896	2,868	2,221	3,064
Auto expense	"	25,913	2,132	2,275	2,397	6,804	6,734	5,165	7,210
Advertising	"	60,000	5,000	5,000	5,000	15,000	15,000	15,000	15,000
Totals		$296,330	$24,613	$25,035	$25,398	$75,046	$74,840	$70,195	$76,249
Southern Sales District									
*Supervisory salaries	"	$ 72,000	$ 6,000	$ 6,000	$ 6,000	$ 18,000	$ 18,000	$18,000	$ 18,000
Travel and entertainment	"	25,279	2,129	2,314	2,184	6,627	6,525	5,466	6,661
Telephone and telegraph	"	9,379	789	847	806	2,442	2,410	2,075	2,452
Commissions	"	84,800	7,200	8,280	7,520	23,000	22,400	16,200	23,200
Freight and express	"	19,198	1,628	1,857	1,696	5,181	5,054	3,738	5,225
Advertising	"	24,000	2,000	2,000	2,000	6,000	6,000	6,000	6,000
Totals		$234,656	$19,746	$21,298	$20,206	$ 61,250	$ 60,389	$51,479	$ 61,538

SCHEDULE 39. (Continued)

	REF.	ANNUAL TOTAL	FIRST QUARTER			QUARTERS			
			JANUARY	FEBRUARY	MARCH	FIRST	SECOND	THIRD	FOURTH
Eastern Sales District									
*Supervisory salaries	(Input)	$ 96,000	$ 8,000	$ 8,000	$ 8,000	$ 24,000	$ 24,000	$ 24,000	$ 24,000
Travel and entertainment	"	30,812	2,470	2,675	2,852	7,997	8,065	6,454	8,296
Telephone and telegraph	"	14,828	1,198	1,277	1,346	3,821	3,848	3,221	3,938
Commissions	"	116,280	9,084	10,356	11,460	30,900	31,320	21,300	32,760
Freight and express	"	19,471	1,530	1,724	1,893	5,147	5,213	3,679	5,432
Advertising	"	36,000	3,000	3,000	3,000	9,000	9,000	9,000	9,000
Totals		$313,391	$25,282	$27,032	$28,551	$ 80,865	$ 81,446	$ 67,654	$ 83,426
Western Sales District									
*Supervisory salaries	"	$ 36,000	$ 3,000	$ 3,000	$ 3,000	$ 9,000	$ 9,000	$ 9,000	$ 9,000
Travel and entertainment	"	11,641	1,001	865	1,045	2,911	2,804	2,580	3,346
Telephone and telegraph	"	4,915	421	371	437	1,229	1,190	1,109	1,387
Commissions	"	42,720	3,732	2,964	3,984	10,680	10,080	8,820	13,140
Freight and express	"	7,844	674	583	704	1,961	1,890	1,740	2,253
Advertising	"	12,000	1,000	1,000	1,000	3,000	3,000	3,000	3,000
Totals		$115,120	$ 9,828	$ 8,783	$10,170	$ 28,781	$ 27,964	$ 26,249	$ 32,126
Summary Totals									
Total all departments		$959,497	$79,469	$82,143	$84,325	$245,942	$244,639	$215,577	$253,339
*Add building services allocated		30,000	2,640	2,460	2,444	7,544	7,276	7,400	7,780
Total company		$989,497	$82,109	$84,608	$86,769	$253,486	$251,915	$222,977	$261,119

*Not controllable in this department.

SCHEDULE 40. Superior Manufacturing Company
Administrative Expense Budgets
For the Year Ending December 31, 1977
Activity Base—Total Sales Dollars

	REF.	ANNUAL TOTAL	FIRST QUARTER			QUARTERS			
			JANUARY	FEBRUARY	MARCH	FIRST	SECOND	THIRD	FOURTH
Administrative Department									
*Supervisory salaries	(Input)	$ 60,000	$ 5,000	$ 5,000	$ 5,000	$15,000	$15,000	$15,000	$15,000
Travel and entertainment	"	9,000	750	750	750	2,250	2,250	2,250	2,250
Telephone and telegraph	"	9,114	750	798	839	2,387	2,364	1,840	2,523
*Depreciation	"	600	50	50	50	150	150	150	150
*Insurance	"	240	20	20	20	60	60	60	60
*Taxes	"	240	20	20	20	60	60	60	60
Stationery and office supplies	"	122	10	11	12	33	32	23	34
Lawyer retainer fee	"	1,800	150	150	150	450	450	450	450
Audit fee	"	2,400	200	200	200	600	600	600	600
Totals		$ 83,516	$ 6,950	$ 6,999	$ 7,041	$20,990	$20,966	$20,433	$21,127
Accounting Department									
*Supervisory salaries	"	$ 48,000	$ 4,000	$ 4,000	$ 4,000	$12,000	$12,000	$12,000	$12,000
Travel and entertainment	"	1,200	100	100	100	300	300	300	300
Telephone and telegraph	"	1,210	100	104	107	311	310	266	323
*Depreciation	"	2,400	200	200	200	600	600	600	600
*Insurance	"	240	20	20	20	60	60	60	60
*Taxes	"	360	30	30	30	90	90	90	90
Stationery and office supplies	"	610	50	54	57	161	160	116	173
Totals		$ 54,020	$ 4,500	$ 4,508	$ 4,514	$13,522	$13,520	$13,432	$13,546

SCHEDULE 40. (Continued)

	REF.	ANNUAL TOTAL	FIRST QUARTER			QUARTERS			
			JANUARY	FEBRUARY	MARCH	FIRST	SECOND	THIRD	FOURTH
Treasurers' Department									
*Supervisory salaries	(Input)	$ 36,000	$ 3,000	$ 3,000	$ 3,000	$ 9,000	$ 9,000	$ 9,000	$ 9,000
Travel and entertainment	"	1,200	100	100	100	300	300	300	300
Telephone and telegraph	"	3,158	260	276	290	826	818	643	871
*Depreciation	"	1,200	100	100	100	300	300	300	300
*Insurance	"	480	40	40	40	120	120	120	120
*Taxes	"	120	10	10	10	30	30	30	30
Stationery and office supplies	"	1,829	151	162	172	485	479	347	518
Loss on bad debts	"	12,190	1,001	1,080	1,148	3,229	3,190	2,316	3,455
Totals		$ 56,177	$ 4,662	$ 4,768	$ 4,860	$14,290	$14,237	$13,056	$14,594
Summary									
Totals all departments		$193,713	$16,112	$16,275	$16,415	$48,802	$48,723	$46,921	$49,267
*Allocated building services cost		30,000	2,640	2,460	2,444	7,544	7,276	7,400	7,780
Total company		$223,713	$18,752	$18,735	$18,859	$56,346	$55,999	$54,321	$57,047

*Not controllable within the department.

of volume) in each expense budget is *sales dollars*. The volume or activity for each department is reflected in the sales plan (Schedule 21, Chapter 5). The selling expense budgets are shown in Schedule 39.

Administrative Expense Budgets Illustrated. The organization chart for the company (Illustration 8) shows three administrative departments (Administrative, Accounting, and Treasurer). The *activity base* for these departments selected by the management is *total* sales dollars as reflected in the sales budget (Schedule 21, Chapter 5). On the basis of past experience and the expected volume of work (activity), the departmental managers developed their expense budgets, which were approved by higher management. The resultant expense budgets are shown in Schedule 40.

The fourteen expense budgets illustrated are used by the director of profit planning and control for consolidation into the overall profit plan as demonstrated in Chapter 13.

DISCUSSION QUESTIONS

1. What are the primary reasons for and focus in planning expenses?
2. Why is it especially important to classify costs in terms of organizational responsibility?
3. Explain the classification of costs as related to changes in volume, output, or activity.
4. Distinguish between controllable and noncontrollable costs.
5. Distinguish between cost control and cost reduction.
6. What are primary classifications of expenses that should be incorporated in the annual profit plan?
7. What are the unique problems related to planning manufacturing expenses or factory overhead?
8. Explain the problem of cost allocation as related to (1) product costing and (2) cost control.
9. What is meant by the activity base? Explain its significance.
10. What is the relationship between the sales budget and distribution expenses?
11. Promotion and advertising costs normally are best planned and controlled on the basis of definite appropriations. Explain this statement.
12. Who should be responsible for the preparation of expense budgets? Explain.

CASE 9-1
Morton Manufacturing Company

Morton Manufacturing Company produces a line of electric heaters that are distributed on a nationwide basis through hardware and similar retail outlets. The heaters are designed primarily for heating small areas and are portable; they generally are plugged in electrical wall outlets. Both 110 and 220 watt heaters are manufactured, and the total lines are represented by fourteen different models of varying sizes, styles, and prices. The heaters are manufactured In a central plant, and the manufacturer sells direct to approximately forty different wholesale outlets who in turn sell the heaters to retail stores. Annual sales during the past year amounted to approximately $38,000,000. The organization of the company is summarized in Exhibit 1. The company has been operating for approximately thirty years, and most of the managers have worked up in the company over many years.

The company employs a traditional cost accounting system (historical absorption basis), and quarterly financial statements are prepared for internal management purposes. Since there are approximately two hundred stockholders, a summarized (and unaudited) financial statement is mailed to them annually. During the past three years the company has dropped behind the industry in both profits and growth. The organization chart shown in Exhibit 1 reflects two major changes that have been made during the past year

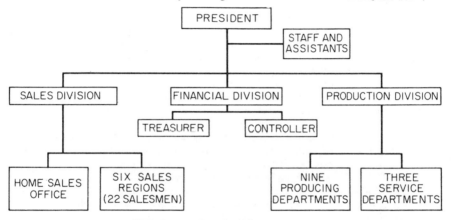

EXHIBIT 1. Organization Chart

by the new president employed from outside the company: (1) The sales division has been reorganized and the six sales regions established (prior to this reorganization all sales supervision was direct from the home office); (2) the financial division was organized (prior to the reorganization the functions were performed separately by a treasurer and chief accountant who were designated as staff assistants). Each division is headed by a vice president including the newly employed financial vice president. The president and the financial vice president are in the process of designing and implementing a comprehensive profit planning and control program. The president stated that a decision has been made to "adopt a responsibility accounting system and to utilize a standard cost system in the factory division." He favors "bottoms up planning and control, fully realizes that due to past precedent it will be difficult to implement in the short run in this company." At a recent meeting of the executive committee (president and the three vice presidents), the president stated that "each division manager shall be responsible for planning and controlling all aspects of his function."

This case focuses on the approaches that should be used in planning and controlling expenses throughout the company.

Required:

    a.   You are to consider all aspects of planning and controlling expenses in the company and to present your recommendations. You should consider such factors as organizational responsibility, accounting approaches, expense clas-sifications, planning expenses, approval of budgets, performance reports, and corrective action. Justify all recommendations that you make.

b. Assume a director of profit planning and control is being appointed. Where should he be placed on the organization chart? What should be his respon-sibilities in respect to planning and controlling expenses?

CASE 9-2
Barden Manufacturing Company

Barden Manufacturing Company is a medium-size company that produces two primary products that are sold in the automotive parts industry. There is a single plant, and manufacturing operations entail a particularly high investment in machinery. Consequently, manufacturing overhead is a significant element of cost; this case focuses on this aspect of operations. The plant is managed by Sam Collins, the manufacturing manager. The plant includes two service and two producing departments (actually there are more departments, but these four are representative and adequate for case purposes). Product X is processed through both producing departments, whereas product Y is processed only through the first department. The two producing departments are designated as 1 and 2 and the two service departments as 3 and 4 for convenience. Direct material and direct labor costs are incurred in both producing departments. During the past year the company initiated a profit planning and control program. The controller stated that "effort are continuing to perfect the program and to coordinate it with the cost accounting system." Over the years the cost system was operated as simply as pos-sible—actual material, labor, and factory overhead costs were accumulated for the month and then allocated on an actual basis to the two products at the end of each month. The management has decided to adopt a standard cost system and to use standard rates for factory overhead."

Management currently is involved in the planning cycle to develop the annual profit plan. The sales plan has been tentatively approved; on the basis of that plan and the inventory policies (for products X and Y) the following production plan has been developed by the manufacturing manager and his staff:

PRODUCT	ANNUAL	JANUARY	FEBRUARY	MARCH	ETC.
X	12,500	1,000	800	1,100	9,600
Y	20,000	1,800	1,400	2,300	14,500

The manufacturing manager working with the controller's department developed the following measures of departmental output:

DEPARTMENT	ACTIVITY BASE
1 Producing	Direct machine hours
2 Producing	Units of product
3 Factory administrative	Number of employees in factory
4 Maintenance	Direct repair hours

The following standards have been established for planning purposes for the up-coming year:

1. Direct machine hours per unit of product in Dept. 1 : X—4 ; Y—5.
2. Direct repair hours : Dept. 1—4 for each 100 direct machine hours ; Dept. 2—.16 for each unit of product.
3. Excerpt from manning table (number of employees planned) : Dept. 1—40 ; Dept. 2—25 ; Dept. 3—10 ; Dept. 4—5.
4. Totals from departmental overhead budgets for year: Dept. 1—$764,000 ; Dept. 2—$330,500 ; Dept. 3—$70,000 ; Dept. 4—$123,000.

Required:

a. Do you agree with the "activity base" selected for each department ? Explain.
b. Translate the production budget into "annual activity" for each of the four departments.
c. Compute the standard overhead rates for each producing department. Assume allocations of service department overhead on the basis of activities determined in b.
d. Develop the planned cost of goods manufactured for the year for each product. Assume the following direct costs : direct material—product X, $62,500 ; product Y, $80,000 ; direct labor—product X, $37,500 ; product Y, $40,000.
e. Outline one approach that could be used by the company to develop the departmental overhead budget amounts given in 4 above.

CASE 9-3
Carter Manufacturing Company

Carter Manufacturing Company produces two products, X and Y. The manu-facturing division consists of two producing (designated 1 and 2) and two service (designated 3 and 4) departments. The company uses a historical (absorption) cost system, except that predetermined (budgeted) overhead rates are used in the producing departments to apportion factory overhead to the products. The rate for Department 1 is based on direct machine hours (DMH) and the rate for Department 2 is based on direct labor hours (DLH). In applying overhead during the year the standard rates are multiplied by actual hours. The following budget and actual data are available:

1. Annual profit plan data :
    a. Factory overhead budgeted for the year: Dept. 1, $85,000 ; Dept. 2, $72,500 ; Dept. 3, $20,000 ; Dept. 4, $15,000. Machine operators' salaries are treated as an overhead cost.
    b. Budgeted units to be produced : product X, 50,000 ; product Y, 30,000.
    c. Budgeted raw material cost per unit of product (all used in Dept. 1) : product X, $4.00 ; product Y, $5.00. No material is added in Dept. 2.
    d. Budgeted time required for production : direct machine hours in Depart-ment 1 for each unit of finished goods—product X, 1½ ; Product Y, 1.

Direct labor hours in Department 2 for each unit of finished goods—product X, 2; product Y, 2½.

e. Average wage rates budgeted in Department 2: product X, $2.40; product Y, $2.50.

f. Allocation of service department cost to producing departments: Dept. 3—allocate ½ to Dept. 1 and ½ to Dept. 2. Dept. 4—allocate ⅔ to Dept. 1 and ⅓ to Dept. 2.

2. January actual data:

a. Units actually produced in January—product X, 4,000; product Y, 3,000.

b. Actual direct machine hours in Dept. 1—product X, 6,100; product Y, 4,150.

c. Actual costs incurred:

DEPT.	OVERHEAD	RAW MATERIAL	DIRECT LABOR HOURS	DIRECT LABOR AMOUNT
1	$7,700	X—$16,300		
		Y— 15,200		
2	6,800		X—8,200	$19,730
			Y—7,400	18,400
3	2,000			
4	1,600			

Required:

a. Compute the predetermined overhead rate for each producing department; show your computations.

b. Use the absorption cost approach and the predetermined overhead rates computed in a to prepare a statement of "Cost of Goods Manufactured—January Actual."

c. Prepare a performance report for January that will reflect the status of cost control for each item of cost by department. Since the company does not develop monthly cost budgets, they use one-twelfth of the annual budget allowance for factory overhead as the monthly budget goal. Explain any reservations that you may have concerning the performance report.

CASE 9-4

Department 21

The monthly performance report for Department 21 (Exhibit 1) was received by the manager of the department, Martin Gaines, on the 12th of February; he quickly noted that "all the variances are unfavorable—and wrong!" The company has been budgeting expenses for the past three years. Monthly performance reports are prepared for each responsibility center; the manager of each responsibility center is expected to discuss his report in detail with his immediate supervisor and to "work out approaches to correct unfavorable variances." An excerpt from the annual profit plan is shown in Exhibit 2.

"Martin, I'm glad you came in. We need to discuss your performance report."
"Well, Jim, that's not what I came in to talk about; I'm all tied up with the special milling machine. It's not working right, and we need to fly in some parts as well as a specialist to help us—can you approve it now? I would like to defer discussing that report until next week (Feb. 26) when we have plenty of time. If you ask me, something needs to be done about those performance reports anyway. "OK, Martin," replied Jim Swanson, his supervisor.

The factory expense budgets reflected in Exhibit 2 were initially prepared in the controller's department, then submitted to the factory manager for "evaluation and recommendations." The factory manager in turn referred them to his departmental managers "for comment." Subsequently, they were approved by the factory manager as reflected in Exhibit 2.

Required:

a. Do you agree with the approach used in developing the expense budgets (Exhibit 2) for the annual profit plan? Explain.

b. Examine all aspects of the performance report (Exhibit 1) very critically. Do you find any basis for the criticisms of Gaines? Explain. Present your recommendations for improvement.

EXHIBIT 1.   Department 21—January Performance Report

PARTICULARS	ACTUAL	BUDGET	VARIANCE
Output	13,000	11,000	2,000
Direct material	$20,000	$19,500	$ 500
Direct labor	32,700	32,500	200
Departmental overhead:			
Salaries	2,500	2,500	
Indirect labor	4,950	4,350	500
Supplies	3,850	3,200	650
Overtime	1,100	1,000	200
Miscellaneous	670	550	
Power (standard charge)	1,090	1,040	50
Totals	$66,860	$64,640	$2,220

EXHIBIT 2.   Department 21—Annual Profit Plan

	ANNUAL	JANUARY	FEBRUARY	ETC.
Output (Units)	120,000	11,000	9,000	
Direct material	$180,000	$16,500	$13,500	
Direct labor	300,000	27,500	22,500	
Departmental overhead:				
Salaries	30,000	2,500	2,500	
Indirect labor	48,000	4,350	3,650	
Supplies	36,000	3,200	2,800	
Overtime	12,000	1,000	1,000	
Miscellaneous	6,000	550	450	
Power	9,600	880	720	
Totals	$621,600	$56,480	$46,120	

CASE 9-5

Walker Food Processing Company

The Walker Food Processing Company employs approximately 375 people and distributes the products in a three-state area. The company had never prepared a budget. To support an increased line of credit the bank has requested the management to furnish a budgeted income statement, a cash flow projection, and a balance sheet covering the next six months. The sales and production budgets have been tentatively approved by the management. No substantial change in inventories is planned.

The sales manager developed the following budget of distribution costs:

	ACTUAL LAST SIX MONTHS		PROPOSED
	AMOUNT	PERCENT	BUDGET
Sales volume	$6,800,000		$7,956,000
Sales expenses:			
Salaries	181,600	15.0	212,400
Commission	340,000	28.1	397,800
Promotion	160,600	13.3	188,300
Travel	275,400	22.8	322,800
Entertainment	40,300	3.3	46,700
Freight	179,200	14.8	209,500
Depreciation, taxes, and insurance			
on autos	17,500	1.4	19,800
Miscellaneous	15,400	1.3	18,400
Totals	$1,210,000		$1,415,700

The production manager developed the following budget of factory costs:

	ACTUAL LAST SIX MONTHS	PROPOSED BUDGET
Direct material	$2,924,000	$3,500,000
Direct labor	1,571,000	1,880,472
Factory overhead:		
Salaries	253,800	253,800
Wages	204,200	224,620
Supplies	87,500	102,375
Utilities	135,100	135,100
Depreciation, taxes, and insurance		
on autos	165,200	165,200
Services	58,400	64,240
Miscellaneous	68,200	79,794
	972,400	1,015,129
Total	$5,467,400	$6,395,601

The management has decided to "budget operations each year from now on in this manner."

Required:

a.   Develop an analysis to determine how the projections were derived.

b.   Evaluate the projections and the approaches used, and make recommendations for improvement.

Development and Application
of Variable Budgets
# of Expense

chapter ten

       The preceding chapter focused on planning expenses and their incorporation into the profit plan, and it focused primarily on problems of planning and coordination. This chapter will discuss the *control* of expenses through a concept known as variable or flexible budgets of expense. The variable budget concept is complementary to the profit plan; it may or may not be used as a complement to the latter depending upon the internal characteristics of the enterprise. Variable expense budgets compare actual expenses incurred with budget allowances that are *adjusted to the level of activity or output* attained. To illustrate, assume the January performance report for Department 42 is being prepared; actual expense data provided by the cost system are to be compared with "budget" and the resultant variances reported. The profit plan for the year specified January output for Department 42 of 9,000 units; the profit plan therefore included a January expense budget for the department at that volume of output. Now, we find at the end of January that the department actually produced 10,000 units of output. For comparison with the actual expenses, we need a budget allowance adjusted to 10,000 units. Obviously, if we were to compare actual expenses incurred at a volume of 10,000 units with budget expense allowances based on 9,000 units, the resultant variances would be unrealistic and unfair to the departmental manager of the responsibility center. The variable budget concept provides a basis for computing an *adjusted expense budget* for inclusion on the performance report. This chapter will present the theory, construction, and application of variable budgets in the profit planning and control program.

CONCEPTS UNDERLYING THE VARIABLE BUDGET

Any attempt to adjust budget allowances for expenses to actual output or activity in a responsibility center must show the effect of output or activity on expenses. The point is, as volume or activity increases or decreases in the responsibility center, what should be the behavior of each expense item incurred in that center. Clearly, there are some fixed expenses, such as monthly salaries, that are not influenced by changes in output or work done. Alternatively, there are some variable expenses, such as direct raw materials used in production, that fluctuate proportionally with changes in production. Then, there are *semivariable* expenses that change but not in direct relationship to changes in volume of work done (see p.262). The central objective of the variable budget approach is specifically to identify how, and to what extent, each item of expense in a responsibility center is influenced by the amount of work done in that center. Variable budgets specify these relationships.[1]

Variable budgets are schedules of costs or expenses indicating how each expense should change with changes in volume, output, or activity—what individual expenses should be at various volumes rather than at one specific or fixed volume. Significantly, variable budgets express short-term cost-volume relationships within a narow *relevant range* of volume. Variable budgets are dynamic in that expense allowances for any particular volume or rate of activity can be computed readily. This type of budget has been variously referred to as variable budget, flexible budget, sliding scale budget, step budget, expense formula budget, and expense control budget. General acceptance of a more descriptive title such as *planned cost-volume relationships* might lead to improved communication and understanding.

A typical variable budget is presented in Illustration 22. Note that it specifies only *controllable* expenses in the responsibility center; it is identified with a particular manager; the method of measuring output or work done is specified as the *activity base* and the relevant range is stated for the amounts applicable. Note also that for each item of expense the (1) constant or fixed component *per period*, and (2) the variable component *per unit of output* are specified (either component may be zero). On a performance report the *adjusted budget allowance* for *indirect labor* at an output of 10,000 units would be

---

[1] Surveys have indicated extensive application of the variable budget concept; see: B. H. Sord and G. A. Welsch, *Business Budgeting, A Survey of Management Planning and Control Practices* (New York: Controllership Foundation Inc.), pp. 158–99.

computed as follows:

$$\$4,000 + (\$2 \times 10,000) = \$24,000.$$

Prior to discussing the approaches for estimating the values included in a variable budget, such as in Illustration 22, we will consider several related concepts.

ILLUSTRATION 22. Variable Budget for Department 42—1977

Supervisor	John Ware		
Activity base	Units of output—Component part X-17		
Relevant range for use	9,000 to 12,000 units inclusive		

CONTROLLABLE EXPENSES	COST BEHAVIOR*	FIXED AMOUNT PER MONTH	VARIABLE RATE PER UNIT OF OUTPUT
Direct material	V	$ 0	$10.00
Direct labor	V	0	8.00
Department overhead:			
Salaries	F	6,000	0
Supplies	V	0	1.00
Indirect labor	SV	4,000	2.00
Total		$10,000	$21.00

*V—Variable
 F—Fixed
 SV—Semivariable

The foundation underlying the variable budget is the *concept of cost variability*. The concept holds that costs can be related to output or activity and that when so related, costs are primarily a function of two factors: (1) the passage of time; and (2) activity. This means that when costs are related to activity, conceptually two classes emerge—fixed costs and variable costs.

Pragmatically, classification of costs according to the concept of cost variability requires three cost categories:

1. Fixed costs.
2. Variable costs.
3. Semivariable (or semifixed) costs.

To classify costs on this basis, it is essential that each category be clearly defined. Throughout accounting and budgeting literature these classes of cost have been variously labeled and defined. The above terminology has been selected for discussion purposes herein; however, each firm should select alternate terminology suitable to its own situation. The definitions and discussions that follow do not purport to be suitable for all situations. The purpose is to develop the significant aspects of each class of cost. These should be kept in mind in defining costs for application in *specific situations*. In applying these concepts, accountants and budget specialists should not let highly theoretical distinctions deter them. Data for management use must be accurate, but this requirement does not forbid the inclusion of realistic estimates. If cost variability is approached from this viewpoint, useful variable budgets can be developed.

In considering the variable budget concept, the following problem areas are important:

1. Definition of costs when related to output or activity.
2. Selection of an activity base that appropriately measures departmental output or activity.
3. Methods of anylyzing costs to identify separately the fixed and variable components of cost.
4. Use and application of the variable budget concept.

Each of these problem areas will be discussed in order.

FIXED COSTS DEFINED

Fixed costs are those that do not vary with output or productive activity. They accrue with the passage of time, that is, they are time costs. They remain constant in amount for a given short-term period within a relevant range of activity. Fixed costs are occasioned by the holding of assets and the other factors of production in a state of "readiness to produce;" hence, they are frequently called capacity costs. Fixed costs are of two principal types. First, prior management decisions set certain fixed costs. Examples of such costs are depreciation, taxes, and insurance. Second, some fixed costs are set by management decisions on a short-term basis. Salaries, advertising expenditures, and research expenditures fall into this category. They may fluctuate by reason of changes in the basic structure of the business, methods of operations, and discretionary changes in management policy. The following list explains the primary factors that a company should consider in establishing a definition of fixed costs.

1. **Controllability**—All fixed costs are controllable over the life-span of the company. Some, but not all, fixed costs are subject to short-run management control. Numerous fixed costs are determined annually by the discretionary management policies.

2. **Relationship to Activity**—Fixed costs result from the *capacity* to produce or to perform some activity; however, they are not a result of the performance of that activity. Fixed costs may be influenced by factors other than the passage of time but not by output or the performance of activity.

3.   Relevant Range—Fixed costs must be related to relevant range of activity. There are few, if any, costs that would remain constant over the wide range of output or activity from zero to full capacity. The fixed costs at one range of activity normally would be different at other ranges because increases or decreases in capacity may change fixed costs. Therefore, in the definition and classification of costs it is essential that a relevant range of activity be specified. The relevant range of activity sets up definite limitations on the validity of the budget amounts.

4.   Management Regulated—The estimation of many fixed costs implies that certain management policy decisions have been made. Many fixed costs are dependent entirely on specific management decisions. They may change if these decisions change. For example, in budgeting salaries, managerial policies on salary changes must be known or anticipated.

5.   Time Costs—Because fixed costs accrue with the passage of time, the amount of the fixed cost must be related to a specified period of time. For budget purposes, fixed costs should be related to the annual accounting period and expressed as a constant amount *per month*.

6.   Fixed in Total but Variable per Unit—A fixed cost is constant in total amount each period; however, when viewed in terms of units of output, it has a variable effect on unit cost. These different effects frequently cause confusion. Assume, for example, fixed costs of $9,600 within a relevant range of 800 to 1,200 units. If 1,200 units are produced, the fixed cost *per unit* is $8.00; however, if 1,000 units are produced, the fixed cost per unit is $9.60. The total cost remains constant at $9,600 regardless of the quantity produced, whereas the unit cost changes inversely with volume.

7.   Practical Application—Practical considerations do not require a cost to be absolutely fixed. In application, a fixed cost is one that is constant for all practical purposes.

The concept of cost variability can be presented graphically. Two types of fixed costs are portrayed in Illustration 23. Graph A illustrates an unusual fixed cost that appears to remain constant over the wide range of volume from zero to full capacity. Graph B presents a more typical fixed cost, constant within specified ranges of activity. In both cases the cost should be included in the variable budget as a fixed cost at $3,000 per period, if it is presumed operations will be within the indicated relevant range.

VARIABLE COSTS DEFINED

Variable costs are those items of cost that vary *in direct proportion* to output or activity in a responsibility center. Variable costs are activity costs because

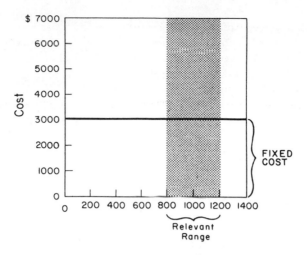

GRAPH A-FIXED COST-CONSTANT AT ALL VOLUMES

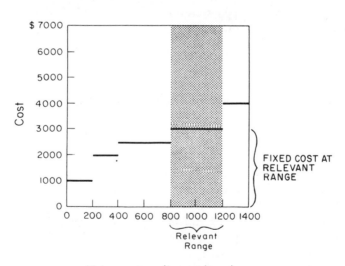

GRAPH B-FIXED COST-RELATED TO RELEVANT RANGE

ILLUSTRATION 23.   Fixed Costs Graphed

they accrue as a result of productive output, activity, or work done. They would not exist were it not for the performance of some activity. A variable cost is necessarily zero at zero activity. Variable costs increase or decrease directly with changes in output; therefore, if output is doubled, the variable cost is doubled; or if output decreases by 10 percent, the cost decreases by 10 percent. The following list sets forth the primary factors a company should consider in establishing a practical definition of variable costs:

1. **Controllability**—Variable costs generally are subject to short-run management control.

2. **Proportionally Related to Activity**—Variable costs vary in proportion to activity or productive output rather than to the passage of time. Because they vary in direct ratio to changes in output (however measured), they are "straightline" costs when related to some measure of activity.

3. **Relevant Range**—Variable costs must be related to activity within a normal or relevant range of operations. Outside this normal range the pattern of variable costs may well change.

4. **Management Regulated**—Most variable costs can be affected by the discretionary policy decisions of management. For example, management may decide to use a less expensive raw material than that currently used, thereby reducing the amount of variable cost, although the cost is still variable but at a different rate.

5. **Activity Costs**—Because variable costs fluctuate in proportion to changes in activity, it is important that some adequate measure of the activity be selected. For example, in a producing department working on several different products simultaneously, units of the several products would not be additive; hence some common measure of effort, such as direct machine or man hours, must be used. The measure of output selected is generally referred to as the activity base.

6. **Variable in Total but Fixed per Unit**—A variable cost is variable when related to total output; however, when viewed as a *unit* cost it is a constant. For example, assume variable cost of $4,000. If 800 units are produced, the variable cost per unit is $5.00. However, if 1,200 units (a 50 percent increase) are produced, the total variable cost would be $6,000 (a 50 percent increase); the variable cost per unit is still $5.00.

7. **Practical Considerations**—A variable cost need not be absolutely variable in application. Many so-called curved costs can be classified as variable as the curve is approximately straight within the narrow relevant range.

The concept of variable costs is portrayed graphically in Illustration 24. Graph A illustrates two different variable costs, each of which varies directly with volume from zero to full capacity activity. Both costs should be shown as variable in the variable budget: A at $5.00 and B at $2.00 per unit. Graph B illustrates a type of variable cost that varies with production within given ranges of activity; however, the rate changes as we move to another relevant range. For relevant range C, this cost should be shown in the variable budget at $2.00 per unit.

SEMIVARIABLE COSTS ANALYZED

Semivariable or semifixed costs are those items of cost that increase or decrease as output or activity increases or decreases, but *not in proportion thereto*. This definition necessarily implies that semivariable costs possess some of the characteristics of both fixed and variable costs. In general the variability of semivariable costs may be attributed to the combined effect of (1) passage of time, (2) activity or output, and (3) discretionary management policy decisions. Semivariable costs frequently represent a significant portion of company expenses.

The concept of semivariable costs is portrayed graphically in Illustrations 25 and 26. In Illustration 25, Graph A portrays the typical semivariable cost with *straightline* characteristics for a fixed component and a variable component. This cost would be included n the variable budget as follows: fixed amount per period $2,000; variable rate per unit produced $2.86. Graph B illustrates the so-called step-cost, showing both the actual cost characteristics and the application of a straightline assumption for budget purposes. Whether or not this straightline assumption can be used depends upon the significance of the steps in the relevant range.

In Illustration 26, curved costs are represented. The actual cost characteristics and the application of a straightline assumption for budget purposes are indicated. For practical purposes step-and curved costs are generally classified as semivariable costs and budgeted on a straightline basis within the relevant range. Semivariable costs are discussed in detail in a subsequent section.

SELECTING THE MEASURE OF ACTIVITY

Fixed costs are time costs and hence are related to a short-time span such as a month. On the other hand, a satisfactory output measurement to which variable costs in a responsibility center can be related is frequently difficult to identify. In the simple case of a department producing one type of output, variable costs can be related directly to the ordinary measure of that

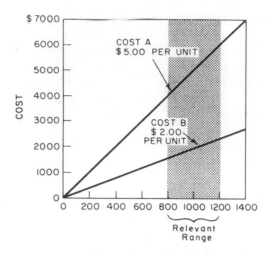

VOLUME – IN UNITS PRODUCED

GRAPH A – VARIABLE COSTS (TYPICAL)

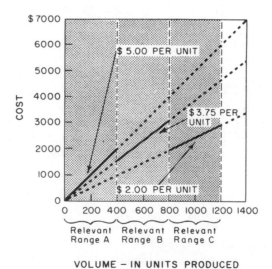

VOLUME – IN UNITS PRODUCED

GRAPH B – VARIABLE COST (REGULATED)

ILLUSTRATION 24.   Variable Costs Graphed

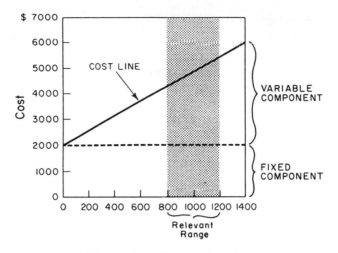

GRAPH A – SEMIVARIABLE COST (STRAIGHT LINE)

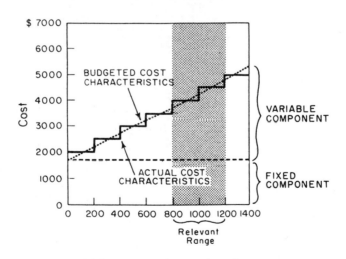

GRAPH B – SEMIVARIABLE COST – (STEP-COST)

ILLUSTRATION 25. Semivariable Costs Graphed

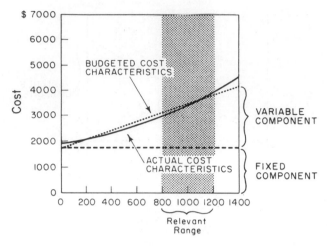

GRAPH A–SEMIVARIABLE COST (CURVED)

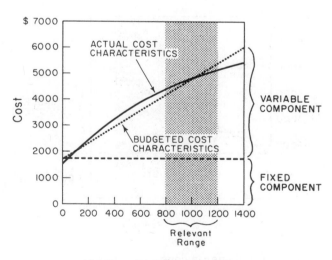

GRAPH B–SEMIVARIABLE COST (CURVED)

ILLUSTRATION 26.   Semivariable Costs (Curved) Graphed

output. For example, the power department produces only kilowatt hours of electricity; hence power department variable costs can be related to kilowatt hours since the latter would accurately measure the activity of the department. In the case of departments producing more than one type of output, such as two or more dissimilar products, some equivalent expression of activity must be established as an activity base. For example, when there are multiple outputs by each department, one department may use direct labor hours, another department may use direct machine hours, and the repair department direct repair hours.

If costs are to be classified according to variability, and if variable budgets are to be used, there exists a serious problem of selecting an appropriate activity base for each department or other responsibility center. The activity base must be the factor that most accurately expresses or measures the *overall activity* of the responsibility center.

Several criteria with respect to selecting a measure of output or activity base should be considered:

1. The activity base must measure fluctuations in the output that cause cost to vary.
2. The activity base selected should be affected as little as possible by variable factors other than output.
3. The base should be easily understood.
4. The activity measurements should be obtainable without undue clerical expense.

The selection of an activity base for each *service* department often presents a special problem. The factor used in the producing departments should not necessarily be carried over into the service departments. Where service departments, such as the power and repair departments, lend themselves to exact measures of activity, these measures should be used. Certain service departments, such as administration, time and motion, and personnel generally do not lend themselves to exact units of measurement. In such cases it might be best to measure activity in terms of overall production of the plant or in terms of the output of producing departments that are most frequently served.

Cost variability analyses frequently are meaningless because an incorrect activity base is used, thereby showing low correlation between cost and activity. Another problem is the tendency of the activity base gradually to become inappropriate. For example, the installation of additional or new machinery in a department may necessitate a change from direct labor hours to direct machine hours as the measure of output.

Selection of an appropriate activity base for each responsibility center is essential in planning expenses (see Chapter 9) even if variable budgets are not used in the firm.

DETERMINING THE RELEVANT RANGE OF ACTIVITY

We have indicated that the relative range concept is important in planning and controlling costs. Although each expense may have its own relative range (that is, points of major change) responsibility center considerations should prevail. As a practical matter, the relevant range—on a monthly basis—should approximate the monthly high (maximum limit) and monthly low (minimum limit) in activity. Obviously, the narrower the range the greater the precision in budget allowances.

METHODS FOR DETERMINING COST VARIABILITY

Let us look again at the variable budget shown in Illustration 22 and consider several approaches that might have been utilized in developing the amounts shown there. Assume that the fixed, variable, and semivariable cost categories used are in accord with the definitions presented in the preceding paragraphs. In that illustration, the activity base was units of output, since Department 42 produces only one product. The next step is through analytical procedures, estimates, and judgments to determine the *variability* of each item of expense incurred in the responsibility center. Determination of variability derives *two components* of each expense: (1) the fixed or constant amount per period; and (2) the variable rate per unit of the activity base. From the definitions and illustrations, recall that a true fixed cost has a zero value for the variable component, and a true variable cost has a zero value for the fixed component.

Clearly, determination of the variability of each expense item in a responsibility center is the most critical problem in the development of variable budgets. Numerous methods have been developed for resolving this difficulty. The purpose of this section is to explain and illustrate the primary methods that have been used. Most of the methods involve an analysis of historical costs to form a basis for estimating the variability of *future* costs. Remember that in the analysis of historical costs the purpose is to develop planned costs for a given period in the future.

The classification of costs by variability should begin with a careful study of each expense account in the responsibility center under consideration; the purpose of the study is to isolate the accounts that are readily identifiable as either fixed or variable. When the fixed and variable expenses are identified, the remaining accounts can be viewed as semivariable. *Each account determined to be semivariable must be analyzed to identify its fixed and variable components.* The procedures discussed in this section are based upon the assumption that semivariable costs can be analyzed and their fixed and variable components determined realistically.

In Department 42, it was clear to the analyst that direct material and direct labor were true variable costs; material usage varies up and down proportionately with production, and direct labor likewise would be incurred only as production occurred. The variable rates for these two expenses included in the variable budget (Illustration 22) were computed from standards as follows:

Direct material: Planned cost per unit of raw material $2.50.
Planned usage—four units of raw material for each unit of output.
Computed variable rate per unit of output:
$2.50 × 4 = $10.

Direct labor: Planned average wage rate in the department $4.00.
Planned labor usage—two direct labor hours for each unit of output.
Computed variable rate per unit of output:
$4 × 2 = $8.

Continuing Illustration 22, it was clear to the analyst that salaries were a true fixed cost; management policies on the number of salaried persons and the amount of their monthly salaries provided the fixed amount (per month) of $6,000.[2] Having made these determinations, the analyst scrutinized the two remaining expenses (Supplies and Indirect Labor) and assumed them to be semivariable and proceeded to determine their fixed and variable components. One or more of the methods discussed in this section were utilized for that purpose. These methods may be classified under three broad categories:

1. Direct estimate methods.
2. Budgeted high and low point method.
3. Correlation methods.

Several variants of each of these methods will be discussed and illustrated.[3] In considering the different methods, we should keep in mind the central objective of each—that is, to determine the fixed and variable

[2] In Illustration 22, we included direct material and direct labor costs in the variable budget. In subsequent illustrations and discussions, these two costs are not included in the variable budget. The latter approach may be followed since these two costs normally are separately planned and controlled as illustrated in Chapters 7 and 8. Recall that in those chapters these two costs were viewed as true variable costs and that the performance reports illustrated reported *adjusted budget allowances* for comparison purposes.

[3] For data on reported practices see: B. H. Sord and G. A. Welsch, *Business Budgeting, A Survey of Management Planning and Control Practices* (New York: Controllership Foundation Inc.), p. 174.

components of individual items of cost. Further, we are interested in future costs rather than historical costs. In discussing each method, we will assume that a suitable *activity base* has been selected. Although the technical aspects of each method will be given primary consideration, realize that management judgment is necessary for their application. In addition, realize that no particular method of cost analysis is appropriate for all situations, nor for all responsibility centers, or items of cost in a firm. Typically, a company should utilize several methods discussed below for varying internal situations.

DIRECT ESTIMATE METHODS

The direct estimate methods involve special techniques of cost analysis used only in special situations. Basically, a direct estimate implies a concentrated attack upon particular cost problem areas. For our purposes we will consider two direct estimate methods: (1) industrial engineering studies; and (2) direct analysis of historical data coupled with interpretation of related managerial policies.

Industrial Engineering Studies.   Many companies rely heavily on industrial engineers for cost data, including the variability of certain costs. Because engineers are intimately involved in the design of products, plant layout, production problems, and the related costs, they are in a particularly favorable position to provide certain cost data for budget purposes. Engineering studies based on analysis and direct observation of processes and operations frequently provide the most reliable variability estimates of certain costs. Industrial engineering studies may best provide such data as rates of material consumption, labor requirements, power usage, and waste and spoilage allowances.

Engineering studies are necessary when historical cost data are not available, but even when they are available, engineering studies are preferable in many situations. In such cases analysis of historical cost data can be used to check the reasonableness of engineering estimates. Conversely, where cost estimates are based principally on an analysis of historical cost data, engineering studies should be made periodically to check the analysis of past experience.

In Illustration 22 we can assume that the direct material and direct labor usage standards were developed through industrial engineering studies.

Direct Analysis of Historical Data and Management Policies.
Generally, the analyst using this approach makes a judgmental estimate of the variability of a particular cost directly from information obtained through

(1) an inspection of the historical activity of the cost, (2) an interpretation of relevant management policies and (3) an evaluation of the nature and cause of the expense. Refined statistical procedures are not used.

The estimate developed is one of two types:

1. An estimate of what the cost should be at certain specified volume levels within the relevant range. This procedure provides information for a *table type* of variable budget.

2. An estimate of the fixed and variable components of the cost. This procedure provides data for a *formula type* of variable budget.[4]

The steps involved in a direct estimate of cost variability of a particular cost in a responsibility center may be summarized as follows:

1. Selection of the activity base for the center.

2. Identification of the relevant range—the maximum and minimum limits of normal volume expectancy.

3. Determination of the various levels within the relevant range for which allowances are to be developed if a table type of budget is being employed.

4. Estimation of cost variability by direct analysis, inspection, and judgment.

The direct estimate approach is usually inappropriate for overall use in the concern; however, it can be quite useful in certain responsibility centers or for individual items of cost requiring special attention.

The direct estimate methods generally are employed when:

1. The expense is not amenable to formalized methods. For example, terminal payments to employees ordinarily would have to be estimated on a direct basis after the employee turnover experience and management policies are taken into account.

2. A new responsibility center is established for which there is no historical experience.

3. A new or nonroutine activity is contemplated that would raise expenses—for example, rearrangement of factory equipment.

4. New machines or additional machines are installed, making historical costs inapplicable for cost estimating.

5. Management decisions are anticipated that will significantly alter the pattern of cost variability.

[4] The formula type of variable budget was shown in Illustration 22; a latter section of this chapter explains and illustrates the table type.

6. Changes in methods of operations are made that significantly alter the pattern of cost variability.

7. Situations where direct observation of processes and operations may provide a basis for reliable cost estimates.

8. A check on the reliability of estimates developed by other methods is desired.

We could logically assume that the salary fixed component of $6,000 shown in Illustration 22 was derived through direct analysis of historical data coupled with management policies with respect to salaries for the planning period.

BUDGETED HIGH AND LOW POINT METHOD

This method is based on the concept of developing *two expense budget allowances at two different assumed levels of activity* for each item of expense in the responsibility center. The fixed and variable components of each cost are computed through an arithmetical interpolation between the two budgets, assuming straightline relationships. The method may be outlined as follows:

1. Select the activity base for the responsibility center.

2. Identify the relevant range for the responsibility center, that is, the minimum and maximum levels within which departmental output will fluctuate during the year.

3. Develop an expense budget for each expense at (1) the maximum level and (2) the minimum level, that is, two expense budgets.

4. Interpolate between the two budgets to determine the fixed and variable components of each expense as follows:

    a. Subtract the minimum volume from the maximum volume.

    b. Subtract the minimum cost from the maximum cost.

    c. Divide the difference in cost by the difference in volume to derive the *variable rate*.

    d. Derive the *fixed component* by subtracting the variable portion (variable rate multiplied by the maximum or minimum volume) from the maximum or minimum cost estimate; the difference is the fixed component.

To illustrate, assume that *indirect labor* is being analyzed and that the activity base is *units of output* as in Illustration 22. Let us see how the $4,000 fixed component and the $2 variable rate for indirect labor in that illustration might have been determined; we will illustrate the above listed steps:

1. Activity base for Department 42—units of output.
2. Relevant range—maximum 12,000 units; minimum 9,000 units.
3. The manager of Department 42 with the assistance of his supervisor and various staff members, developed the following expense budgets for indirect labor:

> At maximum level (12,000 units) $28,000.
> At minimum level (9,000 units)   22,000.

4. Interpolation to compute fixed and variable components of indirect labor:
   a. To compute variable rate:

	BUDGETED COST	VOLUME
At maximum	$28,000	12,000
At minimum	22,000	9,000
Difference	$ 6,000 ÷	3,000 = $2 variable rate per unit.

   b. To compute fixed component (amount per period);

	AT MAXIMUM LEVEL	(OR)	AT MINIMUM LEVEL
Total cost	$28,000		$22,000
Less variable component	(12,000 × $2) 24,000	(9,000 × $2)	18,000
Difference—fixed component	$ 4,000		$ 4,000

Thus, the variable budget would reflect the results as shown in Illustration 22: fixed per month $4,000, and variable rate per unit of output $2. The arithmetical computation illustrated is simply a straightline interpolation between the maximum and minimum values. The critical aspects of this method are the validity of the two budget estimates and whether the cost can be realistically assumed to be straightline in relationship to output. This method is widely used because (a) it is based on budget estimates (rather than historical data directly) and (2) it provides for effective participation by the supervisor of the responsibility center.

CORRELATION METHODS

Correlation techniques are widely used in the analysis of costs. These techniques provide methods for analyzing historical cost data in relation to historical output data to determine how costs *have varied with output in the past,* which is, in turn, the basis for estimating how costs *should vary with output in the future.* Because correlation techniques are based on historical data, a critical problem arises when changes in accounting classifications, methods of manufacturing, management policies, and other such changes tend to make historical data nonrepresentative of future expectations.

Correlation techniques are applied to *monthly historical data*. Monthly information for the past 12 to 18 months is preferable because that generally is not far enough into the past to cause major distortion. Correlation techniques, in general, consist of the following steps:

1. An analysis of the relationship between cost and output as indicated by historical data provided by the accounting records. This analysis indicates how the cost varied with output in the *past*.

2. Following this analysis, an estimate is made of how the cost *should* vary with output in the future, taking into account new conditions that are expected to develop during the budget year, such as changes in management policies, general economic conditions, and methods of operation.

3. The cost estimates are presented to (1) the supervisors of the responsibility centers for their recommendations, and (2) next level of management level for appoval.

4. The revised fixed and variable allowances are formalized in the variable budget that is approved by top management.

The techniques discussed here assume linear relationships; however, some firms have experimented with, and are using, curvilinear regression, such as the logarithmic and reciprocal regression lines. Correlation methods discussed are:

1. Graphic
2. Mathematical.

Graphic Method. This method involves the use of scatter graphs in order to determine *visually* the fixed and variable components of a cost. The analysis involves the preparation of a historical graph with cost plotted on the vertical scale (*Y* axis) and volume or output on the horizontal scale (*X* axis). Historical data are plotted on the graph and a *visual trend line* is drawn through the plotted points. The point at which the trend line intersects the vertical scale (at *zero volume*) indicates the fixed component of the cost and the slope of the trend line represents the variable component.

Historical data to illustrate the method are given on page 321 for Indirect Material in Department Z. The activity base is *direct machine hours*.

From the data presented, a scatter graph was constructed and a trend line was drawn visually through the plotted points as shown in Illustration 27. The numbers on the graph identify the plotted points with the months.

Department Z
Historical Cost and Volume Data

MONTH	POINTS ON CHART	HISTORICAL DATA DIRECT MACHINE HOURS	HISTORICAL DATA INDIRECT MATERIAL COST
January	(1)	44,000	$ 875
February	(2)	41,000	850
March	(3)	45,000	875
April	(4)	43,000	850
May	(5)	36,000	750
June	(6)	22,000	550
July	(7)	23,000	500
August	(8)	15,000	450
September	(9)	30,000	600
October	(10)	38,000	700
November	(11)	41,000	800
December	(12)	44,000	850
Totals		422,000	$8,650

Analyzing Costs—Variable Budgets

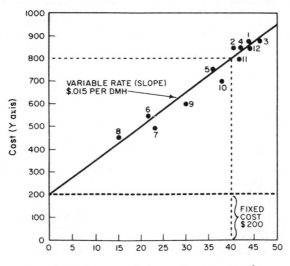

ILLUSTRATION 27.   Graphic Analysis of Costs
Indirect Material, Department Z

The fixed and variable components of the cost as indicated by the trend line are then determined in this manner:

```
Monthly fixed component
(point at which the trend line intersects the Y axis) .........................  $200
Variable component (interpolate between any two points on the trend line)
          Cost at 40,000 DMH                                      $800
          Cost at Zero DMH                                         200
          Cost increase spread over 40,000 DMH                    $600
Variable rate or slope of trend line ($600 ÷ 40,000) = $.015 per DMH
The computations can be checked as follows:
          Fixed cost at 50,000 DMH                                $200
          Variable cost at 50,000 DMH (× $.015)                    750
          Total—(Trend line intersection at 50,000 DMH)           $950
```

The resulting variable budget amounts would be as shown below, *assuming* an adjustment down of 10 percent in the fixed component. The adjustment down represents a *judgment* on the part of management about what the cost *should be* as opposed to *what it was*.

ACCOUNTS	FIXED PER MONTH	VARIABLE RATE PER DMH
$200	$180	$.015

Graphic analysis is relatively simple and provides a visual and readily comprehensible picture of the interrelationships. It is difficult to grasp such relationships in a bare listing of historical data (as in the previous table). Graphic analysis is frequently used as a preliminary study to obtain insights as to additional analyses that should or should not be made. Its principal weakness is lack of objectivity in drawing the trend line; no two individuals would construct precisely the same trend line through the points. However, the margin of error is generally minor for the purposes intended. The procedure can be applied to individual costs, groups of cost, departmental cost totals, and company-wide costs.

Graphic analysis is one of the most useful, yet simple, analytical tools available to the cost analyst. Through use and experimentation, cost accountants and budget experts have found it invaluable. The relationship of cost to volume or output represents only one of the many applications of graphic analysis to cost study. It might be observed that the graphic representation of costs related to *time periods*, traditionally used by accountants, has limited significance other than to portray trends. Semilogarithmic graphs are generally preferable in this latter case. There are several variations of the graphic method.

Mathematical Method.   In the analysis of historical cost and output data, the statistical *method of least squares* may be used to compute the trend line. The method may be adapted for curved costs; however the straightline adaptation is considered by practically all authorities to be sufficiently descriptive of the underlying cost-volume relationship for budgeting purposes.

The method of least squares is a mathematical procedure used to compute a *unique* regression line through a given series of specified points such as those plotted above. In the computation of the trend line, the sum of the deviations of the points from the line will be zero, and the sum of the squares of the deviations will be less than the sum of the squares from any other straight line; thus it is a unique trend line. The method is purely objective in that the same trend line will be developed from the same data, whereas the graphic method trend line's position and slope are subject to the judgment of the analyst.

Fitting a unique mathematical trend line for costs by least squares involves linear correlation analysis of two sets of data—monthly cost and volume. Correlation analysis is a method of defining mathematically the underlying relationship between two variables. The two variables are generally identified in this way:

1. Independent variable (X variable)—The independent series is the one that varies or is thought to vary independently of the other (that is the dependent) series.

2. Dependent variable (Y variable)—The dependent series is the one that changes or is thought to change with changes in the other (that is the independent) series.

In the mathematical definition of a trend line that expresses the relationship between the two variables, the equation for a straight line may be expressed as $Y = a + bX$, where Y represents the dependent variable, a the constant factor, b the slope of the trend line, and X the independent variable. Simply, a expresses the *position of the trend line* and b the *slope* of the trend line. Therefore, b expresses the effect on Y (the dependent variable) of any change in X (the independent variable). The equation may be explained graphically as follows:

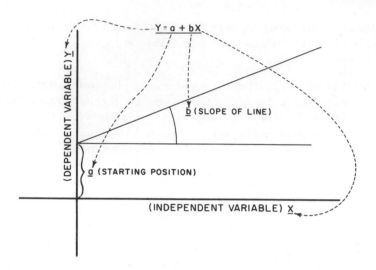

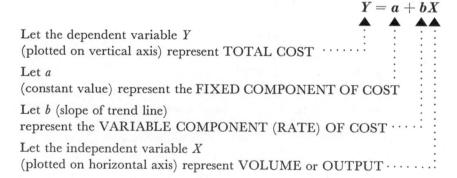

It is readily apparent from the illustration that the technique is adaptable to the analysis of costs to determine their variability or relationship to volume changes. Here, too, we are seeking an expression of the underlying relationship between two variables: cost and volume. Specifically, we want to know the *effect on cost of changes in volume or activity*. Applying the least squares technique to the problem at hand, the equation may be adapted:

$$Y = a + bX$$

Let the dependent variable Y
(plotted on vertical axis) represent TOTAL COST

Let a
(constant value) represent the FIXED COMPONENT OF COST

Let b (slope of trend line)
represent the VARIABLE COMPONENT (RATE) OF COST

Let the independent variable X
(plotted on horizontal axis) represent VOLUME or OUTPUT

It is clear from the adaptation above that the a value represents the *fixed cost per month* and the b value the *variable cost rate per direct machine hour* in the variable budgets as illustrated for indirect material in Department Z. Therefore, the problem is to develop these respective values. We are analyzing historical cost and volume data to determine these values (a and b) that are expressive of cost variability. The a and b values may be computed with the following equations (Note: N represents the number or sets of data, *i.e.*, known points on the graph; $\sum$ denotes summation):

$$a = \frac{\sum X^2 \sum Y - \sum X \sum XY}{N \sum X^2 - (\sum X)^2}$$

$$b = \frac{N \sum XY - \sum X \sum Y}{N \sum X^2 - (\sum X)^2}$$

The equations above require computations best accomplished on a worksheet. To illustrate, a least squares worksheet is presented in Illustration 28. The data concerning Indirect Material for Department Z given on page 321 are used for the worksheet illustration.[5]

ILLUSTRATION 28. Indirect Material—Department Z
Least Squares Worksheet

N	MONTH	HISTORICAL DATA DIRECT MACHINE HOURS (000) X	INDIRECT MATERIAL COST Y	XY	X²
1.	January	44	$ 875	$ 38,500	1,936
2.	February	41	850	34,850	1,681
3.	March	45	875	39,375	2,025
4.	April	43	850	36,550	1,849
5.	May	36	750	27,000	1,296
6.	June	22	550	12,100	484
7.	July	23	500	11,500	529
8.	August	15	450	6,750	225
9.	September	30	600	18,000	900
10.	October	38	700	26,600	1,444
11.	November	41	800	32,800	1,681
12.	December	44	850	37,400	1,936
	Summations (Σ)	422	$8,650	$321,425	15,986

To compute *a* value: $a = \dfrac{\sum X^2 \sum Y - \sum X \sum XY}{N \sum X^2 - (\sum X)^2}$

$$= \frac{(15,986)(\$8,650) - (422)(\$321,425)}{(12)(15,986) - (422)^2}$$

$$= \underline{\underline{\$191.85}}$$

[5] The equations for computing *a* and *b* values may be rearranged in a number of different ways. As a practical matter the equations should be rearranged in such a way to "fit" the preferences of the analyst. The computions frequently are computerized.

To compute b value: $b = \dfrac{N \sum XY - \sum X \sum Y}{N \sum X^2 - (\sum X)^2}$

$$= \frac{(12)(\$321,425) - (422)(\$8,650)}{(12)(15,986) - (422)^2}$$

$$= \$.01504 \text{ per direct machine hour}$$

($15.04 per thousand DMH)

Resulting equation: $Y = a + bX$

$$Y = \$191.85 + \$.01504X$$

The analysis in Illustration 28 shows the fixed and variable components of indirect material for the period covered by the historical data. The next step to develop a variable budget is to adjust the values, derived by the analysis, for conditions or changes anticipated for the future that did not previously exist. For example, assume it is decided that the fixed component as computed is satisfactory but that the variable component should be reduced to $.145 per unit. The variable budget for Department Z would include the following:

ACCOUNTS	FIXED PER MONTH	VARIABLE RATE PER 100 DIRECT MACHINE HOURS
Indirect material	$192.00*	$1.45*

*Practical considerations would suggest that fixed allowances be rounded to even dollars and larger amounts to even tens or hundreds of dollars. Likewise where the number of direct hours is large in a department, the variable rate should be expressed in terms of even tens, hundreds, or perhaps thousands of hours. Rounding on variable rates must be done carefully, especially where the base is large, since the effect of a minor rounding when applied to a large number of hours might be substantial.

Although some people have claimed that the least squares analysis is too involved and troublesome for practical use surveys show that it is frequently used. The method is easy enough when it is realized that the computation may be simplified, because the independent variable (volume or activity) is common to all expense accounts within a particular responsibility center, and one simplified worksheet may provide the analysis for all the accounts in a department (see Schedule 45 for Superior Manufacturing Company). In addition, the computations may be easily computerized.

The least squares method provides a particularly useful and objective method of analyzing historical data. It is important for the analyst to realize, however, that the results are rigid and often misleadingly precise, and therefore must be tempered with experience and management judgment. The underlying mathematical assumptions must be understood. If used properly, this approach to determine expense variability has great potential.

NEGATIVE VALUES IN COST ANALYSIS

Negative fixed values may result from most of the analyses described above. Likewise negative variable values (negative slope) may result from the graphic and least squares methods. Of course, these negative values can be explained mathematically. From a practical viewpoint, however, they generally should not be used. There are a number of factors that may cause negative values: the expense out of control; nonlinear costs; incorrect accounting; nonrepresentative data; incorrect activity base; discretionary cost decisions; inappropriate relevant range; and external influences.

When historical costs are analyzed, it is important that raw data be studied carefully prior to formal analysis. Any months showing unusual or nonrepresentative conditions should not be included in the analysis. For example, assume that during March of the past year the company participated in a trade show at considerable cost. Either the additional expenditures for the trade show, or data for the entire month of March, should be excluded from any analysis of the variability of the costs with volume.

Negative results persisting after adjustments of the raw data indicate the need for further analysis to determine exactly why the expense is following a random pattern. The analyst should identify the causative factors so the expense can be given special treatment with respect to the problem of cost variability. A direct estimate method often should be used in such situations.

PARTICIPATION BY SUPERVISORS IN DEVELOPING VARIABLE BUDGETS

The technical aspects of variable budgets may make it difficult in a particular situation to attain meaningful participation of those responsibility center managers where the concept is applied. Direct estimates, even though developed by industrial engineering studies, should be discussed with the operational managers who use them. The high-low point method is favored in many situations because it does rest fundamentally on the concept that the *two budget estimates* required for each item of expense in the responsibility center should be initiated by the manager of the center and approved by management. The interpolations and development of the variable budget allowances, even though performed at the staff level, thus would be based on a participatory foundation. In contrast, the statistical approaches utilize historical data directly and require technical competence; thus the analytical efforts involved are generally performed at the staff level. In this situation participation is best attained, prior to their approval, by either (1) submitting the proposed variable budgets to the respective responsibility center managers for their evaluation and recommendations (This is feasible only where their level of sophistication is adequate.), or (2) by submitting the expense schedules for the annual profit plan (that were derived from the variable budgets) to those managers for evaluation and recommendations. In view of the importance generally attached to meaningful participation in the planning process, effective ways to achieve it should be developed when the variable budgets are being constructed.

COST-VOLUME CONSIDERATIONS

Some people are skeptical of the classification of cost in relation to activity or volume changes. It is generally recognized that some costs are fixed and others are variable, but there is some doubt as to whether the semivariable costs can be resolved realistically into their fixed and variable components. In addition, there is doubt about the straightline assumption.

Proponents of the concept of cost variability respond to these arguments as follows:

1. Although costs in the past have varied erratically, such behavior should not be taken as normative for the future. Many costs may have been erratic because of poor control, waste, inefficiency, faulty accounting, and unwise management decisions.

2. A large percentage of costs are subject to management policies. The fact that policies were changed during the period under analysis may have caused erratic cost variations. These "policy variations" can be isolated and should be taken into consideration in estimating cost variability for the future.

3. Past costs that have been erratic generally will "shape up" when carefully budgeted and controlled (see Illustration 29).

4. Actual costs that are unlike should be classified separately in the accounting system. For example, certain indirect labor costs may vary in proportion to output; however, management policy may require that any indirect laborer laid off will be paid two weeks' severance pay. This severance pay should be classified, not as a normal indirect labor cost, but as a special expense. Obviously, mixing the two in one account would tend to destroy the pattern of variability for each account. *Direct cost accounting* procedures applied in the accounts significantly simplifies the analysis of cost variability (see Chapter 16).

5. Variable budget procedures do not necessarily require straightline relationships.

6. There will be certain costs in every firm that are influenced by special factors, some external and some internal, which may require special con-

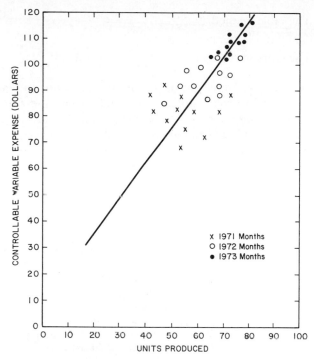

ILLUSTRATION 29.   Typical Improvement in Cost Variability with Budget Control

sideration for planning purposes. The number of such items is considerably smaller than is commonly supposed.

7.   Economic research on the question of whether unit variable costs fall and then rise with expanding output or remain constant in their variability have shown that throughout the relevant ranges of volume total variable costs increase at a constant rate.

8.   Perfect linearity is not required for practical considerations. Approximate linearity is sufficiently accurate as long as sound management decisions may result from the analysis.

9.   Surveys of industry reveal numerous cases where cost variability with volume is identified on a practical and useful basis.

10.   The type of operations engaged in by the firm determines the extent to which cost-volume relationships may be resolved.

METHODS OF EXPRESSING VARIABLE BUDGETS

Variable budgets may be expressed technically in several ways; however, the various methods may be grouped under three principal classifications, namely:

1. The table method.
2. The formula method.
3. The graphic method.

The *table method*, in effect, is a multiple expense budget showing planned allowances for several different volumes or levels of activity within the relevant range. This method of expressing variable budgets is frequently used for illustrative and instructional purposes; however, the formula method appears to be more widely used in actual practice. The table method is shown in Illustration 30. Notice that the activity base is direct machine hours and that budget allowances are given for five different volumes within the relevant range. Also note that the fixed and variable components of each expense are not indicated. Therefore, this form of variable budget makes it possible to accommodate irregular step and curved costs without the straight-line assumption. This feature is shown in Illustration 30 for other Expenses.

ILLUSTRATION 30. Variable Budget—Table Method
(Only Three Typical Accounts Shown)
Bowers Corporation
Variable Budget—Department X
(350,000 to 500,000 Direct Machine Hours Represents
Relevant Range on Monthly Basis)

VOLUME—MACHINE HRS. PERCENT	350,000 70	400,000 80	450,000 90	500,000 100
Foremen salaries	$12,000	$12,000	$12,000	$12,000
Indirect labor	14,000	16,000	18,000	20,000
Other expenses	24,000	27,000	31,000	34,000
Totals	$50,000	$55,000	$61,000	$66,000

Observe in Illustration 30 that foremen salaries is a fixed cost, indirect labor is a variable cost, and other expenses is a semivariable cost.

When the table form is used, a frequent problem arises when budget allowances are desired for some volume between two volume levels for which budget figures are provided. Two approaches to this problem have been suggested:

1. Use the budget allowance nearest the desired volume. For example, if budget allowances for 460,000 direct machine hours were desired, allowances at 450,000 direct machine hours would be used.

2. Determine the budget allowance by straightline interpolation. For example, budget allowances for 460,000 direct machine hours would be computed as follows:

	ALLOWANCE AT 450,000 HOURS	ADD INTERPOLATED INCREASE	ALLOWANCE AT 460,000 HOURS
Foremen salaries	$12,000	(Constant—No interpolation necessary)	$12,000
Indirect labor	18,000	($20,000 − $18,000) × $\left(\dfrac{460,000 - 450,000}{500,000 - 450,000}\right)$	18,400
Other expenses	31,000	($34,000 − $31,000) × $\left(\dfrac{460,000 - 450,000}{500,000 - 450,000}\right)$	31,600
Totals	$61,000	($66,000 − $61,000) × $\left(\dfrac{460,000 - 450,000}{500,000 - 450,000}\right)$	$62,000

Obviously, to determine the allowances at 460,000 hours, the allowances at 450,000 hours must be *increased* by one-fifth of the difference. (10,000 hours represent one-fifth of the increase to the next column).

The *formula method* of expressing the variable budget provides a formula for each expense account in each department. The formula indicates the fixed component of cost and the variable component (rate) of cost. The formula method is more compact and generally more useful because the components of cost are indicated.

The formula method gives *straightline* expression to all costs. Steps within the relevant range may be indicated by footnote as shown in Illustration 31.

ILLUSTRATION 31. Variable Budget—Formula Method
(Only Three Typical Accounts Shown)
Variable Budget—Department X
(Relevant Range—350,000 to 500,000 Direct Machine Hours)

ACCOUNTS	FIXED PER MONTH	VARIABLE RATE PER 100 DIRECT MACHINE HOURS
Foremen salaries	$12,000	
Indirect labor		$ 4.00
Other expenses	4,000*	6.00
Total	$16,000	$10.00

*Decrease to $3,000 at 400,000 (or less) machine hours.

The variable budget for Department X, as expressed under the formula method, is shown in Illustration 31.

The *graphic method* is used primarily for stepped or curved costs as was shown in Illustrations 25 and 26. Budget allowances for all purposes are read directly from the graph. This method is particularly useful where it is not desired to "straighten" curved or stepped costs.

UTILIZATION OF VARIABLE BUDGETS

The primary purpose of variable budgets is to expedite expense control; thus, we can list three specific uses of variable budgets:

1. To facilitate development of the departmental expense budgets for inclusion in the profit plans.
2. To provide expense goals for the managers of responsibility centers during the period covered by profit plan.
3. To provide adjusted budget allowances for comparison purposes (against actual expenses) in the monthly performance reports. This use is generally emphasized.

Variable budgets may be applied in all of the functions in the enterprise—manufacturing selling, and administrative—although they are more frequently used in the responsibility centers in the manufacturing function. They are especially appropriate in responsibility centers where (1) operations tend to be repetitive, (2) there are numerous heterogeneous expenses, and (3) output or activity can be realistically measured.

To comprehend the three uses of variable budgets listed above, understand that the development of variable budgets normally occurs early in the planning cycle. For example, a realistic policy would be to set the target completion date for variable budgets as "prior to completion of the sales plan." Since variable budgets do not relate to a specific level of output, the analytical work essential to their development usually can proceed independently of the other phases of the short-term profit plan. Clearly, when variable budgets are completed early in the planning cycle, they can be used directly in preparing the expense budgets that are to be included in the annual profit plan. To illustrate this particular use, we refer to Illustration 22, which shows the variable budget for Department 42. Now assume that the planned activity for the department has been developed as follows: Year 1977—120,000 units; Janaury—9,000 units; February—11,000 units;

ILLUSTRATION 32. Expense Budget for Department 42
Annual Profit Plan 1977

	ANNUAL	JANUARY	FEBRUARY	ETC.
Output planned (units)	120,000	9,000	11,000	
Direct material	$1,200,000	$ 90,000	$110,000	
Direct labor	960,000	72,000	88,000	
Department overhead:				
Salaries	72,000	6,000	6,000	
Supplies	120,000	9,000	11,000	
Indirect labor*	288,000	22,000	26,000	
Total	$2,640,000	$199,000	$241,000	

*Clerical computations (refer to Illustration 22):
Annual—($4,000 × 12) + ($2 × 120,000) = $288,000
January—$4,000 + ($2 × 9,000) = $22,000
February—$4,000 + ($2 × 11,000) = $26,000

etc. With these two sets of data we can clerically develop the expense budget for the department that would be included in the annual profit plan; this is shown in Illustration 32. Examine that illustration and the computations for each cost.

In the absence of a variable budget for Department 42 the expenses included in Illustration 32 would be estimated in a more time-consuming manner as discussed in Chapter 9.

Now let us turn our attention to the second and third uses of the variable budget by examining a relevant control concept frequently overlooked. *Cost control is possible prior to cost incurrence but not after cost incurrence.* Simply stated, this concept holds that once a cost is incurred (that is, after the decision point) it cannot be controlled; the decision has been made; the money has been spent; it cannot be undone! Therefore, the concept holds that cost goals should be used in two ways:

1. To control costs before incurrence by providing a target in advance. Thus, control before decision point is accomplished by providing operating supervisors with *cost targets* (that is, cost budgets) based on scheduled activity or output, prior to the beginning of such work (the second use).
2. To measure the effectiveness with which costs were controlled during the period. Measurement of cost control is accomplished by comparing actual costs incurred with budget allowances *adjusted* to actual activity or output, thereby gauging cost control performance (the third use).

Now let's return to Department 42 (page 304) to illustrate the second use of variable budgets. First, assume we are ready to start February operations. Note that in Illustration 32 the planned output for February was 11,000. If that planned volume still is valid, the expense goals included in the annual profit plan (Illustration 32) would serve as the *cost targets* for the manager of Department 42 throughout February. Alternatively, assume for various reasons the management now has decided that 12,000 units should be produced in February. In this latter case the expense estimates in the annual profit plan (based on 11,000 units of output) would be inappropriate; the manager of Department 42 needs new estimates at 12,000 units. With the variable budget available (Illustration 22) we can compute the new targets on a dynamic basis as shown in Illustration 33.

The third use of variable budgets relates to the monthly performance report. Performance reports for each responsibility center should be comprehensive along the lines discussed and illustrated in the preceding chapters. They should encompass all controllable items and should compare actual performance with planned performance. With respect to expenses included

ILLUSTRATION 33.   Department 42 Cost Targets for Work
Scheduled for February, 1977
(12,000 Units)

CONTROLLABLE EXPENSES	COMPUTATIONS	COST TARGETS
Direct material	$10 × 12,000	$120,000
Direct labor	$ 8 × 12,000	96,000
Department Overhead:		
Salaries		6,000
Supplies	$ 1 × 12,000	12,000
Indirect labor	$ 4,000 + ($ 2 × 12,000)	28,000
Total	$10,000 + ($21 × 12,000)	$262,000

Note to Department Manager: This projection is based on the output scheduled for your department during February and puts you in a position to control these costs during the month in an effort to meet or better your cost control goals.

on the performance report, one of two basic comparisons may be utilized as follows:

1.   Fixed or Static Budget Procedures.   This approach is utilized when the variable budget concept is not applied. In this situation actual costs are compared with the budget allowances reflected in the annual profit plan. This approach is appropriate in situations where actual output attained is essentially the same as reflected in the annual profit plan. However, when actual output differs significantly from plans, the comparison is apt to be inappropriate. The designation "fixed or static budget procedures" implies that there is no basis for providing *adjusted* budget allowances; the fixed budget amounts are used. Fixed or static budget procedures for cost control quite often are inadequate in a responsibility center because (a) actual output often is significantly different from that reflected in the profit plan and (b) usually variable and semivariable costs are incurred in the responsibility center. Observe that if only fixed costs were incurred there would be no need for variable budget procedures.

2.   Variable or Flexible Budget Procedures.   This approach is utilized when the variable budget concept is applied in the responsibility center. In this situation actual costs incurred are compared with *adjusted* budget allowances based on the actual output attained.

To illustrate use of a variable budget for performance reporting in Department 42, assume at the *end* of February and that actual output attained was 11,500 units. Comparison of actual costs with the profit plan (Illustration 32) would be inappropriate since that plan anticipated 11,000 units of output. The cost target values shown in Illustration 33 likewise are inappropriate since they anticipated an output of 12,000 units. Thus, we must compute *adjusted budget allowances* for comparison with actual costs incurred in producing 11,500 units. The performance report would appear as in Illustration 34.

ILLUSTRATION 34. Performance Report
Department 42

Department	42	Date	February, 1977
Supervisor	John Ware		

CONTROLLABLE EXPENSES	ACTUAL 11,500 UNITS	BUDGET ADJUSTED TO 11,500 UNITS	VARIABLE (UNFAVORABLE)
Direct material	$116,000	$115,000	($1,000)
Direct labor	91,500	92,000	500
Department overhead:			
Salaries	6,000	6,000	0
Supplies	12,100	11,500	(600)
Indirect labor	28,300	27,000	(1,300)
Total	$253,900	$251,500	($2,400)

The more complex operations become, the greater the problem of cost control. In highly complex circumstances costs can be effectively controlled only through planning, continuous effort, and a well-designed system of control. Cost control is a line responsibility, not a staff function. A control system does not and cannot control cost; instead it places within the hands of operating management a tool of control—a tool that can be made effective only by operating management. Operating management will view cost control seriously if top management exhibits an active interest in it. Investigations have clearly shown that lower levels of management tend to view cost control in the same light as do their superiors. If top management is lackadaisical and inconsistent on costs, operating management will be likewise. Merely talking about cost control and "riding" some operating supervisor on occasion will not contribute to effective cost control. Intelligent, organized, and consistent effort is essential to perform this vital managerial function effectively.

The essentials of an effective cost control program may be outlined as follows:

1. Top management must provide active and consistent support.
2. Cost control must be clearly identified as a line responsibility.
3. The control system must be designed to fit the peculiarities of the situation.
4. Realistic cost standards (such as budget allowances) must be developed for use as a basis for gauging performance.

5. There must be provision for adequate performance reporting.
6. Cost standards or allowances should be related to output where possible.
7. The control system must be simple and understandable to operating management.
8. Cost control is effective *prior to cost incurrence* rather than after cost incurrence. Therefore, cost standards should be used for control in two ways:
   a. To control costs before incurrence.
   b. To measure the effectiveness with which costs were controlled.
9. Cost control must be applied to costs prior to their allocation.
10. Adequate follow-up procedures must be developed.

A properly designed and operated budget program will include an effective cost control system. Cost responsibility will have been defined, and cost standards established. The fact that operating supervisors are brought into the entire planning and control program from its inception will in itself tend to generate enthusiasm and cost consciousness.

USE OF THE CONCEPT OF COST VARIABILITY

In this chapter our focus has been on a concept having wide applicability in (1) profit planning, (2) management decision-making, and (3) accounting. The concept is *cost variability* and it is the basic foundation for (1) variable budgets, (2) breakeven analyses, (3) marginal cost analysis, (4) direct costing, and (5) variation analyses. These applications of the concept of cost variability are discussed in succeeding chapters.

COMPREHENSIVE ILLUSTRATION OF THE DEVELOPMENT AND UTILIZATION OF VARIABLE BUDGETS

Recall that Superior Manufacturing Company has fourteen different departments—six factory, four sales, and four general administration departments (including building services). At the end of Chapter 9 the expense budgets for each of these departments were illustrated; they were designed for incorporation into the annual profit plan. For pedagogical reasons it was assumed in that chapter that variable budgets were not available. However, the company utilizes variable budgets in all departments except building services. Variable budgets for each of these thirteen responsibility centers are shown in Schedules 41 to 44 inclusive. These variable budget values were applied to the planned activity (output) in each department to develop the expense schedules included in the annual profit plan (Schedules 33, 34, 39, and 40). For example, the computation of the *January* column for general and administrative factory overhead in Schedule 33 (Chapter 9) was computed as shown below. These expense allowances are based upon total direct labor hours in the factory that were taken from the direct labor budget (Schedule 31 page 8-13). They were applied to the variable budget allowances for general and administrative factory overhead from Schedule 41.

Computations for Expense Schedule 33

ACCOUNT	REF.	FIXED PER MONTH 41		JANUARY DLH (00) 31		VARIABLE RATE 41		JANUARY BUDGET ALLOWANCE
Salaries		$8,000	plus	836	×	$ .00 equals		$8,000
Travel and entertainment		100	″	836	×	.50	″	518
Telephone and telegraph		460	″	836	×	.20	″	627
Depreciation		130	″	836	×	.00	″	130
Insurance		20	″	836	×	.00	″	20
Taxes		30	″	836	×	.00	″	30
Stationery and office supplies		20	″	836	×	.30	″	271
Totals		$8,760	″	836	×	$1.00	″	$9,596

SCHEDULE 41. Superior Manufacturing Company
Variable Budget—Manufacturing Division
(Service Departments)
For the Year Ending December 31, 1977

	SERVICE DEPARTMENTS					
	GENERAL AND ADMINISTRATIVE		POWER		REPAIR	
	FIXED PER MONTH	VARIABLE PER 100 TOTAL DLH	FIXED PER MONTH	VARIABLE PER 1000 KILOWATT HOURS	FIXED PER MONTH	VARIABLE PER DIRECT REPAIR HOUR
*Supervisory salaries	$8,000		$3,000		$300	
Maintenance			100	$ .28		
Fuel				1.20		
Supplies used						$.34
Travel and entertainment	100	$ .50				
Telephone and telegraph	460	.20				
*Depreciation (time basis)	130		450		10	
*Insurance	20		70		3	
*Taxes	30		80		7	
Stationery and office supplies	20	.30				
Wages			3,000		400	
Totals	$8,760	$1.00	$6,700	$1.48	$720	$.34

*Noncontrollable in this responsibility center.

SCHEDULE 42. Superior Manufacturing Company
Variable Budget—Manufacturing Division
(Producing Departments)
For the Year Ending December 31, 1977

| | PRODUCING DEPARTMENTS | | | | | |
| | DEPARTMENT 1 | | DEPARTMENT 2 | | DEPARTMENT 3 | |
	FIXED PER MONTH	VARIABLE PER 100 DEPT. DLH	FIXED PER MONTH	VARIABLE PER 100 DEPT. DLH	FIXED PER MONTH	VARIABLE PER 100 DEPT. DLH
*Supervisory salaries	$10,000		$1,870		$2,920	
Indirect labor	3,000	$22.50		$1.90	800	$ 7.10
Maintenance parts	300	1.50	20	.20	150	.50
Supplies used	450	5.50	40	.50	200	2.50
*Depreciation (output basis)		1.50		.40		.90
*Insurance	100		10		50	
*Taxes	150		20		60	
Totals	$14,000	$31.00	$1,960	$3.00	$4,180	$11.00

*Noncontrollable

In developing the variable budgets for the thirteen departments, Superior utilizes various approaches for analyzing the cost variability of costs. We will illustrates one of these approaches for General Sales Overhead (Schedule 43). The *method of least squares* was used to analyze the expenses in this particular department. Since the variable budgets are constructed during the first part of October, historical cost and sales-volume data cover the twelve months prior to October 1, 1976. Cost-volume data obtained from sales management and the cost department indicated:

General Sales Overhead:

1. Supervisory salaries $12,000 per month (management anticipates no change during the coming year).
2. Travel and entertainment—Cost data as listed on the worksheet, Schedule 45 (Y).
3. Telephone and telegraph—Cost data as listed on the worksheet (Y).
4. Depreciation—Office equipment $50 per month (no change per depreciation schedule).
5. Stationery and office supplies—Cost data as listed on the worksheet (Y).
6. Auto expense—Cost data as listed on the worksheet (Y).
7. Advertising—Budget per advertising schedule (Schedule 38). Total net sales for company—As listed on the worksheet (X).

SCHEDULE 43. Superior Manufacturing Company
Variable Budget—Sales Division
For the Year Ending December 31, 1977

	SOUTHERN		EASTERN		WESTERN		GENERAL SALES OVERHEAD	
	FIXED PER MONTH	VARIABLE PER $100 NET DIST. SALES	FIXED PER MONTH	VARIABLE PER $100 NET DIST. SALES	FIXED PER MONTH	VARIABLE PER $100 NET DIST. SALES	FIXED PER MONTH	VARIABLE PER $100 NET TOTAL SALES
*Supervisory salaries	$6,000		$ 8,000		$3,000		$12,000	
Travel and entertainment	900	$ .683	1,010	$ .643	340	$ .708	916	$ .458
Telephone and telegraph	400	.216	630	.250	180	.258	824	.098
*Depreciation—office equipment							50	
Stationery and office supplies							169	.148
Auto expenses							336	.359
Commissions		4.00		4.00		4.00		
Freight and express	100	.849	140	.612	230	.476		
Advertising	2,000		3,000		1,000		5,000	
Totals	$9,400	$5.748	$12,780	$5.505	$4,750	$5.442	$19,295	$1.063

*Noncontrollable

339

SCHEDULE 44. Superior Manufacturing Company

Variable Budget—Administrative Division

For the Year Ending December 31, 1977

	ADMINISTRATIVE		ACCOUNTING		TREASURERS'	
	FIXED PER MONTH	VARIABLE PER $100 NET SALES	FIXED PER MONTH	VARIABLE PER $100 NET SALES	FIXED PER MONTH	VARIABLE PER $100 NET SALES
*Supervisory salaries	$5,000		$4,000		$3,000	
Travel and entertainment	750		100		100	
Telephone and telegraph	150	$ .120	50	$ .01	60	$ .04
*Depreciation	50		200		100	
*Insurance	20		20		40	
*Taxes	20		30		10	
Stationery and office supplies		.002		.01		.03
Lawyer retainer fee	150					
Loss on bad debts						.20
Audit fee	200					
Totals	$6,340	$ .122	$4,400	$ .02	$3,310	$ .27

*Noncontrollable

From the information given above the following budget allowances were entered on the variable budget (Schedule 43): supervisory salaries, fixed per month $12,000; depreciation, fixed per month $50; and advertising, fixed per month $5,000. The four remaining costs were analyzed by the least squares as indicated in Schedule 45. Observe that the analysis provided fixed and variable components for each individual cost that were entered directly on the variable budget (Schedule 43). It is important to realize that, although these allowances were used directly as computed for illustrative purposes, they should have been tempered with judgment, taking into account new conditions such as revised operations, differing management policies, and changes in the general economic outlook.

DISCUSSION QUESTIONS

1.   Why are variable budgets needed? Explain the principal concept underlying them.

2.   Define fixed costs, variable costs, and semivariable costs.

3.   Distinguish between controllable and noncontrollable costs. Are fixed costs, variable costs, and semivariable costs controllable? Explain.

4.   What is meant by the relevant range of activity? How is it related to the classification of costs as fixed or variable?

5.   What is the relationship of total fixed and total variable costs to unit costs?

6.   What is meant by the factor of variability? Why is it important that the factor of variability be selected with care?

7.   What are "stepped" and "curved" costs? How are they usually analyzed for variable budget purposes?

8.   In developing a variable budget, why is the analysis of semivariable costs especially critical?

9.   There are three major approaches used in the analysis of semivariable costs; identify each, and outline their general approach.

10.   Explain adaptation of the equation: $Y = a + bX$ to the problem of determining cost variability.

11.   Identify the three methods of expressing variable budgets and explain when each would be generally preferable.

12.   What are the three primary uses of variable budgets? Briefly explain each.

CASE 10-1
Mann Manufacturers, Incorporated

Mann Manufacturers, Incorporated, is a medium-size company on the West Coast that has been in business approximately seventeen years. The company operates two manufacturing plants that produce six products distributed throughout the

SCHEDULE 45. Superior Manufacturing Company

Least Squares Worksheet
—General Sales Overhead
(Analysis for 1977 Variable Budget)

MONTHS	REF.	NET SALES (000)		TRAVEL AND ENTERTAINMENT		TELEPHONE AND TELEGRAPH		STATIONERY AND OFFICE SUPPLIES		AUTO EXPENSE	
		X (GIVEN)	X^2	Y (GIVEN)	XY	Y (GIVEN)	XY	Y (GIVEN)	XY	Y (GIVEN)	XY
1975											
October		$ 490	$ 240,100	$ 3,300	$ 1,617,000	$ 1,300	$ 637,000	$ 900	$ 441,000	$ 2,200	$ 1,078,000
November		520	270,400	3,400	1,768,000	1,400	728,000	910	473,200	2,250	1,170,000
December		560	313,600	3,420	1,915,200	1,350	756,000	1,020	571,200	2,300	1,288,000
1976											
January		560	313,600	3,500	1,960,000	1,380	772,800	1,000	560,000	2,300	1,288,000
February		510	260,100	3,200	1,632,000	1,290	657,900	950	484,500	2,150	1,096,500
March		440	193,600	2,950	1,298,000	1,290	567,600	830	365,200	1,950	858,000
April		390	152,100	2,700	1,053,000	1,200	468,000	750	292,500	1,650	643,500
May		350	122,500	2,400	840,000	1,170	409,500	700	245,000	1,550	542,500
June		410	168,100	2,830	1,160,300	1,190	487,900	760	311,600	1,850	758,500
July		500	250,000	3,250	1,625,000	1,350	675,000	870	435,000	2,150	1,075,000

SCHEDULE 45. (Continued)

MONTHS	REF.	NET SALES (000)		TRAVEL AND ENTERTAINMENT		TELEPHONE AND TELEGRAPH		STATIONERY AND OFFICE SUPPLIES		AUTO EXPENSE	
		X (GIVEN)	X²	Y (GIVEN)	XY	Y (GIVEN)	XY	Y (GIVEN)	XY	Y (GIVEN)	XY
August		520	270,400	3,300	1,716,000	1,320	686,400	900	468,000	2,200	1,144,000
September		600	360,000	3,550	2,130,000	1,400	840,000	1,070	642,000	2,450	1,470,000
Summations (Σ)		$5,850	$2,914,500	$37,800	$18,714,500	$15,640	$7,686,100	$10,660	$5,289,200	$25,000	$12,412,000

To compute a and b values:
$$a = \frac{\Sigma X^2 \Sigma Y - \Sigma X \Sigma XY}{N\Sigma X^2 - (\Sigma X)^2} \qquad b = \frac{N\Sigma XY - \Sigma X\Sigma Y}{N\Sigma X^2 - (\Sigma X)^2}$$

Travel and entertainment

$$a = \frac{(2,914,500)(37,800) - (5,850)(18,714,500)}{(12)(2,914,500) - (5,850)^2} = \frac{688,275,000}{751,500} = \$916. \quad \text{Fixed per month}$$

$$b = \frac{(12)(18,714,500) - (5,850)(37,800)}{(12)(2,914,500) - (5,850)^2} = \frac{3,444,000}{751,500} = \$\ .458 \quad \text{Variable per \$100 net sales}$$

Telephone and telegraph:

$$a = \frac{(2,914,500)(15,640) - (5,850)(7,686,100)}{751,500} = \frac{619,095,000}{751,500} = \$824. \quad \text{Fixed per month}$$

$$b = \frac{(12)(7,686,100) - (5,850)(15,640)}{751,500} = \frac{739,200}{751,500} = \$\ .098 \quad \text{Variable per \$100 net sales}$$

Computed in same manner: Stationery and office supplies

$$= \$165. \quad \text{Fixed per month}$$
$$= \$\ .148 \quad \text{Variable per \$100 net sales}$$

Auto expense

$$= \$336. \quad \text{Fixed per month}$$
$$= \$\ .359 \quad \text{Variable per \$100 net sales}$$

343

country. The products are relatively lightweight and compact; therefore, freight is not a particularly limiting factor. The six product lines comprise backyard cooking facilities and are sold to a number of wholesale distributors who, in turn, distribute them to retail outlets. Sales are seasonal, which necessarily reflect on production schedules. This case focuses on the manufacturing plants. Each plant is operated as a separate profit center under the direction of a plant manager. The plants are designated as Plant A and Plant B. The sales function is operated on a centralized basis; therefore, the two plant managers have no direct sales responsibility. Plant output is billed to the sales division at a transfer price set by top management. Each plant manufactures different products, and each plant manager has responsibility for product improvement, meeting sales requirements, production planning, inventory control, cost control, quality, profit planning, and other plant activities.

Due to the diverse products manufactured, the measures of overall plant output are: Plant A—standard direct labor hours; Plant B—standard prime cost of products completed. In Plant A direct labor is a significant element of cost, and labor standards have been used for about five years. These labor standards were developed through engineering analyses, and they specify the number of direct labor hours required for each producing operation in the factory. Standard wage rates have not been developed to date; however, average wage rates for each producing operation are used from time to time for planning and control purposes. These average wage rates represent historical averages adjusted on a managerial judgment basis. In Plant B standard costs for direct material and direct labor have been developed for each product and by operation. In view of the similarity of the products, these standards are considered to be realistic.

Plant A is organized into nine separate departments: three administative; two service (factory); and four producing departments. Plant B is organized to include thirteen separate departments: two administrative; four service (factory); and seven producing departments. Top corporate offices are located at Plant B; they include the central sales division headed by a marketing vice president; the financial division headed by a financial vice president (reporting to him are the controller and the treasurer); the production division headed by a production vice president (the two plant managers report directly to this vice president). At each plant there is a "financial group" comprised of three employees including a plant controller. These financial groups report directly, on a line basis, to the respective plant manager; however, they have functional responsibility to the financial vice president.

For the past four years the management has developed an annual profit plan and a three-year long-range plan. These plans are developed annually; the annual planning cycle extends from around September 1 through December. The accounting period (and the profit plans) agrees with the calendar year. The annual profit plan is divided on a monthly basis when initially developed. Each plant manager is responsible for developing his two plans and is expected to be ready to present them to top management by November 15 each year.

Monthly performance reports are distributed to each department of the company. These performance reports are prepared on the central computer in the central accounting office (controller) and are normally distributed around the 10th of the following month. Since the initiation of the profit planning and control program, these performance reports have shown "actual, month and cumulative to date," "planning budget, month and cumulative to date," and "variances, month and cumulative to date." In view of continuing complaints in respect to the "expense variances" from operating managers in both plants, the management of the company is seriously thinking about adopting variable budget procedures for every department in the company. They would expect that the approach if adopted would be computerized.

Required:

Analyze the situation in light of the contemplated adoption of the variable budget concept, and present your recommendations on the important issues involved. You should analyze and recommend on such issues as: organizational responsibility: accounting requirements; measurement of outputs; cost analysis; responsibilities in developing the variable budgets; variable budget format; and the use of variable budget data.

CASE 10-2
Swanson Company

Swanson Company is developing a variable budget for Producing Department 1, which is a large department having a number of similar machines. The activity base selected is direct machine hours. Because of the diverse nature of costs in the department, several approaches are used in developing the fixed and variable components of each cost. The analyses have been completed with the results indicated below. You are to present the variable budget with the amounts you recommend for inclusion therein; make the budget complete in every detail and provide explanatory comments if needed. The relevant range is 80,000 to 100,000 DMH. Use the formula method.

1. Supervisory salaries last year amounted to $239,984; the management has decided to plan a 10 percent increase for the upcoming year.
2. Least squares analyses of monthly cost data for the past nine months provided the following results (the variable rate given is $ per DMH):
   a. Depreciation $Y = \$9,600 + 0X$
   b. Indirect Materials $Y = 500 + \$.08X$
   c. Power costs $Y = 0 + \$.02X$

   The management has reviewed these results and has decided that indirect materials should be decreased 10 percent and power costs increased 5 percent.
3. Property taxes last year were $1,067; it is estimated that there will be a 12½ percent increase in taxes for the coming year.
4. Indirect supplies are estimated to be $2,000 at a monthly volume of 100,000 DMH; the management and the industrial engineers agreed that this cost should be 60 percent variable and 40 percent fixed.
5. Indirect wages have been estimated to be $42,000 at 100,000 DMH and $36,000 at 80,000 DMH.
6. Maintenance has been estimated as follows:
   At maximum output $20,000
   At minimum output   17,000
7. The method of least squares analysis on a monthly basis indicates that miscellaneous expenses should be: fixed $1,500; variable $.005 per DMH. The economist estimates that a general price increase of 8 percent will occur that will affect this cost; however, management feels that the variable portion is 10 percent too high now (at present prices).

CASE 10-3
Producing Department 9

Producing Department 9 is one of sixteen departments in the factory; it is involved in the production of all of the five products manufactured. The department is highly mechanized, and as a result the output is measured in direct machine hours. Variable budgets are used throughout the factory in planning and controlling costs. This case focuses on the application of variable budgets in Department 9; the following data covering a time span of approximately six months was taken from the various budgets, accounting records, and performance reports (only representative items and amounts are used for case purposes):

1. On September 14, 1976 the following variable budget was approved for the department; it will be used throughout the 1977 operating year. This variable budget was developed through the cooperative efforts of the department manager, his supervisor, and certain staff members from the budget department.

1977 Variable Budget—Producing Department 9

CONTROLLABLE EXPENSES	FIXED AMOUNT PER MONTH	VARIABLE RATE PER DIRECT MACHINE HOUR
Employee salaries	$2,800	$ 0
Indirect wages	5,000	.04
Indirect materials	0	.09
Etc.		
Totals	$7,800	$.13

2. On November 3, 1976 the sales plan and the production budget were completed. In order to continue preparation of the annual profit plan, which was detailed by month, the production budget was translated to planned activity for each of the factory departments. The planned activity for Producing Department 9 was:

	FOR THE TWELVE MONTHS ENDING DECEMBER 31, 1977				
	YEAR	JANUARY	FEBRUARY	MARCH	ETC.
Planned Output in direct machine hours	310,000	20,000	24,000	30,000	236,000

3. On February 26, 1977 the manager of Producing Department 9 was informed that his planned output for March had been revised to 33,000 direct machine

hours. He expressed some doubt whether this volume of work could be attained.

4. At the end of March, 1977 the accounting records reflected the following actual data for the month for the department:

Actual output in direct machine hours	32,000
Actual controllable expenses incurred:	
Employee salaries	$ 2,900
Indirect wages	6,580
Indirect materials	2,830
Etc.	

Required:

The requirements illustrate several uses of the variable budget over the period September, 1976 through March, 1977.

a. What is the factor of variability used in this department? What is the relevant range in the department? Explain.

b. The budgeted high-low point method was used to develop the variable budget for the department; explain and illustrate essentially how this method would be applied in this case.

c. Explain and illustrate with complete schedules how the variable budget would be used at each of the following dates:
   1. November 3, 1976 or shortly thereafter.
   2. February 26, 1977 or shortly thereafter.
   3. March 31, 1977 or shortly thereafter.

CASE 10-4
Department 99—Repair and Maintenance

The manager of the Repair and Maintenance Department, in response to a request, submitted the following budget estimates for his department that are to be used to construct a variable budget to be used during the coming budget year. Only three representative accounts are utilized for case purposes.

CONTROLLABLE COSTS	PLANNED COST AT 6,000 DIRECT REPAIR HOURS	PLANNED COST AT 9,000 DIRECT REPAIR HOURS
Employee salaries	$3,000	$3,000
Indirect repair materials	4,020	6,030
Miscellaneous costs	1,320	1,680
Etc.		

Required:

   a. What is the activity base and the relevant range? Explain.

   b. Prepare a table type of variable budget for the department (use increments of 1,000).

   c. Prepare a formula type of variable budget for the department.

   d. Prepare a graphic type of variable budget for the department.

   e. What would be the budget allowance at 8,500 direct repair hours?

   f. Which form would you recommend for this department? Why?

CASE 10-5
McKay Tool Company

      The stock of McKay Tool Company, a manufacturer of small, specialized tools, was closely held by three members of the McKay family—one brother, Samuel, and two married sisters. Samuel had been president of the company since the death of the senior McKay in 1956. The recent death of Samuel, resulting from a heart attack, came as a shock to the other officers of the company, all who had been hired by the senior McKay before World War II. Samuel McKay's stock passed to his wife and three daughters, none of whom were affiliated with the company. These events resulted in the employment of a new president from the outside. The new president, Richard E. Johnson, brought in two of his former associates who were given the positions (newly created) of executive vice president (Robert Conklin) and controller (Henry Mohle).

      During the first year the new officers succeeded in completing a rather extensive internal reorganization. Simultaneously, the controller revised the accounting system to emphasize the control aspects by adapting it to the new organization structure. The other officers appeared to accept the new officers and the changes instituted. This acceptance was due to three principal factors: (1) the competence of the new officers; (2) company loyalties existing among the old employees; and (3) recognition that the company gradually had become less competitive in the industry.

      Subsequent to the revision of the accounting system, immediate steps were taken to institute a system of sales planning that tied in with the newly adopted quota system whereby monthly quotas would be developed for each salesman.

      With historical cost data for approximately two years, classified in accordance with the new system of accounts now available, Mr. Mohle felt that the next major step was to develop a complete budget program including effective cost control procedures.

      During a conference of supervisors called by Mr. Mohle and the plant supervisor to discuss problems of cost control, Mr. Ralph Mellon, supervisor of Producing Department 5, commented: "I have had no experience with expense budgets, but a friend of mine who works for another plant in the city has warned me about how they work in his company. He is asked to prepare a detailed annual expense budget for his department. When the monthly reports come out, his actual expenses are compared with one-twelfth of the annual budget. Frankly, he says it causes a lot of trouble and is of no use as far as he is concerned. He is trying to get rid of it."

      After some discussion it was suggested that monthly expense budgets for each department might be prepared during each preceding month. Mr. Mohle pointed out that although this procedure might be useful, planning expenses only one month in advance would not meet the planning needs of the management. Another suggestion was to have each supervisor develop an annual expense budget detailed by month. Another supervisor commented that "we cannot guess expenses for December twelve months in advance for a number of reasons. Perhaps the most important one is that we have no idea as to how much work we will be doing in future months. We get production orders about ten days in advance now. I cannot see how guessing expenses will help control them." Another supervisor interjected, "In my department expenses are determined by the work we do more than anything else. I would hate to see my June expenses (when production is at the top) set up against the same budget as my August expenses (when production is at the bottom)."

Mr. Mellon, who had evidenced an appreciation of the need for some new cost control procedures in the company, suggested that "we might establish percentages or rates for each expense in each department so that the budget allowance would be doubled in a month where output was doubled compared with another month."

Mr. Mohle, who had been participating in the discussions on an advisory basis, had indirectly guided the discussions. At this point, he suggested that the company experiment with *variable budget cost control.* He explained that this procedure would require:

1. Identification of the controllable and noncontrollable expenses in each responsibility center.
2. Specification of how the output of each responsibility center should be measured.
3. Identification of the fixed and variable costs.
4. Agreement on variable budget allowances relating the department costs to the measure of department output.
5. Monthly performance reports for the manager of each responsibility center that compare actual costs with *adjusted budget* allowances.

After some preliminary discussion of these ideas, the meeting closed with this comment by Mr. Mellon: "But many of my costs, such as indirect labor, are neither fixed nor variable." Sam Spears, another supervisor, stated: "It appears to me that tying budget allowances to direct labor hours would encourage supervisors to incur more direct labor hours, which itself adds to cost, so that budget allowances would be higher."

Another meeting was scheduled for the following day. In preparation for the next meeting Mr. Mohle decided to use Department 5 costs and production (output) as a basis for discussion of the variable budget concept.

Producing Department 5 was one of the departments that had a high ratio of machines to manpower. Practically all the different types of tools manufactured passed through Department 5; therefore, it appeared that overall productive output in the department was best measured in direct machine hours (DMH). The Accounting Department used DMH as a basis for applying departmental overhead costs to production.

Inspection of the actual controllable expenses in the department for the past year indicated that a few expenses, such as depreciation and salaries, were fairly constant from month to month although DMH varied considerably from month to month during the same period. A few expenses, such as direct material used and direct labor, appeared to vary directly with output. On the other hand, most of the expenses appeared to vary in some degree, although not directly, with the related productive activity. Indirect labor appeared to be typical of the latter type of expense as indicated by the following historical data provided by the Accounting Department (simplified for illustrative purposes):

MONTH (NUMBERED FOR CONVENIENCE)	DEPARTMENT 5	
	DMH'S (000)	INDIRECT LABOR EXPENSE
1	170	1650
2	160	1470
3	160	1480
4	150	1450
5	150	1460
6	140	1450
7	130	1420
8	120	1200
9	130	1440
10	150	1490
11	160	1490
12	170	1500

In preparation for the meeting Mr. Mohle prepared a graph plotting thereon actual indirect labor (vertical scale) against productive activity (horizontal scale). He intended to lead the discussion to two questions: (1) How actual indirect labor cost (in Department 5) changed last year in relation to productive activity; and (2) What should be the planned relation of indirect labor cost to planned production activity?

Required:

a. Be prepared to discuss the five procedures listed by Mr. Mohle related to *variable budget cost control.*

b. Construct a graph of actual indirect labor. Be prepared to present an explanation of the analysis and its application in the analysis of indirect labor cost.

c. What would you recommend as the *variable budget allowance* for indirect labor?

d. What budget variance would be reported for January of the coming year, assuming actual expense of $1,570 and production output of 180,000 DMH?

e. How should the following individuals be involved in setting the variable budget allowances for Department 5: Mr. Mohle, Mr. Mellon, Mr. Mellon's next superior, the executive committee, the president?

f. How would you answer the comment by Mr. Spears?

CASE 10-6
XY Company

The historical data given below were taken from the cost records of the XY Company:

DEPARTMENT X

MONTH	DIRECT LABOR HOURS (THOUSANDS)	INDIRECT LABOR	MAINTE- NANCE	SUPPLIES USED	SALARIES	MISCEL- LANEOUS EXPENSES
1	8.0	$750	$620	$690	$300	$170
2	9.0	820	680	790	300	180
3	9.5	850	685	820	300	195
4	8.1	760	625	700	300	175
5	7.0	690	600	600	300	140
6	6.8	675	590	580	300	125
7	6.0	610	520	490	300	110
8	6.1	600	512	475	300	100
9	6.7	660	585	565	300	120
10	7.2	700	610	625	300	150
11	8.0	740	690	685	300	165
12	9.8	880	685	880	300	200

DEPARTMENT Y

MONTH	DIRECT MACHINE HOURS	MAINTENANCE	SUPPLIES USED
1	19,000	$250	$475
2	18,000	230	450
3	18,000	240	440
4	17,000	225	430
5	17,000	210	420
6	16,000	200	410
7	14,000	190	360
8	14,000	200	350
9	17,000	230	425
10	19,000	240	480
11	20,000	260	510
12	21,000	280	515

Required:

Department X:

a. Prepare a graphic analysis of the above historical data, relating each cost to volume.

b. Using the graphs developed in one, construct a formula type variable budget for Department X. Assume no changes because of management judgment.

c. Prepare a table showing the budget allowances at 7,000 and 9,000 direct labor hours (the relevant range is 6 to 10 thousand DLH) as reflected on the graph.

d. Comment on supplies used if you observe any unusual results.

Department Y:

e. Analyze each cost, using the method of least squares.

f. Prepare a graph plotting the least squares results.

g. What are the variable budget allowances?

CASE 10-7
Texmo Service Company

Texmo Service Company performs services for the oil industry. Texmo is classified as a medium-size firm and has been in operation since 1948. The firm operates in the United States and Canada.

Operations at the field level are under the supervision of division managers who usually are engineers. The typical division covers a wide territory; the extent of the territory depending upon the amount of oil exploration and production activities within it. For example, one state is divided into three divisions whereas another division comprises two states. Similarly, the amount and type of equipment used in a division depend upon the amount of activity in the area and the characteristics of that activity. For example, a district involved in production requires somewhat different services than a district involved in exploration.

Each month's activities are reported on the basis of the (1) number of jobs by type, (2) total revenue by type of job, and (3) average revenue per average job. Expenses are reported by division and by type of job.

Prior to each six-months' period, each division manager is required to prepare a budget (see Exhibit 1 for illustrative figures for one month). At the end of each month a

EXHIBIT 1. Texmo Service Company
Six-Month Budget for the Period Jan. to June, 19B

#5							GCU	
DIVISON C. E. DAVIS		INVESTMENT IN DIVISION $17,050					APPROVED DEC. 10, 19A	
MANAGER							DATE	
PARTICULARS	JAN.	FEB.	MAR.	APR.	MAY	JUNE	TOTAL	
Revenues:								
Type X jobs—No.	10							
$ Amount	8,000							
Type Y jobs—No.	30							
$ Amount	14,000							
Total jobs —No.	40							
$ Amount	22,000							
Av. per job	550							
Expenses:								
Type X jobs (Itemized—$)	3,500							
Type Y jobs (Itemized—$)	7,680							
Division overhead (Itemized—$)	4,000							
Total expenses	15,180							
Division net revenue	6,820							
Percent of total revenue	31%							

performance report is prepared for each division comparing budget (as revised by higher management) with actual (see Exhibit 2).

In discussing the procedure, one division manager commented: "The operating report is not fair as far as I am concerned. For example, in January my jobs were 10 percent above budget, which is a good thing but my expenses show unfavorable variations and although both types of jobs earned more per job the average went down $18. On the other hand, if my jobs are down by say 20 percent, my expense allowances are cut 20 percent. Can't we do something about this?"

EXHIBIT 2. Texmo Service Company

Performance Report, dated Jan. 31, 19B

#5

DIVISION
C. E. DAVIS

MANAGER

| PARTICULARS | MONTH OF JAN. 19B | | | CUMULATIVE _____ MONTHS TO DATE _____ | | |
	ACTUAL	BUDGET	VARIATIONS	ACTUAL	BUDGET	VARIATIONS
Revenues:						
Type X jobs—No.	8	10	2*			
$ Amount	6,580	8,000	1,420*			
Type Y jobs—No.	36	30	6			
$ Amount	16,920	14,000	2,920			
Total jobs —No.	44	40	4			
$ Amount	23,500	22,000	1,500			
Av. per job	534	550	16*			
Expenses:						
Type X jobs						
(Itemized—$)	3,300	$2,800	500*			
Type Y jobs						
(Itemized—$)	8,450	7,680	770*			
Division overhead						
(Itemized—$)	4,050	4,000	50*			
Total expenses	15,800	14,480	1,320*			
Division net revenue	7,700	7,520	180			
Percent of total revenue	33	34	12			

Required:

a. Critically evaluate the approach used in the performance report.

b. Recast the performance report to reflect your recommendations. Assume the following are realistic amounts:

EXPENSE	FIXED PER MONTH	VARIABLE RATE PER JOB
Type X Expenses	$2,000	$150
Type Y Expenses	3,000	156
Division Overhead	3,200	20

CASE 10-8
Dodge Manufacturing Company

Dodge Manufacturing Company produces three different but related products that are distributed nationally through established wholesale channels. The company has always been weak in planning and control. The budget program, although used for over 20 years, has never been "modernized." As a result it has little impact on the management process. The fiscal period ends December 31. Recently the long-time controller retired and a relatively young CPA with industrial experience in a dynamic company was employed as controller. Upon arrival he found what was labelled the "monthly budget report" on his desk. The following excerpt from it, relating to one producing department only, has been selected for case purposes. Producing Department 5 (supervisor, B.E. Careful) produces only one item—a component part that is used in each of the three products. A quick glance by the controller convinced him that it (a) was misleading, (b) was conceptually deficient, and (c) the unit cost amounts were deceptive.

Dodge Manufacturing Company
Department 5
Monthly Budget Report—March, 19XX

	ACTUAL	BUDGET	VARIANCE
Costs:			
Raw material	$14,500	$16,000	$1,500
Direct labor	21,500	22,000	500
Overhead:			
Supervision*	5,300	5,000	(300)
Indirect labor	3,900	4,000	100
Repairs	1,400	1,400	—
Power	2,600	3,000	400
Supplies used	950	1,000	50
Depreciation*	7,000	7,000	—
Taxes*	400	400	—
Insurance*	200	200	—
Allocated costs*	18,000	20,000	2,000
Total	$75,750	$80,000	$4,250
Unit Cost	$4.21	$4.00	

*For case purposes assume that these are fixed costs and that the remaining are variable costs.

Required:

a. Identify and explain the basis for the three conclusions by the controller.

b. List, and briefly explain, your recommendations for improving the report to enhance its potential as a control device.

c. Redraft the report to conform with your recommendations in b. Show your underlying computations separately.

Planning
and Controlling Capital
Expenditures

chapter eleven

The long-range and the short-range profit plans must include the plans of management for expansion and contraction of plant, buildings, equipment, improvements, major renovations, replacements, and other similar resource-demanding decisions. These types of plans comprise the capital expenditures budget. Capital projects normally entail large commitments of funds, and their impact on the enterprise extends over relatively long time spans. They involve both "sunk" and "fixed" costs, which are difficult to amend or retrieve once the initial decision is implemented. In Chapter 2 (Illustraion 6) both *project* and *time period* orientations in the planning process were emphasized. Recall from that discussion that each capital addition preferably should be viewed as an identifiable project (with a specific project number) having its own unique time dimension. For example, some capital additions projects involve a time dimension of two or three years whereas another project may require a thirty-year time horizon. For these reasons, the basic approach to planning capital additions should be on a *project basis*; those projects tentatively approved by the management should then be reflected in the long-range profit plan, and the next annual phase of each project should be reflected in the annual profit plan. The capital expenditures plan is comprised of a series of unique capital projects; therefore, the overall capital expenditures budget normally includes three time dimensions: (1) a time dimension required by the particular project

that extends the farthest into the future; (2) a time dimension in accord with
the long-range profit plan; and (3) a time dimension in accord with the short-
range profit plan. These dimensions in relation to projects are shown graphically for a particular company in Illustration 35.

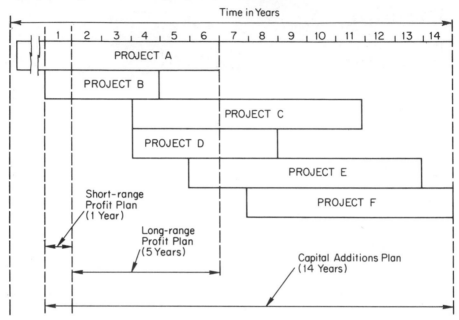

ILLUSTRATION 35. Time Dimensions in a Capital Expenditures Budget
Carter Company

The capital expenditures budget expresses the detailed plans of management concerning asset additions, improvements, replacements, patents,
and funds set aside for these purposes. Capital additions represent assets
purchased, the costs of which are applicable to a number of accounting
periods in the future. The capital expenditures budget does not include
ordinary repairs since they should be included in the current expense budgets.
Major or extraordinary repairs, the costs of which are capitalized, may be
included in the capital expenditures budget or in a separate budget of
extraordinary repairs.

The capital expenditures budget is variously referred to as the capital
additions budget, plant and equipment budget, construction budget, capital
outlay budget, investment budget, or plant additions budget.

The capital expenditures budget has considerable significance from
management planning and control viewpoints. Top management is constantly faced with the problem of determining the amount of funds to be
invested in fixed plant. The basic problems revolve around the necessity

to maintain adequate facilities for growth and for meeting customer demand and competition. On the other hand, considerable planning and control are necessary to prevent (1) idle operating capacity, (2) overinvestment in operating capacity and (3) investment in assets that will produce a *low return on the funds committed.*

There are a number of reasons why management should develop a formal budget of capital additions. The important objectives of a budget program for capital expenditures are:

1. *Planning*—Provides for sound planning of capital expenditures.
2. *Coordination*—Provides for coordination of capital expenditures related to:
    a.   Financing needs—cash requirements.
    b.   Investment committed to the various operational activities.
    c.   Sales potentials.
    d.   Profit potentials.
    e.   Return on investment potentials.
3. *Control*—Provides for control of both minor and major capital additions.

The primary features of a program for planning and controlling capital expenditures may be summarized:

1. Generation of proposals.
2. Collection of data relevant to each proposal.
3. Evaluation of proposals.
4. Selection by the management of the promising proposals and the assignment of project status to those selected.
5. Development of a capital expenditures budget.
6. Control of capital expenditures.
7. Post-completion audits and follow-up evaluations of the actual results from capital additions in periods after completion.

MANAGEMENT PLANNING FOR CAPITAL EXPENDITURES

Because capital expenditures generally involve the more or less permanent commitment of large sums of money, decisions concerning them have a significant, long-term effect on the economic health of the concern. This fact suggests the need for careful analysis and planning on the part of top management. An ill-advised decision concerning capital additions frequently cannot be reversed before it seriously affects the financial health of the concern. Inadequate management attention to capital additions may result in overinvestment or underinvestment and a consequent deterioration of the concern's competitive position in the industry. Because of its importance, systematic procedures and time tables are essential for effective planning of capital additions.

In previous chapters the importance of long-range sales plans was emphasized. Such plans are an essential part of the long-range objectives of the company—where the concern desires to be in the industry five, ten, and fifteen years hence. Development of long-range objectives requires tentative planning of the necessary or desired capital additions and appraisal of the long-range cash and financial position. These long-range budgets must necessarily be developed on broad and tentative plans and policies. Although long-range plans must be flexible, they should be reduced to formal expression—written—in some form, as a part of the confidential files of top management. The plans come to light primarily through the medium of the *short-range profit plan*, at which point the plans become definite to the extent that top management is committed to carry them out. Illustration 36 presents a form used by one company to express its long-term capital expenditures budget.

In developing the short-term profit plan, top management faces the problem of reaching some definite (although tentative) decisions relative to (1) possible changes in capital additions already under way, and (2) capital expenditures that should be included in the short-term profit plan. These decisions are essential so that the short-term capital expenditures budget can be included in the short-term profit plan.

Capital expenditure plans must be consistent with the cash position and financing considerations created. Both the timing of capital expenditures and the amount of funds that can be invested in plant involve serious policy decisions. Sales potential, related costs, and the anticipated profit potential must be carefully appraised for the future. Return on investment (profit divided by investment) is recognized as the chief criterion of the long-run efficiency of management. Capital additions should be analyzed in terms of their probable effect on return on investment. Prudent management ordinarily should not undertake a capital addition unless its analysis indicates that it probably will yield a return equal to, or greater than, the long-range company objective for return on investment.

The capital expenditures budget normally should include two principal types of items. First are the *major projects*, each involving considerable funds, such as buildings, large items of machinery and plant sites. This type of capital expenditure frequently involves construction (and expenditures) covering more than one year. Such projects generally are considered and planned over a number of years before a final decision is reached.

ILLUSTRATION 36. Long-Range Capital Expenditures Budget

The XYZ Corporation—Long-Range Plan

Capital Expenditures Budget—Summary by Project and Years

For the Period January 1, 1977 Through 1981

(Expressed in Thousands of Dollars—Only Representative Amounts Shown)

DESCRIPTION OF PROJECTS	REFERENCE FOR DETAIL	BUDGETED INITIAL DATE	BUDGETED TOTAL AMOUNT	AMOUNT AUTHORIZED TO JAN. 1, 1977	AMOUNT SUBJECT TO AUTHORIZATION	AMOUNT SPENT TO JAN. 1, 1977	UNEXPENDED BALANCE OF APPROPRIATION	1977	1978	1979	1980	1981	SUBSEQUENT YEARS
Approved major projects													
Regular:													
Project A	A-1	1975	$1,000	$800	$ 200	$700	$100	$150	$ 75	$ 50	$ 25		
Etc.													
Special:													
Project E	E-1	1976	$ 500	$200	300	180	20	220	70	30			
Etc.													
Total Approved													
Budgeted major projects—1977*													
Regular:													
Project G	G-1	1977	11	11				11					
Project H	H-1	1977	800		800			100	150	250	200	$ 75	$ 25
Etc.													
Special:													
Project M	M-1												
Etc.													
Undesignated†													
Total budgeted—1977		1977	270					50	50	50	60	60	
Grand total													
For Information:													
Future projects under study:													
Project X	X-1	1978	1,700		1,700			200	200	350	500	400	250
Etc.													

*Detailed in 1977 profit plan.

†To take care of minor capital additions; see annual profit plan for 1977 departmental appropriations.

Observe in Illustration 36 that all of the projects having a specific project designation are of this type.

The second type of capital expenditure includes the *minor* capital additions that cannot or need not be planned in detail far in advance. Capital additions of this type comprise such activities as purchases of relatively low-cost machines and tools, small renovations to buildings, and other miscellaneous items that are essential to operations. This type of capital expenditure normally will not enter into long-range planning, except perhaps as a single amount included in the total funds required. Plans for capital additions for the immediate budget period should be carefully analyzed and presented in as much detail as possible. It is quite obvious, however, that generally it will be impossible to project the minor additions in detail; consequently, the usual procedure is to include in the capital additions budget a *blanket appropriation* and no project identification for each responsibility center for such items. The blanket appropriation should be based on past experience with adjustments for future expectancies. The blanket appropriation should be detailed by *areas of responsibility*. In Illustration 36, this item of capital expenditure is shown on one line as "undesignated." The short-term capital expenditures budget (included in the short-term profit plan) is based upon the decisions of management relative to the *major projects* that will be in process and the requests from the various departments for appropriations to cover the *minor* capital additions. Cash requirements by interim periods during the year should be specified. An annual capital expenditures budget for Superior Manufacturing Company is shown on Schedule 46.

RESPONSIBILITY FOR BUDGETING CAPITAL EXPENDITURES

Policies and procedures should be established to encourage ideas and proposals for capital additions from sources within and even outside the company. However, the primary responsibility for such proposals should rest with all members of management, including divisional and departmental supervisors.

For *major* capital expenditures, the primary responsibility rests with top management. For proposals involving major additions, definite procedures should be established to assure appropriate analysis and evaluation. Many companies report that they must guard against a tendency to disregard a proposal that, on the surface, may not appear to have much potential but, in fact, may be quite desirable upon careful analysis. Procedures should be established for the originator to express his proposal in writing including, (1) a description of the proposal, (2) reasons for the recommendation, (3) sources of relevant data, (4) advantages and disadvantages of the proposal, and (5) recommended starting and completion dates.

On the basis of an analysis along these lines, top management may decide to drop the proposal or to proceed with future analysis and planning on a designated *project* basis as outlined on page 357.

Budget requests for minor capital additions should come chiefly from the managers of the responsibility centers. The executives and supervisors concerned should be primarily responsible for estimates of the needs for their particular operation and their subsequent control.

An executive, such as the chief engineer or financial executive, should be primarily responsible for *coordinating* the development of the capital expenditures budget.

CONTROL OF CAPITAL EXPENDITURES

The importance of control of capital expenditures cannot be emphasized too strongly. Control is not solely, nor even primarily, downward pressure on expenditures. Control must rest upon sound management *planning* that restricts expenditures to economically justifiable additions, yet guards against stagnation in the maintenance, replacement, and acquisition of capital assets.

Control of capital expenditures is best understood and implemented if the distinction between major and minor additions, as mentioned in the preceding paragraphs on planning, is maintained. Major capital additions involve large amounts of funds for single projects, and their economic feasibility normally relates to management strategies. On the other hand, minor capital expenditures relate to ongoing operations involving practically every operating manager; thus, the estimated requirements and week-to-week decisions on actual expenditures should rest primarily with lower levels of management.

Controlling Major Capital Expenditures. Inclusion of major capital expenditure projects in the short-term profit plan indicates that top management has decided to proceed with the project at a specific time. This inclusion, however, should not constitute orders to proceed. A system of control that will indicate to management the progress, cost, and status of capital additions throughout the year is essential.

The first aspect of control involves formal authorization specifically to start a project, including the appropriation of funds, even through the project was included in the annual profit plan. For major capital additions projects, top management should reserve the responsibility for the final go-ahead authorization, which may consist of formal or informal notification, depending upon the internal situation. The usual practice is to give final approval of major capital additions on a *request for capital expenditure* form.

The second phase of current control of major capital expenditures is concerned with accumulating data on costs work progress, and cumulative expenditures on projects in process. As soon as a major capital project is authorized and undertaken, cost records should be set up by project number. This record should provide for accumulation of costs by responsibility and type, and for supplementary information concerning the progress of the work. A *capital expenditure status report* for each project should be prepared for top management at short intervals indicating such items as:

Costs:
Amount budgeted.
Expenditures to date.
Outstanding commitments.
Amount unexpended per budget.
Estimated cost to complete project.
Indicated over- or underexpenditure.

Progress report:
Date started.
Data originally scheduled for completion.
Estimated days needed to complete project.
Estimated date of completion.
Percentage completed to date (in terms of time).
Percentage completed to date (in terms of cost).

Comments for top management:
Quality of work.
Unexpected circumstances.

The final phase of the control of expenditures for major capital additions might be appropriately termed *follow-up*. After the project is completed, the cost records should be completed and the total cost recorded in the accounts as an asset. Underexpenditures on one project should not be offset against the budget excess of other projects without the formal approval of top management; otherwise, control may be lost. A final report on the completed project should be prepared for top management. Follow-up-includes final inspections and related reports.

Another important phase of follow-up should extend several years after a major project is completed. Some companies make regular studies of certain projects at various periods subsequent to completion to determine whether the project is producing the results anticipated in the analysis that led to the management decision to undertake the project. Studies of this type are important for several reasons. In the first place, they provide a good test of the adequacy of the original analysis; and second, they supply valuable information that may constructively influence future management decisions.

Minor Capital Expenditures. Minor capital additions normally are provided for in a "blanket" appropriation for each responsibility center. The manager of the center should be given the authority to issue final authorization for specific expenditures as needed. For example, the authority to approve minor expenditures within the budget appropriation may be delegated along the following lines:

AMOUNTS	APPROVAL REQUIRED
Up to $100	Department manager
$101 to $300	Plant manager
$301 to $1,000	Vice president in charge of manufacturing
Over $1,000	President

Control of minor capital expenditures can be achieved through an authorization procedure similar to this one and through the accumulation of actual expenditures by responsibility center. The actual expenditures are then compared with planning allowances in periodic capital expenditures status report or directly with the monthly performance report for each responsibility center. The report should indicate variations and unexpended balances.

MANAGEMENT EVALUATION OF PROPOSED CAPITAL EXPENDITURES

In the preceding paragraphs we discussed approaches for planning and controlling capital expenditures. It was presumed there that the basic decisions about allocation of funds to specific capital expenditure projects had been resolved. In the framework of a systematized budget program for capital expenditures are the central problems of management choice between numerous alternative capital additions and the allocation of resources to them. The "needs" for capital expenditures developed by executive management, plus those provided by the managers of the responsibility centers, may require more than the available funds. Thus, instrumental in planning and controlling capital additions is the *selection* by executive management of the more promising alternatives. These decisions are critical because once capital is invested in long-lived assets, management's opportunities to change the program are limited since *sunk costs* normally are recoverable through use of the asset rather than through their sale. In view of these considerations, it is quite apparent that management must utilize systematic and reliable approaches in evaluating proposed capital additions. In rationing funds among capital projects, management must necessarily impose an overall budget limitation. Within this limitation expenditures for each of the projects should be made on the basis of an objective evaluation of their *investment worth*. Basically, the problem is to identify and choose those projects having the highest potential *investment worth*—that is, the highest *rate of return* on the investment. Space precludes exhaustive treatment of this subject. The following discussion indicates briefly some of the approaches that have been used. Footnote references are included to direct the reader to comprehensive treatments of the subject.[1]

In making the decision to approve a particular capital expenditure or to select one alternative over another, there are a number of primary factors that management should consider:

1. **Urgency**—The urgency of the operational requirements may preclude extensive analyses, searches for sources of supply, and others. For example, a machine may break down, be beyond practical repair, operations are at a standstill, and urgency dictates that the machine that can be delivered first must be selected.

2. **Repairs**—Availability of spare parts and maintenance experts may be controlling. In some cases this is the important factor that rules out foreign equipment as a practical alternative. For example, many people do not purchase foreign trucks or machines because of the repair problems encountered outside major population areas.

3. **Credit**—Some suppliers provide generous credit terms compared with others; this may be a controlling factor for many companies.

4. **Noneconomic**—Local suppliers, social considerations, and other noneconomic persuasions and preferences.

5. **Investment woth**—The relative return on the investment that can be expected.

Let us focus on the last factor, *investment worth* (that is, the economic evaluation). *Minor* capital expenditures, as defined in the earlier paragraphs, normally are not closely scrutinized in detail since they are necessary for continued operations and involve relatively small amounts of funds. They constitute numerous and varied items needed in most of the responsibility centers. Thus they are best evaluated, planned, and controlled by responsibility through the blanket appropriations for the cost center.

[1] David G. Quirin, *The Capital Expenditure Decision* (Homewood, Ill.: Richard D. Irwin, Inc., 1967). James C. Van Horne, *Financial Management and Policy* (Englewood Cliffs, N.J.: Prentice-Hall, Inc., 1968); Harold Bierman, Jr. and Seymour Smidt, *The Capital Budgeting Decision*, 2nd ed. (New York: The Macmillian Company, 1968); and Charles T. Horngren, *Cost Accounting: A Managerial Emphasis* (Englewood Cliffs, N.J.: Prentice-Hall, Inc., 1972), Chapters 13 and 14.

Analysis of Investment Worth.   Major capital additions, on the other hand, should be accorded special analysis, management evaluation, and judgment. Approaches to determine their *investment worth*   their economic evaluation—should loom large in the decision-making process. Numerous approaches are described in the literature and utilized in practice; we will limit our brief discussion to five as follows:

Payback methods:

1.   Payback.

Average rate of return methods:

2.   Average return on investment.

3.   Average return on average investment.

Discounted cash flow methods:

4.   Net present value.

5.   Internal rate of return (time adjusted rate of return).

In order to illustrate simply the five approaches, we will use the following situation:

A proposal has been made that machine type A be acquired as a capital addition; the following estimates have been developed:

Cost of machine A	$11,000
Economic (useful) life, no residual value	10 years
Earnings and costs over ten-year life (per year):	
Average annual earnings*	$ 4,400
Less depreciation (straightline)	1,100
Earnings subject to income taxes	3,300
Income taxes (assumed rate 50%)	1,650
Average annual earnings after taxes and depreciation	$ 1,650
Indicated cash inflow per year:	
Earnings $1,650 plus depreciation $1,100	= $ 2,750

*Net of expenses except depreciation and income taxes.

Our problem is to determine the *investment worth* of this proposal in terms that can be compared with other proposals (other alternatives).

The Payback or Payout Method.   This method computes the number of years required to recover the *cash* investment from the *cash* inflows generated from the project. The formula for the payback method is:

$$\frac{I \text{ (Net investment outlay)}}{E_c \text{ (Annual cash inflow or cost savings)}} = PB \text{ (Payback in years)}$$

Substituting the illustrative data we have:

$$\frac{\$11,000}{\$2,750} = 4.0 \text{ years}$$

Thus the cash outlay for the investment will be recovered in full in four years. The payback method is easy to compute and understand, yet it has some fundamental weaknesses. It does not measure profitability or investment worth.

It does not consider the *time-value* of money, nor does it distinguish between alternatives having different economic lives. For example, assume we are considering an alternative machine having identical costs and income as the one above *except* that it has an estimated useful life of twenty years instead of ten. In this situation, the two machines would have about the same payback period; however, the alternative machine would be a much better buy since it may generate income twice as long as the other machine. Despite these deficiencies, the payback method is the most widely used. Perhaps the most effective application of the method is as a rough test to determine whether further investigation is warranted.

It is generally useful where (1) precision is not crucial, (2) a large number of proposals are to be screened on a preliminary basis, (3) cash and credit are critical, and (4) the risk is high or the future potentials beyond the payout period are difficult to assess.

Average Return on Investment.   This method simply relates the average annual cash inflow to the investment. The formula is:

$$\frac{E_c \text{ (Annual cash inflow or cost savings)}}{I \text{ (Net investment outlay)}} = R_i \text{ (Average return on investment)}$$

Substituting the illustrative data we have:

$$\frac{\$2,750}{\$11,000} = .25 \text{ (or 25\%)}$$

It is the reciprocal of the payback method (i.e., $1.00 \div 4.0 = .25$)[2] Obviously, this method suffers from the same weaknesses as the payback method plus the fatal weakness that a user may be inclined to compare the result (25 percent in the illustration) with other interest rates that are not comparable because of the time-value of money and averaging factors. The method, since it is based on averages, assumes the earnings are constant over the life of the project. It can be demonstrated mathematically that the

[2] A proposal with an infinite life would reflect a payback reciprocal exactly equal to its rate of return. Payback reciprocal is a good approximation of the rate of return when the useful life is more than twice the payback period.

result will always *exceed* the true rate of return. For these reasons the method cannot be recommended even in simple situations.[3]

Average Return on Average Investment.   This method is identical in concept with the preceding one except that the average investment is utilized; thus the formula is:

$$\frac{E_c \text{ (Annual cash inflow or cost savings)}}{I \text{ (Net investment outlay)} \div 2}$$

$$= R_a \text{ (Average rate of return on average investment)}$$

Substituting the illustrative date we have:

$$\frac{\$2,750}{\$11,000 \div 2} = \frac{\$2,750}{\$5,500} = .50 \text{ (or } 50\%)$$

Clearly, division of the initial investment outlay by two derives the "average" balance of the investment as it is decreased periodically by the depreciation charge. This computation assumes that each annual cash inflow "recovers" a proportionate part of the original investment. The method overstates the true rate of return and suffers from the same deficiencies as enumerated above for the average rate of return. The fundamental weakness again is that it does not consider the *time-value of money*; a dollar of income in the first year is given the same value as a dollar of income to be received in, say, the tenth year. The method has little relevance even in simple situations.

DISCOUNTED CASH FLOW METHODS

The discounted cash flow methods recognize the time-value of money (that is, interest cost); therefore, all future values are discounted to the present so that comparable values may be added, subtracted, and compared. Because they are based on cash flows and adjust for the time-value of money, they clearly are preferable for evaluating major capital expenditure proposals. There are two discounted cash flow methods widely utilized: (1) net present value and (2) internal rate of return. Varying terminology is utilized to identify these two methods. They both focus on the two fundamental concepts of *present value* and *cash flow*. These two concepts must be clearly understood in order to comprehend the discounted cash flow methods.[4]

---

[3] A variation of this method divides the income amount (or cost savings) on a noncash basis by the investment cost. In the illustration the computation would be: $1,650/$11,000 = .15 or 15%). For obvious reasons this is sometimes referred to as the financial statement method.
[4] Ezra Solomons, "The Arithmetics of the Capital-Budget Decision," *Journal of Business*, 29, no. 2 (April 1956), 124–29.

First, look at the concept of *present value* in a general way, then relate it to our specific problem of evaluating the investment worth of machine A. The present value concept may be illustrated simply: What is the present value of, say, $1,000 to be received one year hence, assuming an interest rate of 10 percent? The present value may be computed as follows:

$$PV = F\left(\frac{1}{1+i}\right)^n$$

where
$$\begin{aligned} PV &= \text{Present value} \\ F &= \text{Future sum of money} \\ i &= \text{Interest rate per period} \\ n &= \text{Number of periods} \end{aligned}$$

Substituting:

$$PV = \$1,000\left(\frac{1}{1+.10}\right)^1$$

$$= \$\ \ 909.09$$

Proof:

Present value	$ 909.09
Interest ($909.09 × .10)	90.91
Value one year hence	$1,000.00

Rather than making the computation as illustrated above, we may refer to a "Present Value of $1" table (Table A, p. 369) and obtain the *present value factor* for 10 percent for one year. This factor (0.909) multiplied by the $1,000 gives the same present value, $909.09, computed above.[5] Similarly, we may determine the present value of $4,500 to be received three years hence, assuming an interest rate of 6 percent. Reading from the table (the 6 percent column, the line for three years) we find the factor 0.840. The present value is: ($4,500 × 0.840) = $3,780. The following table indicates the correctness of the computation:

YEAR	PRINCIPAL INVESTED AT BEGINNING OF YEAR	ADD EARNINGS (6% × COL. 1)	PRINCIPAL PLUS EARNINGS INVESTED AT END OF YEAR
1	$3,780.00	$226.80	$4,006.80
2	4,006.80	240.41	4,247.21
3	4,247.21	254.83	4,502.04*

*$2.04 due to rounding error since table is carried to only three places.

[5] Tables may be based on several assumptions, viz.: that the cash flow occurs (1) at year end, (2) in uniform monthly installments, or (3) continuously during the year. For purposes of illustration herein, tables under assumption one are used, although the second and third assumptions often are more representative of actual conditions.

TABLE A. Present Value of $1 (Symbol p)

YEARS HENCE	1%	2%	4%	6%	8%	10%	12%	14%	15%	16%	18%	20%	22%	24%	25%
1	0.990	0.980	0.962	0.943	0.926	0.909	0.893	0.877	0.870	0.862	0.847	0.833	0.820	0.806	0.800
2	0.980	0.961	0.925	0.890	0.857	0.826	0.797	0.769	0.756	0.743	0.718	0.694	0.672	0.650	0.640
3	0.971	0.942	0.889	0.840	0.794	0.751	0.712	0.675	0.658	0.641	0.609	0.579	0.551	0.524	0.512
4	0.961	0.924	0.855	0.792	0.735	0.683	0.636	0.592	0.572	0.552	0.516	0.482	0.451	0.423	0.410
5	0.951	0.906	0.822	0.747	0.681	0.621	0.567	0.519	0.497	0.476	0.437	0.402	0.370	0.341	0.328
6	0.942	0.888	0.790	0.705	0.630	0.564	0.507	0.456	0.432	0.410	0.370	0.335	0.303	0.275	0.262
7	0.933	0.871	0.760	0.665	0.583	0.513	0.452	0.400	0.376	0.354	0.314	0.279	0.249	0.222	0.210
8	0.923	0.853	0.731	0.627	0.540	0.467	0.404	0.351	0.327	0.305	0.266	0.233	0.204	0.179	0.168
9	0.914	0.837	0.703	0.592	0.500	0.424	0.361	0.308	0.284	0.263	0.225	0.194	0.167	0.144	0.134
10	0.905	0.820	0.676	0.558	0.463	0.386	0.322	0.270	0.247	0.227	0.191	0.162	0.137	0.116	0.107
11	0.896	0.804	0.650	0.527	0.429	0.350	0.287	0.237	0.125	0.195	0.162	0.135	0.112	0.094	0.086
12	0.887	0.788	0.625	0.497	0.397	0.319	0.257	0.208	0.187	0.168	0.137	0.112	0.092	0.076	0.069
13	0.879	0.773	0.601	0.469	0.368	0.290	0.229	0.182	0.163	0.145	0.116	0.093	0.075	0.061	0.055
14	0.870	0.758	0.577	0.442	0.340	0.263	0.205	0.160	0.141	0.125	0.099	0.078	0.062	0.049	0.044
15	0.861	0.743	0.555	0.417	0.315	0.239	0.183	0.140	0.123	0.108	0.084	0.065	0.051	0.040	0.035

A somewhat different situation involving the concept of present value is posed when the present value of a *series of equal annual future payments* is involved. To illustrate, what is the present value of three $1,000 payments, one to be received at the end of each of three years, assuming an interest rate of 6 percent? Stated differently, what would you have to pay in lump sum at the beginning of year one for an annuity contract that pays you in return $1,000 at the end of each of three years, assuming an interest rate of 6 percent? The situation can be presented graphically as follows:

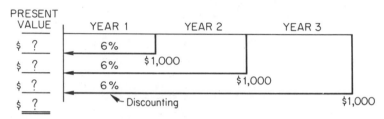

The cost of the annuity contract (present value of the future receipts) may be computed by a formula. However, if a table of "Present Value of $1 Received Annually for *N* Years" (Table B, p. 371) is available, the computation is quite simple. From the table we obtain the discount factor of 2.673 (6 percent column, line for three years). The present value may be directly computed: $(2.673 \times \$1,000) = \$2,673$. The computation may be verified as follows:

YEAR	PRINCIPAL INVESTED AT BEGINNING OF YEAR *a*	YEAR END EARNINGS (6% × COL. *a*) *b*	ANNUITY PAYMENTS AT YEAR END *c*	BALANCE INVESTED AT YEAR END *a + b − c*
1	$2,673.00	$160.38	$1,000.00	$1,833.38
2	1,833.38	110.00	1,000.00	943.38
3	943.38	56.62	1,000.00	0

Now let's look briefly at the *cash flow concept*. It involves *excluding depreciation* and all other noncash costs. Fundamentally, the analysis of present value must exclude depreciation as a cost because the present value concept itself *automatically* provides for the return of the initial investment over its useful life. To illustrate, when you purchase an automobile on the installment plan, the cash down payment is a cash outflow. Similarly each *equal monthly* payment is a cash outflow that includes both interest and principal. Obviously, the early payments include more interest and less principal than the later payments. Present value formulas and tables incorporate both principal and interest. Thus, depreciation, which is also amortized principal, but not a cash flow, must be omitted when using the present value concept.

TABLE B. Present Value of $1 Received Annually for N Years (Symbol P)

YEARS (N)	1%	2%	4%	6%	8%	10%	12%	14%	15%	16%	18%	20%	22%	24%	25%
1	0.990	0.980	0.962	0.943	0.926	0.909	0.893	0.877	0.870	0.862	0.847	0.833	0.820	0.806	0.800
2	1.970	1.942	1.886	1.833	1.783	1.736	1.690	1.647	1.626	1.605	1.566	1.528	1.492	1.457	1.440
3	2.941	2.884	2.775	2.673	2.577	2.487	2.402	2.322	2.283	2.246	2.174	2.106	2.042	1.981	1.952
4	3.902	3.808	3.630	3.465	3.312	3.170	3.037	2.914	2.855	2.798	2.690	2.589	2.494	2.404	2.362
5	4.853	4.713	4.452	4.212	3.993	3.791	3.605	3.433	3.352	3.274	3.127	2.991	2.864	2.745	2.689
6	5.795	5.601	5.242	4.917	4.623	4.355	4.111	3.889	3.784	3.685	3.498	3.326	3.167	3.020	2.951
7	6.728	6.472	6.002	5.582	5.206	4.868	4.564	4.288	4.160	4.039	3.812	3.605	3.416	3.242	3.161
8	7.652	7.325	6.733	6.210	5.747	5.335	4.968	4.639	4.487	4.344	4.078	3.837	3.619	3.421	3.329
9	8.566	8.162	7.435	6.802	6.247	5.759	5.328	4.946	4.772	4.607	4.303	4.031	3.786	3.566	3.463
10	9.471	8.983	8.111	7.360	6.710	6.145	5.650	5.216	5.019	4.833	4.494	4.192	3.923	3.682	3.571
11	10.368	9.787	8.760	7.887	7.139	6.495	5.988	5.453	5.234	5.029	4.656	4.327	4.035	3.776	3.656
12	11.255	10.575	9.385	8.384	7.536	6.814	6.194	5.660	5.421	5.197	4.793	4.439	4.127	3.851	3.725
13	12.134	11.343	9.986	8.853	7.904	7.103	6.424	5.842	5.583	5.342	4.910	4.533	4.203	3.912	3.780
14	13.004	12.106	10.563	9.295	8.244	7.367	6.628	6.002	5.724	5.468	5.008	4.611	4.265	3.962	3.824
15	13.865	12.849	11.118	9.712	8.559	7.606	6.811	6.142	5.847	5.575	5.092	4.675	4.315	4.001	3.859

Earnings must be reduced by income taxes because the latter require cash. As a result of these adjustments, the present value computation is based on a strictly *cash flow* concept of income for the project.

Now we can return to our problem of evaluating the *investment worth* of machine A. Application of the cash flow and present value concepts to this problem may be diagrammed as shown in Illustration 37.

Net Present Value Method. This method requires the selection of a *minimum desired or target* rate of return for discounting purposes. The cash flows are discounted at this rate of return for the periods involved. The sum of the present values of the *outflows* (investment in machine A) is compared with the sum of the present values of the *inflows* (periodic cash earnings from machine A); if the difference is favorable to the inflows, the project will earn more than the minimum rate of return. Alternatively, if the difference is unfavorable to the inflows, the project will not earn the minimum rate. The present value method may be applied to machine A as follows, assuming a minimum desired rate of return of 15 percent:

Net Present Value Method
Machine A

Data summarized:			
Outflows—investment in machine A		$11,000	
Useful life, no residual value		10 years	
Annual cash inflows (net of income taxes)		$ 2,750	
Minimum desired rate of return		15 percent	

	CASH FLOWS	PRESENT VALUE FACTOR (TABLE B)	PRESENT VALUE
Computation of Present Value:			
Outflow—initial investment	$11,000	0	$11,000
Inflows—equal annual cash inflow	2,750	5.019	13,802
Difference—favorable to inflows			$ 2,802

Since the inflows were *equal each year*, we could utilize Table B, Present Value of $1 Received Annually for *N* Years. The value from the table at 15 percent for ten years was 5.019. The present value of the ten equal annual revenues (cash inflows) of $2,750 multiplied by the table factor indicated a present value of $13,802. The $2,802 favorable difference between the present value of the cash inflows and the cash outflow for the investment in machine A reveals that this proposal will pay substantially more than the 15 percent minimum required by the management. On the basis of *investment worth* it appears to be a desirable investment. If we were comparing machine A with another machine, say machine B, a similar analysis would be applied to the latter as well. If the *difference* on machine B were greater in amount than the $2,802 on machine A, machine B would be the preferable

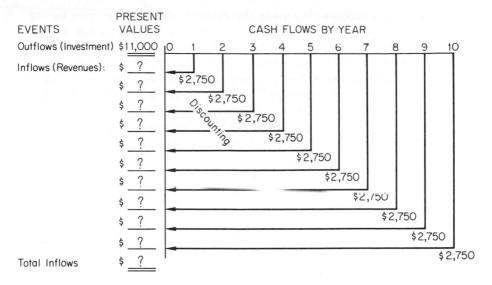

ILLUSTRATION 37. Present Value Analysis—Machine A

alternative. On the other hand, if the difference were less than $2,802, then Machine A would be preferable.[6]

You should observe that the net present value method does not derive the rate of return that the proposal will generate; rather it tests its economic feasibility against a minimum target rate of return selected by the management. Selection of the minimum rate of return is a critical problem since it will affect the results in subtle as well as obvious ways. Generally viewed, the minimum desired rate of return should not be less than the *cost of capital* to the enterprise.

The net present value method is relatively easy to apply procedurally, especially when compared with the next method illustrated. When the periodic cash inflows are unequal, different discounting values from Table A must be selected for each period. The central problem in all determinatons of investment worth is reaslistic projection of the *future* cash flows over the life of the proposal.

Internal Rate of Return. In direct contrast to the preceding method, this method determines the *discounted rate of return* that the proposal will generate. Instead of selecting a minimum rate of return (15 percent in the preceding situation), we must find the exact rate that will discount the future inflows so that their discounted sum will equal the outflows. That is, we want to find the rate that will cause the difference illustrated in the preceding method to be zero. For machine A we will invest $11,000 cash; now what

[6] Harold Bierman, Jr. and Seymour Smidt, *The Capital Budgeting Decision* (New York: The Macmillan Company, 1960).

discount rate is necessary to equate the $2,750 cash inflow per year for ten years to that amount? The concept holds that: *The rate of return that a project earns is that rate of interest that will discount the future cash earnings of the asset so that their sum exactly equal the present value of the cash investment in the asset.*

The discounted rate of return cannot be computed directly; therefore it must be determined by trial and error. There are two distinct situations: (1) when the cash inflows are *equal* in amount each period; and (2) when the cash inflows are *unequal* each period. The former situation where the cash flows are *equal* is much simpler. To illustrate the first situation, we can return to machine A. You will recall cash investment of $11,000, no residual value, a life of ten years, and an equal annual cash inflow of $2,750. The computational steps shown below can be used when the annual inflows are equal:

Step 1:   State the data in the following equation:

I (investment) $= E_c$ (cash earnings per period) $\times P_n$ (discount factor from Table B)

i (interest rate)

$$\$11,000 = \$2,750 \qquad\qquad \times P_n = 10 \text{ years}$$
$$i = ?$$

Step 2:   Determine relevant Table B factor (P):

$$P_n = 10 = \frac{\$11,000}{\$\ 2,750} = 4.0 \text{ (Table B Factor)}$$
$$i = ?$$

Step 3:   Enter Table B, Present Value of $1 Received Annually for N Years (on the line "ten years") and find the discount factor closest to 4.0. In this case the 4.0 falls between 20 percent (4.192) and 22 percent (3.923). From this we can deduce that the rate of return is approximately 21 percent.[7]

In the second situation, where the periodic cash inflows are *unequal* each period, determination of the interest rate (internal rate of return) is more complex since each period is different. In this situation we must use Table A, Present Value of $1, and obtain therefrom a different discounting value for each period. We must use the discount values for a specific interest

---

[7] If more precision is desired, we can interpolate between 20 and 22 percent as follows:

22% — 3.923 ┐
                  ├ .077 ┐
 ? — 4.000 ┘   ├ .269
                            │
20% — 4.192 ──────┘

$$\frac{.077}{.269} \times 2\% = .572\%$$

$$22\% - .572\% = 21.428\% \text{ rate of return}$$

rate, but for a different number of periods for each inflow. To illustrate we will utilize the following proposal for machine X:

Cost of machine X (cash outflow)	$15,000
Residual value	0
Estimated useful life	5 years

Annual Cash Inflows
(Earnings After Income Taxes and Before Depreciation)

Year 1	$ 5,050
2	4,550
3	4,050
4	3,550
5	3,050
Total	$20,250

Some students may find it useful to "chart" this situation in a manner similar to that shown in Illustration 37. It is clear from the data that the discounting must be as follows: $5,050 discount for one period; $4,550 discount for two periods; $4,050 discount for three periods; and so on—that is, each annual cash inflow must be discounted separately. In this situation we must simply *estimate* the rate by inspection, then test it. Let's assume we estimate that the rate will be 15 percent.[8] We will test at that rate; if it misses the mark, we will test again and so on until the true rate is pinpointed. Our three tests could be as follows:

COST OF MACHINE X—$15,000
(five-year life)

		FIRST TRIAL @ 15%		SECOND TRIAL @ 14%		THIRD TRIAL @ 12%	
YEAR	EARNINGS (CASH INFLOW ESTIMATED)	DISCOUNT FACTOR FROM TABLE A	PRESENT VALUE	DISCOUNT FACTOR FROM TABLE A	PRESENT VALUE	DISCOUNT FACTOR FROM TABLE A	PRESENT VALUE
1	$ 5,050	.870	$ 4,394*	.877	$ 4,429	.893	$ 4,510
2	4,550	.756	3,440	.769	3,499	.797	3,626
3	4,050	.658	2,665	.675	2,734	.712	2,884
4	3,550	.572	2,031	.592	2,102	.636	2,258
5	3,050	.497	1,516	.519	1,583	.567	1,729
Totals	$20,250		$14,046		$14,347		$15,007

*$5,050 × .870 = $4,394

[8] Numerous suggestions have been made for making an estimate "in the ball park." Although none of them are particularly useful in all cases, one that is simple and in many cases helpful follows:

$$\frac{\text{Average periodic cash flow} - \text{depreciation}}{\text{Average investment}} = \frac{(\$20,250 \div 5) - \$3,000}{\$15,000 \div 2} = 14\%$$

Our first trial demonstrated that 15 percent rate was too high since the sum of the discounted cash inflows was below $15,000; the second trial demonstrated that 14 percent also was too high. The third trial at 12 percent equates the investment cost of $15,000 with the sum of the present values of the earnings for the five years; thus, the rate of return for the proposal is 12 percent.[9]

The two discounted flow methods are superior conceptually; they automatically provide for the time-value of money and automatically provide for recoupment of the investment. The *internal rate of return method* has the distinct advantage over the net present value method in that it (1) avoids the arbitrary choice of a minimum rate of interest, and (2) the *true interest rate* generated by the proposal is computed. The interest rate computed is comparable in every respect to all other interest rates since it is conceptually consistent with the conventional understanding of interest. Thus, in selecting between several alternatives on the basis of *investment worth*, we would always select the proposal that shows the highest interest rate. The rate computed for a proposal (such as the 22 percent for machine A and the 12 percent for machine X) might be: (1) compared with a minimum standard rate for projects established by the management; (2) used to rank a series of proposals; (3) compared with the return on investment objective of the overall enterprise; and (4) compared with interest rates on other types of investment alternatives (such as stocks, bonds, mutuals).

In contrast, the *net present value method* has distinct advantages in that it (1) avoids the detailed trial and error method of searching for the rate, (2) it is easier to apply particularly when the cash inflows are unequal, (3) it is easier to apply for sensitivity analysis purposes, and (4) it is more susceptible to algebraic manipulation. Nevertheless, the internal rate or return method is more widely used. Canned computer programs often are used to facilitate the computations.

Computation complexity and the difficulty of developing reliable estimates of future cash flows for a proposal have deterred some firms from utilizing the discounted cash flow approaches. On the other hand, many firms have found with experience that these constraints are not severe in most instances and that the adoption of sophisticated approaches tends to force a more careful analysis of proposals and a consequent improvement in the resultant decisions.

Some firms follow the practice of developing all the analyses listed above; most firms using the discounted cash flow analyses also compute payback. In comparing and ranking various proposals, consideration may

[9] The reader should realize that the computation is more complex when such factors as salvage value, multiple investment dates, partial disinvestment, and cost savings (rather than earnings) are involved. Compelling arguments have been presented in recent years that the Net Present Value Method is superior for ranking capital projects; see footnote reference 6.

be given to a number of analyses, practical considerations, and value judgments.

In using the results of the various evaluation techniques discussed in this chapter, the role of *judgment* must not be overlooked. Because all the evaluations are based upon *estimates* of future potentials, the result can be no better than the estimates. In large measure the estimates themselves are subjective. In addition there may be numerous factors related to a proposal that cannot be quantified. For example, the effect of a particular proposal on employee morale, and hence output, cannot be expressed in figures; yet it may be an overriding factor in the decision. In many cases the nonquantitative factors may be clearly controlling. A keen appreciation of the assumptions underlying the computations in each technique is essential.[10] In decision-making we must guard against accepting a quantitative expression as being infallible and thus allowing ourselves to be lulled into a false sense of confidence. The role of management judgment and experience still looms large despite the mathematical results obtained through techniques such as those discussed above.

CAPITAL EXPENDITURES BUDGET ILLUSTRATED

Executive management of Superior Manufacturing Company develops a long-term capital expenditures plan that is reviewed and revised annually. Although the long-term plan is not illustrated (it is structured by projects), the annual capital expenditures budget shown in Schedule 46 reflects the 1977 segment. This segment of the overall capital expenditures plan is included in the annual profit plan. In this particular company, only major capital expenditures are included; the company has defined them as "any capital expenditure $100 or over." In view of this definition, minor capital additions are viewed as "not material," hence they are incorporated in the planning of repair costs and thus included in the departmental expense budgets.

Since one facet of planning expenses and capital expenditures is the analysis of "book" depreciation on present assets, the company prepares a related schedule of depreciation for inclusion in the annual profit plan. Schedule 47 reflects this facet of planning; you should note that the depreciation is reflected by time period, by item, and by function during the year. Reference to the departmental expense budgets (both variable budgets and expense budgets for the annual profit plan illustrated in preceding chapters)

---

[10] Robert N. Anthony, "Some Fallacies in Figuring on Investment," *NAA Bulletin* (December 1960), pp. 5–13, and Eugene M. Lerner and Alfred Rappaport, "Limit DCF in Capital Budgeting," *Harvard Business Review* (September–October 1968), p. 133.

SCHEDULE 46. Superior Manufacturing Company
Annual Capital Expenditures Budget
For the Year Ending December 31, 1977

ITEMS	ESTIMATED STARTING DATE	ESTIMATED COMPLETION DATE	ESTIMATED COST	ANNUAL TOTAL	1977 BUDGET—DATE OF CASH PAYMENTS						
					FIRST QUARTER			QUARTERS			
					JAN.	FEB.	MARCH	FIRST	SECOND	THIRD	FOURTH
Major items for 1977:											
Repair tools	1977	1977	$ 200	$ 200	$200	$	$	$200	$	$	
Power motor	1977	1977	8,500	8,500							$ 8,500
Totals			$ 8,700	$ 8,700	$200			$200			$ 8,500
Assets funded:											
New building				20,000							20,000
Cash required by time period				$ 28,700	$200			$200			$28,500
Information on items tentatively planned for 1978:											
New building	1978	1978	$120,000	$120,000							
Machinery—Dept. 1	1978	1978	10,000	10,000							

	ESTIMATED DEPRECIABLE LIFE	SCRAP VALUE
Depreciation information:		
1977:		
Repair tools	5 years	—
Power motor (Power Dept.)	10 years	—
1978:		
New building	Undecided	—
Machinery—Dept. 1	Undecided	—

NOTE: Minor capital expenditures are not reflected in this schedule; they are directly incorporated in the departmental expense budgets as repair costs in view of their immateriality.

SCHEDULE 47. Superior Manufacturing Company

Schedule of Budgeted Depreciation

For the Year Ending December 31, 1977

ITEM	REF.	DEPRE-CIATION RATE	ASSET BALANCE 1/1/77 (INPUT)	ASSETS ACQUIRED 1977	ASSET BALANCE 12/31/77	ACCUMU-LATED DEPRE-CIATION BALANCE 1/1/77 (INPUT)	DEPRE-CIATION CHARGED 1977	ACCUMU-LATED DEPRE-CIATION BALANCE 12/31/77	DEPRECIATION CHARGED—1977 FIRST QUARTER JAN.	FEB.	MARCH	QUARTERS SECOND	THIRD	FOURTH
Building		30 yrs.	$1,800,000	—	$1,800,000	$360,000	$60,000	$420,000	$5,000	$5,000	$5,000	$15,000	$15,000	$15,000
General purpose tools		5 yrs.	7,800		7,800	4,680	1,560	6,240	130	130	130	390	390	390
Power machinery		10 yrs.	54,000	$8,500	62,500	21,600	5,400	27,000	450	450	450	1,350	1,350	1,350
Repair tools		5 yrs.	400	200	600	200	120	320	10	10	10	30	30	30
Machinery—Dept. 1		$.015*	100,000		100,000	20,000	7,320	27,320	522	588	594	1,860	1,761	1,995
Machinery—Dept. 2		.004*	20,000		20,000	12,000	768	12,768	56	64	64	192	184	208
Machinery—Dept. 3		.009*	72,000		72,000	13,500	4,392	17,892	313	353	356	1,116	1,057	1,197
Sales office equipment		8 yrs.	4,800		4,800	2,400	600	3,000	50	50	50	150	150	150
Accounting office equipment		5 yrs.	12,000		12,000	6,000	2,400	8,400	200	200	200	600	600	600
Treasurer's office equipment		5 yrs.	6,000		6,000	2,000	1,200	3,200	100	100	100	300	300	300
Administrative office equipment		5 yrs.	3,000		3,000	1,000	600	1,600	50	50	50	150	150	150
Subtotals			$ 280,000	$8,700	$ 288,700	$ 83,380	$24,360	$107,740	$1,881	$1,995	$2,004	$ 6,138	$ 5,972	$ 6,370
Grand totals			$2,080,000	$8,700	$2,088,700	$443,380	$84,360	$527,740	$6,881	$6,995	$7,004	$21,138	$20,972	$21,370
Depreciation expense analysis by function:														
Manufacturing							$19,560		$1,481	$1,595	$1,604	$ 4,938	$ 4,772	$ 5,170
Selling							600		50	50	50	150	150	150
Administration							4,200		350	350	350	1,050	1,050	1,050
Totals							$24,360		$1,881	$1,995	$2,004	$ 6,138	$ 5,972	$ 6,370

*Per direct labor hour.

379

will reveal that those budgets reflect, on a departmental basis, the amounts shown in Schedule 47.

DISCUSSION QUESTIONS

1.   Define and indicate the scope of the capital expenditures plan.

2.   What are the primary features of a budgetary program for planning and controlling capital expenditures?

3.   Distinguish between major and minor capital additions, and indicate why the distinction is important in planning and controlling.

4.   Outline the appropriate responsibilities for capital expenditure planning in a typical company.

5.   Explain what is meant by investment worth, and relate it to the planning and control of capital expenditures.

6.   Explain and evaluate the payback method of evaluating proposed capital expenditures.

7.   Define and evaluate the two "average rate of return methods."

8.   Explain and evaluate the discounted cash flow methods of evaluating proposed capital expenditures.

9.   In applying the discounted cash flow methods, explain why depreciation is not considered a cost and why the analysis is based on a cash flow concept.

CASE 11-1
Auburn, Incorporated

Auburn, Incorporated, is a rapidly growing manufacturer of parts for the aircraft industry. It manufactures approximately fifteen different parts that are sold direct to users. The parts are similar; however, they are manufactured to specifications provided by the purchaser. Orders are in the form of contracts for large numbers of items to be delivered over a specified period of time. Auburn uses a number of different machines and related equipment in the manufacturing function. Frequent changes in parts manufactured and new models require numerous changes and adaptations in the manufacturing departments. Consequently, there are numerous capital expenditures of relatively small cost; however, the total amount each year is significant.

The company is organized into three major divisions: sales, production and finance, each managed by a vice president. The production division is comprised of separate departments for administration, engineering, production planning and scheduling, and purchasing. Also there are three plants. In each plant there are three service departments and nine producing departments. Each plant is operated as a "profit center" although sales are handled by the sales division. There is a controller at each plant who reports to the plant manager and, functionally, to the financial vice president. The company uses an up-to-date cost accounting system for the plants and for the past three years has developed an annual profit plan on a "bottoms up approach." In addition, a five-year broad plan is developed and revised each year. The accounting and calendar year coincide.

The five-year plan is developed during April-June, and the planning cycle for the annual profit plan extends from September 1 through December 20 each year. The executive committee, comprised of the president, executive vice president, and the three functional vice presidents, exercises the overall budgetary evaluation; the president gives final approval to all budgets. The financial function is subdivided into four subfunctions: accounting; planning and control; internal auditing; and treasurer.

Executive management is seriously considering three major capital expenditures: (1) renovation of Plant 1 (oldest plant); (2) building a new plant that will produce a new line of products; and (3) replacing two identical machines (essential to operations and very expensive) in Plant 2. With respect to the machines, two competing suppliers have made tentative, although quite different, proposals. The competing machines are different—different cost and operating characteristics; however, either kind will meet the needs of the department. They incorporate major improvements over the two old machines; they will produce at a faster rate and will attain higher tolerances. In terms of urgency, the management has tentatively ranked the three expenditures in inverse order to the listing above.

Upon inquiry the case writer learned that on the five-year plan "a single line represents capital expenditures and that no particular procedures are used to develop and evaluate long-range needs; we just include a dollar judgment." In recent years there have been no large capital expenditures such as the three now under consideration. The annual profit plan incorporates an estimate for each plant for the small capital additions; plant managers control them. The president responded to a question that "I feel that we have not yet come up with appropriate budgetary approaches to cope with the problems that are evolving in the area of capital expenditures."

Required:

Evaluate the situation, and present your recommendations to the company with respect to planning and controlling capital expenditures. Be specific about the approach, and include planning procedures, responsibilities, control procedures, analytical requirements, and follow-up. Justify your recommendations.

CASE 11-2
A Debate

At a recent conference attended by educators and successful administrators from a wide range of industries, the topic was: Why is it that economic analysis and business practice do not coincide more closely? The discussions revealed that the educators were insistent that the management should, without exception, rely on the results of discounted cash flow techniques in making major capital expenditure decisions. The businessmen tended to feel that these techniques were quite useful "when applicable, but there were many situations where managerial judgment can provide the only practical answer." Finally, the discussions turned to a consideration of the reasons for the divergence in opinion on this important point.

Required:

Briefly explain what you consider to be the basis for the divergence of opinion.

CASE 11-3
Simmons Company

The management of Simmons Company is faced with the necessity to replace an old machine. They are considering the purchase of a new machine that incorporates the latest developments. Three competing manufacturers have machines that would satisfy the specifications of the management. Data collected to date on each of the three competing machines are:

	MACHINE A	MACHINE B	MACHINE C
List price	$12,000	$14,600	$20,000
Trade in allowance on old machine (fully depreciated)	$ 1,000	$ 1,100	$ 1,200
Estimated useful life (yrs.)	5	5	5
Estimated residual (scrap) value	$ 1,000	$ 1,500	$ 2,000
Average annual earnings before deducting depreciation and income taxes	$ 4,500	$ 5,400	$ 8,100

The management has requested an analysis of investment worth and a ranking of the three machines on this basis. They have always utilized payback and average return analyses for these purposes. The company uses straightline depreciation for tax purposes; the average income tax rate is 40 percent.

Required:

Rank the investments on the basis of the following analyses:

a. Payback.
b. Average return on investment.
c. Net present value (assume a 15 percent minimum desired rate of return; treat the residual value discounted as a reduction in the investment).

Explain the reasons for any differences in rankings between the three analyses. Which ranking should be recommended to the management?

CASE 11-4
Base Manufacturing Company

The management of Base Manufacturing Company is purchasing a machine required for a special operation. They are considering two different machines. The following data have been developed to provide a basis for selecting one alternative over the other.

	MACHINE A	MACHINE B
Cost of machine	$120,000	$120,000
Estimated life-years (straightline)	8	15
Estimated average annual income		
(before deducting income taxes)	$ 24,000	$ 16,800
Residual value	0	0
Income tax rate—40%		

You are requested to develop the following analyses; assume a 15 percent cost of capital:

a. Payback.
b. Average return on investment—(a) on average investment and (b) on original investment.
c. Discounted cash flow—(a) net present value and (b) internal rate of return.
d. Evaluate the results.

CASE 11-5

XYZ Company

XYZ Company is considering the acquisition of one of two machines. As a basis for selection of one of them, the following date were developed:

	MACHINE A	MACHINE B
Investment (original cost)	$26,563	$26,563
Annual estimated income after		
depreciation and income taxes		
Year 1	$ 687	$ 4,687
Year 2	1,687	3,687
Year 3	2,687	2,687
Year 4	3,687	1,687
Year 5	4,689	689
Total	$13,437	$13,437
Estimated life—straightline (years)	5	5
Estimated residual value	0	0
Estimated average income tax rate	40%	40%
Minimum desired rate		
of return—16 percent.		

Required:

a. Compute the cash inflow on each machine.
b. Compute payback.
c. Compute the average return on investment (two approaches).

d. Compute the discounted cash flow return (two methods).

e. Evaluate the results.

CASE 11-6
Ajax Company

Management of Ajax Company is considering replacing an old machine used in the manufacture of products for sale. Data on the old machine follows:

	PURPOSE	
	BOOK	TAX
Annual cash operating costs	$60,000	$60,000
Cost	40,000	40,000
Accumulated depreciation-straight line	25,000	25,000
Remaining useful life—years	5	5

Residual value—no residual value has been used for book and tax purposes. The machine can be sold now for $6,000; however, it is now estimated that five years hence the machine can be sold for only $400 cash. Assume that any gain or loss on sale would be subject to ordinary tax rates (that is, not a long-term capital gain).

The new machine under consideration has the following economic effects:

	PURPOSE	
	BOOK	TAX
Annual cash operating costs	$65,000	$65,000
Cost	45,000	45,000
Residual value	7,000	0
Useful life—years	5	5
Method of depreciation	Straightline	Sum of years digits (no residual value used)

The minimum desired rate of return, after income taxes, is 12 percent and assume an ordinary tax rate of 40 percent.

Required:

a. Use net present value computations to compare the two alternatives: (1) Keep the old machine and (2) Replace the old machine.

b. Explain your recommendations and indicate which alternative appears to be preferable.

Planning
and Controlling
Cash

chapter twelve

From the management point of view, two major kinds of flows through a business must be planned and controlled. One is the flow of physical goods and services; the preceding chapters have discussed planning and controlling this flow. The other flow is cash; this chapter focuses on cash flow and its relationship to the flow of physical goods and services both into and out of the enterprise. Cash budgeting involves projection of cash inflows, outflows, and financing needs coupled with cash control. Cash budgeting is directly concerned with the lag between transactions and the related cash flows, with cash needs, and with excess cash. Excess cash involves an opportunity cost, that is, the interest that could be earned on excess cash. The timing of cash flows can be controlled in many respects by the management. Credit and collection activities, payments by time drafts rather than check, payments on last day of discount periods, batching certain payments, and discount policies on sales; all are ways of influencing the timing of cash inflows and outflows. Thus, "money management" is vital to enterprises, whether large or small. Many lending agencies require cash flow projections before granting large loans.

A comprehensive profit planning and control program establishes the foundation for a realistic cash budget. There must be a balance between available cash and the cash-demanding activities—operations, capital expenditures, and so on. Too often the need for additional cash is not realized until the situation becomes critical.

A cash budget is the planned cash position by interim periods for a specific time span. Most firms should develop both long-term and short-term projections of their financial position. The short-term projection is included in the annual profit plan. A cash budget consists of two parts: (1) the planned cash receipts (inflows); and (2) planned cash disbursements (outflows).

Determination of probable cash inflows and outflows permits an evaluation of the probable cash position for the budget period. Evaluation of the cash position in this manner may indicate (1) the need for financing to cover projected cash deficits or (2) the need for management planning to put excess cash to profitable use. Clearly, the cash budget is closely related to the sales plan, expense budgets, and capital expenditures budget. Nevertheless, planning and control of these factors do not automatically establish an optimum cash position. This statement suggests an essential distinction between the cash budget and other budgets. The cash budget is concerned with the *timing* of cash inflows and outflows (cash basis), whereas the other budgets are concerned with the timing of the basic transactions (accrual basis).

The principal purposes of the cash budget may be outlined as follows:

1. To indicate the probable cash position as a result of planned operations.
2. To indicate cash excess or shortages.
3. To indicate the need for borrowing or the availability of idle cash for investment.
4. To coordinate cash with (1) total working capital, (2) sales, (3) investment, and (4) debt.
5. To establish a sound basis for credit.
6. To establish a sound basis for continuing control of the cash position.

Preparation of the cash budget should be a responsibility of the executive (usually the treasurer) assigned the responsibility for cash management. Since the cash budget is based on the other plans and budgets originating throughout the firm, the treasurer must work closely with the other executives.

TIME HORIZONS IN CASH PLANNING AND CONTROL

To generalize, cash planning and control normally should relate to three different time horizons:

1. **Long-range**—The timing is in accord with (a) the time dimensions of the capital expenditure projects and (b) the time dimension of the long-range profit plan (usually five years). Projection of long-range cash inflows (primarily from sales and services) and long-range cash outflows (primarily for expenses and capital expenditures, including expansion projects) is fundamental to sound financing decisions and to the development of long-term credit needs. Long-range cash planning focuses only on the major outflows and inflows.

2. **Short-range**—The timing is in accord with the profit plan. Short-range cash planning for this time horizon entails detailed estimation of cash inflows and outflows as generated by the annual profit plan; thus it rests directly on the formal budgets discussed in the preceding chapters. It forms the basis for assessing short-term credit needs and for cash control during the year.

3. **Operational Cash Planning**—Cash inflows and outflows are projected for the ensuing month, week, or even day. This activity is primarily directed toward dynamic control of cash balances to minimize *interest cost* on loans and *opportunity cost* deriving from idle cash.

METHODS OF DEVELOPING THE CASH BUDGET

Two principal approaches can be used to develop the cash flow budget. First is the *cash receipts and disbursements method* (sometimes referred to as the integrated method). This method is based on a detailed profit plan, and essentially projects the cash account as it would reflect such items as sales, expenses, capital expenditures. It is simple, and it is appropriate where a comprehensive profit plan is well established. It is especially useful for short-term cash budgeting (annual profit plan); the method is not appropriate for the more generalized long-term profit plans. The underlying plans causing short-term cash inflow and the budgets causing cash outflows are carefully analyzed to translate them from an *accrual basis to cash basis*. This method will be illustrated in this chapter for Superior Manufacturing Company.

The second approach is *income statement cash flow method* (sometimes referred to as the adjusted net income method). The starting point in this approach is *projected net income* reflected on the budgeted income statement. It is similar to the familiar "analysis of working capital." Basically, projected net income is converted from an accrual basis to cash basis (that is, adjusted for changes in inventories, receivables, accruals, and deferrals); then other cash sources and requirements are projected. The method requires less supporting detail and predictably provides less detail in its projection. It is especially appropriate for making long-range cash projections. For a common set of underlying projections, both methods will derive identical cash flow results that differ only with respect to the amounts of detail.

CASH RECEIPTS AND DISBURSEMENTS METHOD OF ESTIMATING CASH RECEIPTS

Cash inflows arise from cash sales, collections of accounts and notes receivables, interest on investments, sales of capital assets, and miscellaneous income sources. If these amounts have been estimated as discussed and illustrated up to this point, estimating cash receipts is simplified.

Receipts from cash sales generally can be planned on the basis of historical ratios of cash to credit sales, with adjustments for expected changes in the general business trend and for other relevant conditions. Cash sales generate immediate cash; therefore, there is no problem of lag between point of sale and realization of cash.

In the case of credit sales, the lag between point of sale and realization of cash causes a problem. The principal approach to the problem is based on past collection experience—the average period between the date of sale and the date of collection. The manager in charge of credit and collections should regularly determine, for example, the efficiency of collections. Data such as the percentages of credit sales collected in thirty days, sixty days, and so forth, are invaluable in estimating the cash receipts from accounts receivable. It may be advisable to accumulate such information for various sales districts, products, or different classes of customers.

The treasurer usually will not encounter much difficulty in estimating miscellaneous cash receipts from sources such as royalties, rent income, interest income, and dividend income.

ESTIMATING CASH RECEIPTS ILLUSTRATED

To illustrate the cash budget, Superior Manufacturing Company derives cash from two sources: sales and miscellaneous incomes. First, look at sales. Bad debts experience provided the basis for projected expected losses from bad debts of $.20 per $100 total net sales; this estimate was incorporated in the variable budget (see Schedule 44, Chapter 10). Collection experienced also provided a basis for projecting expected collections on total sales. The following decisional inputs were computed for planning collections for during 1977; the percents relate to total sales:

82% collected in month sold
10% collected in the first month following sale
5% collected in the second month following sale
3% collected in the third month following sale
Quarterly basis—92% collected in quarter sold
8% collected in next quarter

SCHEDULE 48. Superior Manufacturing Company
Cash Inflow from Sales and Accounts Receivable
For the Year Ending December 31, 1977

	REF.	SALES	LESS ALLOWANCE FOR DOUBTFUL ACCOUNTS	BALANCE TO BE COLLECTED	ESTIMATED COLLECTIONS—1977 FIRST QUARTER JANUARY	FEBRUARY	MARCH	QUARTERS SECOND	THIRD	FOURTH	BALANCE UNCOLLECTED 12/31/77
Balance in accounts receivable and allowance for doubtful accounts 12/31/76:											
Prior accounts	(Given)	$ 10,000	$ 6,000	$ 4,000						$ 4,000	
October, 1976	(Given)	20,000	$ 400	19,600	$ 19,600						
November 1976	(Given)	40,000	800	39,200	24,500	$ 14,700					
December, 1976	(Given)	90,000	1,800	88,200	49,000	24,500	$ 14,700				
		160,000	9,000								
1977 budgeted sales:	21										
January		500,400	1,001	499,399	409,507	49,940	24,970	$ 14,982			
February		540,000	1,080	538,920		441,914	53,892	43,114			
March		574,100	1,148	572,952			469,821	103,131			
1st Quarter		1,314,500	3,229								
2nd Quarter		1,595,000	3,190	1,591,810				1,464,465	$ 127,345		
3rd Quarter		1,158,000	2,316	1,155,684					1,063,229	92,455	
4th Quarter		1,727,500	3,455	1,724,045						1,586,121	137,924
Total year		$6,095,000	$12,190								
Totals		$6,255,000	$21,190	$6,233,810	$502,607	$531,054	$563,383	$1,625,692	$1,190,574	$1,682,576	$137,924
Less bad debts to be written off in 1977		3,000	3,000								
Budgeted balance in allowance for doubtful accounts, end of 1977			$18,190								
Less net uncollected on 12/31/77				137,924							
Budgeted cash receipts for 1977		6,095,886		6,095,886	$502,607	$531,054	$563,383	$1,625,692	$1,190,574	$1,682,576	
Balance in accounts Receivable Dec. 31, 1977		$ 156,114									

To derive the cash inflow from sales and accounts receivables, the treasurer referred to the sales plan (Schedule 21, Chapter 5) and predicted the receivables that would be uncollected on the first day of the budget year (January 1, 1977). An analysis of current accounts receivable and expectations for the balance of the current year provided the following estimates:

Actual Balances in Accounts Receivable Anticipated
January 1, 1977

MONTH OF SALE	UNCOLLECTED ACCOUNTS RECEIVABLE ON 1/1/77	BALANCE IN ALLOWANCE FOR DOUBTFUL ACCOUNTS 1/1/77
Prior to October, 1976	$ 10,000*	$6,000
October, 1976	20,000	400
November, 1976	40,000	800
December, 1976	90,000	1,800
Totals	$160,000	$9,000

*It is anticipated on the basis of current collection activities, that $4,000 of this amount will be collected in 1977 and that $3,000 will be written off as a bad debt; the balance will be held "open" although collection is uncertain at this date.

With these data, the treasurer planned the *cash inflow from sales and receivables* shown in Schedule 48. Note the following features: (1) effect of the planned ratio for bad debt losses; (2) utilization of the collection percentages; (3) derivation of the *interim* cash inflows; and (4) reconciliation of the planned balances in accounts receivable.[1]

Analysis of miscellaneous sources of "other incomes" provided the cash inflow estimates shown in Schedule 49. The results of these two schedules

SCHEDULE 49.   Superior Manufacturing Company
Planned Cash Inflows from Other Incomes
For the Year Ending December 31, 1977

	BUDGETED AMOUNT
January	$ 3,390
February	2,950
March	3,620
Total 1st Quarter	$ 9,960
2nd Quarter	9,510
3rd Quarter	8,220
4th Quarter	9,430
Total for year	$37,120

[1] Note that this company assumes all sales are on credit and that bad debt losses are related to total sales. Generally it is preferable to relate bad debts and collection experience to credit sales.

are summarized in Schedule 50. Note that cash inflows are developed for interim periods throughout the year in harmony with the overall profit plan.

SCHEDULE 50. Superior Manufacturing Company
Summary of Budgeted Cash Inflows
For the Year Ending December 31, 1977

| | | | SOURCES OF CASH | |
| | | | ACCOUNTS RECEIVABLE | OTHER INCOMES |
	REF.	TOTAL	48	49
January		$ 505,997	$ 502,607	$ 3,390
February		534,004	531,054	2,950
March		567,003	563,383	3,620
Total 1st Quarter		$1,607,004	$1,597,044	$ 9,960
2nd Quarter		1,635,202	1,625,692	9,510
3rd Quarter		1,198,794	1,190,574	8,220
4th Quarter		1,692,006	1,682,576	9,430
Total for year		$6,133,006	$6,095,886	$37,120

ESTIMATING CASH PAYMENTS

Cash disbursements are made principally for raw materials, direct labor, out-of-pocket expenses, capital additions, retirement of indebtedness, and dividends. The budgets for these items (already prepared at this point in the planning cycle as illustrated in prior chapters) provide the basis for projecting the cash requirements. The *cash receipts and disbursements approach* requires elimination of *noncash items*, such as depreciation, from the appropriate budget schedules of expense previously prepared. Experience and company policy on purchase discounts must be taken into account in estimating the time lag between the incurrence of accounts payable and the payment. Accruals and prepayments must be taken into account to determine the timing of related cash disbursements. Interest payments on indebtedness and property taxes can be estimated. Cash requirements for dividends may present a problem; but in many firms a consistent dividend policy simplifies this matter. In other cases, cash requirements for dividends must be estimated by top management on the basis of whatever information is available at the time. Then, too, the amount of dividends may depend upon the availability of cash. Income taxes cannot be estimated until the pretax income is planned. Borrowing and repayment of principal and interest influences both cash flow and income taxes. Thus there is a sequence (unique to each situation) that usually must be followed in planning cash outflows.

ESTIMATING CASH PAYMENTS ILLUSTRATED

Superior Manufacturing Company credits all purchases of raw material to accounts payable. The company takes all cash discounts; hence, purchases and payables are recorded in the accounts at *net of purchase discount*. Payments are made as a general policy on the last day of the discount period. The result is that, on the average, *one-third* of the purchases for a particular month are carried over to the next month for payment. The treasurer estimated that one-ninth of the purchases for each quarter will not be paid until the following quarter.

It is estimated that the December 31, 1976 balance in accounts payable will be $52,100. Based on these data inputs and data from the *raw material purchases budget* (Schedule 26, Chapter 7), a schedule of *budgeted cash required for purcahses of raw materials* was prepared as shown in Schedule 51. The computations are rounded to the nearest $10, and cash requirements are developed by interim periods. As with some of the previous schedules, the format shown in Schedule 51 is primarily computational. Certain schedules, such as this one, should be recast for inclusion in the formal profit plan.

SCHEDULE 51.   The Superior Manufacturing Company
Budgeted Cash Required for Purchases of Raw Materials
For the Year Ending December 31, 1977

	REF	BEGINNING BALANCES ACCOUNTS PAYABLE	RAW MATERIAL PURCHASES 26	TOTAL PAYABLE	ESTIMATED BALANCE OF PURCHASES TO BE PAID NEXT MONTH	CASH REQUIRED (INVOICES PAYABLE)
January		$52,100	$ 97,900	$150,000	$32,630*	$ 117,370
February		32,630	129,700	162,330	43,230	119,100
March		43,230	118,900	162,130	39,630	122,500
Total 1st Quarter			$ 346,500	$474,460		$ 358,970
2nd Quarter		39,630	373,000	412,630	41,440	371,190
3rd Quarter		41,440	321,850	363,290	35,760	327,530
4th Quarter		35,760	377,650	413,410	41,960	371,450
Total for Year			$1,419,000			$1,429,140
Ending balance in Accounts Payable 12/31/77					$41,960	

*One-third of $97,900.

Next, focus on the development of the cash outflow required for budgeted expenses by interim period for Superior Manufacturing Company. The expense budgets were illustrated in Schedules 32, 33, 34, 39, and 40. These schedules show planned expenses for each department by interim periods. The *treasurer* working with the accounting department must convert these values to a *cash basis* by excluding the *noncash items of expense* (including those that will not be paid on a current basis). Schedule 52 illustrates the *budgeted cash required for expenses*. Note in particular the "less noncash items"; included are such items as depreciation (a noncash expense), taxes, insurance and audit fee (paid annually or less often). For example, the $2,160 exclusion on the first line in Schedule 52 is comprised of the following items obtained from Schedule 33, Factory Expense Budget:

Depreciation	$1,560
Insurance	240
Taxes	360
Total	$2,160

In developing Schedule 52 the treasurer included the following special items planned:

Lawyer retainer fee—Paid monthly.

Audit fee—Paid annually on March 1, that is, the 1976 audit fee is paid on March 1, 1977.

Supplies used—Purchases when made are placed in inventory and debited to the supplies inventory account; the expense reflects usage. Therefore, this item was treated as a noncash item in Schedule 52.

Stationery and office supplies—Purchases are recorded when made directly as an expense; there is no inventory. Therefore, this item was treated as a cash outflow according to the expense schedule.

The capital expenditures budget previously illustrated (Schedule 46, Chapter 11) reports the cash requirements for that purpose.

The next items that the treasurer had to consider were deferrals, accruals, dividends, and income taxes that require cash. In large measure these items reflect the results of the account process; therefore, the treasurer and the controller jointly developed the following data for planning purposes:

1. Unexpired insurance—Balance on December 31, 1976, $2,532 (four months of remaining premium). Policy renewal date May 1, 1977; $22,788 cash paid for three-year premium.
2. Accrued property taxes—Unpaid taxes as of December 31, 1976, $4,982, payable during February, 1977. Estimated taxes for 1977 as indicated in the expense schedules previously prepared from the various budgets.

3. Federal income taxes—1976 income taxes payable on April 15, 1977, $279,400. (Assume for simplicity that the 1977 income tax rate is 30 percent of net income.)

4. Accrued interest expense—Balance on December 31, 1976, $7,000. (Represents ten and one-half months' interest on $200,000, 4 percent long-term notes. Interest payable each February 15.) $150,000 of these notes are due and payable on February 15, 1977.

5. Dividends—An annual dividend of $12,000 is anticipated in June, 1977, payable in August, 1977.

6. Interest income—There will be no accrued interest income on December 31, 1976; however, on December 31, 1977, the bank will credit $2\frac{1}{2}$ percent interest on the building fund ($20,000) to the fund.

7. Direct labor and other wages—No accruals.

8. Stationery and office supplies—No inventory.

9. Supplies used—Inventory on December 31, 1976, $13,700. Budgeted purchases during 1977: January, $3,400; February, $3,300; March, $3,500; 2nd Quarter, $10,400; 3rd Quarter, $10,400; and 4th Quarter, $10,140. Supplies used as indicated on expense schedules previously prepared. Supplies paid for as purchased.

10. Annual audit fee—The 1976 audit fee of $2,400 is payable on March 1, 1977 and the 1977 fee of $2,400 is payable on March 1, 1978.

11. Contingent liabilities—Court litigation currently in progress may result in a payment of approximately $620,000 as an adjustment of prior years' federal income taxes.

These data were used to develop Schedule 52. Observe that, because of the simplified illustration, numerous items are included in the one schedule. This is not typical; generally, separate schedules and computations would be necessary for each separate type of expenditure. Although the estimates and requirements for income taxes are indicated on the schedule, the schedule must be constructed initially without this item. The schedule generally should be completed with a rough estimate of income taxes so that the probable cash position can be determined. As soon as net income is computed and the tax estimate prepared, the schedule can be recast as illustrated.

The cash requirements indicated in Schedules 46, 51, 52, and 53 are summarized in Schedule 54. Notes payable, to be paid during the upcoming budget year, are also included.

SCHEDULE 52. Superior Manufacturing Company
Budgeted Cash Required for Expenses
For the Year Ending December 31, 1977

	REF.	TOTAL EXPENSE	LESS NONCASH	TOTAL CASH REQUIRED	CASH REQUIREMENTS						
					FIRST QUARTER			QUARTERS			
					JANUARY	FEBRUARY	MARCH	FIRST	SECOND	THIRD	FOURTH
Manufacturing Division:											
General and Administrative overhead	33	$ 116,800	$ 2,160	$ 114,640	$ 9,416	$ 9,524	$ 9,532	$ 28,472	$ 28,700	$ 28,548	$ 28,920
Power Department	33	110,000	7,200	102,800	8,246	8,468	8,468	25,182	25,848	25,404	26,366
Repair Department	33	10,000	1,600	8,400	700	700	700	2,100	2,100	2,100	2,100
Department 1	34	319,280	42,560	276,720	21,652	22,708	22,804	67,164	69,660	68,076	71,820
Department 2	34	29,280	2,568	26,712	2,184	2,226	2,226	6,636	6,678	6,636	6,762
Department 3	34	103,840	20,312	83,528	6,515	6,849	6,880	20,244	21,034	20,532	21,718
Totals		$ 689,200	$ 76,400	$ 612,800	$ 48,713	$ 50,475	$ 50,610	$149,798	$154,020	$151,296	$157,686
Buildings Services	32	150,000	66,000	84,000	7,700	6,800	6,720	21,220	19,880	20,500	22,400
Sales Divisions:											
Southern District	39	234,656		234,656	19,746	21,298	20,206	61,250	60,389	51,479	61,538
Eastern District	39	313,391		313,391	25,282	27,032	28,551	80,865	81,446	67,654	83,426
Western District	39	115,120		115,120	9,828	8,783	10,170	28,781	27,964	26,249	32,126
General Sales Overhead	39	296,330	600	295,730	24,563	24,985	25,348	74,896	74,690	70,045	76,099
Totals		$ 959,497	$ 600	$ 958,897	$ 79,419	$ 82,098	$ 84,275	$245,792	$244,489	$215,427	$253,189
Administrative Division:											
Accounting	40	54,020	3,000	51,020	4,250	4,258	4,264	12,772	12,770	12,682	12,796
Treasurer	40	56,177	13,990	42,187	3,511	3,538	3,552	10,611	10,587	10,290	10,689
Administrative	40	83,516	3,480	80,036	6,660	6,709	6,751*	20,120	20,096	19,563	20,257
Totals		$ 193,713	$ 20,470	$ 173,243	$ 14,421	$ 14,505	$ 14,577	$ 43,503	$ 43,463	$ 42,535	$ 43,742
Grand Totals		$1,992,410	$163,470	$1,828,940	$150,253	$153,878	$156,182	$460,313	$461,852	$429,753	$477,017

* Does not include 1976 audit fee; see Schedule 53.

395

SCHEDULE 53. Superior Manufacturing Company
Cash Requirements for Accrued Items, Deferred Items, Dividends, and Income Taxes
For the Year Ending December 31, 1977

	BALANCE 12/31/76	RENEWALS AND PAYMENTS 1977	TOTAL	EXPIRATIONS AND ACCRUALS 1977	BALANCE 12/31/77	JANU-ARY	FEBRU-ARY	MARCH	FIRST	SECOND	THIRD	FOURTH	TOTAL
						FIRST QUARTER			QUARTERS				
Unexpired insurance	(Given) $ 2,532	(Given) $ 22,788	$25,320	$ 7,596	$ 17,724	$	$	$	$	$22,788	$	$	$ 22,788
Accrued property taxes	4,982*	4,982		7,284*	7,284*		4,982		4,983				4,982
Federal income taxes	279,400*	279,400		258,318*	258,318*			279,400	279,400				279,400
Accrued interest Expense	7,000* (10½ Mos.)	8,000 (12 Mos.)	1,000	2,750* (12 Mos.)	1,750* (10½ Mos.)		8,000		8,000				8,000
Interest income on building fund ($20,000 at 2½% credited to building fund on December 31)													
Supplies inventory	13,700	41,140	54,840	49,640*	5,200	3,400	3,300	3,500	10,200	10,400	10,400	10,140	41,140
Audit fee	2,400*	2,400		2,400*	2,400*			2,400	2,400				2,400
Dividends											12,000		12,000
Total cash requirements						$3,400	$16,282	$285,000	$304,982	$33,188	$22,400	$1C,140	$370,710

*Credit.

Note: Notes payable will be included in Schedule 54.

SCHEDULE 54. Superior Manufacturing Company
Summary of Cash Requirements
For the Year Ending December 31, 1977

	REF.	ANNUAL TOTAL	1ST QUARTER				QUARTERS		
			JANUARY	FEBRUARY	MARCH	FIRST	SECOND	THIRD	FOURTH
Material	51	$1,429,140	$117,370	$119,100	$122,500	$ 358,970	$ 371,190	$ 327,530	$ 371,450
Labor	30	1,752,000	125,400	141,600	142,800	409,800	444,000	421,200	477,000
Expense	52	1,828,940	150,253	153,878	156,182	460,313	461,852	429,758	477,017
Capital additions	46	28,700	200			200			28,500
Accrued and deferred items	53	370,710	3,400	16,282	285,300	304,982	33,188	22,400	10,140
Notes payable	(Input)	150,000		150,000		150,000			
Totals		$5,559,490	$396,623	$580,860	$706,782	$1,684,265	$1,310,230	$1,200,888	$1,364,107

DETERMINATION OF FINANCING NEEDS

Cash inflows and outflows must next be compared to assess the planned cash position throughout the period. To make this comparison, the treasurer had to develop another input—the probable starting cash balance (actual) on January 1, 1977. He estimated it at $54,000 and proceeded to develop Schedule 55, Comparison of Estimated Cash Receipts and Disbursements, prior to financing.

SCHEDULE 55. Superior Manufacturing Company

Comparison of Estimated Cash Receipts and Disbursements
(Prior to Financing)
For the Year Ending December 31, 1977

| | BEGINNING CASH BALANCE | CASH RECEIPTS | TOTAL | CASH DISBURSEMENTS | ENDING CASH BALANCE |
REF.		50		54	
January	$ 54,000	$ 505,997	$ 559,997	$ 396,623	$163,374
February	163,374	534,004	697,378	580,860	116,518
March	116,518	567,003	683,521	706,782	23,261*
2nd Quarter	23,261*	1,635,202	1,611,941	1,310,230	301,711
3rd Quarter	301,711	1,198,794	1,500,505	1,200,888	299,617
4th Quarter	299,617	1,692,006	1,991,623	$1,364,107	627,516
Totals		$6,133,006		$5,559,490	

*Credit balance indicated.

The last column, "ending cash balance," indicates a favorable cash position for each period except one. March has a cash deficit of $23,261, indicating a need for some form of financing. Estimated cash balances for the following periods suggest that a short-term bank loan would protect the cash position. After consideration of all factors involved, the treasurer decided that the following short-term financing should be included in the cash budget:

Date needed :	March 1, 1977
Amount needed :	$100,000
Repayment date :	April 30, 1977
Interest rate :	6%
Type of financing :	Interest bearing note

The short-term financing, its interest thereon, and effect on cash is presented in Schedule 56, Budgeted Short-Term Financing Requirements. Determination of budgeted financing completes all aspects of the cash budget. Utilizing the data in Schedules 55 and 56, the treasurer prepared the *final cash budget* indicated in Schedule 57. Of the cash flow schedules illustrated, only this last one is needed in the *formal* profit plan.

It may be reemphasized that the schedules concerning the cash budget as illustrated in this chapter are primarily computation schedules. The form included in the planning budget should be adapted to the peculiarities of different concerns and managements. There is no single universal application.

SCHEDULE 56.   Superior Manufacturing Company

Budgeted Short Term Financing Requirements*
For the Year Ending December 31, 1977

	REF.	BEGINNING ACCOUNT BALANCE	CASH RECEIVED (LOAN INCURRED)	SUBTOTAL	CASH PAYMENT (LOAN PAID)	ENDING ACCOUNT BALANCE
a NOTES PAYABLE—SHORT TERM						
January		—				—
February		—				—
March		—	$100,000	$100,000		$100,000
1st Quarter			$100,000	$100,000		$100,000
2nd Quarter		$100,000		$100,000	$100,000	—
3rd Quarter		—				—
4th Quarter		—				—
Total		—	$100,000	$100,000	$100,000	—

*In view of the fact that only *one* loan is contemplated, this schedule is superfluous. It is included simply to indicate one possible format for situations involving numerous loans and repayments.

	REF.	BEGINNING ACCOUNT BALANCE	EXPENSE INCURRED	SUBTOTAL	CASH PAYMENTS	ENDING ACCOUNT BALANCE
b INTEREST EXPENSE ON SHORT-TERM NOTES						
January		—				—
February		—				—
March		—	$ 500	$ 500		$500
1st Quarter		—	$ 500	$ 500		$500
2nd Quarter		$500	$ 500	$1,000	$1,000	—
3rd Quarter		—				—
4th Quarter		—				—
Total		—	$1,000	$1,000	$1,000	—

SCHEDULE 57. Superior Manufacturing Company
Final Cash Budget
For the Year Ending December 31, 1977

	REF.	BEGINNING CASH BALANCE	CASH RECEIPTS 50	TOTAL	CASH PAYMENTS 54	ENDING CASH BALANCE
January		$ 54,000	$ 505,997	$ 559,997	$ 396,623	$163,374
February		163,374	534,004	697,378	580,860*	116,518
March		116,518	667,003†	783,521	706,782	76,739
2nd Quarter		76,739	1,635,202	1,711,941	1,411,230**	300,711
3rd Quarter		300,711	1,198,794	1,499,505	1,200,888††	298,617
4th Quarter		298,617	1,692,006	1,990,623	1,364,107	626,516
Totals			$6,233,006		$5,660,490	

*Includes $150,000 payment on long-term note payable.
†Includes $100,000 short-term note payable.
**Includes payment of short-term bank loan and interest $101,000.
††Includes $12,000 dividend payment.

INCOME STATEMENT CASH FLOW METHOD

The *income statement cash flow method* of planning cash is used by some firms for the short run; however, it is used more frequently for long-term cash planning. The method requires less detail and fits the more general projections common in long-range planning.

Basically, this method develops cash flows staring with *net income*; adjustments are made for noncash items affecting reported net income. Essentially, net income is converted from the *accrual* basis to a cash basis. The other cash inflows and outflows are estimated for nonprofit items such as sale of fixed assets, capital additions, and payment of debt and dividends. These estimates are computed much like the cash receipts and disbursements method. Technically, the income statement cash flow method is similar in approach to that commonly utilized in the analysis of working capital.[2]

To illustrate the income statement cash flow method and its potential applications in a broader context, adaptations from the procedures of two well-known companies are presented. Illustration 38 shows how one company develops its cash flow analysis as a supplement to the income statement. Note that (1) the cash flow analysis *starts* with net income ($250,000), (2) this amount is "adjusted" for the accrual to a *cash basis* ($350,000), and (3) "nonincome statement" inflows and outflows of cash are included. You

[2] For a technical treatment of the method see: G. A. Welsch, C. T. Zlatkovich, and J. A. White, *Intermediate Accounting* (Homewood, Ill.: Richard D. Irwin, Inc., 1976), Chapter 21.

ILLUSTRATION 38. Income Statement Cash Flow Method—Short Term

AK Corporation—Budgeted Net Income and Cash Flow
for the Year Ending December 31, 19XX

(In Thousand Dollars: Only 100% Column Partially Completed with Hypothetical Amounts for Illustrative Purposes)

	AT 80% CAPACITY		AT 90% CAPACITY		AT 100% CAPACITY		AT 110% CAPACITY		AT 120% CAPACITY	
	AMOUNT	PER CENT	AMOUNT	PER CENT	AMOUNT	PER CENT	AMOUNT	PER CENT	AMOUNT	PER CENT
PART 1—INCOME STATEMENT:										
Sales	$8,000		$9,000		$10,000	100	$11,000		$12,0C0	
Variable costs:										
Direct material										
Direct labor										
Factory overhead										
Distribution cost										
General administrative cost					7,000	70				
Total variable Costs					3,000	30				
Marginal income										
Fixed costs:										
Factory overhead										
Distribution										
General administrative					2,500	25				
Total Fixed costs					500	5				
Operating income					250	2.5				
Provision for income taxes					250	2.5				
Net income					$ 250					

ILLUSTRATION 38. (Continued)

	AT 80% CAPACITY		AT 90% CAPACITY		AT 100% CAPACITY		AT 110% CAPACITY		AT 120% CAPACITY	
	AMOUNT	PER CENT	AMOUNT	PER CENT	AMOUNT	PER CENT	AMOUNT	PER CENT	AMOUNT	PER CENT
PART 2—CASH FLOW ANALYSIS:										
Beginning cash balance					$ 40					
Cash sources:										
Net income					250					
Add: Depreciation and amortization					100					
Decrease in inventory					12					
Deduct: Increase in prepaid expenses					(5)					
Increase in receivables					(7)					
Net income converted to cash inflow basis					350					
Financing					100					
Total cash inflow					450					
Total cash available					490					
Cash requirements:										
Dividends					40					
Decrease in long-term liabilities					30					
Net increase in fixed assets					300					
Total cash required					370					
Ending cash balance					$ 120					

should analyze the adjustments to net income to comprehend their treatment. For example, the $7,000 increase in receivables is a deduction since income includes this amount of credit sales awaiting the cash inflow. Two broader features of this illustration should be noted: (1) this company develops a *flexible* income statement and cash flow analysis for several capacity levels; and (2) the budgeted income statement and cash flow analysis are presented as a "single package."

Illustration 39 reflects the income statement cash flow method in its usual setting as an important facet of long-range planning; one column is completed. The illustration reflects that less detail and broader projections are implicit in this approach.

CONTROL OF THE CASH POSITION

The company financial officer is directly responsible for control of the cash position, subject, of course, to the decisions of the chief executive. Actual cash receipts and payments will be somewhat different from those anticipated in the profit plan. This discrepancy may result from (1) variation in factors affecting cash, (2) sudden and unexpected circumstances influencing operations, or (3) lack of cash control.

A good system of cash control is especially important because of the potential consequences. Frequently, it is possible for management to make decisions or to alter existing policies so that the cash position is enhanced. For example, an unexpected change in operations may create a serious cash shortage, but management may be able to avoid, or at least to minimize, the undesirable situation by (1) increasing efforts to collect receivables, (2) reducing out-of-pocket expenses, (3) deferring capital expenditures, (4) deferring payment of selected liabilities, (5) reducing inventories, and (6) altering timing of operations that affect cash. Obviously, the effect of these decisions on the cash position is contingent upon their timing. Often the earlier the decision, the greater the potential effect on the ultimate cash position. Therefore, it is essential that management be fully informed as far in advance as possible about the *probable* cash position.

Assuming adequate planning, continuing control of the cash position generally should be based upon two procedures. First, an adequate and continuous evaluation of both the present and the probable cash position should be made. This procedure involves a periodic evaluation and reporting, usually monthly, of the actual cash position to date. This report is coupled with a *reprojection* of the probable future cash flows for the remainder of the period, taking into account budgeted conditions affected by unexpected developments not originally anticipated. Assume, for example, that at the end of February there was an actual cash balance of $11,000,

ILLUSTRATION 39. Income Statement Cash Flow Method—Long Term

RB Company Long-Range Plans—Analysis of Cash Flow

ITEMS	CURRENT YEAR	FUTURE PROJECTIONS				
	1977	1978	1979	1980	1981	1982
Beginning cash position (000's)	160					
Cash inflows:						
Net income planned (after tax)	400					
Adjustments:						
Add: Depreciation and amortization	70					
Deduct: Increase in working capital other than cash	(10)					
Net income on cash basis	460					
Other sources of cash:						
Capital stock sold	100					
Long-term loans	80					
Sales of fixed assets	30					
Total cash inflow	670					
Cash outflows:						
Sinking fund requirements	20					
Dividend payments	40					
Payment on long-term debt	550					
Additions to fixed assets	150					
Total cash outflow	760					
Ending cash position	70					

whereas the original budgeted balance was $32,000. The factors causing the $21,000 unfavorable variation in cash should be carefully analyzed, with particular emphasis given to the probable future effect. Next, the budgeted cash receipts and payments for the *remainder* of the year should be carefully evaluated and *adjusted for any new conditions* that may affect them. The final step, then, in evaluating the probable future cash position is to start with the $11,000 actual cash balance at the end of February by adding to it the reprojected budget receipts for each time period during the rest of the budget year and by deducting the reprojected budget payments for the same period. In this way a completely new evaluation of the probable future cash position can be developed for top management. This dynamic approach gives management a *continuous budget* evaluation of the cash position. This continuous monitoring gives control through policy decisions that, by the very nature of the situation, must be made some time in advance to have the maximum effect on the cash position. This procedure is indicated in Illustration 40, which was adapted from the procedures of a medium-size firm.

The other aspect of cash control maintains data on the day-to-day (or week-to-week) cash position. In order to minimize interest costs, to assure adequate cash, some financal executives develop a daily evaluation of the current cash position as indicated in Illustration 41. This approach is particularly useful in companies having widely fluctuating cash demands and widely dispersed branches through which large amounts of cash flow. Many companies are aware of the reduced interest costs that can be attained through *daily* control of cash. For example, one company estimated that daily control saved approximately $140,000 in interest during one year. Prior to instituting daily control it was not uncommon for one division of the company to have excess cash of several million dollars while another division was borrowing substantial amounts on a short-term basis and paying $10\frac{1}{2}$ percent interest.

Many companies control cash with their comprehensive budget program, which includes (1) systematic planning of the cash flows for both the long range and short range, (2) daily evaluation of the cash position, and (3) monthly reprojection of the cash position as discussed above.[3]

DISCUSSION QUESTIONS

1. Define the cash budget, and explain its scope and objectives.

2. What manager, or managers, should be responsible for planning and controlling cash?

3. What are the two principal approaches used to develop cash flow budgets? Explain each briefly.

[3] "Cash Flow for Managerial Control," *NAA Bulletin,* Research Report No. 38.

ILLUSTRATION 40. Monthly Report of Cash Position

X Company
At March 31, 19XX

PARTICULARS	ACTUAL CASH POSITION		REPROJECTION OF CASH POSITION FOR REMAINDER OF YEAR				
	MONTH OF MARCH	CUMULATIVE JAN. 1–MAR. 13	APRIL	MAY	JUNE	3RD QUARTER	4TH QUARTER
Cash receipts:							
Accounts receivable							
Trade notes receivable							
Cash sales							
Other sources							
Total cash inflow							
Cash payments:							
Raw material							
Accounts payable							
Current expenses							
Dividends							
Other payments							
Total cash outflow							
Indicated cash position from							
operations							
*Financing required (net of interest):**							
Short-term							
Long-term							
Total							
Indicated cash position							
(after financing)							

*Indicates payment of debt.

ILLUSTRATION 41. Daily Report of Cash Position

Y Company
For the Month of _____

DATE	DAY	RUNNING CASH BALANCE	CASH INFLOW			TOTAL CASH OUTFLOW	CASH OUTFLOW			
			TOTAL CASH INFLOW	COLLECTION ON RECEIVABLES	OTHER SOURCES OF CASH		PAYMENT CURRENT LIABILITIES	PAYROLL REQUIRE-MENTS	OPERATING EXPENSE	OTHER DISBURSE-MENTS
1	Th									
2	Fri									
3	*									
4	*									
5	Mon									
6	Tue									
7	Wed									
8	Th									
9	Fri									
Etc.										

End of month balances:

Actual:
  Amount $_____
  Average daily balance** $_____

Budgeted:
  Amount $_____
  Average daily balance** $_____

*Nonworking day.
**Based on number of working days in the month.

4. In projecting cash outflows, budgeted expenses must be "adjusted." Explain the general approach and the nature of the adjustment.

5. The income statement cash flow method involves the "adjustment" of accrual net income to a cash flow basis. Explain the nature of the adjustment required for each of the following: depreciation; amortization; inventory change; changes in accounts receivables; changes in prepaid items; and changes in accrued items.

6. Assuming adequate planning, continuing control of each position generally should be based upon two procedures; identify the two procedures and explain each.

CASE 12-1
Eaton Corporation

Although Eaton Corporation has been operating more than thirty years, its most dynamic growth has occurred in the past five years. A new line of products based on a patent developed by the company caused sales volume to increase more than 400 percent during the past five years. Consequently, the company has been operating at capacity while trying to increase plant capacity. The growth of the company has posed serious management problems; the management was hardly capable of handling the problems incident to rapidly expanded operational levels. Although the sales function generally has kept pace with the growth, the manufacturing function was inefficient, and top management talent was needed. During the past year, two vice presidents (production and finance) were employed from the outside; these were new positions in the company. The president and executive vice president are long-time employees (and large stockholders); recently the retirement age was set at seventy and they both have four years before retirement. It was clear to any perceptive observer that, although these two men stated that they had employed the new officers to "introduce the latest management techniques," they were reluctant to make major changes.

The commitments of resources for plant expansion, increased working capital, and expanded operations created serious cash problems. The two new vice presidents have prevailed on the president to institute a program of "dynamic profit planning and control." The financial vice president currently is designing a comprehensive five-year profit plan, a detailed annual profit plan, and monthly performance reports. This approach is new to the old management. The annual profit plan will be detailed by month since the seasonality of monthly sales does not vary more than 15 percent (except during the August vacation period).

The financial vice president currently is considering an approach for planning and controlling cash. In the past approximately one-third of the sales were cash sales; the balance on terms of 2/10, n/30. The 2 percent discount, of course, is allowed on all cash sales. Credit has been extended rather generously, and bad debt losses for the past five years averaged 2.1 percent of total sales. Collections, as reflected by a recent analysis of the records, are irregular. The financial vice president has concluded that the credit and collection experience reflected by the records is untenable and was due largely to the lack of planning and control of these functions; accordingly, these functions have recently been transferred from sales to the financial function. The sales executive stated that he was "glad to get rid of that problem." Due to the recent expansion in operations it was said that "capital additions have been a nightmare." Since even greater expansion is expected in the future, the financial vice president has outlined a planning and control approach to capital expenditures including (1) project planning, (2) long-range and short-range capital expenditure budgets (revised annually), (3) discounted cash flow evaluations, and (4) monthly performance reports.

Direct raw material accounts for approximately 20 percent of product cost. Raw materials are purchased from three different suppliers, each of whom grants cash and volume discounts. Eaton purchases on sixty-day credit terms. The financial vice president, in reviewing the purchase and payment records of the company, found that cash discount was taken on about 15 percent of the purchases and that payment was beyond the sixty-day period on approximately 25 percent of the purchases. These delayed payments were usually made following a "special reminder from the supplier," and included an extra charge for late payment. Quantity discounts were allowed on approximately 60 percent of the purchases.

The financial vice president concluded that the cash problems were due to a number of factors such as credit and collections, discounts, dividend policies, lack of cost control, and the absence of planning. However, the president stated that they all go back to "our sudden problem of having to build more capacity." The company has not established a line of credit; the local bank that carries the company accounts makes short-term loans as needed. Funds to finance expansion of plant and operations thus far were obtained by revising the charter to permit the sale of more stock to present shareholders. This source of expansion funds was inadequate and created problems because some shareholders did not want to invest additional cash in the company; yet they did not want their ownership diluted.

Required:

Assuming the financial vice president will establish the profit planning and control on a sound foundation, present your recommendations for the related cash planning and control approaches in this company.

CASE 12-2

CD Company

Based on the budget data given below for the CD Company, determine the estimated cash receipts from collections of accounts receivable by time period.

1. Balance in accounts receivable as of December 31, 19A, $1,000.
2. Balance in allowance for doubtful accounts as of December 31, 19A, $600.
3. Budgeted sales for 19B:

January	$10,100
February	12,120
March	11,110
2nd Quarter	30,300
3rd Quarter	33,330
4th Quarter	32,320

4. Estimated losses on accounts receivable due to bad debts—1 percent of sales, rounded to even $10.

5. Experience indicates collections, after provision for bad debts, should be: 80 percent in month sold; 10 percent in first month following sale, and 10 percent in second month following sale. On quarterly basis, assume 90 percent will be collected in the quarter sold and the balance in the next quarter. One-fourth of the net balance in accounts receivable as of December 31, 19A, will probably be collected in June; the balance is uncertain.

CASE 12-3
Feder Company

Feder Company prepares an annual profit plan covering all phases of operations. The plan is broken down by quarter and the first quarter is detailed by months. The following planning data have been developed to date:

1. Capital additions budget—Cash requirements as follows: machinery to be purchased: March, $2,500, 3rd Quarter, $6,000. Contribution to building fund: $30,000 on December 15. Blanket appropriations for minor capital additions: 1st Quarter, $600; 2nd Quarter, $500; 3rd Quarter, $500; 4th Quarter, $700.

2. Sales budget (average 70 percent cash sales)—January, $90,000; February, $85,000; March, $85,000; 2nd Quarter, $250,000; 3rd Quarter, $230,000; 4th Quarter, $300,000.

3. Collections on credit sales, after allowance for bad debts, are expected to be as follows: 80 percent in month sold, 10 percent in first month following sale, 7 percent in second month following sale, and 3 percent in third month. On a quarterly basis, 94 percent collected in the quarter sold and 6 percent in the next quarter.

4. Estimated balance at beginning of the budget year:
   Accounts receivable $20,000   (Estimated collections: 2nd
   Allowance for doubtful accounts   7,000   Quarter $5,000, 4th Quarter
   Cash   15,000 $7,000)

5. Estimates of Other Incomes and Other Expenses (cash basis):

	OTHER INCOMES	OTHER EXPENSES
January	$1,500	$2,000
February	1,000	2,000
March	1,000	1,500
2nd Quarter	3,000	5,000
3rd Quarter	3,000	5,000
4th Quarter	4,000	6,000

6. Allowance for bad debts is one-half of 1 percent of credit sales. (Round to even $10.)

7. Cash required for purchases is estimated to be as follows : January, $14,408; February, $16,272; March, $15,230; 2nd Quarter, $46,380; 3rd Quarter, $39,370; and 4th Quarter, $48,496.

8. Expense budget totals are as follows (assume exclusions for noncash items such as depreciation total $4,500 per month) : January, $70,900; February, $67,710; March, $70,120; 2nd Quarter, $200,620; 3rd Quarter, $174,630; and 4th Quarter, $212,010.

9. Estimated miscellaneous cash requirements :
    a. Insurance policy to be renewed on June 1, cost $750.
    b. Property taxes to be paid in February, $1,400.
    c. March 15, annual payment of interest (4 percent) on long-term notes payable, principal $50,000. $20,000 is also paid on the principal at this time.
    d. Dividends $20,000 (June).
    e. Legal retainer fees $150.00 per month.*
    f. Audit fee payable $2,500 (February).
    g. Federal income taxes : April, $21,000; November, $3,000; and December, $3,000.

*Not included in (8)

Required :

Prepare the following schedules for the annual profit plan :
a. Estimated cash collections from receivables.
b. Summary of cash receipts detailed by source and time periods.
c. Summary of cash payments—detailed by reason and time periods.
d. Tentative cash budget.
e. Schedule of short-term financing recommended. (Assume 5 percent interest rate.)
f. Final cash budget—set out financing and repayment separately.

CASE 12-4
Moore Manufacturers

Moore Manufacturers is a medium-size manufacturer of a limited line of retail items sold through hardware stores. Production is carried on in an old plant; however, the management is planning the construction of a new plant in 1979. The management currently is developing a five-year long-range plan (1977 through 1981). The following projections and estimates have been developed thus far :

1. Sales for 1977, $800,000; the sales objective is to increase sales $40,000 per year through 1981.
2. Variable cost objective is 40 percent of sales; fixed cost objective for 1977 is $380,000 with a 10 percent increase in 1980.

3. Depreciation and amortization will constitute 30 percent of the $300,000 fixed costs.

4. Actual cash balance at the start of 1977 will be $70,000; working capital other than cash at this date will be $150,000. The planned objective for working capital other than cash is to hold the same rate of increase as sales.

5. Income tax rate will be 52 percent.

6. Sources of cash:
   Sale of old assets: 1977, $5,000; 1978, $5,000; 1979, $50,000; 1980, $4,000; and 1981, $4,000.
   Sale of treasury stock in 1979, $100,000.
   Long-term loan and mortgage in 1978, $200,000.

7. Cash requirements:
   The sinking fund has a balance at the start of 1977 of $150,000 and $50,000 must be added to it in 1977.

   Payment of bonds amounting to $600,000 from sinking fund and cash in 1978.
   Capital expenditures: 1977, $40,000; 1978, $50,000; 1979, $350,000 (plant); 1980, $50,000; and 1981, $50,000.
   Dividends: 1977 and 1978, $20,000 per year; 1979, 1980, and 1981, $24,000 per year.
   Miscellaneous requirements: 1977, $4,500; 1978, $6,020; 1979, $6,540; 1980, $6,220; and 1981, $6,740.

Required:

a. Prepare a long-range income projection.

b. Prepare a long-range cash flow projection (use income statement cash flow approach).

c. Comment on any particular problems or suggestions with respect to the income and cash flow projections.

CASE 12-5

Riley Company

The executive committee of the Riley Company is developing a profit plan for the company. This is the company's first experience in profit planning and control. Some estimates for the upcoming year have been made; now attention has been turned to an evaluation of the cash position. The controller requested Sid Pearce, his latest employee, a recent MBA, to "develop a cash flow analysis." After considerable effort and numerous discussions, Sid collected the following data from various sources:

From the tentative sales budget—Planned sales, $400,000 (normal capacity).
From the accounting department—Payment on bonds payable to be made during the upcoming year, $55,000 plus $5,000 bond interest; annual dividends per year for the last seven years, $12,000; probable beginning balances at start of upcom-

ing year—cash, $22,000, accounts receivable, $32,000, and inventory, $62,000; variable costs 55 percent of sales; fixed costs per year, $120,000 (including depreciation of $40,000, amortization of intangibles, $10,000, and bond interest for the year, $5,000).

From the controller—Idle assets to be sold during upcoming year for $10,000 cash (net of tax); accounts receivable at year end should be approximately 10 percent of sales and inventory 15 percent of sales.

From the company engineer—Estimated cost of new plant addition during coming year $200,000.

From the executive vice president—A $140,000 long-term mortgage loan will be obtained in March of the upcoming year.

Convinced that these were the best data he could obtain at this time, Sid proceeded to develop a tentative cash flow analysis at three levels of operations, that is, at the "normal" level specified in the tentative sales budget and at levels 10 percent above and 10 percent below the sales budget.

Required:

a. Develop a combined income statement and cash flow analysis for each of the three levels in the way that you think Sid would have done. Assume a flat 40 percent income tax rate.

b. Explain all assumptions that you make, and indicate appropriate management action for each. No major events are anticipated during the year except construction of the new plant; it will not go "on stream" during the upcoming year.

c. Evaluate the indicated cash position.

CASE 12-6

Conway Company

Conway Company uses a comprehensive budget program. The profit plan is developed on a semiannual basis and is detailed by months. The company has had considerable difficulty with working capital, especially cash. Payments on a serial bond issue constitutes a heavy drain on cash; the last payment is to be made in 19A. Certain data as of March 31, 19A, are given below.

1. The cash budget for the six months ending June 30, 19A, is shown in the schedule below.

2. Actual results of operations in respect to cash for three months ending March 31, 19A:

Cash receipts—Cash sales: Jan.-Feb., $173,000; March, $81,000. Receivable collections: Jan.-Feb., $61,000; March, $34,000. Notes collected: Jan.-Feb., $8,000; March, $3,000. Other incomes: Jan.-Feb., $6,200; March, $3,400.

Cash payments—Raw material purchases: Jan.-Feb., $36,000; March, $18,000. Accounts paid: Jan.-Feb., $51,000; March, $28,000. Notes paid:

CONWAY COMPANY CASH BUDGET

	JANUARY	FEBRUARY	MARCH	APRIL	MAY	JUNE	TOTAL
Beginning cash balance	$ 20,000	$ 33,500	$ 40,800	$ 47,500	($21,300)	($15,300)	$ 20,000
Cash receipts:							
Cash sales	80,000	90,000	90,000	75,000	70,000	65,000	470,000
Receivable collections	30,000	35,000	36,000	25,000	20,000	20,000	166,000
Notes collected	5,000	2,000	3,000	8,000	3,000	6,000	27,000
Other incomes	3,000	3,000	3,500	3,000	2,500	2,500	17,500
Sale treasury stock				18,000			18,000
Total receipts	$118,000	$130,000	$132,500	$129,000	$ 95,500	$ 93,500	$698,500
Total cash available	$138,000	$163,500	$173,300	$176,500	$ 74,200	$ 78,200	$718,500
Cash payments:							
Raw material purchases	$ 15,000	$17,000	$ 16,000	$ 8,000	$14,000	$13,000	$ 83,000
Accounts paid	25,000	28,000	26,000	12,000	17,300	25,000	133,300
Notes paid	10,000		10,000				20,000
Expenses paid	48,500	61,700	66,600	54,800	52,700	49,500	333,800
Dividends						15,000	15,000
Bonds				40,000			40,000
Other expenses	5,000	6,000	6,000	4,500	4,500	4,000	30,000
Income taxes				78,000			78,000
Capital additions	1,000	10,000	1,200	500	1,000	500	14,200
Total payments	$104,500	$122,700	$125,800	$197,800	$ 89,500	$107,000	$747,300
Ending cash balances (before financing)	$ 33,500	$ 40,800	$ 47,500	($ 21,300)	($15,300)	($28,800)	($ 28,800)
Budgeted financing				35,000†			35,000
Ending cash balances (after financing)	$ 33,500	$ 40,800	$ 47,500	$ 13,700	$ 19,700	$ 6,200	$ 6,200

†Six months bank loan $35,000 @ 5%.

Jan.-Feb., $10,000; March, $10,000. Expenses paid: Jan.-Feb., $115,700; March, $68,200. Other expenses: Jan.-Feb., $13,000; March, $5,500. Capital additions: Jan.-Feb., $10,500; March, $900.

Required:

a. Prepare a performance report of cash receipts and disbursements as of March 31, 19A (March and cumulative). Provide comments where appropriate.
b. Prepare an analysis of the probable cash position for the remainder of the period, including your recommendations for additional financing. The present line of credit is $50,000. Provide comments where appropriate.

Completion and Application
of The Profit Plan

chapter thirteen

The planning process as we have characterized it coordinates a long-range profit plan and a short-range (annual) profit plan. We have discussed a planning process, based on well-defined responsibilities. Chapters 4 through 12 focused on the various components of profit plans; therefore, at this point we will discuss completion of the formal planning cycle. The *planned financial statements* are developed to report the net financial results of the various functional subplans and commitments. On this point, one authority stated:[1]

> The planning process which increasingly characterizes the medium to large-size corporation today is summarized and systematized in three financial statements: the projected operating statement, the projected balance sheet, and the projected flow-of-funds statement. Each of these may be constructed for several time periods—a short run, which includes time segments of up to one year, the intermediate span, which may range from one to five years, and the long run, which looks into horizons more distant than five years. The precision of each statement usually varies inversely with the nearness of time, with detailed statements correlated with short runs and vice versa.

This chapter discusses three facets of profit planning and control deferred until this point. These facets are presented in the following order:

[1] Neil W. Chamberlain, *The Firm: Micro-Economic Planning and Action* (New York: McGraw-Hill Book Co., Inc., 1962), p. 249.

416

1. Completion of the profit plan.
2. Analysis, evaluation, and choice among alternatives in developing a profit plan.
3. Implementation of the completed profit plans.

COMPLETION OF THE ANNUAL PROFIT PLAN

The development of an annual profit plan ends with the planned income statement, the balance sheet and the planned statement of changes in financial position. These three statements summarize and integrate the details of plans developed by management for the period. They also report the primary impacts of the detailed plans on the financial characteristics of the firm.

At this point in profit planning, the budget director has a heavy responsibility. Up to this point, aside from designing and improving the overall system, the budget director has been described as an advisor to the various executives and supervisors to help develop plans for their particular areas of responsibility. Now the parts must be put together as a complete profit plan, and this is the responsibility of the budget director. Other essential subbudgets not discussed earlier are:

1. Planned cost of goods manufactured.
2. Planned cost of goods sold.
3. Planned income statements.
4. Planned statement of changes in financial position.
5. Planned balance sheet.

Each of the subbudgets, which have been only *tentatively* approved, must be combined by the budget director to compute *net income*, assets, liabilities, and owners' equity. These are the final tests of the detailed plans. The last section of this chapter demonstrates the combining process for Superior Manufacturing Company.

Before distributing the completed profit plan, it is generally desirable to recast certain budget schedules (some of which were previously illustrated as worksheets) so that technical accounting mechanics and jargon are avoided as much as possible.

The redesigned budget schedules should be assembled in a logical order, reproduced, and distributed before the first day of the upcoming budget period. When assembled and bound, the completed plan is variously referred to as *the profit plan, the planning budget, the plan, the master budget, the forecast budget, the financial budget, the operating plan,* or *the plan of operations.* Throughout this text the phrases short-term, and long-term, profit plans have been used.

The current trend is to drop the word "budget" entirely and to use instead such terms as *the profit plan* or simply *the plan*. There are good psychological reasons for this trend. Over the years, many people have tended to associate the word "budget" with restrictions, pressure devices, and limitations. This unfavorable attitude can be traced to a misunderstanding of the purposes and to misuses of budgets. Aside from these considerations, terms such as *profit plan* are more descriptive of the characteristics and objectives of comprehensive profit planning and control.

In arranging the schedules to be included in the final profit plan, the budget director should consider management preferences, as well as the principles of good presentation. No one arrangement is preferable in all situations. As a general rule, however, it is desirable to place the *planned financial statements* ahead of the supporting subbudgets such as the sales, expense, cash, and capital additions budgets. Arrangement should re-emphasize responsibility centers.

The budget director should have a limited number of copies of the profit plan appropriately bound. It may be desirable to use loose-leaf binding, because the budget should be viewed as a flexible document to be revised as circumstances warrant. Revision may involve one or more subbudgets, depending upon the nature of the revision.

The profit plan completion date is important. Issuance of a profit plan after the beginning of the budget period is one sure way of destroying much of the budget potential. Timely completion of the planning budget suggests the need for a *budget calendar* (see Chapter 4).

CONSIDERATION OF ALTERNATIVES IN DEVELOPING THE PROFIT PLAN

The *mechanical aspects* of profit plan development might suggest that once the sales executives develop the sales plan this can be followed by simple clerical activities that produce the production, inventory, purchases, labor, materials, and other components of the profit plan. Throughout the preceding discussions we have emphasized the fundamental importance of decision-making, policy formulation, and consideration of alternative actions throughout the planning process. We have emphasized the importance of participation by all members of the management in providing the *decisional inputs*. The development of the decisional inputs and the preparation of a subbudget by the manager of each responsibility center is the heart of a comprehensive profit planning and control program.

Management choices from numerous alternatives are essential to building a realistic plan of operations. References were made throughout the preceding chapters to *tentative approval* of the various subbudgets by the executive committee and the president. To make these tentative decisions, there must be a step-by-step consideration of various alternatives. Tentative approvals are given in most cases because the full impact of a selected alternative may not be realized until the profit plan has developed into the financial statements.

The buildup of a profit plan normally will not, and probably should not, involve a smooth flow of planning and decision-making from one phase to another. Subsequent development of other parts of the plan may indicate that a previously selected alternative should be discarded and other alternatives considered. Through this process of building, tearing down, and rebuilding, a realistic profit plan usually can be developed. It frequently happens that a plan almost completed has to be torn down, restudied, and rebuilt. This may be the result, for example, of an unsatisfactory profit margin, return on investment ratio, or cash flow. Management then must face one or more factors that might "turn the plan around." Of course, to be realistic, there may be circumstances where a *loss* must be planned. Various procedures such as ratio analysis, breakeven analysis, differential cost analysis, and return on investment analysis should be used to help management *test* and *evaluate* proposed courses of action.

Numerous situations have been cited to show how management, in the process of developing the profit plan is faced with alternative decisions. Some illustrations demonstrated how to evaluate alternatives and select from among them. Other important areas where planning alternatives must be considered and choices made are:

1. **Sales Prices to be Budgeted**—Management must set pricing policy and estimate the quantities of gools that can be sold at given prices. Evaluation of such factors as product cost, the market, economic trends, and competitor prices is essential in selecting the best price.

2. **General Advertising Policies**—Financial limitation of advertising expenditures—local versus national, and product versus institutional advertising—represents areas where alternative choices must be made early in the planning process.

3. **Sales Territory and Sales Force Expansion or Contraction**—Decisions in these areas should be based on careful studies of market potentials either by company personnel or outside professional help.

4. **Sales Mix**—Sales mix refers to the relative sales emphasis to be given the various products sold by the concern. The relative profitability of products must be assessed because the more profitable products should be given more emphasis. These decisions must be based necessarily upon cost analysis by product. In this respect, it is important that the product costs be accurate. Fixed and variable cost identification, as in the variable budgets,

provides a valuable tool for differential cost analysis by product and, in addition, makes possible a more accurate allocation of indirect costs to products. Cost allocation generally can be more accurate, because fixed costs ordinarily should be allocated on a different basis than variable costs.

5.   Balance between Stable Production and Inventory Levels— Mathematical models and computer applications are particularly useful in selecting the most desirable alternative in this critical area (see Chapter 5).

6.   Research Expenditures—This is one of the alternative decision areas that must be based upon long-range objectives, judgment, competition, and the ability of the concern to finance research.

7.   Capital Additions—Cost and income analyses, evaluation of cost and income differentials, and discounted cash flow computations represent the principal considerations for sound capital budgeting decisions.

8.   Testing Alternative Decisions—Perhaps the principal aspect of alternative decisions has to do with evaluating the probable profit result *while the profit plan is being built*, rather than waiting until the budgeted financial statements are finally determined.

Breakeven analysis represents a technique that is especially valuable for testing alternative decisions. It facilitates evaluation of the effect of varying combinations of (1) sales prices, (2) sales volumes, (3) sales mix, (4) fixed costs, and (5) variable costs. The effect on profits, breakeven points, and margins of safety can be evaluated in general terms concurrent with planning budget development. The application of breakeven analysis is discussed in the next chapter. Also, variable budgets should be completed early in the budget development period so they can be used to evaluate the concurrent impacts of the subbudgets on profit.

To illustrate, assume that the sales plan, production plan, materials budget, direct labor budget, and the variable expense budgets have been tentatively approved. From these data for Superior Manufacturing Company, the *probable profit* is readily determinable as shown in Illustration 42. Note in particular the utilization of the variable budget *totals* to derive the summary expense allowances. Trace the data back to the original sources as indicated in the source column. This procedure illustrates another important use of variable budgets to test alternatives. In the absence of variable expense budgets, estimating expense allowances at *various volumes* would present a burdensome task. Illustration 42 shows additional columns frequently developed to estimate profit for a series of assumed sales levels (for another example, see Illustration 38, Chapter 2).

The analysis in Illustration 42 may also be presented graphically as a breakeven chart (see Chapter 14). As a matter of fact, many budget directors

ILLUSTRATION 42. Worksheet to Estimate Probable Profit
Superior Manufacturing Company

SOURCE SCHEDULE NO.				
1	Sales			$6,095,000
	Costs for year:			
29	Direct material	$1,416,600		
30	Direct labor	1,752,000		
	Manufacturing overhead:			
42 and 31	Dept. 1 ($14,000 × 12) + ($31. × 4,880)	319,280		
42 and 31	Dept. 2 ($1,960 × 12) + ($3. × 1,920)	29,280		
42 and 31	Dept. 3 ($4,180 × 12) + ($11. × 4,880)	103,840		
41 and 31	General and Administrative			
	($8,760 × 12) + ($1.00 × 11,680)	116,800		
41 and Estimate	Power ($6,700 × 12) + ($1.48 × 20,000)	110,000		
41 and Estimate	Repair ($720 × 12) + ($.34 × 4,000)	10,000		
Estimated	Building services	90,000		
	Total	$ 779,200		
Estimated	Add inventory decrease	106,800	4,054,600	
	Indicated gross margin		2,040,400	
	Distribution costs:			
21 and 43	Southern district			
	($9,400 × 12) + ($5.748 × 21,200)	234,656		
21 and 43	Eastern district			
	($12,780 × 12) + ($5.505 × 29,070)	313,391		
21 and 43	Western district			
	($4,750 × 12) + ($5.442 × 10,680)	115,120		
21 and 43	General sales overhead			
	($19,295 × 12) + ($1.063 × 60,950)	296,330		
Estimated	Building services	30,000		
	Total	$ 989,497		
	Administrative costs:			
21 and 44	Administrative Department			
	($6,340 × 12) + ($.122 × 60,950)	83,516		
21 and 44	Accounting department			
	($4,400 × 12) + ($.02 × 60,950)	54,020		
21 and 44	Treasurer's Department			
	($3,310 × 12) + ($.27 × 60,950)	56,177		
Estimated	Building services	30,000		
	Total	$ 223,713	1,213,210	
	Estimated operating profit		$ 827,190	

maintain informal *planning worksheets* and *breakeven graphs* throughout the profit planning process. These are continually revised as the numerous sub-budgets are received from the various executives and supervisors—each one's effect on the final income figure is tested. This informal step-by-step pretesting may save considerable revision later.

Returning to Illustration 42, at this point the indicated operating profit of $827,190 should be evaluated to determine whether it is satisfactory in terms of:

1. Past profit trends.
2. Long-range profit objectives.
3. Industry high and average profits.
4. Retun on investment and earnings per share objectives.
5. Breakeven analysis.

If profit is satisfactory, preparation of the profit plan can be continued. If the profit is unsatisfactory, management should re-examine the alternatives.

Ratios also may be very useful in testing alternative decisions. The *ratio test* compares selected ratios, based on budget data, with the past ratios (1) for the firm, (2) for the industry (when available) and (3) with the objectives of the company. Any significant difference between the ratio reflected by the budget data and the trend should be carefully investigated to determine the cause since the basic ratios of a company often are difficult to change in the short run. If the cause can be related to specific planning decisions, policies, or assumptions that influence projected results, the ratio has passed the ratio test. On the other hand, should there be no identifiable factors that would affect the planned results, the assumption should be that some facet of the plan is wrong.

The budget director should apply the ratio test step-by-step during development of the profit plan. When the test shows a particular ratio to be out of line with company objectives the executive responsible for the particular projection should be informed so that he can study the problem. Should a preferable alternative develop, action can be taken to revise all affected aspects of the plan. The ratio tests are generally represented by an informal worksheet maintained by the budget director. One type of worksheet adapted from the procedures of a well-managed company is shown in Illustration 43. Although in this company the budget director applies the tests using a total of sixty-three ratios, only three representative ratios related to operating profit are illustrated. We might note at this point that the ratio test is even better to evaluate the plausibility of the quantified results of *long-range planning* (see Illustration 13, Chapter 4).

ILLUSTRATION 43. Worksheet for Ratio Tests
Worksheet for Ratio Tests on 1977 Budget

ITEMS TESTED RATIO		HISTORICAL				ANNUAL PROFIT PLAN 1977	LONG-RANGE PROJECTION			
		1973	1974	1975	1976		1978	1979	1980	1981
Sales Ratios:										
Growth trend	%									
Operating Profit Ratios:										
Profit/sales		6.33	6.51	6.08	5.92	7.21*	6.20	6.20	6.40	6.40
Sales/investment		2.12	2.23	1.97	1.96	2.14	2.26	2.25	2.30	2.30
Return on investment		13.42	14.52	11.98	11.60	15.43*	14.01	13.95	14.72	14.72
Earnings per share										

*Ratio appears to be out of line; potentially indicates (1) an error or (2) a deficiency in planning. Projected profit primarily is suspect.

IMPLEMENTING THE PROFIT PLAN

In preceding chapters, considerable attention was given to the various segments of the annual profit plan, particularly for control purposes. The final test of whether the effort and cost in developing a profit plan are worthwhile is its usefulness to management; thus, some fundamental questions are posed. How should the plans be implemented? Should the plans be followed under all circumstances? Should the profit plan be used as a pressure device? How should it be used by the lower levels of management?

In the early chapters it was emphasized that a profit plan should represent potentially attainable goals yet the goals should present a challenge to the firm. The plan should be developed with the conviction that the enterprise is going to meet or exceed all major objectives. Participation enhances communication (both downward and upward). If this principle is to be effective, the various executives and supervisors should have a clear understanding of their responsibilities.

After approval of a profit plan, the next step is to distribute it to various segments of the firm. In Chapter 4, *distribution instructions* were illustrated as an important part of the *budget manual*. Recall that a limited number of copies of the *complete* profit plan should be prepared. The copies of the complete plan should be distributed to the members of executive management. Normally, distribution of the complete plan should be limited to vice presidents and to the heads of certain staff groups. The guiding principle in establishing the distribution policy might be expressed to provide one copy to each member of the management team according to their overall responsibilities, taking into account the problem of *security*. Some companies have discovered that a copy of their profit plan found its way into the hands of unauthorized parties, a competitor, for example. Most companies number each copy of the complete profit plan and keep a record of its distribution. At year end the copies are returned to the budget director for destruction.

The distribution policy should allow distribution of *parts*, or segments, of the profit plan to middle and lower management. For example, a sales district supervisor would not be given a copy of the entire budget, but should receive those parts that apply to his particular responsibility, such as the sales budget, expense budget, and advertising budget for his district. In preceding discussions we suggested that the budget format should coordinate with related segments, but at the same time the various subbudgets should be complete and stand alone.

After distribution of the profit plan, a series of *profit plan conferences* should be held. The top executives discuss comprehensively the plans, expectations, and steps in implementation. At this top-level meeting the importance of *action*, *flexibility* (see Chapter 19), and *continuous control* may well be emphasized. In particular, it must be realized by each manager that the budget is a *tool* for their use. The profit plan, no matter how well designed and how carefully drawn, cannot *manage*; in the final analysis people, not budgets (or other similar tools), perform the management functions. Use of the profit plan as a guide to action and performance, directed toward attaining or bettering the goals quantified in the annual profit plan requires continuous management effort and attention.

Similar conferences should be conducted until all levels of management are reached. Each executive and supervisor must clearly understand his particular responsibilities. These conferences should induce "profit awareness" throughout management and, if conducted properly, will tend to ensure active support for the objectives. Basically this is a phase of communication from the top down—a generally neglected phase in management.

The profit plan provides the manager of each responsibility center an approved operating plan for his center. For example, the advertising director has an approved advertising plan related to company objectives. Within this plan he can make decisions from day to day and month to month to execute the advertising function. Similarly, the financial executive has information concerning such things as expected cash receipts, cash disbursements, and capital additions. Thus the planning budget becomes the basis for current operations and exerts considerable coordinating and controlling effects.

Performance must be measured and reported to management. Execution of the plan is assured through control. Procedures must be established so that accomplishment, or failure, is immediately known. On this basis action can be taken to correct or minimize any undesirable effects. Short-term performance reporting is essential. For example, one facet in the control of sales is a comparison of actual sales with planned sales by areas of responsibility. Such a comparison at the end of the year would be of little value, because it is then too late to take effective action. On the other hand, daily, weekly, or even monthly sales reports may serve as a basis for timely action by the management action. If January sales are below the quota reflected in the sales budget, management should determine the reasons. It may be that the condition is due to circumstances over which the management has no control and little can be done to compensate for it. On the other hand, it may be that management can correct the condition, or action may be taken to increase the sales volume beyond budget figures for subsequent months of the year. It is important that management know about the trouble spots as they occur so that immediate attention can be given to them. Actual figures standing alone do not indicate weak spots; they must be compared with a standard (budget) to be properly evaluated. Chapter 15 is devoted to a discussion of performance reporting to management.

One key aspect of budget implementation is the principle of *flexibility*. To view the profit plan as an inflexible blueprint of operations is to invite trouble. Obviously, it is impossible during the planning phase to anticipate all contingencies; each day may present contingencies not anticipated in the plans. Therefore, current adjustments must be made in operating plans despite the original budget. The budget should not be viewed as a restrictive influence but rather as a specification of the goals of the entity. Certainly every advantage should be taken as it arises despite its not having been anticipated in the budget. Taking advantage of favorable opportunities as they arise is a primary responsibility of the management.

A budget program viewed and administered in a sophisticated way does not hamper or restrict management; instead, it provides definite goals around which day-to-day and month-to-month decisions are made. It aids effective implementation of the exception principle discussed in Chapter 2. Flexibility in the use and application of both the profit plan and the variable budgets also were considered in detail in most of the other chapters. Flexibility in budget application is essential, and it increases the probabilities of achieving or bettering the objectives as laid down (also see Chapter 19).

DEVELOPMENT OF THE BUDGETED FINANCIAL STATEMENTS ILLUSTRATED

To illustrate development of the *planned financial statements* and completion of the short-range profit plan in a typical situation, return to Superior Manufacturing Company. We strongly recommend that the student return to the appropriate subbudgets and trace the development of the following statements for Superior Manufacturing Company (note that the "Ref." column on the schedules provides tracing data).

SCHEDULE NO.	DESIGNATION
58	Estimated cost of goods manufactured—detailed.
59	Estimated cost of goods manufactured—summary.
60	Worksheet—cost of goods sold and finished goods inventory.
61	Budgeted cost of goods sold—detailed.
62	Budgeted cost of goods sold—summary.
63	Finished goods inventory budget.
64	Budgeted income statement by time periods.
65	Budgeted income statement by sales districts (responsibility).
66	Budgeted income statement by product.
67	Budget worksheet (for income statement and balance sheet).
68	Budgeted balance sheet—January.
69	Budgeted changes in working capital.
70	Budgeted statement of changes in financial position.

To develop the budgeted financial statements, the first logical step for Superior is preparation of the *estimated cost of goods manufactured*. Budgets for raw materials (Schedule 28), direct labor (Schedule 30), factory overhead applied (Schedule 36), and production (Schedule 22), together with work in process inventory provide data that may be assembled in a schedule of cost of goods manufactured. This procedure is illustrated in Schedule 58. Beginning work in process inventories (January 1, 1977) were assumed to be as follows:

Product X—No work in process inventory throughout the year.
Product Y—10,000 units valued at $13,800. (This inventory is Department 3 and remains relatively constant throughout the year.)

Observe the division by product and by time periods. The cost of goods manufactured is summarized in Schedule 59.

Budgeted cost of goods sold may be developed next from the data on cost of goods manufactured and finished goods inventories. Superior Manufacturing Company uses first-in, first-out in pricing issues of finished goods. To compute cost of sales by sales district, assume that withdrawals from initial inventories are in the ratio of district *unit* sales to total unit sales for each period. Initial inventories (January 1, 1977) of finished goods are estimated to be:

	PRODUCT X	PRODUCT Y
Units	240,000	100,000
Valuation	$806,400	$138,000

Cost of goods sold is developed by product, by time period, and by sales district. A worksheet (Schedule 60) is used for this purpose. Detailed results are shown in Schedule 61 (budgeted cost of good sold) and in summary in Schedule 62.

Schedule 23, Chapter 6, illustrated the *finished goods inventory budget*. At that point *units only* were known. Data developed in Schedule 60 (budget worksheet) make possible the completion of the finished goods inventory budget, which is illustrated in Schedule 63.

At this point the compilation of the budgeted income statements (Schedules 64, 65, and 66) assembles appropriate estimates from schedules already developed.

The budgeted balance sheet may be developed directly from prior schedules much like the income statement. The budgeted balance sheet requires the application of the cash budget, capital additions budget, and other budgets to the estimated balances in the real accounts at the beginning of the budget year. Thus, the process is more involved than is the development of the income statements. Although it is possible to develop the balance sheet directly, it is usually desirable to set up a special worksheet for this purpose. Such a worksheet for Superior Manufacturing Company is illus-

SCHEDULE 58. Superior Manufacturing Company
Estimated Cost of Goods Manufactured—Detailed
For the Year Ending December 31, 1977

	REF.	ANNUAL TOTAL	FIRST QUARTER JANUARY	FIRST QUARTER FEBRUARY	FIRST QUARTER MARCH	QUARTERS FIRST	QUARTERS SECOND	QUARTERS THIRD	QUARTERS FOURTH
Product X:									
Materials used	28	$1,156,600	$ 85,400	$ 97,600	$ 97,600	$280,600	$288,000	$276,000	$ 312,000
Direct labor	30	1,440,000	105,000	120,000	120,000	345,000	360,000	345,000	390,000
Prime cost		2,596,600	190,400	217,600	217,600	625,600	648,000	621,000	702,000
Overhead applied	36	633,600	46,200	52,800	52,800	151,800	158,400	151,800	171,600
Cost of goods manufactured		3,230,200	236,600	270,400	270,400	777,400	806,400	772,800	873,600
Units produced	22	960,000	70,000	80,000	80,000	230,000	240,000	230,000	260,000
Unit cost		$3.38	$3.38	$3.38	$3.38	$3.38	$3.36	$3.36	$3.36
Product Y:									
Materials used	28	$ 260,000	$ 17,000	$ 18,000	$ 19,000	$ 54,000	$70,000	$ 63,500	$ 72,500
Direct labor	30	312,000	20,400	21,600	22,800	64,800	84,000	76,200	87,000
Prime cost		572,000	37,400	39,600	41,800	118,800	154,000	139,700	159,500
Overhead applied	36	145,600	9,520	10,080	10,640	30,240	39,200	35,560	40,600
Cost of goods manufactured		717,600	46,920	49,680	52,440	149,040	193,200	175,260	200,100
Units produced	22	520,000	34,000	36,000	38,000	108,000	140,000	127,000	145,000
Unit cost		$1.38	$1.38	$1.38	$1.38	$1.38	$1.38	$1.38	$1.38
All products:									
Materials used	28	$1,416,600	$102,400	$115,600	$116,600	$334,600	$358,000	$339,500	$ 384,500
Direct labor	30	1,752,000	125,400	141,600	142,800	409,800	444,000	421,200	477,000
Prime cost		3,168,600	227,800	257,200	259,400	744,400	802,000	760,700	861,500
Overhead applied	36	779,200	55,720	62,880	63,440	182,040	197,600	187,360	212,200
Total manufacturing cost		$3,947,800	$283,520	$320,080	$322,840	$926,440	$999,600	$948,060	$1,073,700
Add initial work in process inventory		13,800	13,800	13,800	13,800	13,800	13,800	13,800	13,800
Deduct ending work in process inventory		(13,800)	(13,800)	(13,800)	(13,800)	(13,800)	(13,800)	(13,800)	(13,800)
Cost of goods manufactured		$3,947,800	$283,520	$320,080	$322,840	$926,440	$999,600	$948,060	$1,073,700

SCHEDULE 59. Superior Manufacturing Company

Estimated Cost of Goods Manufactured—Summary

For the Year Ending December 31, 1977

		ANNUAL	1ST QUARTER			QUARTERS			
	REF.	TOTAL	JANUARY	FEBRUARY	MARCH	FIRST	SECOND	THIRD	FOURTH
Product X:									
Cost of goods manufactured	58	$3,230,200	$236,600	$270,400	$270,400	$777,400	$806,400	$772,800	$ 873,600
Units produced	22	960,000	70,000	80,000	80,000	230,000	240,000	230,000	260,000
Unit cost	58	$3.38	$3.38	$3.38	$3.38	$3.38	$3.36	$3.36	$3.36
Product Y:									
Cost of goods manufactured	58	$ 717,600	$ 46,920	$ 49,680	$ 52,440	$149,040	$193,200	$175,260	$ 200,100
Units produced	22	520,000	34,000	36,000	38,000	108,000	140,000	127,000	145,000
Unit cost	58	$1.38	$1.38	$1.38	$1.38	$1.38	$1.38	$1.38	$1.38
All products:									
Cost of goods manufactured	58	$3,947,800	$283,520	$320,080	$322,840	$926,440	$999,600	$948,060	$1,073,700

SCHEDULE 60. Superior Manufacturing Company

Budget Worksheet—Cost of Goods Sold and Finished
Goods Inventory
(First-In, First-Out)
For the Year Ending December 31, 1977

| | TOTAL | | | SALES DISTRICTS | | | | | |
| | | | | SOUTHERN | | EASTERN | | WESTERN | |
	UNITS	UNIT COST	COST	UNITS	COST	UNITS	COST	UNITS	COST
Product X:									
January									
Initial inventory	240,000	$3.36	$ 806,400						
Production	70,000	3.38	236,600						
Total	310,000		$1,043,000						
Sales at cost	85,000	3.36	285,600	30,000	$ 100,800	40,000	$ 134,400	15,000	$ 50,400
Inventory	155,000	3.36							
	70,000	3.38	757,400						
February production	80,000	3.38	270,400						
Total	155,000	3.36							
	150,000	3.38	$1,027,800						
Sales at cost	90,000	3.36	302,400	35,000	117,600	45,000	151,200	10,000	33,600
Inventory	65,000	3.36							
	150,000	3.38	725,400						
March production	80,000	3.38	270,400						
Total	65,000	3.36							
	230,000	3.38	$ 995,800						

| | TOTAL | | | SALES DISTRICTS | | | | | |
| | | | | SOUTHERN | | EASTERN | | WESTERN | |
	UNITS	UNIT COST	COST	UNITS	COST	UNITS	COST	UNITS	COST
Sales at cost	65,000	3.36	218,400	20,526*	68,967	34,211	114,949	10,263	34,484
	30,000	3.38	101,400	9,474	32,022	15,789	53,367	4,737	16,011
Inventory	200,000	3.38	676,000						
2nd Quarter production	240,000	3.36	806,400						
Total	200,000	3.38							
	240,000	3.36	$1,482,400						
Sales at cost	200,000	3.38	676,000	69,231†	234,000	103,846	351,000	26,923	91,000
	60,000	3.36	201,600	20,769	69,784	31,154	104,677	8,077	27,139
Inventory	180,000	3.36	604,800						
3rd Quarter production	230,000	3.36	772,800						
Total	410,000	3.36	$1,377,600						
Sales at cost	190,000	3.36	638,400	65,000	218,400	90,000	302,400	35,000	117,600
Inventory	220,000	3.36	739,200						
4th Quarter production	260,000	3.36	873,600						
Total	480,000	3.36	$1,612,800						
Sales at cost	280,000	3.36	940,800	90,000	302,400	140,000	470,400	50,000	168,000
Inventory	200,000	3.36	672,000						
Total sales at cost	1,000,000		$3,364,600	340,000	$1,143,973	500,000	$1,682,393	160,000	$533,234
Product Y:									
January									
Initial inventory	100,000	$1.38	$ 138,000						
Production	34,000	1.38	46,920						
Total	134,000		$ 184,920						
Sales at cost	34,000	1.38	46,920	15,000	$ 20,700	11,000	$ 15,180	8,000	$ 11,040

SCHEDULE 60 / (continued)

| | TOTAL | | | SALES DISTRICTS | | | | | |
| | | | | SOUTHERN | | EASTERN | | WESTERN | |
	UNITS	UNIT COST	COST	UNITS	COST	UNITS	COST	UNITS	COST
Inventory	100,000	1.38	$ 138,000						
February production	36,000	1.38	49,680						
Total	136,000		$ 187,680						
Sales at cost	41,000	1.38	56,580	16,000	$ 22,080	14,000	$ 19,320	11,000	$ 15,180
Inventory	95,000	1.38	131,100						
March production	38,000	1.38	52,440						
Total	133,000		$ 183,540						
Sales at cost	45,000	1.38	62,100	19,000	26,220	15,000	20,700	11,000	15,180
Inventory	88,000	1.38	121,440						
2nd Quarter production	140,000	1.38	193,200						
Total	228,000		$ 314,640						
Sales at cost	135,000	1.38	186,300	55,000	75,900	45,000	62,100	35,000	48,300
Inventory	93,000	1.38	128,340						
3rd Quarter production	127,000	1.38	175,260						
Total	220,000		$ 303,600						
Sales at cost	95,000	1.38	131,100	40,000	55,200	35,000	48,300	20,000	27,600
Inventory	125,000	1.38	172,500						
4th Quarter production	145,000	1.38	200,100						
Total	270,000		$ 372,600						
Sales at cost	150,000	1.38	207,000	65,000	89,700	50,000	69,000	35,000	48,300
Inventory	120,000	1.38	165,600						
Total sales at cost	500,000		$ 690,000	210,000	$ 289,800	170,000	$ 234,600	120,000	$165,600

Computations:

$*$ March sales costing \$3.36 $\times$ $\dfrac{\text{March sales in dist.—Sch. 5}}{\text{March total sales—Sch. 5}}$ = Allocation to district $\dfrac{30,000}{95,000} \times \dfrac{65,000}{1}$ = 20.526

$\dagger$ $\dfrac{90,000}{260,000} \times \dfrac{200,000}{1}$ = 69,231

SCHEDULE 61. Superior Manufacturing Company
Budgeted Cost of Goods Sold
For the Year Ending December 31, 1977

	REF.	TOTAL ALL DISTRICTS UNITS 21	COST 60	SOUTHERN DISTRICT UNITS 21	COST 60	EASTERN DISTRICT UNITS 21	COST 60	WESTERN DISTRICT UNITS 21	COST 60
Product X:									
January		85,000	$ 285,600	30,000	$ 100,800	40,000	$ 134,400	15,000	$ 50,400
February		90,000	302,400	35,000	117,600	45,000	151,200	10,000	33,600
March		95,000	319,800	30,000	100,989	50,000	168,316	15,000	50,495
Total 1st Quarter		270,000	907,800	95,000	319,389	135,000	453,916	40,000	134,495
2nd Quarter		260,000	877,600	90,000	303,785	135,000	455,677	35,000	118,138
3rd Quarter		190,000	638,400	65,000	218,400	90,000	502,400	35,000	117,600
4th Quarter		280,000	940,800	90,000	302,400	140,000	470,400	50,000	168,000
Total Product X		1,000,000	$3,364,600	340,000	$1,143,974	500,000	$1,682,393	160,000	$538,233
Product Y:									
January		34,000	$ 46,920	15,000	$ 20,700	11,000	$ 15,180	8,000	$ 11,040
February		41,000	56,580	16,000	22,080	14,000	19,320	11,000	15,180
March		45,000	62,100	19,000	26,220	15,000	20,700	11,000	15,180
Total 1st Quarter		120,000	165,600	50,000	69,000	40,000	55,200	30,000	41,400
2nd Quarter		135,000	186,300	55,000	75,900	45,000	62,100	35,000	48,300
3rd Quarter		95,000	131,100	40,000	55,200	35,000	48,300	20,000	27,600
4th Quarter		150,000	207,000	65,000	89,700	50,000	69,000	35,000	48,300
Total Product Y		500,000	$ 690,000	210,000	$ 289,800	170,000	$ 234,600	120,000	$165,600
All Products:									
January			$ 332,520		$ 121,500		$ 149,580		$ 61,440
February			358,980		139,680		170,520		48,780
March			381,900		127,209		189,016		65,675
Total 1st Quarter			1,073,400		388,389		509,116		175,895
2nd Quarter			1,063,900		379,685		517,777		166,438
3rd Quarter			769,500		273,600		350,700		145,200
4th Quarter			1,147,800		392,100		539,400		216,300
Total for year			$4,054,600		$1,433,774		$1,916,993		$703,833

SCHEDULE 62. Superior Manufacturing Company

Budgeted Cost of Goods Sold—Summary

For the Year Ending December 31, 1977

| | | TOTAL ALL DISTRICTS | | SALES DISTRICTS | | | | | |
| | | | | SOUTHERN | | EASTERN | | WESTERN | |
	REF.	UNITS	COST	UNITS	COST	UNITS	COST	UNITS	COST
Products:									
X	60	1,000,000	$3,364,600	340,000	$1,143,974	500,000	$1,682,393	160,000	$538,233
Y	60	500,000	690,000	210,000	289,800	170,000	234,600	120,000	165,600
Total Cost			$4,054,600		$1,433,774		$1,916,993		$703,833

SCHEDULE 63. Superior Manufacturing Company

Finished Goods Inventory Budget

For the Year Ending December 31, 1977

	TOTAL COST	PRODUCT X			PRODUCT Y		
		UNITS 23	UNIT COST 60	TOTAL COST	UNITS 23	UNIT COST 60	TOTAL COST
January 1, 1977	$944,400	240,000	$3.36	$806,400	100,000	$1.38	$138,000
January 31, 1977	895,400	225,000	*	757,400	100,000	1.38	138,000
February 28, 1977	856,400	215,000	†	725,400	95,000	1.38	131,100
March 31, 1977	797,440	200,000	3.38	676,000	88,000	1.38	121,440
End of 2nd Quarter	733,140	180,000	3.36	604,800	93,000	1.38	128,340
End of 3rd Quarter	911,700	220,000	3.36	739,200	125,000	1.38	172,500
End of 4th Quarter	837,600	200,000	3.36	672,000	120,000	1.38	165,600

*70,000 units at $3.38, and 155,000 units at $3.36.

†150,000 units at $3.38, and 65,000 units at $3.36.

SCHEDULE 64. Superior Manufacturing Company
Budgeted Income Statement—By Time Periods
For the Year Ending December 31, 1977

| | REF. | ANNUAL | FIRST QUARTER | | | | QUARTERS | | |
			JANUARY	FEBRUARY	MARCH	FIRST	SECOND	THIRD	FOURTH
Sales	21	$6,095,000	$500,400	$540,000	$574,100	$1,614,500	$1,595,000	$1,158,000	$1,727,500
Less cost of goods sold	61	4,054,600	332,520	358,980	381,900	1,073,400	1,063,900	769,500	1,147,800
Gross margin		2,040,400	167,880	181,020	192,200	541,100	531,100	388,500	579,700
Less:									
Selling expenses	39	989,497	82,109	84,608	86,769	253,486	251,915	222,977	261,119
Administative expenses	40	223,713	18,752	18,735	18,859	56,346	55,999	54,321	57,047
Totals		1,213,210	100,861	103,343	105,628	309,832	307,914	277,298	318,166
Operating profit		827,190	67,019	77,677	86,572	231,268	223,186	111,202	261,534
Add:									
Interest income	53	500	42	41	42	125	125	125	125
Other income	49	37,120	3,390	2,950	3,620	9,960	9,510	8,220	9,430
		864,810	70,451	80,668	90,234	241,353	232,821	119,547	271,089
Less interest expense	53	3,750	667	416	667	1,750	1,000	500	500
Profit before income tax		$ 861,060	$ 69,784	$ 80,252	$ 89,567	$ 239,603	$ 231,821	$ 119,047	$ 270,589
Per cent of sales		14.13	13.9	14.8	15.6	14.8	14.5	10.3	15.7
Federal income taxes	53	258,318							
Net income		$ 602,742							

SCHEDULE 65. **Superior Manufacturing Company**
Budgeted Income Statement—By Sales Districts
For the Year Ending December 31, 1977

	REF.	TOTAL	SALES DISTRICT		
			SOUTHERN	EASTERN	WESTERN
Sales	21	$6,095,000	$2,120,000	$2,907,000	$1,068,000
Cost of goods sold	61	4,054,600	1,433,773	1,916,993	703,834
Gross margin		2,040,400	686,227	990,007	364,166
District sales expenses	39	663,167	234,656	313,391	115,120
District direct operating profit		1,377,233	451,571	676,616	249,046
Per cent of net sales		22.6	21.3	23.3	23.3
Allocations:					
General sales overhead	39	296,330			
Administrative expenses	40	193,713			
Building services	32	60,000			
To be allocated		550,043	191,305	262,370	96,368
Allocation basis*			(34.78%)	(47.70%)	(17.52%)
District operating profit		827,190	$ 260,266	$ 414,246	$ 152,678
Per cent of net sales		13.57	12.3	14.2	14.3
Add net of other incomes and expenses	49 & 53	33,870			
Profit before income tax		861,060			
Federal income tax	53	258,318			
Net income		$ 602,742			

*On basis of net sales.

trated in Schedule 67. The worksheet is developed from the *estimated trial balance* as of December 31, 1976 as reflected in the first two columns of the budget worksheet. The reader is reminded that this trial balance (December 31, 1976) is needed *before* the end of the current operating period if the budget is to be completed and distributed before the beginning of the budget year. This requirement does not deter completion of the planning budget. The trial balance generally can be estimated with reasonable accuracy by the budget and accounting departments by using the November actual balance and the current December forecast. In some cases it becomes necessary to revise parts of the planning budget after initial distribution. This revision should be made if the estimated year-end trial balance is materially incorrect. Immaterial differences should cause no concern.

The resulting annual balance sheet for Superior Manufacturing Company was shown in Schedule 17 (Chapter 4). Monthly budgeted balance sheets may be prepared. Since they require little time to prepare, they may

SCHEDULE 66. Superior Manufacturing Company

Budgeted Income Statement—By Product
For the Year Ending December 31, 1977

	REF.	TOTAL	PRODUCT X	PRODUCT Y
Sales	21	$6,095,000	$5,066,000	$1,029,000
Cost of goods sold	61	4,054,600	3,364,600	690,000
Gross margin		2,040,400	1,701,400	339,000
Allocations:				
District sales expenses	39	663,167		
General sales overhead	39	296,330		
Administrative expenses	40	193,713		
Building services	32	60,000		
Total to be allocated		1,213,210	1,008,420	204,790
Allocation basis*			(83.12%)	(16.88%)
Operating profit		827,190	$ 692,980	$ 134,210
Per cent of sales		13.57	13.68	12.07
Add net of other incomes and	49&			
expenses	53	33,870		
Profit before income tax		861,060		
Federal income tax	53	258,318		
Net income		$ 602,742		

*On basis of net sales.

be justified. The January balance sheet is illustrated in Schedule 68. Note the contingent liability indicated in the footnote and the treatment of *manufacturing overhead, over- and under-applied* on the monthly balance sheet. The latter item does not appear on the annual balance sheet. Preparation of the monthly balance sheets may be facilitated through the use of a worksheet similar to Schedule 67.

Superior Manufacturing Company prepares an estimated statement of changes in financial position (working capital basis). The statement includes two parts:

1. Budgeted changer in working capital balances (Schedule 69). These data were taken directly from the worksheet, Schedule 67.
2. Budgeted flows of working capital (Schedule 70). Preparation of this statement is facilitated by a special worksheet similar to that illustrated in many accounting textbooks.[2]

[2] G. A. Welsch, C. T. Zlatkovich, and J. A. White, *Intermediate Accounting* (Homewood, Ill.: Richard D. Irwin, Inc., 1976), Chapter 21.

SCHEDULE 67. Superior Manufacturing Company
Budget Worksheet
For the Year Ending December 31, 1972

	TRIAL BALANCE DEC. 31, 1976		ENTRIES 1977 BUDGET		WORK IN PROCESS		PROFIT AND LOSS		BALANCE SHEET DEC. 31, 1977	
	Dr	Cr	Dr	Cr	Dr	Cr	Dr	Cr	Dr	Cr
Cash	$ 54,000		17-$6,133,006	17-$5,560,490					$ 626,516	
Accounts receivable	160,000		1-6,095,000	1-6,095,886 11-3,000					156,114	
Allowance for doubtful accounts		$ 9,000		9-12,190						$ 18,190
Raw material inventory	257,600		11-3,000 2-1,419,000	3-1,416,600					260,000	
Work in process inventory	13,800				$ 13,800	$ 13,800			13,800	
Finished goods inventory	944,400						$ 944,400	$ 837,600	837,600	
Prepaid insurance	2,532		15-22,788	5-3,600 6-3,036 9-960					17,724	
Supplies inventory	13,700		15-41,140	6-49,640					5,200	
Land	25,000								25,000	
Building, machinery and equipment	2,080,000		14-8,700						2,088,700	
Allowance for depreciation		443,380		5-60,000 6-19,560 8-600 9-4,200						527,740
Building fund	20,000		14-20,000 18-500						40,500	
Accounts payable		52,100	13-1,429,140	2-1,419,000						41,960
Audit fee payable		2,400	15-2,400	9-2,400						2,400
Accrued interest expense		7,000	15-8,000	19-2,750						1,750
Property taxes payable		4,982	15-4,982	5-2,400 6-4,164 9-720						7,284

SCHEDULE 67. (continued)

	TRIAL BALANCE DEC. 31, 1976		ENTRIES 1977 BUDGET		WORK IN PROCESS		PROFIT AND LOSS		BALANCE SHEET DEC. 31, 1977	
	Dr	Cr	Dr	Cr	Dr	Cr	Dr	Cr	Dr	Cr
Income taxes payable		279,400	15-279,400	20-258,318						258,318
Notes payable—Long-term		200,000	15-150,000							50,000
Common stock		2,000,000								2,000,000
Retained earnings		522,770	15-12,000							510,770
Premium on stock		50,000								50,000
	$3,571,032	$3,571,032								
Sales				1-6,095,000				6,095,000		
Raw material used			3-1,416,600		1,416,600					
Building services			5-150,000	7-150,000						
Factory overhead			6-689,200							
			7-90,000		779,200					
Direct labor			4-1,752,000		1,752,000					
			7-30,000							
Selling expenses			8-959,497				989,497			
			7-30,000							
Administrative expenses			9-193,713				223,713			
Interest expense			16-1,000				3,750			
			19-2,750							
Interest income				18-500				500		
Other income				12-37,120				37,120		
Income tax expense			20-258,318				258,318			
Cost of goods manufactured						3,947,800	3,947,800			
					$3,961,600	$3,961,600				
Net income							602,742			602,742
							602,742			
							$6,970,220	$6,970,220	$4,071,154	$4,071,154

SCHEDULE 68. Superior Manufacturing Company

Budgeted Balance Sheet—January*

For the Month Ending January 31, 1977

ASSETS

Current assets:			
Cash	$	$ 163,374	
Accounts receivable	157,793		
Less allowance for doubtful accounts	10,001	147,792	
Raw material inventory		253,100	
Work in process inventory		13,800	
Finished goods inventory		895,400	
Prepaid insurance		1,899	
Supplies inventory		13,457	1,488,822
Funds:			
Building fund			20,042
Fixed assets:			
Land		25,000	
Building	1,800,000		
Less allowance for depreciation	365,000	1,435,000	
Machinery and equipment	280,200		
Less allowance for depreciation	85,261	194,939	1,654,939
Deferred charges:			
Factory overhead under-applied			6,637
Total assets			$3,170,440

LIABILITIES AND CAPITAL

Current liabilities:			
Accounts payable	$	$ 32,630	$
Audit fee payable		2,600	
Property taxes payable		5,589	
Accrued interest expense		7,667	
Federal income taxes payable†		300,335	348,821
Fixed liabilities:			
Long-term notes payable			200,000
Capital:			
Common stock		2,000,000	
Premium on common stock		50,000	
Retained earnings	522,770		
Add January net income	48,849	571,619	2,621,619
Total liabilities and capital			$3,170,440

*See Schedule 17, page 122 for Annual Balance Sheet.

†Litigation currently in progress may result in payment of approximately $620,000 as an adjustment of prior years' federal income taxes.

SCHEDULE 69. Superior Manufacturing Company

Budgeted Changes in Working Capital Balances

For the Year Ending December 31, 1977

	BALANCES 1/1/77	BALANCES 12/31/77	WORKING CAPITAL INCREASE OR DECREASE*
Current assets:			
Cash	$ 54,000	$ 626,516	$572,516
Accounts receivable (net)	151,000	137,924	13,076*
Raw material inventory	257,600	260,000	2,400
Work in process inventory	13,800	13,800	—
Finished goods inventory	944,400	837,600	106,800*
Unexpired insurance	2,532	17,724	15,192
Supplies inventory	13,700	5,200	8,500*
Total current assets	$1,437,032	$1,898,764	$461,732
Current liabilities:			
Accounts payable	$ 52,100	$ 41,960	$ 10,140
Audit fee payable	2,400	2,400	—
Accrued interest expense	7,000	1,750	5,250
Property taxes payable	4,982	7,284	2,302*
Income taxes payable	279,400	258,318	21,082
Total current liabilities	$ 345,882	$ 311,712	$ 34,170
Working capital	$1,091,150	$1,587,052	$495,902

SCHEDULE 70. Superior Manufacturing Company

Budgeted Flows of Working Capital

For the Year Ending December 31, 1977

Working Capital provided:			
From operations:			
Net income		$602,742	
Add nonfund charges:			
Depreciation		84,360	
Total funds provided			$687,102
Working Capital Applied:			
Cash dividends paid		$ 12,000	
Cash transferred to building fund	$20,000		
Add interest credit	500	20,500	
Notes paid—long term		150,000	
Purchases of equipments and tools		8,700	
Total funds applied			$191,200
Budgeted increase in working capital			$495,902

After completion of these summary schedules, the annual profit plan is presented to the executive committee and then to the chief executive for approval. Upon final approval, the budget director reproduces it for distribution to specified executives.

DISCUSSION QUESTIONS

1. Why should planned financial statements be developed as a part of the annual profit plan?

2. Briefly, what should be the responsibility of the budget director in completing and assembling the components of the annual profit plan?

3. During the planning process, why should the various subbudgets usually be given tentative, rather than final, approval?

4. Explain the way that variable expense budgets may be used in "testing" the appropriateness of the profit plan during the process of its development rather than at the end of the planning process when the budgeted income statement, flow statement, and balance sheet are completed.

5. What is meant by the ratio test? Explain its applicability with respect to (a) development of the annual profit plan and (b) long-range planning.

6. The annual profit plan should be completed prior to the beginning of the period for which the budget is being made. To complete it, the trial balance as of the end of the current year is needed before that period ends. What can be done to resolve this apparent inconsistency?

7. Outline the distribution of the annual profit plan in a typical situation.

8. Why should the annual profit plan and the variable expense budgets be assembled under separate covers?

9. Discuss the advantages of two alternatives concerning distribution of the annual profit plan: Alternative 1—distribute through company mail. Alternative 2—distribute through line channels supplemented with conferences.

10. Why is it essential that management apply the annual profit plan in a flexible manner?

CASE 13-1
Superior—Distribution

The annual profit plan for 1977 for Superior Manufacturing Company was completed on December 17, 1976 as illustrated in the present and preceding chapters. The president and his assistant are developing a distribution policy for the plan and security precautions to be observed. Assume you are his assistant, and you have been asked to give him your recommendations on the following:

a. General:

   1. What responsibilities should be assigned for distribution of the profit plan?

   2. How should it be distributed?

   3. On what date should it be distributed?

   4. What special management activities should be initiated for the distribution?

b. What should be included in the packages for the various managers? In response to this problem, the president has requested you to "indicate for each of the" following groups the package by schedule numbers (one through seventy). Thus, you are to list the following and indicate after each the appropriate schedule numbers:

   1. President.

   2. Vice presidents.

   3. Controller.

   4. Treasurer.

   5. Sales district supervisor (list each district separately).

   6. Factory supervisors (list each department separately).

   7. Other individuals or groups (list each).

   8. Schedules not to be distributed.

You should review the organization chart for the company, the budget manual, and each of the seventy schedules previously illustrated to develop your recommendations.

CASE 13-2

Napko Company

Napko Company is currently developing a budget for 19A. Certain plans developed to date are given below.

1. Budgeted cost of goods manufactured.

	PRODUCT A	
	UNITS	UNIT COST
January	20,000	$1.00
February	20,000	1.00
March	21,000	1.00
April	23,000	1.00
May	23,000	1.00
June	23,000	1.00

2. Sales budget (units).

	PRODUCT A	
	DISTRICT 1	DISTRICT 2
January	10,000	7,000
February	12,000	8,000
March	13,000	11,000
April	15,000	12,000
May	14,000	11,000
June	9,000	8,000

3. Beginning inventories: product A, 20,000 units @ $.90. The company uses fifo.

Required:

a. Prepare a worksheet to compute cost of goods sold by product, by sales district. Assume shipments to districts from stock to be in the ratio of budgeted sales on a unit basis.

b. Prepare a budgeted cost of goods sold by product, district, and time.

c. Prepare a budget of finished goods inventories by product and time period.

d. Indicate the sources of the input budget data utilized in requirements (a), (b), and (c). Is the assumption in one sound? Why?

CASE 13-3
Monroe Company

Monroe Company manufactures a medium-priced line of furniture that is sold in a four-state area. Twenty-one different items are manufactured, and there are several variations in about one-half of the items. For example, there are four different styles of "TV-Lounger" chairs, although they are all built around the same chassis. The variations are principally in the type and design of the covering used on the chairs, although one type utilizes a more expensive material for the padding.

The company has been in operation for more than twenty years and is owned by thirty-one stockholders. The board of directors, consisting of four members of the active management and three other stockholders, meets monthly to review operations and to formulate basic policy. Since World War II the company has experienced a steady growth in sales volume, having increased approximately 180 percent to an annual volume of about 18 million dollars.

For several years the company has budgeted sales and, to a limited extent, the cash position. During the past year a complete profit plan was used for the first time. The management was generally pleased with the results despite the fact that some aspects of the plan appeared to have been unrealistic. During the year there had been numerous suggestions that some part of the budget be revised. The president had taken the posision that no changes should be made in the plan of operations under any circumstances.

This policy caused some concern especially when the monthly performance reports were distributed.

The budget for the coming year has just been completed and is being considered by the executive committee (composed of the four top operating executives who were also on the board of directors). The company followed what they considered good budget procedure in bringing intermediate members of the management into the budget planning activities. It appeared that these supervisors were quite interested in the program although they were frank to admit that they needed to know more about the whole picture.

The executive committee first considered the sales budget, which had been discussed previously by them and tentatively approved. In view of the experience during the past several years, it was generally agreed that the sales budget was realistic. The inventory policy seemed sound, consequently there were only a few minor questions about the production budget. The expense budgets were considered next. At this stage of the discussions Ray Crandall, the executive in charge of manufacturing, remarked that "the production budget looks OK; however, these expense budgets still bother me as they did last year. My supervisors who worked on them have recommended that our revision policy be relaxed. Once we set the budget there appears to be an inflexible policy that it cannot be changed. It seems to me that we should establish a more flexible policy on this matter. Now as to production, we can plan it on a week-to-week basis; the production budget is merely a guide. But for expenses the budget is the master." "Well, Ray, we have held the line on all revisions (and not only expense) in the past year because requests for budget changes can very quickly become a habit; every time someone falls down on the job we get a request for a change in the budget. Before long the budget means nothing, particularly since some supervisors can anticipate an unfavorable report of their operations and, for self-protection, request a budget change before the report is prepared. We have operated under the concept that we will build a good sound plan and that we should know where and when we fall down. As top management, we need a clear-cut plan with some force behind it; we need to know where we are heading. If we continually change the budget, our plan becomes so vague and changeable that it will be of little use to us. If we keep changing our goals, we will lose sight of where we should be going; in fact we will be wandering in the dark just as if we had no plan. Besides we can't be revising the budget at every whipstitch; we have other things to do," replied the president, Harry Rapides. "What do you think, Rich?" "I'm not sure just what we should set as policy on this matter, Harry," replied Glen Richards, the executive in charge of sales. "We spend a lot of time developing our budget; obviously we can't foresee all events and conditions; yet we can't be changing our plans all the time. If conditions get too far from that anticipated in our budget, comparisons won't mean much. If we are willing to look carefully at the variations to determine those causes beyond our control and those due to inefficiency, we might get along without too much revision." Benny Hughes, the executive in charge of finance and accounting, had responsibility for coordinating the budget activities; consequently, he had very definite ideas about the matter. He observed that "We should be very reluctant to change the budget; only when major events that were unforeseen occur should we consider revision." Mr. Rapides, noting that it was about lunch time, stated: "Let's knock off until tomorrow at 2:00. At that time let's get together and agree on a basic policy relative to budget revision for the coming year. Remember we are experimenting; we can always change the policy for the next year. In the meantime, I would like for each of you to do some serious thinking on the matter."

Required:

What policy would you recommend for this situation relative to budget revision? Provide the basis for your recommendations.

CASE 13-4
Central Company

The executive committee of Central Company has had one meeting to discuss the sales budget proposed by the sales division. During the meeting there was considerable discussion concerning potential profits. Profits for the past several years have been rather low, averaging 4 percent of sales, whereas the industry average is 6 percent. Tentative planning data already developed are as follows:

1. Annual sales projection:

DISTRICT	AMOUNT
1	$6,000,000
2	4,000,000

2. Raw material cost averages 21 percent of sales.
3. Direct labor cost averages 30.6 percent of sales.
4. Variable budget totals:

	FIXED PER MONTH	VARIABLE
Producing Dept. 1	$50,000	$2.00 per 100 direct machine hours
Producing Dept. 2	40,000	$1.00 per 100 direct machine hours
Service Dept. 21	20,000	$ .20 per 100 total direct machine hours
Administrative Dept. 30	30,000	$ .003 per total sales dollar
Sales:		
Home office	40,000	$ .004 per total sales dollar
District 1	15,000	$ .06 per district sales dollar
District 2	10,000	$ .07 per district sales dollar

5. Inventory changes—none.
6. Assume federal income tax average rate of 52 percent.
7. Volume data:

	AT SALES PROJECTION
Direct machine hours (hundreds):	
Department 1	150,000
Department 2	120,000

Required:

a. Prepare a tentative income statement (summarized) at the projected volume. Detail the expenses by department.

b. What would be the profit if sales volume (not price) were increased 10 percent? Assume direct machine hours will increase by the same percent.

CASE 13-5

Hill Company

Hill Company is a manufacturer of a line of durable goods distributed in a ten-state area. Sales are relatively stable throughout the year and consequently, the company has been able to maintain a stable labor force and plant capacity. Three years ago the plant capacity was substantially increased; however, the company has not been able to utilize more than 60 percent of that capacity although there has been a 7 percent increase in volume each year since the plant expansion. The company prepares an annual profit plan detailed by months and distributes internal performance reports to each responsibility center on a monthly basis. These performance reports compare actual revenues, costs, and other quantitative performance measurements with the original profit plan.

The company is in the fourth month of the year and sales valume is approximately 20 percent above the level anticipated in the annual profit plan. This unexpected increase in sales developed as the result of a contract with a new distributor in a new sales area. Although the sales people had been working on this distributor for some time, they were not optimistic; consequently, they did not anticipate this new development when the profit plan was developed. As a result of this significant increase in sales volume, variations between actual and profit plan reflected on the monthly performance reports are "becoming somewhat ridiculous." In view of the stability of operations in the past, the company had not faced this particular budget problem. Several suggestions have been made to resolve the problem. One vice president has suggested, "We should completely revise the profit plan for the remainder of the year." Another vice president has suggested that "I see no reason for taking all the time that is required to revise the profit plan. My suggestion would be that we continue reporting as we have in the past and then consider the variations as explained; that is, we can't pay much attention to the variations because they are caused by an event that is certainly in our favor." The financial vice president has not made a recommendation although he made the following statement at the last meeting of the top management: "We must not get in the habit of changing the profit plan at every whipstitch and on the request of any and everyone, because our goals cease to have meaning and the profit planning approach to managing would be undermined."

Required:

Evaluate this situation, and indicate what recommendation you think the financial vice president should make in respect to this particular problem. Justify your recommendations.

Techniques and Managerial
Application of Cost-Volume-Profit
Analysis (Breakeven Analysis)

chapter fourteen

Although an adequate profit planning and control program may be developed without cost-volume-profit (breakeven) analysis its use may enrich the application.

These is a close relationship between budgeting and cost-volume-profit analyses. Although the analyses may be applied to historical data, its best application is to *budget estimates*. The latter application suggests its importance in comprehensive profit planning and control. If variable budgets are used, as illustrated in Chapter 10 and in the Superior Manufacturing Company case, the basic data for cost-volume-profit analyses are available. If variable budgets are not used, the variability of expenses is not known (that is, the identification of the fixed and variable components); consequently, cost-volume-profit analysis involves careful expense analysis. Current literature is replete with discussions of breakeven analysis. Most of these discussions are concerned with its arithmetic, and *assume that the variability of expenses has been determined* but the latter is the critical problem. It is important to realize that breakeven analyses rest upon a valid identification of cost variability, that is, an identification of the fixed and variable cost components.

A more descriptive title of the underlying concepts is *cost-volume-profit analysis*. The breakeven point, defined as that volume level at which revenue exactly equals total cost, is somewhat incidental to the broader scope of cost-volume-profit analysis. This analysis is directly concerned with the effect on profits of changes in (1) fixed costs. (2) variable costs, (3) sales quantities, (4) sales prices, and (5) sales mix. An analysis offering relevant insights into these effects and their interrelationships in the enterprise has obvious merit. If breakeven analyses can be made with reasonable accuracy, its importance cannot be overlooked by the controller, budget director, by management in general.

The purposes of this chapter are to (1) explain the basic concepts underlying cost-volume-profit analysis, (2) indicate some of its applications and (3) consider its relationship with profit planning and control.

THE CONCEPT OF COST-VOLUME-PROFIT ANALYSIS

Understanding cost-volume-profit analysis requires appreciation of the *underlying concepts*, which are best indicated in the familiar breakeven chart shown in Illustrations 44, 45, and 46. These illustrations are based on the following budget data.

ANNUAL PROFIT PLAN—XYZ COMPANY

	FIXED	VARIABLE	
Budgeted sales (200,000 units @ $25)			$5,000,000
Budgeted costs:			
Direct material		$ 900,000	
Direct labor		1,000,000	
Factory overhead	$ 700,000	300,000	
Administrative expenses	600,000	100,000	
Distribution expenses	500,000	300,000	
Totals	$1,800,000	$2,600,000	4,400,000
Budgeted profit			$ 600,000
(Capacity production 240,000 units)			

The vertical scale on the chart (Illustration 44) represents dollars of revenue and cost. The horizontal scale represents the activity base, the volume or output—in this case, *units of volume*. The three lines representing total fixed costs, total costs, and sales may be located readily by placing the *profit plan* vertically at the budgeted volume of 200,000 units and marking the budget level of (1) fixed costs ($1.8 million), (2) total costs ($4.4 million), and (3) sales dollars ($5.0 million). The fixed cost line is drawn *horizontally* through the fixed cost point of $1.8 million. The total cost line is drawn through (1) the total cost point of $4.4 million and (2) the intersection of the fixed cost line with the left vertical scale. The sales line is drawn through the budget sales point ($5.0 million) to the origin point at the lower left. If the same

Cost-Volume-Profit Analysis

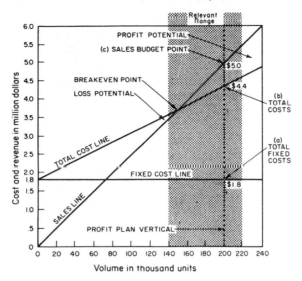

ILLUSTRATION 44.   Breakeven Chart, XYZ Company

distance is used on the horizontal scale for volume of sales as on the vertical scale for the revenue realizable from that volume, the sales line will connect opposite corners of the graph.

The point at which the *sales* and *total cost* lines intersect is the breakeven point ($3.75 million). The area between the line to the right of this point represents the profit potential, and the area between the two lines to the left represents the loss potential.

From the point of view of graphing technique, there are two additional variations of the breakeven chart. In Illustration 44 fixed costs were charted below variable costs. Another variation frequently used shows fixed costs charted *above* variable costs, as in Illustration 45. This method has the advantage of indicating the recovery of fixed costs at various volume levels before profits are realized. It may be observed also from Illustration 44 that output or volume is expressed in *budgeted sales dollars* rather than in units, the units were converted to sales dollars at the budgeted unit sales price of $25.

A third method shows the various fixed and variable costs in a particular sequence: for example, in the order found on the income statement for major classifications such as manufacturing, distribution, and administrative expenses, as shown in Illustration 46.

Obviously, the breakeven point is the same in each of the three methods of graphing. Illustration 44 indicates the breakeven volume in both units (150,000) and dollars ($3.75 million), whereas Illustrations 45 and 46 show the breakeven volume in dollars only.

Cost-Volume-Profit Analysis

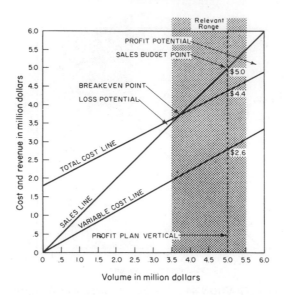

ILLUSTRATION 45. Breakeven Chart, XYZ Company

The breakeven point, as well as other important information, may be determined through the use of simple mathematical procedures. There are a number of formulas that may be used for these computations; the two usually employed are as follows:

1. Breakeven computation based on budget totals:

$$BES = \frac{\text{Fixed Costs}}{1 - \dfrac{\text{Variable Costs}}{\text{Corresponding Sales}}}$$

Substituting the illustrative data we have

$$BES = \frac{\$1.8 \text{ million}}{1 - \dfrac{\$2.6 \text{ million}}{\$5.0 \text{ million}}} = \frac{\$1.8 \text{ million}}{1 - .52} = \frac{\$1.8 \text{ million}}{.48}$$

$$= \$3.75 \text{ million (breakeven point in dollars)}$$

$$= \$3.75 \div \$25 = 150,000 \text{ (breakeven point in units)}$$

The above formula provides an insight into the characteristics of breakeven analysis. Dividing variable costs by sales results in the *variable cost ratio*. For example, the .52 (that is, $2.6 \div \$5.0$) derived above indicates that variable costs are 52 percent of sales, or to express it differently, $.52

Cost-Volume-Profit Analysis

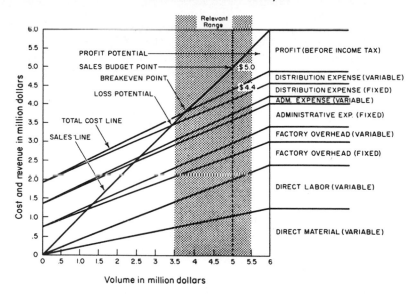

ILLUSTRATION 46.   **Detailed Breakeven Chart, XYZ Company**

of every sales dollar is necessary to recover exactly the variable costs. Subtracting the variable cost ratio from one gives the *profit-volume ratio*. For example, the .48 (that is, 1 — .52) derived in the illustration above indicates that 48 percent of sales are available to cover fixed costs (and generate profits), or to express it differently, $.48 of each sales dollar is available to cover fixed costs and make a profit. Since profit at breakeven is zero, dividing fixed costs by the profit-volume ratio (.48) (also referred to as the P/V ratio) gives the number of dollars of sales revenue necessary to exactly recover fixed costs ($2.8 million ÷ .48 = $3.75 million).[1] The computations can be verified as follows.

[1] The formula is derived as follows:

(1) Sales = Fixed Costs + Variable Costs + Profit

(2) Adapted:

$$\frac{\text{Breakeven}}{\text{Volume}} = \text{Fixed Costs} + \frac{\text{Variable Costs}}{\text{at Breakeven}} + \frac{\text{Profit}}{\text{at Zero}}$$

(3) Therefore:

$$\text{BE} = \text{FC} + \frac{\text{VC}}{\text{S}}(\text{BE}) + \text{Zero Profit}$$

(4) Rearranged:

$$\text{BE} = \frac{\text{FC}}{1 - \dfrac{\text{VC}}{\text{S}}}$$

Breakeven sales (as computed)		$3,750,000
Deduct budgeted:		
Fixed costs	$1,800,000	
Variable costs ($3,750,000 × .52)	1,950,000	
Total		3,750,000
Profit		Nil

2. Breakeven computation based on budgeted unit price and costs:

Unit sales price ($5.0 million ÷ 200,000 units)	$25
Unit variable cost ($2.6 million ÷ 200,000 units)	13
Contribution of *each unit* sold to cover fixed costs and profits	$12

Fixed costs of $1.8 million to be recovered divided by $12 recovery per unit gives a breakeven volume of 150,000 units. The breakeven point in dollars then is: $150,000 \times \$25 = \$3.75$ million.[2] These computations may be set in equation form as follows:

(1)   Sales = Variable costs + Fixed costs + Profit

(2)   Adapted:

Let X = units at the breakeven point

Therefore: $\$25X = \$13X + \$1,800,000 + 0$

$$\$12X = \$1,800,000$$

$$X = 150,000 \text{ (units at the breakeven point)}$$

Obviously computations based on unit prices and costs can be used only for a single product or, in the case of multiple products, for each product separately.

BASIC ASSUMPTIONS UNDERLYING COST-VOLUME-PROFIT ANALYSIS

The simplified breakeven charts and the illustrative computations presented above indicate the assumptions underlying cost-volume-profit analyses. These underlying assumptions are:

1. That the concept of cost variability is valid; therefore, costs can be classified realistically as fixed and variable.

[2] Note that computations based on *total cost* give the breakeven point in dollars of sales whereas the unit cost approach gives the breakeven point in units.

2. That there is a relevant range of validity for all facets of the analysis that must be observed.

3. That selling price does not change as physical volume of sales changes.

4. That there is only one product, or, in case of multiple products, that sales mix remains constant.

5. That basic management policies on operations will not change materially in the short run.

6. That the general price level will remain essentially stable in the short run.

7. That sales and production levels are synchronized; that is, inventory remains essentially constant or is zero.

8. That efficiency and productivity per person will remain essentially unchanged in the short run.

THE PRINCIPLE OF COST VARIABILITY AS APPLIED TO COST-VOLUME-PROFIT ANALYSIS

In the illustrations in this chapter all costs are identified by their fixed and variable components. Obviously, the reliability of cost-volume-profit analysis depends upon the accuracy of the variability estimates. The principle of cost variability was discussed in Chapter 10 with respect to variable budgets. Also fixed and variable costs were defined and illustrated there. The concepts of cost variability, fixed costs, and variable costs discussed in Chapter 10 are the same concepts as in cost-volume-profit analysis.

Cost-volume-profit analyses are developed under the assumption that the concept of cost variability is valid and, further, that it is possible to identify fixed and variable components of cost. Many leading firms have shown that this concept and its application are valid.

IDENTIFICATION OF FIXED AND VARIABLE COST COMPONENTS

A rough estimate of cost variability and the breakeven point may be derived by plotting past revenue and cost data for several successive periods. Such an estimate may give a general idea of the economic characteristics of a firm. However, this unsophisticated approach must be viewed skeptically because, in most cases, each set of historical data represents varying conditions such as changes in the general price level, management policies, accounting classification, productivity, methods of manufacturing, and products. Because this approach uses the *historical* relationship, there is the implicit assumption that past trends will continue in the future as in the past. Some firms use this approach to approximate competitor breakeven points for comparison with their own.

Since cost-volume-profit analysis should focus on the future, a careful analysis of each cost must be made. Preliminary analysis will usually indicate certain costs to be fixed for all practical purposes and certain other costs to be variable. There will also be a group of costs possessing the characteristics of both fixed and variable costs, that is the semivariable costs. These are the costs that require special analysis, the objective being to identify and measure the separate fixed and variable components. Generally the logical starting point to resolve this problem is an analysis of past data. Numerous methods have been suggested for determining cost variability. The principal approaches are discussed in Chapter 10 in connection with variable budget construction. These same approaches may be applied here.

Remember that, if variable budgets have been constructed, cost variability is already determined and may be readily used for breakeven analysis. This relationship of variable budgets and breakeven analysis suggests that, once reliable variable budgets are constructed, numerous cost-volume-profit analyses can be developed with little effort and cost. This application is illustrated at the end of the chapter for Superior Manufacturing Company.

STRAIGHTLINE VARIABILITY

The fixed and total cost lines on the breakeven chart normally are drawn as *straight* from zero to capacity. The assumption that the fixed costs remain constant at all volume levels, and that the variable costs vary *proportionally* at all volume levels, is seldom, if ever, literally true. A casual glance at the breakeven chart may convey this impression; however, a practical analyst will readily note that such is not the case. In Illustrations 44-46 a portion of the breakeven chart was shaded to indicate a *relevant range*. The concept of relevant range was discussed in Chapter 10 in connection with variable budgets. The relevant range may be thought of as the area of significance. Although the lines may be extended to the left and right of the relevant range, the analysis has meaning only within this range. The analysis purports to show what fixed costs *should be* and how variable costs *should vary* within the relevant volume range *determined by existing policies*. Within this relevant volume range, operational conditions and management policies can be assumed to be relatively consistent; hence, the results should be predictable on a straightline basis. Outside this range, different operational conditions and management policies usually will cause a completely new pattern of cost variability and, consequently, new cost-volume-profit relationships. To apply the analysis outside the relevant range will lead to erroneous conclusions. The analysis purports to show what would happen at the various volume levels within the relevant range, assuming that conditions and policies remain stable.

SALES PRICE AND SALES MIX CONSIDERATIONS

Cost-volume-profit analysis assumes a constant unit sales price; hence, the revenue line is straight. This simplifying assumption is necessary for two reasons. First, the effect of the budgeted sales price should be shown. Second, since the sales line expresses the combined results of *volume* and *sales price*, any attempt to show the effect of changes in unit selling prices on sales volume would involve price and demand theory. If it is possible to make a reliable estimate of the net effect of a price increase or decrease on total sales revenue, the breakeven analyst could easily include a nonlinear estimate in his analysis. There is no reason why the sales line cannot be expressed as a curve or in steps, provided a realistic determination can be made of what the expression should be.

A cost-volume-profit analysis may be developed for each product separately or for multiple products. If only one product or similar products are involved, the complication of *sales mix* is avoided. Sales mix refers to the relative quantities of the various products making up the "sales line." To illustrate the analysis of sales mix, assume the following budget data are available concerning two products.

| | PRODUCT A | | PRODUCT B | | |
	UNITS	AMOUNT	UNITS	AMOUNT	TOTALS
Sales planned	10,000	$10,000	7,500	$10,000	$20,000
Costs budgeted:					
Fixed		2,000		5,500	7,500
Variable		6,000		3,000	9,000
Total		8,000		8,500	16,500
Profit		$ 2,000		$ 1,500	$ 3,500

The breakeven chart and computation of the breakeven point are shown in Illustration 47, Graph A. The *sales line* and *total cost line* assume a 10 to 7.5 *quantity* ratio between the two products at all points up and down the volume scale. Observe that, although the profit per unit can be computed from the above data at $.20 for each product, this figure would be different for each product at all other sales volumes due to the effect of fixed costs.

Assume top management is considering the effect of a change in sales mix, one objective being to determine which product should be pro-

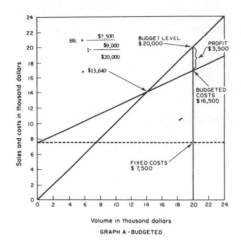

GRAPH A - BUDGETED

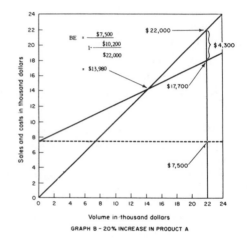

GRAPH B - 20% INCREASE IN PRODUCT A

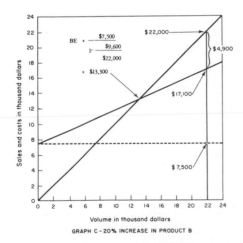

GRAPH C - 20% INCREASE IN PRODUCT B

ILLUSTRATION 47.   Breakeven Charts

Sales Mix: (a) Budgeted; (b) 20 Percent Increase in Product A; (c) 20 Percent Increase in Product B.

moted more. Casual observation of the budget data provides no direct clue to which product is potentially more profitable; in fact, it may appear that they are equal in profit potential ($.20 profit per unit for each product) and that the budgeted sales mix is appropriate. To demonstrate the effect of a change in sales mix, assume the controller prepared the following analyses:

Assumption 1: Twenty percent quantity increase in product A, no change in product B.

	PRODUCT A			PRODUCT B			
	UNITS	PER UNIT	AMOUNT	UNITS	PER UNIT	AMOUNT	TOTALS
Sales	12,000	$1.00	$12,000	7,500	$1.33⅓	$10,000	$22,000
Costs:							
Fixed			2,000			5,500	7,500
Variable		.60	7,200		.40	3,000	10,200
Total			9,200			8,500	17,700
Profit			$ 2,800			$ 1,500	$ 4,300

Assumption 2: Twenty percent quantity increase in product B, no change in product A.

	PRODUCT A			PRODUCT B			
	UNITS	PER UNIT	AMOUNT	UNITS	PER UNIT	AMOUNT	TOTAL
Sales	10,000	$1.00	$10,000	9,000	$1.33⅓	$12,000	$22,000
Costs:							
Fixed			2,000			5,500	7,500
Variable		.60	6,000		.40	3,600	9,600
Total			8,000			9,100	17,100
Profit			$ 2,000			$ 2,900	$ 4,900

The analysis may be summarized as follows:

	RESULTS AT PRESENT BUDGET	RESULTS OF 20% INCREASE IN PRODUCT A	RESULTS OF 20% INCREASE IN PRODUCT B
Profit	$ 3,500	$ 4,300	$ 4,900
Percentage profit change (increase-decrease)		23%	40%
Breakeven point	$13,640	$13,980	$13,300

The analysis above indicates that it would be desirable to push product B, because in the second assumption (1) greater profits result, and (2) the breakeven point is lowered. The analysis is graphically illustrated and the effects demonstrated in Illustration 47, Charts B and C. Notice that a new cost-volume-profit analysis should be developed for each new sales mix ratio, wherein both the sales and cost lines are based upon the new sales mix or quantity ratio between the two products at all points up and down the volume scale. Obviously, this application provides a good management tool that clearly indicates the effect on the profit and loss picture (and the breakeven point) of promoting the more profitable products. Therefore, the sales mix assumption inherent in breakeven analysis, if viewed properly, is an advantage rather than a disadvantage. Observe that the breakeven points summed for the two products computed separately (which assumes independence) will not equal the breakeven point on combined data (which assumes a dependence imposed by the budgeted sales mix).

MANAGEMENT POLICIES

Cost-volume-profit analysis carries implicit assumptions about the basic management policies. The revenue data used in the computations implies definite policies on such items as sales prices, sales mix, and products. The fixed cost data implies specific policies on such items as salary scales, number of indirect employees on fixed salaries, depreciation methods, insurance coverage, research, advertising, and plant capacity—that is, those policies that determine the fixed cost structure of the company. The variable cost data imply specific policies that determine the variable cost structure of the firm, such as quality of raw materials, production technology, wage rates for direct labor employees, and sales commissions.

Because cost-volume-profit analysis implies a definite set of management policies affecting the revenue and cost characteristics of the firm—and this is one of its most important applications—it tells management in effect, "Here are the approximate results to be expected at varying volume levels of operations presuming a *specific set* of policies and decisions." For example, if the firm is approaching the breakeven point in operations or profits are dropping, management action should be taken to lower the breakeven point *before it is reached*. This distinction is important, because management must know what the financial effect of present policies is in order to know when and why they should be changed, how they should be changed, and what the probable effect would be. A series of breakeven analyses under varying management policy assumptions can help decision-making.

EVALUATION OF ASSUMPTIONS

The last three assumptions listed on page 455, concerning price stability, stable inventory levels, and worker efficiency, generally matter little in cost-volume-profit analysis, because it is a short-term analysis. The analysis generally assumes a stable price level. This assumption, of course, is not completely valid, but for periods of one year or less (and the analysis must be kept current) the change generally is not significant. Should there be a significant price level change affecting revenue or costs, as was the case particularly in 1974, the entire analysis should be reconstructed.

The assumption of efficiency and productivity per individual is particularly important in the long run; however, these seldom change materially in the short run. If they do, the existing relationships between volume and costs will change and, hence, a new analysis is required.

Should a material change in the inventory be anticipated during the budget period, appropriate adjustment must be made in the computations for the inventory increase or decrease along the lines suggested in a later section of this chapter.

Most criticisms of cost-volume-profit analyses are directed at one or more of the eight assumptions listed above. Although some of them are justified in specific situations, none is beyond reasonable resolution under most circumstances. Whether they can be validated in a particular situation will depend to a large degree upon the abilities and judgment of the analyst.

SPECIAL PROBLEMS IN BREAKEVEN ANALYSIS

In the previous examples in this chapter, volume was expressed in product units or net sales dollars. The usual *activity base* is net sales dollar, as the best measure of overall activity in a company. Product units are preferable if the analysis is applied to one product. For multiple products, the activity factor must be in additive units using a common denominator of volume. For the concern as a whole, net sales dollars are generally the only satisfactory common denominator because manufacturing, selling, and administrative activities are expressed in combination.

If variable budgets are available, they may be summed for cost-volume-profit purposes. This process may cause some complications because the different departmental variable budgets are related to different activity bases. For example, selling expenses may be related to sales dollars, factory overhead related to direct labor or machine hours, and power department costs related to kilowatt hours. In adding the variable budget allowances, it is assumed that the departmental activity factors correlate reasonably with the overall base selected for breakeven purposes. The usual procedure in constructing breakeven analysis based on variable budgets is to add the *fixed* cost component shown in the variable budgets and to treat the remaining costs (determined by subtraction from total costs) as variable. This procedure will be illustrated subsequently for Superior Manufacturing Company. Selection of an appropriate activity base for different types of cost centers was discussed in Chapter 10.

Other incomes and other expenses, if significant, present another special problem in cost-volume-profit analyses. Preferably nonoperating items should be omitted from the analysis; however, if they are included, it is best to include the *net* of other income and other expenses. If the excess is expense, it should be added to fixed expense, whereas if the excess is income, it should be deducted from the fixed expense. When graphed, the effect of these amounts should be indicated with additional lines, thus showing the economic characteristics of the firm before and after the nonoperating items. The computations may be illustrated simply. Assume the following budget data are available:

Budgeted sales (10,000 units @ $3)		$30,000
Less:		
Fixed costs	$18,000	
Variable costs	9,000	27,000
Operating profit		3,000
Add:		
Other incomes	$ 3,000	
Less other expenses	1,000	2,000
Budgeted net income		$ 5,000

To compute the breakeven points:
    Case A—Omitting other incomes and expenses;

$$\text{BES} = \frac{\$18,000}{1 - \dfrac{\$9,000}{\$30,000}} = \underline{\underline{\$25,714}}$$

    Case B—Including other incomes and expenses:

$$\text{BES} = \frac{\$18,000 - \$2,000}{1 - \dfrac{\$9,000}{\$30,000}} = \underline{\underline{\$22,857}}$$

The computations may be verified for Case B as follows:

Sales		$22,857
Less:		
Fixed costs	$18,000	
Variable costs (.30 × $22,857)	6,857	24,857
Operating loss		($ 2,000)
Add:		
Other incomes	$ 3,000	
Less other expenses	1,000	2,000
Net income		Nil

Case C—Assuming other incomes of $1,000 and other expenses of $3,000; that is, excess expense of $2,000:

$$\text{BES} = \frac{\$18,000 + \$2,000}{1 - \dfrac{\$9,000}{\$30,000}} = \underline{\$28,571}$$

The graphic analyses for each of the three cases are shown in Illustration 48.

Cost-Volume-Profit Analysis

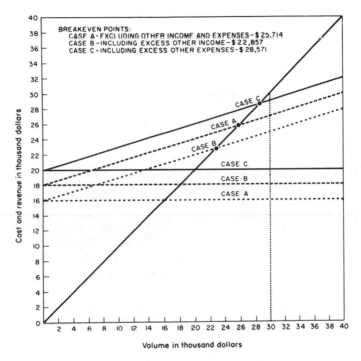

ILLUSTRATION 48.   Breakeven Chart
With Other Incomes and Expenses

BREAKEVEN ANALYSIS AND INVENTORY CHANGE

Usually budgeted changes in inventories (that is, finished goods and work in process) are immaterial and thus may be disregarded in cost-volume-profit analyses. On the other hand, when the budgeted change in inventory is significant, the analyst usually should include this factor in the computations. In this respect it is appropriate to note that when *direct costing* (only variable costs are considered as production and inventory costs), is used, inventory changes have no effect on the breakeven computations as they do in *full costing*. This fact is often cited as an advantage of direct costing.

Introducing the effect of inventory change in cost-volume-profit analyses (1) requires subjective judgment about what management might do (relative to inventory change) at different levels and (2) the theoretical precision that the analyst desires. Let us examine one practical approach frequently used although it does overlook some theoretical distinctions in the interest of pragmatic simplicity.[3]

The following simplified data are used:

Budgeted sales (90,000 units @ $2)		$180,000
Budgeted production (100,000 units):		
Fixed costs	$ 80,000	
Variable costs ($.60 per unit)	60,000	
Total costs	140,000	
Less inventory increase (10,000 units @ $1.40)	14,000*	126,000
Gross margin		54,000
Less administrative & distribution costs:		
Fixed costs	10,000	
Variable costs ($.10 per unit)	9,000	19,000
Budgeted income		$ 35,000

*This amount is composed of:	
Variable costs (10,000 units × $.60)	$ 6,000
Fixed costs ($80,000 × 10%)	8,000
	$14,000

Note that (1) only one product is involved (so that the effects may be seen clearly), and (2) there is a budgeted *increase* in inventory amounting to 10 percent of production. It is also assumed that the increase in inventory is at the same unit cost as budgeted production ($1.40 per unit).

Inventory change disregarded—If it is desired to *disregard* the inventory change in computing the breakeven point (which is a common practice), the breakeven point may be computed as follows:

Based on budget totals:

$$\text{BES} = \frac{\$80,000 + \$10,000}{1 - \dfrac{\$60,000 + \$9,000 - \$6,000^4}{\$180,000}}$$

[3] For excellent discussions of this problem see: R. Lee Brummet, *Overhead Costing* (Bureau of Business Research, School of Business Administration, University of Michigan, 1957), and Roy E. Tuttle, "The Effect of Inventory Change on Breakeven Analysis," *NAA Bulletin* (January 1959), pp. 77–87.
[4] The *variable costs* and the *sales figure* must always relate to the same level of activity. The subtraction of $6,000 (10,000 units at $.60) reduces the variable costs to a 90,000 unit basis, which is necessary in this case since the $180,000 sales figure is based on 90,000 units, whereas the production costs are based on 100,000 units.

$$= \frac{\$90,000}{1 - .35}$$

$$= \frac{\$90,000}{.65}$$

$$= \$138,462 \text{ or } 69,231 \text{ units (that is, } \$138,462 \div \$2)$$

Because there is only one product, the following computations give the same results.

Based on budgeted unit prices and costs:

Unit sales price		$2.00
Less unit variable costs:		
Factory	$.60	
Administrative and selling	.10	.70
Contribution to cover fixed costs and profit		$1.30

Fixed cost to be recovered $90,000 divided by unit recovery of $1.30 gives 69,231 units at breakeven or $138,462.

The computations may be verified by omitting the inventory change, viz.

Breakeven sales (69,231 units at $2)		$138,462
Less production costs:		
Fixed	$80,000	
Variable (69,231 × $.60)	41,539	121,539
Gross margin		16,923
Less administrative and selling:		
Fixed	10,000	
Variable (69,231 × $.10)	6,923	16,923
Profit or loss		Nil

Inventory change included—If we regard the inventory change material and therefore we introduce it in the analysis, we must assume either: (1) that management will maintain a constant *ratio* of inventory change to production—that is, in the above example the inventory increase will approximate 10 percent of production at various levels of operations, or (2) that the inventory change will be constant for each unit change—that is, in the above example management will maintain the 10,000 unit increase in inventory regardless of the level of operations. We may also assume (1) that a beginning inventory is, in effect, a fixed cost or (2) that it is in part a fixed cost and in part a variable cost. The theoretical aspects are complicated by these assumptions and the additional factor of factory *overhead over- or underapplied.*

To avoid complexity, yet to derive a reasonable approximation, many firms simply assume (1) that the inventory increase or decrease will be proportional to changes in production, and (2) that the inventory change carries the same ratio of fixed and variable costs to total cost as is budgeted for current production.

Returning to the illustrative data, the inventory change (increase of 10,000 units or 10 percent of production) may be analyzed as follows:
Costs in the inventory increase:

$$\text{Fixed component:} \qquad \frac{10{,}000 \text{ units}}{100{,}000 \text{ units}} \times \$80{,}000 = \$\ 8{,}000$$

$$\text{Variable component:} \quad \frac{10{,}000 \text{ units}}{100{,}000 \text{ units}} \times \$60{,}000 = \underline{\quad 6{,}000}$$

$$\text{Total (10,000 units)} \qquad\qquad\qquad\qquad\qquad\quad \underline{\underline{\$14{,}000}}$$

Accepting the two simplifying assumptions listed above, the breakeven point may be computed as follows:
Based on budget totals:

$$\text{BES} = \frac{\$80{,}000 + \$10{,}000 - \$8{,}000}{1 - \dfrac{\$60{,}000 + \$9{,}000 - \$6{,}000}{\$180{,}000}}$$

$$= \frac{\$82{,}000}{.65}$$

$$= \$126{,}154 \text{ or } 63{,}077 \text{ units (that is, } \$126{,}154 \div \$2)$$

Because there is only one product, the following computations give the same results:
Based on budgeted unit prices and costs:

Unit sales price		$2.00
Less unit variable cost:		
Factory	$.60	
Administrative and selling	.10	.70
Contribution to cover fixed costs and profit		$1.30

$$\text{BES} = \frac{\$80{,}000 + \$10{,}000 - \$8{,}000}{\$1.30}$$

$$= 63{,}077 \text{ units or } \$126{,}154 \ (63{,}077 \times \$2)$$

Note that the $8,000 (computed above) subtracted from fixed costs in both computations represents the *fixed cost* component of the inventory change. It is subtracted because the inventory is *increased* and this fixed cost belongs to inventory rather than to cost of sales.

The computations may be verified in terms of the two simplifying assumptions as follows:

Breakeven sales (63,077 units @ $2)		$126,154
Less costs:		
Production (63,077 ÷ .90 = 70,085 units)		
Fixed costs	$ 80,000	
Variable costs (70,085 × $.60)	42,051	
Total production costs	122,051	
Less inventory (10% of production)	12,205	
Cost of goods sold		109,846
Gross margin		16,308
Less selling and administrative costs		
Fixed	$ 10,000	
Variable (63,077 × $.10)	6,308	16,308
Net income		Nil

Alternatively, if we assume the budget presented above, with the exceptions that (1) budgeted sales are 110,000 units and (2) production is 100,000 units, a 10,000 *decrease* in inventory results. The breakeven point under the two simplifying assumptions would require that the $8,000 fixed costs *withdrawn* from inventory be added to fixed costs as follows:

$$\text{BES} = \frac{\$90,000 + \$8,000}{\$1.30}$$

$$= 75,385 \text{ units (or } \$150,769)$$

Application of this *practical* method is illustrated for Superior Manufacturing Company at the end of the chapter. When dealing with the somewhat heterogeneous and detailed data common to an actual situation, some practical approach is generally preferable to a complicated, theoretical approach, assuming that the practical approach provides a reasonable approximation of the results.

USE AND APPLICATION OF COST-VOLUME-PROFIT ANALYSIS

Where cost-volume-profit analyses are reasonably accurate, they can help management decision-making. Essentially, cost-volume-profit analysis offers greater insight into the *economic characteristics* of a company and may be used to determine the approximate effect of various alternatives. Cost-volume-profit analysis is based on *estimates*; however, and the arithmetical manipulations generally involve *averages*; hence the results should never be interpreted as precise. Rather, the analysis may be characterized appropriately as a "slide-rule" approach that may be used to develop and test, with a minimum of effort, the approximate effect on costs and profits of several types of management decisions.

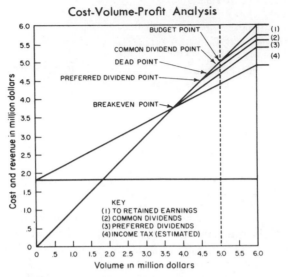

ILLUSTRATION 49.   Breakeven Chart—Economic Characteristics

Illustration 49 indicates a few of the *economic characteristics* of a business, viz :

1. Fixed costs, variable costs, and total costs at varying volumes.
2. The profit and loss potential, before and after income taxes, at varying volumes.
3. The margin of safety—the relationship of budget volume to breakeven volume.
4. The breakeven point.
5. The preferred dividend or danger point—the point below which preferred dividends are not earned.
6. The dead point—the point where management earns only the "going" rate on the investment.
7. The common dividend or unhealthy point—the point below which earnings are insufficient to pay the preferred dividends and the expected dividend on the common stock.

All these points, and as others, can be computed if data are developed for cost-volume-profit purposes. The remaining paragraphs of this chapter indicate some of the more important applications of breakeven analysis.

EVALUATING THE EFFECT OF CHANGING VARIABLES

An important aspect of cost-volume-profit analysis is the relative ease with which the effect of a contemplated management decision can be evaluated even when more than one factor is changed. This is a key aspect of cost-volume-profit analyses during the development of the annual profit plan, because it allows early and continuous *testing* to determine the probable over-all effect of the alternatives under consideration.

The methods of identifying the effect of a change in sales mix were illustrated earlier in this chapter. This section considers the evaluation of changes in (1) fixed costs, (2) variable costs, and (3) sales price.

Returning to the earlier illustration in this chapter (p. 450) concerning the XYZ Company, let's evaluate the effect of a contemplated 10 percent increase in *fixed costs*. The computation would be:

1. Effect on BES:

$$ \text{BES} = \frac{\$1.8 \text{ million} \times 110\%}{1 - \dfrac{\$2.6 \text{ million}}{\$5.0 \text{ million}}} = \$4.125 \text{ million} $$

2. Sales necessary to earn the budgeted profit of $600,000:

$$ \text{BES} + \text{``Profit'' sales} = \frac{(\$1.8 \text{ million} \times 100\%) + \$.6 \text{ million}^5}{1 - \dfrac{\$2.6 \text{ million}}{\$5.0 \text{ million}}} $$

$$ = \$5.375 \text{ million} $$

The computations may be verified:

	AT BREAKEVEN		TO EARN $.6 MILLION PROFIT	
Sales (millions)		$4,125		$5.375
Fixed costs	$1.8		$1.8	
10 percent increase	.18		.18	
	1.98		1.98	
Variable costs (52% rate)				
$4.125 × 52%	2.145	4.125		
5.375 × 52%			2.795	4.775
Net income		Nil		$ .600

---

[5] Note that the desired profit figure is merely added to the fixed costs because the contribution of sales above variable costs is to "cover fixed costs and profits."

Now assume instead that it is desired to evaluate the effect of a contemplated 10 percent increase in *variable costs*. The computation could be made as follows:

1. Effect on BES

$$\text{BES} = \frac{\$1.8 \text{ million}}{1 - \dfrac{\$2.6 \text{ million} \times 110\%}{\$5.0 \text{ million}}} = \$4.2 + \text{million}$$

2. Sales necessary to earn the budgeted profit of $600,000.

$$\text{BES} + \text{``Profit'' sales} = \frac{\$1.8 \text{ million} + \$.6 \text{ million}}{1 - \dfrac{\$2.6 \text{ million} \times 110\%}{\$5.0 \text{ million}}}$$

$$= \$5.6 + \text{million}$$

Cost-Volume-Profit Analysis

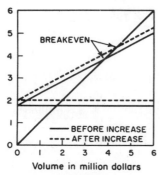

GRAPH A
EFFECT OF 10% INCREASE IN FIXED COSTS

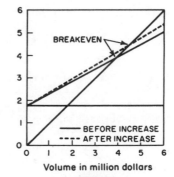

GRAPH B
EFFECT OF 10% INCREASE IN VARIABLE COSTS

ILLUSTRATION 50 / CHANGE IN COST STRUCTURE

ILLUSTRATION 50. Change in Cost Structure

Finally, evaluate the effect of a contemplated 10 percent increase in *sales price*. The computations are:

1. Effect on BES:

$$\text{BES} = \frac{\$1.8 \text{ million}}{1 - \dfrac{\$2.6 \text{ million}}{\$5.0 \text{ million} \times 110\%}} = \$3,413,795 \text{ or } 124,138 \text{ units}$$

2. Sales necessary to earn the budgeted profit of $600,000; assume further that the price increase will reduce units sold by approximately 5 percent:

$$\text{BES} + \text{``Profit''} \text{ sales} = \cfrac{\$1.8 \text{ million} + \$.6 \text{ million}}{1 - \cfrac{\$2.6 \text{ million} \times 95\%}{\$5.0 \text{ million} \times 95\% \times 110\%}}$$

$$= \$4,551,720 \text{ or } 165,517 \text{ units}$$

Significantly, the effect of decisions such as those illustrated above may be graphed as in Illustration 51. Special care is necessary to plot the effect of a price change (see Illustration 51).

Note that when volume is expressed in *units*, a price change may merely raise or lower the *sales line*. In contrast, when volume is expressed in *sales dollars* the *total cost* line, rather than the sales line, must be changed.

These illustrations should indicate the wide application of cost-volume-profit analyses for *testing* the effect of proposed alternative management decisions. For example, the technique can help determine the profit potential of replacing old machinery with new machinery, which change may result in a shift of fixed and variable costs.

COST-VOLUME-PROFIT ANALYSIS BY ORGANIZATIONAL SUBDIVISION OR PRODUCT

In many instances it is useful to develop cost-volume-profit analyses by product, plant, or other subdivision. An actual incident may dramatize this kind of application. A particular sales division executive, whose variable costs to sales ratio was 75 percent, was contemplating an increase in divisional *fixed* costs. The president asked how much sales would have to be to maintain the present profit position after the increase in fixed costs. The sales executive replied that for each dollar increase in fixed cost, sales volume would have to be increased one dollar to maintain the same dollar profit. Needless to say, the sales executive was not nearly so enthusiastic about increasing fixed costs when told by the controller (based on the cost-volume-profit analysis) that "for cash $1 increase in fixed costs, sales volume must be increased by $4, in order to maintain exactly the present dollar profit position ($1 \div 25\% = $4)."

Breakeven analysis by organizational subdivisions or by products presents a special problem to the analyst because of indirect costs. It is generally preferable to develop an analysis (1) before and (2) after allocation of the indirect costs. Better allocations frequently can be obtained if the allocation basis for fixed costs differs from the one used for variable costs. One application of breakeven analysis by sales districts is shown in Illustration 52.

For preparation of breakeven charts, the analyst may want to plot the data on the same chart for before and after cost allocations.

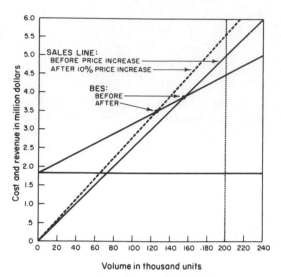

PLOTTING 10% PRICE INCREASE
WHEN VOLUME SCALE IS IN UNITS

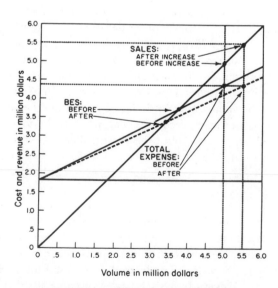

PLOTTING 10% PRICE INCREASE
WHEN VOLUME SCALE IS IN SALES DOLLARS

ILLUSTRATION 51.   Change in Unit Sales Price

ILLUSTRATION 52. Breakeven Analysis by Sales Districts
Budget Data

	EASTERN DISTRICT			WESTERN DISTRICT			COMPANY		
	FIXED	VARIABLE	TOTAL	FIXED	VARIABLE	TOTAL	FIXED	VARIABLE	TOTAL
Sales			$300,000			$200,000			$500,000
Cost of goods sold	$36,000	$ 84,000	120,000	$24,000	$ 56,000	$ 80,000	$ 60,000	$140,000	200,000
Gross margin			180,000			120,000			300,000
Direct district sales expenses	30,000	99,000	129,000	20,000	64,000	84,000	50,000	163,000	213,000
Direct district operating profit			51,000			36,000			87,000
Cost subtotals	66,000	183,000		44,000	120,000		110,000	303,000	
Allocated general sales and administrative costs*	21,600	14,400	36,000	14,400	9,600	24,000	36,000	24,000	60,000
Total costs	87,600	197,400		58,400	129,600		146,000	327,000	
Net income			$ 15,000			$ 12,000			$ 27,000

Breakeven computation:

Before allocations:

EASTERN DISTRICT

$$BE = \frac{\$66,000}{1 - \frac{\$183,000}{\$300,000}} = \$169,231$$

WESTERN DISTRICT

$$BE = \frac{\$44,000}{1 - \frac{\$120,000}{\$200,000}} = \$110,000$$

COMPANY

$$BE = \frac{\$146,000}{1 - \frac{\$327,000}{\$500,000}} = \$421,965$$

After allocations:

EASTERN DISTRICT

$$BE = \frac{\$87,600}{1 - \frac{\$197,400}{\$300,000}} = \$256,140$$

WESTERN DISTRICT

$$BE = \frac{\$58,400}{1 - \frac{\$129,600}{\$200,000}} = \$165,909$$

*Allocated on same basis for simplicity.

MARGIN OF SAFETY

The margin of safety is the relationship of budgeted volume (or actual volume) to the breakeven volume. It can show management how close to the breakeven point the concern is operating. For example, assume the following data for two companies:

	COMPANY A	COMPANY B
Budgeted sales	$100,000	$100,000
Budgeted costs:		
Fixed	70,000	20,000
Variable	20,000	70,000
Budgeted income	$ 10,000	$ 10,000
Indicated breakeven points	$ 87,500	$ 66,667

Although the two companies budgeted the same income amount, there is a basic difference in their economic characteristics. Company A is much closer to the breakeven point than Company B. Whereas Company A will operate at a loss if volume drops more than $12^1/_2$ percent, Company B will profit until volume drops more than $33^1/_3$ percent; in other words, they have different margins of safety. The margin of safety may be expressed (1) as a ratio of budget to the breakeven point or (2) as the ratio or percent of the difference between sales and breakeven to budgeted sales. The following figures illustrate this concept for companies A and B:

	COMPANY A	COMPANY B
1. Margin of safety expressed as a percent of budget to breakeven:		
($100,000 ÷ $87,500)	114.3%	
($100,000 ÷ $66,667)		150.0%
2. Margin of Safety expressed as the percent of the difference to budgeted sales		
($12,500 ÷ $100,000)	$12\frac{1}{2}$%	
($33,333 ÷ $100,000)		$33\frac{1}{3}$%

COST-VOLUME-PROFIT ANALYSIS ILLUSTRATED FOR SUPERIOR MANUFACTURING COMPANY

The annual income statement for Superior Manufacturing Company is recast for cost-volume-profit purposes in Schedule 71. Assume that the inventory contains the same ratio of fixed to variable cost as in current production.

The fixed and variable components of the inventory change were derived on Schedule 71 as follows:

1. Determine percents on line—"Percent of fixed and variable to total" from the data on the preceding line ($525,840 ÷ $3,947,800 = 13%).

2. Determine *total* change in inventory (last column) as "Total manufacturing costs" minus "Cost of goods sold" ($4,054,600 − $3,947,800 = $106,800).

3. Determine fixed and variable components of inventory change on the line — "Add decrease in finished goods inventory" using the percents developed on the preceding line ($106,800 × 13% = $13,884).

Data now are available on Schedule 71 for computing four different breakeven points, each with different assumptions:

1. Omit inventory change, but include other incomes and expenses.
2. Omit both inventory change and other incomes and expenses.
3. Include inventory change, but omit other incomes and expenses.
4. Include both inventory change and other incomes and expenses.

Representative computations are shown below for the first and second assumptions. The related breakeven chart is shown in Schedule 72. Note that for practical reasons the volume scale at the left does not extend to zero.

Computation of breakeven point:

Assumption 1—Omit inventory change but include other incomes and expenses.

$$BE = \frac{\$1,309,140 - \$33,870}{1 - \dfrac{\$3,851,870 + \$92,916}{\$6,095,000}}$$

$$= \frac{\$1,275,270}{1 - .6472}$$

$$= \$3,614,710$$

Assumption 2—Omit both inventory change and other incomes and expenses.

$$BE = \frac{\$1,309,140}{1 - \dfrac{\$3,851,870 + \$92,916}{\$6,095,000}}$$

$$= \frac{\$1,309,140}{1 - \dfrac{\$3,944,786}{\$6,095,000}}$$

$$= \frac{\$1,309,140}{1 - .6472}$$

$$= \$3,710,714$$

SCHEDULE 71. Superior Manufacturing Company
Income and Cost Data for Cost-Volume-Profit Analysis
For the year ending December 31, 1977

	REF.	TOTAL	REF.	FIXED COSTS COMPUTED AMOUNT		VARIABLE COSTS (TOTAL MINUS FIXED)
Budgeted sales	1	$6,095,000				$1,416,600
Manufacturing costs:						
Material	29	1,416,600				1,416,600
Labor	30	1,752,000				1,752,000
Prime cost		3,168,600				3,168,600
Factory overhead:						
General factory	33	116,800	41	$ 8,760 × 12 = $	105,120	11,680
Power	33	110,000	41	6,700 × 12 =	80,400	29,600
Repair	33	10,000	41	720 × 12 =	8,640	1,360
Producing Dept. 1	36	319,280	42	14,000 × 12 =	168,000	151,280
Producing Dept. 2	34	29,280		1,960 × 12 =	23,520	5,760
Producing Dept. 3	34	103,840		4,180 × 12 =	50,160	53,680
Building services	32	90,000			90,000	
Total factory over head costs		779,200			525,840	253,600
Total manufacturing costs		3,947,800			525,840	3,421,960
Per cent of fixed and variable to total		100%			13%	87%
Add decrease in finished goods inventory		106,800			13,884	92,916
Cost of goods sold	60	4,054,600			539,724	3,514,876
Gross margin		2,040,400				

	REF.	TOTAL	FIXED COSTS COMPUTED		VARIABLE COSTS (TOTAL MINUS FIXED)
			REF.	AMOUNT	
Distribution:					
General sales overhead	39	296,330		$19,295 \times 12 =$ 231,540	64,790
District	39	663,167		$26,930 \times 12 =$ 323,160	340,007
Building service	32	30,000		30,000	
Total distribution		989,497		584,700	404,797
Administrative:					
Administrative Department	40	83,516		$6,340 \times 12 =$ 76,080	7,436
Treasurer's Department	40	56,177		$3,310 \times 12 =$ 39,720	16,457
Accounting Department	40	54,020		$4,400 \times 12 =$ 52,800	1,220
Building services	32	30,000		30,000	
Total administrative		223,713		198,600	25,113
Total selling and administrative expenses		1,213,210		783,300	429,910
Operating profit		827,190			
Add net of other income and expense	13	33,870			
Net profit before income taxes	13	861,060			
Less federal income taxes	13	258,318			
Net income	13	$ 602,742			
Total fixed costs *excluding*					
Inventory decrease				$1,309,140	
Total variable costs *excluding*					
Inventory decrease					$3,851,870

477

Points plotted on Schedule 72 for Assumption 2:

Sales	$6,095,000
Fixed costs	1,309,140
Total costs	
($1,309,140 + $3,944,876)	5,253,926

SCHEDULE 72. **Breakeven Chart of the Superior Manufacturing Company**

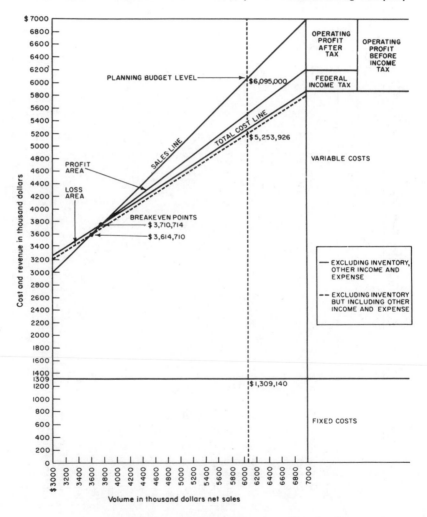

DISCUSSION QUESTIONS

1.   Explain the relationships between budgeting and cost-volume-profit analysis.

2.   Explain the fundamental concept of cost-volume-profit analysis.

3.   Discuss the advantages and disadvantages of the three principal methods of graphic presentation of breakeven analysis.

4.   Explain (1) the variable cost ratio and (2) the P/V ratio, and relate them to breakeven analysis.

5.   List and briefly explain the eight assumptions underlying breakeven analysis.

6.   Why is it important to define clearly the relevant range in breakeven analysis?

7.   Why is the assumption of straightline variability of cost usually considered sufficiently valid for cost-volume-profit analyses?

8.   What is the relationship between management policies and cost-volume-profit analysis?

9.   Should "other" incomes and expenses be included in the breakeven analysis? Explain.

10.   When a breakeven analysis is being prepared from budget data that reflect an inventory change in finished goods, what recognition should be given to the change?

11.   What is meant by the economic characteristics of a company?

12.   What is meant by the margin of safety? Why is it important to management?

13.   What are the primary uses of cost-volume-profit analysis?

CASE 14-1
Baker Company

This case was designed to review the basic concepts used in the development of breakeven analysis. For this purpose, we assume a single product and that the variability of costs for the firm has been determined. The 1977 annual profit plan is essentially complete; the sales objective for the year is $500,000 and a unit sales price of $50. Budgeted fixed costs for the year total $240,000 and a profit of $6.00 per unit. The company sales reflect a definite seasonal pattern that varies above and below the monthly average by 15 percent.

Required:

   a.   Reconstruct the 1977 budgeted income statement in summary form to compute breakeven analysis.
   b.   What is the breakeven point in dollars? In units? Show computations (a) based on total costs and (b) based on unit costs.
   c.   Prove your computations in item (b) above.

d. What is the variable cost ratio? Show computations. How is this ratio used in computing the breakeven point?

e. What is the P/V ratio? Show computations. How is the P/V ratio used in computing the breakeven point?

f. Did the income statement prepared in (a) above reflect the variable cost and P/V ratios? Explain.

g. What is the "profit pickup" above the breakeven point?

h. What is the unit sales price? Unit variable cost? Unit fixed cost? Unit profit? What would each of these be, assuming the number of units budgeted for sale were increased 10 percent? What is the new breakeven point? State any assumptions you make.

i. What is the activity base and the relevant range in this situation? Explain.

j. Construct a breakeven chart to conform to your responses to (a) and (b) above. Identify all important facets of the chart.

CASE 14-2
Duncan Company

The Duncan Company profit plan for the year is summarized below.

Sales (400,000 units)		$20,000,000
Manufacturing costs:		
Material	$1,700,000	
Labor	1,600,000	
Fixed overhead	2,650,000	
Variable overhead	4,050,000	
Distribution costs:		
Fixed	3,400,000	
Variable	1,900,000	
Administrative costs:		
Fixed	1,750,000	
Variable	350,000	
Total costs		17,400,000
Profit (before income taxes)		$ 2,600,000

Required:

a. Compute the breakeven point using total costs.

b. Compute the breakeven point using unit costs.

c. What is the variable cost ratio and the P/V ratio?

d. What is the activity base and the relevant range?

e. How much will the company earn per unit above the breakeven point?

f.   Assume management is considering revising the profit plan downward on sales volume by 10 percent. Develop a table to show unit sales price, unit variable cost, unit fixed cost, and unit profit before and after the percent drop. What would be the new breakeven point? State any assumptions you make.

g.   Using the results in item (a) construct a breakeven chart and identify all important facets of it.

CASE 14-3
K Corporation

The executives of K Corporation are developing the annual profit plan. The effect on profit of several contemplated decisions are being assessed. Some of these decisions will affect fixed costs; others will affect variable costs; and still others relate to sales price and sales volume (number of units). The profit target adopted by the management calls for $15,000. The following income statement data (summarized) has been tentatively developed:

Sales (@ $20)		$100,000
Costs:		
Fixed	$49,600	
Variable	38,000	87,600
Profit		$ 12,400

Required:

(Each alternative is independent unless specifically stated otherwise.)

a.   Compute the breakeven point.

b.   Compute the breakeven point and profit assuming management makes a decision that will cause fixed costs to increase 10 percent.

c.   Compute the breakeven point and profit assuming instead that the decision will cause only variable costs to increase 10 percent.

d.   Compute the breakeven point and profit assuming a decision is made to increase sales price by 10 percent.

e.   Compute the breakeven point and profit assuming the projection of sales volume is increased by 10 percent.

f.   There is the possibility that all of the above alternatives will be included in the final profit plan—that is, a 10 percent increase in fixed costs, a 10 percent increase in variable costs, and a 10 percent increase in sales price. What would be the new breakeven point considering the combined effect of these three changes? How many units would have to be sold under these conditions to meet the profit target?

g.   Be prepared to explain the comparative results between the six alternatives, a through f.

CASE 14-4
Borden Company

The executives of Borden Company, a small manufacturer of one product, are developing the annual profit plan. They have just reviewed the "first cut" at the annual income statement and are concerned with the $11,000 indicated profit on a sales volume of 20,000 units. The fixed cost structure of $99,000 appears to be high, and they have some doubts about departing from the unit sales price of $10. There is general agreement that the "profit target should be $22,000." This case deals with several tentative alternatives suggested during the meeting of the executive committee that just reviewed the tentative profit plan.

Required:

    a. Prior to considering the suggested alternatives under consideration, respond to the following questions (show detailed computations):
        What is the budgeted breakeven point in dollars and in units? How many units would have to be sold to earn the target proft?

    b. You are to respond directly to each of the following alternatives under consideration by the management. Consider each independent of the others, and state any assumptions that you make.

        Alternative 1—A sales price increase of 20 percent is contemplated; the sales executive estimates that this will cause a drop in units that can be sold by approximately 15 percent. What would be the new breakeven point? What would be the new profit figure? How many units would have to be sold to earn the target profit?

        Alternative 2—A decrease in fixed costs of $5,500 is contemplated. What would be the breakeven point and new profit?

        Alternative 3—A decrease in variable costs of 6 percent is contemplated. What would be the new breakeven point and profit?

        Alternative 4—A decrease in fixed costs of $5,500 and a decrease in variable costs of 6 percent are contemplated. What would be the new breakeven point? How many units must be sold to earn the target profit?

CASE 14-5
Cording Company

Cording Company prepares a cost-volume-profit budget analysis for each plant. The profit plan for Plant 1 shows: annual budgeted fixed costs are $120,000; variable costs, $84,000; and sales value of production, $220,000. Allocated home office budgeted fixed costs are $32,000.

Required :

a.   You are asked to prepare an analysis indicating the breakeven points before and after cost allocations. Explain why the breakeven point change (in dollars) is greater than the allocated amount.

b.   Plant 2 produces a product that sells at $4.00 and costs $4.25 when produced in quantities of 15,000 and $3.8125 per unit when produced in quantities of 20,000. What is the breakeven point in dollars and in units?

c.   Plant 3 budgeted income and cost estimates are as follows:

Sales (annual)		$100,000
Costs:		
Fixed	$ 40,000	
Variable	30,000	
Home office allocated	35,000	105,000
Loss		$ 5,000

Sale of Plant 3 is under consideration; what is your recommendation based on the data given? Justify your recommendation. What is the breakeven point for the plant? Explain.

d.   Plant 4 produces one product; the budgeted income and cost estimates are as follows:

Sales (annual) @ $20		$200,000
Costs:		
Fixed	$ 74,750	
Variable	135,000	
Home office allocated	50,250	260,000
Loss		$ 60,000

How many additional units must be manufactured in the plant in order to break even? What would be the profit pickup per unit above breakeven? Explain.

CASE 14-6
Short Company

        Short Company manufactures two products, A and B. The company is having difficulty attaining a sales volume sufficient to employ present plant capacity. A new customer offers a large repeating contract for product A at $10 each and for product B at $18 each. The following budget data are available (assume the old market will not be affected) :

	PRODUCT A	PRODUCT B
Direct labor	$ 6,000	$15,000
Direct material	3,000	5,000
Variable factory overhead	3,000	4,000
Fixed factory overhead	12,000	20,000
Packing, shipping, and other variable costs	4,800	1,000
Administrative and sales overhead	9,000	15,000
Current planned sales: Average quantity	4,000 units	2,500 units
Unit sales price	$ 14	20

Assume the new contract will not increase fixed costs and administrative and selling overhead.

Required:

a. Compute the breakeven point for each product separately.

b. Based on the data given, should the contract be accepted? Support your conclussion with computations.

c. What is the minimum price and volume for each product that could be accepted under the new offer?

CASE 14-7
Smith Printers

Smith Printers, a small job-printing firm, is preparing a bid for 10 to 15 thousand advertising pamphlets, to which the following budget amounts relate:

Estimated cost of setting up and fixed overhead	$390
Estimated cost of material and variable overhead	$5.00 per hundred
Estimated cost of labor	$3.00 per hundred
Estimated selling price	$ .11 each

Required:

a. How many pamphlets must be sold to break even?

b. What is the profit per pamphlet above breakeven?

c. What should be the bid price for 10,000 pamphlets if a 10 percent profit on sales is desired? On 14,000 pamphlets?

CASE 14-8
Companies A & B

Certain annual budget data for two similar companies are as follows:

	COMPANY A		COMPANY B	
Sales		$200,000		$200,000
Costs:				
Fixed	$120,000		$ 60,000	
Variable	60,000	180,000	120,000	180,000
Income		$ 20,000		$ 20,000

Required:

Evaluate and compare the economic characteristics of the two companies.

CASE 14-9
Egon Corporation

Egon Corporation, in evaluating profit potentials for the sales objective of $24,000, is analyzing the effect of sales mix. Budgeted fixed costs are $3,312; and budgeted variable cost ratios are: product A, 70 percent; product B, 80 percent; and product C, 90 percent. Two sales-mix alternatives are being considered: Alternative 1—A, 50 percent; B, 30 percent; and C, 20 percent; Alternative 2—A, 70 percent; B, 20 percent; and C, 10 percent.

Required:

Evaluate the two alternatives. Select the preferable one, and justify your choice.

CASE 14-10
Hill Company

The income statement of the Hill Company for the past year showed the following statistics:

Sales		$5,000,000
Cost of sales:		
Fixed	$1,600,000	
Variable	1,750,000	3,350,000
Gross margin		$1,650,000
Selling and general expenses:		
Fixed	$ 556,000	
Variable	800,000	1,356,000
Income		$ 294,000

In developing the plans and policies for the coming year the executive in charge of sales estimated a potential sales volume of $7,500,000. The executive in charge of manufacturing realized that this volume of sales would necessitate major additions to fixed plant. The controller and other executives estimated that the expansion required would have the following effects:

Increase in depreciation, taxes, and insurance on factory	$220,000
Increase in superintendence salaries	20,000
Increase in miscellaneous fixed factory overhead	60,000
Increase in monthly sales salaries	200,000
Increase in annual advertising appropriation	100,000
Increase in interest cost.	50,000

Required:

1. Prepare an estimated income statement for the contemplated plan.
2. Compare the breakeven points before and after the expansion.
3. Compare profits, before and after the expansion at present sales levels.
4. Compute the sales needed after the expansion to yield $1,000,000 profit assuming, Case (a) no change in selling prices, and Case (b) the additional sales revenue is derived solely by means of a price increase.

Performance Reports for Management Control

chapter fifteen

We have discussed long-range and short-range profit plans. In those discussions, problems and approaches relating to control were also considered. Performance reports for internal management use constitute an important part of a comprehensive profit planning and control system. This chapter will focus on the fundamentals that should be observed in establishing a system of performance reports. The performance reporting phase of a comprehensive budget program may determine the extent to which the planned goals and objectives are attained.

To indicate the extensive reporting requirements a business must fulfill and to focus on performance reporting, the following broad classification of reports is presented and briefly explained:

1. **External Reports**—These are reports to government agencies, regulatory commissions, creditors, investigative agencies, and other groups external to the active management. Frequently, these reports are quite extensive and comprise a significant portion of the overall reporting activities of the business. These reports are costly and consume a lot of management attention.

2. **Report to Owners**—These are the traditional annual report to the owners (to stockholders in case of a corporation) and other special reports

prepared for the owners concerning special problems or items of interest. These reports, by and large, are based upon "generally accepted accounting principles" and generally report data that have been subject to audit by an independent C.P.A.

3. **Internal Reports**—These are reports prepared within the company for internal use only; they may be considered *confidential* reports. They do not have to meet the needs of external groups, nor the test of "generally accepted accounting," but rather the test of *internal management needs*. For purposes of discussion this category of reports is subdivided into three distinctly different subclassifications.

a. **Statistical Reports**—These are accounting reports that show the vital historical statistics concerning all phases of operations. The data included in these reports constitute the detailed financial and operating history of the firm. The accumulation of these data is essential on a continuing basis for both contemplated and unknown uses in the future. These statistics include the basic data for the two categories of reports outlined above; they also provide the basic data for special-purpose studies that are made from to time. Separate reports of this type are common in better-managed companies and are made on a repetitive basis (usually monthly).

b. **Special Reports**—These are internal reports prepared irregularly, each one being related to a specific management problem. Their design, scope, and comprehensiveness depend upon the particular problem at hand.

c. **Performance Reports**—These reports are generally prepared on a monthly basis and follow a fairly standardized format from period to period (but not standardized among companies or industries). These reports are specifically designed to facilitate internal control by the management. They should comprise carefully selected series of data related to specific responsibility centers. Fundamentally, they report actual results compared with goals or budget plans. Frequently, they identify a problem that requires a special report, since they are designed to pinpoint both efficient and inefficient performance.

All companies, regardless of size have reporting requirements for all the categories listed above. In the smaller company most of the basic reporting needs may be accomplished with a *single* general purpose report. However, as the size and complexity of the company increases, there is greater need for segmentation of the reporting as suggested above. Many companies make the mistake of mixing these several categories despite the increasing size and complexity of operations. As a company changes and grows, the overall system of financial reporting must be adapted to meet the changing needs. It is common to find an antiquated accounting and financial reporting system; in such cases, it is safe to say that the full potentials of the management (and the company) are jeopardized. The usual accounting report prepared for external use has limited application for internal management purposes. Accountants who attempt to meet the internal problems of management with reports designed for external purposes are failing in their responsibilities.

We are concerned here specifically with *performance reports* (3c above). This particular phase of reporting is an integral part of a comprehensive budget program. We will first discuss some of the essential characteristics of performance reports. In the latter part of the chapter we will discuss a typical monthly performance report related to the annual profit plan.

PERFORMANCE REPORTS AS A COMMUNICATION TOOL

Performance reports constitute an important phase of the control process. The prior discussions of the control process can be summarized as follows:

THE CONTROL PROCESS SUMMARIZED

In most business situations, management must rely to a great extent upon information contained in reports developed within the business. The internal reports, therefore, serve as an important means of communication. On this point one study stated:

In order to be useful to management, accounting information must be communicated to management personnel. Communication implies that a person receiving the information understands the nature and significance of material contained in the reports he receives. When communication is genuinely effective, management's actions and decisions are likely to be based on the facts which they receive rather than on untested impressions and guesses. However, there is reason to believe that accounting reports to management have not always achieved their intended purpose because the reports were not understood, recipients lacked time required to grasp the meaning, or the content of reports was not relevant to problems facing the persons who received them.[1]

Reports that communicate effectively to all levels of management stimulate action and influence decisions. Those charged with the design and preparation of reports for management, to be effective, must know and understand the problems and approaches used, and attitudes of the management.

ESSENTIAL FEATURES OF PERFORMANCE REPORTS

A great deal of management effort and time is required to develop realistic profit plans for an enterprise. This effort is justified primarily on the grounds that the activities of all subunits must be focused on enterprise objectives; each component of an enterprise fulfills a prescribed and necessary role in attaining the enterprise objectives. Thus fulfillment of the profit plan is vital. To assure performance of the objectives, control is a vital part of effective management. Control has many facets; among the more important are internal performance reports. Thus, in comprehensive profit planning and control, one focus is on performance reports. Performance reports have as their central objective the communication of performance measurements and operational data. In addition to control implications, performance reports offer management essential insights into all facets of operational efficiencies. Clearly, performance reports pose critical behavioral problems since inefficiencies, as well as efficiencies, of individuals are pinpointed and reported. Performance reports must be tailored to the characteristics of each particular environment; however, we may generalize about certain relevant criteria in their design and application. Thus, performance reports should be:

1. Tailored to the organizational structure and controllability (that is, by responsibility centers).
2. Designed to implement the exception principle in management.
3. Repetitive and relate to short time spans.
4. Adapted to the requirements of the principal user.
5. Simple, understandable, and report only essential information.
6. Accurate and expressive of significant distinctions.
7. Prepared and presented promptly.
8. Constructive in tone.

[1] "Reports Which Management Find Most Useful," *NAA Bulletin*, Accounting Practice Report, no. 9, sec. 3.

THE BASIC FORMAT OF PERFORMANCE REPORTS

The first three criteria listed above suggest the basic format in the design and application of performance reports. The performance report system should be tailored to the organizational structure of the enterprise in the same way that we have emphasized for budgeting and the accounting systems. There should be a separate performance report for each *responsibility center*, starting with those at the lowest level, which in turn feed into summary reports for each higher level. Performance reports must clearly distinguish between controllable and noncontrollable items. Performance measurement requires that actual results be compared with plans, objectives, and standards so that differences (exceptions) call management attention to high, low, and satisfactory performance. The variances from plans signal to those in authority that there is a need for investigation and possible action. The action may be corrective, commendatory, or revisory. Favorable variances justify investigation as well as unfavorable variances. Unfavorable variances may signal danger; further investigation generally is necessary to pinpoint the precise cause. Performance reports should be repetitive, generally on a monthy basis, although certain problems may suggest the need for weekly or even daily reports that focus on a particular problem.

A hypothetical manufacturing company is assumed to illustrate the manner in which reports may be (1) related to the organizational structure, (2) designed to identify the exceptional items that are controllable, and (3) related to specific time horizons. The organization chart for SP Manufacturing Company is shown in Illustration 53. Note the four levels of management indicated and the line organization from president down to the departmental foreman (the manager) of Machining No. 2. The blocked out segment of the chart is used to illustrate the concepts. Illustration 54 shows the February *performance report* for each level of management and their integration. Observe that the lower report (for Machining No. 2) indicates the *status of cost control* for the month and year to date for each controllable cost in the department. This report is designed especially for the foreman of Machining No. 2. Similar reports would be prepared for the other producing departments (Machining 1, Drill Press, Assembly, and Others). Obviously, the foreman of each department would normally receive the performance report that relates only to his department.

Moving one step up the organizational ladder (to the production manager), a *productive department cost summary* is prepared. This performance report is simply a summary of the five producing department reports (Illustration 54). The report is designed especially for the production manager and clearly pinpoints, *by department*, weaknesses in cost control. Should the production manager desire to trace the source of either favorable or unfavor-

Performance Reports for Managerial Control

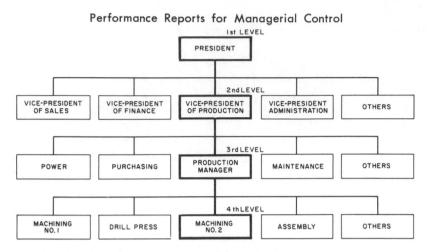

ILLUSTRATION 53. Organization Chart—SP Manufacturing Company

able cost control performance to *accounts* within the department involved, he can refer to the appropriate departmental performance reports, each of which should be attached to his summary. For example, the *productive department cost summary* (last column) calls attention to two departments (Machining No. 2 and Assembly) that have unfavorable cost variances. Tracing the $130 unfavorable variance in Machining No. 2, one can immediately identify the specific cost (direct labor) as the primary problem that needs attention.

Noncontrollable costs (see Chapter 9) are not reported in this simplified example. A policy problem exists in this respect—that is, whether to show all costs chargeable to the particular responsibility center or to show only the controllable costs. Although may companies report only controllable costs on the departmental performance reports, others prefer to show all costs chargeable to the department (as explained in Chapter 9) on the theory that the supervisor should be aware of the full cost of operating his department. The former procedure is generally preferable. In addition to costs, the performance report for a responsibility center should report all controllable items as illustrated in Chapters 6, 7, 8, 9, and 10.

This simplified illustration for SP Manufacturing Company also shows the application of the *management by exception principle*. For example, the production manager does not have to delve into numerous figures to identify the source of trouble (the exception); he can check the last column of the summary for *significant variations*. The exception principle cannot be applied to actual (historical) figures standing alone; there must be some standard (budget in this case) against which actual figures may be compared in order to identify the exceptions.

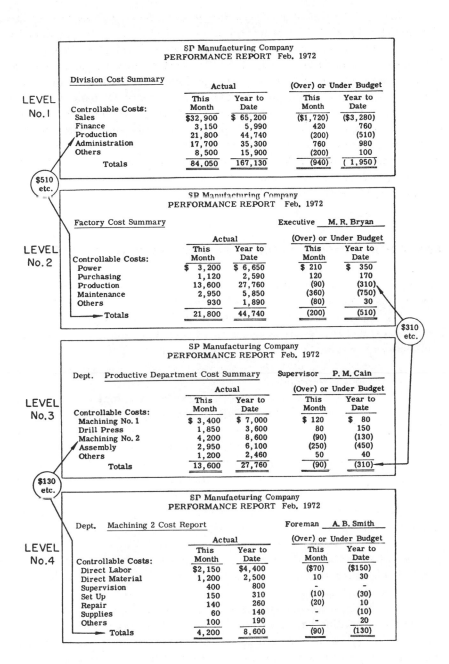

LEVEL No. 1

SP Manufacturing Company
PERFORMANCE REPORT Feb. 1972

Division Cost Summary

Controllable Costs:	Actual		(Over) or Under Budget	
	This Month	Year to Date	This Month	Year to Date
Sales	$32,900	$ 65,200	($1,720)	($3,280)
Finance	3,150	5,990	420	760
Production	21,800	44,740	(200)	(510)
Administration	17,700	35,300	760	980
Others	8,500	15,900	(200)	100
Totals	84,050	167,130	(940)	(1,950)

$510 etc.

LEVEL No. 2

SP Manufacturing Company
PERFORMANCE REPORT Feb. 1972

Factory Cost Summary Executive M. R. Bryan

Controllable Costs:	Actual		(Over) or Under Budget	
	This Month	Year to Date	This Month	Year to Date
Power	$ 3,200	$ 6,650	$ 210	$ 350
Purchasing	1,120	2,590	120	170
Production	13,600	27,760	(90)	(310)
Maintenance	2,950	5,850	(360)	(750)
Others	930	1,890	(80)	30
Totals	21,800	44,740	(200)	(510)

$310 etc.

LEVEL No. 3

SP Manufacturing Company
PERFORMANCE REPORT Feb. 1972

Dept. Productive Department Cost Summary Supervisor P. M. Cain

Controllable Costs:	Actual		(Over) or Under Budget	
	This Month	Year to Date	This Month	Year to Date
Machining No. 1	$ 3,400	$ 7,000	$ 120	$ 80
Drill Press	1,850	3,600	80	150
Machining No. 2	4,200	8,600	(90)	(130)
Assembly	2,950	6,100	(250)	(450)
Others	1,200	2,460	50	40
Totals	13,600	27,760	(90)	(310)

$130 etc.

LEVEL No. 4

SP Manufacturing Company
PERFORMANCE REPORT Feb. 1972

Dept. Machining 2 Cost Report Foreman A. B. Smith

Controllable Costs:	Actual		(Over) or Under Budget	
	This Month	Year to Date	This Month	Year to Date
Direct Labor	$2,150	$4,400	($70)	($150)
Direct Material	1,200	2,500	10	30
Supervision	400	800	-	-
Set Up	150	310	(10)	(30)
Repair	140	260	(20)	10
Supplies	60	140	-	(10)
Others	100	190	-	20
Totals	4,200	8,600	(90)	(130)

ILLUSTRATION 54.   Performance Reports—SP Manufacturing Company

Moving to level two, the development of the *factory cost summary* for the vice president of production is accomplished by listing the summary data for each of the five organizational subdivisions (Power, Purchasing, Production, Maintenance, and Others). Similarly, the performance summary for the president is developed. The reports are repetitive with monthly and cumulative data. The result of these procedures is an *integrated* performance reporting system built around (1) the organization structure, (2) the budget objectives and the exception principle, and (3) specific time dimensions. The system is simple, easily understood, and enables the executives to keep their fingers on the performance pulse of the company with a minimum of time and study. Obviously, this same system should be applied to sales performance reporting and other operational areas.

ADAPT PERFORMANCE REPORTS TO REQUIREMENTS OF USER

The extent to which the various managers utilize their performance reports depends upon many factors, some behavioral and some technical. One important factor is the extent to which the performance reports serve the evaluation and decision-making needs of the user. Communication is a subtle problem, and it is enhanced by performance reports, if the different needs and experiences of the user are taken into account. A foreman responds differently than a vice president.

Top management must have reports that give a complete and readily comprehensible summary of the overall aspects of operations and an identification of major events. The summaries must be supported by sufficient detail to facilitate tracing unfavorable situations to their source.

Middle management is usually defined as those members of management in charge of the major subdivisions of the business, such as sales, production, and finance. Middle management is responsible for carrying out the responsibilities assigned to the subdivisions within the broad policies and objectives established by top management. Middle management is closer and more concerned with operations than top management, although it also has important planning functions. Performance reports for middle management, although including summary data, also are characterized by detailed data on day-to-day operations.

Lower level management (supervisors and foremen) is principally concerned with coordination and control of day-to-day operations; therefore, control reports must be designed accordingly. These reports are principally concerned with production and cost control. Reports to foremen and supervisors must be detailed, simple, understandable, and limited to items having a direct bearing on the supervisors' operational responsibilities.

The presentation media for financial data may be broadly classified as follows:

1. Written:
   a. Formal financial statements.
   b. Tabulated statistics.
   c. Narration and exposition using words.
2. Graphic:
   a. Charts.
   b. Diagrams and pictures.
3. Oral:
   a. Group meetings.
   b. Conferences with individuals.

A company should use a variety of media for presentation of reports to management. In most companies all of the media listed above should be employed from time to time. Selection of the appropriate method should depend upon such factors as type of report, data involved, level of management using the report, purpose of the report, background of the principal user, and the nature of the operations. Some executives are chart-minded, others are figure-minded. Because accountants by training and tradition are figure-minded, financial reports have been predominantly tabulations of financial statistics. Those preparing performance reports must remember that financial reports are generally used by nonaccountants with varied backgrounds. In view of these considerations some companies have adopted combination forms. A useful combination of media for recurring reports employs both charts and figures. To illustrate, assume the following data were taken from a conventional report:

Trend Report of Profits and Sales 1967 to Date

YEAR	OPERATING PROFITS	SALES
1967	$14,000	$150,000
1968	14,000	147,000
1969	14,500	154,000
1970	14,700	160,000
1971	14,400	158,000
1972	14,800	161,000
1973	14,600	164,000
1974	14,500	165,000
1975	14,500	165,000
1976	18,000*	166,000
1977	14,600†	168,000†

*Includes fixed assets sold at a gain of $4,000.
†Budgeted.

Performance Report—Sales March 31, 1977

MONTH	ACTUAL SALES	BUDGETED SALES	VARIATION FROM BUDGET (UNDER)
January	$11,800	$ 12,000	($200)
February	12,100	12,000	100
March	14,300	14,000	300
April		15,000	
May		16,000	
June		15,000	
July		14,000	
August		12,000	
September		13,000	
October		14,000	
November		15,000	
December		16,000	
Total		$168,000	

Although the trend report accurately presents past profits and sales for a period of years, comparisons and trends are not readily understandable. The same data are presented in a more understandable way in Illustrations 54a and 54b. Similarly, the performance report is presented more clearly in Illustrations 56a and 56b. The procedure suggested by this simple example indicates the advantages of presenting certain types of information both graphically and in figures. The charts effectively communicate the overall aspects of the data; the figures provide exact data when needed. Some companies maintain a "performance report book" for individual executives. The book is generally a loose-leaf binder containing the performance and related reports for the particular executive. If the combined procedure is used, the graphs might be printed on the back of the page and the corresponding tabulations on the front of the next page so that, when the report is opened at any particular page, the graphs are always on the left and the figures on the right. Illustrations 55 and 56 are presented in this manner.[2]

Many top executives have a strong preference for narrative summaries of internal reports. Words frequently tell the story much more effectively than bare figures. Analyses of the causative factors involved, for example, in a performance report showing significant exceptions, generally should be presented in narrative form.

Oral presentation should be a significant part of the internal reporting system in all companies. Controllers and budget directors should encourage the use of executive conferences where the performance report is presented, explained, and discussed. Oral presentation is important because

[2] Robert A. Blake, "The Management Data Book," *NAA Bulletin* (May 1962), pp. 43–50.

interpretation and emphasis are possible that are lacking in other forms. In addition, the managers have the opportunity to pose questions and bring up points that are not clear, thus assuring understanding and communication.

KEEP REPORTS SIMPLE AND ESSENTIAL

In the design and preparation of performance reports, keep in mind that the user generally is not an accountant and that the report is to serve a user other than the report-maker. Careful attention to form is important. Titles and headings should be descriptive, column headings and side captions should clearly identify the data, and technical jargon should be avoided.

Reports should not be too long; complex tabulations should be avoided. Reports should be carefully screened to eliminate all nonessential information. Many performance reports include too much data rather than too little. Illustration 54 shows how a report can be simplified. Actual costs and budget variations are reported and the budget allowances omitted. The "Budget Allowance" column may add little understanding and tends to make the report bulky. Another technique to simplify reports is to round amounts to the nearest significant figures.

Performance reports should be standardized. Executives become accustomed to certain terminology, forms, and methods of presentation and know where to look to find the specific information. Thus, changing report forms indiscriminately can be a source of annoyance. Despite the desirability of standardizing performance reports, constant attention must be given to improving them. Improvement necessarily involves changes; but desirable changes, if made at an opportune time and adequately presented, can be accomplished usually with a minimum of confusion.

Reports must be kept relevant. It is not uncommon to find data in some performance reports (or even entire reports) that serve no useful purpose. Such data are there, frequently, because someone in upper management, months or even years before, requested it for a special purpose. Although there is no further use for the information, no one has taken the initiative to discontinue it. It is not surprising that busy executives, in requesting special information, may not give a date beyond which it will no longer be needed; nor do they necessarily remember to tell someone to discontinue presenting the special data.

Surveys reveal that a considerable percentage of the data on internal financial reports are not used. Continuous effort to simplify reports should supplement periodic surveys to divulge the extent of nonrelevant information being presented to the various levels of management.

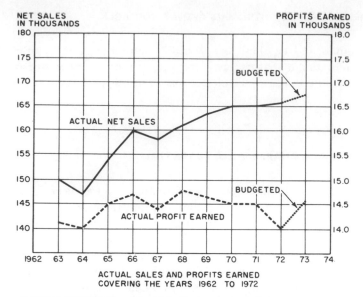

ILLUSTRATION 55a.   Graphic Presentation—Sales and Profits

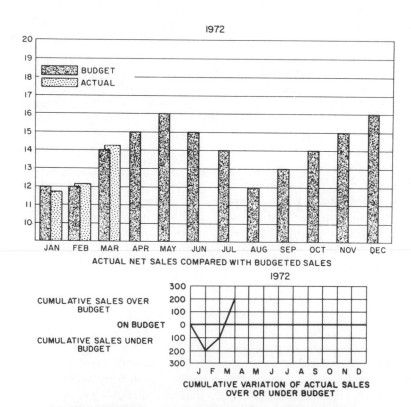

ILLUSTRATION 56a.   Graphic Presentation—Sales and Profits

ILLUSTRATION 55b

Summary of Actual Sales and Profits
Earned from Operations Covering
the Years 1967 to 1977

YEAR	ACTUAL NET SALES	PROFITS EARNED (EXCLUDING UNUSUAL OR NONOPERATING ITEMS)	PROFITS AS PERCENT OF SALES
1967	$150,000	$14,000	9.3
1968	147,000	14,000	9.5
1969	154,000	14,500	9.4
1970	160,000	14,700	9.1
1971	158,000	14,400	9.1
1972	161,000	14,800	9.2
1973	164,000	14,600	8.9
1974	165,000	14,500	8.8
1975	165,000	14,500	8.8
1976	166,000	14,000	8.4
1977 (Budgeted)	168,000	14,600	8.7

ILLUSTRATION 56b

Summary of Actual Net Sales Compared with
Budgeted Sales for Three Months
Ending March 31, 1977

MONTH 1977	ACTUAL NET SALES	BUDGETED NET SALES	VARIATION OF ACTUAL SALES FROM BUDGET (AMOUNTS BELOW BUDGET*)	
			MONTHLY VARIATION	CUMULATIVE VARIATION
January	$11,800	$ 12,000	($200)	($200)
February	12,100	12,000	100	(100)
March	14,300	14,000	300	200
April		15,000		
May		16,000		
June		15,000		
July		14,000		
August		12,000		
September		13,000		
October		14,000		
November		15,000		
December		16,000		
Total		$168,000		

MINIMIZE THE TIME GAP BETWEEN THE DECISION
AND THE REPORTING

As a rule, executives, supervisors, and foremen are very busy tending to their respective responsibilities. They are continually (daily) making deasions, varying from major decisions to relatively insignificant ones. It is the sum total of these decisions that determines the success or failure of the firm and its various segments. Because of the significance of the decision-making process and its immediate and continuous effect on efficiency, the gap between the point of decision and the reporting of the results of such decisions must be minimized. In any situation both good and bad decisions must be expected; the degree of overall efficiency depends upon the *ratio* of the good decisions to the total. Advance planning minimizes the risk of an excessive number of bad decisions; likewise a sound system of performance reporting minimizes this risk. The time gap between the decision point and performance reporting must be minimized because (1) unfavorable situations and problems are most significant to the supervisor at the time they occur; as time passes the supervisor becomes more concerned with new events and less concerned with past; (2) the longer an unfavorable situation continues before correction, the greater the financial loss to the company; and (3) with the passage of time there is a tendency to regard inefficiency as "normal" or "the best we can do under the circumstances." Here we may observe a parallel with Gresham's law that "bad money drives out the good money," similarly, inefficiency tends to drive out efficiency.

Consistent with the cost of detailed record-keeping and reporting, performance reports should be available on a timely basis. To achieve a realistic balance between immediate reporting and the costs of detailed reporting, monthly performance reports are widely used by industry. When special problem areas are involved, weekly and even daily reporting may be necessary, at least for a time.

The tendency of some accountants to hold up the issuance of performance reports until all the "facts are in" frequently detracts from the usefulness of the reports. Because accounting data can seldom be exact (there will always be some estimation, such as depreciation), those preparing such reports should not hesitate to make reasonable estimates of "actual" items, so that an early report is possible. Even in simple situations monthly performance reports often are issued after the twentieth of the following month. Objective analysis will usually show no valid reason for the reports being issued later than the fifth to seventh day in the following month. Some accuracy may have to be sacrificed, but not enough to impair the effectiveness of the resulting information for *management purposes*. It bears repeating that external reporting presents communication problems that are entirely different from those of internal reporting.

MANAGEMENT FOLLOW-UP PROCEDURES

Better-managed companies issue monthly performance reports covering all aspects of operations. These reports indicate favorable and unfavorable variations between actual performance and planned performance for the month just ended and, cumulatively, for the year to date. Executives should examine the monthly report carefully to be fully knowledgeable about both *high* and *low* performance in their respective responsibility centers. High and low performances should be given immediate priority to determine the causes. However, the process should not stop at this point. *Follow-up procedures* constitute a key aspect of effective control. Some companies require written explanations of significant variances. The follow-up procedures preferred by other companies involve constructive conferences where the causes are discussed and corrective action is decided upon. Follow-up procedures should begin at the top management level—in the executive committee meeting, for example, where both unsatisfactory and satisfactory conditions are discussed and analyzed. Decisions should be made concerning ways and means of correcting unsatisfactory conditions. Favorable variances should be accorded equivalent study (1) to determine whether the goals were realistic, and (2) to give recognition to those responsible for high performances, and (3) possibly to transfer some "know-how" to other subdivisions of the company.

Group and individual conferences should be held at the various management levels for effective corrective action. Follow-up procedures should embody constructive action to correct unfavorable conditions rather than punitive action for failures, the results of which obviously cannot be erased. Another important aspect of follow-up procedure is that the resulting *action* is strictly a *line* responsibility rather than a staff responsibility. The budget director, controller, or other staff officer should not undertake, nor be assigned, the responsibility for *enforcing* the budget.

TECHNICAL ASPECTS OF CONTROL REPORTS

A few concerns issue separate internal "accounting" and "budget" reports; however, because separation of these two reports for internal managerial purposes seems illogical; we assume in this book that they are combined into a single performance report.

Performance reports are variously called internal reports, financial and operating reports, accounting reports, budget reports, or simply financial reports. Performance reports primary value is in the comparison of actual results with budget objectives and in the analysis of the resulting variations. There are numerous methods of expressing variances. The expression of variances as absolute amounts are not always satisfactory because an absolute amount standing alone frequently means little. Variations should also be expressed in relative terms; that is, as a percent or ratio of the budget allowances. Although *satistical control limits* can be developed, most companies find it entirely satisfactory to establish a general "rule-of-thumb" policy concerning the significance of variation. For example, a medium-size business might establish a policy that variations up to $25 or 5 percent of budget are to be considered insignificant. A realistic policy along this line should be established because neither actual figures nor budget objectives will be absolutely accurate.

In Illustration 54, the report contains columns for actual results and budget variations budget objectives are not included. Many companies prefer to show actual, budget, dollar variations, and percentage variations. The mechanics for several methods of reporting variations may be illustrated as follows:

	1	2	3	RELATIVES		
				4	5	6
			VARIATION	PERCENT OF VARIATION	PERCENT OF BUDGET	PERCENT OF ACTUAL
	ACTUAL	BUDGET	IN DOLLARS	TO BUDGET	REALIZATION	TO BUDGET
			(1 − 2)	(3 ÷ 2)	(2 ÷ 1)	(1 ÷ 2)
Expense	$ 110	$ 100	$ 10*	10%*	90.9%	110%
Sales	$11,000	$10,000	$1,000	10%	110 %†	110%

*Unfavorable.
†For incomes the dividend and divisor must be reversed.

Reports normally should carry *actual* (column 1); however, there is a serious question as to which of the remaining columns would be preferable in a particular situation. In most cases it would seem desirable to report data shown in columns 1, 3, and either 4, 5, or 6. Column 4 is more generally used than 5 or 6, because it relates the variation directly to the objective. In the illustration column 4 indicates that expense was 10 percent over budget (unfavorable). Sales were also 10 percent over budget, which is favorable. To compute this column, the mathematical process is the same for incomes or expenses, that is, column 3 divided by column 2. If the budget variation is negative (unfavorable), the resulting percentage will be negative (unfavorable). Column 5, "Percent of Budget Realization," is used by some companies because it is easily understood. In the above case the budget realization of 90.9% ($100 ÷ $110) indicates that the efficiency of cost control was only 90.9 percent; had actual expense been $100, budget realization would have been 100 percent; that is, exactly "par." On the other hand, had actual expense been $90, budget realization would have been 111 percent. When dealing with incomes, the mathematical process must be reversed, that is, actual is divided by budget. Thus budget realization for sales in the illustration is 110 percent because actual sales were 10 percent above budgeted sales. The latter method is simple to understand, because a percentage figure above 100 percent always indicates a favorable condition, whereas a percentage figure below 100 percent indicates an unfavorable condition. The method illustrated in column 6 is seldom used.

Monthly performance reports covering operations should generally show (1) variations for the month being reported and (2) cumulative variations to date. Those preparing performance reports should make judicious use of footnote comments where the reasons for specific variations are known. In addition, footnotes should be used to direct the attention of management to specific conditions that may require attention.

THE INTEGRATED PERFORMANCE REPORT

A comprehensive performance report for Producing Department X in the Stanley Company is shown in Illustration 57 (the related variable budget is given on p. 16-11). Note in particular the following features: (1) identification of responsibility; (2) distinction between controllable and noncontrollable items; (3) specific time dimensions—month and cumulative to date; (4) method of reporting variances; (5) adjustment of the "planned" amounts to actual outputs (that is, the variable budget approach); (6) detail on each category (including service usage in units); and (7) explanatory comments and suggestions. This illustration will be continued in the next chapter where the analysis of variances is discussed.

This chapter focuses primarily on *repetitive performance reports*. To be of maximum usefulness, the monthly performance report should be carefully designed to indicate the performance of each individual having supervisory responsibility. A well-designed control report should be completely *integrated*; that is, each schedule should link, on a responsibility basis, as in Illustration 54. Integration is particulary important so that (1) major variations may be traced to the source of the problem and (2) the various segments comprise, within themselves, a complete report. The latter aspect is essential for distribution of the performance report and its segments to the respective responsibility centers.

Distribution of the various segments of the annual profit plan was discussed in Chapter 13. Distribution of the monthly performance report (and its segments) should follow essentially the same pattern. The financial

ILLUSTRATION 57. Departmental Performance Report

Stanley Company Performance Report

DATE JANUARY, 1977 RESPONSIBILITY OF B. R. SPEER

| | DEPT. PROD. DEPT. X CURRENT MONTH—JANUARY | | | | | YEAR TO DATE | | |
	ACTUAL	PLANNED	VARIANCE* AMOUNT	VARIANCE* %	DESCRIPTION	ACTUAL	PLANNED	VARIANCE* AMOUNT	VARIANCE* %
					CONTROLLABLE:				
	87,500	100,000	12,500*	13*	Dept. output in units				
					Raw material A:				
	176,000	175,000	1,000*	1*	Units				
	$ 35,200	$ 35,000	$ 200*	1*	Cost				
					Direct labor:				
	35,357	35,000	357*	1*	Hours				
	$ 1.96	$ 2.00	$ .04	2	Average wage rate				
	69,300	70,000	700	1	Cost				
					Controllable dept. overhead:				
	10,000	10,000	—	—	Salaries				
	3,740	3,800	60	2	Indirect materials				
	7,550	7,250	300*	4*	Indirect labor				
	560	1,000	440	44	Miscellaneous				
	$ 21,850	$ 22,050	$ 200	1	Subtotal				
					Service usage:				
	530	480	50*	10*	Kilowatt hours (000's)				
	72	60	12*	20*	Direct repair hours				
	$126,350	$127,050	$ 700	1	Grand total				

ILLUSTRATION 57. (Continued)

	DEPT. PROD. DEPT. X				DATE JANUARY, 1975			RESPONSIBILITY OF B. R. SPEER		
	CURRENT MONTH JANUARY							YEAR TO DATE		
			VARIANCE*						VARIANCE*	
ACTUAL	PLANNED	AMOUNT	%	DESCRIPTION	ACTUAL	PLANNED	AMOUNT	%
				NONCONTROLLABLE:				
				Dept. Overhead:				
$ 2,000	$ 2,000	—	—	Depreciation				
500	500	—	—	Insurance				
200	200	—	—	Taxes				
$ 2,700	$ 2,700	—	—	Total—non-controllable				

*Unfavorable variance.

COMMENTS:

1. Output was 13 per cent below the planned level due to production scheduling pull back to accomodate 5,000 unit unfavorable sales volume variation; the department met its production schedule as adjusted.

2. Unfavorable variances in service usage should be carefully investigated to determine the underlying causes.

officer or budget director should develop (as a part of the budget manual) a *performance report distribution schedule*. Certain executives need the complete monthly performance report. Other members of management need only those schedules related to their particular responsibility centers. The tendency to provide everyone with a complete copy of the monthly report should be discouraged. The receipt of a bulky financial report by a department supervisor discourages interest in even the part that directly relates to his department. Lower levels of management may receive only one of the *detailed segments*. On the other hand, the higher the level of management, the greater the need for *summaries*, yet these summaries must be supported by adequate detail to identify particular aspects of operations. The distribution of reports to the various levels of management is indicated simply in Illustrations 53 and 54. The distribution schedule could be as follows:

POSITION AND NAME	REPORT TO BE RECEIVED
Foreman, A. B. Smith	Cost Report, Machining No. 2
Supervisor, P. M. Cain	Cost Report, Productive Department Summary
	Cost Reports, All Productive Departments
Executive, M. R. Bryan	Factory Cost Summary
	Productive Department Summary
	Cost Reports, All Productive Departments
	Service Department Summary
	Cost Reports, All Service Departments
President	Complete Report.

JANUARY PERFORMANCE REPORT FOR SUPERIOR MANUFACTURING COMPANY

Space limitations preclude inclusion of this company's monthly performance report. The report is completely integrated and includes two types of comparisons: (1) actual results compared with the annual profit plan; and (2) actual results compared with adjusted budget allowances for costs (that is, variable budget allowances). The report carries actual, budget, and variations for the month and cumulative for the year to date. Schedules 19 and 20 and Illustration 57 represent the general format and composition of the various segments of the integrated report.

Illustration 58 lists the various segments of the complete performance report. Note that the schedule identification (first column) indicates the relationship of the detailed and summary schedules. For example, Schedule G2 is a *summary* performance report of distribution expenses that is supported by Schedules G2.1, G2.2, G2.3, and G2.4, which are the individual expense performance reports for the four sales districts. The column to the right, "Order of Preparation," is included to suggest that there is a necessary

ILLUSTRATION 58. Superior Manufacturing Company

Performance Report—List of Schedules

January Report—Schedules

SCH. NO.	TITLE	DEPARTMENT	SUPERVISOR	ORDER OF PREPARATION
A	Balance Sheet with Budget Comparisons (with Original Plan)			26
B	Income Statement (compared to Original Plan and Adjusted Budget)			23
C	Cost of Goods Sold			—
D	District Income Statements (compared with Adjusted Budget)	By district		25
E	Sales Control Report	By district		22
F	Summary of Manufacturing Costs (by product)	Mfg.	A. B. Works	24
G	Departmental Expense Control Report (summary)	Company	Gen. Management	20
G1	Departmental Expense Control Report (summary)	Gen. Adm.	B. R. Taylor (Ex. VP)	7
G1.1	" " " " (dept. only)	Adm.	P. A. Johnson	4
G1.2	" " " " "	Accounting	H. H. Harrison	5
G1.3	" " " " "	Treasurer	I. M. Cash	6
G2	" " " " (summary)	Sales	G. A. Beloit	12
G2.1	" " " " (dept. only)	Southern	Ray C. Nixon	8
G2.2	" " " " "	Eastern	C. C. Campbell	9
G2.3	" " " " "	Western	W. W. Anderson	10
G2.4	" " " " "	Gen. Sales	T. K. Rielly	11
G3	" " " " (summary)	Factory	A. B. Works	19
G3.1	" " " " (dept. only)	1	K. R. Mason	13
G3.2	" " " " "	2	A. B. Ross	14
G3.3	" " " " "	3	W. E. Cox	15
G3.4	" " " " "	Repair	C. R. Medford	16
G3.5	" " " " "	Power	K. W. Haus	17
G3.6	" " " " "	Gen. Fac.	A. R. Carson	18
G4	" " " " "	Bldg. Serv.	Sam Adams	3
G5	Report of Noncontrollable Expenses at Dept. Level (summary)	Company	Gen. Man.	21
H	Report of Material Purchases	Pur.	T. E. Merton	2
I	Report of Other Income and Expenses (compared with Orig. Plan)	Treasurer	I. M. Cash	1
J	Analysis of Mfg. O. H. Over/Under Applied	Factory	Gen. Man.	27

sequence that usually must be followed in developing the various detailed reports, the summaries, and finally the complete performance report. Notice the structure of the complete report in terms of organization responsibilities.

DISCUSSION QUESTIONS

1. Outline and briefly explain the reporting structure for a medium to large-size firm that recognizes the needs of the major interested parties.

2. Why should financial reports for internal purposes be significantly different in structure and content from those for external purposes?

3. What are the principal purposes of internal performance reports?

4. What are the fundamental foundations that should underlie performance reports?

5. Why should performance reports be tailored to the organizational responsibilities in the enterprise?

6. Relate the management exception principle to performance reports.

7. Distinguish between internal reports for (1) top management, (2) middle management, and (3) lower management.

8. Why is it advisable that several different media be used in performance reports?

9. What criteria might be used to determine whether a variation is significant?

10. Why is it generally undesirable to distribute the entire monthly performance report for the company to all supervisory personnel?

11. Assume that a particular performance report shows for item A a $500 unfavorable variation and for item B a $500 favorable variation. Should equal consideration be given to the two variations? Discuss.

12. Explain the time gap in performance reporting. Why is it critical?

13. What is meant by integration in the design of the monthly performance report? Is it significant? Why?

CASE 15-1

Frankel Company

Frankel Company produces five different products that are distributed widely throughout the United States. Annual sales approximated $43,000,000 last year. There are two plants in widely separated sections of the country. The manufacturing division is composed of fifteen different departments (seven in each plant) including central plant administration. The country is divided into five sales districts, each headed by a district sales manager. The company has approximately 9,000 shareholders, and the stock is sold on one of the national stock exchanges. The latest balance sheet reflected that approximately 40 percent of the total assets were provided by creditors. Internal management has been changed in recent years so that now it is dynamic, and the company is expecting a 12 percent increase in sales for the coming year. The annual profit plan and the five-year profit plan incorporate this planned increase although a slower average rate was anticipated for the next four years (long-range). Management tentatively plans to incorporate a new plant to be constructed in about five years. In planning for dynamic changes and to keep up with "special problems," the management has frequently requested special studies by the controller and other functional executives. The accounting system is well-organized and the organization structure of the company is set up on a sound basis. Due to seasonality and dynamic growth, monthly projections in the annual profit plan frequently are materially different from actual, particularly in planned output, although the annual projection has been pretty much on target.

Although the profit planning and control program appears to be functioning effectively and is generally accepted by the mangers at all levels, there is a continuing concern about the reporting structure of the company. The financial vice president stated that he had decided that "a comprehensive analysis of the reporting in the company as it is now carried on must be undertaken. On the basis of that analysis, and following sound theory and procedures, we will completely overhaul the reporting structure taking into considetation all actual and potential users of our reports." Casual conversation and observation convinced the case writer that the present reporting structure "just grew."

Required:

Assuming that the statement by the financial vice president confirmed the conclusions reached by the case writer, present your recommendations for a broad and comprehensive approach to financial reporting for the company. Focus on important concepts, approaches, and issues.

CASE 15-2
Canning Company

Canning Company is a medium-size manufacturer of parts; its major customer is a large automotive manufacturer. Seven different products are produced, three of which are sold to outlets other than the major customer. Sales and production necessarily follow the seasonal patterns experienced by the major customer. The company has developed a comprehensive profit planning and control program that incorporates a five-year long-range plan, an annual profit plan (detailed by month), variable expense budgets in the factory departments, and a comprehensive performance reporting system. The performance reports are developed and distributed on a responsibility basis each month. The supervisor concerned has the direct responsibility to investigate causes of all significant variances (both favorable and unfavorable) and to report the results to his immediate supervisor. He is expected to recommend specific follow-up actions with respect to all significant variances; when approved by his immediate supervisor, these recommendations are implemented.

There are a number of service and production departments in the factory. This case specifically relates to one of the productive departments—21, supervised by John Campbell. Of the seven products, this particular department works on three of them: A, B, and C. The output of Department 21 is measured in standard direct machine hours. The department uses one raw material, designated material X. The following data relates to the operations of this department:

Profit plan data:
1. Planned output in January—A, 800 units; B, 400 units; and C, 500 units.

2. Budgeted rates and cost:
   Raw material X—Standard purchase price per unit $3.
                   —Standard usage rates per unit of finished product:
                       A requires one unit of raw material X.
                       B requires three units of raw material X.
                       C requires two units of raw material X.
   Direct labor—Average wage rate in Department 21, $5 per hour.
               —Standard labor times per unit of finished product:
                   A requires three direct labor hours.
                   B requires two direct labor hours.
                   C requires one and one-half direct labor hours.

Variable budget for Dept. 21:

	FIXED PER MONTH	VARIABLE PER STANDARD DIRECT MACHINE HOUR
Indirect materials		$.10
Indirect labor	$ 400	.75
Miscellaneous	200	.05
Supervisory salaries*	6,000	
Productive salaries	4,000	
Depreciation*	1,000	
Insurance and Taxes*	400	

   *Noncontrollable in the department.

Service usage planned for January:

Kilowatt hours (000's)	650
Direct repair hours	20

Direct machine hours at standard for: product A, 4; product B, 6; and product C 10.

3. Actual data provided by the Accounting Department at the end of January:
   Actual output in January—A, 800 units; B, 300 units; and C, 400 units.
   Actual purchases of raw material X in January—9,000 units at $3.05 per unit.
     Actual units issued to Dept. 21 in January, 2,640.
   Actual direct labor costs for January: 3,580 hours, cost $18,616.
   Actual overhead costs for January:

Indirect materials	$ 940
Indirect labor	7,000
Miscellaneous	690
Supervisory salaries	6,000
Productive salaries	4,200

   (Two supervisors resigned and were replaced with a salary increase of $100 each.)

Depreciation	1,000
Insurance and taxes	400

   Actual service usage for January:

Kilowatt hours (000's)	640
Direct repair hours	28
Actual direct machine hours for January	9,100

Required:

Use the above data to prepare a complete and comprehensive performance report for January for Department 21. State any assumptions that you make.

CASE 15-3
Lelon Company

Lelon Company manufactures a line of products processed through five production centers. Selected actual and budget data for the month of June are presented below. Utilize these data to illustrate an integrated performance report system for the company. Identify the primary features of the system that you design.

| | JUNE | |
COSTS	ACTUAL	BUDGET
Divisions:		
Sales	$65,000	$60,000
Financial	7,000	7,100
General Administrative	16,000	15,700
Research	21,000	22,000
Factory		
Departments (factory only):		
Purchasing	6,000	5,600
Maintenance	4,000	3,500
Factory Administrative	9,000	8,800
Production (five cost centers)		
Production Cost Centers:		
1	18,000	17,700
2	27,000	26,000
3	32,000	30,500
4 (see below)		
5	11,000	10,000
Cost Detail for Production Cost Center 4:		
Salaries	2,500	2,500
Wages	8,000	7,800
Material used	4,500	4,500
Supplies	420	380
Maintenance	200	160
Depreciation*	100	100
Taxes*	20	20
Insurance*	50	50
Power	120	115
Miscellaneous	80	90

*Noncontrollable in this cost center.

CASE 15-4

Rambler, Incorporated

Rambler, Incorporated, manufactures three lines of products that are sold to the oil industry. The company has been in operation for approximately twenty years; annual sales for the past year approximated $60,000,000. The company is organized into three basic functions: production, sales, and finance. Each is under the direction of a vice president. There are forty-two departments and five sales regions, each headed by a departmental manager. Since its organization the company has experienced a relatively stable growth; profits and return on investment in recent years have leveled off. As a matter of fact, the results for the past two years have been disappointing to the management and to the approximately three thousand shareholders. The stock is sold over the counter, and there has been little turnover. The management of the firm is undergoing gradual change due to retirement of executives who started with the company. Two years ago, a new financial vice president was employed from the outside. He was determined to institute a comprehensive profit planning and control program, but he has encountered a lackadaisical, though not hostile, attitude throughout the management. He fully realizes the behavioral problems to be overcome. He is not discouraged; rather he stated, "I will keep pushing the program, improving it, and through education and demonstration of its usefulness make a very effective management tool." The annual profit plan for the upcoming year has been completed and "distributed to selected managers; appropriate component parts have been provided each manager throughout the firm. Our planning and implementation conferences were reasonably successful."

The financial vice president has turned his attention to improving the performance reporting system. Monthly performance reports, disaggregated by responsibilities, will be prepared and distributed. Actual performance will be compared with budgeted performance for each responsibility center. With respect to the performance reports, the vice president and his staff are concerned about the following issues:

a. Specific data that should be included in the performance report: actual; budget; variances; monthly; and cumulative.
b. The method to be used for expressing the variances: dollar amounts; percentage of budget; budget realization; and percentage of actual.
c. What to report for productive departments about usage of services from the nonproductive departments: actual dollars of cost allocation; allocation of standard dollars of cost; actual units of service used.
d. How to define significant variances; policy with respect to favorable variances.
e. Policy on rounding of amounts on the performance reports.
f. Policy with respect to the financial staff providing comments on the performance reports.
g. Extent of "graphing" that should be utilized on the performance report; this could be a costly endeavor.
h. Deadline date for distribution of the monthly performance report.
i. Distribution schedule for the performance report.
j. Responsibilities for investigation of significant variances and "explanation" of such variances.

Required:

What recommendations would you make on each of these items? Justify your position.

Analysis of Budget Variances

chapter sixteen

Comparison of actual results with budgeted objectives has been stressed as an important part of the control process. The monthly performance report was discussed in the last chapter. A distinguishing feature of the performance report was the *variances* between actual results and budget standards. It was also indicated that a variation if significant, should lead to a careful management investigation to determine the *underlying causes*; for the causes rather than the results need remedies through appropriate corrective action by the management.

In evaluating and investigating a variance to determine the underlying causes, the following possibilities should be considered:

1. The variance is immaterial.
2. The variance was due to reporting errors—both the budget goal and the actual data supplied by the accounting department should be examined for clerical errors. For example, a single accounting entry charging the wrong department may cause unfavorable variance in one department and a favorable variance in another department.
3. The variation was due to a specific management decision— to improve efficiency or to meet certain exigencies management

often will make decisions that create variations. For example, it may be decided to raise a salary, to meet competitive efforts by another firm to attract a key employee, or to undertake a special advertising project not previously planned. Such discretionary decisions will result in reported variations. Variations of this type must be identified because, once identified, they need no further investigation. When the decision was made it was recognized that a variance from plans was caused.

4. Many variations are explainable in terms of the effect of *uncontrollable* factors that are identifiable. An example would be a storm loss.

5. Those variations for which the precise underlying causes are not known should be of primary concern and should be carefully investigated. In other words, we must give special attention to the variations that "need explaining;" these are the exceptions that generally require corrective action.

There are numerous ways to investigate variances to determine the underlying causes. Some of the primary approaches are:

1. Conferences with supervisors, foremen, and sometimes other employees in the particular responsibility centers involved.

2. Analysis of the work situation including the flow of work, coordination of activities, effectiveness of supervision, and other prevailing circumstances.

3. Direct observation.

4. On-the-spot investigations by *line* officials.

5. Investigations by *staff* groups (specifically designated as to responsibilities).

6. Audits by the internal audit staff.

7. Special studies.

8. Variance analysis.

The discussions present the concept of variance analysis and relate the analysis to the monthly performance report. Variance analysis is a mathematical manipulation of two sets of data in order to gain some insights into the underlying causes of a variation. One amount is treated as the base, standard, or reference point. Variance analysis has wide application in financial reporting; it is frequently applied in the following situations:

1. Investigation of variations between actual results of the current

period with the actual results of a prior period; the prior period is considered as the base.[1]

2. Investigation of variations between actual results and standard costs; the latter is treated as the base. (See Chapter 17.)

3. Investigation of the variations between actual results and budget goals; the latter is treated as the base.

In each of these three uses of variation analysis, the same analytical approach is used—the arithmetic is essentially the same—the only difference is in the data being analyzed. This chapter is concerned only with the analysis of budget variances. We will consider variance analysis related to (1) sales, (2) raw material, (3) direct labor, and (4) manufacturing overhead.

ANALYSIS OF SALES VARIANCES

An appreciation of both the significance and limitations of the results of variance analysis is enhanced if its arithmetic is understood. The following simplified example is used to present the arithmetic of variance analysis and to suggest how the analysis of certain *variances between actual results and budget goals* may give management greater insights into the causes underlying the symptoms. First, we will consider sales variances. Assume executive management of the Stanley Company received the following performance report:

Stanley Company
Sales Performance Report—Summary
For the month of January, 19XX

SALES DISTRICTS:	ACTUAL RESULTS	GOALS (FROM THE PROFIT PLAN)	VARIATION UNFAVORABLE*
1	$ 481,500	$ 500,000	$18,500*
2	198,800	200,000	1,200*
3	402,100	400,000	2,100
Total	$1,082,400	$1,100,000	$17,600*

Management attention should be drawn immediately to the *exceptional* items, that is, the $17,600 total sales variance, then to the $18,500 unfavorable variation in District 1 monthly sales. Since each variation is identified with a specific sales district, responsibility is pinpointed; in this instance, the

[1] Horngren, C. T., *Cost Accounting: A Managerial Emphasis*, 3rd ed. (Englewood Cliffs, N.J.: Prentice-Hall, Inc., 1972).

manager of District 1. However, the *cause* of the unfavorable situation is not apparent. Assume management pursues the issue further and examines another schedule in the performance report that "details" the $18,500 variance as follows:

Stanley Company
Sales Performance Report—District 1
For the Month of January, 19XX

PRODUCTS	ACTUAL RESULTS		PROFIT PLAN		VARIATION UNFAVORABLE*	
	UNITS	AMOUNT	UNITS	AMOUNT	UNITS	AMOUNT
M	35,000	$182,000	40,000	$200,000	5,000*	$18,000*
N	49,900	299,500	50,000	300,000	100*	500*
Total		$481,500		$500,000		$18,500*

Again an exceptional item stands out—product M in District 1. An alert executive would ask what caused the $18,000 unfavorable variance in product M. At this point, variance analysis of the $18,000 may provide additional insight for management. The first analytical step is to compute both the actual and budgeted *average* sales prices, viz.:

$182,000 ÷ 35,000 units = $5.20 actual average sales price

$200,000 ÷ 40,000 units = $5.00 budgeted average sales price

We can see that the *quantity* sold was below the budget goal and that the sales *price* was above the budget goal. The dollar effects of these two factors—quantity and price—are computed in the following table.[2]

[2] Some students may prefer to organize "graphically" the mathematical computations in the following way:

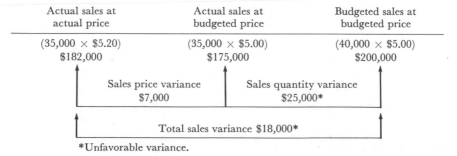

Actual sales at actual price	Actual sales at budgeted price	Budgeted sales at budgeted price
(35,000 × $5.20) $182,000	(35,000 × $5.00) $175,000	(40,000 × $5.00) $200,000

Sales price variance $7,000   Sales quantity variance $25,000*

Total sales variance $18,000*

*Unfavorable variance.

Sales quantity variance
Sales price held constant:

Actual sales at budget sales price (35,000 × $5)	$175,000	
Budget sales at budget sales price (40,000 × $5)	200,000	$25,000*

(The computation may be simplified:
(40,000 − 35,000) × $5 = $25,000*)

Sales price variance
Sales quantity held constant:

Actual sales at actual sales price (35,000 × $5.20)	182,000	
Actual sales at budgeted sales price (35,000 × $5.00)	175,000	7,000

(The computation may be simplified:
35,000 × ($5.20 − $5.00) = $7,000)

Total sales variance		$18,000*

---

*Indicates unfavorable variance.

Interpretation of the results of the above analysis may be briefly explained:

There is an $18,000 unfavorable variance for product M, in District 1, when actual sales are compared with the goal in the profit plan. Analysis of this variance indicates that the number of units sold was 5,000 below plan; when valued at the budgeted sales price, an unfavorable *sales quantity variance* of $25,000 resulted. This unfavorable quantity variance was offset in part by a favorable *sales price variance* of $.20 per unit on the 35,000 units actually sold; the offset totaled $7,000. The factors causing the large quantity variance should be investigated further.

Note that: (1) in computing the quantity variance the budget *price* factor is held constant and the quantity is variable; (2) in computing the price variance the actual *quantity* factor is held constant and the price is variable.[3]

ANALYSIS OF RAW MATERIAL VARIANCES

Raw material variances may be shown on two performance reports: (1) one that reports the performance of the *purchasing manager*, and (2) one (or

---

[3] Some analysts prefer a three-way analysis rather than the two-way analysis illustrated above. The three-way analysis is computed as follows:

Quantity variance (40,000 − 35,000) × $5	$25,000*
Price variance ($5.20 − $5.00) × 40,000	8,000
Combined quantity-price variance (40,000 − 35,000) × ($5.20 − $5.00)	1,000*
Total variance	$18,000*

*Unfavorable variance.

more) that reports the performance(s) of the *manager*(s) of the *using* department(s) (review Chapter 7).

First, let's discuss the performance report of the purchasing manager. He is responsible for controlling (1) the purchase *price* of raw materials, and (2) the *timing* and *quantity* of raw material purchases. Recall from Chapter 7 that he also is responsible for developing the purchases budget that is incorporated in the annual profit plan. The performance report on the purchase function will show a comparison of *actual purchases* with *planned purchases*; the resultant variance can be analyzed in a manner similar to that illustrated for sales, since there are two factors operating—quantity and price. To illustrate, assume the January performance report for the Stanley Company showed the following:

Stanley Company
Purchasing Department
Performance Report for the Month of January, 19XX
(Partial)

	ACTUAL	PLANNED	VARIANCE
Purchases of raw material A:			
Units	210,000	200,000	
Average price	$ .224	$ .20	
Total cost	47,040	40,000	$7,040*

*Unfavorable (Asterisks will indicate unfavorable variance unless footnote indicates otherwise.)

The following *variance analysis*, to reflect two subvariances, could be shown on the performance report to provide the management with additional insights:

Variance analysis—raw material A:	
Purchase price variance ($.224 − $.200) × 210,000	$5,040*
Purchase quantity variance (210,000 − 200,000) × $.20	2,000*
Total purchase variance	$7,040*

*(Unfavorable)

Second, let's discuss the performance report of the *using* department(s). The manager of a using department is responsible for the quantity of raw materials used in producing a given quantity of output; however, he has no responsibility for the cost of that material. Management policy determines the *quality*, and hence the planned unit cost, of the raw materials he uses. Thus, the using department should be "charged" for the actual number of units used during the period valued at the standard or budgeted price per unit; the resultant amount represents "actual" on his performance report. In contrast, his budgeted goal should reflect the number of units that should have been utilized in the actual output of his department. These units must be valued at the budgeted unit price. To illustrate, we return to the Stanley Company and Producing Department X, which uses raw material A. Illustration 57 shows the performance report for this department. The data from that performance report on raw material A are extracted for your convenience as follows:

	ACTUAL	PLANNED GOAL	VARIANCE
Units of finished goods (output)	87,500	100,000	
Raw material A:			
Units (budgeted two units of raw material per unit of finished goods)	176,000	175,000	
Average unit cost (budgeted $.20)	$ .20	$ .20	
Cost	$ 35,200	$ 35,000	$200*

*Unfavorable variance.

The $200 unfavorable variance represents one factor only—material *usage* variance: thus, further arithmetical analysis is unnecessary. The usage variance can be verified: (176,000 − 175,000) × $.20 = $200*. In summary, the purchasing officer is responsible for two subvariances—purchase price and purchase quantity, whereas the *using* manager is responsible for only one variance—material usage.

The material *price* variance is identified at the time of purchase and is based on the quantity purchased during the period. In contrast, some firms "charge" the using department with "actual units of raw material used multiplied by the actual price per unit." This procedure creates two effects, both of which are inconsistent with sound control theory since the material price variance is consequently reflected on the performance report of the using department. First, the material price variance is identified at the point of *usage* rather than at the point of purchase; obviously, the latter is the decisional control point. Identification at point of usage also relates the price variance to the number of units used rather than to the number of units purchased. Second, the procedure incorrectly "charges" the *using* manager rather than the purchasing manager with the material price variance.[4]

ANALYSIS OF DIRECT LABOR VARIANCES

The performance report of each department using direct labor usually will reflect a direct labor variance. As with sales and direct materials the variance reflects the effect of two factors—*quantity* (direct labor hours) and *price* (average wage rate). Therefore, the direct labor variance may be analyzed mathematically to reflect two subvariances that may add some insights in management evaluation of the underlying causes. To illustrate, we return to the Stanley Company and the January performance report for Producing Department X shown in Illustration 57, Chapter 15. The direct labor data from that report are:

	ACTUAL	PLANNED GOAL	VARIANCE
Units of finished goods (output)	87,500	100,000	
Direct labor:			
Direct labor hours (budgeted .4 DLH per unit of finished goods)	35,357	35,000	
Average wage rate (budgeted $2.00 per DLH)	$ 1.96	$ 2.00	
Cost	69,300	70,000	$700

[4] Occasionally, only for special reasons, it may be useful to compare (or reconcile) actual cost of materials used for the period with the planned cost of materials reflected in the *original* profit plan. This comparison introduces an additional subvariance to the analysis of the *using* department. To illustrate, the amount of the variance to be analyzed in Department X (Stanley Company) for January would be:

	Actual	Original profit plan	Variance between actual and original profit plan
Units of finished goods (output)	87,500	100,000	12,500*
Raw material A:			
Units	176,000	200,000	
Cost	$ 35,200	$ 40,000	$ 4,800

The variance analysis for the using department necessarily would identify two subvariances: (1) usage variance, and (2) a profit plan volume variance, as follows:

Usage variance 176,000 − (87,500 × 2) × $.20	$ 200*
Profit plan volume variance (200,000 − 175,000) × $.20	5,000
Total variance	$4,800

The profit plan volume variance simply reflects the amount of material that was not utilized because actual output was 12,500 units less than originally planned, that is, (12,500 × 2) × $.20 = $5,000. This analysis is seldom utilized.

The following variance analysis, to reflect the two subvariances, could be shown on the performance report as additional data:[5]

Variance analysis—direct labor:	
Labor efficiency (usage) variance (35,357 − 35,000) × $2.00	$ 714*
Labor wage rate variance ($2.00 − $1.96) × 35,357	1,414
Total labor variance .	$ 700

*Unfavorable.

The results of the variance analysis may be explained as follows:[6]

The monthly performance report showed a favorable direct labor variance for Department X of $700. This variation resulted from comparing labor costs actually incurred in producing 87,500 units of output with a budget goal adjusted to this output. Although the overall variance is favorable, further analysis indicates an *unfavorable* labor usage or efficiency variance of $714. This unfavorable condition was because the department used 357 more direct labor hours than the budget standard. This unfavorable condition should be discussed with the supervisor concerned. On the other hand, there was a *favorable* wage rate variation of $1,414 since the average wage rate per hour in the department was $.04 below the standard. This favorable variance should be investigated to determine the cause. It is possible that the supervisor of the department was able to maintain a higher proportion of lower paid employees, which is desirable assuming product quality and

[5] Graphic representation of the computations would be:

(Inputs) Actual labor hours at actual cost	Actual labor hours at budgeted cost	(Outputs) Budgeted labor hours at budgeted cost
(35,357 × $1.96) $69,300	(35,357 × $2.00) $70,714	(35,000 × $2.00) $70,000

Labor wage rate variance $1,414 | Labor usage variance $714*

Total labor variance $700

[6] Some analysts prefer a three-way analysis of the direct labor variance as follows:

Labor usage variance (35,357 − 35,000) × $2.00	$ 714*
Labor wage rate variance ($2.00 − $1.96) × 35,000	1,400
Combined usage-rate variance (357 × $.04)	14
Total labor variance	$ 700

employee relations are not adversely affected. This latter factor may have been the cause of the excess hours used.[7]

ANALYSIS OF MANUFACTURING OVERHEAD VARIANCES

The analysis of manufacturing overhead variances is somewhat more complex than for sales, raw materials, and direct labor, and it has been a primary concern of cost accountants for many years. As a result, practically every book discussing cost accounting and management accounting describes this analysis. Although the mathematical analysis of manufacturing overhead variances is fairly simple, the analysis itself is imprecise because of the numerous opportunities for theoretical and practical distinctions in manipulating the data. The problem is further complicated by a lack of standardization in terminology; almost every writer on the subject has his own "pet" terms. The student pursuing this subject may be understandably confused by the maze of terminology, theoretical distinctions, practical differences, and the resulting alternative procedures. Another factor adds to the complexity; that is the type of data available for the analysis—specifically, the type of *budget data* available. If *variable budget* data (where overhead expreses are identified by their fixed and variable components) are available, a realistic analysis of overhead variances generally can be computed. Alternatively, when only *static* budget data are used (that is, where the fixed and variable components of overhead expenses are not differentiated), attempts to develop a useful analysis are difficult at best. Some analysts, however, actually try to support an illogical result! Our discussions and illustrations will be limited to the general case where cost variability is known.

---

[7] In those special instances where actual direct labor costs are to be reconciled with the original profit plan (as illustrated in a previous footnote for direct materials) direct labor would be analyzed as follows:

Total variance to be analyzed:		
Actual direct labor: 35,357 hours @ $1.96 =	$69,300	
Original profit plan: 100,000 × .4 × $2.00 =	80,000	
Total variance		$10,700
Variance analysis:		
Labor efficiency variance (computed as illustrated above)		714*
Labor wage rate variance (computed as illustrated above)		1,414
Profit plan volume variance (12,500 × .4 × $2.00)		10,000
Total variance		$10,700

We do not dwell on theoretical distinctions, but rather stress the relationship of the analysis of manufacturing overhead variations to the monthly performance report as applied to a comprehensive profit planning and control program.[8]

To illustrate (1) the mathematical aspects, (2) the interpretation of the results, and (3) the relationship of variance analysis of manufacturing overhead to a comprehensive profit planning and control program, Department X of Stanley Company. Focus on January performance report, and refer again to Illustration 57. That performance report for Department X reports the variances for each item of controllable and noncontrollable manufacturing overhead; there is an overall variance for January of $200 (favorable). To understand and illustrate the analysis of overhead variance, the following additional data are needed:

1. From the annual profit plan:

   a. Computation of the annual overhead rate for Department X (see Chapter 9 for discussion of this feature):

	FACTORY OVERHEAD BUDGETED	VOLUME IN DLH BUDGETED[9]	FACTORY OVERHEAD RATE BUDGETED (PER DLH)
Fixed costs	$192,000	480,000	$.40
Variable costs	120,000	480,000	.25
Total	$312,000	480,000	$.65

   b. Output in units planned for January   100,000

   c. Planned direct labor hours for January output   40,000

---

[8] Readers interested in in-depth analysis of manufacturing overhead are referred to one or more of the textbooks on cost accounting, for example, C. T. Horngren, *Cost Accounting, A Managerial Emphasis*, 3rd ed. (Englewood Cliffs, N. J.: Prentice-Hall, Inc., 1972).

[9] Throughout this discussion of variation analysis of manufacturing overhead, assume that productive volume (output) is measured in terms of direct labor hours (DLH). Other measures of productive volume might be more appropriate, depending on the circumstance. Assume also that annual predetermined overhead rates are used for accounting purposes and that overhead is applied by multiplying the standard rate by the *standard hours* for the output of the period. This latter point suggests the standard cost approach. In absorption costing the standard rate is frequently multiplied by the actual hours for the output. In either case, a useful variation analysis of the overhead over/underapplied is possible. The reader is referred to leading cost accounting books for further considerations of this product costing problem.

2. From the variable budget for Department X:

EXPENSES	FIXED PER MONTH	VARIABLE PER DLH
Salaries	$10,000	
Indirect materials	1,000	$.08
Indirect labor	2,000	.15
Miscellaneous	300	.02
Depreciation	2,000	
Insurance	500	
Taxes	200	
Total	$16,000	$.25

3. Actual Department X data for January from Accounting Department:

    a. Units produced in January in Department X   87,500

    b. Actual direct labor hours incurred in January   35,357

    c. Standard direct labor hours for January actual output (87,500 × .4 DLH)   35,000

    d. Actual departmental overhead incurred in January (debited to the manufacturing overhead account) $24,550

    e. Manufacturing overhead applied in January (credited to the manufacturing overhead applied account) (35,000 × $.65) $22,750

With these data we can pinpoint the manufacturing overhead variance that is to be analyzed for January for Department X; specifically, it is the $1,800 *underapplied overhead* computed as follows:

Actual overhead incurred in the department during January	$24,550
Overhead applied in the department during January	22,750
Underapplied overhead in the department in January	$ 1,800

The objective of overhead variance analysis is to develop a reasonable explanation of why there was $1,800 underapplied overhead in Department X in January. The total overhead variance can be analyzed by either a two-way or a three-way approach. Both approaches produce a *budget variance* and an *idle capacity variance*. The three-way approach also produces an *efficiency variance*. In the two-way approach the efficiency variance is buried in the budget variance. We will illustrate and compare these approaches.

Two-way approach:

(1) Budget variance:		
Variable budget allowance adjusted to standard hours in		
production $16,000 + ($.25 × 35,000)	$24,750[10]	
Actual departmental overhead incurred	24,550	
Budget variance		$ 200
(2) Idle capacity variance:		
Departmental overhead applied (35,000 × $.65)	22,750	
Variable budget allowance adjusted to standard		
hours in production (computed immediately above)	24,750[10]	
Idle capacity variance		2,000*
Total overhead variance analyzed		$1,800*

*Unfavorable.

The two variations may be evaluated and interpreted as follows:[11]

Budget variation—The budget variation is a valid measure of the effectiveness of overhead *cost control* because actual costs are compared with budget allowances *adjusted to actual work*. The variation can be reconciled with departmental variations reported on the departmental performance report. For example, this variation agrees with the $200 favorable variation shown on the January performance report for the department (Illustration 57); that report provides the subvariances comprising the $200 total variance.

Idle capacity variation—The variation measures the *cost of idle plant capacity*. In the illustration, the annual profit plan anticipated that the average monthly potential capacity was 40,000 standard DLH (480,000 ÷ 12). Actual production volume was equivalent to only 35,000 standard direct labor hours; thus there was idle plant capacity amounting to 5,000 DLH. The varriation shows the portion of monthly *fixed cost* related to the idle plant capacity. The 5,000 direct labor hours of idle plant capacity multiplied by the *fixed* component of the overhead rate ($.40) gives the variation ($2,000). This point may be further clarified by computing the variation as follows:

$$\frac{5,000 \text{ DLH}}{40,000 \text{ DLH}} \times \$16,000 \text{ (monthly fixed costs)} = \$2,000$$

[10] Some analysts prefer to utilize for this value the variable budget allowance adjusted to *actual* hours in production, $16,000 + ($.25 × 35,357) = $24,839.
[11] In some cases adjustments may have to be made for service department volume differentials.

Three-way Approach:

(1) Budget (or spending) variation:		
Variable budget allowance adjusted for *actual*		
hours worked $16,000 + ($.25 × 35,357)	$24,839	
Actual overhead incurred (at 35,357 DLH)	24,550	$ 289
(2) Efficiency variation:		
Variable budget allowance adjusted for standard		
hours in production $16,000 + ($.25 × 35,000)	$24,750	
Variable budget allowance adjusted for actual		
hours worked 16,000 + ($.25 × 35,357)	24,839	89*
(3) Idle capacity variation (volume variation):		
Overhead applied (35,000 DLH × $.65)	$22,750	
Variable budget allowance adjusted for *standard*		
hours in production $16,000 + ($.25 × 35,000)	24,750	2,000*
Total overhead variance analyzed		$1,800*

The third variance may be explained as follows:

Overhead efficiency variation—This variation measures the *excess overhead costs* that were incurred because more direct labor hours were used than the budget standard (357 DLH). Since variable costs (but not fixed costs) increase and decrease as direct labor hours increase and decrease, the efficiency variation should be expressed as variable costs only. The variation precisely fits these specifications and may be demonstrated as follows:[12]

Standard hours in production	35,000
Actual hours incurred	35,357
Difference—Inefficient hours	357*
Multiply by variable portion of overhead rate	$.25
Overhead efficiency variation (wholly variable)	$ 89

To systematize the analysis, the computations may be conveniently organized in either a worksheet or a graphic format as illustrated below for both the two-way and the three-way approaches:

[12] It may be convincingly argued that overhead efficiency variation should include some fixed costs since workers who waste time also waste the cost of space, machinery, supervisory effort, and so forth, which they occupy, use, and require. If this position is accepted, the computations in the example could be made so that the portion of fixed costs related to the 357 hours of inefficiency also are included in the efficiency variation and excluded from idle capacity or volume variation. This amount of fixed costs (to be taken from the idle capacity variance and added to the efficiency variance) may be readily computed:

$$\$16,000 \times \frac{357}{40,000} = \$143$$

(a) Worksheet format:

Computation of the required amounts :

1. Actual overhead incurred (given)	$24,550
2. Variable budget allowance adjusted to *actual* hours in production $16,000 + ($.25 × 35,357)	24,839
3. Variable budget allowance adjusted to *standard* hours in production $16,000 + ($.25 × 35,000)	24,750
4. Overhead applied (35,000 × $.65)	22,750

Computation of the variances :

	TWO-WAY ANALYSIS		THREE-WAY ANALYSIS	
	COMPUTATION	AMOUNT	COMPUTATION	AMOUNT
Budget variance	3–1	$ 200	2–1	$ 289
Efficiency variance			3–2	89*
Idle capacity Variance	4–1	2,000*	4–1	2,000*
Total variance		$1,800*		$1,800*

(b) Graphic format:

	ACTUAL OVERHEAD INCURRED	VARIABLE BUDGET ADJUSTED TO ACTUAL HOURS	VARIABLE BUDGET ADJUSTED TO STANDARD HOURS	OVERHEAD APPLIED
COMPUTATIONS	(GIVEN)	$16,000 + ($.25 × 35,357)	$16,000 + ($.25 × 35,000)	35,000 × $.65
	$24,550	$24,839	$24,750	$22,750

Two-way analysis	Budget variance $200	Idle capacity variance $2,000*

Three-way analysis	Budget variance $289	Efficiency variance 89*	Idle capacity variance $2,000*

Total overhead variance $1,800*

USE OF VARIANCE ANALYSIS

In developing and reporting the analyses discussed in this chapter, the analyst should remember that the *results* must: (1) deal with relevant distinctions; (2) be understandable; (3) measure with reasonable accuracy what they are supposed to measure; and (4) be presented and explained concisely. It is unrealistic to expect top executives to devote time and attention to esoteric and technical analyses.

Whether the additional analyses discussed in this chapter are useful depends upon the situation. These analyses can be quite helpful when carefully developed, interpreted in a practical way, and wisely used. However, these analyses involve distinctions that are often difficult to express simply and concisely; therefore, they should be used with caution.

To present the results of variance analyses, two approaches are available. First, the results of the analyses may be reported in a *special report* that focuses on specific (but not recurring) problems with which the management is concerned. Second, the results may be included on the *monthly performance report*. These results generally are best reported as supplementary comments in the performance report.

DISCUSSION QUESTIONS

1. Explain the relationship of the analysis of budget variations to the monthly performance report.
2. What are some of the more important techniques to determine the underlying causes of variances?
3. Define (1) sales quantity variance, and (2) sales price variance.
4. Assume that a performance report showed the following data for product T:

		ACTUAL	PLANNED	VARIANCE
Sales		$9,690	$10,000	$310*
Average sales price		.95	1.00	
Volume variation	$200			
Price variation	$510*			

*Means unfavorable.

Explain how the quantity and price variations were computed, and give the interpretation of each.

5. Identify and explain the nature of the two different basic responsibilities involved in the analysis of raw material variances.
6. Why should the using department be "charged" for the actual number of units of raw material used multiplied by the standard or budgeted unit cost rather than by the actual unit cost of the raw material?
7. Explain labor usage variance and wage rate variance.
8. In the analysis of manufacturing overhead variances, what particular amount is normally subject to variance analysis? Explain.
9. Define the following: (1) budget variance; (2) idle capacity variance; and (3) efficiency variance.
10. Why should technical variance analysis be used with caution?

CASE 16-1
Lyles, Incorporated

Lyles, Incorporated, is a medium-size manufacturer of a single line of products, although there are four different models in the line. There are two plants (located widely apart), and the country is divided into seven sales districts. The manufacturing vice-president stated that "The Eastern plant (an old plant) has been experiencing difficulty in getting costs in line with the budget." The monthly performance report in some of the departments has consistently shown significant variances. The management has undertaken a number of steps to get at this cost problem. Included was a recent decision to utilize variable budgets for overhead expenses throughout the plant. The vice president remarked that "The performance report approaches are being reviewed and improved, and more attention will be given to determination of the underlying causes of significant variances; we have too many excuses now." This case focuses on a suggestion made by a newly employed accountant in the Controller's Department that "variance analyses should be incorporated in the monthly performance report of each department." Simplified data from one of the producing departments are provided below for illustrative purposes.

Required:

    a.   Develop a two-way variance analysis of materials, labor, and departmental overhead.

    b.   Evaluate the results of your analysis and identify any weaknesses in the departmental performance report illustrated.

Performance Report

DEPT. PRODUCING NO. 4	DATE JANUARY, 19XX	SUPERVISOR K. W. MASON	
	ACTUAL	PLANNED	VARIANCE
Department output—in direct machine hours:			
Actual hours in output	18,400		
Standard hours in output		18,000	
Direct material A	6,300 @ $2.15=$13,545	6,000 @ $2.00=$12,000	$1,545*
Direct labor	4,160 @ $5.10= 21,216	4,000 @ $5.00= 20,000	1,216
Department overhead	$23,000	$21,000†	2,000*
Over/underapplied overhead:			
Actual incurred	$23,000		
Applied ($1.10×18,000 DMH)**		$19,800**	
Underapplied for month			$3,200*
Service usage			
Etc.			

*Unfavorable variance.
†Computation based on variable budget: fixed $12,000 + ($.50 × 18,000) = $21,000.
**Computation of overhead rate: $264,000 ÷ 240,000 DHM = $1.10 per DMH.

c. Explain and illustrate your recommended method of incorporating the variance analysis developed in a monthly performance report of the department.

d. Should Lyles incorporate the variance analysis in the regular performance report? Explain the advantages and disadvantages involved.

CASE 16-2
Hudson Wholesalers

Hudson Wholesalers is a major distributor of three products in a fourteen-state region; there are four sales districts, each headed by a district sales manager. The company utilizes a comprehensive profit planning and control program including monthly performance reports. Recently the financial vice president decided that "variance analyses will be incorporated into the monthly performance report." The following data for one of the sales districts (Inland) for June has been developed for performance report purposes:

	INLAND DISTRICT		
	PROD. X	PROD. Y	PROD. Z
Budget data:			
Units	15,000	30,000	50,000
Average unit price	$ 2.00	$ .70	$ 1.10
Actual data:			
Units	14,000	25,000	62,000
Amount	$28,560	$18,750	$62,620

Required:

Utilizing the above data for illustrative purposes you are to prepare appropriate sales schedules for the June performance report; indicate by illustration, integrative relationships and the variance analysis that should be reflected in the report; limit your illustration to sales. Include a brief evaluation of the results of your variance analysis.

CASE 16-3
Super-Beam Company

Super-Beam manufactures two major products, "Super" and "Beam." The company uses a comprehensive profit planning and control program including monthly performance reports. This case relates to one responsibility center—Production Department 8, which works only on Super. The following data are available to develop the Departmental Performance Report for March (third month in the fiscal period):

Budget data for March:	
Units to be manufactured	150,000
Units of raw material 1 required (based on standard rates)	495,000
Planned purchases of raw material 1—units	540,000
Average unit cost of raw material 1—$.80	
Direct labor hours per unit of finished good	$\frac{3}{4}$
Direct labor cost (total)	299,250
Actual data at the end of March:	
Units actually manufactured during March	160,000
Raw material 1 cost (purchase cost based on units actually issued)	$434,190
Raw material 1 (purchase cost based on units actually purchased)	$451,000
Average unit cost of raw material 1—$.82	
Total direct labor hours for March	125,000
Total direct labor cost for March	$337,500

Required:

a. Design a Performance Report for March for Department 8. Enter March data and variances. (Manufacturing overhead and service usage are not included in the above data; therefore, you should indicate how they would be reported without illustrative amounts.) Also develop a variance analysis of direct materials and direct labor and incorporate the results in the performance report.

b. Compute and explain any implied variances that would appear on the performance report of another department.

CASE 16-4
Nelson, Incorporated

Nelson, Incorporated, manufactures a line of products distributed through local hardware stores. The company utilizes comprehensive profit planning and control including monthly performance reports. This case focuses on Productive Department 3 in the factory. The activity factor (measure of output) in the department is direct machine hours (DMH) since it processes a number of products simultaneously. Departmental overhead is applied to production on the basis of standard productive hours. This case focuses on the analysis of departmental overhead variance; therefore, the following data relating to Department 3 have been extracted from the company records and reports:

From the annual profit plan:

Departmental overhead:

Fixed per year	$1,080,000
Variable for year (from the variable budget)	$ 720,000
Direct labor hours planned for the year	144,000
Direct machine hours planned for the year	2,400,000
Direct labor hours planned for January	12,000
Direct machine hours planned for January	200,000

From the accounting records for January (actual data):

Departmental overhead incurred:	Fixed	$ 90,500
	Variable	$ 64,500
Direct labor hours in January:	Actual	13,000
	Standard hours in actual output	12,500
Direct machine hours in January:	Actual	207,000
	Standard hours in actual output	205,000

Required:

An analysis of the departmental overhead variance is to be developed; to establish the background for this analysis answer to the following (show computations in each instance):

a. What is the annual overhead rate for the department?

b. How much overhead was applied in January?

c. What is the amount of over-underapplied overhead in the department for January? Is it favorable or unfavorable?

d. What is the amount of the "total departmental overhead variance" to be analyzed for January? Explain.

e. Present a two-way analysis of the total departmental overhead variance identified in d.

f. Present a narrative explanation of the two subvariances developed in e.

g. How would the two variances developed in e be reflected on the January performance report for Department 3?

CASE 16-5

Cord Company

The January performance report for the Cord Company is being developed; it is complete except for the variance analyses. Based upon the extracted data given below from the performance report, develop the variance analyses for each schedule (show your computations). Also evaluate each analysis.

SCHEDULE A—SALES PERFORMANCE REPORT—CENTRAL SALES DIVISION

	ACTUAL		PROFIT PLAN		VARIANCE
	UNITS	AMOUNT	UNIT	AMOUNT	(UNFAVORABLE*)
Product AK	109,000	$182,030	100,000	$180,000	$2,030
Variance analysis					
Evaluation					

SCHEDULE B—PURCHASING DEPARTMENT PERFORMANCE REPORT

	ACTUAL		PROFIT PLAN		VARIANCE
	UNITS	AMOUNT	UNITS	AMOUNT	(UNFAVORABLE*)
Purchases material X	7,000	$ 11,410	6,000	$ 10,200	$1,210*
Variance analysis					
Evaluation					

SCHEDULE C—PRODUCING DEPARTMENT No. 1 PERFORMANCE REPORT

	ACTUAL	BUDGET ADJUSTED TO ACTUAL OUTPUT	VARIANCE (UNFAVORABLE*)
Departmental output:			
Actual DLH in output	2,900		
Standard DLH in output		2,500	
Raw material	5,300 units $ 9,010	5,000 units $8,500	$ 510*
Direct labor	2,900 DLH 11,310	2,500 DLH 10,000	1,310*
Departmental overhead:			
Controllable:			
Productive salaries	$ 2,600	$ 2,500	$ 100*
Indirect material	4,180	4,000	180*
Indirect labor	3,120	2,900	220*
Noncontrollable:			
Depreciation	2,600	2,600	
Insurance and taxes	400	400	
Supervisory salaries	1,600	1,600	
Total overhead	$14,500	$14,000	$ 500*
Variance Analysis:			
Raw material X			
Evaluation			
Direct labor			
Evaluation			
Departmental overhead:			
Predetermined overhead rate per DLH	$		
Actual overhead incurred		$	
Overhead applied		$	
Difference—over-underapplied		$	
Variance Analysis of overhead (two-way)			
Evaluation			

Additional data are available:

1. From the annual profit plan—Department 1:

Budgeted annual output in DLH		36,000
Budgeted annual overhead:	Fixed	$108,000
	Variable	$ 72,000

2. Department 1 variable budget:

	FIXED PER MONTH	VARIABLE PER DLH
Productive salaries	$2,500	
Indirect material	500	$1.40
Indirect labor	1,400	.60
Depreciation	2,600	
Insurance and taxes	400	
Supervisory salaries	1,600	
Totals	$9,000	$2.00

Profit Planning and Control Related to the Accounting System

chapter seventeen

The preceding chapters emphasized that the accounting system provides much historical data to support a profit planning and control program. Historical data are especially relevant for planning purposes; the immediate operational and financial history of the enterprise, in effect, provides a launching pad for the planning function. It is unusual to find a company where successes and failures of the immediate past are not indicative of reasonable future potentials, particularly the short run. We repeatedly stressed the importance of accurate and relevant accounting data as one key to effective control. We also emphasized that the accounting system should be tailored to the special planning and control requirements of the management. This means that accounting must be established on a responsibility basis.

Profit planning and control requires (1) a long-range profit plan and (2) a short-range profit plan of the anticipated financial implications of various *decisional inputs* to the planning process. Expression of the expected financial impacts must harmonize with the format of the internal accounting (financial) reports. Thus, since the "profit planning and control" format and the internal "accounting" format must be in harmony; realistic compromises must be adopted. However, we must recognize (as we did in the chapter on performance reports) that the several reporting needs—external, internal, and others—normally should be satisfied with essentially different types of reports. This requirement necessitates organization of the accounting function to meet those diverse needs.

Industry characteristics can determine to some extent the profit planning and control approach and the accounting approach adopted in a given enterprise. However, whatever the industry or the "system" used, the concept of responsibility accounting dominates the management planning and control point of view. There are numerous designations of accounting "systems" such as: retail accounting; oil and gas accounting; financial accounting; actual costing; full costing; direct costing; contribution accounting; manufacturing; and standard costing. Obviously, these designations are not parallel, and it would be impractical to attempt to deal with them here. Clearly, both the accounting and the profit planning and control systems must be tailored to industry and enterprise characteristics, and an appropriate conceptual framework. This chapter focuses on two accounting "approaches" that apply in practically all industries and are important to planning and control—that is, variable or direct costing and standard costs. We will concentrate on the underlying concepts rather than on the accounting procedures; we will also emphasize their relationships to a profit planning and control system previously described in this book.[1]

VARIABLE COSTING RELATED TO PROFIT PLANNING AND CONTROL

Throughout several preceding chapters we have emphasized the concept of *cost variability*, that is, the relationship of cost to output. This concept shows how changes in the output of a responsibility center affect cost. Cost variability was discussed in Chapter 10; definitions of fixed and variable costs were provided. Chapters following Chapter 10 emphasized applications of variable expense budgets in (1) developing the annual profit plan, (2) preparation of performance reports and, (3) variation analyses. In Chapter 14 cost variability was identified as the foundation for cost-volume-profit (breakeven) analyses. In recent years the concept of cost variability has had a significant impact on accounting. Perhaps the most pervasive effect has been the development of *direct costing* (also referred to as variable costing, marginal costing, and contribution accounting). As with any new concept that affects traditional procedures, a lot of controversy has arisen over direct costing. Our purpose here is not to enter the controversy; rather, it is to outline primary features and to relate them to a comprehensive profit planning and control system. We do think; however, that variable costing is

---

[1] For a comprehensive treatment see: C. T. Horngren, *Cost Accounting*, 3rd ed. (Englewood Cliffs, N.J.: Prentice-Hall, Inc., 1972).

especially significant to accounting since it dovetails perfectly with the dynamic approach to planning and control presented throughout this book.

THE DISTINCTIVE FEATURES OF VARIABLE COSTING

Variable costing has four distinct features, viz.:[2]

1.   The fixed and variable components of all costs (manufacturing, administrative, and distribution) are *formally segregated* in the accounts at initial recording. This segregation of fixed and variable cost components requires special provision in the chart of accounts. For example, the manufacturing expense control accounts might appear as follows:

14191 Variable manufacturing expense control.

14192 Fixed manufacturing expense control.

2.   Only variable costs (direct material, direct labor, and variable manufacturing overhead) are treated as costs of production; therefore, cost of goods sold, inventories of work in process, and finished goods are accounted for and reported at *variable cost* only. Fixed costs are viewed as *period costs* rather than production costs. Consequently, all fixed costs are written off and reported as a direct deduction on the income statement for the period in which they are incurred. No fixed costs are carried to cost of goods sold or capitalized in inventory.

3.   The income statement is rearranged to emphasize the *contribution margin* —that is, the excess of sales revenue over *variable* production, distribution, and administrative costs. The fixed costs are deducted in full as period costs.

4.   Reported net income fluctuates directly with increases and decreases in sales revenue from period to period. This effect contrasts with full costing (absorption costing) where reported net income is significantly affected by the amount of increase or decrease in inventories. For example, one company reported the following comparative results (amounts simplified for illustrative purposes) where inventory of finished goods changed significantly from month to month:

| | | REPORTED NET INCOME UNDER | |
	NET SALES	ABSORPTION COSTING	VARIABLE COSTING
January	$30,000	$ 5,000	$ 5,000
February	27,000	5,600	3,200
March	27,000	800	3,200
Total for Quarter		$11,400	$11,400

[2] For a comprehensive treatment of the subject of variable costing see: Wilmer Wright, *Direct Standard Costs* (New York: McGraw-Hill Book Co., Inc., 1962).

Variable costing features are shown in the proforma income statment using simplified amounts shown in Illustration 59.

The data in Illustration 59 show that 60 percent (that is, the variable cost ratio) of each sales dollar is required to pay variable costs and that 40 percent (the P/V ratio) is available to "cover fixed costs and make a profit." Clearly, the breakeven point is: $70,000 ÷ .40 = $175,000. The income statement shown in Illustration 59 could be extended to report the contribution margin by major segments of the company (say, by divisions or by products). Variable costing, then, gives useful information to management for decisions in areas such as:

1. Selecting the more profitable products.
2. Identifying the more profitable divisions.
3. Computing minimum selling prices.
4. Developing cost-volume-profit analyses by division and by products.
5. Increased sales volume required to offset reduced sales price.
6. Volume of sales required to earn a target profit.
7. Whether to make or buy.
8. Evaluation of plant expansion proposals.
9. Evaluation of a profit plan.

The above discussions outline the key impacts of variable costing on an accounting system and its outputs of historical financial data. To repeat, cost variability should be applied throughout a comprehensive profit planning and control program. Thus, we come to a basic distinction and a vital complementary relationship: in the accounting system, the concept of cost variability is applied to historical data; in the budgeting system, the concept is applied to planned data. The latter application is more relevant since all management decisions are prospective (they deal with futures) rather than retrospective. However, the complementary relationships are important because: (1) conceptually the two systems harmonize and (2) the cost-behavior distinctions maintained in the accounting system provide a strong basis for applying the concept in planning and control. We may summarize the primary features of the relationships between variable costing and dynamic profit planning and control as follows:

1. In long-range planning, costs are best projected separately in fixed and variable categories; variable costing provides a sound foundation for this distinction in planning.
2. In short-range profit planning, a distinction between fixed and variable costs is imperative; variable costing provides historical data on this basis, which facilitates projections.

ILLUSTRATION 59. Income Statement
Variable Cost Approach

Net sales			$200,000	100%	
Less variable costs:					
Beginning inventory (at variable cost)		$ 10,000			
Variable costs:					
Direct material	$50,000				
Direct labor	40,000				
Variable factory overhead	20,000				
Variable administrative costs	5,000				
Variable distribution costs	6,000	121,000			
Total		131,000			
Less ending inventory (at variable cost)		11,000			
Total variable costs			120,000	60	(variable cost ratio)
Marginal income (or contribution margin)			80,000	40	(P/V ratio)
Less period (fixed) costs:					
Fixed factory overhead		$ 10,000			
Fixed administrative cost		25,000			
Fixed distribution costs		35,000			
Total period (fixed) costs			70,000		
Operating income (pretax)			$ 10,000		

539

3. The financial statements provided by the accounting system harmonize (format and results) with those developed in the planning process.

4. Income statements, both planned and actual, can be developed and compared on a contribution margin basis.

5. Troublesome allocations of fixed costs to products are largely avoided for both planning and accounting purposes.

6. Control is enhanced; if variable expense budgets are used, the problem of determining the variability of planned expenses is simplified, because the historical expense data will be differentiated between fixed and variable components.

7. The accounting system must be evaluated, and an appropriate activity factor (that is, measure of output) for each responsibility center must be chosen.

8. The comparison of actual costs with planned or budgeted costs by responsibility is enhanced, because allocation of indirect costs is deemphasized in the accounting system, as it must be in the budget program.

9. The historical data from the accounting system emphasize cost-volume-profit relationships; therefore, these relationships can be projected.

10. Perhaps most important, cost variability provides management with information on the diverse effects of fixed and variable costs on the financial outcomes. The fact that both *planned* and *actual* financial data focus on the behavior of costs enhances management's sophistication in considering alternatives when volume varies.

The primary disadvantages of direct costing are (1) the difficulty in realistically segregating actual costs into fixed and variable categories, and (2) the public accounting profession has not accorded general acceptability to the direct cost method of valuing inventories. Nevertheless, we may say, in summary, that application of the direct costing concept in an accounting system, regardless of the other characteristics of the accounting system, can be vital for internal management. For this reason, the variable cost concept will probably continue to gain increasing acceptance. Thus, the approaches and techniques discussed in the preceding chapters and in particular in Chapters 10 (variable expense budgets) and 14 (cost-volume-profit analyses) will assume greater relevance.[3]

[3] *Current Applications in Direct Costing,* N.A.A. Research Report No. 37 (January 1961); also see Research Reports Nos. 22 and 23, and Wright, *Standard Costs.*

STANDARD COSTS RELATED TO PROFIT PLANNING AND CONTROL

Standard cost "systems" have developed to the point where there is general agreement on the underlying concepts and their application. Standard costs can be utilized in a wide variety of industries; however, they are applied more often in manufacturing situations. Fundamentally, in a standard cost accounting system, the costs *recorded* are predetermined or target costs; and the *variances* between them and the actual amounts are recorded in *separate variance accounts*. The latter amounts are described as "losses due to inefficiencies." Thus, a standard cost system, at the time a transaction is recorded, compares actual with targets, similar to the process used in budgetary control.

To focus on the complementary relationships between standard costs and profit planning and control, let us review the distinctive features of standard costs as applied in an accounting system. Standard costs are predetermined costs that, presumably, represent what costs should have been as opposed to historical costs that represent what costs *were*. Proponents of standard cost systems view the standard cost as the *true* costs of activity or production, whereas actual costs generally represent the true cost *plus* losses due to inefficiency, faulty operations, and inadequate control.

Cost systems may also be broadly classified either as job order or process costing systems. The type of operation generally determines the system used. For example, a machine shop would normally use a job order cost system, whereas a flour mill would use a process cost system. Standard costs do not represent "another system"; they may be used with either a job order or a process cost system, or some combination thereof.

In a standard cost system, the standard costs are recorded directly in the accounts; separate accounts are established for recording the *variations* between actual costs and standard costs. Thus, both the standard costs and the standard cost variations are an integral part of the recorded accounting values. Recall that budget figures are *not* incorporated in the accounts. The flow of data through a standard cost system is graphically shown in Illustration 60; note the recording of *standards* and *variances*.

THE STANDARD COST SPECIFICATION

The standard cost specification represents a basic component of a standard cost system. Basically, it specifies the standard costs of material, labor, and overhead for each product or job. The standard cost specification generally emerges from a series of cost analyses and engineering studies to develop reliable standards. In the case of standardized products there would be a standard cost specification for each product. In job order situations a stan-

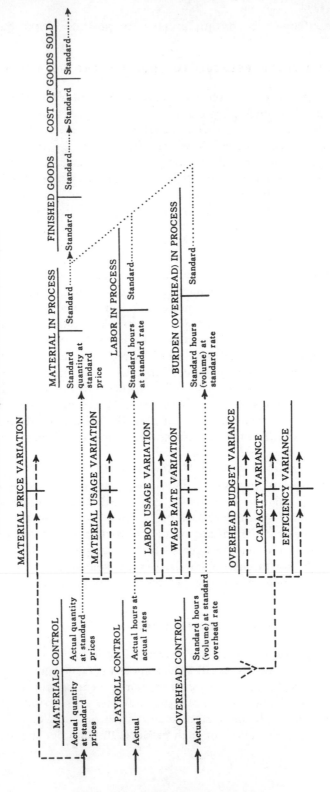

ILLUSTRATION 60. Simplified Standard Cost Flow Chart

dard cost specification is developed for each job. The procedure for each job involves predetermination of the requirements for raw material, labor, and overhead, taking into account the various responsibility centers through which the work must flow from start to completion. Many companies find it more practicable to develop a separate standard specification for each major component, operation, or assembly so that the total standard cost may be determined by summing the various standard costs for the components. Obviously, the standard cost specification should be designed to fit each particular situation.

A simplified standard cost specification for a standardized product is shown in Illustration 61. Observe that the product passes through two departments (1 and 2). Raw material R is used in Department 1 and raw material M is used in Department 2. Direct labor is required in both departments. Standard overhead rates based on departmental direct labor hours are used to allocate manufacturing overhead to the product in each department.

ILLUSTRATION 61. Able Company
Standard Cost Specification

Product: _____ P _____		Date ____ 1/1/— ____
Specifications ____ Attached ____		
Department 1:		
Material R	2 Units @ $1.50	$3.00
Direct labor	3 Hours @ 2.00	6.00
Overhead	3 Hours @ 1.00[4]	3.00	$12.00
Department 2:		
Material M	4 Units @ $ .50	2.00
Direct labor	2 Hours @ 3.00	6.00
Overhead	2 Hours @ 2.50[4]	5.00	13.00
Total standard cost		$25.00

STANDARD COSTS FOR MATERIAL—ACCOUNTING AND BUDGETING PROCEDURES

Standard quantities of material required for each unit of product and standard raw material unit cost must be determined; then—

$$\begin{array}{c}\text{Standard} \\ \text{Number of} \\ \text{Units of} \\ \text{Material}\end{array} \times \begin{array}{c}\text{Standard} \\ \text{Price Per} \\ \text{Unit of} \\ \text{Material}\end{array} = \begin{array}{c}\text{Standard Raw} \\ \text{Material Cost} \\ \text{Per Unit of} \\ \text{Product}\end{array}$$

[4] See page 551 for computation of these overhead rates.

Development of standard quantities of each raw material for each unit of product requires an analysis, in terms of product specifications, drawings, and blueprints. This is essentially an engineering problem that might involve procedures such as chemical analyses, mechanical analyses, and test runs. Such procedures should be utilized also for developing budget costs, even though standard costs are not employed.

The development of standard material prices is a responsibility of the purchasing manager. Standard material prices should represent expected actual conditions and should be developed in the same manner as budgeted material costs (see Chapter 7). Because material prices are frequently affected by the quantities of raw material to be purchased, production and raw materials budgeting are generally essential to the establishment of meaningful standard material prices.

In situations where material quantities and prices have been established for standard cost purposes they should be used to build the materials and purchases budgets.

To illustrate accounting with standard costs for raw materials, assume that during January Able Company purchased 2,100 units of material R at $1.55 per unit and 4,200 units of material M at $.49; refer to Illustration 61 for the standards. These purchases would be recorded in the accounts of a standard cost system as follows:

FOR MATERIAL R PURCHASE

Raw materials control (2,100 units @ $1.50)	3,150	
Material price variance (2,100 units @ $.05)	105	
Cash (2,100 units @ $1.55)		3,255

FOR MATERIAL M PURCHASE

Raw material control (4,200 units @ $.50)	2,100	
Material price variance (4,200 @ $.01)		42
Cash (4,200 @ $.49)		2,058

The Raw Materials Control account is debited with the *standard cost of material purchased* the difference between standard cost and actual cost is debited or credited to a Material Price Variance account. Referring to the above entries, the Material Price Variance Control account shows a debit balance for the month of $63, which represents an unfavorable standard cost variation. Detailed records supporting the control account would indicate the amount of variance for *each item or class of raw material* and specifically which purchases caused the variation. It is not necessary to wait until the end of the reporting period to determine the material price variance. Variations on weekly or even on individual purchases may be determined and reported to management so that appropriate corrective action may be taken when necessary. The responsibility for controlling material price variances rests with the purchasing manager. The Material Price Variance account is usually closed at the end of the period to the Income Summary account because it represents a *loss* due to inefficiency rather than a cost of production.[5] The price variance would be shown on the monthly performance report of the purchasing manager.

Materials used in production may be charged to the Materials in Process account for standard quantities valued at standard prices. For example, assume that 1,000 units of product P (Illustration 62) were produced in January and that raw material issues were: 2,050 units of raw material R; 4,020 units of raw material M. Entries in the accounts would be:

FOR RAW MATERIAL R

Material in process—Dept. 1 (2,000 units @ $1.50)	3,000	
Material quantity variance (50 units @ $1.50)	75	
Raw materials control (2,050 units @ $1.50)		3,075

FOR RAW MATERIAL M

Material in process—Dept. 2 (4,000 units @ $.50)	2,000	
Material quantity variance (20 units @ $.50)	10	
Raw materials control (4,020 units @ $.50)		2,010

In the above entries, the Work in Process account is charged with standard quantities of raw material requied for 1,000 units of product produced, whereas the Material account is credited with actual quantities used; both quantities are valued at the standard material prices given.[6] The material *quantity* variance account has a debit balance of $85, which represents the standard cost of excess material used. This variance measures the effectiveness with which raw materials were used. The variance is expressed in terms of the standard material unit cost rather than of the actual material unit cost, since the departmental supervisors (factory Departments 1 and 2) have no control over material prices but do have control over material *usage*. The Raw Materials Control account carries the final inventory of raw materials costed at standard prices. The Material Quantity

[5] Another, although deficient, method of entering standard material costs in the accounts debits the Raw Material Control account at actual cost for purchases and, for issues, credits the Material Control account at actual cost, the Materials in Process account is debited at standard. The effect of this procedure is to record both price and quantity variations at the time the material is issued. The result of this procedure is that the material price variance is based on issues, and the price variance is "charged" to the using department (which is inconsistent with the control responsibility for unit cost) rather than on purchases; the Raw Material Control account is carried at actual unit material prices rather than at standard.
[6] Another method debits the in-process account at actual, and credits it at standard, thereby drawing off the variances at the point of completion. The reader is referred to cost accounting books.

Variance account is closed at the end of the period to the Income Summary account on the assumption that the balance represents a *loss* due to inefficiency, therefore it is not a proper cost of production.

If standard costs for material were used for budget purposes also, then obviously standard cost variations and budget variations for material would be the same and the usage variance would be reported on the monthly performance report.

A distinct advantage resulting from standard material costs is that the accounting is simplified for inventories of raw material and work in process. If raw material purchases are recorded in the Materials Control account at standard unit prices, the problem of costing individual issues on inventory record (using some method such as first-in, first-out) is avoided. Perpetual inventory records can be kept in terms of units only, because both issues and inventories are valued at the standard unit material price. The use of standards for material reduces the cost of the accounting function and at the same time increases the potentials of control through accounting and budgeting.

STANDARD COSTS FOR DIRECT LABOR—ACCOUNTING AND BUDGETING PROCEDURES

Establishing standard costs for direct labor generally is more complex than for material. Standard costs for labor may be developed according to the discussions in Chapter 8. Just as it is generally necessary to develop separately standard quantities and standard unit prices for material, it is likewise generally desirable to develop hourly labor requirements and standard wage rates per hour for different classes of direct labor in each responsibility center. Labor standards sometimes require further subdivision into cost centers so that each kind of direct labor is segregated. For example, cost centers may be established for such activities as drilling, grinding, polishing, assembly, and painting. Direct labor standards are then developed for each cost center. Standard labor hour requirements in a cost center are usually developed by the engineering department, using time and motion studies. If standard times for the various operations are developed, the standard time for any item to be processed through the cost center can be determined by adding the standard time required for each operation involved. Obviously, if standard direct labor costs have been developed, they should be used directly for budgetary purposes.

A typical standard cost accounting procedure for direct labor may be illustrated. Refer to Illustration 61 for typical labor standards. Continuing the assumption that 1,000 units of product P are produced in January, assume further that actual direct labor data were: Department 1, 3,100 actual direct labor hours at an average hourly actual rate of $2.05; Department 2, 1,960 direct labor hours at an average hourly actual rate of $3.10. The accounting entries would be:

FOR DEPARTMENT 1

Labor in process—Dept. 1 (3,000 DLH @ $2.00)	6,000	
Labor usage variance (100 DLH @ $2.00)	200	
Wage rate variance (3,100 DLH @ $.05)	155	
Accrued payroll (3,100 DLH @ $2.05)		6,355

FOR DEPARTMENT 2

Labor in process—Dept. 2 (2,000 DLH @ $3.00)	6,000	
Wage rate variance (1,960 DLH @ $.10)	196	
Labor usage variance (40 DLH @ $3.00)		120
Accrued payroll (1,960 DLH @ $3.10)		6,076

The in-process accounts are charged (debited) with the standard cost of direct labor, the difference between actual and standard cost is debited or credited to appropriately titled *variance accounts*. The labor variance accounts are closed at the end of the period to the Income Summary—just like the material variance accounts. Observe that the standard cost variations for labor are identical with the related budget variations. Thus, the wage rate and labor usage variances would be reported on the monthly performance report of the responsibility center. Inclusion in the ledger accounts (and reports) of standard costs for labor and the resulting variances tends to increase management attention. The responsibility for direct labor *usage* variances rests directly on the managers of the productive responsibility centers. Labor usage variances should be analyzed by cost center, shifts, or groups of workers. Labor usage variances can be measured and reported on a monthly, weekly, or even daily basis for control purposes. Daily and cumulative reports of labor variances often are posted on bulletin boards or charts in the factory.

The analysis of standard cost variations for either material or labor should not stop with the identification of time and responsibility. Significant variations should be carefully investigated to determine precisely *what caused the variations* so that timely management action is possible.

STANDARD COSTS FOR OVERHEAD—ACCOUNTING AND BUDGETING PROCEDURES

Standard costs for manufacturing overhead must be based on the budget program for the manufacturing function. Budgeting is essential because *standard overhead rates* must be developed in advance for each responsibility center. The problem is analogous to that encountered in absorption (actual) cost systems when overhead is apportioned to production by predetermined overhead rates. Recall that a predetermined overhead rate is computed as follows (see Chapter 9):

$$\frac{\text{Budgeted overhead for year}}{\text{Budgeted volume for year}} = \text{Standard overhead rate per unit of volume}$$

The formula requires that (1) annual volume (output) and (2) annual overhead costs be budgeted for each responsibility center. It is generally thought that these estimates should be more carefully analyzed when standard costs are being developed than when they are to be used in historical cost systems. There is no real logic for the distinction. When a budget program is used, the volume projections and overhead cost budgets should be used as the basis for computation of the standard overhead rate for accounting purposes.

Standard cost accounting procedures for factory overhead may be shown by referring to Illustration 61 for budget data and standard overhead rates. Continuing the assumption that 1,000 units of product P are produced in January, assume further the following data for overhead: actual overhead incurred for January in Department 1, $3,500; in Department 2, $5,373. Direct labor hours are given on page 547. Accounting entries for a standard cost system would be:

FOR ACTUAL OVERHEAD INCURRED

Overhead control—Department 1	3,500	
Overhead control—Department 2	5,373	
Various accounts		8,873

FOR OVERHEAD APPLIED—DEPARTMENT 1

Overhead in process (3,000 DLH @ $1.00)	3,000	
Overhead control—Department 1		3,000

FOR OVERHEAD APPLIED—DEPARTMENT 2

Overhead in process (2,000 DLH @ $2.50)	5,000	
Overhead control—Department 2		5,000

FOR OVERHEAD VARIANCES—DEPARTMENT 1
(see next page for computation)

Overhead budget variance	200	
Overhead idle capacity variance	300	
Overhead control—Department 1		500

FOR OVERHEAD VARIANCES—DEPARTMENT 2
(see next page for computation)

Overhead budget variance	40	
Overhead idle capacity variance	333	
Overhead control—Department 2		373

Observe that, as with material and labor, the Overhead in Process account is charged (debited) at standard cost. The three Work in Process accounts (material, direct labor, and overhead) are *credited* at standard cost for goods completed, leaving the work in process inventory valued at standard. In the above example the overhead *under-applied* for January was $500 (that is, $3,500 — $3,000) for Department 1, and $373 (that is, $5,373 — $5,000) for Department 2. In standard cost systems overhead over/ underapplied is analyzed and recorded in separate variance accounts as illustrated. Either the two-way or three-way analysis may be used (see Chapter 16).

The overhead variances recorded in the last two entries were computed as follows:[7]

	DEPT. 1	DEPT. 2
1. Actual overhead incurred	$3,500	$5,373
2. Variable budget adjusted to actual hours		
$2,100 + (3,100 × $.40)†	3,340	
$2,333 + (1,960 × $1.50)		5,273
3. Variable budget adjusted to standard hours		
$2,100 + (3,000 × $.40)	3,300	
$2,333 + (2,000 × $1.50)		5,333
4. Overhead applied	$3,000	$5,000
Variations:		
Overhead budget variance (1—3)	$ 200*	$ 40*
Overhead idle capacity variance (4—3)	300*	333*
Total variance (4—1)	$ 500*	$ 373*

*Unfavorable.
†See Section on variable budgets.

Because the budget variance represents a loss due to inefficiency, it is reported on the performance report for the responsibility center. On the income statement it is deducted similar to an expense. The idle capacity variance tends to balance out during the year; therefore, on a monthly reporting basis it is usually reflected on a deferred basis on the balance sheet rather than as an income statement item.

[7] This analysis is identical conceptually and mathematically with the analysis discussed and illustrated in Chapter 16. The interpretations given there are appropriate for the standard cost variations illustrated above.

We may reemphasize that, if *expected actual standards* for overhead are used, the resulting standard cost variations are identical with those obtained by budget variation analysis procedures, as illustrated in Chapter 16. Computation procedures are identical in both situations.

THE STANDARD COST INCOME STATEMENT

To complete the illustration developed thus far for Able Company, a simplified income statement reflecting the standard cost concept is presented in Illustration 62.

ILLUSTRATION 62. Able Company
Income Statement—Standard Cost Approach
(Based on Standard Cost Data)
For the Month of January 19—

Sales—product P (1,000 units @ $40)		$40,000
Less: standard cost of goods sold (1,000 units @ 25)		25,000
Standard gross margin		15,000
Deduct standard cost variances (unfavorable*):		
Material price variance—material R	$105*	
Material price variance—material M	42	
Material quantity variance—material R	75*	
Material quantity variance—material M	10*	
Labor usage variance—Department 1	200*	
Wage rate variance—Department 1	155*	
Labor usage variance—Department 2	120	
Wage rate variance—Department 2	196*	
Overhead budget variance—Department 1	200*	
Overhead budget variance—Department 2	40*	
		819*
Actual gross margin		$14,181
Selling and administrative costs		9,261
Net income		$ 4,920

(Note: On monthly statements idle capacity variance is usually shown as a deferred item on the balance sheet.)

Observe that the variances, except for idle capacity, are written off as a loss in the period in which they were incurred; thus the losses due to inefficiency do not affect cost of goods sold nor are they carried forward in inventory as an asset. The monthly performance report would incorporate this income statement, and the variances would therefore be reflected by a responsibility center in a manner similar to that illustrated in the preceding chapters.

VARIABLE EXPENSE BUDGETS RELATED TO STANDARD COSTS

Variable expense budgets, as discussed and illustrated in Chapter 10, complement standard cost procedures; they provide data (1) for computation of the predetermined overhead rates and (2) for overhead variance analyses.

Predetermined overhead rates were discussed and illustrated in Chapter 9. The same procedures apply to standard costs. For example, the standard overhead rates shown on the cost specification (page 548) and used in the illustrations on page 543 were computed as follows:

	DEPT. 1	DEPT. 2
Budgeted data:		
Direct labor hours budgeted for the year	42,000	28,000
Variable budgets:		
Fixed cost per month	$ 2,100.00	$ 2,333.33
Variable rate per DLH	.40	1.50

Computation of standard overhead rates for the year:
Dept. 1

$$\frac{(12)(\$2,100) + (42,000 \times \$.40)}{42,000} = \$1.00 \text{ per DLH}$$

Dept. 2

$$\frac{(12)(\$2,333.33) + (28,000 \times \$1.50)}{28,000} = \$2.50 \text{ per DLH}$$

In the analysis of standard cost overhead variances, data from the variable budget were utilized in the computations on page 548. The procedures used there are identical with those discussed and illustrated in Chapter 16.[8]

INTEGRATION OF STANDARD COSTS AND BUDGETING

An appraisal of standard costs and budgeting reveals that there is a considerable amount of overlapping of purposes, advantages, and internal applications. There are, nevertheless, distinct and important aspects of each procedure that are not common to the other.

The preceding chapters suggest that budget costs should represent

---

[8] In Chapter 16 the discussions and illustrations indicated that the relevance of variance analysis (whether budget data or standard cost data) depends upon whether the fixed and variable components of cost are known.

potentially attainable goals under expected operating conditions. Budget costs should be fairly "tight," because efficient operations should be assumed in establishing budget allowances. Budget costs, then, should represent *expected actual costs* under normal operating conditions, assuming a high yet realistic efficiency level.

There are numerous theories (and opinions) about what level of efficiency standard costs should represent.[9] It is generally recognized that *when expected actual standards are developed for use in the standard cost system, these same standards should be used for cost estimates in the annual profit plan and also for cost control purposes.* Obviously, then, expected actual standards and budget costs are *identical*; thus, the budget variations and standard cost variations should be identical.

On the other hand, if standards other than expected actual are used in the standard cost system, differences will occur between standard costs and budget costs. As a general rule, standards other than expected actual will be "tighter" than is desirable for budget purposes. Even so, standard costs calculations may still be used for budget construction. In that event, the budget should include amounts for *budgeted variations between expected actual and standard costs.*

There are situations where it may be desirable to have a standard cost system in addition to a complete budget program. Whereas a comprehensive budget program is concerned primarily with a coordinated plan of operations covering a given period as well as control of all aspects of operation, the primary objectives of a standard cost system are (1) to control manufacturing costs and (2) to simplify certain cost accounting procedures.

Clearly, effective budgeting must precede realistic determinations of standard costs for material, labor, and factory overhead. This is true because of the levels of output, managerial policies, and other variables affecting cost be havior.

Haphazard cost estimates for budgets are not unusual. Careful development of standard costs for material, labor, and even administrative and distribution costs can greatly improve budget accuracy. Certainly the two procedures complement one another in many ways.

In addition to the budget aspects of standard costs, there are numerous accounting aspects involved. Standard costs simplify the cost accounting procedures in several ways,—the principal ones have already been indicated, such as the accounting for raw materials, work in process, and finished goods inventories at standard cost.

In systems integrating standard costs and budgeting, it is common to find standard cost procedures used for manufacturing costs and to find

[9] Refer to leading cost accounting books for discussions of the relative theoretical and pragmatic implications of basic standards, ideal standards, normal standards, and expected actual or current standards.

budget procedures used for distribution and administrative costs. Standard cost systems almost always also incorporate direct costing.

The integration of direct costing and standard costs, as a part of the accounting system with a comprehensive budget program, represents a progressive, dynamic, and systematic approach to comprehensive planning, coordinating, and controlling.

DISCUSSION QUESTIONS

1. Why should the accounting system be in harmony with the profit planning and control program?
2. Define variable costing, and explain its primary features.
3. Explain the relationships between variable costing and profit planning and control.
4. What are standard costs? Conceptually compare them with historical costs.
5. What is a standard cost specification?
6. What are the two standard cost variations with respect to raw materials? Relate them to budget variations for raw material.
7. What are two standard cost variances with respect to direct labor? Relate them to the budget variances for labor.
8. Briefly explain the standard cost procedure for handling manufacturing overhead.
9. What are the variances usually associated with manufacturing overhead in standard costing? Relate them to budget variances for overhead.
10. Explain the integration of standard costs and budgeting.

CASE 17-1

Bowman Company

Bowman Company is a small manufacturer of a single product sold through auto parts stores in a five-state region. Manufacturing is relatively simple and only five producing departments are required in the one plant. Manufacturing operations are repetitive, and production is fairly stable throughout the year. The company has experienced steady growth since organization in 1948, and profits have been slightly above average for the industry. The company utilizes a full absorption cost system for plant operations; the accounting department (comprised of three individuals) each year computes a predetermined overhead rate for the plant. This rate is multiplied by actual plant output to apply overhead for each month. Over the years the accounting department has developed some "informal" standards for material and labor; these standards were not a part of the accounting system but were slated to have been used as a "gauge of actual performance" on the monthly financial report that was prepared for the management.

The company is organized into a sales division and a manufacturing division. The sales division is comprised of a home office and seven sales districts. Including sales districts, plant departments (four producing and three service), and administrative departments, there are a total of twenty responsibility centers. The company is owned by ten stockholders, and the shares are not for sale. The accounting department develops a quarterly summarized financial statement for the shareholders.

Two years ago the long-time president retired at the age of seventy-two, and Martin Bowman, son of the founder of the company, was appointed president. He had received a college degree in engineering and two years later an MBA from a large midwestern university. He stated that he has numerous plans to "expand the company and to introduce the latest managerial approaches." He perceived that the accounting function was "solid but not up-to-date in its approaches." The three employees in that department are long-time employees without formal education in management and accounting. The head of the department will retire in two years. Rather than waiting, Bowman decided to employ a recent MBA graduate as his "first assistant," and among other responsibilities asked him to "develop a dynamic profit planning and control program." Ron Baker, the newly employed first assistant, has just completed the first draft of the annual profit plan for the upcoming year. He has worked closely with the managers of the twenty responsibility centers; however, he found that he had to "do much of the work since this was an entirely new concept to them." The historical accounting data and the informal standards were useful; however, there had never been any effort to categorize costs as fixed and variable. Baker decided that he would establish the planning process for the plant on the "variable-standard cost basis." His conversations with the plant supervisors and the head of the accounting department convinced him that it would be best not to insist on major changes in the accounting system prior to the retirement of the present accounting manager. After the manager's retirement, he anticipated that the accounting system would be placed on a variable-standard basis in harmony with the profit planning approach. In the meantime, he decided to concentrate on improving the accounting on a responsibility basis and revising the performance reports to be issued monthly, to reflect, by responsibility, *actual, planned,* and *variances* (based on the variable budget concept). The president of the firm agreed with this approach; it was progressive, and, in his opinion, it would not unduly upset the long-time employees.

In order to illustrate the approach taken initially in the annual profit plan, the planned income statement for January of the first budget year is presented in Exhibit 1 including some explanatory data (amounts have been simplified for case purposes).

Additional data from annual profit plan:

1. Annual output planned—120,000 units of product (including 10,000 planned for January).

2. Annual predetermined overhead rate per unit of output:

	AMOUNT	UNITS	RATE PER UNIT
Fixed costs	$144,000	120,000	$1.20
Variable costs	156,000	120,000	1.30
Total	$300,000	120,000	$2.50

3. No idle capacity variance was budgeted for January since planned output was one-twelfth of the annual planned output.

EXHIBIT 1. Bowman Company
Planned Income Statement—January, 19XX (Only)

	UNITS	UNIT PRICE	AMOUNT	PERCENT
Sales	9,000	$10.00	$90,000	100%
Variable standard costs:				
Material	10,000	.90	$ 9,000	
Labor	10,000	1.20	12,000	
Plant overhead	10,000	1.30	13,000	
Total variable mfg. costs @ std.	10,000	3.40	34,000	
Less: inventory increase	1,000	3.40	3,400	
Variable cost of goods sold @ std.	9,000	3.40	30,600	
Variable distribution costs	9,000	.40	3,600	
Variable administrative costs	9,000	.20	1,800	
Total variable costs	9,000	4.00	36,000	40
Contribution margin	9,000	$ 6.00	54,000	60
Fixed costs:				
Plant overhead			12,000	
Distribution costs			14,000	
Administrative costs			16,000	
Total fixed costs			42,000	
Variances from standard			None	
Total fixed costs and variances			42,000	
Income (pretax)			$12,000	13%

At the end of January of the budget year, the accounting department, following the old approach, prepared the financial report; the income statement portion of it is shown in Exhibit 2, including their comments.

Additional actual data for the month of January:

1. Material usage variance, $80.
2. Labor variance: efficiency, $120; rate, $160.
3. Overhead incurred, $26,750; applied, 9,900 units × $2.50 = $24,750. Under-applied includes $120 idle capacity variance.
4. Inventory valuation on average basis: $47,900 ÷ 9,900 units = $4.84 per unit.
5. There were no changes in the fixed costs for distribution and administration during the month.

Required:

1. Baker has just received the report (Exhibit 2) from the accounting department and has decided to prepare an income statement for January that compares *actual* results with *planned* following the format utilized in the profit plan.

EXHIBIT 2.   Bowman Company

Income Statement for the Month of January, 19XX

	JANUARY, 19XX OF				INCREASE DECREASE*
	CURRENT YEAR		LAST YEAR		
Sales (9,200 units)	$92,000	100%	$88,000	100%	$4,000
Cost of goods sold:					
Initial inventory	None		1,450		1,450*
Manufacturing costs (9,900 units mfg.)					
Material	8,990	10	8,920	10	70
Labor	12,160	13	11,940	14	220
Plant overhead applied	24,750	27	23,870	27	880
Plant overhead underapplied	2,000	2	600	1	1,400
Total manufacturing costs	47,900	52	46,780	53	1,120
Final inventory—700 units @ $4.84	3,388	4	None		3,388
Cost of goods sold	44,512	48	46,780	53	2,268*
Gross profit	47,488	52	41,220	47	6,268
Operating costs:					
Distribution costs	17,880	19	15,900	18	1,980
Administrative costs	17,940	20	17,100	19	840
Total operating costs	35,820	39	33,000	37	2,820
Net profit (pretax)	$11,668	13%	$ 8,220	10%	$3,448

You have been asked to prepare this report. You should set up side captions similar to Exhibit 1 then enter in the first money column the "actual" amounts *converted* to that basis; for example, for materials you should enter the following:

LINE	ACTUAL
Variable standard costs:	
Material	$8,910
Variances from standard:	
Material variance	80

After completing the "actual" column in this manner you should then complete the "planned" column by "adjusting" the budget to actual output. Finally, the variances should be entered in the third column. Add any comments that appear appropriate. At this point it is anticipated that the statement would be appropriate for managerial use. Hint: The "income" amount shown in your "actual" column should be $10,660, which is the same as in Exhibit 2 except for the effect of the difference in the inventory valuation.

2. Evaluate the approach to introducing profit planning and control adopted by Baker. Do you agree with his approach to the "accounting problem?" Compare and evaluate the two income statements.

CASE 17-2
Moore Company

Moore Company is a small manufacturer of five products. This case focuses on one of the products that has been of considerable concern to the management. Although there is a wide market for this particular product, the company has tended to stay within a three-state region with all its products. The company has been earning low profits for the last four or five years. Two years back the president asked the accounting department to develop a budget. The accounting department was comprised of four individuals headed by the chief accountant who had been with the company since its organization thirty-two years earlier. Neither he nor the others had formal training in accounting. The second budget for the company was recently completed and included the following income statement related to product A (summarized):

	UNIT BASIS	TOTAL COST	PER CENT
Sales (10,000 units)	$20	$200,000	100%
Cost of goods manufactured and sold	12	120,000	60
Gross profit	8	80,000	40
Selling and administrative costs	6	60,000	30
Profit	$ 2	$ 20,000	10%

The company utilizes a full absorption cost system and allocates actual overhead at the end of each month (predetermined overhead rates are not used). Monthly performance reports are prepared; actual expenses are compared with one-twelfth of the annual budgeted amount.

Immediately after a recent meeting of the president and the two vice presidents (production and sales), the president asked the chief accountant several questions; the chief accountant told the president that he would need some time, otherwise his answers would be "off the cuff." The president wanted "some estimates now." Essentially, the questions by the president and "off the cuff" answers by the chief accountant were as follows:

Question 1: Horn (Vice President, Sales) says we should accept a 2,000 unit order at $10.50 per unit; I said no, our cost is $12 per unit. What do you think?

Answer. I agree with you; of course, if we produced 12,000 instead of 10,000, our unit cost would go down some but not that much—I would estimate that it might drop to $11 per unit.

Question 2. What do you think our minimum price should be on this offer? It is from a state outside our market, and they are talking to our number one competitor.

Answer. Well, offhand, I would say we should not sell for less than $18, or maybe $17.

Question 3. Horn also mentioned our breakeven point on this item; I suggested it was around 9,000 units. How was that?

Answer. Well, we would have to do a lot of analysis to compute it, but your answer makes sense. We make approximately $20,000 on 10,000 units, that is, 1,000 units for the profit. The 9,000 was a good rough estimate.

Question 4. I feel that we need $30,000 profit on this product. As I read it we pick up $8 per unit; therefore, to pick up another $10,000 profit, we need to sell 1,250 additional units. Blue (Vice President, Manufacturing) says we would have no production problems, although Horn says we would have to reduce the price to increase the volume. I also proposed a 10 percent price increase; Horn says that will knock volume down by 15 percent. What do you think?

Answer. Well, there are a lot of factors working here. I suspect Horn is right about the 15 percent drop. If we could hold the price and sell the 1,250 units, your profit target would be all right.

Question 5. Blue wants to produce 15,000 units instead of 10,000; he says the unit cost will go way down and profits up. What would be the effect of this plan? Horn insists on the 10,000 volume at our present price.

Answer. Well, let's see; our unit cost might go down to the $10 I mentioned earlier. On the 10,000 units budgeted we would pick up $2 each; so our profits would go up to $40,000. However, we might have an inventory problem next year.

Required:

    a.   Evaluate the responses of the chief accountant.

    b.   What changes would you recommend in (1) the budget system and (2) the accounting system? Explain.

    c.   Following your recommendations in b, develop responses to each of the questions posed by the president. Use the following additional data if it will be helfpul:

        Fixed costs included in cost of goods sold, $40,000.

        Fixed costs included in selling and administrative expenses, $50,000.

CASE 17-3

Straus Company

    Straus Company produces and distributes twenty-three different items; each item is relatively low cost, and all are distributed through the same channels. Although the products are fairly standardized, their number has precluded separate planning and accounting for each product; they are grouped into five classifications for several purposes. The company is considered a small manufacturer and has been only moderately successful in terms of profit margin. The company controller stated that they "utilize an average cost system; materials and labor are accounted for at actual as used and are charged directly to the using department without regard to product. Factory overhead is accumulated by department during the month, and the actual amounts of service department costs are allocated to the producing departments at the end of each month. The unit cost of producing each product is not determined by the cost system, since we can estimate very closely the material and labor costs; overhead is handled for this purpose as a load factor related to prime cost." Each year the company controller, at the request of the president develops an annual projected (budgeted) income statement that follows the traditional income statement format. The projection for the upcoming year has just been completed and is under consideration by the president and the two vice presidents (sales and production); it is as follows:

BUDGET OF INCOME AND EXPENSES

For the twelve months ending December 31, 19XX

	THIS YEAR		BUDGET	
Sales	$727,272	100%	$800,000	100%
Manufacturing costs:				
Direct material	73,113	10	$ 80,000	10
Direct labor	146,121	20	156,000	19.5
Overhead	341,698	47	360,000	45
Total manufacturing costs	560,932	77	596,000	74.5
Gross profit	166,340	23	204,000	25.5
Selling expenses	109,100	15	120,000	15
General administrative expenses	51,120	7	60,000	7.5
Total selling and administrative	160,220	22	180,000	22.5
Pretax net profit	$ 6,120	1%	$ 24,000	3.0%

Notes: 1. Projected a 10 per cent increase in sales volume; no change in sales price.
2. Projected a slight decrease percentage-wise in manufacturing costs; push managers to keep costs in line.
3. Projected same percentage for sales costs; Vice President of Sales says this is necessary to raise sales volume; administrative costs kept in line percentage-wise with this year.

Although the budget reflected a 3 percent profit margin, compared with 1 percent last year, the president insists on a 5 percent margin; the industry average reported by the trade association is 5.21 percent. The discussions centered on steps that might be taken to "get the 5 percent profit margin." During the discussions the controller was called in to "listen." Incidentally, the controller actually served only as the company accountant; he had been with the company many years having been initially employed as a bookkeeper. His training in accounting consisted of some correspondence courses; due to the depression he had started working immediately after graduation from high school. The following ideas were proposed during the meeting although no definitive decisions were made.

1. The president proposed a price increase. "To get the 5 percent profit margin ($40,000) we need $16,000 more profits; now all we need to do is to raise prices 2 percent." However, Mason (Vice President of Sales) reflected that volume would "drop off by 3 or 4 percent if we did that."

2. Mason felt that he should be given "$15,000 more for selling expenses so that I can get you about $50,000 more in sales at the same price; the way I figure it, that would about do the trick."

3. The assistant to the president (a recent college graduate with a mathematics undergraduate degree and an MBA degree) said that he "doubted that the expenses as reflected in the budget were realistic; no one here has complained about them so they must be plenty high; they appear to be straight extrapolations from last year, which was unsatisfactory. Perhaps a sophisticated analyses would reveal some avenues for savings." This drew absolutely no comments; just a few moments of noticeable silence! (At least, this was the way he reported it to the case writer.)

4. Justin (Vice President of Production) suggested that "the more profitable items should be pushed; if those allocations of overhead weren't so troublesome to the accountants, we would be sure which ones are the best."

5. Mason speculated that at present prices "we would breakeven at about $700,000 sales, since we made a little profit on last year's sales. The president has stated that we should earn $40,000 next year, I still think we can do it on $850,000 sales, if we hold all costs as budgeted all costs except for the material, direct labor, and the additional $15,000 that I need."

6. Mason also proposed that "if we drop prices by 2 percent, 1 can pick up 5 percent more volume with no increase in costs. Let's see, that would reduce sales revenue by $16,000, and the volume would increase it by $40,000. Thus sales would be $824,000, which should give us about $16,000 additional profit; 30 percent of the $24,000 sales would go to pay material and labor costs."

Required:

a. In general, would you say that the estimates made by the several participants were approximately correct? Explain.

b. Evaluate the budget approach. What basic changes would you recommend with respect to the budget program and the accounting system?

c. On the basis of your recommendations, recast the budgeted income statement for internal purposes. For illustrative purposes, if you need additional information, assume that fixed costs included in the expenses are: manufacturing overhead, $240,000; selling expenses, $84,000; and administrative expenses, $60,000.

d. On the basis of your response to (c), develop responses to each of the six proposals discussed in the meeting.

CASE 17-4

A Fable

Once upon a time a company was losing money; although its plant had a normal capacity of 30,000 widgets, it was selling only 10,000 a year, and its operating figures looked like this:

Price per unit	$ 1.00
Total fixed cost	$ 6,000.00
Fixed cost per unit	.60
Variable cost per unit	.65
Total unit cost	1.25
Total manufacturing cost	$12,500,00
Value of closing inventory	0
Cost of goods sold	$12,500.00
Sales income	10,000.00
Operating loss	(2,500.00)

Then one day a bearded stranger came to the board of directors and said: "Make me president, pay me half of any operating profit I produce, and I'll put you on easy street." "Done," they said.

So the bearded stranger set the factory running full tilt, making 30,000 widgets a year. So his figures looked like this:

Total fixed cost	$ 6,000.00
Fixed cost per unit	.20
Variable unit cost	.65
Total unit cost	.85
Total manufacturing cost	$25,500.00
Value of closing inventory	17,000.00
Cost of goods sold	8,500.00
Sales income	10,000.00
Operating profit	1,500.00

"Pay me," said the bearded stranger.
"But we're going broke," said a director.
"So what?" said the stranger. "You can read the figures, can't you?"
WHAT IS YOUR REPLY?

* Adapted from *Business Week*, January 15, 1955.

CASE 17-5
Christy Company

Christy Company is a small manufacturer of a single product that has been successful in a two-state distribution area. The company utilizes a comprehensive budget program, including variable expense budgets for factory overhead and monthly performance reports. Since the product is standardized and the operations repetitive, a standard cost system is utilized by the accounting department. The budget and standard cost projections are identical. The monthly performance report (by responsibility) includes a monthly income statement prepared on the basis of standard costs. Predetermined overhead rates per direct machine hour are used; overhead is applied on the basis of standard machine hours in actual output.

The following data were taken from annual profit plan and related documents:

1. From the variable budget:

	FIXED PER MONTH	VARIABLE PER DIRECT MACHINE HOUR
Indirect materials	$ 1,000	$ .30
Indirect labor	3,000	.50
Salaries	9,000	
Depreciation	1,500	
Insurance and Taxes	400	
Etc.	100	.20
Totals	$15,000	$1.00

2. From the annual profit plan:
    a. Annual production scheduled: in units, 7,500; in direct machine hours, 90,000.
    b. One raw material is used in producing the one product; it costs (at standard) $2.00 per unit, and 10 units are used for each unit of finished product.
    c. Each unit of finished product is budgeted to require four direct labor hours at a budgeted average rate of $4.00 per hour.
    d. Planned output for January, 625 units.

The following data relate to actual transactions completed in January, the first month of the budget year:

1. Sold 590 units at $110 per unit during January.
2. Manufactured 600 units of product.
3. Purchases of raw material, 6,600 at $2.07 per unit.
4. Issues of raw material, 6,150 units.
5. Direct labor incurred, 2,500 hours amounting to $9,950.
6. Actual overhead incurred during January (actual direct machine hours, 7,500):

Indirect materials	$ 3,460
Indirect labor	7,200
Salaries	9,300
Depreciation	1,500
Insurance and taxes	400
Etc.	1,740
Total	$23,600

7. Actual selling and administrative expenses, $12,000.

Required:

    a. Compute the annual predetermined overhead rate.

    b. Develop a standard specification per unit of product.

    c. Present the accounting entries for January assuming a standard cost system. The company utilizes a two-way variance analysis. Assume cash transactions.

    d. Prepare a standard cost income statement for January for internal purposes.

    e. Prepare a performance report for manufacturing costs for January that reflects detailed variances.

    f. Be prepared to discuss the interrelationships between the budget program and the accounting system reflected in the above requirements.

CASE 17-6

Standard Products

    Standard Products manufactures a line of products known as "Packers:" There are eleven different designs and sizes in the line. The company distributes the line over a wide geographical area, and seasonality of sales is a minor factor. The manufacturing operations are primarily repetitive; consequently, the company utilizes standard cost accounting procedures, profit planning, and variable budgets for factory expenses (selling and administrative expenses are all fixed for all practical purposes). This case focuses on one product designated as Packer X-1. The following data relative to this item were extracted from the annual profit plan:

    1. Planned costs for one unit of Packer X—1:

		PRODUCING DEPARTMENTS		
		X	Y	Z
Raw materials:	1 ($1.00 per unit)	2 units		
	2 ($1.20 per unit)		3 units	
	3 ($1.50 per unit)		1 unit	4 units
Direct labor:	Hours	3	2	4
	Average wage rate	$4.00	$4.20	$5.00

    2. Planned output for year (all products)

	X	Y	Z
in direct labor hours	120,000	50,000	144,000

    3. Planned overhead costs for year

(all products):	X	Y	Z
Fixed	$120,000	$36,000	$ 86,400
Variable	60,000	50,000	201,600

    The following actual data pertain to transactions that were completed during the month of January (the first month of the budget year):

    1. Actual number of units of X—1 manufactured during January, 2,000.

    2. Actual number of units of X—1 sold during January, 1,900 at $110 each.

3. Actual raw material purchases:
   Material 1—4,200 units @ $1.05.
   Material 2—5,800 units @ $1.20.
   Material 3—10,000 units @ $1.45.

4. Actual issues of raw materials:
   Dept. X—4,100 units of material 1.
   Dept. Y—6,150 units of material 2.
             1,900 units of material 3.
   Dept. Z—8,200 units of material 3.

5. Actual direct labor incurred:
   Dept. X—6,250 hours @ $4.12.
   Dept. Y—3,900 hours @ $4.10.
   Dept. Z—8,000 hours @ $5.05.

6. Actual overhead incurred:
   Dept. X—$14,000.
   Dept. Y—$ 7,480.
   Dept. Z—$18,600.

7. Departmental overhead is applied on the basis of standard direct labor hours in actual output.

8. The company utilizes two-way analysis of variances for materials, direct labor, and overhead.

9. Selling and administrative expenses actually incurred, $34,000.

The variable budgets for the three departments (summarized) were:

	FIXED PER MONTH	VARIABLE PER DIRECT LABOR HOUR
Dept. X	$12,000	$ .50
Dept. Y	3,000	1.00
Dept. Z	7,200	1.40

Required:

1. Compute the annual overhead rates for each of the three departments; maintain a distinction between the fixed and variable costs.

2. Prepare a *standard specification* (cost per unit) for Packer X—1.

3. Record the actual transactions and overhead application for January; use the standard cost format, and record the variances in appropriate accounts. Assume cash transactions.

4. Prepare a simplified income statement utilizing the standard cost format.

5. Be prepared to discuss the interrelationships in this case between the profit planning and control program and the standard cost system.

Budget Planning
and Control
for Nonmanufacturing Concerns

chapter eighteen

The preceding chapters have emphasized profit planning and control procedures for manufacturing concerns. This chapter discusses some of the particular problems and procedures involved in budgeting for wholesale and retail firms. Instead of converting raw materials into finished products, a merchandising business purchases goods and resells them in essentially the same form. A nonmanufacturing business would not develop budgets covering production, raw materials, purchases, direct labor, or manufacturing overhead. Alternatively, nonmanufacturing companies focus on the *merchandise budget.*

Although industrial budgeting has received much more attention in business literature, comprehensive budgeting has been employed more in retailing than in manufacturing situations. The reason is that the operating margin (that is, profit as a percentage of sales) in merchandising business is typically very low. In addition, purchasing is particularly critical. While it is not unusual for a manufacturing business to make 10 percent profit on net sales, a 2 to 3 percent profit on net sales is considered good in many retail businesses. Another factor is that, historically, the financial control function in retail companies (particularly in department stores) has been emphasized more than in manufacturing companies.

Effective profit planning and control for wholesale and retail companies comprises the same basic procedures as for manufacturing companies; viz.:

1. The development of realistic profit plans.
2. Continuous effort to assure attainment of the goals expressed in the profit plans.
3. The development of a control system based upon performance reports for the various responsibility centers.

GENERAL CONSIDERATIONS

The essentials discussed in Chapters 1–4 have equal application to wholesale and retail situations. As in manufacturing companies the controller or budget director should be assigned the responsibility for supervising and designing the program, but the decisional inputs to the profit plan should be provided by the managers responsible for the performance. Departmental managers, buyers, divisional merchandise managers, and other executives should be included in budget planning.

Well-defined organizational structure is as essential to effective profit planning and control in nonmanufacturing concerns as to manufacturers and for the same reasons. The simplified organization chart in Illustration 63 shows how department stores are typically organized.

Most retail companies set up their budgets on a six months' basis with a breakdown by months within the period. The budget periods frequently are February through July and August through January because they represent the two major merchandising seasons: spring-summer and fall-winter. Where practicable the budget should cover a twelve-month period, with a breakdown by months.

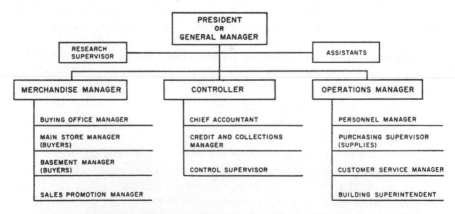

ILLUSTRATION 63. Simplified Organization Chart of a Department Store
(Buying and Selling Functions Integrated)

THE MERCHANDISE BUDGET

The term *merchandise budget* is frequently used in nonmanufacturing situations. The term merchandise budget usually includes planning of sales, stocks (inventory), reductions, markdowns, employee discounts, stock shortages, purchases, and gross margins.

Sales Planning.   The first basic item to be planned in a nonmanufacturing company is sales. Two general approaches are used in nonmanufacturing situations. One approach is to estimate *unit* sales by price lines. This approach is practicable only in situations where there are a limited number of relatively high-value items. Another approach, extensively employed, estimates sales by appropriate classifications in *sales dollars*.

Frequently two sales projections are developed independently, viz.:

1.   On a departmental (or merchandise line) basis.
2.   On a total sales basis.

If the two projections are approximately equal, the departmental sales estimates are generally used. In case of significant differences, both estimates should be carefully studied to reconcile the discrepancy. It is often desirable to subdivide the sales into cash, charge, and C.O.D.

In budgeting sales a number of factors should be given consideration, such as:

1.   Outside Conditions.
    a.   The general business conditions expected to prevail during the coming period.
    b.   Local business conditions expected to prevail.
    c.   The trend of population in the trading area.
    d.   Probable changes in purchasing power.
    e.   Expected changes in the competitive situation.
    f.   Fashion movements expected.
2.   Inside Conditions.
    a.   Changes in promotional policies.
    b.   Changes in location and space.
    c.   Changes in personnel policies.
    d.   Changes in physical arrangement and merchandise layout.
    e.   Changes in price policy.
    f.   Changes in credit policy.

To illustrate sales planning, assume that the overall sales estimate for the six-month period beginning February 1 is $590,000 net sales (after discounts and other reductions). When the *total sales approach* is used, the total amount is usually disaggregated by the time periods and by merchandising departments on the basis of *projected experience percentages*. For example, the total may be broken down by months as shown in Illustration 64.

ILLUSTRATION 64. **Distribution of Planned Net Sales**
by Month

MONTH	PROJECTED EXPERIENCE PERCENTAGES BY MONTH	PLANNED NET SALES BY MONTH (ROUNDED)
February	15.25%	$ 90,000
March	16.10	95,000
April	17.29	102,000
May	18.98	112,000
June	18.65	110,000
July	13.73	81,000
Total	100.00%	$590,000

Similarly, the projected sales may be further categorized by month for each department. The projected experience percentages should be carefully developed on the basis of local conditions and past experience and adjusted for future expectations. Distribution of net sales by department for each month is shown in Illustration 65. Note that the *input* data are (1) the overall sales estimate ($590,000) and (2) the projected experience percentages by time periods, for each department.

Stock and Purchase Planning. After sales are planned, three additional projections are required, viz.: (1) the amount of stock (inventory) that should be on hand at the beginning of the month (BOM); (2) the goods that should be purchased during the period; and (3) the desired inventories of stock at the end of the month (EOM). Since the end of the month inventory for one month is the beginning of the month inventory for the next month, consideration focuses on the BOM monthly stock levels and purchase requirements.

Planning and controlling inventory levels are on going and critical problems. When sales and stock requirements have been projected, purchase requirements can be computed as a residual quantity.

Principal factors to be considered in determining beginning of the month (BOM) stock levels have been stated as follows:

1. Basic stock requirements, that is, the investment necessary to maintain adequate assortments of those items for which the demand is relatively stable.
2. Promotional merchandise needed to reach planned volume for the month.

ILLUSTRATION 65. Distribution of Planned Net Sales by Department

DEPARTMENT	FEBRUARY		MARCH		APRIL		MAY		JUNE		JULY		TOTAL
	%	AMOUNT	%	AMOUNT	%	AMOUNT	%	AMOUNT	%	AMOUNT	%	AMOUNT	AMOUNT
Women's Coats and Suits	9	$ 8,100	7	$ 6,650	5	$ 5,100	5	$ 5,600	4	$ 4,400	4	$ 3,240	$ 33,090
Women's Dresses	33	29,700	35	33,250	40	40,800	38	42,560	39	42,900	40	32,400	221,610
Men's Furnishings	18	16,200	20	19,000	21	21,420	19	21,280	20	22,000	18	14,580	114,480
Draperies, Curtains, Etc.	12	10,800	15	14,250	15	15,300	12	13,440	13	14,300	10	8,100	76,190
Others	28	25,200	23	21,850	19	19,380	26	29,120	24	26,400	28	22,680	144,630
Totals—Amount	100	$90,000	100	$95,000	100	$102,000	100	$112,000	100	$110,000	100	$81,000	$590,000
Totals—%		15.25		16.10		17.29		18.98		18.65		13.73	100.00

3. Policy on the department: Is it to be a dominant policy so far as competition is concerned?

4. What is the relation of stock to sales? Does this relation insure maximum turnover and at the same time afford complete stocks?

5. Outlook for prices.[1]

Planning Inventory Levels. Retailers and wholesalers must determine the amount of stock that should be on hand at the beginning of the month. BOM plus the planned inflow of goods during the month must be adequate to support planned sales. On the other hand, inventory levels must be kept at levels to minimize the risk of losses through style changes, obsolescence, and excess capital tied up in inventory. The delicate balance of stock levels requires sound judgment in addition to sophisticated analytical and computerized approaches. Nonmanufacturing companies rely to a considerable degree on *stock-sales ratios* to determine suitable stock levels. Two methods of computing the stock-sales ratio are:

At retail:

$$(1) \qquad \frac{\text{Average inventory at retail}}{\text{Net sales}} = \text{Stock-sales ratio}$$

At cost:

$$(2) \qquad \frac{\text{Average inventory at cost}}{\text{Cost of sales}} = \text{Stock sales ratio}$$

The two methods will provide the same result only when the markups on sales and inventories are the same. The usual practice in retail companies is to base the computation on retail rather than on cost. Trade publications provide useful information on past industry averages for the stock-sales ratio.

To illustrate application of the BOM stock-sales ratio, assume that a BOM stock-sales ratio of 2 for February is projected in the Women's Coats and Suits department (Illustration 65). Because planned sales for February are $8,100, the BOM planned stock at the beginning of February would be $16,200 at retail. The planned February BOM for each department may be computed as shown in Illustration 66. Stock levels and stock-sales ratios should be developed separately for each department or kind of merchandise.

Planning Purchases. The following formula is usually employed to compute the required purchases at *retail value*:

$$\begin{array}{l}\text{Planned} \\ \text{Purchases} \\ \text{(at retail value)}\end{array} = \begin{array}{l}\text{Planned} \\ \text{Net Sales}\end{array} + \begin{array}{l}\text{Planned} \\ \text{Reductions}\end{array} + \begin{array}{l}\text{Planned} \\ \text{EOM Stock}\end{array} - \begin{array}{l}\text{Planned} \\ \text{BOM Stock}\end{array}$$

---

[1] *The Buyer's Manual*, rev. ed. (New York: National Retail Dry Goods Association, Merchandising Division, undated), p. 178.

ILLUSTRATION 66.   Computation of BOM Stock Levels

DEPARTMENT	PROJECTED BOM STOCK SALES RATIO DESIRED	PLANNED NET SALES (FEB.)	PLANNED BOM STOCK (AT RETAIL)
Women's Coats and Suits	2	$ 8,100	$ 16,200
Women's Dresses	3	29,700	89,100
Men's Furnishings	2.5	16,200	40,500
Draperies, Curtains, Etc.	1.5	10,800	16,200
Others	3.5	25,200	88,200
Totals	2.78 (average)	$90,000	$250,200

The logic of the formula is that purchases must be equivalent to sales, plus or minus changes in the inventory of goods on hand, assuming all are priced at retail. In addition, enough goods must be purchased to include all reductions in goods.

Reductions include (1) markdowns, (2) discounts given to employees, (3) discounts given to certain types of customers such as clergymen, and (4) inventory shortages due to theft and other causes. The formula may be further clarified by illustration:

ITEMS—PRICED AT RETAIL	CASE A	CASE B	CASE C
Planned sales	$10,000	$10,000	$10,000
Add planned reductions	—	1,000	1,000
Total	10,000	11,000	11,000
Add planned final inventory (EOM Stock)	—	—	5,000
Total	10,000	11,000	16,000
Less planned beginning inventory (BOM)	—	—	4,000
Purchases required at retail value	$10,000	$11,000	$12,000

The formula may be applied to a stock classification, department, or to an entire store. The purchases (priced at retail value) for February for the planned net sales shown in Illustration 65 may be computed as shown in Illustrations 66 and 67.

In Illustration 67 *planned purchases were* computed at *retail* price; and the amount that should be budgeted for purchases *at cost* is not indicated. The conversion of purchases at retail price to purchases at cost is made by multiplying the retail amount by the "cost multiplier," which is the complement of the planned *initial* markup percentage on sales price. Computation of purchases at cost is shown in Illustration 68.

The last column in Illustration 68 represents the *purchases budget at cost*. These amounts are used as the basis for buying merchandise for the several

ILLUSTRATION 67. Computation of Purchases at Retail

DEPARTMENT	1 PLANNED NET SALES (ILLUSTRATION 66)	2 PLANNED REDUCTIONS (ASSUMED)	3 PLANNED EOM STOCK (BOM FOR FOLLOWING MONTH)	4 PLANNED BOM STOCK (ILLUSTRATION 67)	5 PLANNED PURCHASES (1 + 2 + 3 − 4)
Women's Coats and Suits	$ 8,100	$ 500	$ 16,200	$ 16,200	$ 8,600
Women's Dresses	29,700	2,000	87,100	89,100	29,700
Men's Furnishings	16,200	1,000	41,500	40,500	18,200
Draperies, Curtains, Etc.	10,800	800	17,000	16,200	12,400
Others	25,200	1,200	86,000	88,200	24,200
Totals	$90,000	$5,500	$247,800	$250,200	$93,100

ILLUSTRATION 68. Computation of Purchases at Cost

DEPARTMENT	PLANNED PURCHASES (ILLUS. 67— AT RETAIL)	PLANNED INITIAL MARKUP ON SALES PRICE	COST MULTIPLIER	PURCHASES (AT COST)
Women's Coats and Suits	$ 8,600	60%	40%	$ 3,440
Women's Dresses	29,700	70%	30%	8,910
Men's Furnishings	18,200	50%	50%	9,100
Draperies, Curtains, Etc.	12,400	40%	60%	7,440
Others	24,200	50%	50%	12,100
Totals	$93,100			$40,990

departments. The illustrative data were developed for only one month (February); the procedure would be identical for every month.

The planned purchases are incorporated in the other budgets, such as the cash budget in a manner similar to that previously illustrated for manufacturing costs in manufacturing situations.

MARKUP CONSIDERATIONS

In the preceding discussions (see Illustration 68), the *planned initial* markup was based on retail value (that is, sales price). The term *markup* refers to the difference between cost and the selling price of an article. Markup is variously expressed as a dollar amount or as a percentage of either (1) cost or (2) retail price. For example, if 100 items costing $60 were marked to sell for $100, the markup would be $40, or $.40 each. The markup as a percentage could be expressed either:

(1)   On cost $\frac{\$40}{\$60} = 66\frac{2}{3}\%$

(2)   On retail price $\frac{\$40}{\$100} = 40\%$

In nonmanufacturing situations, it is particularly important to distinguish between *initial markup* and *maintained markup*. This distinction is especially vital for pricing, budgeting, and accounting purposes. Initial markup represents the difference between the cost and the original or first retail price placed on goods. The initial markup figure in the preceding paragraph was $40, or $.40 each. Maintained markup is the difference between cost and the actual sales price. For example, if, in the case above, the 100 articles were marked down from $100 to $90 and then sold, the maintained markup (also called the gross margin) would be $30, or $.30 each. The examples may be summarized in this way:

	INITIAL MARKUP	MAINTAINED MARKUP (GROSS MARGIN)
Sales (100 units)	$100	$90
Cost of sales	60	60
Initial markup	$ 40 (40% on sales)	
Maintained markup		$30 (33⅓% on sales)

The difference between initial markup and maintained markup is due to the effect of additional markups and reductions, which includes markdowns, discounts, and stock shortages.

In planning careful consideration must be given to developing (1) the planned initial markup and (2) the planned maintained markup. The procedure may be illustrated by the following example:

Planned *net* sales	$5,000
Planned *reductions*	400
Total goods required at retail (before reductions)	$5,400
Planned maintained markup on net sales 60 percent; that is, $5,000 × 60% =	$3,000

Question. What should be the planned *initial markup* on the goods required, ($5,400 in this instance) in order to attain the 60 percent maintained markup planned ($3,000 in this instance)?

Response. The initial markup must be equal to the maintained markup of $3,000 *plus* the deductions of $400. Therefore, the initial markup percentage (on retail) must be:[2]

$3,400 ÷ $5,400 = 62.9629% on retail (or 170% on cost).

Verification:

Sales (gross retail value)	$5,400
Deductions	400
Net sales	5,000
Cost of goods sold $5,400 × (1.0 − .629629)	2,000
Maintained gross margin	$3,000
Maintained markup: $3,000 ÷ $5,000 = 60%.	

[2] A shortcut approach that can be demonstrated algebraically for computing the required initial markup is:

$$\frac{60\% + 8\%*}{100\% + 8\%} = 62.9629$$

$$*(\$400 \div \$5,000 = 8\%)$$

Also see next section for conversion of the 62.9629 on retail to 170% on cost.

Markup Conversion. Although markups are usually expressed on retail price, when the goods arrive a markup on cost must be applied to derive the desired markup on retail. For example, an item costing $.60 must be marked up $66\frac{2}{3}$ percent *on cost* to sell at a price that will give 40 per cent *on retail* price, viz.:

Markup based on cost price:			
1. Cost	$.60		
2. Sales price ($.60 × 166⅔%)		$1.00	
3. Markup on cost ($.60 × 66⅔%)			$.40
Markup based on sales price:			
1. Sales price		$1.00	
2. Markup on retail price ($1.00 × 40%)			$.40
3. Cost ($1.00 × 60%)	$.60		

Tables giving equated markup figures may be available; however, a simple procedure may be used to convert from markup on retail to markup on cost, or *vice versa*. Observe the relationship between the two columns below:

EQUATED MARKUP

	MARKUP BASED ON RETAIL (RETAIL FRACTION ALWAYS SMALLER)	MARKUP BASED ON COST (COST FRACTION ALWAYS LARGER)
⅓ on retail	$\frac{1}{3}$ (33⅓%)	$\frac{1}{2}$ (50%)
40% on retail	$\frac{40}{100}$ (40%)	$\frac{40}{60}$ (66⅔%)
30% on retail	$\frac{30}{100}$ (30%)	$\frac{30}{70}$ (42.8%)
50% on retail	$\frac{50}{100}$ (50%)	$\frac{50}{50}$ (100%)

Conversion from the retail fraction to the cost fraction merely involves carrying over the numerator and taking the *difference* between the retail numerator and denominator for the cost denominator. Converting from the cost fraction to the retail fraction may be accomplished in the reverse procedure: the retail denominator is the sum of the cost numerator and denominator. The method is easily remembered when it is realized that the cost fraction must always be a larger fraction than the retail fraction.

OPEN-TO-BUY PLANNING

Open-to-buy is a term generally used in nonmanufacturing firms to refer to that amount that a buyer can spend for goods during specified period.

For example, if the cost of planned purchases for a particular department for the month is $2,000, open-to-buy is $2,000 before any purchases are made. If by the 15th the buyer has spent $1,200, he is then open-to-buy $800.

Control of purchases is frequently exercised through open-to-buy reports. Computation of open-to-buy throughout a specific period may be a function of several factors. For example, assume the following data for Women's Coats and Suits (from Illustration 67):

	AT RETAIL
Planned sales for February	$ 8,100
BOM inventory	16,200
Planned EOM inventory	16,200
Planned reductions for the month	500
Actual sales to date (February 20)	5,000
Actual reductions to date	300
Merchandise received to date (at retail)	6,000
Planned initial markup 40 percent on retail (i.e., $66\frac{2}{3}$% on cost)	

The open-to-buy at February 20 may be computed as follows:

NEEDED STOCK

Planned EOM inventory			$16,200
Planned sales for remainder of February:			
Planned sales for February		$ 8,100	
Less actual sales to Feb. 20		5,000	3,100
Planned reductions for remainder of February			
Planned reductions for February		500	
Less actual reductions to Feb. 20		300	200
Total stock needed			$19,500

AVAILABLE STOCK

Stock on hand at Feb. 20				
BOM inventory	$16,200			
Goods received to Feb. 20	6,000	$22,200		
Less:				
Actual reductions to Feb. 20	300			
Actual sales to Feb. 20	5,000	5,300	$16,900	
Stock on order for February delivery			2,000	
Total				$18,900
Open-to-buy at retail (on Feb. 20)				600
Cost multiplier (100% − 40%)				60%
Open-to-buy at cost (on February 20)				$ 360

If available stock were in excess of needed stock, the department would be "overbought."

Up to this point in the chapter we have discussed the primary issues involved in developing the *merchandise budget*; its development has been simply illustrated as follows:

PLAN	ILLUSTRATION NUMBER	BASIC MANAGEMENT (DECISIONAL) INPUTS
Sales Plan by Month	64	1. Projection of total company sales—dollars.
		2. Projected seasonal sales cycle—percents.
Sales Plan by Department	65	3. Projected departmental share of total sales by month—percents.
Inventory Plan (BOM)	66	4. Planned BOM stock/sales—ratios.
Purchases Budget (at retail)	07	5. Planned reductions by department dollars or percent of net sales.
Purchases Budget (at cost)	68	6. Planned initial markups on retail—percents.

BUDGETING EXPENSES

In nonmanufacturing situations, expenses typically are broken down into natural classifications such as salaries, taxes, repairs, and insurance. In addition, and certainly more significantly for control, they should be further classified by operating responsibilities determined by the organizational structure. Like that described for manufacturing concerns, each individual having cost-incurring responsibilities should actively participate in planning the expenses for his particular department or function. Expenses should be classified as fixed and variable. Variable expense budgets similar to those discussed in Chapter 10 should be used as much as possible. Again, the key concern in variable budgets is selection of appropriate measures of departmental activity to relate to variable costs. Net-sales dollars are appropriate for some expenses, while the number of transactions may be more appropriate for others.

To evaluate and adjust expense budgets prepared by the supervisors and executives, a computation similar to the following may be used:

Planned February sales (Illustration 65)	$90,000
Planned cost of sales, at cost (Illustration 68)	40,990
Planned gross margin (maintained markup)	49,010
Necessary *net profit margin* (3% of net sales)	2,700
Expense Limitation	$46,310

Should the detailed expense budgets total more than $46,310, they must be restudied to reduce them to that limit. Since the profit margin is generally small in nonmanufacturing situations, expense control through budget planning is very important.

When the expense budgets are finally pared down to the expense limitation, they are incorporated into the profit plan and provide essential data for budgeting cash, and the like, in the manners previously discussed and illustrated.

BUDGETING CAPITAL ADDITIONS

Budgeting capital additions in nonmanufacturing situations presents essentially the same problems as those encountered in a manufacturing situation. The procedures discussed in Chapter 11 relating to budgeting capital additions are equally appropriate for retail and wholesale concerns. The capital additions budget as finally approved is incorporated into the profit plan and provides essential data for planning cash requirements and the budgeted financial statements.

BUDGETING CASH

In companies of all types, good cash management is vital. In retail and wholesale firms particularly, cash management may be critical because large and costly inventories must frequently be maintained. In addition, extensive credit is used to maintain these inventories. A complete plan of operations covering a definite period is essential in developing a realistic cash budget. A line of credit with lending agencies is frequently dependent upon an adequate cash forecast supported by a well-conceived plan of operations. The cash budget in retail and wholesale companies may be developed in a manner similar to that previously discussed and illustrated for manufacturing concerns. Control of the cash position may be exercised in a similar manner.

BUDGET SUMMARIES

Although some retail firms budget only sales, stock levels, and purchases, a comprehensive profit planning and control program extending to all phases of operations is desirable. In such cases the several subbudgets (sales, stock, purchase, expense, capital additions, cash, and so on) are summarized in budgeted income statements, balance sheets, and statements of changes in financial position.

BUDGET CONTROL

A realistic profit plan constitutes one of the primary functions of management in retail and wholesale companies. Nevertheless, it is equally true that the planning activities must be complemented with an adequate system of control, geared to the planned objectives.

A control system in all but very small operations must necessarily be based upon a performance reporting system that provides a running account of operations. Budgeted goals permit the evaluation of actual operations as the business moves through the planned period. The performance reports should (1) cover all significant aspects of operations, (2) be consistent with assigned responsibilities, and (3) implement the management by exception principle. The discussion of performance reports in Chapter 15 is equally applicable to nonmanufacturing companies.

DISCUSSION QUESTIONS

1. There are two primary aspects of department store budgeting that distinguish it from manufacturing situations; briefly explain these two distinguishing features.

2. Define the term "merchandise budget."

3. Briefly explain the general procedures utilized in developing a sales budget for a typical department store.

4. Assume the following budget data are available for a particular department of X Department Store: sales, $70,000; EOM stock, $120,000; planned reductions, $3,000; BOM stock, $140,000; planned initial markup on sales price, 40 percent. Compute the amount of goods that should be purchased: (1) at retail value; and (2) at cost. Explain the logic of the formula that you utilize.

5. Define reductions. Why must they be considered in computing purchases?

6. Distinguish between (a) initial markup and (b) maintained markup.

7. An item that cost $70 is marked to sell for $100. What is the markup: (a) on retail; and (b) on cost?

8. Why is the problem of expense control especially critical in nonmanufacturing concerns?

CASE 18-1
Duncan Department Store

The Duncan Department Store is currently developing the budget for the period August through January. The budget is detailed by months. Planned net sales for the six months total $900,000, distributed 13 percent to Jewelry, 43 percent to Men's

Furnishings, 41 percent to Women's and Misses' Coats and Dresses, and Miscellaneous, 3 percent. Distribution of sales targets by months are as follows:

	JEWELRY	MEN'S FURNISHINGS	WOMEN'S AND MISSES' COATS AND DRESSES	MISCELLANEOUS
August	8.0%	8.2%	14.4%	12.1%
September	9.8	8.3	20.8	16.3
October	11.3	9.1	18.9	15.7
November	18.5	20.7	16.7	18.2
December	45.3	47.4	13.7	27.3
January	7.1	6.3	15.5	10.4

Planned BOM stock sales ratios for August are: Jewelry, 3.9; Men's Furnishings, 4.8; Women's and Misses' Coats and Dresses, 2.0; and Miscellaneous, 3.1.

Planned reductions for August are: Jewelry, $700; Men's Furnishings, $2,500; Women's and Misses' Dresses, $3,600; and Miscellaneous, $100.

Planned BOM stocks for September are: Jewelry, 3.6; Men's Furnishings, 4.6; Women's and Misses' Coats and Dresses, 2.0; and Miscellaneous, 3.0.

Planned initial markups on retail are: Jewelry, 45 percent; Men's Furnishings, 40 percent; Women's and Misses' Coats and Suits, 40 percent; and Miscellaneous, 50 percent.

Required:

    a.   Prepare a summary sales budget by department.

    b.   Prepare a sales budget by department, by months.

    c.   Compute the planned August stock levels (BOM) for each department.

    d.   Schedule August purchases budgeted at retail and cost.

    e.   Compute the budgeted maintained markup by department (per budget).

    f.   Prepare a list of managerial "decisional inputs" to the above plans identified by schedule.

CASE 18-2

Miet Department Store

Assume you are working on the sales budget for the fall season for the Miet Department Store. The following data are available:

Actual sales for the same period last year	$400,000
Expected decrease in consumer prices	2%
Expected decrease in number of transactions	1%

Planned distribution of Sales:
By department:

Dept. X	40%	
Dept. Y	50%	
Dept. Z	10%	

By department, by months:

	DEPT. X	DEPT. Y	DEPT. Z
August	15%	13%	10%
September	17	18	12
October	18	12	12
November	16	14	18
December	24	30	27
January	10	13	21

Required:

a. Prepare appropriate sales budget schedules.

b. Evaluate the approach used to budget sales by the company.

CASE 18-3

Department A

Budget objectives for Department A (Men's Furnishings) during a particular period are as follows (assume no inventory change):

Planned sales	$10,000	
Planned markdowns	100	
Planned discounts	400	
Planned stock shortage	200	

Required:

a. Compute the planned initial markup percent that should be budgeted to attain a planned gross margin of 55 percent on sales.

b. Compute the resulting budgeted gross margin percent assuming a planned initial markup of 60 percent.

CASE 18-4

Tex Department Store

The following data are for Departments X and Y of the Tex Department Store. The period covered is March 1 through March 15.

	DEPARTMENT X	DEPARTMENT Y
Planned sales for the month	$25,000	$ 7,000
Actual sales to date	11,000	3,700
BOM nventory	55,000	18,000
EOM inventory	58,000	17,000
Merchandise received to date	16,000	4,500
Merchandise ordered for March delivery	6,000	2,500
Planned reductions	2,000	400
Actual reductions to date	800	300
Planned initial markup	30%	35%

Required:

Compute the open-to-buy amount as of March 15 for each department.

An Overview

chapter nineteen

Throughout this book we have emphasized profit planning and control as an integral part of the broad management process. We have emphasized its conceptual and practical applications in decision-making, planning, and controlling. We stressed particularly (1) broad management participation, (2) its application to all phases of operations, and (3) the long-range and short-range planning explicit in a comprehensive system of profit planning and control. Throughout the discussions we also emphasized that it is not a financial (or accounting) exercise but rather that it must rest upon a firm foundation of management leadership evidenced by realistic objectives, motivational approaches, and dynamic control. This chapter summarizes some of the primary aspects in applying profit planning control.

BUDGET ADAPTATION

A central problem in developing and applying an effective profit planning and control program is selecting appropriate concepts and techniques for different situations. Further, as the enterprise grows, changes, and becomes more complex, there is the continuing problem of discarding less useful approaches and replacing them with more appropriate ones. Both the budgeting and the accounting systems must be revised as the enterprise changes. It is not uncommon to find a situation where these two systems are internally inconsistent and do not effectively serve the needs of the enterprise. This result usually occurs when a "system" developed in another enterprise is literally transplanted without change. It is doubtful that any two profit planning and control systems should be identical because no two companies are identical.

Prior to initiating a profit planning and control program, management should conduct studies designed to collect factual information on the strengths and weaknesses of the enterprise and to assess the economics involved in potential changes. One type of study, or survey, called *factual* studies, requires in-depth analysis of present operations; it should constitute critical self-analysis and introspection to determine internal strengths and weaknesses of the enterprise and of each of its subdivisions. This self-audit provides factual and oftentimes unpleasant information essential to development of a constructive profit improvement program and the implementation of changes. Another type of study, frequently characterized as *economic feasibility* studies, focuses on alternatives to correct or minimize the inefficiencies pinpointed in prior *factual studies*. Economic feasibility studies develop alternative courses of action and their economic assessment. Many decisions to pursue selected alternatives are based on persuasion rather than on facts. To prevent this situation, these two types of studies go hand in hand. Studies of these types are fundamental not only in the design but also in the continuing implementation and improvement of a comprehensive profit planning and control program.

Appropriate methods of planning sales and other revenue vary between companies depending upon (1) certain external factors that affect the enterprise, (2) the internal characteristics, and (3) the level of management sophistication. Likewise, the approach to plan expenses allowances should necessarily vary. For example, variable budget procedures for expenses do not have universal application, but the concept of adjusting budget expense allowances to output (that is, the volume of work) should be given serious consideration by every management. The variable budget concept may not have application with respect to all costs in a business yet it may be particularly useful in certain responsibility centers. Cost-volume-profit analyses may have considerable application in one situation but not in another. The design of the performance reports should be based upon the characteristics of the situation and particular needs of the principal users. A profit planning and control system should not be static; for example, contribution margin analysis may not be useful currently in a particular company, yet five years later it may be imperative. The system of planning sales that is appropriate today may be entirely inadequate a few years hence.

SYSTEM INSTALLATION

System installation can be troublesome for a number of reasons. In the first place, there is a natural tendency on the part of many individuals, regardless of their position in the organization, to resist major changes of any type. This tendency may be due to several factors, such as, insecurity, lack of understanding, and fear of the unknown. Second, as a result of unfortunate misuse, budgeting has acquired bad connotations for some people. Some supervisors may think of budgeting as another "infernal device" used by management to increase pressure. In the third place, budgeting, properly viewed, requires time and effort on the part of executives, supervisors, and foremen. These reasons make it imperative that a profit planning and control program be carefully designed and intelligently implemented.

It has been said that a company should not expect to develop an adequate profit planning and control program in less than two years; generally, by the end of the third year, the program should be satisfactory. Although the size and characteristics of the company are the determining factors, it may be undesirable to attempt to budget all phases of operations the first year. Sales clearly is one of the best areas in which to initiate budget procedures. Many companies, through necessity, have initiated budget procedures for capital additions, subsequently extending budget procedures to other phases of operations. Where practicable, however, it is advisable to start on company wide profit planning and control the first year.

Once the program is started, its development must be aggressively supported by top management. Initial resistance may be overcome only through active and continuous *budget education* conducted at all levels of management. The objectives of the profit planning and control program should be made clear to executives and supervisors alike. Adequate understanding and appreciation of the program can best be accomplished through conferences and discussions to explain how the program may not only benefit the firm but also how it may help the executives and supervisors in meeting their responsibilities. A common mistake is to hire a budget director to "come in and set up a budget program in the shortest possible time." The mistake is compounded when top management fails to follow through to assure (1) a positive internal climate, (2) management participation, and (3) effective budget eduction. In budget eduction, the idea of some executives that "everyone but me" needs to be educated must frequently be overcome. Line executives should actively participate in conducting budget education within their particular areas of responsibility.

The way in which the system is initiated will have a marked effect upon its acceptance throughout the enterprise. Psychological factors are important.

Careful planning by top management prior to budget initiation is essential. It is generally desirable that a committee of top management officials be appointed to analyze the budgetary needs of the enterprise, to develop the specific objectives of a budget program for the business, and to recommend an approach to budget initiation and implementation (refer to the discussion above of *factual* and *feasibility* studies).

In designing and implementing a profit planning and control program the following steps are recommended:

1. Appoint a high-level management committee to provide broad recommendations.
2. Analyze the internal environment based upon factual studies.
3. Conduct economic feasibility studies.
4. Specify the broad objectives of the program.
5. Specify management responsibilities in planning and controlling (line versus staff).
6. Decide on the basic budgetary approach.
7. Select appropriate concepts, techniques, and approaches.
8. Plan the implementation of the system.
9. Institute budget eduction.
10. Establish procedures for monitoring the system to assure its appropriateness and to provide for improvements.
11. Establish guidelines to assure effective utilization of the system by all levels of management.

MANAGEMENT FLEXIBILITY IN USING PROFIT PLANS

Profit planning and control is an approach for managing future performance consistent with specified management responsibilities. The profit plan results from critical evaluation of many alternatives. These alternatives affect the future of the enterprise under conditions of uncertainty and risk. In accomplishing the management task, broad enterprise objectives must be established—such as target rates of return, profit margins, growth rates, and social programs. The enterprise is seldom involved in profit maximization in the theoretical sense; rather, its broad objectives represent judgments by the management that are generally founded on the firm's past performance, comparisons with other companies, and to some extent the ambitions and personal whims of executive management.

The profit planning and control concept, if adopted, imposes a self-discipline on the management—that is, to specify plans, to evaluate precisely their probable effects on the resource flows of the firm (that is, the financial impacts), and to measure and evaluate performance critically on a continuing basis.

Management attitudes, the key to flexiblity—Profit planning and control requires a high level of management sophistication. Broad problems of leadership, motivation, judgment, and technical competence are generally encountered. The profit plan should be viewed as a guideline to action; realistic goals and objectives are specified and buttressed with strategies and policies. There must be a strong management commitment to attain the specified objectives and goals. On the other hand, the plans must not be administered inflexibly. One of the most important facets of dynamic management is *rational flexibility* designed to take advantage of all favorable opportunities and to minimize the impact of unfavorable events. At the micro level, flexibility is as much a matter of management attitudes as anything else. The willingness to listen, to evaluate alternatives not covered in the plans, and to change positions are elements of management flexibility. Obviously, a plan cannot anticipate all events; thus, a dynamic approach is needed to cope with a dynamic environment.

Reprojections to attain flexibility—A good approach to flexibility utilized by better-managed companies may be designated as *current estimates of future performance*. Under this approach when unanticipated events occur or previously anticipated events become unlikely, the emphasis is not on mechanical revision of the profit plan; rather, each manager of the responsibility center(s) directly affected should submit by the end of the current month a reprojection of his expectations, taking into account the altered situation. Should this reprojection be materially different in any respect from the original profit plan, a complete explanation of the expectations should be required. In addition to flexibility, this procedure should be used to provide top management with information concerning all developments expected in the immediate future that may have a significant financial effect. It puts management in a position to take effective advance action to cope with a changing situation. This concept meets a need that the annual profit plan and the end-of-the-month performance reports do not fully satisfy.

Applied on a broader basis, estimation of future performance constitutes a reappraisal of the primary variables and economic effects in light of present conditions so that the probable results for the remainder of short-range planning period can be recast. The concept is demonstrated in Illustrations 69 and 70. Observe in the illustration that, at the end of August, sales were *reprojected* for the remainder of the planning period. The reprojection is significantly different from the original plan. Thus, by combining the "actuals" for the first eight months with the *reprojection* for the remaining four months, management has a realistic and valuable estimate of "how we will probably come out by year end." Obviously, the application illustrated for sales suggests the potentialities of applying the concept to all major areas

ILLUSTRATION 69.   Illustrative Data for Estimation of Future Performance
(Illustrative Data Simplified)

	ANNUAL PROFIT PLAN (SALES PLAN)		ACTUAL		REEVALUATION	
	MONTHLY	CUMU-LATIVE	MONTHLY	CUMU-LATIVE	MONTHLY	CUMU-LATIVE
Jan.	10	10	14	14		
Feb.	14	24	16	30		
March	16	40	12	42		
April	10	50	7	49		
May	20	70	19	68		
June	40	110	32	100		
July	30	140	28	128		
Aug.	10	150	7	135		
Sept.	10	160			13	148
Oct.	20	180			20	168
Nov.	40	220			34	202
Dec.	20	240			23	225
Totals	240	240				225

of operations. The reprojection concept has been neglected in literature dealing with planning and control, despite its powerful potential.

Techniques to introduce flexibility—In addition to management attitudes and behavior, flexibility may be introduced into a profit planning and control program by a number of techniques: estimation of future performance; variable expense budgets; contribution costing; cost-volume-profit analyses; continuous budgeting; variance analysis and interpretation; and budget revision. Each of these approaches has been discussed in preceding chapters.

If unanticipated opportunities arise, this fact should not deter immediate management action to take advantage of the situation. Likewise, should conditions change so that it appears undesirable to carry out planned projects such as a costly capital addition, there should be no hesitancy to violate the budget. All these suggestions imply that the budget should not be a rigid, inflexible plan, but rather should be used as a viable tool that should be adjusted as circumstances warrant. On the other hand, it is essential that the budget not be changed with every whim, nor that it be taken lightly. Implemented properly, the budget becomes an important tool in the management kit permitting effective management by exception.

In summary—Although there are many techniques that tend to add flexibility to a profit planning and control program, we must reemphasize again that it is the human element, the attitudes of higher manager, that fundamentally reflects the real and perceived flexibility so vital to dynamic

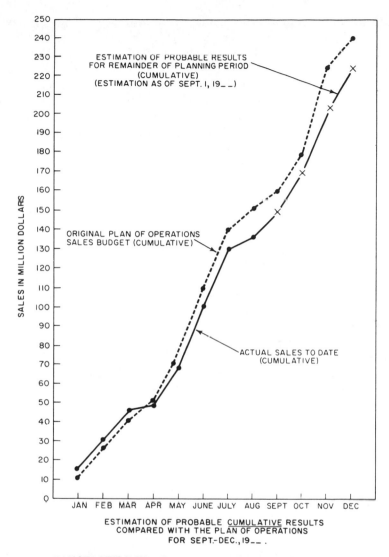

ILLUSTRATION 70.   Estimation of Future Performance

management. Remember also a statement made early in the book: budgets do not manage; only people manage.

SOME BEHAVIORAL IMPLICATIONS

We have emphasized the importance of human relations in profit planning and control. Many of the shortcomings attributed to budget programs can be directly identified with defective management attitudes and other behavioral errors. In the case of a weak or unsophisticated management, techniques such as budgeting frequently are used as the "whipping boy." Obviously, a technique by itself can do nothing—the individuals using it determine its worth; it is the individual manager who commits the error, exerts unfair pressure, establishes unrealistic standards and who is inflexible. Clearly, the overriding factor in the management process is behavioral, that is, the interrelationships between individuals and groups. A key function of the manager is the positive motivation of people through enlightened leadership. The behavioral implications of a profit planning and control program offer both opportunities and problems. In designing and administering the program the emphasis should be on maximizing positive motivations of managers at all levels. Focusing on the behavioral impacts, it may be helpful from time to time to distinguish between the viewpoints of the individual manager and the enterprise. Each has its own peculiarities, motivations, goals, and impacts. A common error is to always blame the problems on someone else. Self-evaluation can solve many problems. Also, on certain issues, it is helpful to view separately the managers and nonmanagers; they occupy essentially different roles in the enterprise.

Critical areas of behavioral implications of a comprehensive profit planning and control program were noted and briefly discussed in prior chapters. By way of summary, it is appropriate to pinpoint selected areas and to suggest that those who may become involved in management should give them further study and reflection. Some of the more critical areas are:

1. **The System**—Management is a leadership or directive effort that sets objectives and goals and measures performance. Profit planning and control is a system to help management accomplish these responsibilities. Individual managers quickly identify the management approach with the enterprise; the system, as they perceive it, will affect them both positively and negatively. In the case of excessive negative motivations they will become discouraged, resign, or often sabotage the system. They will go to the extent of soliciting help from others in sabotage. Alternatively, if the system gains their favor they will reflect enthusiasm, creativity, and productivity. Thus, the interface between the system and the managers at all levels is loaded with behavioral implications. This point suggests the importance of applying sound behavioral judgment in developing, administering, and improving the management system.

2. **Goal Orientations**—There are goal orientations that must be harmonized, those of the enterprise and those of the individual manager. The enterprise goals must be understood and must be in accord with the ethical and economic goals of the manager. The manager must be able to

reconcile the goals of the enterprise with his own personal goals—reward, recognition, social, and ethical.

3. Attitudinal—The attitudes of the higher manager permeate from top management down through the organization. The lower manager adopts certain attitudes of the manager above. A critical aspect is the ease with which lower managers distinguish between the *claimed* and *real* attitudes of the higher manager. Attitudes of importance relate to such factors as participation, flexibility, fairness, openess, goal accomplishment, cost consciousness, productivity, and diligence.

4. Participation—An important behavioral facet is the opportunity of each manager to participate meaningfully in planning, as opposed to pseudo-participation. To be effective, participation must be systematic.

5. Line v. Staff—Many management problems arise because of conflicts between line and staff; the staff is accused of usurping the authority of the line managers and the line managers are viewed as ineffective by the staff. The solution to this behavioral problem is clear understanding and observance of the respective roles of the two groups and yet assure that each group contribute its full potential.

6. Aspirational Level—The level of performance that an individual manager will personally accept is related to many factors, including his own immediate past performance; successes and failures significantly affect his attitudes. Top management should strive to raise the: aspiration levels of the individual managers and of the enterprise as a unit.

7. Pressure—Individuals and groups react to pressure variously. Systems such as profit planning and control are pressure inducing. Pressure, depending upon its characteristics, may create positive or negative motivations. Numerous subtle behavioral implications are involved.

8. Resistance to Change—This reaction is rooted in fear of the effects of change, uncertainty, lack of information, and lack of confidence in the leadership. It can be largely resolved.

9. Performance Measurement—This activity implies a knowledge of what is good and bad performance and the measurement of actual performance. Fairness, relevance, consistency, and rewards (positive and negative) are implicit. There are broad and pervasive behavioral problems in this area, and much additional research is needed.

10. Padding the Budget—This behavioral problem frequently is attributed to "self-protection;" however, it is more apt to be rooted in unenlightened human relations and faulty administration.

11. Budget Approval—The approach used in approving profit plans is loaded with potentials for positive and negative motivation.

12. Follow-up on Variances—Management policies, attitudes, and actions on favorable and unfavorable variables have many behavioral implications.

This list suggests the scope and pervasiveness of the behavioral implications of a profit planning and control program. Several of the items listed above indirectly relate to the responsibilities of the budget director. The controller and budget director are staff personnel, and as such, they are concerned principally with service. Staff personnel should not usurp line authority, nor give that impression. Staff personnel should not be directed to exercise authority over operating line personnel. The controller and budget director should not provide the decisional inputs to the profit plan because this is strictly a line function. Neither should the controller or budget director reprimand operating personnel for unfavorable results reflected on performance reports. The duties of the budget director have been outlined; basically he should design and direct the budget program; he should not provide decisional inputs; and he should have no responsibility for enforcing the budget. It is important to make a clear-cut distinction between (1) enforcing the budget and (2) reporting actual results compared with budget goals. The controller and budget director are responsibile for reporting to all levels of management the results of operations related to budget goals. Corrective action resulting from either favorable or unfavorable results is strictly a line function. The controller or budget director should not be put in the position of approving budgets or taking line action concerning efficient or inefficient operating results outside his particular department. The controller and budget director should not be responsible for cost control, rather, they may be properly charged to design an effective system of cost control. In the final analysis, line executives and supervisors should be charged with the direct responsibility for implementing cost control. A careful distinction between line and staff is essential to good management; the distinction must not only be drawn by top management, but there must also be assurance that the distinction is being *practiced* throughout the firm. The responsibilities for budget planning and control should be carefully specified in written instructions distributed to all managers. A company budget manual is important for disseminating general budget responsibilities and policies.

The behavioral implications of both accounting and profit planning and control are complex. This general area has been given scant attention, particularly in terms of meaningful research, although active interest has been increasing for the past several years. Students and others interested in the subject are encouraged to look into these implications in much greater depth than is possible within the scope of this book.[1]

---

[1] William J. Bruns, Jr., and Don T. DeCoster, *Accounting and Its Behavioral Implications* (New York: McGraw-Hill Book Inc., 1969).

IMPACT OF MATHEMATICAL MODELS AND DATA
PROCESSING SYSTEMS

The scope of this book precluded detailed discussion of mathematical models and data processing systems important to profit planning and control. In the management context, the development of operational mathematical models and computerized data processing systems has imposed an even greater significance on the quantification of management objectives and standards. Since the typical business enterprise is complex and must adapt to change, it requires sophisticated conceptual approaches and information processing. The dynamics of the relevant variables with which a firm must cope also frequently demand extensive conceptual and data processing capacities. Simulation can serve as a partial, although valuable, substitute for actual experience. Quantitative objectives and standards required for profit planning and control are basic foundations for effective application of mathematical models and computer technology. Thus, as the sophistication of these two developments increases, the greater the need for the development by executive management of enterprise objectives and standards of performance. Greater data-processing capacities as well as the related conceptual developments makes available background data and current information important to the planning and control functions. However one of the critical problems facing the researcher is to develop decision models that can be realistically operationalized.

Computers have led a number of enterprises to adapt these techniques to many facets of the budget process. The replacement of manual procedures and computations by these new approaches is significant. It is not unusual to find companies that have "computerized" their budgeting; a few are experimenting with the adaptation of these methods to long-range planning problems and to the "total system." However, it must be realized that the computer cannot substitute for the judgment and unique decision-making role of the manager.

In viewing the budget process, as in accounting, one quickly observes the necessity for testing the financial effect of numerous alternatives and processing large quantities of data. The modern computers and tabulating equipment are especially useful for these two purposes. The computer may be thought of as a machine that can perform arithmetic calculations in tremendous quantities at fantastic speeds. It can store vast quantities of data. On the other hand, the computer can only do what it is told to do—that is, a program must tell the computer what data to select and what operations to perform on the selected data. Thus, we have two basic sets of input data: (1) programming input (instructions); and (2) basic data to be used by the computer in connection with the programmed instructions. The latter data are enhanced by the computer only to the extent that mathematics can improve it. Fundamentally, the output data can be no better than the basic input data and the programmed instructions.

Electronic data processing (EDP) aids budgeting by (1) handling the burden of mass calculations, (2) reducing the time span required for such calculations, (3) testing the probable effects of numerous alternatives, and (4) providing more time for executive consideration of the basic decisions underlying the budget. On the other hand, several disadvantages may be cited, viz.: (1) equipment cost may be prohibitive for the smaller firms; (2) tendency of the mathematical exactness of the results to restrict the imagination of the planners; (3) the necessity to follow "exact rules of the game;" and (4) the cost of programming. Despite these disadvantages, computer implications for managerial profit planning and control are enormous and, consequently, EDP applications will receive increasing attention and use.

Index

Accounting system, 535–564
  adaptation of, 584
  standard costing, 4, 37, 214, 243, 541–553
    for direct labor, 546–547
    income statement, 550
    integration of budgeting and, 551–553
    for manufacturing overhead, 547–550
    for material, 543–546
    related to profit planning and control, 541
    specification, 541–543
    variable expense budgets related to, 551
  variable costing, 328, 536–540
    distinctive features of, 537 540
    inventory change and, 463–464
    related to profit planning and control,
      536–537
Ackoff, Russell L., 9n, 11, 12, 16n
Activity base:
  net sales dollars as, 461
  selection of, 268–269, 277
  variable budgets of expense and, 309, 313,
    314, 316
Adjusted expense budget, 302–303
Adjusted net income method, see Income
    statement cash flow method
Adjusted sales values, 159, 161
Administrative expense planning:
  development of, 265, 276–277
  illustrated, 115, 117, 118, 290, 293–294
Advertising plan, 143, 145, 146, 272, 274–275,
  419

Alternatives, consideration of, 16–17, 49–50,
  146–147, 418–423
Anthony, Robert N., 3n
Average direct labor wage rates, 242, 244–246
Average return on average investment method,
  365, 367
Average return on investment method, 365–367

Balance sheet, 417, 427, 437–441
Behavioral aspects, 46–49, 589 592
Blake, Robert A., 496n
Blanket appropriations, 360
Boodman, David M., 186n
Breakeven analysis, see Cost-volume-profit
  (breakeven) analysis
Breakeven capacity, 197
Breakeven graphs, 422
Brummet, R. Lee, 464n
Bruns, W. J., 49n, 592n
Budget adaptation, 583–584
Budget approval, 591
Budget calendar, 44, 418
Budget director, duties of, 77–78
Budget education, 585
Budget estimates, 449
Budget manual, 94–97, 424
Budget variance, see Variance analysis
Budgeted balance sheet, 417, 427, 437–441
Budgeted cost of goods sold, 427, 430–434

Budgeted high and low point method, 318–319
Building services budget, 111–112
Building supervisor, 111

Capital, sales plan and, 165
Capital additions budget, *see* Capital
 expenditures planning and control
Capital expenditure status report, 362
Capital expenditures planning and control,
 197–198, 355–384, 421
 control, 361–363
 discounted cash flow methods, 367–377
  cash flow concept, 367, 370, 372
  internal rate of return method, 373–377
  net present value method, 372–373,
   376–377
  present value concept, 367–371
 illustrated, 116, 119, 377–380
 management evaluation, 363–367
 management planning, 357–360
 nonmanufacturing concerns, 578
 responsibility for, 360–361
Cash flow concept, 367, 370, 372
Cash planning and control, 385–415
 cash receipts and disbursements method,
  387–400
  determination of financing needs, 398–400
  estimating cash payments, 391–397
  estimating cash receipts, 388–391
 control, 403, 405
 income statement cash flow method, 387–388,
  400–404
 nonmanufacturing concerns, 578
 time horizons in, 386–387
Cash receipts and disbursements method of
 planning cash, 387–400
 determination of financing needs, 398–400
 estimating cash payments, 391–397
 estimating cash receipts, 388–391
Chamberlain, Neil W., 9n, 416n
Change, resistance to, 591
Chart of accounts, 36
Communication, 15–16
 defined, 37
 full, 37–38
 See also Performance reports
Comprehensive performance reports, *see*
 Performance reports
Comprehensive profit planning and control,
 defined, 3–4
Comprehensive sales planning, 142–146
Confidential reports, 488
Continuous control, 424
Continuous profit planning, 74–76
Contribution accounting, *see* Variable costing
Control, 5–6, 16–19
 See also Performance reports; Profit planning
  and control
Controllable expenses, 262–263
Controllable variables, 7–8, 62
Coordination, 19–20
 capital expenditures plan and, 357

Coordination (*cont.*)
 production plan and, 199–200
 raw materials plan and, 221
Correlation analysis, 155, 160, 319–326
Cost accounting, *see* Accounting system
Cost behavior, 262
Cost centers, 34, 245
Cost control, 263, 264
Cost of goods manufactured, 426–429
Cost of goods sold, 427, 430–434
Cost of materials used budget, 212, 219–220,
 225, 228, 230–232
Cost reduction, 263–264
Cost by responsibility, 261–262
Cost variability, *see* Cost-volume-profit
 (breakeven) analysis; Variable budgets
 of expense
Cost-volume-profit (breakeven) analysis, 68,
 420–422, 449–486
 basic underlying assumptions, 454–455
 concept of, 450–454
 cost variability applied to, 454–457
 economic characteristics of company and,
  467–468
 evaluating effect of changing variables,
  469–471
 evaluation of assumptions, 460–461
 illustrated, 474–478
 inventory change and, 463–467
 management policies, 460
 margin of safety, 474
 by organizational subdivision or product,
  471–473
 sales price and sales mix considerations,
  457–460
 special problems in, 461–463
 straitline variability, 456–457
Cowden, Dudley J., 158n
Cross-cut method of projecting sales, 155, 162
Croxton, Frederick E., 158n
Customer classification, 142
Cyclical forecast, 160, 161
Cyclical sequence method of projecting sales,
 155, 160

Data processing systems, 593–594
Dauten, Carl A., 158n
Dean, Joel, 275n
Decision centers, 34
DeCoster, D. T., 49n, 592n
Direct costing, *see* Variable costing
Direct estimate methods, 316–318
Direct labor, standard costs for, 546–547
Direct labor cost planning and control, 240–259
 approaches in, 241–242
 direct labor hours, 242–244, 249, 252
 illustrated, 248–252
 organizing, 246
 performance report, 247–248
 planning and control features of budget,
  246–248
 wage rates, 244–246

Direct labor hours, planning, 242–244, 249, 252
Direct labor variance analysis, 520–522
Direct machine hours, 268
Direct materials budget, 108–110, 213–216
Directing, 5–6, 11
Discounted cash flow methods, 367–377
  cash flow concept, 367, 370, 372
  internal rate of return method, 373–377
  net present value method, 372–373, 376–377
  present value concept, 367–371
Distribution expense planning:
  development of, 265, 272–276
  illustrated, 113, 114, 289–292
Dollar-cost estimates, 113
Dynamic cost control, 70
Dynamic performance reports, 72

Economic feasibility studies, 584
Economic order quantity, 218–219
Economic rhythm method of projecting sales, 155, 159–161
End-use analysis, 155, 163
Enterprise objectives, see Objectives
Estimated cost of goods manufactured, 426–429
Estimated statement of changes in financial position, 438
Estimated trial balance, 437
Estimates:
  of cash payments, 391–397
  of cash receipts, 388–391
  direct, 243, 316–318
  of future performance, 587–589
  statistical, 243–244
Executive committee, duties of, 78–79
Executive management instructions, 66
Executive opinion method of projecting sales, 157–158
Expense control, see Variable budgets of expense
Expense planning, 260–301
  administrative expenses, 265, 276–277
  cost concepts, 261–264
  distribution expenses, 265, 272–276
  illustrated, 111–118, 277–294
  manufacturing overhead, 265–272
    activity base selection, 268–269, 277
    control of, 266–267
    factory overhead budgets, 265, 269–272
    product costing, 266–268
  nonmanufacturing concerns, 578
External reports, 72, 487

Factory cost summary, 494
Factory overhead, standard costs for, 548–549
Factory overhead budgets, 184
  developing, 265, 269–272
  illustrated, 112–114
Factory overhead performance report, 123, 125
Factual studies, 584

Fayol, H., 5
Feedback, 16, 17
Feedforward process, 11, 16, 17, 37
Financial performance, 65
Financial and physical resources, 65
Financial statements, planned, 416, 417, 418, 426–443
Financing needs, determination of, 398–400
Finished goods inventories, see Production planning
Fiscal concept, 32
Fixed costs, 106, 262, 276
  defined, 304–307
  See also Cost-volume-profit (breakeven) analysis; Variable budgets of expense
Fixed or static budget procedures, 334
Flexibility, 3, 45, 72, 424–426, 586–589
Follow-up, 16, 49, 72–73, 363, 501, 592
Formalization of planning and control functions, 20–22
Formula method of expressing variable budgets, 331
Frey, Albert W., 274n
Full costing, 464
Fulmer, Robert M., 68n

Gellerman, Saul W., 49n
Geographical breakdown, 142
Goal orientation, 46–47, 590–591
Goals, 10, 13–14, 34–35
  establishment of, 64–65
  illustrated, 99–100
  realistic expectations, 38–39, 46
Graphic analysis, 320–323, 331
Greene, M. Whitney, 159n

Historical data analysis, 155, 160, 162, 316–318
  See also Correlation methods
Horngren, Charles T., 3n, 523n, 536n

Idle capacity variance, 524–527
Implementation of plans, 71–72
Income statement cash flow method, 387–388, 400–404
Income statements:
  planned, 115–116, 417, 578
  standard cost, 550
Indirect material, 213
Industrial engineering, 243
Industrial engineering studies, 316
Industry analysis, 155, 162
Initial markup, 573–574
Integrated performance report, 494, 503–506
Internal performance reports, 222–224
Internal rate of return method, 373–377
Internal reports, 72, 222–224
  See also Performance reports
Inventory changes, 463–467

Inventory policies:
  nonmanufacturing concerns, 568, 570–573
  raw material, 217–219
  setting, 192–196
  See also Production planning
Investment center, 34
Investment worth:
  analysis of, 365–377
    average rate of return methods, 365–367
    discounted cash flow methods, 367–377
    payback methods, 365–366
  defined, 364

Jablonski, Ronald, 168*n*
Jain, Subhash, 61*n*
Judgmental methods of projecting sales,
    155–158

Kayesh, R. A., 144*n*
Klein, Sidney, 158*n*
Koontz, Harold, 5–6, 10–11, 19*n*, 33*n*, 37

Labor:
  indirect, 240–241
  direct, *see* Direct labor cost planning and
      control; Direct labor variance analysis
  production planning and availability of, 198
Lerner, Eugene M., 377*n*
Letter of instruction, 71
Line management, 73, 76–80, 591
Linear programming models, 68
Lippitt, Vernon G., 144*n*, 145*n*, 158*n*, 159*n*
Long-range planning, *see* Strategic planning
Lower level management, performance reports
    for, 494

Magee, John F., 186*n*
Maintained markup, 573–574
Management by exception, 18, 221, 492
Management by objectives, 3
Management process, 1–27
  comprehensive profit planning and control,
      defined, 3–4
  control function, 16–19
  coordination, 19–20
  formalization of, 20–22
  management planning function, 11–16
  role of management, 4–11
Management quality, 17
Managerial activity, 5
Managerial involvement, 15, 30–32, 327–328,
    591
Managerial sophistication, 152
Manning tables, 242
Manufacturing facilities, production planning
    and, 197–198

Manufacturing overhead, standard costs for,
    547–550
Manufacturing overhead planning, 265–272
  activity base selection, 268–269, 277
  control of, 266–267
  factory overhead budgets, 265, 269–272
  illustrated, 111–112, 277–289
  product costing, 266–268
Manufacturing overhead variance analysis,
    522–527
Margin of safety, 474
Marginal costing, *see* Variable costing
Market effectiveness, 65
Market penetration plan, 142–146
Market research group, 154
Market theory, 8–9
Marketing plan, 143, 145, 146, 182–183
Marketing responsibility, 141–142
Markup, 573–575
Materials, *see* Raw materials; Raw materials
      planning and control
Materials budget, 184, 213–216, 225–226
Materials inventory budget, 212, 217–219, 229
Mathematical analysis, 323–326
Mathematical models, impact of, 593
Maximum capacity, 197
Mechanical design, 151
Mechanics, distinguished from fundamentals, 29
Mellman, Martin, 272*n*
Merchandise budget, 567–573
  sales planning, 567–569
  stock and purchase planning, 568, 570–573
Method of least squares, 338
Middle management, performance reports for,
    494
Miller, Ernest C., 32*n*
Monthly historical data, 320
Monthly performance report, *see* Performance
    reports

Negative values in cost analysis, 327
Net present value method, 372–373, 376–377
Noncontrollable expenses, 262–263, 492
Noncontrollable variables, 7–8, 62
Nonmanufacturing concerns, planning and
      control for, 565–582
  budget control, 519
  budget summaries, 518
  cash budgeting, 578
  expense budgeting, 578
  general considerations, 566
  markup considerations, 573–575
  merchandise budget, 567–573
    sales planning, 567–569
    stock and purchase planning, 568, 570–573
  open-to-buy planning, 575–577

Objectives, 6–7, 10, 13, 31
  realistic expectations, 38–39
  sales plan and, 143, 144

Objectives (*cont.*)
  specification, 63-64
  statement, illustrated, 97–98
O'Donnell, Cyril, 5–6, 19*n*, 33*n*, 37
Open-to-buy planning, 575–577
Operational cash planning, 387
Optimum balance, *see* Distribution expense
  planning
Organizational adaptation, 33
Organizing, 5-6, 10
Other expenses, 462–463
Other incomes, 462–463
Overformalization, 21
Overhead, *see* Manufacturing overhead
  planning
Overhead efficiency variation, 524, 526, 527

Padding the budget, 39, 591
Participation, managerial, 15, 30–32, 327–328,
  591
Parts production budget, 198
Payback method, 365–366
Performance concept, 32
Performance expectations, 32
Performance measurement, 591
Performance reports, 4, 17–18, 72, 425, 487–512
  basic format of, 491–494
  classification of reports, 487–489
  as communication tool, 489–490
  direct labor control and, 247–248
  essential features of, 490
  expense control and, 263
  follow-up procedures, 501
  illustrated, 123–126, 506–508
  integrated, 494, 503–506
  nonmanufacturing concerns, 579
  presentation media for, 495–499
  raw materials control and, 222–224
  relevancy in, 497
  sales control and, 166–167
  simplicity in, 497
  technical aspects of, 501–503
  time gap minimization, 500–501
  utilization of, 494–499
  variable budget and, 333–335
  See also Variance analysis
Performance variations, 72
Periodic profit planning, 41–43, 74
Planned cost of goods manufactured, 266–269,
  271, 286
Planned cost-volume relationships, 303
Planned financial statements, 416, 417, 418,
  426–443
Planned income statements, 115–116, 417
Planned statement of changes in financial
  position, 417
Planning, 5–6, 10–16
  See also Profit planning and control
Planning calendar, 44, 418
Planning and control theory, 8–9
Planning cycle, 44
Planning horizons, 41

Planning model simulations, 68
Planning premises, 66, 101–103
Planning projection, 12–13
Planning worksheets, 422
Plant capacity, sales plan and, 165
Practical capacity, 197
Predetermined overhead rates, 270
Present value concept, 367–371
Pressure, effects of, 47, 591
Pricing policy, 147–149
Prime cost, 241
Probable profit, 420, 421
Producing departments, 266, 268, 270–271
Product costing, 266–268
Product detail, 142
Product line:
  analysis, 155, 162–163
  sales plan and, 149, 150
Product and service quality, 65
Production planning, 182–210
  adequacy of manufacturing facilities and,
    197–198
  availability of raw materials and labor and,
    198
  development of, 186–191
  general considerations in, 185–186
  illustrated, 108, 109, 201–203
  length of production period, 198–199
  production budget as planning, coordinating
    and control tool, 199–201
  responsibility for, 183–184
  setting inventory policies, 192–196
  setting production policies, 196–197
  time dimensions of, 186
Productive department cost summary, 491–493
Productivity improvement, 65
Profit center, 34
Profit margin, 106
Profit plan conferences, 71–72, 424–425
Profit planning and control:
  accounting system and, *see* Accounting system
  capital expenditures, *see* Capital
    expenditures planning and control
  cash, *see* Cash planning and control
  completion of plans, 417–418, 426–443
  direct labor costs, *see* Direct labor cost
    planning and control
  expenses, *see* Expense planning; Variable
    budgets of expense
  fundamentals, 28–59
    advantages and disadvantages of, 50–53
    application to various types of firms, 50
    behavioral viewpoint, 46–49
    establishment of foundation, 53–54
    evaluation of alternatives, 49–50
    flexible application, 45–46
    follow-up, 49
    full communication, 37–38
    managerial involvement, 30–32
    mechanics distinguished from, 29
    organizational adaptation, 33–35
    realistic expectations, 38–40
    responsibility accounting, 35–37
    techniques distinguished from, 29–30

Profit planning and control (*cont.*)
  time dimensions, 40–45
  illustrated, 92–138
    broad objectives statement, 97–98
    case background, 92–97
    enterprise strategies statement, 100–101
    performance reports, 123–126
    planning premises, 101–103
    project plans, 103
    relevant variables evaluation, 97
    specific goals statement, 99–100
    strategic and tactical profit plans, 103–120
    variable expense budgets, 120, 122–123
  implementing the plan, 424–426
  management process and, 1–27
    comprehensive profit planning and
      control, defined, 3–4
    control function, 16–19
    coordination, 19–20
    formalization of, 20–22
    management planning function, 11–16
    role of management, 4–11
  materials usage and purchases, *see* Raw
      materials planning and control
  nonmanufacturing concerns,
      see Nonmanufacturing concerns,
      planning and control for
  outlined, 60–91
    broad objectives statement, 63–64
    enterprise strategies statement, 65–66
    financial plan, defined, 82
    follow-up actions, 72–73
    frequency in, 74–76
    implementation of plans, 71–72
    line and staff responsibilities, 76–80
    long-range planning, 80–81
    periodic performance reports, 72
    planning premises, 66
    project plans, 66–67
    relevant variables evaluation, 62–63
    specific goal statement, 64–65
    strategic and tactical profit plans, 67–68
    substantive plan, defined, 82–83
    supplemental analyses, 68–71
    time dimensions, 74–76
  overview, 583–584
    behavioral implications, 589–592
    budget adaptation, 583–584
    data processing systems, impact of, 593–594
    management flexibility, 586–589
    mathematical models, impact of, 593
    system installation, 585–586
  production, *see* Production planning
  sales, *see* Sales Planning
Profit planning and control manual, 79–80,
      94–97, 424
Profitability indices, 106
Project plans, 34–35, 43
  illustrated, 103
  periodic plans distinguished from, 41–43
  preparation and evaluation of, 66–67
Projected balance sheet, 119, 121
Promotion and advertising plan, 113, 114, 117,
      272, 274–275

Public acceptance, 65
Purchase planning, nonmanufacturing
      concerns, 568, 570–573
Purchase budget, 110, 212, 217–220, 225–228
Purchasing manager, 110
Purposive managerial decisions, 7, 10–11
Pyhrr, Peter A., 62*n*

Rappaport, Alfred, 377*n*
Ratio test, 422, 423
Rational flexibility, 587
Raw materials:
  production planning and availability of, 198
  sales plan and adequacy of, 165
  standard costs for, 543–546
  variance analysis, 517–520
Raw materials planning and control, 211–239
  coordination and, 221
  cost of materials used budget, 212, 219–220,
      225, 228, 230–232
  illustrated, 224–228
  materials budget, 184, 211, 213–216, 225–226
  materials inventory budget, 212, 217–219
  performance reports, 222–224
  purchases budget, 110, 212, 217–220, 222,
      225–228
Reference projection, 12
Reichard, Robert S., 144*n*, 158*n*
Relevant range concept, 306, 308, 314
Relevant variables, 3, 7–8, 10, 62–63, 97
Repetitive performance reports, *see* Performance
      reports
Report to owners, 487–488
Reports:
  classification of, 487–489
  See also Performance reports
Request for capital expenditure form, 361
Research expenditures, 420
Responsibility accounting, 4, 35–37
Return on investment, 68, 106
Richard D. Irwin, Inc., 3*n*
Rue, Leslie W., 68*n*

Sales budget, 145, 146
Sales budget summary, 107
Sales division supervisors composite, 157
Sales force composite, 155–157
Sales forecast, 143–145, 152–153
Sales mix, 419–420, 457–460
Sales performance report, 123, 124
Sales planning, 139–181, 584
  alternatives, 146–147
  capabilities of concern and, 165–166
  comprehensive, 142–146
  control of sales and related costs, 166–167
  illustrated, 107–108, 167–169
  long-and short-range compared, 140–142
  managing, 150–151
  methods of projecting, 154–164
    combination of methods, 163–164

Sales planning (*cont.*)
    judgmental, 155–158
    specific purpose, 162–163
    statistical, 158–162
  nonmanufacturing concerns, 567–569
  pricing policy in, 147–149
  product line considerations, 149–150
  selecting approaches, 151–152
  steps in, 152–154
Sales price, 419, 457–460
Sales variance analysis, 515–517
Schiff, Michael, 272*n*
Schoennauer, Alfred W., 64*n*
Selling expense budgets, 143, 145, 146,
    272–274, 289–292
Semivariable costs, 262, 303
  analysis, 304, 309, 311–312
  See also Variable budgets of expense
Service departments, 266, 269, 270–271
Short-range profit plan, *see* Tactical planning
Short-term performance report, 72
Sighvi, Surendra, 61*n*
Sord, B. H., 303*n*, 315*n*
Special reports, 488
Staffing, 5–6, 10, 76–80
Standard costing, 4, 37, 214, 243, 541–553
  for direct labor, 546–547
  income statement, 550
  integration of budgeting and, 551–553
  for manufacturing overhead, 547–550
  for material, 543–546
  related to profit planning and control, 541
  specification, 541–543
  variable expense budgets related to, 551
Standard labor times, 243
Standard overhead rates, 547–548
Statement of planning premises, 66
Statistical control limits, 502
Statistical estimates of direct labor costs,
    243–244
Statistical methods of projecting sales, 158–162
Statistical reports, 488
Stedry, Andrew C., 46*n*
Steiner, George A., 5*n*, 61*n*, 63*n*, 68*n*
Strategic planning, 14, 34, 43, 49, 80–81
  cash, 387
  developement and approval, 67–68
  illustrated, 103–120
  production, 186
  sales, 140–142
  specific goals statement, 65
Strategies, 10, 65–66
  defined, 14
  illustrated, 100–101
  sales plan and, 143, 144
Sunk costs, 362
Supplemental analyses, 68–69
System installation, 585–586

Table method of expressing variable budgets,
    330
Tactical planning, 11–12, 34, 42, 49–50

Tactical planning (*cont.*)
  cash, 387
  cost planning for, *see* Expense planning
  development and approval, 67–68
  illustrated, 103–120
  production, 186
  sales, 140–141
  specific goals statement, 65
Thompson, Stewart, 64*n*
Time dimensions, 40–45, 75–76
  capital expenditures planning, 355–356
  cash planning, 386–387
  production planning, 186
  sales planning, 152
Time and motion studies, 243
Top management, performance reports for, 494
Trend analysis, 155, 159–161
Tuttle, Roy E., 464*n*

Unit material usage rates, 109

Variable budgets of expense, 277, 302–354, 584
  concepts underlying, 303–305
  cost-volume considerations, 328–329
  fixed costs, 304–307
  illustrated, 120, 122–123, 336–343
  measure of activity, 309, 313
  methods for determining cost
  methods of expressing, 329–331
  participation by supervisors, 327–328
  relevant range of activity, 314
  semivariable costs, 304, 309, 311–312
  utilization of, 331–336
  variability, 314–326
    budgeted high and low point, 318–319
    correlation, 319–326
    direct estimate, 316–318
  variable costs, 304, 306, 308–310
Variable costing, 68, 328, 536–540
  distinctive features of, 537–540
  inventory change and, 463–464
  related to profit planning and control,
    536–537
Variable costs, 106, 262
  defined, 304, 306, 308–310
  ratio, 452–453
  See also Cost-volume-profit (breakeven)
    analysis; Variable budgets of expense;
    Variable costing
Variable expense budgets, 4, 68–71, 551
Variable or flexible budget procedures, 334
Variance accounts, 541
Variance analysis, 513–534
  applications, 514–515
  defined, 514
  direct labor, 520–522
  manufacturing overhead, 522–527
  raw materials, 517–520
  sales, 515–517
  use of, 527–528

Wage rates, planning, 242, 244–246
Warren, E. Kirby, 80*n*, 81–82
Welsch, Glenn A., 3*n*, 303*n*, 315*n*, 400*n*, 438*n*,
   515*n*
White, J. A., 400*n*, 438*n*, 515*n*
Wishful projection, 12

Work in process inventories, *see* Production
   planning

Zlatkovich, C. T., 400*n*, 438*n*, 515*n*